The Palgrave Handbook of Everyday Digital Life

Hopeton S. Dunn • Massimo Ragnedda
Maria Laura Ruiu • Laura Robinson
Editors

The Palgrave Handbook of Everyday Digital Life

palgrave
macmillan

Editors
Hopeton S. Dunn
University of Botswana
Gaborone, Botswana

Massimo Ragnedda
Northumbria University
Newcastle upon Tyne, UK

Maria Laura Ruiu
Northumbria University
Newcastle upon Tyne, UK

Laura Robinson
Santa Clara University
Albany, CA, USA

ISBN 978-3-031-30437-8   ISBN 978-3-031-30438-5 (eBook)
https://doi.org/10.1007/978-3-031-30438-5

© The Editor(s) (if applicable) and The Author(s), under exclusive licence to Springer Nature Switzerland AG 2024

This work is subject to copyright. All rights are solely and exclusively licensed by the Publisher, whether the whole or part of the material is concerned, specifically the rights of translation, reprinting, reuse of illustrations, recitation, broadcasting, reproduction on microfilms or in any other physical way, and transmission or information storage and retrieval, electronic adaptation, computer software, or by similar or dissimilar methodology now known or hereafter developed.
The use of general descriptive names, registered names, trademarks, service marks, etc. in this publication does not imply, even in the absence of a specific statement, that such names are exempt from the relevant protective laws and regulations and therefore free for general use.
The publisher, the authors, and the editors are safe to assume that the advice and information in this book are believed to be true and accurate at the date of publication. Neither the publisher nor the authors or the editors give a warranty, expressed or implied, with respect to the material contained herein or for any errors or omissions that may have been made. The publisher remains neutral with regard to jurisdictional claims in published maps and institutional affiliations.

Cover illustration: Gremlin / Getty Images

This Palgrave Macmillan imprint is published by the registered company Springer Nature Switzerland AG.
The registered company address is: Gewerbestrasse 11, 6330 Cham, Switzerland

Paper in this product is recyclable.

Foreword

Everyday life in the title of this volume signals an important emphasis on how people experience their digitally mediated lives. This is in contrast to discussions in both the global North and South on the expected impacts of investment in digital technologies and services on economies. These discussions are often accompanied by forecasts of how all countries will benefit from adopting the latest technology infrastructures and gain access to the big tech company platforms and their services.

Following in the critical research tradition on digitalisation and datafication where there are many concerns about the proliferating monetisation of individuals' data with little or no regard for their fundamental rights, the first special feature of this volume is its shift of analytical focus away from a neoliberal view. In this view, individuals are treated simply as agents who are assumed to express their demand in a market where big tech companies respond by supplying social media, audiovisual and other digital commercial services. In this volume, individuals are contextualised—they have agency, but they are also subject to powerful corporate, and often state, pressures aimed at shaping their behaviours.

The second special feature is a focus on individual and group experiences in the broader context of their everyday experiences and their capacities to embrace or resist the digital technologies on offer. In focusing on everyday life, this collection calls attention to how media and communication technologies are interwoven with the fabric of the everyday—with routines, rituals and behaviours. This approach signposts what comes to be normalised culturally, socially, politically and economically when people are immersed in a digital ecology—an ecology that comes with specific affordances and implications for people's social, cultural, political and working lives.

In this volume, the authors do not treat digital technologies as being 'out there'. Instead, they examine how these technologies are implicated in people's 'ways of operating' as Michel de Certeau might have put it. They illustrate the many everyday practices through which digital technology users can shape or reappropriate digital technologies in their own interests, instead of in the interests of often distant providers of digital platforms and services. The authors acknowledge the multiple harms and sometimes alienating conditions of digitally mediated everyday life, but they also look to the potentials, if new practices can be put in place and if governments are able to introduce policies and regulations that curtail harmful practices.

While the companies and governments that are investing in artificial intelligence and the algorithms that increasingly monitor and govern the lives of people in the global South and North exert their power and hegemony through overt and covert (nudging) strategies and practices, the contributors to this volume refreshingly draw attention to the fact that digital dominance is not uniformly experienced. Many chapters highlight resistance strategies and everyday tactics. Instead of focusing exclusively on what the digital world does to people, the great strength of this collection is its focus on what people do with or make of the digital world and how they go about changing it.

When digital technologies are not contributing to more equitable societies, the challenge for researchers is to uncover why this is so and what can be done about it. Even as technology designers and business strategists contain and constrain people's behaviour in multiple ways, it is crucial to reveal and protect local ways of 'knowing' or indigenous epistemologies as Sohail Inayatullah might argue. As the authors show, insights can then be deployed as a means of countering exploitative visions and practices associated with a commercially datafied future.

The contributors to this volume also acknowledge that access to, and participation in, a system of mediated digital communication is becoming a precondition for full participation in society. If the distribution of access is unfair, action is needed. Values, actions, interests and constraints all need to be revealed through empirical study. When the prevailing digital services business models operate by surveilling individuals when they go online, the implications are felt by all—in the labour force, in education, in social service, and in the media. In this sense, the relations of digital production and consumption are always political, and they are often discriminatory.

Structuring this collection around five themes—Social Media and Digital Lifeworlds; Digital Affordances and Contestations; Digital Divides and Inclusion Strategies; Work, Culture and Digital Consumption; and New Media and Digital Journalism—the opportunities, but also the exclusions and harms, linked to digital technologies are addressed. The reader will find insight into the varying types of platform architectures or 'grammars of action', following Philip Agre, that influence the way digital platforms shape cultural, social and political norms. The reader will also find chapters which critique the always persistent discourse about digital transformation as if it is necessarily universally beneficial for all.

Attention is given in this volume to developments in artificial intelligence that are infusing societies, conditioning ways of interpreting and acting in the world. The chapters illustrate how digital technologies are enabling the pervasive monetisation of data and how both adults and children manage to navigate their everyday lives, their socialisation, their identities and their access to education as well as their jobs and their increasingly precarious working lives.

Several chapters focus on how digital systems provided by big tech companies—especially in response to the Covid-19 pandemic—have influenced data collection and led to new forms and intensities of population surveillance. Also highlighted are pressures to adopt new forms of working in paid employment, new approaches to humanitarian responses to crises and novel strategies to sustain local industries such as tourism. The authors show how new practices of governance have been introduced from above and that sometimes they can be resisted from below. They highlight creative and beneficial adaptations to a changing digital ecology such as the introduction of robots or the gamification of work tasks, but importantly, they do not neglect maladaptive outcomes which mean that workers and volunteers face new pressures to perform more efficiently. In all these instances, the authors emphasise the need for digital technology applications to be designed and implemented consistent with the contexts in which they are applied and with human well-being in mind.

Importantly, the authors stress the way digital apps and social media may be empowering for some, but lead to risks and harms that are incompatible with people's rights to safety and to live in a just world. From abusive online communication about intimate relationships to cybercrime and mis- or disinformation, as well as the changing, often idealised, representations of cities online, the contributors demonstrate how their digital ecologies are producing new inequalities and perpetuating existing societal injustices, both for the excluded and disadvantaged and for the included.

Everyday lives are increasingly also mediated by digital journalism which is implicated in representing a close and distant world. Several chapters emphasise how mainstream journalism tends to marginalise certain perspectives on issues like climate change, the need to consider what public service journalism can mean when it is owned and operated by the state, and whether alternative modes of critical journalistic practice are feasible in the face of persistent underfunding.

In this volume, the contributors do not set out simply to describe a changing digital landscape. Also addressed is what can be done to achieve radical change. Several chapters highlight the need to enhance individual and collective agency and responsibility, to engage in activism through involving children in the design and development of digital services, to use digital resources to support local or regional languages, and to develop trusted digital services to support local and national economic activities. They also highlight strategies of formal governance such as the Convention on the Rights of Persons with Disabilities (CRPD) and the need for governments to introduce digital strategies that aim to indigenise digitalisation agendas.

Just as Roger Silverstone's work on the everyday life experience of digital technologies emphasised attending to both the over- and under-determination of relationships involved in the development and use of innovative digital technologies, the contributors to this volume succeed in demonstrating that digitally infused everyday lives are both historically situated and contingent upon institutional forces and individual actions. This dialectic creates ambiguity in the outcomes of digitalisation and the exercise of power from below and from above. From above, as Shoshana Zuboff argues, in today's digital environments 'illegitimate knowledge' is being transformed into 'illegitimate power'. From below, this volume succeeds in demonstrating that options for resistance exist and that, through action, opportunities can be created for mitigating the harms of digitalisation and, in some instances, bringing the benefits of digitalisation into the experience of people's everyday lives.

In short, this book may be about digital technologies, but its focus on the 'everyday' means that is—as it should be—principally about 'the conceptions, interests and ideals from which human ways of treating one another spring, and the systems of value on which such ends of life are based'.[1]

Department of Media and Communications Robin Mansell
London School of Economics and Political Science
London, UK

---

[1] Berlin, I. (1959/2003) *The Crooked Timber of Humanity*. London: Random House, p. 1.

Acknowledgements

The publication of this Handbook is the labour of many hands and minds and involved long hours of work and sacrifices. The editors would like to thank everyone who has assisted in making this book possible. We thank the large number of contributors who responded positively to our invitation to prepare a chapter and who worked tirelessly and within rigorous deadlines to ensure the timely publication of the Handbook.

We are also indebted to the commissioning editors, unknown reviewers and production assistants from Palgrave Macmillan for their painstaking reviews and meticulous attention to detail in the production and publication of this volume. We are grateful to Professor Robin Mansell for expertly producing the Foreword and to other distinguished colleagues who offered testimonials on the quality of the book's ideas and overall content. To our colleagues at the University of Botswana in Southern Africa, Northumbria University in the United Kingdom and Santa Clara University in the United States, the editors say thank you for your encouragement and active support.

The editors are joined by our wide-ranging group of contributors in thanking our families and other loved ones who allowed us time and space to generate and document our research and ideas for the chapters and for all elements of the book. We thank them sincerely for their patience, love, understanding and support.

To all others who assisted, we extend our profound appreciation, even as we assume full responsibility for any errors, weaknesses or omissions in the book. We trust that readers all over the world will find value, as well as resonance with their own digital experiences, as they traverse the pages and navigate the concepts of everyday digital life presented in this book.

Contents

1. Living Digitally: Mapping the Everyday Contours of a Still-Emerging Data-Driven Era ... 1
   Hopeton S. Dunn, Massimo Ragnedda, Maria Laura Ruiu, and Laura Robinson

Part I Social Media and Digital Lifeworlds ... 21

2. Artificial Intelligence and Everyday Knowledge ... 23
   Veridiana Domingos Cordeiro and Fabio Cozman

3. Economic Aspects of Social Media: Facebook's Potential for Generating Business in Iran ... 37
   Hamid Abdollahyan and Mahin Sheikh Ansari

4. The Digital Shaping of a City: A Biography of 'Cyberabad' in Three Acts ... 61
   Usha Raman and Aditya Deshbandhu

5. Social Media, Space and Place in South Africa: #egoli (Johannesburg) on Instagram ... 77
   Tanja Bosch

6. Mapping the Digital Fabric of Cities: 'Site Codes' as Spatial Identifiers in Urban China in the COVID-19 Pandemic ... 91
   Deqiang Ji and Xiaomei Jiang

Part II Digital Affordances and Contestations — 107

7 Hidden Abodes: Digital Lives and Distant Others — 109
Graham Murdock

8 The Din and Stealth of the Digital Revolution — 125
Renata Włoch

9 Contentious Content on Messaging Apps: Actualising Social Affordances for Normative Processes on Telegram — 143
Nathalie Van Raemdonck and Jo Pierson

10 Glimpses of the Greek 'Me Too' Movement on Facebook: Tracking Digital Interactivity and the Quest for Equity and Empowerment — 169
Sophia Kaitatzi-Whitlock

11 Non-Consensual Intimate Image Sharing on the Internet: Regulating Betrayal in Jamaica and India — 187
Allison J. Brown

Part III Digital Divides and Inclusion Strategies — 203

12 Indigenizing a Developing Country's Digitization Agenda: Re-visioning ICTs in Ghana — 205
Kwaku O. Antwi and William Asante

13 Nurturing the Transformative Agency and Activism of Children Through Digital Technology — 223
Netta Iivari and Marianne Kinnula

14 The Challenges of Gamification in Brazil's Educational Delivery During Covid 19 — 245
Julia Stateri

15 Re-thinking Critical Digital Literacies in the Context of Compulsory Education — 261
Anastasia Gouseti, Liisa Ilomäki, and Minna Lakkala

16 Universal Design and Assistive Digital Technologies: Enhancing Inclusion of Persons with Disabilities — 283
Floyd Morris

17 Digital Divides and Policy Interventions in a Pandemic World: Issues of Social Inclusion in Argentina 307
Bernadette Califano

Part IV Work, Culture and Digital Consumption 325

18 The Changing Nature of Work in Digital Everyday Life 327
Jessica S. Dunn and Hopeton S. Dunn

19 Indigenous People and Digital Misinformation in the Brazilian Amazon 347
Cristian Berrío-Zapata, Monica Tenaglia, and Sheyla Gabriela Alves Ribeiro

20 Regenerating African Languages and Cultures Through Information Technology Strategies 363
Thapelo J. Otlogetswe

21 Dancing in the Digital Domain: Mas, Media and Covid 19 in Caribbean Carnival 379
Alpha Obika

22 Digital Transformation in Development Settings: Remote Volunteering and Digital Humanitarianism 397
Bianca Fadel and Thiago Elert Soares

Part V New Media and Digital Journalism 415

23 Digital Journalism: The State of Play in Russia and in Global Academia 417
Elena Vartanova, Anna Gladkova, and Denis Dunas

24 Digital Climate Newsletters: The New Alternative for Climate Journalism? 439
Hanna E. Morris

25 Public Service Broadcasting in Transition: The Rise of Digital Non-State Public Service Media in Southern Africa 451
Khulekani Ndlovu and Peter Mutanda

26 **A Typology of Digital Leaks as Journalistic Source Materials**   469
Philip Di Salvo

27 **Gig Labour and the Future of Freelance Journalism in South Africa and Zimbabwe**   489
Dumisani Moyo and Allen Munoriyarwa

Index   507

Notes on Contributors

Hamid Abdollahyan is a professor in the Department of Communication in the Faculty of the Social Sciences at the University of Tehran and a visiting scholar at the Faculty of Arts at the University of British Columbia in Canada. In addition to teaching research methods at BA, MA and PhD levels, Adollahyan's main areas of interest include addressing changes that are affecting human communications in the context of historical sociology.

Kwaku O. Antwi is an ICT policy analyst and researcher at the Ghana Institute of Management and Public Administration in Accra, Ghana. He holds an MA from the University of the West Indies, Jamaica. He provides consulting support for government reform projects and international businesses. He is a PhD candidate in Public Administration at the Ghana Institute of Management and Public Administration.

William Asante is a lecturer in the Department of Public Policy and Management of the Simon Diedong Dombo University of Business and Integrated Development Studies (SDD-UBIDS) in Ghana. He has a keen interest in public policy change dynamics, natural resource and environmental politics, public management and sustainable development. He is working in the areas of public service delivery at the local government level and the politics of harnessing Ghana's renewable energy for sustainable development.

Cristian Berrío-Zapata is in the Faculty of Archival Science (Institute of Applied Social Sciences) at the Federal University of Pará (UFPa), Brazil. He is acting as a postdoctoral researcher at the Department of Library and Documentation at Carlos III University (UC3M), Spain, with a project about digital sustainability in the Amazon. He holds a PhD in Information Science from Universidad Estadual Paulista (UNESP), Brazil.

Tanja Bosch is Associate Professor of Media Studies and Production at the Centre for Film and Media Studies at the University of Cape Town. Her monograph, *Social Media and Everyday Life in South Africa* (Routledge, 2021), explores how South Africans use social media apps for personal and group identity formation. Bosch has also published in the area of social media activism and campaigns in South Africa.

Allison J. Brown is a PhD candidate and Associate Instructor in the Media School at Indiana University, Bloomington, US. She is Managing Editor of *Black Camera: An International Film Journal*. She holds a BA in Media and Communication and an MA in Communication Studies, both from the University of the West Indies. Her central focus for research is on technology policy and access issues, particularly, emerging media, changing environments and digital divides. She is also interested in representation of race and gender in film and on television.

Bernadette Califano (PhD) is a professor at the University of Buenos Aires (UBA) in Media and Communication Policies. She holds a PhD in Social Sciences (UBA). She is a member of the National Scientific and Technical Research Council (CONICET), researcher at the National University of Quilmes, Argentina, and former Fulbright Visiting Scholar at University of California San Diego (UCSD) in the US. Her research focuses on media regulation and the political economy of communication, as well as advisory work on communication policies and rights.

Veridiana Domingos Cordeiro is a Postdoc at the Center for Artificial Intelligence at the University of São Paulo, Brazil. Cordeiro holds a BA in Social Sciences; an MS degree in Sociology from the University of São Paulo, Brazil; and a PhD in Sociology from the University of São Paulo. She has also completed graduate work at the University of Chicago. Her research is on the sociology of knowledge, digital sociology and distributed cognition.

Fabio Cozman holds BA and MS degrees in Mechatronic Engineering from the University of São Paulo, Brazil, and a PhD in Robotics from Carnegie Mellon University. He is Professor of Artificial Intelligence at the University of São Paulo and Director of the C4AI—Center of Artificial Intelligence (IBM—São Paulo Foundation). He develops research on knowledge representation, reasoning and probabilistic logics.

Aditya Deshbandhu is Lecturer in Communications and Digital Media Sociology at the University of Exeter. A researcher of video game studies, new media and the digital divide, Deshbandhu examines how people engage with digital artefacts and seeks to understand how these interactions shape everyday lives. Deshbandhu's research has examined social media and Over-the-top (OTT) platforms alongside video games and digital cultures. Deshbandhu is the author of *Gaming Culture(s) in India: Digital Play in Everyday Life* and *the Twenty-First Century in a Hundred Games*.

Philip Di Salvo is a postdoctoral researcher in the School of Humanities and Social Sciences at the University of St. Gallen (HSG) Switzerland. Philip's main research interests are investigative journalism, Internet surveillance, the relationship between journalism and hacking, and black box technologies. At

HSG, Philip is involved in the Human Error Project, dealing with the fallacies of algorithms in reading humans. Previously, he was a Visiting Fellow at the London School of Economics and Political Science (LSE)'s Department of Media and Communications (2021–2022) and he held different research and teaching positions at Università della Svizzera italiana (USI)'s Institute of Media and Journalism (2012–2021).

Denis Dunas (PhD in Philology) is a leading researcher at the Faculty of Journalism, Lomonosov Moscow State University, and an associate professor at the Russian Academy of Education. His research interests include media theory, Russian media studies, anthropology of media and media consumption by youth.

Jessica S. Dunn is an occupational psychologist and a senior lecturer at Nottingham Trent University in the UK. She studied at the University of the West Indies, Jamaica, and the University of Nottingham, UK. Dunn has published in higher education and applied psychology. Her research interests relate to socio-cognitive factors in technology applications and the changing nature of work.

Hopeton S. Dunn is Professor of Communications Policy and Digital Media at the University of Botswana and senior research associate at the School of Communication, University of Johannesburg, South Africa. Dunn is the former Director of the Caribbean School of Media and Communication (CARIMAC) (UWI Jamaica), where he also headed the Mona ICT Policy Centre (MICT). His extensive research spans such areas as technology policy reforms, new media in the Global South, telecommunications for development and broadcasting regulation.

Bianca Fadel is a research fellow in the Centre for International Development at Northumbria University, UK. She is an interdisciplinary academic involved in policy-focused initiatives, with particular interests in community development in the Global South. Her work focuses on local volunteering, as well as on agency and belonging in humanitarian and development settings. As a practitioner, she has previously worked as advisor for humanitarian diplomacy at the Ministry of Foreign Affairs in Brazil. Her work has also involved the implementation of local youth engagement in voluntary projects with the Brazilian Red Cross.

Anna Gladkova is a leading media researcher and the Director of International Affairs Office at the Faculty of Journalism, Lomonosov Moscow State University. She is co-chair of the International Association for Media and Communication Research's (IAMCR's) Digital Divide Working Group. She has published and edited collections on ethnic media, multicultural affairs, digital inequalities and digital divides. Her most recent books include *Digital Inequalities in the Global South* (Palgrave Macmillan, 2020), co-edited with Massimo Ragnedda, and *Ethnic Journalism in the Global South* (Palgrave Macmillan, 2021), co-edited with Sadia Jamil.

Anastasia Gouseti is Lecturer in Digital Education at the University of Hull, UK. Her research interests include the use of digital media in educational settings and the role of new technologies in promoting teaching, learning and collaboration. She has been involved in various funded research projects in the field of educational technologies and has published widely in this area. She is the Principal Investigator for the Erasmus+ DETECT project which focuses on supporting educators with developing critical digital literacies.

Netta Iivari is Professor of Information Systems at the University of Oulu, Finland. She has a background in cultural anthropology as well as in information systems and human-computer interaction. Her research interest concerns understanding and strengthening people's participation in shaping and making their digital futures. Recently, her research has addressed empowerment of children through critical design. Her research is strongly influenced by interpretive and critical research traditions.

Liisa Ilomäki is a researcher at the University of Helsinki, Finland. Her research interests are in learning and teaching with digital technology, changes within school and teaching communities, and knowledge work competencies in education. She has been involved in several projects and activities in technology-enhanced learning, as either principal investigator or a member of a research team.

Deqiang Ji is a professor and Deputy Dean of the Institute for Community with Shared Future, at Communication University of China in Beijing. He has served as the Vice Chair of the International Communication Section of the International Association for Media and Communication Research (IAMCR) since 2016. He has been a Program Council Member of Dialogue of Civilizations Research Institute (Berlin) since 2020. He is also Commissioning Editor of *Global Media and China* (Sage) since 2016, and Editorial Board Member of *Annals of the International Communication Association* (Routledge) since 2020.

Xiaomei Jiang is a media and communication researcher and a PhD candidate at Communication University of China. She has been a media researcher for several years. Her most recent research addresses crucial interfaces between digital platforms, cities and citizen participation.

Sophia Kaitatzi-Whitlock is Professor of Politics and Political Communication at Aristotle University of Thessaloniki, Greece. She holds a PhD in Communication from the University of Westminster, London, and an MA in Communications Policy Studies from City, University London. She has written extensively on European digital policymaking, global and EU technology and cultural policies, the implications of WTO agreements for key media sectors. Kaitatzi-Whitlock is also interested in crisis reporting, the political economy of knowledge, and symbolic goods and the media.

Marianne Kinnula is Associate Professor of Human-Centred Design and Digitalisation at University of Oulu, Finland, as well as the research unit vice-leader of the group INTERACT. Her research is in the fields of information systems and human-computer interaction with inter- and transdisciplinary approaches. Kinnula's interests are in social sustainability of technology in terms of social inclusion, empowerment and ethical stances.

Minna Lakkala is a postdoctoral researcher in the Department of Education at the University of Helsinki, Finland. She specialises in technology-enhanced teaching and learning, knowledge creation pedagogy and competence learning at all educational levels. Her main research interest is in educators' pedagogical expertise in implementing collaborative practices and digital technologies in teaching. One of her projects is 'Argumentative Online Inquiry in Building Students' Knowledge Work Competences' (ARONI).

Floyd Morris is a Caribbean communications researcher and advocate in the field of disability rights and access. He is the Director of the University of the West Indies Centre for Disability Studies (UWICDS). His recent publications include the book *Political Communication Strategies in Post-independence Jamaica, 1972–2006*, as well as an autobiography titled *By Faith, Not by Sight*. Morris, who is blind, served as President of Jamaica's Senate between 2013 and 2016. He was the 2020 recipient of the UWI's Vice Chancellor's Award for Excellence in Public Service. Morris was elected to the United Nations Committee on the Rights of Persons with Disabilities for the term 2021–2025.

Hanna E. Morris (PhD, University of Pennsylvania) is Assistant Professor of Climate Communication at the School of the Environment at the University of Toronto where she researches and teaches interdisciplinary courses on media, culture and the politics of the climate crisis. She is writing a book entitled *Apocalyptic Authoritarianism: Climate Crisis, Media, and Power* and has recently co-edited the book entitled *Climate Change and Journalism: Negotiating Rifts of Time*.

Dumisani Moyo is Executive Dean, Faculty of Humanities at North-West University, South Africa. His research interests include media policy and regulation, and media, politics, culture and technology in Africa. His major works include co-edited books on radio in Africa, media policies in Southern Africa and global reforms in media practice. In 2020 he published the volume *Mediating Xenophobia in Africa: Unpacking Discourses of Migration, Belonging and Othering*. He is a co-editor of the 2021 book *Re-imagining Communication in Africa and the Caribbean*.

Allen Munoriyarwa is a Senior Lecturer in the Department of Media Studies at the University of Botswana. His research interests are in journalism, news production practices, and social media platforms. He has also researched widely on data journalism, big data and digital surveillance.

Graham Murdock is Professor Emeritus of Culture and Economy at Loughborough University. Murdock's own research focuses on the changing organisation and impact of contemporary communication systems. It ranges from studies of institutional structures to research on cultural forms and everyday practices. He is widely known for his work in the critical political economy of culture and communications and for his scholarly explorations of the relations between the organisation of communication systems, the exercise of power and the dynamics of change.

Peter Mutanda is a filmmaker, writer, visual artist and educator. He is a lecturer in the Media Studies Department at the University of Botswana. His creative works in video installations include an award-winning project, 'The Besiegement—Advocating Mental Health'. He is actively engaged in 'new media' productions and in analysing the digital media landscape through creative lenses. Mutanda holds an MA in Theatre and Global Development from the University of Leeds, UK.

Khulekani Ndlovu is a media and communication studies lecturer at the University of Botswana's Media Studies Department. His research interests include critical media studies, journalism and 'post-truthism', youth and media, digital media in the global south and the ethics of mediation. Ndlovu holds a PhD in Media Studies from the University of Cape Town, South Africa.

Alpha Obika is a Caribbean Social Scientist and Policy Analyst located at the Mona Campus of the University of the West Indies (UWI), Jamaica. Obika lectures in new media, digital communication, cultural policy and events management at the Caribbean School of Media and Communication (CARIMAC), UWI. He holds a PhD in Communication Studies from UWI and an MA in Cultural Policy and Management from City, University of London.

Thapelo J. Otlogetswe is Professor of Linguistics and Lexicography at the University of Botswana (UB). His research is in lexical computing and corpus lexicography, with particular reference to the Setswana language. He serves as Deputy Dean, Faculty of Humanities, University of Botswana. He is a recipient of the Presidential Order of Honour, Botswana. Otlogetswe is a member of the African Academy of Languages and African Association of Lexicography and sits on the editorial boards of *Lexikos* and *Marang* journals.

Jo Pierson is Professor of Digital Technologies and Public Values in the Department of Media and Communication Studies at the Vrije Universiteit Brussel (VUB) in Belgium. He is also the Principal Investigator at the SMIT research centre at VUB. He is in charge of the research unit 'Data, Privacy & Empowerment', working in close cooperation with 'imec', the R&D and innovation hub in nanoelectronics and digital technology. He is affiliated with Hasselt University. Pierson's main research interests are in data privacy, digital platforms, algorithms, user innovation and value-based design.

Massimo Ragnedda is Associate Professor of Media and Communication at Northumbria University, Newcastle, UK, and a visiting professor at the Faculty of Journalism, Lomonosov Moscow State University. He is co-chair of the Digital Divide Working Group of the International Association for Media and Communication Research (IAMCR), co-convenor of NINSO (Northumbria

Internet and Society Research Group), co-editor of the Palgrave Studies in Digital Inequalities book series, and ambassador for the Digital Poverty Alliance. He has authored or edited 15 books. His articles appear in numerous peer-reviewed journals, and many of his book chapters are published in English, Spanish, Italian, Portuguese and Russian texts. His most recent book is titled *Enhancing Digital Equity: Connecting the Digital Underclass* (Palgrave, 2020)

Usha Raman is a professor in the Department of Communication, University of Hyderabad, India. Her research interests include digital cultures, science and technology studies, feminist media studies and journalism pedagogy. She is co-founder of FemLab, a feminist futures of work initiative. Before joining the University, she headed the communications department at L V Prasad Eye Institute. She has written for the popular press on topics related to health, technology, women's issues, education and digital culture.

Sheyla Gabriela Alves Ribeiro is a researcher and documentalist at the Federal Rural University of the Amazon (UFRA) in Brazil. Ribeiro was trained in Librarianship at the Faculdades Integradas de Jacarepaguá (FIJ) and holds a BA degree in Information Systems from the Universidade Federal Rural da Amazônia (UFRA). She has conducted graduate research work in Information Science at the Universidade Federal do Pará (UFPA).

Laura Robinson is a professor in the Department of Sociology at Santa Clara University and faculty associate at the Harvard Berkman Klein Center for Internet & Society. She holds a PhD from UCLA, where she held a Mellon Fellowship in Latin American Studies. Robinson's other affiliations include the UC Berkeley Institute for the Study of Societal Issues, the Cornell University Department of Sociology, Department of Sociology at Trinity College Dublin, USC Annenberg Center and the École Normale Supérieure.

Maria Laura Ruiu is Senior Lecturer in Sociology at Northumbria University (UK). Her first PhD in Sociology (University of Sassari, Italy, 2014) focused on community development, whilst her second PhD, in Media and Communication (Northumbria University, 2019), explored media construction of climate change narratives. Her research interests include environmental and media sociology, management and governance of climate change communication, social capital and digital media, new forms of digital vulnerability in times of pandemic, and management of COVID-19 in Italy. She has investigated digital inequalities in the UK and is exploring the Bourdieusian concept of habitus in relation to the combination of technological competencies, environmental awareness and existing socio-economic-cultural backgrounds.

Mahin Sheikh Ansari is a lecturer at Payame Noor University, Tehran, Iran, and Postdoc at Tehran University. Ansari holds a PhD from the Department of Sociology at Payame Noor University of Tehran and also degrees in Sociology from the Islamic Azad University and in Engineering from the Shahid Beheshti University.

Thiago Elert Soares is a development professional with work experience at the United Nations and the Deutsche Gesellschaft für Internationale Zusammenarbeit (GIZ). He holds an MSc degree in Development Studies from the London School of Economics and Political Science (LSE) as a Chevening scholar and an MPP degree from the Hertie School in Berlin as a Helmut-Schmidt scholar.

Julia Stateri is a faculty member at the Institute of Technology and Leadership in São Paulo, Brazil, as well as the Founder and Creative Director at Oficina Lúdica. Stateri holds a PhD in Visual Arts from the Institute of Arts at UNICAMP, an MA in Education, Art and Cultural History from the Universidade Presbiteriana Mackenzie, and a BA in Graphic Design from the Faculty of Communication and Arts at Senac in São Paulo.

Monica Tenaglia holds a doctorate in Information Science from the University of Brasília in Brazil. She lectures at Federal University of Pará (UFPA), Brazil. Her PhD explored the relationship between the military dictatorship archives and truth commissions in Brazil. She is a postdoctoral researcher at the University of Brasília and investigates the training of archivists for the identification, use and access to archives on human rights violations. She has previously worked in a variety of roles as an archivist in England and Brazil, including with the Brazilian National Truth Commission.

Nathalie Van Raemdonck is a PhD candidate at the Vrije Universiteit Brussel (VUB). She is part of the imec-SMIT research group and is affiliated with the Brussels School of Governance (BSoG). She works with the Hannah Arendt Institute on projects concerning online polarisation. Her research interests are disinformation and the influence of platform affordances on group dynamics and information flows.

Elena Vartanova is Professor, Dean and Chair in Media Theory and Economics at the Faculty of Journalism, Lomonosov Moscow State University, Russia. She is also Academician of the Russian Academy of Education and President of the National Association of Mass Media Researchers (NAMMI). Her research focuses on the Russian media system, media economics, media theory, journalism education in Russia, digital inequalities, digital capital and other topics.

Renata Włoch is a Polish sociologist focusing on digital transformation and global studies. She is Chair of Digital Sociology in the Faculty of Sociology at the University of Warsaw, Poland. She is involved in knowledge-exchange with public institutions and business and is co-creator of DELab (Digital Economy Lab) at the University of Warsaw. Włoch is Scientific Director and Coordinator of the project 'Developing Digital Sociology at the UW'.

List of Figures

Fig. 3.1	Economic aspects of social media	42
Fig. 3.2	Social media statistics in Iran 2009 to 2020	55
Fig. 3.3	Social media statistics in Turkey 2009 to 2020	56
Fig. 3.4	Social media statistics in the world 2009 to 2020	56
Fig. 5.1	Expansion of city specific hashtags	81
Fig. 5.2	Coding categories	82
Fig. 9.1	The interactability in a one-to-many isolated & directed Channel	154
Fig. 9.2	The interactability in a one-to-many Channel with discussion	155
Fig. 12.1	Digital inclusion pyramid. (Source: Author construct from the literature)	211
Fig. 13.1	Framework for mapping projects on children's agency and activism through digital technology development. (Source: Figure generated by the authors)	239
Fig. 14.1	Increased interest in gamification in Brazil. (Source: Figure generated using Google Trends (2022))	247
Fig. 14.2	Regional section of searches. (Source: Figure generated using Google Trends (2022))	248
Fig. 14.3	Related searches in 2019. (Source: Figure generated using Google Trends (2022))	249
Fig. 14.4	Related Searches in 2020. (Source: Figure generated using Google Trends (2022))	249
Fig. 14.5	Related searches in 2021. (Source: Figure generated using Google Trends (2022))	250
Fig. 15.1	Critical digital literacies framework—Biblioteca UOC. (Figure generated by the authors)	264
Fig. 15.2	Critical digital literacies (DETECT Project). (Figure generated by the authors)	265
Fig. 17.1	Individuals using the internet and fixed broadband subscriptions per 100 inhabitants in Argentina (2000–2010). Source: Own analysis with data from ITU Database, 2021	312
Fig. 17.2	Fixed internet penetration rates per 100 households by province (2°Q 2020–2°Q 2021). Source: Own analysis, with data from ENACOM	312

List of Tables

Table 3.1	Validity of Scales	44
Table 3.2	Frequency distribution of sample age and location	44
Table 3.3	T-test to evaluate the difference between the mean of grafted bridging social capital in the control and experimental groups	45
Table 3.4	Pearson correlation test between social capital of Facebook users and the intensity of usage	45
Table 3.5	Names of five brands that had the highest growth rates in Iran in June 2014, 2015 and 2016	47
Table 3.6	Names of 5 brands in terms of number of followers in June 2014; Iranians are at the top of the list	47
Table 3.7	Names of the 5 brands with the highest growth rates in June 2014 in Turkey	48
Table 3.8	The names of the 5 brands that are at the top of the list in June 2014, 2015 and January 2016 in terms of the number of followers in Turkey	48
Table 3.9	The 5 brands that have the highest frequency in the world in terms of the number of likes on Facebook in June 2014, 2015 and January 2016, the first rank and February 2022	49
Table 3.10	Comparison between the number of Facebook followers of Iran, the World and Turkey re airlines in the pages in June 2015 and January 2016	50
Table 3.11	An example of some small Iranian businesses on Facebook in June 2014 and 2015	51
Table 3.12	Small Iranian businesses on Facebook, Telegram and Instagram in February 2022	54
Table 3.13	Businesses Active in e-commerce	55
Table 5.1	General city-specific hashtags	80
Table 13.1	Presentation of the analyzed projects	228
Table 13.2	Summary of the results	238
Table 13.3	Guidelines for projects aiming at nurturing children's agency and activism in and through digital technology development	241
Table 18.1	Illustrative examples of changing jobs, work processes and services derived from digital automation and artificial intelligence	332

Table 20.1	World Internet Statistics	366
Table 20.2	African countries—internet access 2022	367
Table 22.1	Overview of different types of remote volunteering engagement	402
Table 22.2	Critical questions towards sustainable digital ecosystems in humanitarian and development work	408
Table 26.1	A summary of the case studies	478

CHAPTER 1

Living Digitally: Mapping the Everyday Contours of a Still-Emerging Data-Driven Era

Hopeton S. Dunn, Massimo Ragnedda, Maria Laura Ruiu, and Laura Robinson

Digital living is about *creating new experiences and new value* by using neural networks and evolving data applications for a wide range of everyday activities. This process occurs within the context of people's lives, as they use newly acquired literacies in a changing cultural milieu. At the heart of digital life are the interlinked technologies of generative artificial intelligence, the internet itself, the world-wide web, global social media platforms, and so-called 'smart' mobile phones.

To consider the latter, anthropologists now contend that for a high proportion of humans, the smart phone is now 'the place where we live'. According to a year-long global study conducted by a team from University College London (UCL), "the smartphone is no longer just a device that we use, it's become the place where we live." According to Daniel Miller, the leader of the study, "...at any point, whether over a meal, a meeting or other shared activity, a person we are with can just disappear, having 'gone home' to their smartphone." (Hern, 2021, np). The UCL study argues further that it is not

H. S. Dunn (✉)
University of Botswana, Gaborone, Botswana

M. Ragnedda • M. L. Ruiu
Northumbria University, Newcastle upon Tyne, UK

L. Robinson
Santa Clara University, Albany, CA, USA

© The Author(s), under exclusive license to Springer Nature Switzerland AG 2024
H. S. Dunn et al. (eds.), *The Palgrave Handbook of Everyday Digital Life*, https://doi.org/10.1007/978-3-031-30438-5_1

unreasonable to consider that "we now live in a placeless world" (Miller et al., 2021, p. 220). Connectivity is enabled anywhere, anytime, by broadband access that, if available, ensures content can be quickly retrieved, stored and managed from remote locations 'in the cloud'.

Digital everyday life, therefore, involves *new ways of operating, seeing and doing things*. The enabling technologies of AI, the internet and their online resources and applications combine with archived digital data-bases and non-broadcast processes to help deliver this experience for the connected. These digital technologies generate, store and process digital pulses of information signals in positive and non-positive states of zeros and ones, to create a seamless world of content, productivity tools and social interactions.

However, well beyond technical definitions, 'the digital' has now acquired the connotation of *a new way of twenty-first Century life*, pre-shadowed by such twentieth century legacy technologies as wired, wireless and mobile systems, satellites, digital fibre and computing. This accumulation of enhanced and interlocking digital applications has accelerated the pace of human interchange and global productivity (Dunn, 2021). 'The Digital', as a concept, has help to transform commerce, manufacturing, governance and society, enabling society to operate at a more agile pace than ever before.

The Internet

While the digital ecology is not confined to internet-based applications, it is its online association that gives this digital world, perhaps, its greatest utility. In this context, understanding the beneficial functions, disruptive role and global gaps of the internet is key to grasping the power and potential of the digital domain.

Daily internet activities are expanding exponentially. Millions of online messages, e-mails and texts are sent, reviewed and uploaded, and hundreds of thousands of hours of content are consumed by users globally. According to Statista, every 60 seconds a total of one million hours of internet content was exchanged by users worldwide (Statista, 2022).

In a global population that has now topped 8 billion, it remains the case that a third of humanity or about 3 billion people, were still left outside of digitally networked communities and remote from the everyday online workstreams that others often take for granted.

At the same time, internet usage continues to grow (ITU, 2022). While questions inevitably linger as to the quality of people's online connectivity and experiences, and about what exactly is being counted as access, it is undeniable that a majority of people globally are engaged in digital life, as their content creation and use of new digital applications continue unabated.

Yet, as we have noted, the digital extends beyond its immediate **human reality**. In contrast to an analogue past, the affordances of digital life have become integrated with a virtual reality existence. Being digital can now mean forging a personal 'avataric' life linked to the *metaverse*, lived concurrently in real and virtual spaces. It can be the building of new networks of remotely located 'friends', and creating the ability to complete work tasks and educational goals using re-imagined or remote intellectual tools. For many, digital everyday life means being in constant contact with messaging on versatile mobile devices, while also making use of evolved VR entertainment and media services. Such digital users also benefit from smart new robotic AI appliances that make domestic chores, work assignments and personal appointments immeasurably quicker and easier to manage.

Digital Communities

To be more meaningful, digital life is often lived in community, through mobile networks or platforms connected to family, work colleagues and strangers with shared interests who we now call 'friends'. New virtual reality tools enable us to reinvent ourselves and our careers in ways that are limited only by our imaginations and resources. We are able to gain access to seemingly limitless sources of information, in a world that is dominated by an abundance of images, voice, text and other forms of readily available big data. We can better manage issues of health, wealth and well-being through access to connected professionals, using dynamic devices that are operated from home, from work or *in-transit*, in an 'anywhere-anytime world' where these locational distinctions are becoming increasingly less relevant.

Yet, the above scenario is more akin to an idealised notion of digital everyday life. The reality is often much more complex and challenging. This book is about the multifaceted nature and human realities of a more nuanced digital life, lived everyday by people of different backgrounds and nationalities, of varied abilities, with differing digital access levels, reflecting relative scarcity or abundance. This version of digital everyday life can mean living with constant internet access deficits, sometimes restricted to a few minutes daily on a mobile device, or none at all. It can mean facing the uncertainty of electrical power outages or spotty internet access from unreliable service providers.

Everyday life in the digital world can mean the risk of toxic social media experiences, such as online hate speech, trolling and revenge porn. It is a world in which computer systems are frequently affected by various forms of cyberattacks, including through ransomware, hacking, surveillance and espionage. It is one in which we wrestle with issues of junk mail, unsolicited propaganda, mis-information and disinformation. It can be a lifeworld that fosters alienation, misogyny, depression, child abuse and even suicide. For many, the promise of an improved life in a digital environment can be a source of frustration, demoralisation and confusion for communities and potential users who are denied its affordances through poverty, or are made into victims by the insensitive policies of some of its providers and the abhorrent conduct of some digital inhabitants.

This Handbook of Everyday Digital Life is about mapping the contours of these diverse digital experiences, as experienced on an individual level, on a community basis, or as a nation, region or continent.

Digital Disruption

Varied forms of digital disruption are happening around the world in virtually all sectors, every day. As we have seen, the decades-old shift from analogue legacy systems to digital and online technology applications encompasses new ways of working, communicating and interacting across disciplines, communities, businesses and boundaries. So pervasive are the everyday changes generated by artificial intelligence systems such as ChatGPT and Bard, that we are at risk of failing to grasp how intensively human civilization is being transformed, for better or worse. This transformation takes place in homes, in educational institutions, in professional careers, in economic and social institutions, and in the financial and banking sectors. It is also felt in popular culture, as well as in the communication and media industries, just to name a few of the areas that are being 'disrupted' by emerging digital and AI innovations.

While the internet is a forum for education, commerce, social interactions and empowerment, it is also a site of cultural and linguistic loss and content imbalance, within various indigenous groups and from remote regions of the world. It is beset, as we have seen repeatedly, with the constant challenge of criminality and misuse, whether through ransomware, identity theft, falsifications of news, creation of deceptive 'deep fakes' images, and promoting commercial forgeries. Digital spaces can be appropriated by political demagogues and military adventurists, and can also be subject to unwarranted controls by authoritarian regimes. Disparities in digital resources and data literacy among users globally can facilitate cultural hegemony and empower military adventurists. The data divide can disproportionately privilege large platform private conglomerates, run by corporate megalomaniacs with deep pockets.

Use of the internet and other digital tools in everyday life is, therefore, not unproblematic. The internet represents a form of globalisation than can be a two-edged sword (Dunn, 1995). However, despite its dysfunctionalities and risks, it has also created vast new opportunities for minorities, engendered countless start-ups, and increased the number of voices that can be heard locally and globally. Online applications have enabled the adoption of new business approaches, including fintech, block chain applications, and analytics in corporate marketing and networking. The widespread use of digitally connected utilities and appliances online, dubbed the Internet of Things (IoT), has enhanced domestic and civic life. At the same time, the rise of new applications in robotics and machine learning is changing the face of industry, military and government administration.

Our electrical grids, water supply systems, urban transport and traffic management services, electoral and voting systems, agricultural and food processing systems, as well as media and entertainment networks all now operate on digital platforms that are managed or delivered digitally. The combined effect of these established or emerging online innovations is to create new everyday experiences, as well as newly imagined domestic lifestyles and professional work environments. In analysing them historically and collectively, it becomes clear that there are many ways to characterise the still emerging digital era.

Alternative Periodisation

Many cultural and development analysts have provided alternative perspectives and classifications of emergent technologies during their phases of interaction with people. In this volume, we have mostly referred to the emergence of a 'Digital Era'. However, in the broader sweep of human history and development analysis, there are other perspectives that can inform our thinking about alternative historical or technology periodisations.

It is clear that classifications of industrial era or periods of human civilization are not mutually exclusive. They are often overlapping or they offer alternative ways of seeing and addressing similar issues and times. In some instances, they focus on the broad sweep of mankind through history, while others seek to characterize the significance of a single event, technology or epoch. Understanding these alternative ways of looking at human and technological interactions helps us to locate and deconstruct the innovations of the present, and to see them as part of a historical continuum.

For example, it was said that we are living in the Fourth Industrial Revolution (4IR), having navigated three previous industrial epochs. In his 2016 book, Schwab invited his readers to "think about the staggering confluence of emerging technology breakthroughs covering wide-ranging fields such as artificial intelligence (AI), robotics, the internet of things (IoT), autonomous vehicles, 3D printing, nanotechnology, biotechnology, materials science, energy storage and quantum computing, to name a few." (Schwab, 2016, p. 1).

According to Schwab, "major technological innovations are on the brink of fuelling momentous change throughout the world, **inevitably so**." (Schwab, 2016, p. 1) In this somewhat techno-determinist conception, Schwab runs the risk of advancing the technological over the social and thereby undermine notions of human agency and its historical role in directing and controlling our futures. Such technology driven approaches can be problematic, especially if they appear primarily to serve the interests of wealthy global elites in a renewed hegemonic process of what has been variously called data colonialism and 'globalization from above' (Dunn, 2012, p. 157).

However, while 4IR presents us with its vision of the present era, there are yet other ways of understanding these moments in time.

The first decades of the twenty-first century have also been described as reflecting a **platform society**, (Van Dijck et al., 2018) given the prevalence of social media platforms that are used extensively among certain demographic groups globally. Of the over 100 online platforms that are said to be in existence in 2022, the 30 largest such sites support at least 100 million active users per month (Statista, 2022). The top four western social media platforms: Facebook, YouTube, WhatsApp and Instagram, account for an average of 2 billion active user per month. Comparable Chinese-owned digital social media platforms, such as TikTok, Weibo and WeChat are also growing at a rapid rate. The indication here is that a large part of human communication and digital interactions now take place on dedicated digital platforms. In the West, these platforms are less mediated and more unregulated than traditional media and communication channels, with myriad social implications and concerns.

One such concern is the virtual impunity conferred on US based platforms by Section 230 of the US Communication Decency Act. Under Section 230 of the Act, platforms like Facebook, Instagram, Twitter and YouTube enjoy immunity from prosecution for so-called 'third party' content. This means that they are granted protections in the US against legal liability for any content that users post on their websites. The Act, while requiring the platforms to police their own content, does not require them to remove any offensive or hateful posts, and it protects them from legal liability if they choose not to.

According to Smith and Van Alstyne of the Harvard Business Review (August, 2021, np), while social media do provide a plethora of positive social and societal benefits, the world has also learned about "how much social devastation these platforms can cause", forcing us to "confront previously unimaginable questions about accountability." Continuing, these writers pointedly ask a number of relevant questions: "to what degree should Facebook be held accountable for the [US 2021] Capitol riots, much of the planning for which occurred on their platform? To what degree should Twitter be held accountable for enabling terrorist recruitment? How much responsibility should Backpage and Pornhub bear for facilitating the sexual exploitation of children? What about other social media platforms that have profited from the illicit sale of pharmaceuticals, assault weapons and endangered wildlife?" (Smith & Van Alstyne, 2021, np).

Smith and Van Alstyne also argue that Section 230 of this 1996 law is no longer fit for purpose. "Let's just say that we have learned a lot since 1996." Despite the many positive benefits of social media, they conclude that, "today, there is a growing consensus that we need to update Section 230" in order to establish some liability and to offer the common law standard of "a duty of care" to not cause harm. (Smith & Van Alstyne, 2021, np). This is especially the case as younger users are the most active on these platforms, which many find to be an appealing way to interact with and understand the world in which they inhabit as digital natives.

Other analysts have claimed that we are living in the **Era of Amazon and Ali Baba** (Wu & Gereffi, 2019), where virtually everything can be commodified and marketed online: a world in which we should just shut up and shop, ultimately to the benefit of foreign mega-corporations. We have also seen writers, such as Brynjolfsson and McAfee, speak of the present era as **"the second machine age"**, with digital software and mobile devices of the present succeeding the heavy industrial equipment of factory and transport mechanizations of past times. (Bryjolfsson & McAfee, 2014)

Still others, such as the writers of one of UNESCO's World Reports, speak about the creation and existence of a "**knowledge society**", building on the outcomes of the 2003 and 2005 phases of the World Summit of the Information Society (WSIS). In that 2005 UNESCO report, called 'Towards Knowledge Societies', the distinction is made between knowledge societies and the information society. It explains that "[W]hile the **information society** is based on technological breakthroughs, knowledge societies encompass broader social, ethical and political dimensions." (UNESCO, 2005, np)

The UNESCO Report cogently argues that knowledge can serve as a new springboard for development in the countries of the South. It also presents a detailed analysis of the factors blocking the access of many countries to the opportunities offered by information and communication technologies, especially the growing digital divide and restrictions on freedom of expression in many jurisdictions. It is tempting to think that the digital AI society, with its vast information endowments and deficits, is at core, a knowledge society. But only for some. The reality is that although the digital and knowledge domains may intersect, in certain global contexts their combined affordances are far from epoch-making.

Digital Transitioning and Sharing

As the preceding discussion has made clear, the current era can mean different things to different people. However, dissecting the global digital experience so far can identify some typical and uncontested features.

In their 2019 book 'Transitioning to a Digital World', Malter and Rindfleisch observed that the digital world was still in its early stages. They note that "we live in a world that is increasingly digital, but not yet completely digital, which makes it quite interesting. The transition from the pre-digital age, just a few short years ago, to a new digital reality provides fertile ground for scholars to study a landscape that is shifting before our eyes." They observe further that users are "participant-observers in this great transformation, both recording changes as they occur while contributing to new waves of change." For these authors, the next generation of not-yet-imagined digital technology and software applications "will further transform markets, society, and everyday life." (Malter & Rindfleisch, 2019, pp. 1–2)

An opportunity for *sharing* is deemed by some to be one of the defining features of living digitally. The introduction of 'Wikimedia' applications that enable multiple users to share and make concurrent inputs, has seen the rise of such landmark sharing innovations as Wikipedia, Wiktionary and Google Docs. An extension of this emergent sharing culture is reflected in the concept of 'crowd-sourcing', or creating shared value from multiple contributors online.

The neighbouring notion of crowd-funding enables financial and other resource inputs to be gathered from a diversity of sources, online.

Crowd-funding has been widely used to finance causes deemed by contributors as worthy of support, such as innovative start-ups around the world. Zaffiro and Mourgis (2018) argue that this collective way of resource accumulation is a major achievement of the digital era. "The creation of a sharing movement …could be an instrument to revitalize and harness the less market-oriented transformative power of the sharing economy for building social solidarity, democracy and sustainability." (Zaffiro & Mourgis, 2018, p. 26). While calling for more transparent regulation to govern online crowdsourcing transactions, Zaffiro and Mourgis suggest that in future, "it is likely that the most successful companies will operate based on crowd solutions." (Zaffiro & Mourgis, 2018, p. 26)

Caution and Contestation

Not everyone sees a silver lining in the accelerated pace of technology growth and datafication globally. Writing in 1992, at the very dawn of what has become our contemporary digital world, US scholar Neil Postman sounded a word of caution about embracing everything technological. Postman observed that the world was, at that time, entering what he called a 'technopoly'. He defines a technopoly as a totalitarian version of a technocracy, where technology reigns supreme over all other aspects of life. In a technopoly, he argues, efficiency is the primary goal of all labor, technical calculations are superior to human judgment, and anything that cannot be measured is either ignored or devalued. Precision and objectivity are valued above all else.

In criticizing 'technopolies' Postman argued that the frequent focus on measurement and data over feeling and subjectivity destroys everything that makes us human. In his book *Technopoly: The Surrender of Culture to Technology*, he contends that any hyper-focus on technology creates a culture without moral foundations. He sees science as becoming the new moral authority in this type of society, but argues that science is designed to be objective, not to form the basis of what is right or wrong. Postman feared for the future of the American society as one that was already being affected by an inundation of what he saw as unmediated information, presented without context: information that serves no purpose. That information glut, he writes, may become dangerous to societies and cultures that focus predominantly on technology and less on human agency (Postman, 1993).

A contrasting viewpoint postulates that digital technology is in fact an enabler of traditional culture, providing a platform for the globalization of varied cultural practices and for preserving some indigenous ways of life. While there is doubtless merit in much of Postman's analysis, the digital era has shown that we can embrace both caution and the opportunity. While not debunking moderation in how we approach culture and technology, Barnabas and Bodunrin (2021), for example, demonstrate how digital tools can empower and support exponents of traditional culture. They cite the use of digital media and new forms of entertainment by some young members of the traditional

San people of South Africa's Northern Cape province, to keep themselves engaged.

> The bedroom studio has become their digital classroom, a space to collectively experience and access technology and its requisite skills. Software and digital sharing platforms have allowed for the global democratization of music-making. What we are witnessing with [indigenous] hip hop artists in Platfontein is their entry into this exciting space. It is a space in which they find belonging to the imagined communities of hip hoppers across the globe, a space of a new and evolving literacy, a platform through which to voice their everyday struggles. (Barnabas & Bodunrin, 2021, p. 169)

Other perspectives on digital everyday life speak to its implication for vulnerable sections of the human population, including ethnic minorities, children, disadvantaged women, sexual minorities and persons with disabilities. Such issues of intersectionality, digital literacy and the digital divide have become important challenges in global online environments (Ragnedda & Ruiu, 2020). In contributing to on-going initiatives towards a deeper understanding of these digital era challenges, Ignatow and Robinson employed a Bourdieusian conceptual framework to help unravel how differently situated individuals relate to IT resources. They argue that "disparities in the level of Internet skills originate in inequalities of access, but are mediated by orientations that can only be understood in relation to total life contexts." (Ignatow & Robinson, 2017, pp. 7–8)

In their analysis, digital literacy provides a distinct advantage to varied users of the internet. They found that "skills related to finding and assessing information constitute one of the building blocks of information literacy. Mastery of digital skills is a precondition for the acquisition of informational advantage. Not only do more skilled Internet users reap benefits by obtaining desired information with less effort, but they also use the Internet in a more flexible and versatile manner than less-skilled users." (Ignatow & Robinson, 2017, pp. 7–8). In addressing one of the factors in a lack of adequate digital skills and resources in some societies, Ignatow and Robinson conclude that the internet ecosystem can reinforce pre-existing social inequalities.

DIGITAL ACCESS AND NATIONAL DEVELOPMENT

As we have seen, an absence of digital access and information literacy can be among the greatest impediments to national economic development and personal aspirations within our twenty-first century digital lifeworld. In its special briefing on internet access, the World Bank endorses this perspective as it observed that broadband (or high-speed internet access) is not a luxury, but a basic necessity for economic and human development in both developed and developing countries.

It is a powerful tool for the delivery of essential services such as education and healthcare, offers increased opportunities for women's empowerment and environmental sustainability, and contributes to enhanced government transparency and accountability. It also helps foster the social development of communities, including within the broader global context. The challenge is to expand broadband access to all. Only about 35 percent of the population in developing countries has access to the Internet (versus about 80 percent in advanced economies). Broadband has also become a foundation for smart infrastructure (e.g. Intelligent Transport Systems and Smart Electric grids) that is facilitated by new wireless technologies. It can help create jobs in information and communication technology (ICT), engineering and other sectors, as well as help catalyze job skills development, an important avenue toward poverty reduction and shared prosperity. (World Bank, 2018, np)

The Bank indicates further that broadband can help expand the reach of task-based work through online outsourcing platforms, which are projected to provide millions of jobs and billions of dollars in revenue over the coming years. "Raising Internet penetration to 75 per cent of the population in all developing countries (from the current level of approximately 35 per cent) would add as much as US$2 trillion to their collective gross domestic product (GDP) and create more than 140 million jobs around the world". (World Bank, 2018, np)

Other strategic development organizations have underlined the universal development benefit of affordable digital access. The global Internet Society (ISOC) states that the internet has immense potential to improve the quality of education, which it regards as one of the pillars of sustainable development. Over many years ISOC has recommended ways in which policymakers can unlock that potential of ICTs through an enabling framework for access to the internet. In that regards, ISOC has identified five development priorities for policymakers: expanding infrastructure and access, clarifying and improving government's vision and ICT policy, increasing inclusion, building capacity through enhanced training and literacy, and focusing on wholesome content and lower-cost devices and services. (ISOC, 2017). This analysis advocates an integrated approach, which is consistent with the findings of a study by Ruiu and Ragnedda, which concluded that "digital inequalities cannot be tackled by considering access and competence separately. By contrast, the adoption of measures that synthesise the two dimensions might help simplify policy-making's initiatives to tackle digital inequalities." (Ruiu & Ragnedda, 2020, p. 1)

These strategies represent key considerations to help unlock sustainable economic development in global digital contexts. Operationally, ISOC maintains that the best results are likely to be achieved through cooperation among the key stakeholders, including government, internet business specialists, technical experts, and development sector specialists such as educators and educational administrators.

If large sections of the global population are not to be left behind, credible transformational processes must include strategies for greater access by low-income groups, women and especially the girl child, as well as rural citizens and persons with disabilities. For a wider community of beneficiaries of the digital endowments of our era, specific policy measures are required. This should involve more widespread low-cost access to the internet and the provision of more stable electricity supplies in many underserved countries of the world. The process also requires the deployment of more extensive training programmes in digital literacy, data analytics, technology innovation and digital enterprise. These are essential in the search for inclusive digital futures among people worldwide.

FEATURES OF THE HANDBOOK

In this opening chapter, we have sought to shine a light on the many and varied features, issues and facets of 'living digitally'. It is part of a volume that attempts to deepen our understanding of the impacts, scenarios, concepts and contestations inherent in the still emerging digital era and its everyday life. It is written against the backdrop of the over two-year long Covid 19 pandemic that inescapably figures in many of the contextual analyses and empirical studies that make up the content of the book. The additional context is the exponential rise of generative artificial intelligence as a major part of the on-going techno-global transformation. The book's 27 chapters explore the key innovations and lifestyles that underpin human and technology aspects of our emerging Twenty First century societies. It offers various angles and approaches, delivered within an extensive yet thematically integrated compendium.

Chapter contributions come from a wide range of geographical, conceptual, gender and economic perspectives. The book is interdisciplinary in nature, with chapters from scholars in applied science, the humanities, the social sciences, professional disciplines and practical occupational pursuits.

It is edited by a diverse team drawn from different regions of the world, with varied research emphases, perspectives and specialisations. Together, these research interests encompass new media technologies, digital inclusion, technology divides, technology history, educational equity, climate change, digital sociology, digital humanities, telecommunications policy and broadcasting.

BOOK STRUCTURE AND CHAPTER SUMMARIES

The book is structured into five sections, each bringing together chapters that are broadly linked thematically, and which explore crucial aspects of the digitalisation of everyday life. These include the transformation of knowledge, social life and urban spaces; digital affordances and contestations; inclusion-related challenges, especially as experienced by the most vulnerable users; digital consumption, culture and work practices and impacts of digital technologies on media and journalism practice. In the text that follows, we provide overviews of the five sections of the book and synopses of the chapters within them.

Section 1: Social Media and Digital Lifeworlds

The cognitive and special issues under discussion in this section seek to tackle the meaning of digital governance and participation. The chapters reflect the pervasive character of society's digital everyday life by exploring both challenges and opportunities within this evolving domain. The Covid 19 pandemic often forms the catalyst for technological acceleration in these digital lifeworlds. The pandemic can, therefore, be regarded as a circumstantial factor in the more rapid digitalisation of almost every aspect of everyday life. The emphasis in these chapters is on the effects of various forms of digital technology, including artificial intelligence, on human processes of knowing, doing and socialising.

More specifically, in Chap. 2, Cordeiro and Cozman used a sociological lens to examine the integration of artificial intelligence into modern systems and societies, emphasising the importance of reflecting on the incorporation of such innovations into daily practice. This chapter connects with the other chapters in this section by underscoring the linked relationships between technologies and everyday activities. This also contributes to shaping of digital contexts and how individuals socialise and live in public spaces.

In Chap. 3, Hamid Abdollahyan and Mahin Sheik Hansari discuss the *Economic Aspects of Social Media: Facebook's Potential for Generating Business in Iran*. They analyse the insufficiently appreciated affordances of social media in facilitating business-generating activities in that country. This chapter underlines the importance of Facebook, not just as a casual interactive platform, but also as a bridging capital in both education and socialization in Iran.

Building on these emerging digital knowledge systems, the section then focuses on the digital processes at play in urban settings in India, South Africa and China.

In its Chap. 4, Raman and Deshbandhu offer an in-depth analysis of the digital shaping of a city, by exploring the growth of Hyderabad, India's "second electronic city", in order to accommodate a new digital economy. The chapter deals with the dilemmas that digitalising of urban contexts can pose due to power shifts away from traditional economic and cultural centres and a new dependence of inhabitants on networked devices and services. The chapter highlights the effects of such reshaping of the city on ways of working, learning, entertaining, and socialising.

Chapter 5 also addresses digital urban transformation by taking a bottom-up approach to investigating how Instagram users map their daily lives through photo-sharing apps. These narratives analysed by Tanja Bosch in discussing space and place in Johannesburg, contribute to the evolution of digital urban storytelling. These narratives also reveal specific discourses of South Africa's black middle class, while making social inequalities invisible.

Chapter 6 draws further on the urban digitalisation context while also referencing the Covid 19 pandemic responses and its related techno-acceleration role. Authors Ji and Jiang address the mapping of the digital fabric of urban contexts in China. They emphasise the profound social transformation and risks related to such digitalisation processes. The example of the introduction of Site Codes, as analysed in this chapter, poses crucial questions about the purpose and governance of these technologies, which are not only overseen by governments, but also managed by tech companies.

Section 2: Digital Affordances and Contestations

The five chapters in Sect. 2 deal with affordances and contestations of digital life. They highlights many of the new possibilities and offerings of a digital environment, while providing systemic critiques of inappropriate technology deployments and some adverse consequences of the human technology interface.

The Section begins with a compelling analysis by Graham Murdock, titled "Hidden Abodes: Digital Lives and Distant Others". As Chap. 7, the author spells out the stark environmental challenges and options faced by humanity and our problematic relationships with some of the related dire consequences of digital technologies. Murdock contends that humanity must choose between embarking on a fundamental transformation toward a sustainable future or one that allows the negative and adverse effects of mindless exploitation of the natural environment and digital tools to doom our destiny.

The critique continues in Chap. 8 in which Renata Wloch identifies multiple ways in which the adoption of digital technologies has affected the new digital economy. The chapter, titled, *The Din and Stealth of the Digital Revolution*, analyses how the digital revolution is both directly and indirectly supporting and disrupting its constituent parts, whether as households or businesses. Wloch's chapter discusses the impact of digital technologies on the labour market and how this, in turn, affects the education system. It tracks the new skills that will become in-demand competences over the next few years, as many jobs are stripped of their security of tenure. It examines how people socialise and interact in these new conditions.

Chapter 9, by Van Raemdonck and Pierson, discusses '*Contentious Content on Messaging Apps*', in seeking to actualise social affordances for normative processes on the 'Telegram' platform. The chapter develops a socio-technical taxonomy of group dynamics for digital platforms, argues that Telegram's social affordances provide insights into how the platform offers users the possibilities to influence the normative process within networked publics. Based on these findings, the authors suggest that future research could investigate which affordances are most impactful in the self-moderation of users on the platform.

In Chap. 10, Sophia Kaitatzi-Whitlock offers '*Glimpses of the Greek 'Me Too' Movement on Facebook*'. The chapter provides insights into interactions and posts among 20 Facebook users, as sparked by two pivotal 'MeToo' rape cases, and assesses the respective posted content relating to gender violence and society. The Facebook posts enabled an assessment of online reactions to these cases and crises. Kaitatzi-Whitlock discusses them in terms of their symbolic impacts and potential benefits as influencers in the struggle for gender equity in Greek society.

In Chap. 11, Allison Brown exposes the harm associated with *non-consensual sharing* of intimate images online. She does so by critically reflecting on the violation and abuse that can arise from the malicious use of digital communication technologies in intimate relationships. In line with the contents of key parts of this Section, this chapter focuses on those who are subject to the wider risks and inequalities that vulnerable groups, such as women, often face in their everyday digital lives.

Section 3: Digital Divides and Inclusion Strategies

The six chapters in this third section of the book delve into the issue of digital exclusion and limitations in access. The section documents the experiences of specific categories of users with digital technologies, and discusses the efforts to bridge divides and promote inclusion. Its scope includes developing frameworks to educate children on how to use digital technologies in meaningful ways, improving the inclusion of people with disabilities, and addressing digital inequalities in specific national contexts. The section provides context-specific recommendations, policies, and frameworks that can support policymaking to tackle digital inequalities and ensure more meaningful use of technologies by the most vulnerable users.

In Chap. 12, Antwi and Asante reflect on both the first and second levels of the digital divide, focusing on gaps in household internet access and digital data literacy, aggravated by the Covid 19 pandemic. Referring to the Ghana context, this chapter emphasises that digitalisation has created disparities that enlargen the risk of leaving people behind. It argues that comprehensive policy interventions are needed to address challenges of access, affordability, knowledge, and capacity.

In Chap. 13, Iivari and Kinnula discuss theories on the agency and activism of children and explore a set of digital technology projects that they organised with children, aged 7 to 16. The project outcomes emphasise the need to shift the debate on children's use of digital technologies and the nurturing role that society should play in orienting the use of technologies for meaningful purposes. The authors propose a framework to facilitate civic engagement education to nurture children's agency and activism in and through digital technology development.

In Chap. 14, Julia Stateri further analyses the processes of digitalisation of learning practices by problematising the processes of gamification in education. She discusses inclusion-related issues, especially in the context of distance learning and other adaptations imposed by the problematic handling of the

Covid 19 pandemic in Brazil. This chapter deals with the effects of neglecting intersectionality issues of marginalised groups when adopting collaborative learning and teaching methods.

Directly connected to the education issues raised in previous chapters, Chap. 15, by Gousetti, Ilomäki and Lakkala, reflect on the differentiated effects of technology use on everyday teaching and learning. The authors discuss the need to frame critical digital literacy through a multidimensional approach. The role of policymaking is further emphasised in terms of promoting digital competencies which are not merely based on basic technical skills. Policymakers are urged to develop more comprehensive strategies to address the complexity of learning and teaching practices in a digital era. In this regard, the authors propose a critical digital literacy framework that adopts a diverse competence-oriented approach, based on the proactive participation of educators and learners.

Chapter 16 continues the focus on vulnerable users of evolving technologies. Floyd Morris discusses the benefits of digital assistive technologies for people with disabilities, and makes five recommendations consistent with the UN Convention on the Rights of Persons with Disabilities. The chapter calls for greater sensitivity to the needs of persons with disabilities, including greater attention to universal design and to the need for wider access to the rapidly changing digital applications in assistive devices.

Digital inequalities are also the focus of Chap. 17, in which Califano reviews public interventions to address digital interventions during the Covid 19 pandemic in the specific context of Argentina. The chapter highlights how public interventions must address the effects of technological acceleration imposed by eventualities such as pandemic restrictions that disrupt traditional systems of work, education, domestic lives, and communication practices.

Section 4: Work, Culture and Digital Consumption

Section 4 deals with digital practices related to data consumption, new work practices, and the impact of digital technologies on culture. It discusses the ongoing transformation in the work environment and foregrounds the need for an adaptive psychology in coping with change. The challenge of spreading misinformation and the mitigating role of ICTs in preserving and recovering valued linguistic and cultural assets are also highlighted. The section explores some new strategic challenges in humanitarian aid provision, as well as how failing to regulate the transformation process can lead to inefficiency, misinformation and exclusion.

In Chap. 18, Dunn and Dunn critically examine the implications of a decisive shift towards digital and AI applications in work practices. They discuss the implication of these changes for organisational learning and for cognitive, psychosocial, and affective behaviours. The chapter refers to the pandemic as a trigger for the technological acceleration and digitalisation of work methods, practices which could become the new normal. Pre- and intra-pandemic developments are examined in terms of changes in organisational efficiency, working culture and community responses to social and industrial problems.

In Chap. 19, Berrío-Zapata, Tenaglia, and Alves Ribeiro explore the information access factors that influence behaviours and cultural change among the indigenous people in Brazil's Amazon. The limits imposed by access to the online arena have caused the spread of misinformation during the COVID-19 pandemic, including the proliferation of conspiracy theories. The chapter argues that such misinformation highlights the role played by a lack of digital tools for correcting and filtering vital information, practices that could change the way users perceive problems and react to them.

In Chap. 20, Otlogetswe analyses the role of ICTs and digitalisation in regenerating African languages and cultures. The author examines the risks for minority languages that come with the digitalisation and globalisation processes. These risks are primarily represented by the potential extinction of certain linguistic and cultural traits. However, the use of digital tools such as speech-to-text-to-speech translation technologies, digital spellcheckers, and mobile dictionaries can mitigate the cultural loss and lower the risk of marginalisation that has shifted from the offline to the online arena.

Continuing in the cultural sector, Obika explores the resilience of the Caribbean creative environment to adapt to changes imposed on one of the region's primary cultural events by the Covid 19 pandemic. In Chap. 21, he discusses the eventual success of temporarily shifting Trinidad and Tobago's annual Carnival to an online mode, despite some initial resistance. This chapter speaks to an inherent versatility in promoting new digital forms of cultural consumption and global reach, despite resistance by some traditional stakeholders.

Directly connected to the topic of resilience and adaptation, Fadel and Soares conclude this section by critically assessing the role of digital technologies in reforming voluntary work and what the authors describe as 'digital humanitarianism'. Chapter 22 thus examines the acceleration of many forms of humanitarian assistance to online networks. However, despite the benefits of greater flexibility and multiple forms of engagement, the authors conclude with a call to address the inequalities and exclusion often caused by digitalisation.

Section 5: New Media and Digital Journalism

The final section of the book turns the spotlight on one of the professional disciplines whose everyday practices have been among those most affected by the emergence of digital technologies. Section 5 focuses on Media and Journalism, with the rise of new infrastructures of digital communication, as well as new risks to content credibility and accuracy. The construction of alternative narratives is the common ground of these chapters. They analyse varied understandings of the rationale and processes through which digital and citizen journalism have changed the profession and media practices overall.

Opening this Section with Chap. 23, Vartanova, Gladkova and Dunas focus on the rise of de-institutionalization and de-professionalisation in the field of digital journalism with specific attention to the Russian context. The chapter emphasises the necessity to reconcile the variety of conceptualisations of digital journalism by focusing on increased participation and the value of personal agency.

In Chap. 24, Hanna Morris foregrounds climate journalism in the US by exploring Climate Newsletters as a key outlet for environmental journalism. This form of media outlet is analysed in light of its power to be counter-hegemonic and to contrast with the mainstream narrative that, she argues, privileges sensational frames and neglects environmental justice.

Alternative narratives and new media channels are also the focus of Chap. 25, in which Ndlovu and Mutanda explore the rise of digital non-state public-service media in Southern Africa. In circumstances where public service media have traditionally been state-owned, the authors contend that the resulting state narratives have failed to address issues of inclusiveness and egalitarianism in post-colonial societies. The chapter discusses the rise in digital non-state outlets as a way of meeting the need for more diverse and credible public service content. It draws on the experience in four Southern African countries to demonstrate this pattern, while reflecting on the global implications.

The analysis of alternative digital journalism remains the focus in Chap. 26 that follows. Di Salvo investigates the role of information leaks and whistle-blowers in informing digital journalism. This emerging journalistic trajectory is facilitated by new digital practices and the multiplicity of informants emerging in this scenario, beyond traditional sources. By creating typologies of different expressions of digital leaks, Di Salvo shows how leaks have become an integral component of present-day online journalism.

In the final chapter of the book, Moyo and Munoriyarwa analyse new frontiers in freelance journalism, and look to reforms in the future. They discuss the rise of gig labour as part of a global trend in informal occupational pursuits that are facilitated by a digital environment. Drawing on interviews with practising freelance journalists in South Africa and Zimbabwe, the chapter explores the implications of digital technologies for the future of freelance journalism and discusses the reality and challenges of what they term 'journalistic nomadism'.

Overall, the 27 Chapters of this handbook bring together close to 50 contributors and co-authors, combining their knowledge and expertise from across the globe. In common, the chapters address how the rise of new digital technologies and AI have changed some of the most fundamental aspects of our daily domestic and professional lives. In tracking these changes, and in mapping their manifestations and implications for society, the book begins to open up new vistas in understanding the human side of present and future digital applications, in a wide range of sectors globally.

This handbook provides diverse scholarly resource for established and emerging researchers, as well as offering a key data source for graduate and undergraduate students in many disciplines. In sharing insights into everyday lived experiences, the book also creates a point of reference for ICT policymaking, whilst implicitly suggesting future research directions in the field.

References

Barnabas, S.B. and Bodunrin I. (2021). Indigenous Hip Hop: Digital media Practices Among Youth of the South African San People, in Dunn H. S., Moyo D., Lesitaokana W. and Barnabas S.B. (Eds), Reimagining Communication in Africa and the Caribbean: Global South Issues in Media, Culture and Technology, Palgrave Macmillan, London.

Bryjolfsson E. and McAfee A. (2014). The Second Machine Age: Work, progress and Prosperity in a Time of Brilliant Technologies, Norton, New York.

Dunn, H.S. (2021). Globalisation from Within: Enhancing Digital Productivity and Technology Transformation in the South, in Dunn H., Moyo, D., Lesitaokana W. and Barnabas, S. Re-imagining Communication in Africa and the Caribbean: Global South Issues in Media, Culture and Technology, Palgrave Macmillan, London.

Dunn H.S. (2012). Ringtones of Opportunity: Policy, Technology and Access in Caribbean Communication. Ian Randle Publishers, Kingston and Miami.

Dunn, H. S. (1995). Globalization, Communication and Caribbean Identity, St Martin's Press, New York.

Hern, A. (2021). Smartphone is now 'the place where we live', anthropologists say. The Guardian Newspaper, May 10, 2021.

Internet Society (2017). Policy Paper 20—Internet Access and Education: Key considerations for policy makers, ISOC. https://www.internetsociety.org/resources/doc/2017/internet-access-and-education/.

Ignatow G. and Robinson L. (2017). Pierre Bourdieu: Theorizing the Digital. Information, Communication and Society 20 (7) 1–7, March 2017. https://www.researchgate.net/publication/315325169_Pierre_Bourdieu_theorizing_the_digital.

International Telecommunications Union (ITU) (2022). Measuring Digital Development: Facts and Figures, ITU Development Division, Geneva.

Malter A. and Rindfleisch A. (2019). Transitioning to a Digital World. In Marketing in a Digital World, pp. 1–11, Emerald, United Kingdom. https://www.researchgate.net/publication/335589004_Transitioning_to_a_Digital_World [accessed Nov 29 2022].

Miller D., Abed Rabho L., Awondo P., de Vries M., Duque M., Garvey P., Haapio-Kirk L., Hawkins C., Otaegui A., Walton S., and Wang, X. (2021). The Global Smartphone: Beyond a Youth Technology, UCL Press, May 6, 2021.

Postman, N (1993). Technopoly: The Surrender of Culture to Technology, Vintage Books, New York.

Ragnedda, M, and Ruiu M.L. (2020). Digital Capital: A Bourdieusian approach to Digital Divide, Emerald Publishing.

Ruiu, M.L. and Ragnedda M. (2020). Digital Capital and Online Activities: An Empirical Analysis of the Second Level of Digital Divide. First Monday, 25 (7).

Schwab, K. (2016). The Fourth Industrial Revolution, Penguin Books, London.

Smith, M.D. and Van Alstyne M. (2021). It's Time to Update Section 230. Harvard Business Review, August 12, 2021, HBR, Boston.

Statista (2022). User-generated Internet Content per Minute 2022. https://www.statista.com/topics/1716/user-generated-content/#topicHeader__wrapper.

UNESCO (2005). Towards Knowledge Societies: UNESCO World Report, Paris.

Universidade Estadual de Campinas. (2020). *Unicamp inicia empréstimo de equipamentos para atividades não presenciais durante quarentena.* https://www.unicamp.br/unicamp/noticias/2020/04/06/unicamp-inicia-emprestimo-de-equipamentos-paraatividades-nao-presenciais

Universidade Federal do Rio Grande do Sul. (2020). *Pesquisa da UFRGS revela impacto das desigualdades de gênero e raça no mundo acadêmico durante a pandemia.* https://www.ufrgs.br/coronavirus/base/pesquisa-da-ufrgs-revela-impacto-dasdesigualdades-de-genero-e-raca-no-mundo-academico-durante-a-pandemia/.

Van Dijck, J., deWaal, M. and Poell T. (2018). The Platform Society: Public Values in a Connective World, Oxford University Press, Oxford.

World Bank (2018). Brief: Connecting for Inclusion—Broadband Access for All, World Bank.org, Washington DC. https://www.worldbank.org/en/topic/digitaldevelopment/brief/connecting-for-inclusion-broadband-access-for-all.

Wu X. and Gereffi G., (2019). Amazon and Alibaba: Internet Governance, Business Models and Internationalization Strategies, chapter 14 (np), in Piscitello, L., Van Tuldar R. and Verbeke, A. International Business in the Information and Digital Age. Dukumen.pub.

Zaffiro, G and Mourgis, I. (2018). How Digital Life Changes our Personal Economy—A Market Analysis. *Journal of Innovation Management* 6(1): 13–31. https://www.researchgate.net/publication/325059362_How_Digital_Life_Changes_our_Personal_Economy_-_A_Market_Analysis [accessed Nov 29 2022].

PART I

Social Media and Digital Lifeworlds

CHAPTER 2

Artificial Intelligence and Everyday Knowledge

Veridiana Domingos Cordeiro and Fabio Cozman

INTRODUCTION

Artificial intelligence is not a strange term for us anymore. It is not a mere scientific or engineering issue as a few decades ago. Artificial intelligence can no longer be treated as an independent object of social life since it has flooded every corner of contemporary society. As we become more dependent on the digital affordances of the world, AI is increasingly being integrated into the everyday life of contemporary societies. It has completely changed how we interact, purchase, and consume culture. Behind these multiple daily practices, AI has increasingly changed how we acquire, produce, and interact with knowledge. Even though artificial intelligence was originally crafted inside the scientific environment, it is in daily life that artificial intelligence has made (and is making) deeper impact on how we deal with knowledge.

This chapter discusses how artificial intelligence is changing everyday socio-epistemic relations. By 'everyday', we mean social relations established in everyday life that involve non-scientific knowledge. And, by 'socio-epistemic relations', we mean the relation between subject(s), knowledge, and object(s). Many artificial intelligence applications are detached from social life, such as the ones for sorting out rotten coffee beans. However, in this chapter, we lean toward discussing the impact of artificial intelligence applications embedded in social life and its consequences. When dealing with such an issue, we can elaborate on the biases, mediation, enhancements, and replacements that artificial intelligence may engender throughout social life.

V. D. Cordeiro (✉) • F. Cozman
University of Sao Paulo/Center for Artificial Intelligence (C4AI), Sao Paulo, Brazil
e-mail: veridiana.cordeiro@usp.br; fgcozman@usp.br

© The Author(s), under exclusive license to Springer Nature
Switzerland AG 2024
H. S. Dunn et al. (eds.), *The Palgrave Handbook of Everyday Digital Life*,
https://doi.org/10.1007/978-3-031-30438-5_2

Usually, the term 'artificial intelligence' encompasses any computational system that can sense its relevant context and react intelligently to any input (data or information) (Elliot, 2019). By 'react intelligently', Elliot probably means the software returns correct decisions when executed based on input data. In this paper, specifically, we adopt an exceptionally broad view of artificial intelligence considering any system/device with decision-making, reasoning or learning abilities. When dealing with everyday knowledge, we will see that we highly consider (social or cultural) platforms that hold some dimension of artificial intelligence.

However, when discussing about artificial intelligence in everyday life, we consider "pieces of artificial intelligence outside medical laboratories or factories". That is, pieces of artificial intelligence that play logic games, "choose" cultural contents, "remember", "write" and do other knowledge-related activities made by humans. In that vein, introducing the real-world applications of artificial intelligence teases the debate around the possibility/probability of "automation of the mental sphere" (Andrejevic, 2020, p. 4).

Researchers have not failed to debate this technological novelty's contradictions, risks, and consequences of this technological novelty from the very onset of artificial intelligence introduction in specialized areas, such as factories and labs. However, less has been said and unraveled about introducing artificial intelligence in biasing and producing everyday knowledge. Therefore, this chapter discusses how artificial intelligence and knowledge interact in science, especially in everyday life. While the use of artificial intelligence in science is much more evident and circumscribed, in "everyday life," artificial intelligence is enmeshed in platforms we interact with while engaging interfaces.

Just as a reminder, it is worth mentioning that although sociology has been discussing algorithms often, here, we take a broader conception of artificial intelligence in which 'algorithms' is just a unitary level of it. An algorithm is "a well-defined computational procedure that takes a certain value or set of values as input and produces a certain value, or set of values, as output" (Cormen et al. 2009, p. 5). They are commands written in computational language instructing how the computer should proceed, mostly optimally. It does not necessarily mean that an algorithm is always an artificial intelligence, but it artificial intelligence may be composed of some algorithms.

Artificial Intelligence and Scientific Knowledge: An Old Relationship

As we will briefly discuss, the application of artificial intelligence in scientific processes is evident as its users (the scientists) are quite acquainted with its dynamics and purposes. The use of artificial intelligence in everyday life started later, and up to now, its dynamics are still opaque for lay people. It is muffled behind social media, translators, and other "services" that we use on a daily basis.

Let us start from where the waters are less muddy. An unquestionable form of knowledge is what we call "scientific knowledge". This term loosely comprises theories, hypotheses, conjectures, proofs, datasets, etc. In other words, every input and output are related to what we employ in the scientific method. When it comes to this kind of knowledge, people may not be aware that artificial intelligence has supported the scientific enterprise in various areas, from pure to applied research, for a long time. Actually, scientific work has been pioneering the application of artificial intelligence. For instance, we can trace back the application of artificial intelligence to the 1980s and 1990s when the so-called expert systems ruled. Roughly speaking, an expert system emulates the decision-making ability of a human expert because they are designed to solve complex problems by reasoning through bodies of knowledge, represented mainly as "if–then" rules.

Today, it is not hard to see significant breakthroughs in scientific knowledge aided by artificial intelligence. A recent case in the news headlines was the first-ever "picture of a supermassive black hole" at the center of the M87 galaxy. A black hole is called "black" because it is everything, including light, so getting a direct image of a black hole is impossible. This is/was a significant issue proving these galactic objects' existence. The image of the black hole was generated from an algorithm called CHIRP, for Continuous High-resolution Image Reconstruction using Patch priors, devised by Katie Bouman, a Ph.D. student at that time, and her team. With the combination of data from 8 telescopes across the globe, Bouman prepared an extensive database of synthetic astronomical images and their measurements from these different telescopes. They trained the algorithm on three different sets of data. First with some expected sizes of a black hole, second with some other galactic images, and third with general images (cats, dogs, people, etc.) The algorithm was fed with many galactic and other images to make it learn how things look in the universe. As a result, it performed better than previous algorithms which preceded it. Artificial intelligence helped not only the production of a relevant scientific piece of knowledge and also became the only way to achieve such a piece of knowledge. It is an essential immaterial tool analogously to the telescopes.

Besides the pure scientific enterprise, artificial intelligence has also been deployed in several industries dealing with knowledge. During the 1980s, one could find artificial intelligence in the form of expert systems in the oil extraction industry, medical diagnosis, and in the discovery of organic molecules, to name a few. All of them have been relying on artificial intelligence since then. For instance, in the oil industry, one could see expert systems in the form of exploration advisors first. Expert programs would already assist oil professionals in drilling rigs in remote areas. It acted as a specialist, asking questions to advise what to do to avoid or correct accidents. One can also find semantic networks that allowed oil and gas companies to understand the critical concepts of the oil drilling enterprise in context, and they were related to each other. Today, artificial intelligence is used on massive amounts of data to evaluate better the impact of good attributes, reservoir characteristics, and production behavior. Artificial intelligence has become essential for knowledge validation and acquisition in many scientific fields.

Another good example is how Machine Learning is helping to develop new drug discoveries (Brown, 2021). One of the most significant challenges in synthetic organic chemistry is designing and planning new chemical syntheses. Recently, more modern deep learning artificial intelligence, in addition to symbolic artificial intelligence methods, "take advantage of the vast repositories of reaction data held in public databases, proprietary data held by publishers, and internal data sources at chemical companies to rapidly synthesize options of synthetic routes that have been demonstrated to be competitive with human experts (Brown, 2021). "Discovering" means the production of new knowledge. Interacting with the data we have, our specialized 'AI-algorithmic industries' can output something new, from scientific pieces of knowledge to the creation of new substances.

Unquestionably science and industry were the early adopters of artificial intelligence. As we have seen, artificial intelligence has been used as a tool to assist various processes. However, it did not change the scientific method in the process. Artificial intelligence becomes a tool that enables the development of further research, as a microscope would allow researching the microscopic world, or the telescope allows us to observe the universe.

The interaction, acquisition, and production of knowledge with artificial intelligence and algorithms are not circumscribed only in scientific knowledge but also in daily life practices. In daily life practices, these human-technological interactions profoundly impact our actions requiring some knowledge production or comprehension. Since the outset of Sociology, intellectuals have highlighted how the human-technological relationship impacts human cognition since the invention of these disciplines. As sociologist and philosopher Stephen Turner, draws on Thorstein Veblen, a classic German sociologist: "Thorstein Veblen thought that the experience of working with machine technology fundamentally changed people's mental outlook (…) This discipline (sociology) falls more immediately on the workmen engaged in the mechanical industries, and only less immediately on the rest of the community (1904, p. 307)" (Turner, 2021, p. 100). Before, the relationship between machines and humans was in the spotlight of Sociology. Nowadays, artificial intelligence has become one of the central issues. Digitalizing of life powered by artificial intelligence became a "new industrial revolution" for Sociology. However, artificial intelligence is less evident, palpable, and understandable as a factory machine. Sometimes artificial intelligence is disguised by friendly interfaces precluding us to see it as a "thing". In the same way, scientific knowledge is much more evident and circumscribed than 'everyday or common sense' knowledge. However, artificial intelligence and everyday knowledge pervade our lives and constantly interact. More than that, the ways we acquire, produce, and interact with knowledge every day have substantially changed with the current level of AI and the ubiquity of algorithms that we have.

Unpacking the Concept of "Knowledge" Besides Scientific Knowledge

Knowledge is a concept challenging to define, and epistemology, which is an entire branch of philosophy, is dedicated to this matter. There is also no consensus on what knowledge is. However, there has been a classical definition around since Plato's Theaetetus (Gettier, 1963), in which knowledge would be a judgment with an account. Contemporary theories of knowledge would add to the classical definition specifying that knowledge is a statement that must be believed, justified, and true. In other words, a justified true belief. To say that it is a "statement" means that it is language-dependent. Consequently, it points to the social nature of knowledge, which transmutes epistemology into social epistemology.

Different conceptions of knowledge became real alternatives for characterizing knowledge since the classic conception of knowledge was challenged by Edmund Gettier, who proved that "true" factor of the classic conception of knowledge is due to sheer chance. One alternative some philosophers and social scientists adopt is Wittgenstein's definition of knowledge as an ability expressed within a language game (Wittgenstein, 1998). A direct consequence of that is that knowledge is context-based and dependent on a community of participants of that game. Also, knowledge would be useful and serve to achieve something else, i.e., it would be a means of action. In a classic sociological theory of action such as Max Weber's—a paradigm in sociology—knowledge would be required for the means of rational social actions, either axiomatic or teleological. In addition, the ends defined in the teleological action would also require knowledge (Weber 1921b). This broad definition matches what we say as having "everyday knowledge" in various situations.

With this conception of knowledge in mind, we can derive that it cannot be identified solely as "scientific knowledge". Instead, any knowledge, especially everyday life knowledge, should be considered. In many aspects, everyday knowledge and scientific knowledge do not differ fundamentally. The main difference is that scientific knowledge is under an industrial process of creating, validating, and revising of such pieces of knowledge.

From here on, we can go on discussing how artificial intelligence has been changing fundamentally changing how we interact, produce, and interact with knowledge, once the environment that supports contemporary knowledge has changed dramatically. It has changed because of the world's digitalization and artificial intelligence development. Without this environmental change, the impact of artificial intelligence and algorithms in everyday life would still be weak. Since artificial intelligence and algorithms are constitutive of our knowledge environment, they are fully integrated with it and with our lives.

Artificial Intelligence and "Everyday" Knowledge: An Emerging Relationship

Differently from science/scientists doing science that employs artificial intelligence as a tool or as a functional piece in the research process, artificial intelligence, in daily life, is entirely disguised behind screens and interfaces we interact with. We have become so used to live relying on the use of artificial intelligence (or programs that embody artificial intelligence) and algorithms that sometimes we do not perceive them. Also, at odds with science, we do not have any control over artificial intelligence's uses in everyday life.

The number of daily actions we do relying on artificial intelligence and algorithms is remarkable. This list ranges from navigating across the cities, writing an email (and even a whole narrative), knowing, and socializing with others, listening to music, searching for information, or creating a piece of art, either music or a picture, and even helping us recall memories. Before getting into these real examples, we shall first question how that is possible and what enabled it?

In consonance with previous studies (Elliot, 2019; Van Djick, 2018), the short answer is the rise and domination of digital platforms. It is also perfectly possible to argue that they are just an inevitable internet development and the "culture of connectivity" that emerged with it (Van Dijck 2013). The development of hardware technology, such as faster computers and processors, buttressed this process. Before, the technological development of artificial intelligence was secluded in a scientific or industrial environment. When the internet gained the world, it started changing people's everyday lives.

Tim Berners-Lee, the legendary mastermind behind the Web, wrote a 2009 paper for the *Artificial Intelligence Journal* expressing the following: "from the very beginning ... the Web was designed to create a network of humans changing society empowered using this shared infrastructure" (Hendler & Berners-Lee, 2009). The keyword here is infrastructure, and the internet is the digital infrastructure for AI and most algorithms to happen.

In the beginning, the Web was a repository of information. When the internet started to host more complex systems, such as SaaS (Software as a Service) or social media, it entangled other elements (i.e., algorithms) capable of binding people through technology. This way, the web became part of a "socio-technical network" (Latour, 2007). According to Latour (2007), a "socio-technical network" bound not only human beings within themselves but also non-human elements, such as animals and machines, and elements without any physical existence, such as digital content, algorithms, cultural items, etc.

When the web became popular and spread worldwide, artificial intelligence started to be deployed in many areas of social life. Artificial intelligence transcends the scientific debate or specific application in this historical moment. It reaches people who have never paid for a device powered by artificial intelligence or those who have never wanted to be in touch with artificial intelligence. Without realizing it, artificial intelligence invades everyday life through some algorithms deployed on the web.

We have a turning point here: "non-human elements" become part of the everyday social world and acquire some action. In this text, we will not discuss some ontological issues regarding the nature of the action or artificial intelligence, and this discussion may be better explored by Philosophy of Mind, Artificial Intelligence, and Cognitive Sciences (Thagard 1982; Searle, 1980). Sociologists must pay attention to how artificial intelligence behaves inside groups and societies. As Donati (2021) puts it: "the issue is not whether AI or robots can assume human-like characteristics, but how they interact with humans and affect their social identities and relationships" (p. 214).

As aforementioned, artificial intelligence appears in society through its many interfaces, such as digital platforms that range in various areas, from translation assistants to pure entertainment. This phenomenon called "platformization" in the specialized literature (Nieborg & Poell, 2018; Van Djick, 2018; Poell et al., 2018). Nieborg and Poell (2018) argue that platformization can be defined as the penetration digital platforms' economic, governmental, and infrastructural extensions into the web and app ecosystems, fundamentally affecting the operations of the cultural industries. So far, this process has been examined from three perspectives: business studies, political economy, and software studies. Platformization has been responsible for providing massive and real-time data for feeding machine learning models, more precisely deep learning neural networks, which are our contemporary algorithms. AI and algorithms were put in action on the output side, outputting effectively in the social world.

Digital platforms differ according to their primary purposes. Some years ago, we could point out precisely their goals. Recently, platforms such as Instagram entangles many different features and purposes inside the same platform. If we stick to these "ideal-types" classifications, we may divide them into a.) Over-the-top (OTT) service platforms (e.g., Netflix), b.) social network site platforms (e.g., Facebook), c.) user-generated content platforms (e.g., YouTube), and d.) searching platforms (e.g., Google).

Over-the-top service platforms are video or streaming media that provide access to movies or TV shows by sending the media directly through the internet, e.g., Netflix, Amazon Prime Video, Hulu, Spotify, and Deezer. *Social networks* may be the first kind of platforms on the internet. Step by step, they started implementing artificial intelligence within them. Their primary purpose is to connect people and enable them to interact through short texts or reactions, e.g., Orkut (inactive), Facebook, and Instagram. The *users feed customer-generated content (CGC) platforms* to create some content for their followers, e.g., YouTube and Instagram may also be classified as CGC platforms. And *searching platforms* e.g., Google Search, Google Maps, CC search, Bing. All these platforms embody algorithms powered by artificial intelligence techniques, such as recommendation systems, clustering, and prediction. These algorithms are fundamental for the functioning of these platforms. However, each of these platforms will impact our relation to "knowledge" or how we know differently.

Considering *over-the-top service platforms*, already by 2015, 80% of what was consumed on Netflix came from the recommendation system; consequently, only 20% was due to the free choice of individuals (Gomez-Uribe and Hunt 2015). When the recommendation system becomes so essential to our cultural consumption, we realize that our process of knowing the world is cut by something else besides our cognitive capacity, aesthetic judgment, or preferences. These recommendation shortcuts become part of our process of searching and filtering knowledge. Thus, platforms shape how we produce and consume cultural content, particularly music and movies. Morris (2020) shows how the phonographic industry has changed since the advent of music platforms such as Spotify, Apple Music, and Deezer. On the one hand, artists are producing music in more "suitable" formats to the platform dynamics, and they optimize musical content as a strategy to circulate and be delivered by these platforms quickly. On the other hand, platforms such as Spotify and YouTube mediate the circulation of cultural commodities and end up influencing and shaping, through algorithmic recommendations, how users discover, listen to, and share cultural content (Morris, 2020, p. 2).

If those digital environments rose as the main space of creation and access to cultural items in our days, algorithms and artificial intelligence would become a constituent pillar of our cultures. Following Bruno Latour's idea, Elliot argues that "technology and society are mutually constitutive, and the agency is best conceived as distributed among people and machines. From this angle, the condition of modernity is distinguished as a folding of humans and non-humans into ever deeper and more intimate imbroglios (Elliot, 2019, p. 41)." In a sense, we may push forward the claim stating that we have an "algorithmic culture" since most of our cultural items interact with an algorithm at some point.

In this sense, artificial intelligence is shaping our cultural judgment and appreciation. We have explored cultural consumption as existent on Netflix and YouTube algorithms so far. However, many other platforms and digital services impact us more profoundly than we realize. "As society becomes informationalized as never before, digitization emerges as the operating backcloth against which everything is coded, tagged, scanned, and located. Complex automated digital technology systems emerge as the 'surround' to both everyday life and modern institutions" (Elliot, 2019, p. 31).

As we know, if culture changes, the mental outlook or social cognition changes. As Turner (2021) puts it, "one can readily recognize the importance of objects as an anchor of social life. The digital experience is also, at least intermittently, liminoid, and the digital experience is also a powerful means of inducing cognitive reorganization" (p. 106). If digital technologies transfigure institutions, they also reach profoundly into individual identities. The digital is both around us and inside us (Elliot, 2019, p. 18). Some social media, such as Facebook, impact us in deep subjective aspects, such as our identity. When we access it, the first thing pops up is the famous question on the top of the feed: "what's on your mind?". We make Facebook a real diary by posting shorts comments, places we have been, pictures or suggestions. Who we are (or at least a hint of it) is expressed there. Connected to that, how we remember changed when Facebook introduced its "memory feature". The idea was simple but powerful. It displays what you have done on the same day and month in past years. We are then automatically nudged by an algorithm, triggering our memories. The idea picked up, and other providers started to offer similar services. OneCloud or Microsoft's cloud service does precisely the same, sending emails showing what you have uploaded on that day. Finally, for Apple's iPhone users, one of the newest features of the Photos app compiles and clusters pictures and clips taken with the camera into automatically generated larger clips, even adding soundtracks. Without doing much, we receive "stories of our life" automatically.

The photos algorithms leverage the metadata produced when the camera is used. Thus, artificial intelligence voluntarily becomes part of our cognitive performance and does part of our mental work for us. Consequently, algorithms that populate digital services we use every day leverage our data, and they output both triggers of actions and cognitive triggers to us.

These simple AI architectures, however, are becoming outdated when we get into Generative AI possibilities. Platforms such as Chat GPT and Midjourney are not social network services (SNS) but will quickly be comprehended by them. Generative AI represents a significant advancement in AI technology compared to three years ago. Generative AI models have made remarkable progress in understanding and generating human-like text or images. They can produce coherent and contextually relevant text at a level unattainable with previous AI technologies. Many SNS (such as Facebook, Twitter and LinkedIn) are already testing to integrate chatbot technology and AI-powered conversational agents into their platforms, including some based on GPT-like models. Some generative AI models can process and generate multiple types of content, including text, images, and audio. This enables them to perform tasks that involve multiple modalities, such as generating image descriptions or translating between text and speech. More than that, some generative AI create content, including art, music, and storytelling, often blurring the line between human and AI-generated creativity. It means that more than doing part of our mental work (or coupling with our mental work), generative AI is sometimes doing almost all our mental work. Previous works broadly discuss the relationship between cognition and social media (Cordeiro, 2021; Cordeiro & Neri, 2019). In these works, we draw from some Philosophy of Mind arguments (Carr, 2010; Heersmink, 2017; Sutton et al., 2010) on how some cognitive tasks (such as the way we remember past events and, consequently, who we were) have been supported, coupled with, and enhanced by external things (in this case the technologies as mentioned above). These philosophical strands usually relate to the "hypothesis of external mind". From that main hypothesis, many different arguments and philosophical branches discuss how the external world (in contemporaneity, especially online technologies) becomes part of our own mind and its cognitive processes, such as knowing the world.

Two or three years ago, we discussed how artificial intelligence implemented in everyday platforms have changed how we relate to everyday knowledge. The discussion was around the "platformization phenomenon". And, sociology has been concerned about how our social actions "social actions" (Weber, 1921b) were transformed into quantified data. People do not act freely within platforms. Platforms limit social actions to convert them into quantified data, which platform owners (companies) explore commercially. Zuboff (2019) states that this is precisely the characteristic of current capitalism.

Of course, the main goal of these platforms is getting most of the customer lifetime value (CLV)—a concept used within venture capital environments. However, as the Calvinists did not want to create the moral structure of capitalism (Weber 1921a), these startup companies and venture capitalists (the main characters propelling the platformization) did not want to change the "knowledge dynamics" or our mental outlook fundamentally. In the same way Calvinists did not intend to shape the moral structure of capitalism, but they did it, these venture capitalists actions also have unforeseen consequences: if they wanted to promote autonomy, contrariwise they promoted technological dependency. The discussion on "algorithm power" and "algorithm authority" (Beer, 2009) has been hot, and the concerns about knowledge and truth are already at the center of the debate. Browsing on the web has become our main form for validating our knowledge.

"Google it," the daily expression, is a synonym for getting accurate information. If there is any knowledge that may be wrong, it will be displayed in search results and believed to be true. For example, if you think that Brazil's capital is Rio de Janeiro, but you are not sure, you search it on google. Suppose the first article (which may be the most read) or a paid article says that São Paulo is Brazil's capital. If you do not go deeper, you will probably believe it and take it for granted. After all, Google is saying it. Who is Google? It does not matter; it has what we call the "algorithmic authority." We legit our beliefs and hypothesis through Google, which may be wrong because Brazil's capital is Brasilia. In this case, we transfer our epistemological judgment to an algorithmic authority.

Nowadays, the discussion has reached another level because algorithms and the bias they often produce are not the only concern anymore. The whole production of knowledge has been impacted by the emergence of generative AI. The creation of texts, songs, sounds, and images or paintings has completely changed. Our texts are not "corrected and reviewed" anymore; they are created (almost) from scratch. We used to "cut & paste" from a text editor (such as "word") to an AI text reviewer (such as "grammarly"), in this context, the AI assistance (i.e. grammarly) couple and enhance the cognitive tasks we perform to write a text. With generative AI, we need a good "prompt", and the text or image is instantaneously created. They will rely less on mere copy-pasting and more on honing their skills in crafting effective prompts and adeptly organizing information. In this reality, the discussion around "algorithm power" and "algorithm authority" couples with the issue of "authenticity and truth". If before AI likely blurred (or biased) our interaction with reality, now, generative AI blurs the created reality. This blurred line between human-generated and AI-generated content leads us to ponder authenticity, misinformation, and digital trust issues. Looking for knowledge on Google sparked the problem, now we have an alarming issue: How does the prevalence of generative AI affect our perceptions of truth and reality? If we do not pay attention to it, readers may not necessarily notice or mind the authorship of texts, images, and other knowledge contents. It is worth mentioning that these latest developments do not cease the discussion on the limits and potentialities of AI. AI is still unaware of what it is doing; it performs even faster than a human in specific tasks (Esposito, 2017); it still does not represent the replacement of human intelligence because we still do not fully know the extent and limitations of artificial intelligence. Furthermore, it is human intelligence itself that still conceptualizes and implements artificial intelligence. As argued by Norvig and Russell (1995), an airplane flies without having to imitate a bird exactly; that is, although the airplane can also perform one of the main functions of the bird—flying—it operates in a very different way.

Both human and artificial intelligence look alike in some situations. However, their nature diverges.

Human beings grasp the sense and meaning without necessarily mapping, sorting, and parsing out every possible scenario—as the computer does. Whenever there are new situations and interactions, humans rapidly try to understand them in terms of events we have already understood (Schank, 2000); that is, we set analogies.

Conclusion

We've explored how artificial intelligence has become intertwined with contemporary epistemological processes, both within and beyond the realm of scientific inquiry. In the scientific sphere, the application of artificial intelligence is relatively transparent and confined, owing to the distinct nature of knowledge forms within this domain. Conversely, in everyday life, the presence and impact of artificial intelligence often remain diffuse and may even elude the awareness or comprehension of its users. Regardless of the context, it's indisputable that artificial intelligence and algorithms have significantly altered the landscape of knowledge production and understanding processes in modern social existence. Artificial intelligence has assumed a pivotal role in filtering, selecting, and even generating knowledge, reshaping the very environment in which we engage and interact. It has seamlessly integrated into the fabric of our social interactions, mediating many epistemologically rooted social relationships. Integrating these digital cultural artifacts into our digital environment and our methods of accessing them elevates platforms beyond mere intermediaries; they emerge as active mediators and creators in their own right. Generative

AI is swiftly infiltrating social platforms and is becoming an integral part of our daily lives. As we scroll through our favorite social media feeds, we may encounter posts, comments, or messages that appear to be human-crafted but are, in fact, products of AI algorithms. From chatbots offering personalized customer support to AI-generated content recommendations, generative AI is reshaping the landscape of online communication and content creation. However, it's crucial to emphasize that AI remains unable to replace human beings in the realm of knowledge production fully. Humans continue to supply the data upon which generative AI is trained and formulate the prompts necessary for generating final knowledge content. AI remains reliant on human agency and lacks independent intentionality. It lacks the capacity to grasp the intricacies of meaning and intentions inherent in human interactions, necessitating human input to provide context, data, and specify desired outcomes. For example, Chat GPT was trained on data available on the internet up to 2021. If human knowledge production were to cease beyond that point, Chat GPT would likely become outdated in its creative outputs.

References

Andrejevic, M. (2020). Shareable and un-sharable knowledge. *Big Data and Society*, June.

Beer, D. (2009). Power through algorithm? *New Media and Society*. 11: 985.

Brown, N. (2021). Introduction to Artificial Intelligence and Chemistry. In.: Brown, Nathan (ed.). *Artificial Intelligence in Drug Discovery*. Royal Society of Chemistry.

Carr, Nicholas (2010). *The Shallows: What the Internet Is Doing to Our Brains*. New York: W. W. Norton & Company.

Cordeiro, V. (2021). To which past do we belong: Self and narrative in a Brazilian mnemonic community of former institutionalized children. *Memory Studies*, vol 14 (5), pp. 987–1001.

Cordeiro, V. & Neri, H. (2019). Placing the subjective locus in the environment: How social media are enhancing the autobiographical remembering and identity processes. In.: Gouvea, Steven & Curado, Manuel. *Automata's Inner Movie*. Wilmington: Vernon Press.

Cormen, et al. (2009). *Introduction to algorithms*. Cambridge, MA: MIT press.

Donati, P. (2021). Impact of AI/Robotics on Human Relations: Co-evolution Through Hybridisation. In.: Von Braum, Joachim, Archer, Margaret, Reichberg, Gregory & Sorondo, Marcel. *Robotics, AI and Humanity*. Cham: Springer.

Elliot, A. (2019). *The Culture of AI: everyday life and the digital revolution*. London: Routledge.

Esposito, Elena (2017). Organizing without understanding. Lists in ancient and in digital cultures. *Zeitschrift für Literaturwissenschaft und Linguistik*, Lili, v. 47, n. 3, pp. 351–9.

Gettier, E. L. (1963). Is Justified True Belief Knowledge? *Analysis*. 23 (6), pp. 121–123. https://doi.org/10.1093/analys/23.6.121.

Gomez-Uribe, C., & Hunt, N. (2015). *The Netflix recommender system*. ACM Transactions on Management Information Systems.

Heersmink, Richard (2017). The narrative self, distributed memory, and evocative objects. *Philosophical Studies*, 175 (8), pp. 1829–1849.
Hendler, J. & Berners-Lee, T. (2009). From the Semantic Web to social machines: A research challenge for AI on the World Wide Web. *Artificial Intelligence Journal*. https://doi.org/10.1016/j.artint.2009.11.010.
Latour, B. (2007). *Reassembling the social: an introduction to the actor-network theory*. Oxford: Oxford University Press.
Morris, J. W. (2020). Music Platforms and the Optimization of Culture. *Social Media + Society*, July–September, pp. 1–10.
Nieborg, D. & Poell, T. (2018). The platformization of cultural production: Theorizing the contingent cultural commodity. *New Media & Society*, April.
Norvig, P. & Russell, S. (1995). *Artificial Intelligence: A Modern Approach*. New York: Pearson.
Poell, T.; Van Dijck, J. & De Waal, M. (2018). *The Platform Society*. Oxford: Oxford University Press.
Schank, R. (2000). *Tell me a story*. Evanston: Northwestern.
Searle, John (1980). Minds, Brains, and Programs. *Behavioral and Brain Sciences*, 3, pp. 417–424.
Sutton, John et al. (2010). The Psychology of memory, extended cognition and socially distributed remembering. *Phenom Cognitive Science*, 9, pp. 521–560.
Thagard, P. (1982). *Artificial intelligence, psychology, and the philosophy of discovery*. Proceedings of the Biennial Meeting of the Philosophy of Science Association, pp. 166–175.
Turner, S. (2021). Digital Affordances and the liminal. In.: O'Connor, P. & Benta, M. *Technologisation of the social*. London: Routledge.
Van Djick, J. (2013). *The culture of connectivity: A critical history of social media*. Oxford: Oxford University Press.
Van Djick, J. (2018). *The Platform Society*. Oxford: Oxford University Press.
Veblen, T. T. (1904). *The theory of business enterprise*. Martino Fine Books.
Weber, M. (1921a). *The Protestant ethics and the spirit of capitalism*. New York: Dover Publication.
Weber, M. (1921b). *Economy and Society*. Cambridge, MA: Harvard University Press.
Wittgenstein, L. (1998). *Philosophical Investigations*. New Jersey: Willey-Blackwell.
Zuboff, S. (2019). *The age of surveillance capitalism*. London: Profile Books.

CHAPTER 3

Economic Aspects of Social Media: Facebook's Potential for Generating Business in Iran

Hamid Abdollahyan and Mahin Sheikh Ansari

INTRODUCTION

In light of the major theme of this volume which focusses on everyday digital life and Futures, here we focus on the economic aspect of digital life. This is, therefore an attempt to show the economic potential of Facebook and to evaluate the situation of Iranian businesses on social media. It seeks to do so in the context of an assessment of the impact of social media on businesses. When academics and marketers discuss the 'digital transformation of marketing', of necessity they will consider such issues as online commerce, online advertising tactics, live chat services and mobile services; all of which have become part of the daily lives of billions of people (Yogesh & Ismagilova, 2021).

The number of global internet users reached 4.7 billion in 2021,[1] and is expected to reach 5 billion in 2022 and 5.3 billion in 2023. In 2021, Facebook was reported as having 2.895 billion users, YouTube reported 2.291 billion, WhatsApp with 2 billion, and Instagram with 1.393 billion monthly-active

---

[1] https://www.statista.com/statistics/1190263/internet-users-worldwide/.

H. Abdollahyan (✉) • M. Sheikh Ansari
University of Tehran, Tehran, Iran
e-mail: habdolah@ut.ac.ir

© The Author(s), under exclusive license to Springer Nature Switzerland AG 2024
H. S. Dunn et al. (eds.), *The Palgrave Handbook of Everyday Digital Life*, https://doi.org/10.1007/978-3-031-30438-5_3

users. Telegram was reported as having 550 million[2] users and was ranked 11th among major social media platforms.. According to these statistics, virtual space has now become an integral part of the lives of people worldwide. Such statistics also show that the internet and social media provide a good market platform for advertising and for attracting customer attention to brands and businesses. Social media was strategically and technologically based on Web 2.0 (Kaplan & Haenlein, 2010). These media include virtual social networks (Facebook and LinkedIn, etc.), Wikipedia-shared multimedia sites (YouTube and Flickr), ranking sites (Yelp, etc.) and bookmark sites (Cray, 2012). Brands, websites, blogs and communities have launched themselves in cyberspace and have used various methods to attract the attention of their users and subscribers.

Performance of corporate brand on social media is currently a measure of their success (Moffitt & Dover, 2011). In this regard, statistics show that companies and brands have spent a high percentage of their advertising payments on social networks. For example, Coca-Cola with 106.96 million[3] followers on Facebook spent USD 3.96 billion online in 2017. This figure moved to USD 4.11billion in 2018; USD 4.25 billion in 2019; USD 2.77 billion in 2020 and USD 4.098 billion in 2021 for advertising on social networks. Samsung, with 159.82 million followers on Facebook is reported to have spent about 1.81 billion US dollars on advertising on social networks[4] in 2020.

According to the latest statistics published in Iran, the number of mobile internet subscribers in the country in 2021 reached 90 million 354 thousand; and the internet penetration rate reached 106.36 percent.[5] Social media penetration rate in Iran in 2021 was estimated at 71 percent,[6] with an 11 percent growth index. Also, the number of Iranian internet users in 2021 reached 67,602,731.[7] The number of Facebook users in 2017 reached 17.2 million,[8] but there is no exact data on the number of Iranian Facebook users in 2022, although according to the ISPA survey,[9] 73.6% of Iranians over the age of 18 use social media. Although Facebook, Twitter, YouTube and Telegram have been filtered, Iranian users have access to these social media through virtual private networks (VPNs). Of the total users, 64.1% use WhatsApp, 45.3% use Instagram, 36.3% use Telegram, 3.3% use Facebook, 2% use Twitter, 0.3% use LinkedIn, and 0.3% use Tic Tok (Dogres, 2021). The number of Facebook users in in Iran in 2021 was about 2.3 million people.

---

[2] https://www.statista.com/statistics/272014/global-social-networks-ranked-by-number-of-users/.
[3] It reached 109 million in February 2022.
[4] https://www.statista.com/statistics/621999/samsung-ad-spend-usa/.
[5] www.irna.ir/news/84527797.
[6] https://www.tasnimnews.com/fa/news/1400/08/15/2602617.
[7] www.Internetworldstats.com/top20.htm.
[8] www.Internetworldstats.com.
[9] This is a short name for and Iranian research institution.

The Iranian standards organization, BRC, reports that forty-nine million Iranian users of the Persian-language Telegram channels have posted five hundred million posts in one year, despite the fact that the social media channel had been banned since 2018. The same organization claims that forty-eight million Instagram users annually post one billion items of content. In addition, there were fifty Persian language accounts on Instagram that had more than three million followers. Some six hundred accounts were said to have more than one million followers. This data shows that social media represents a good domestic market for advertising and for attracting customers for Iranian corporate brands and businesses.

Hypothesis: Facebook users in Iran provide part of the social capital required by the new economy.

For the purpose of operationalization of the hypothesis we broke it down into two workable hypotheses as follows:

1. Considering that being a Facebook user results in an increase in social capital, it is expected that the average social capital of Facebook users will be higher than those who are not Facebook members.
2. The higher the intensity of Facebook use, the more the social capital develops. In other words, Increasing the intensity of Facebook use results in an increase in the social capital of Facebook users.

Research Question

Is the status of Iranian small businesses on social media equal to its potential?
Or;
What is the position of Iranian brands, companies and small businesses in terms of using Facebook's capabilities for advertising and sales? And how has filtering affected businesses?

Research Background

The first issue is related to social capital and economic growth (intra-organizational dimension). In the contemporary capitalist economy, the process of producing goods and services has become more complex, and the need for informal and normative exchange has increased. For this reason, the new capitalist economy creates a constant demand for social capital (Fukuyama, 2006 [1385 Iranian Calendar], p. 92). "The increasing importance of social capital in the new capitalist economy is due to the shift of low trust to high trust in production and the service sector" (Fukuyama, 2006, p. 79). Fukuyama argues that the answer to the question of the social capital required by the new capitalist economy can be found in sociology.

Coleman believes that social capital is inherently present in the structure of actors' relations with each other and the relationship between them (Tajbakhsh, 2010]1389 Iranian Calendar], p. 49). Granovetter distinguishes between "strong ties such as bonds between people and their close friends and weak ties such as bonds between people and their acquaintances" (in Ritzer, 2003, p. 577). He believes that weak ties function as "a bridge that exist between two groups that have strong internal ties". Without such a weak tie, the two groups may be completely disconnected (Ritzer, 2003, p. 578). Putnam also names two types of social capital and considers bridging social capital as useful for the transfer and dissemination of information. Bonding social capital (within the group) is seen as useful for the transmission of relationships (Field, 2009, p. 56).

Putnam (Field, 2009, p. 56) and Fukuyama (2006, pp. 71–76) believe there is a large amount of knowledge in social networks and these networks accelerate the flow of information by establishing weak ties between people. Fukuyama (2006) believes that these weak ties between corporate employees reduce transaction costs and lead to economic prosperity (Fukuyama, 2006, p. 79). He points out that informal relationships between employees do not destroy authority in organizations, but "internalize authority and provide the possibility of self-organization and self-management" (Fukuyama, 2006, p. 80). Putnam also considers dense social networks as a guarantee of economic and political success of governments and civil society (Tajbakhsh, 1389, p. 99). Also, Zhang et al. (2011) compared the results of the US National Family and Neighborhood Survey (1987–1988) with the results of the same survey, five years later (1992–1994) and concluded that bridging social capital affects economic development and prosperity (Zhang et al., 2011).

In this regard, Ellison et al. (2007) has redefined bridging social capital in cyberspace, stating that bridging social capital in virtual social networks refers to unstable relationships between individuals and the acquisition of information through virtual social networking sites, which often are very large in number and quantity (Steinfield et al., 2008). The results of research in the United States (Ellison et al., 2007; Steinfield et al., 2008), and the United Kingdom (Lewis & West, 2009) indicate that in all cases there is a positive correlation between the intensity of Facebook use and an increase in the bridging social capital of Facebook users. Accordingly, it seems that social media can contribute to economic prosperity by expanding weak ties and accelerating the flow of information.

The results of Lee Sing's (2009) research in this regard have shown that the relationships among employees of Serena Software Company on Facebook are in line with the goals of the company's management. Facebook enabled employees of its branches in various countries to share information with each other. "I can communicate with all Serena employees in the world," said one employee. Another employee stated that I really enjoy being able to find information about other employees and connect with them through Facebook. Another employee said that social media has made me know my co-workers better. Employee communication through social networks seems to increase trust and satisfaction among employees (Lee Sing, 2009). The research results of Munene and Nyaribo's (2013) study on the impact of social media on employee productivity show that the use of social media has led to the exchange and sharing of information between employees and has increased employee productivity. The results of Ashraf's (2014) research in Pakistan also show that the use of social networks results in a positive increase in skills, knowledge and efficiency of banking employees.

Social Media and the External Dimension

In the business world, the relationship between business to business, and businesses to customers alone, is no longer the issue. Social media has created the connection of people to people or customers to customers. The major trait of people's interaction with people, assuming that the internet and virtual networks are not censored, lies in the fact that information control is no longer in the hands of businesses. It is the customers who determine what information is important and outstanding (Mangold & Faulds, 2009). The role of customers in sales has increased and customers' interaction with brands has gone far beyond transactions (Yogesh & Ismagilova, 2021). This feature has created opportunities and threats for companies. One of these threats is that if previously a dissatisfied customer could tell ten people their opinion, now he/she can share his opinion with more than ten million other customers. But social media has also brought opportunities for brands and companies. Companies can get acquainted with customer perspectives and use them to solve problems and improve the quality of their products, as well as support them by interacting with dissatisfied customers. Another characteristic is that customers trust other customers' opinions about the quality of a product more than advertising, and companies can use it to attract customers and increase their sales (Cray, 2012). Qualman (2011) states that 34% of bloggers write about products and brands, and 90% of customers trust each other's writing, while only 14% of customers trust advertising (Cray, 2012).

Advertising is no longer a source for vertical interaction, but a means of creating and maintaining a regular presence of a brand in the virtual social media space with customers (Cray, 2012). In a study by Cone (2008), 93% of users believed that companies should be present on social media and 85% of them believed that companies should interact with their customers through virtual social networks (Michaelidou et al., 2011). Qualman (2011) argues that the question that companies need to answer is not about whether they should use virtual social media. Rather, the question and the issue they are facing is how to use social media in the best way (Cray, 2012). Most organizations and brands have changed their advertising strategies and tactics, directing their efforts at customer participation as it is considered as a key element in the structure and design of organizations. Accordingly, the structure of the marketing department of most brands has changed and is composed of both traditional and internet departments, where social media is considered as a suitable marketing platform that can be used to attract customers. 'Customer engagement' has become so important in marketing that the acronym (CEBs) has been assigned to 'customer engagement behaviors' (Yogesh & Ismagilova, 2021).

Conceptual Model of Research

In summary, the role of virtual social networks in the new capitalist economy is twofold and can be evaluated from two dimensions. The first one is intra-organization dimension in which the role of these networks is to create informal relationships between employees within organizations and production units that meet the demand of the new capitalist economy for social capital. The second one is external or inter-organization dimension and is related to the capacity of these networks in marketing and interaction between companies. It also extends to the relationship of businesses to customers and customers with customers, which provide another part of the social capital required by the new capitalist economy. We illustrate the economic aspects of social media in Fig. 3.1.

Research Methodology

The methodological strategy here is based on a mixed method using three techniques including survey, focus group interviews, and direct observation to collect data. In addition, a longitudinal study of businesses on social media was implemented.

Data were collected in the survey method online and offline (using a questionnaire). The unit of analysis or statistical population included Iranian Internet users of which some 2437 samples were drawn.

A focus group interview technique was launched, during which four focus groups were formed, each consisting of 6 interviewees. Being an internet user and familiarity with Facebook were among the prominent criteria to be included in the group. Of course, each focus group was conducted one week apart. It should be noted that for one of the focus groups, we selected people who were

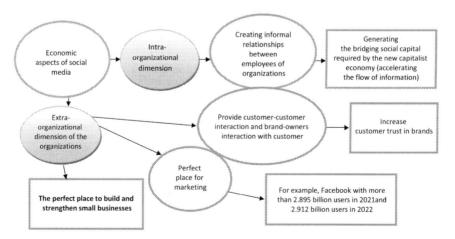

Fig. 3.1 Economic aspects of social media

Facebook members. The interviewees of the other group were selected from among non-Facebook members. Focus groups were also selected from students or staff aged 25 to 36 years. Using direct observation method and using the Social Bakers site, we collected the desired data about companies and brands on Facebook. We also created a page with our name on Facebook, and using the "search option" and entering a keyword such as jewelry, restaurant, book, clothes, rice, tea, etc., we viewed the pages that were in the grouping of these titles, then we randomly selected several of them for evaluation in the longitudinal studies and brands.

Operationalization of Variables

Intra-organizational dimension: It should be noted that due to the filtering of Facebook, it was not possible to assess the impact of an organization's employees' relationships while active on Facebook. In the same token, we were not able to assess the impact of such relationships on accelerating information and/ or boosting the economy. That is the reason that we evaluated the impact of Facebook users on the bridging social capital of Facebook users. We used the Ellison's model (Ellison et al., 2007) to measure the bridging social capital and the intensity of Facebook use.

Extra-organizational or inter- organization dimension: There seems to be a significant relationship between the number of likes that a company on social media receives and the amount of sales and income of the company. In the same vein, Asur and Huberman (2010) from the University of California launched an "analysis of emotions" in 3 million tweets on the Twitter site and showed there is a correlation between the conversations that users have on Twitter about a movie and the sales of the movie at the box office.

Here, we also measured the success rate of businesses on Facebook by the number of their likes. We did a comparative analysis of sales between Turkish brands, Iranian brands and world-famous brands in terms of the number of followers on Facebook, as well as the position of Iranian brands and businesses on Facebook. This longitudinal study took place in 2014, 2015, 2016 and then in 2021–2022.

Validity and Reliability of Scales

A Kaiser-Mayer-Olkin (KMO) test can determine the validity of the measuring tools. If the KMO size is greater than 0.75 (Hooman, 2001, p. 384) and Cronbach's alpha coefficient is greater than 0.73 then it means the scales are valid and reliable (Table 3.1).

Table 3.1 Validity of Scales

Variables	KMO	Bartlett Test	Alpha Cronbach's Coefficient
Intensity of Facebook use	875	801/2518	73/0
Bridging social capital	781/0	472/4112	803/0

Table 3.2 Frequency distribution of sample age and location

Age	Frequency	Percent	Residential area	Frequency	Percent
16 and lower	272	2/11	Tehran	2085	6/85
17 to 36	2046	84	Other cities	282	8/11
Over 36 years old	119	9/4	Abroad	62	5/2

Research Findings

Here we first discuss the frequency distribution of age and location of respondents in the sample as described. The age range of some 84% of the respondents is between 16 and 36 years. And 85.6% of the respondents live in Tehran (Table 3.2).

Testing Hypothesis 1: The average bridging social capital of Facebook users is higher than those who are not members of Facebook.

We performed the t-test of two independent groups to assess the difference in the average social capital between the control (non-Facebook member) and experimental (Facebook member) groups. Findings show that the average bridging social capital of Facebook members (1028 people) is equal to 27.74 which is more than 26.43 of the average bridging social capital of non-Facebook members (1131 people) and this difference is significant (Table 3.3).

Evaluation of Hypothesis 2: Increasing the intensity of Facebook use increases the bridging social capital of Iranian users.

Findings indicate that there is a correlation between " the intensity of Facebook use " and "bridging social capital" with a correlation coefficient of 0.171 and a significant level of 0.000 (Table 3.4). This means when the intensity of Facebook use increases, the bridging social capital increases among Facebook users. This means Facebook expands weak ties between people and facilitates the flow of information, which in turn contributes to the prosperity of the economy.

The results of the focus group interviews also confirm findings of the quantitative research data and the observations show that there is a significant difference between Facebook member groups and Facebook non-member groups, in the following four cases:

1. Scope of Relationships (Bridging Social Capital)
2. The radius of trust towards others for the purpose of friendship (one of the indicators of bridging social capital)

Table 3.3 T-test to evaluate the difference between the mean of grafted bridging social capital in the control and experimental groups

Social Capital type	T test	Significance
Bridging social capital	641/7-	000/0

Table 3.4 Pearson correlation test between social capital of Facebook users and the intensity of usage

Variables	Type of Test	Intensity of Facebook use
Bridging social capital	Pearson	171/0
	Two-tailed significance	**000/0**

3. Circulation and breadth of information (Bridging social capital)
4. Finding and reconnecting with old friends who did not know the whereabouts of each other due to relocation.

One of the most striking differences is the rapid and widespread flow of information among Facebook members. Information resources of people who are not members of Facebook are limited to official sources, media, colleagues or classmates. While Facebook members were fully aware of the social events of the day. This was achieved by asking questions about a number of social events that were to be reported to Facebook members and non-Facebook members that week. The results showed that those who were not Facebook members were unaware of the events, while all Facebook members were aware of the events and shared them with their acquaintances and commented on the Facebook page.

Another point is that when Facebook members accepted a friend's invitation, his/her circle of acquaintances can be seen for this person as well. In this way, Facebook users make new friends and make friends with their friends and colleagues, or friends or colleagues of their siblings. Several Facebook members who posted their portfolios (design, tailoring, etc.) on the Facebook page had found several co-workers or business partners through Facebook.

In this regard, Maleki Minbash Razgah and Shahriari (2017 [1396 Iranian Calendar], p. 90) in interviews with business experts and based on their research results, indicate that interaction and establishing two-way communication with the customer are opportunities of social networks for businesses to expand their activities. The results of Feizi and Ghaffari Ashtiani's (2018 [1397 Iranian Calendar], p. 14) study on the effect of social media content on the intention to buy, indicate that among customers of Novin Charm who use Instagram, the social interactions affect the intention to buy through customer relationship.

DelAfrooz et al. (2019 [1398 Iranian Calendar], p. 83), try to identify the factors influencing the development of e-commerce, by emphasizing the role of social networks. They come up with some suggestions to managers. They suggest to them to create personal pages on social networks so to enable their customers to communicate with the organization and their colleagues.

Evaluation of the Research Question

What is the position of Iranian brands, companies and small businesses in terms of using Facebook's capabilities for advertising and sales?

To answer this question, we have compared the brands and companies in Iran and Turkey that had the highest growth rate in terms of number of likes on Facebook in June 2014, June 2015 and 2016, as well as the brands that have the most likes in the world. We then re-evaluated the situation of these businesses in 2020 to depict the phenomenon of 'migration' of Iranian brands on social media. It should be noted that when a social media is filtered, businesses are forced to leave this social media and continue their economic activities in other social media. This is what we call the migration of Iranian brands in social media.

Iranian Brands and Companies on Facebook

In addition to creating a private page with their name, Facebook users can create public pages on Facebook. The number of likes indicates the popularity of a page, in other words, the number of followers of that page on Facebook. Facebook has divided public pages into the following subgroups.

1. Local jobs and businesses
2. Companies, organizations and institutions
3. Brands, industries
4. Art groups
5. Entertainment
6. Association

Here, by comparing the names of the brands that are in the highest rank in Iran, Turkey, and the world, we show that due to the filtering of Facebook in Iran, famous industries and brands in Iran have not been able to use Facebook. Facebook had nearly 1.591 billion users in 2016 and it now has 2.912 billion monthly-active users in 2022. This is a good market and platform for advertising and customer attraction.

Table 3.5 presents the names of 5 brands that had the highest growth rate in increasing the number of followers on Facebook (number of likes) in June 2014, June 2015 and January 1995 in Iran. By looking at these pages, it is clear that they are unprofessional in creating and designing business pages due to the filtering of Facebook. The Media world page, which is formed under the brand subgroup, is about football and has nothing to do with commercial companies (Table 3.5). Zarrin Home porcelain and "Mim" design and printing

Table 3.5 Names of five brands that had the highest growth rates in Iran in June 2014, 2015 and 2016

Five brands that had the highest growth in June 2014	Number of likes in 2014	Five brands that had the highest growth in June 2015	Number of likes in 2015	Five brands that had the highest growth in December 2016	Number of likes in 2016
Media world	776,000	Media world	1,000,400	Be-ruz-resani	627,259
System professional Sp	65,000	Be-ruz-resani	584,088	Net berg	196,764
Mim team	63,000	What do I wear?	324,900	BF GF	194,036
Zarrin home	64,000	Mim team	73,300	Kia gallery	110,846
Smirnoff	50,000	System professional	65,300	System professional	77,172

Table 3.6 Names of 5 brands in terms of number of followers in June 2014; Iranians are at the top of the list

Five Brands	Total number of Likes	Iranian followers
BMV	17,766,085	299,004
ZARA	21,772,983	226,442
Mercedes- BNZ	14,603,344	224,262
Snickers	11,003,410	207,806
Adidas originals	24,207,871	205,244

companies are the Iranian team, which have about 63,000 to 64,000 followers. The fifth brand in June 2014 is an alcoholic beverage company with more than 50,000 Iranians. The number one brand is "Be-ruz-resani[10]", which had more than 600,000 likes in December 2016.

Here, we evaluate the names of the 5 brands that in terms of the number of Iranian followers are in the highest rank (Table 3.6). The 5 brands are all foreign brands and up to the rank of more than 50. The names of any Iranian brands were not seen in the list.

It is also important to pay attention to the names of the 5 brands that had the highest growth rate in Turkey in June 2014 (Table 3.7). The first rank in terms of growth rate in June 2014, belongs to Turkish Air with 4,200,000 likes on Facebook, and 200,000 people were added to its followers in June 2014. The number of "likes" in favor of Turkish Air reached 6,000,000 in 2015 (Table 3.9). The second brand is the representative of the American Polo brand in Turkey with 2,500,000 likes in June 2014. Of course, in June 2014, more than 125,000 likes were added to the number of likes. The other three businesses are all Turkish brands or shops with more than 1,000,000 likes. Comparing figures of Table 3.7 and Table 3.5, it is clear that the number of Kish Air "likes" is more than 40 times that of the Iranian brand Mim-Team and

---

[10] It means "updating".

Table 3.7 Names of the 5 brands with the highest growth rates in June 2014 in Turkey

Brands	Number of likes	The increase in June
Turkish Airlines	4,200,000	225,032
U.S. polo Assn.	2,500,000	125,963
HiSLeR AYNaSı	1,500,000	123,791
DeFacto	1,300,000	114,163
Grupfoni	139,000	109,767

Table 3.8 The names of the 5 brands that are at the top of the list in June 2014, 2015 and January 2016 in terms of the number of followers in Turkey

Five brand names in June 2014	Number of likes in June 2014	Increase rate in June 2014	Five brand names in June 2015	Number of likes in June 2015	Brand names in December 2016	Number of likes in June 2016
VolkswagenTürkiye	3,120,104	3,029,554	Turkish airline	6,463,400	Turkish airline	9,508,497
Turkcell	3,070,423	2,920,341	Sefamerve	4,076,400	Sefamerve	4,664,142
Avea	2,825,737	2,743,814	Volkswagen Türkiye	3,325,800	KAYRA	4,266,796
bukombin.com	2,320,487	2,213,669	Turkcell	2,883,200	Volkswagen	4,040,339
Nokia Türkiye	2,161,153	2,095,029	KAYRA	2,841,300	Turk Telekom	3,348,379

the growth rate of the Turkish Air brand is more than 50 times higher than the Iranian brand Mim-Team in June '93.

We also analyzed the names of the 5 brands that were at the top of the list in terms of the number of followers in Turkey in June 2014, June 2015 and January 1995 (Table 3.8). There are 5 Turkish brands and more than 90% of the likes are from Turkish users and the rest of the likes are from other countries including the USA and Germany. Comparing Iran and Turkey in terms of the position of brands on Facebook, it reveals that both the number of likes of brands in Turkey is higher and that the brands belong to Turkey. This is while up to the rank of 50, no Iranian brand name can be seen in the list of brands that have been ranked in the highest rank by Iranian followers.

The names of the 5 brands that have the highest frequency in terms of the number of likes on Facebook in the world in June 2014, June 2015, January 2016 and February 2014 are listed in Table 3.9. It can be seen that the number of Coca-Cola followers on Facebook in June 2014 was 84 million, to which about 5 million people were added in the six months of 2014. The number of Coca-Cola followers reached more than 90 million in June 2015 and more than 100 million on January 19, 2016. Samsung Mobile with more than 38 million followers on Facebook ranks second in June 2014. This is while the second rank in June 2015 belonged to the McDonald brand with more than 57 million followers. On January 28, 2016, McDonald still retained second place with more than 68 million followers. Coca-Cola ranked first with 109 million openers in 2021–2022.

Table 3.9 The 5 brands that have the highest frequency in the world in terms of the number of likes on Facebook in June 2014, 2015 and January 2016, the first rank and February 2022

Brands-2014	Number of likes-2014	Number of comments	Increase rate in during 6 months-2014	Brands-2015	Number of comments-June 2015	Brands-December 2016	Number of likes in 2016	Brands -2021	Number of like-2021
Coca-Cola	84,280,185	1,401,948	5,000,000	Coca-Cola	90,523,356	Coca-Cola	101,104,908	Coca-Cola	109,195,018
Red bull	43,811,276	–	1,500,000	McDonald	57,111,904	McDonald	68,523,245	McDonald	81,452,871
Converse	40,185,036	–	2,000,000	Red bull	43,048,504	Red bull	47,009,350	Netflix	80,182,951
Samsung mobile	38,238,556	1,000,000	5,000,000	Nike football	41,951,200	Microsoft Lumia	46,869,618	Red bull	47,715,644
Play station	37,438,932		1,000,000	Oro	40,127,100	Windows	45,298,767	Samsung	47,676,628

As we know, Iran produced 75%[11] of the world's saffron in 2016 while it has no page on Facebook This is despite the fact that Iranian saffron controlled 94%[12]of the world market in 2020. Ghaen Saffron, is an exception as it formed a small group with 1516 members on Facebook with the purpose of introducing the product. In addition to saffron, Iranian carpet industry with a 7.9 percent share in the export of hand-woven carpets in the world in 2020, and Iranian leather brands such as Dersa Leather, Novin Leather, Mash-had Leather, etc. do not have any pages on Facebook either.

Turkish Air ranks third among airlines worldwide and first in Turkey in terms of the number of likes on Facebook in 2015. Meanwhile, the airline symbol for Iran was not activated until June 2015 due to economic sanctions. But then, with the lifting of economic sanctions in January 2016, the symbol of airlines for Iran was activated (Table 3.10). Iran Air had 11,584 likes in February 2022, while the number of likes and followers of Turkish Air had reached more than 10,000,000 in the same year.

SMALL BUSINESS ASSESSMENT ON FACEBOOK

In evaluating the small businesses, the first issue observed in 2014, 2015 and 2016 was that Iranian users created these pages without knowing exactly the features and groupings that Facebook had provided for the pages. For example, Golestan or ZarIran Saffron, which are brands, chose the options of associations or local businesses instead of choosing the brand option. As we can see, ZarIran Saffron's page did not have more than 24 likes in June 2014 and 32 likes in June 2015. Also, the title of some pages is different from the ads inside

Table 3.10 Comparison between the number of Facebook followers of Iran, the World and Turkey re airlines in the pages in June 2015 and January 2016

Iran-June 2015		World-June 2015		Turkey-June 2015	
Inactive airline symbol		KLM	6,043,351	Turkish Airlines	4,283,729
		Southwest Airlines	4,304,493	PegasusHavayollari	1,047,248
		Turkish Airlines	4,283,729	Türk Hava Yollari	865,009
Iran-December 2016		World-December 2016		Turkey-December 2016	
Iran air	9547	QATAR airways	12,320,323	Turkish Airlines	9,508,497
		KLM Royal Dutch Airlines	11,705,285	Türk Hava Yollari	1,964,708
		LATAM airline	9,816,963	PegasusHavayollari	1,340,995
Iran-February 2022		World-February 2022		Turkey-February 2022	
Iran air	11,584	QATAR airways	25,447,246	Turkish Airlines	10,628,142
		LATAM airlines	13,580,593		

[11] http://iraneconomist.com/fa/news/78262/75.
[12] https://tn.ai/2137233.

them. For example, a page called The Ideal Bag and Shoes, has chosen a photo that belongs to a women's fragrance. Or the page of buying and selling domestic dogs opens under the title of education. Perhaps one of the reasons these pages are unprofessionally created is because Facebook is filtered. Of course, some pages have a good name and design and have coded for their goods that customers can order the desired product by sending a message. Examples of these pages are Mitis or Sahebqaranieh Jewelry, the number of likes of which is more than 28,000 in June 2014. However, this decreased by June 2015 as reflected in Table 3.11.

Some pages on Facebook were created and designed in 2015, 2016 and used the taste and interest of users to advertise a restaurant or a product. For example, a page called "shekam-bazhaye Restorangard"[13] selects the title and design of the page in accordance with the interest of some people in a variety of foods, and promotes famous restaurants in Tehran or other cities. The number of likes on this page is more than three hundred thousand. Also, Firoozi Publications, based on the interest of some users in books, has created a book cafe page, which has more than 28,000 likes, and in that way, introduces the books that have been published (Table 3.11). Some of the pages are related to a specific place such as a cafe, pastry shop, etc., such as Bibi Cookies with more than 350,000 likes or Kafka cafe in Kermanshah, which have been very successful.

Of course, some users employed Facebook filtering in 2014 and 2015 and used it for illegal businesses such as prostitution and marijuana sales. For example, several pages in the field of prostitution were observed, one of which had 56,861 likes and the other 11,799 likes in June 2014. There also seems to be a new fake job called buying and selling high-liking pages on Facebook. In summary, it can be said that some businesses such as handicraft and pets selling,

Table 3.11 An example of some small Iranian businesses on Facebook in June 2014 and 2015

Pages	Number of Likes. in June 2014	Number of Likes. June 2015	Pages	Number of likes. 2014	Number of likes. 2015
Sahebqaranieh Jewelry	28,350	26,670	BiBi chocolate cake	353,253	324,041
Amitis Jewelry	31,077	28,263	Café-ketab	289,609	317,871
ZarIran saffron	24	34	Ideal shoes	1226	1597
Shekam-bazhaye Restorangard	321,774	342,402	Viana evening dress	153,000 2396	152,417 9237
Golestan	17,275	–	Dogs store	3622	4071

[13] Belly-worshipers who spend a lot of time in restaurants.

although limited, have been able to use Facebook to advertise and sell their products by the end of 2016 as shown on Table 3.11.

An assessment of small businesses on Facebook in 2021–2022 shows that these businesses have almost become inactive on the platform, migrating from Facebook to Telegram and after filtering Telegram they migrated to Instagram. We address this issue below.

Business 'Migration' from Social Media to Other Social Media

After imposition of filtering on Facebook and the disruption of Line and Viber, Telegram quickly became the most popular social media among Iranians, reaching more than 45 million users in 2017. But in January 2017, Telegram was filtered for one month, and then filtered permanently in May 2017. After filtering Telegram that had more than 45 million Iranian users, businesses that had migrated from Facebook to Telegram gradually migrated to Instagram and some family and friends migrated to WhatsApp. Our assessment of the Telegram groups[14] on February 1st, 2022 indicates that most of the Telegram groups had a negative growth rate, including the Song World Group,[15] which was ranked first with 4.6 million people, but now had a negative growth rate of -2.7. The second group named the Channel of Persepolis followers also had a growth rate of -24.2 k with 3.7 million followers. Only a few news channels, music or proxies had a positive growth rate.

Telegram filtering has imposed a great deal of costs on Iranian businesses. Mousavi, the head of the Information and Digital Media Development Center of the Ministry of Guidance, talked about the number of businesses on Telegram. The official statistics show 19,000 channels with " Shamad Code"[16] were registered on Telegram, of which 9000 channels were related to the sale of goods or services.[17] Their businesses were affected by Telegram filtering. Also, Azari Jahromi, the Minister of Communications at the time, estimated the number of jobs in Telegram at 35,000, which were to be affected by filtering of Telegram.[18] According to another report, after filtering Telegram, about 100,000 shops, service providers, buyers and customers experienced problems with buying and selling and providing online services in Telegram media. According to published statistics, 19,000 channels were operating in the field of business in Telegram. Revenue from Telegram's annual operations are as follows, based on a field report by the Iranian Research Institute.

---

[14] Ir.tgsta.com.
[15] Ahangifaye Donyaye Taraneh.
[16] Shamad is the official code that businesses in Iran have to have it in order to be able to continue their business online.
[17] Click.ir/news/internet-businesses-telegram/ 1397/10/17.
[18] www.yic.news/fa/6549297/.

- Telegram channels with more than 1 million members, had about 80 million Tomans in revenues (22,222 US dollars).[19]
- Telegram channels with 500 thousand to 1 million members, earned about 50 million Tomans (13,888 US dollars).
- Telegram channels with 100 thousand to 500 thousand members, earned about 25 million Tomans (6950 US dollars)
- Telegram channels with 50 to 100 thousand members, earned about 5 million Tomans[20] (1389 US dollars)

It should be noted that each channel with more than 500,000 members usually had 5 content administrators who received salaries, overtime, etc., and also the hundreds of millions of content files that were produced and had a high value, are no longer valuable due to Telegram filtering[21] and are all gone.

In order to provide a better picture of the migration of small businesses from social media to other media, we have re-evaluated the situation of small businesses in 2014 through 2016 and in 2021–2022 (Table 3.12).

In this regard, many Iranian businesses that are active in the field of e-commerce, and incurred a great deal of capital loss following filtering Facebook and then Telegram, made the most sales through their websites. Our evaluation results show that these businesses do not invest in social media for sales and advertising. It should be noted that economic sanctions against Iran have been effective in this situation as well. Below we show the status of some e-commerce companies that are in the highest rank in terms of e-commerce, on Facebook, Telegram and Instagram. Five stars is the sign of the highest ranking in e-commerce (Table 3.13).

Perhaps a line graph comparison of Fig. 3.2 with Figs. 3.3 and 3.4 below, which show the state of social networks in Iran, Turkey and the world, respectively, from 2009 to 2020, indicates more clearly the migration of Iranian businesses.

As shown in Fig. 3.2 after filtering Facebook (marked in dark blue) in 2009, the number of Iranian Facebook users has fallen sharply and then increased again with the use of VPN users, in 2017. The number of Facebook users was about 17,200,000, which in 2021 (Dogres, 2021) dropped down to 2,200,000. The number of Telegram users in January 2016 had reached 45,000,000, which with the Telegram filter in May 2018, including 36.3 per cent of total users (Dogres, 2021) has reached 24,500,000 in 2021. The number of Instagram users (marked in brown), on the other hand, has increased significantly, and with 45.3% of the total (Dogres, 2021), users have reached more

---

[19] Rate of US dollar was about 3600 Tomans at the end of 2016.
[20] www.eghtesadnews.com/fa/tiny/news-262052.
[21] https://www.bmsd.net/fa-ir/blogs/telegram-filtering-side-effects/.

Table 3.12 Small Iranian businesses on Facebook, Telegram and Instagram in February 2022

Name of page	Facebook	Telegram	Instagram	Name of page	Facebook	Telegram	Instagram
Sahebqaranieh jewelry	There is no longer a page with this name	There was no page	There is no longer a page with this name	BiBi chocolate cake	There was no page	There was no page	There was no page
Amitis Jewelry	Only one like	13 members. Latest post on March 2020	122 followers. Average likes 23	Café-Ketab	136 members and 3 likes	75,157 Members Latest post on Jabuary 23rd, 2022	1955 followers, 1730 Post and 230 Views
ZarIran saffron	There was no page	235 Members No post, created onb April 2020	55,300 followers, 1200 Likes and 233 Post	Ideal shoes	Latest post in 2014	231 members Latest post on January 25, 2022	3301 followers 261 post and 41 Likes
Shekam-bazhaye Restorangard	There is no longer a page with this name	62 members, latest post in 2016	7685 followers, 70 likes and 166 post	Viana evening dress	Last post on February 2015 And 5 likes	22 Members, inactive since January 2019	17,900 followers, 90 post and 578 likes

than 30,000,000 in 2021. In conclusion, it can be said that Iranian brands have not occupied any significant place in the global virtual market of Facebook that has more than 2.912 billion monthly active users in 2022. It is hoped that with any future lifting of economic sanctions against Iran, the presence on social media, especially Facebook, which connects businesses to the global market, will regain its importance for Iranian brands.

Conclusion

The process of producing goods and services in the new economy has become more complex and the need for informal and normative exchange has increased. For this reason, the new capitalist economy creates a constant demand for social capital (Fukuyama, 2006, p. 92). Social networks, including virtual social networks, are a good place to provide and produce the social capital needed by the new capitalist economy. Here, an evaluation of the economic aspects of social media was offered both from internal and external dimensions. The results of the survey research in a sample of 2437 proved the hypotheses of this

Table 3.13 Businesses Active in e-commerce

Ranking	Name of the Business	Facebook	Telegram	Instagram
Five star	Zanbil E-store Zanbil.Ir	Inactive, used to have 1872 followers, latest post on June 21, 2015	3100 members, latest post on December 2021	105,000 followers, 2150 post, latest post had 139 likes
Five star	Hostiran.net	Active, 7600 followers, latest post on January 1st did not have any likes	Inactive	7276 followers, 66 post and the latest post gained 144 likes
	Digikala.com	Inactive, 6277 followers, last post on April 26, 2014 gained 8 likes	90,092 member, latest post on January 21, 2022	56 followers, 11 posts, latest post gained 5 likes
Five star	Esam.Ir	Inactive, last post on November 2, 2014	14,100 members, latest post on December 21, 2021	96,800 followers, 1055 posts, last post gained 659 likes and 100 comments
Four star	Divar.Ir	Inactive	17,172 members, latest post on February 1, 2022	420,000 followers, 519 posts. Latest post with 36,686 likes and 107 comments
Three star	Avajang.com	Active, latest post on December 4th, 2021	94 members and last post on May 2018	19,500 followers, 592 posts. Latest post gained 7401 likes and 120 comment

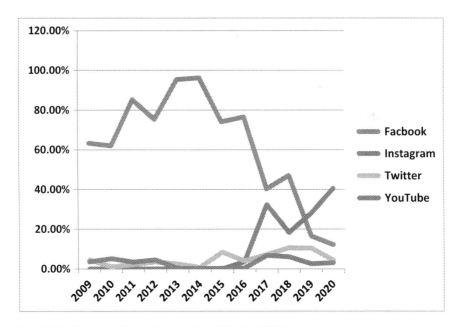

Fig. 3.2 Social media statistics in Iran 2009 to 2020

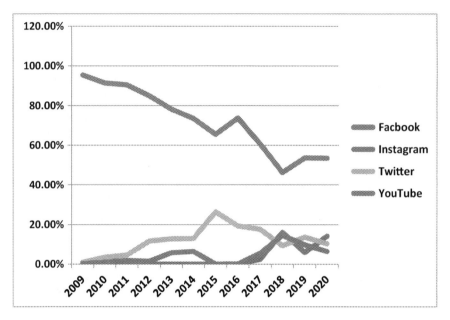

Fig. 3.3 Social media statistics in Turkey 2009 to 2020

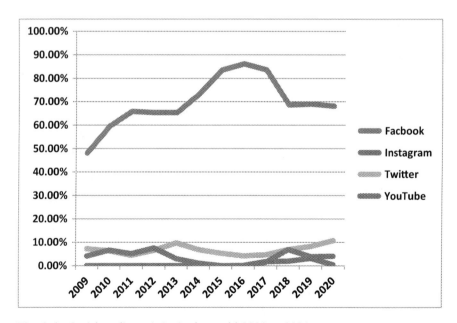

Fig. 3.4 Social media statistics in the world 2009 to 2020

research (hypotheses 1 and 2). In other words, the results show that being an Iranian Facebook user results in an increase in the bridging social capital of the Facebook user and accelerates the flow of information.

Here we will explain that if Facebook was not filtered, how this social capital would have contributed to the economic prosperity of brands and companies in the internal and external sectors.

If Facebook was not filtered in Iran and every organization had a page on Facebook through which employees interacted with each other, the information circulation in various categories of the organization would have been easier. This facilitation of information circulation would have likely led to economic prosperity (Fukuyama, 2006, p. 92; Zhang et al., 2011). In addition, Facebook could provide a platform for interaction between employees and managers of the organizations, which in turn could cause managers to be familiar with the views and opinions of employees and be informed about the issues and problems of the organization. All of these as Fukuyama argues (2006, p. 80) could result in an increase in trust among employees of the organization and could contribute to self-management and self-organizational authority.

From an external point of view, the nature of people's interaction with people and industry owners has caused information control to no longer be in the hands of companies. It is now the customers who determine what information is important and prominent (Mangold & Faulds, 2009) and the success of famous brands is measured by how they appear on social media and how they interact with customers. Facebook also has a large global market for advertising and marketing for brands with 2.912 billion users in 2022. However, due to Facebook filtering, Iranian businesses lost this global market and have not been able to use this global market for marketing and economic prosperity.

The research results showed that success can be achieved by corporate brands that manage to maintain a strong presence online on Facebook. Turkish Air, for example, with more than 4 million likes in June 2014 and 6 million in June 2015, ranked first in Turkey and third in the world in terms of the number of "likes" received on Facebook in 2015. The number of Turkish Air followers reached 10,600,000 in February 2022, while Iran Air had only 11,584 likes on Facebook in February 2022. Other famous Iranian brands do not have a page on Facebook in products such as saffron, carpets and leather industries.

The results of the longitudinal study also showed that small businesses have also gradually migrated from Facebook and Telegram as a result of filtering which had a devastating effect on Iranian business performance online in the periods studied.

References

Ashraf, N. (2014). Impact of Social Networking on Employee Performance. *Business Management and Strategy, 5(2),139–150.*

Asur, S. & Huberman, B. (2010). Predicting the Future with Social Media. *IEEE/WIC/ACM International Conference on Web Intelligence and Intelligent Agent Technology,* 492–499.

Cone (2008). Business in social media study. Retrieved from: http://onesocialmedia.com/wpcontent/uploads/2010/03/2008_business_in_social_media_fact_sheet.pdf.

Cray, E. (2012). The Social ROI: Successful Social Media Measurement from an Agency Standpoint. *The Elon Journal of Undergraduate Research in Communications.* 3(1), 43–52.

DelAfrooz, Narges, Taghavi Amir Ali, et al. (2019) Identifying Factors Affecting the Development of E-Commerce with Emphasis on the Role of Social Network, Business Management Quarterly No. 43 Fall 2017 70–87.

Dogres, Holly (2021), Iranian on social Media https://www.atlanticcouncil.org/in-depth-research-reports/report/iranians-on-socialmedia/

Ellison B. N. & Steinfield, S. & Lamp, C. (2007). The Benefits of Facebook "Friends" Social Capital and College Students' Use of Online Social Network Sites. *Journal of Computer-Mediated Communication, 12,* 1143–1163.

Feizi, Zahra, Peyman Ghaffari Ashtiani (2018) Investigating the Impact of Social Media Content on Purchase Intention Considering the Mediating Role of Normative and Information Social Influence and Customer Relationship (Customers of Novin Charm Store through Instagram Social Network), Journal of Marketing Management No. 41 Winter 1397, 1–20.

Field, J. (2009). *Social Capital.* trans. Qafari, Q. & Ramezani, H. 2nd Ed. Tehran: Kavir Publication.

Fukuyama, F. (2006). *The End of the Order.* trans. Tavassoli, Q. Tehran: Hekayate Qalame Novin Publications.

Hooman, H. (2001) *Multivariate Data Analysis in Scientific Research.* Tehran: pars.

Kaplan, A. & Haenlein, M. (2010). Users of the world, unite! the challenges and opportunities of social media. *Business Horizons,* 53(1), 59–68.

Lee Sing, R. (2009). Social Network Websites and intra-organizational relationships: Using Facebook to Build Employee Relationships at Serena Software, University of South Florida.

Lewis, Jane and Anne West (2009), 'Friending': London-based Undergraduates' Experience of Facebook, **New Media Society** at: http://nms.sagepub.com/content/11/7/1209; also available at: New Media& Society, http://nms.sagepub.com.

Mangold, W. & Faulds, D. (2009). Social media: The New Hybrid Element of the Promotion Mix. *Business Horizons,* 52, 357–365.

Maleki Minbash Razgah, Morteza; Mehri Shahriari (2017) Using Social Networks for Business in Iran: Challenges and Opportunities, World Media Magazine Volume 12 Issue 2 Published in Fall and Winter 1996, 108–89

Michaelidou, N. & Siamagka N. & Christodoulides, G. (2011). Usage, barriers and measurement of social media marketing: an exploratory investigation of small and medium B2B brads. *Industrial Marketing Management,* 40 (2011), 1153–1159.

Moffitt, S. & Dover, M. (2011). Wikibrands: Reinventing your Company in a Customer-Driven Marketplace. *New York: McGraw-Hill, c2011.*

Munene, A. Nyaribo, Y. (2013). Effect of Social Media Pertication (sic) in the Workplace on Employee Productivity. *International Journal of Advances in Management and Economics*. 2(2), 141–150.

Qualman, E. (2011, Jun 18). Social media revolution video 2011 (Motion picture). Retrieved April 4th, 2022, from: Qualman, E. (2011, Jun 18). Social media reviolution video 2011 (Motion picture). http://www.socialnomics.net/2011/06/08/social-media-reviolution-video-2011/.

Ritzer, G. (2003). *Sociology Theory in Modern Age*. trans. Solasi, M. 7th Ed. Tehran: Elmi Publications.

Steinfield, C., Ellison, N. B., & Lampe, C. (2008). Social capital, self-esteem, and use of online social network sites: A longitudinal analysis. *Journal of Applied Developmental Psychology, 29*(6), 434–445.

Tajbakhsh, K. (2010). Social Capital: Trust, Democracy, and Development. trans. Khakbaz, A. & Pouyan, H. Tehran: Shirazeh Publication.

Yogesh, K. Dwivedi, Elvira Ismagilova (2021), Setting the future of digital and social media marketing research perspectives and research propositions, International Journal of Information Management 59 (2021) 102168

Zhang, S. A., Anderson S. & Zhan, M. (2011). The Differentiated Impact of Bridging and Bonding Social Capital on Economic Well-Being: An Individual Level Perspective. *Journal of Sociology & Social Welfare*, XXXVIII (1), 119–143.

CHAPTER 4

The Digital Shaping of a City: A Biography of 'Cyberabad' in Three Acts

Usha Raman and Aditya Deshbandhu

INTRODUCTION

The growth over the past three decades of the city of Hyderabad, India's 'second electronic city' after Bangalore, has paralleled the vision and the aspirational policies of a newly liberalised India. In the process it has created both opportunities and disruptions in the lives of its inhabitants. The last three decades have seen the city steadily expand both in terms of its geographical borders and population size, as a large migrant community takes up residence, in pursuit of work in the city that has now been dubbed "Cyberabad". This transformation has seen the city's loci of power shift as traditional economic and cultural centers have either been reconfigured or have made way for new quotidian infrastructures that mark the environs of a "Hi-Tech City" or the new IT corridor. For the city's inhabitants, the digital has shaped everyday life not only because of the growing dependence on networked devices, but also through 'covid' inspired business adjustments and changes in the infrastructures of daily living. These include the routing of urban transport, the availability and distribution of white-, blue- and no-collar jobs, security

U. Raman (✉)
University of Hyderabad, Hyderabad, India
e-mail: usharaman@uohyd.ac.in

A. Deshbandhu
University of Hyderabad, Hyderabad, India

University of Exeter, England, UK
e-mail: aditya.deshbandhu@exeter.ac.uk

© The Author(s), under exclusive license to Springer Nature Switzerland AG 2024
H. S. Dunn et al. (eds.), *The Palgrave Handbook of Everyday Digital Life*,
https://doi.org/10.1007/978-3-031-30438-5_4

considerations, road networks, and waste management, not to mention patterns of life and leisure outside of work.

This chapter attempts to make sense of these ongoing transformations by framing them not only as geographical or urban developments but also as sites that reconfigure and shape the way a city's population routinely works, learns, lives, performs acts of leisure, and of course relates and communicates. Underlying these transformations are policy decisions and governance approaches that emphasise the digital as essential development infrastructure—such as the Narendra Modi government's much-touted Digital India initiative.[1] Using a multi-sited ethnography of three historically and socio-economically distinct parts of Hyderabad, this chapter traces the manner in which these sites have transformed to accommodate and be accommodated by the city's re-creation as a hub of the new (digital) economy. In an ever-expanding urban frame that seeks to make the digital a key part of the everyday life of the city's residents, we explore how these locations, from their rise to their current resolution, as three acts in a dramatic urban transformation that acquires new meanings and forges new relationships and ways of being.

THE DIGITAL (RE)MAKES THE CITY

The nature of urban growth and its impact on the various aspects of city life has been studied from multiple vantage points and across different disciplines, from economics to geography to sociology and more recently, information systems, cultural studies, and media studies. The growth of the information economy and the parallel network society, has also been described and analyzed by several scholars, perhaps most notably Manuel Castells (1996). Swapna Banerjee-Guha's extensive body of work on the "new" and "belligerent urbanism" (Banerjee-Guha, 2009) is premised on the assertion that "neoliberal projects, pursued at diverse scales, are often found tangled with the contradictions and tensions of everyday life." (p. 95). This is in line with Saskia Sassen's exhortation to attend to the dynamics of place: the "local" in global cities (Sassen, 2018). She notes, for instance, that "[the] vast new economic topography that is being implemented through electronic space is one moment, one fragment, of an even vaster economic chain that is in good part embedded in non-electronic spaces." (p. 13). For Sassen, the global city carries a particular conceptual weight predicated on economic, political and social dynamics that drive the formation of a "certain type of urban environment" (Sassen, 2004, p. 29). This urban environment, arguably, has a character that allows it to be linked with a transnational imaginary while cleverly also exploiting those aspects of the local that serve to give it either a historical or cultural patina.

Cities have at their core been economic and political entities, designed to create efficient flow and management of capital and resources, but they are undeniably also social agglomerations. They allow for individuals and communities to connect in new ways, exchanging culture and simultaneously

[1] https://digitalindia.gov.in.

reinforcing continuities and disrupting ways of life as new connections are made. The physicality of life in the city–the roads, transport networks, organization or zoning of living and work spaces–and the governance structure, mark its parts in specific ways. Arguably, the information technology sector, in its broadest formulation, has had a major impact on cities across the world, but particularly visibly in countries like India (which have become offshore labour pools for the IT industry).

Several scholars have examined the ways in which cities like Hyderabad and Bangalore have been transformed along with the growth of the Information Technology and associated services sector (ITES). (Kennedy & Zerah, 2009; Liang, 2006). Gayatri Spivak, in an evocative narrative, describes the growth of a "secessionist culture" in Bangalore, represented by individuals who have "very good telecom links overseas, traveling abroad incessantly, making a dollar salary but living in India, free to be globally mobile in skills, with corresponding aspirations." (Spivak, 2000, p. 11) She links this to what she terms "electronic capitalism", which "steps in to manage the affairs of the state as it helps build an infrastructure for its own optimal functioning and no more" (p. 16). In this view, globalization, as evidenced in the growth of urban centres, remakes the relationship of the city to its various parts, and in doing so, remakes the relationship of its inhabitants to city spaces, its economy, culture, and social and civic life. As new forms of capital enter to create new forms of work infrastructures that in turn spawn civic and governance infrastructures, cities reorient their spatial configurations. What was the centre–in all aspects, of cultural, civic, business and political life–becomes peripheral as the logic of work and its management forces the creation of new spaces of deemed prosperity. In a detailed critique of Hyderabad's transformation into Cyberabad (detailed further in the following section), Isa Mirza, drawing on a range of literature, points to the rapid withdrawal of public investment in existing/historical commercial hubs in favour of the new globalised part of the city–one that represented its connection to the transnational digital economy:

> In an article on global cities in National Geographic, Naidu's Secretary P.K. Mohanty explained that the transformation of Hyderabad was a visual process in which the role of the government was to "show that something was happening" (Greenspan, 2004, p. 51). Naidu's team embarked on a range of tasks from improving infrastructure to a "greening" of the city, all with an obsessive commitment to information technology. Many of these tasks were done through privatisation and private investment schemes ... (Mirza, 2013, p 157)

Even as new space is made for the city to turn global–and digital–a new set of coordinates emerge pushing other parts of the city to be rendered old, their economies less relevant, and alongside, their occupants forced to re-map their spatial relationships. Sociologist Sujata Patel exhorts us to understand these new forms of urban [hyper]development that have emerged in otherwise less developed countries such as India, asking "How do urban structures and forms, characteristic of pre-capitalist cities of India, reorganize as capitalist relations enter into these cities?" (Patel, 2009, p.32) Hyderabad is one of these "pre-capitalist" cities, its growth mirroring the journey of India across pre-modern, modern and globalised (neoliberal) phases, thus an apt site of study to examine these and other related questions.

Traversing the City, Wired and Unwired

Hyderabad was established around 1591 by the Qutb Shahi sultans of Golconda as the capital of a Deccan sultanate subservient to the Mughal rulers of Delhi (Britannica, 2022), and in the four and a half centuries since, has grown into India's sixth largest urban agglomeration (area 650 sq. km; population in 2021, 10.4 million).[2] It is considered to be a geographical and cultural bridge between north and south India, and was developed in the first few decades after the country's independence into an important industrial, research and education center. Since the late 1980s the city has firmly positioned itself as a hub for the computer and IT services industry, taking on from the economic vision of former chief minister of the undivided state of Andhra Pradesh, Chandrababu Naidu (Das, 2015; Kennedy & Zerah, 2009), under whom it began to be referred to as 'Cyberabad'. Today this is the name of one of the three major zones that make up the city (the other two being the traditional urban demarcations of the twin cities of Hyderabad and Secunderabad), a region that houses most of the large IT and IT Services companies and the residential colonies inhabited by the associated workers (Das, 2010, 2012). The city has however grown (and changed) not only in relation to these new spaces, but also in terms of how other, older economic/commercial zones have accommodated the influx of new forms of capital, new kinds of consumers, and new categories of workers. Since the 1940s, there has been a gradual shift of economic power from the old city (the seat of power in India's pre-Independence times) to the newer city of Hyderabad (representing the new republic), to the birth of liberalization and mass consumption, to finally, the era of the digital economy (Mohan et al., 2012). These shifts have resulted in the emergence of new infrastructures including roads, public facilities, and the growth of associated services, and the accompanying decay—or repurposing--of older establishments and structures. Depending on where one lives and works in Hyderabad, like perhaps in most urban spaces in South Asia, IT is present in varying degrees—as economy, as materiality (gadgets, wires, screens of different kinds), as infrastructure (connectivity, mobile apps), as discourse (advertising), and as practice. (For a discussion of civic infrastructure and security for women workers in neoliberal Indian cities, see Raman & Komarraju, 2018). In some pockets of this post-colonial technopolis (Mohan et al., 2012; Postman, 1992), it is the source of control and power, while in others it offers an aspirational path, a firm commercial anchor, or a structuring force.

The chapter draws on a multisite ethnography of three locations in Hyderabad namely; The Financial District and the new IT corridor; the old

[2] https://www.populationu.com/cities/hyderabad-population The 2011 Census records the population at 7.7 million.

business districts of Abids and Koti; and the "assembly and maintenance" market at Chenoy Trade Center in Secunderabad. These sites were chosen because the first is symbolic of the new city and its shiny new centre, while the second is emblematic of its decentered past. The third offers an interesting story of survival and continued relevance.

The sites were examined using a rapid fieldwork approach (Eden et al., 2019) that allowed us to amplify our own deep familiarity with the city. Both co-authors are long-time residents of the city, having watched it grow and change over the years. Hyderabad's entry to the IT space may roughly date back to the early 1980s, when early non-resident Indian (NRI) entrepreneurs with links to the city set up small ventures, noting the presence of a technical workforce with adequate English language skills. (Rediff, 1997; Williamson, 2007; Das, 2010) These companies—mostly computer/hardware resellers and software service providers located themselves in the existing business centres, requiring no more than a few hundred square feet of office room and some storage space. But as the appetite for computing and associated machinery expanded, the outsourcing market grew, and western IT majors began looking at India as a significant offshore location from which to operate. Labour and land were relatively cheap, and skills were available—or possible to develop.

Between the early 1990s and the early 2000s, Hyderabad, along with other Indian cities like Bangalore and Gurgaon, experienced a boom in IT-related workforce and land area occupied by the industry (Gordon & Gupta, 2005; Sharma, 2015). No longer confined to the small shops dotting the old business districts, these new enterprises, both local and multinational, moved to new spaces on the outer fringes of the city, taking with them people, aspirations, and capital. While the governance centers of the city[3] remained where they were (at the time of writing), what changed was where people went to work—and with this, gradually, where people lived, and shopped too. There were new roads, new shopping complexes, and new residential high-rises. Following them were new schools with the promises of curricula that could match the city's global ambitions, and finally, in 2008, a new airport and subsequently a network of "ring roads" that allowed flyers traveling to and from Hyderabad to bypass the old city to reach the new one. The daily life of the city, and its people, had changed, irrevocably.

The authors charted these changes across three sites of the city using rapid ethnographic methods where observations were made in a time-sensitive frame and analysed in conjunction to understand the city's transformation. Existing literature on methodology indicates that ethnographies conducted in short time spans have also been called by other names like 'quick', 'focused', and 'short-term' and have been used in a variety of disciplines where timeliness is an essential part of answering the questions at hand (Eden et al., 2019,

---

[3] The state machinery—the Telangana State Assembly and Legislative Council, the High Court, and the Income Tax Offices—remained in the same location. By 2020 the Income Tax Office had opened a new set of offices in the Madhapur area of Cyberabad.

pp. 1–2). In the social sciences rapid ethnographies are generally performed alongside long time-frame ethnographies or other qualitative data collection tools to supplement and/or complement the observations made and the data gathered (Knoblauch, 2005; Pink & Morgan, 2013). In the context of this study, the researchers used rapid ethnography to understand the contextual realities prevalent in a post-pandemic Hyderabad while at the same time observing and making note of the latest transformations in the city's urban landscape. These observations are then used to explore the central premise of this chapter's argument, namely that everyday lives in the city of Hyderabad have been irrevocably reconfigured owing to the ongoing transformations in the city wrought mainly by the IT economy.

The sections that follow compile observations made by the authors during field visits in February and March, 2022, and are placed in the context of our intimate knowledge of these sites. Both authors have lived in Hyderabad for the large part of their lives, and while the first author has witnessed first-hand the transformations of a "historic city" over the past four decades, the second author grew up in what had become a rapidly emerging global metropolis. Our examination of these locations was framed by a set of questions that sought to understand how the digital in these various forms had impinged on their topography and character, and the ways in which this had shifted perceptions and experiences of these sites in relation to the city. Our analytical framework draws from the existing literature discussed above, on global cities, urban neoliberalism, and the political economy of information technology.

The Commercial Center of Old: Dismantled, Silenced and Empty

It is a hot Wednesday morning in early April 2022 as I hail an Uber to Abids, located in the city's southeastern quadrant in the area known as Gunfoundry. I had not visited this area since 2016. Abids and its neighboring area of Koti are known to be perennially busy, populated by banks, wholesale and retail businesses in multiple sectors, representing some of Hyderabad's oldest family businesses. This area housed the treasury of the erstwhile princely state and later the government of Andhra Pradesh, as well as the head offices of the State Bank of Hyderabad[4] and the General Post Office (GPO). It was for many years the city's financial center and carried the iconic postal index number (PIN) of 001 (500001); in postal terms it was Hyderabad's point of origin. Gunfoundry also housed one of Hyderabad's oldest computer shops, Youdan Marketing, a firm that sold computers, components, and software since the early nineties. This trip to Abids, in a bid to trace Hyderabad's tryst with digitality, was supposed to start at Youdan owing to its location and history. As the cab makes its

---

[4] The State Bank of Hyderabad (SBH) was one of the seven associate banks of the world's largest banking institution the State Bank of India (SBI). On 31st March 2017 the associate bank merged with its parent SBI in a move that was part of a larger merger.

way from the IT corridor to Abids, I note billboards and street signage carrying bright ads from e-commerce and platform companies like *Zepto* and *Swiggy* promising deliveries of groceries in a matter of minutes or emergent ride hailing services like *Whiprides* and *Rapido* offering discounts to first time users. As the cab driver discusses *Uber's* pricing policies in a time when India's fuel prices have soared to newfound heights, Gunfoundry appears in the distance and my eyes scan for Youdan as I prepare to get off.

Ten minutes along the main road and side streets of Gunfoundry, my search for Youdan was to no avail. The location on Google Maps translates offline to a site under construction and as I look for answers on the deserted road, not many people had them. As I speak to owners of surrounding shops, the story begins to fall into place; one of them points out that the building was demolished last year and another tells me that a residential complex is to take its place. As my mind struggles to comprehend how a residential structure could be built in the heart of what was once considered Hyderabad's prime commercial center, I realize that with the closure of Youdan this study has lost its ontological entry point.

It is nearly noon as I decide to visit Koti, some 2 kilometers away, and I hail an autorickshaw (tuk-tuk) to traverse the short distance. I find one willing to ferry me, and the driver, a man in his seventies, is already carrying another passenger but is happy to accommodate me. As I board the auto and listen to a Hindi song from the nineties, my co-passenger inquires if the song was being played off a USB drive or an audio cassette. Ten minutes later I am on the famous Bank Street and I walk towards Koti's widely known electronic market, which spans four streets with over two hundred shops that sell and service electronic appliances. I am mentally prepared for an enormous pre-lunch Wednesday crowd with Covid-19 lockdown restrictions having been earlier lifted in entirety across the nation. Instead, I am greeted by an eerie silence that catches me unprepared. The market is almost empty as shop staff wait for customers who are nowhere in sight. Some of the shopkeepers are immersed in their phones while others rummage through their wares—but the silence is unfamiliar and disorienting. The only place with customers is the pharmacy further down the road.

Further inside the electronics market is a sub-section called Haridas Market, known for great deals on electronic gadgets like digital cameras, video game consoles, home theatre systems. Here too, the shops are empty and the shopkeepers look at me as a prospective customer. Haridas Market, once the epicenter of the "cracking economy" in Hyderabad with numerous video game stores, not only lacks the usual hustle and bustle but also seems to have lost its characteristic air of urgency. In previous work (Deshbandhu, 2020, pp. 137–139) I had observed how some of these stores were filled with gamers from the city who sought inexpensive ways to access their favourite games. In 2017, these shops boasted tall stacks of the latest games and scores of customers thronging the counters through the week. Here I was, six years later, finding the store completely bereft of customers. The stairs leading to one of the popular stores,

Ambrit, are heavily stained with betel juice and the corridors littered. The shopkeepers of the various gaming stores at the market discuss the drawbacks of the ongoing global chip shortage as most of their investments in the latest games haven't translated into sales. At most of the gaming stores as the conversation progresses the sellers try to sell me scalped versions of the hard to come by PlayStation 5 at INR 65,000 –nearly USD180 above its list price. In the three hours I spend wandering the electronics markets at Koti, there are no customers in any of the shops I visit.

High-Tech City: A Node in the Planetary Economy

It is early evening on a Monday. I make my way by DLF Centre, one of the large corporate buildings in the Gachibowli sector of Hyderabad, the western part of the city, now known as Cyberabad. The road alongside it is usually lined by food stalls that in pre-Covid times served an unending crowd of workers from Hyderabad's IT sector. Today, I see just a few people seeking their daily fix of "cutting chai" (Rangaswamy & Sambasivan, 2011). The once brightly lit DLF Centre has several floors of commercial space cloaked in darkness.

From DLF, I drive to the heart of the financial district as the once busy traffic checkpoints have just a few cars waiting for the signal to go. The 50 meter (160 feet) wide road that leads to the campuses of IT majors like Microsoft, Wipro, Infosys and ICICI Bank was once impossible to navigate on weekday evenings and here I was cruising along, taking my time, making observations in the soft orange light cast by the innumerable streetlights. At the (post-Covid) time of writing, most of Hyderabad's IT workforce continues to work from their homes. Local media sources estimate that close to 240,000 workers have left the city in the last two years as the remote working option has allowed them to return to their hometowns and villages, thus saving on rent (Venugopal, 2022). The city of Hyderabad is estimated to house an IT workforce of 600,000 and a further 400,000 additional workers that are dependent on the sector (Venugopal, 2022). Despite the temporary emptiness of the 'district' and the surrounding IT corridor, the gleam of the tall concrete and glass structures is hard to miss as they rise along the broad rivers of black tar that await the inevitable traffic. I drive to the other end of the IT corridor, an area marked by gigantic structures under construction, including a long winding overpass that promises to bring in an even larger workforce.

The contrast between the old commercial centers of Abids and Koti and the IT corridor is stark; one is cloaked in the gloomy silence of inactivity with commerce giving way to residences, while the other is expanding in towers of glass, steel and concrete, making space for more business. Everything here is on a much larger scale, as if in continuity with the global in both space and time (Castells, 1996). Flyovers and skywalks introduce a rhythm and speed more suited to the transnational companies, and the traffic lights are busy even at 2 a.m., as people and businesses meet the temporal requirements of a globalized economy. In this part of the city, gigantic malls stand at convenient distances from the huge business centres, interspersed with gated communities of multistoried apartments; work, leisure, life, all stitched together in a patchwork with wide, well-lit roads and criss-crossing overpasses.

SECUNDERABAD'S CTC: THE NERVE CENTER OF THE LOCAL DIGITAL ECONOMY

The Chenoy Trade Center is a market place in Secunderabad (Hyderabad's twin city) that is based in a squarish plot the size of a conventional city block. CTC as it is generally known, houses over fifty shops that are dedicated to the sale, service, and maintenance of computers, computing hardware, related peripherals and specialized software. Located across from the street that houses one of the city's most renowned Chinese restaurants, CTC is the perfect example of the "other information city" that Lawrence Liang describes in his exploration of Bangalore's IT industry (2006). As I walk into CTC, which, like other parts of the city, is certainly less crowded than usual, I find the shops and showrooms were still abuzz with activity. Sales people were on their phones sharing price quotes with potential clients and negotiating deals while others were ensuring availability of devices and hardware due to the ongoing global chip shortage. However, the smaller shops to the rear of the complex were less busy, their staff either playing games on their phones or waiting for customers to show up.

The few dedicated stores that specialize in service and repair were mostly empty because the number of walk-ins had dropped significantly since the pandemic. As I make my way to the heart of the CTC, I see some activity in the Asus Republic of Gamers store where a clutch of teenage boys admire the RGB-lit dedicated gaming machines while talking specifics with the salesperson. At the heart of CTC also lies its only restaurant, the *Golden Dragon,* a restaurant that serves South Indian, North Indian, Mughlai, and Chinese cuisine, despite its name. A regular haunt for the various employees at CTC, the restaurant is empty at peak lunchtime and the person at the billing desk tells me that most orders are now delivered to the various stores across the complex. I make my way to the end of the complex as I take note of the various stores offering "back to school" discounts at the end of the academic year. The shopkeepers tell me "Anything to increase sales and get a customer into the store." A place once teeming with an endless crowd of people now seems entirely devoid of customers and tech enthusiasts making me wonder if the way these places were doing business had fundamentally changed. Business seemed to be going on, yet there were few customers in sight.

I exit CTC and go towards a predominantly residential area just a few hundred yards away. This place is a lot calmer and greener, and there are no obvious signs of commercial activity. I enter an apartment building, take the flight of stairs to the third floor and a door on the left is my destination: a hardware computer shop that goes by the name of Navya Solutions. As I walk into the three-room office it's clear that a residence has been repurposed into a site of commercial activity. Two women are clacking away on their keyboards in a cabin on the left as Moolchand, the proprietor, rises to greet me. We exchange brief pleasantries as I take in the cartons of processors, GPUs, RAM chips and motherboards. Two men are in another room, assembling CPUs and checking their performance. Even before I can ask Moolchand some basic questions, he jumps on a call promising a client that they will receive a price quotation for an order in a minute. And even before he ends the call, the quotation has been emailed. The calls are unending. Navya Solutions is one of the largest suppliers of computing hardware in the country, providing several IT and ITES organizations with workstations, terminals, and enterprise hardware and then maintaining and upgrading them as part of annual maintenance contracts. In the hour I spend in his office, Moolchand fields close to twenty calls and sends over a dozen purchase orders. Deals are being made on the phone, while the women in the cabin to the left are sending emails, processing orders, and receiving payments.

Taking a break from work, Moolchand invites me to have lunch with him. We sit in his cabin across a wooden plank balanced on a cardboard box that once housed a CPU cabinet. The food is from the *Golden Dragon*. Two of Moolchand's colleagues join us as the phones continue to ring. During lunch they collectively make deals to the tune of 40 lakh rupees (about 52,000 USD), all without a single face to face meeting. They were agreed upon over calls, the details confirmed via messaging services like WhatsApp and then formalized via email. As the three of them squabble over the last of the meal, I realize that at places like CTC the way business is done has indeed forever changed, and that digitality and mobility are at the core of this transformation.

It's [Not] Business as Usual in the City

The observable decay of Hyderabad's old commercial centers in Abids and Koti contrasts with the rapid expansion of the IT corridor on the city's western arm. What were once the epicenters of brick-and-mortar business as well as financial activity now wear a forlorn look, even as the traffic would suggest that conventional trade still continues. Textile showrooms, construction materials, and jewelry stores in these areas are still patronised by older residents of the city. Many of these merchants have set up new shops in Cyberabad's malls, while some shopkeepers and proprietors point out that their potential and returning customers are now shopping online as India's adoption of ecommerce platforms like *Amazon* and *Flipkart* continues unabated (Economic Times, 2022; Dayalani, 2022). Even Youdan, once among the city's primary suppliers of business computers and software, could not sustain a shopfront as customers moved online and elsewhere, to more integrated and diverse marketplaces with a larger range of products and even services. This also reflects the precarious nature of the global IT supply chains and shifting demands.

At Haridas market in Koti, the PlayStation 5 console offers a case in point; a device that has continued to remain challenging to find 18 months after launch (at the time of writing) due to the chip shortages occasioned by pandemic related manufacturing disruptions (Howley, 2022; Martin, 2022). The device was never sold through retailers in India and the only way to obtain the console is through time sensitive sales on ecommerce platforms. Similarly, mobile phones, televisions, sound systems, and computing hardware have all been launched in recent years in India on e-commerce platforms making commercial centers like the Koti electronics market redundant and forcing stores like Youdan to shutter down. Things seem more challenging for centralized video game, electronics and photography markets like Koti's because of the smartphone revolution that has characterized India's digital journey. As most first-time users of the internet access it through smartphones, most digital acts of leisure are performed on these handheld devices. Casual gaming, free to play games and mobile photography become increasingly relevant in the SNS rendered reality of the digital every day, and places like Haridas market and Ambrit seem out of place in this socio-technological imaginary (Jasanoff & Kim, 2015; Ferrari, 2020). For the newer, more affluent customer base, the shopping centres in Cyberabad (where other forms of leisure converge), or the convenience of online ecommerce platforms are the natural destinations.

This reconfiguration of how Hyderabad is doing business needs to be understood both as a social and an urban phenomenon. It is a phenomenon that manifests itself when one situates the construction of a residential complex on the most prominent location of Gunfoundry (the former commercial center) in the context of a Hyderabad that has realigned itself to support its IT workforce and the digital capital that it accrues in a globalized economy through the process. It makes little sense for computer machinery to be sold through a single retailer in Gunfoundry when customers can get everything they stocked—and more—online, or from the many suppliers still doing business at different scales of operation in Secunderabad's CTC. The new IT corridor on the other hand is where the human resources throng to, for jobs in the sector and in the many support structures it requires. Even as shops shut down and yield their real estate to residences, the IT corridor continues to see a steady expansion in facilities and infrastructure. This realignment of the city's locus signals a shift that is not just commercial and financial but also digital and aspirational.

The Chenoy Trade Center (CTC) however, stands as a stark contrast to this transformation of the city as it remains a site of business that has only specialized further with time. When Liang conceptualizes the other information city of Bangalore (Liang, 2006) he views it as a covert site that specializes in the gray areas of the digital economy and works alongside Bangalore's IT publics. The CTC on the other hand is overt and transparent, a site that is accessible by all willing to seek it. Most people who do business at the CTC and its surrounding areas talk about the availability of the best possible prices and service. Moolchand says that it's got to do with the centralization of the business and its capability bolstered by the collective and cooperative ethos of the many vendors in the complex. He says "I don't mind one bit sending new clients to people I think can serve them better. There is enough in Hyderabad as a market for everybody here." He elaborates on the unique nature of how CTC as a collective operates:

> Our logic is simple; we sell in high volumes with razor thin margins and thus we need a direct connect with both the manufacturers and the customers. No single business can achieve both of those connections but CTC's businesses together can. When I started Navya (my firm), I thought about situating it in Cyberabad but there was simply no such network there and it made no commercial sense.

The connection between the city's financial district and IT corridor to CTC is increasingly visible when you look further and find that most of the large volume clients at CTC are the firms and offices operating on the other side of the city (Raman et al., 2014). Moolchand says that his clients are mostly businesses and educational institutions[5] located in Cyberabad, a side he hasn't visited in the last two years. The digital logic of the everyday though, ensures that his business and the businesses of several others at CTC bridge that purported divide between Cyberabad and the CTC every day as they enable the technological capabilities of Cyberabad while being fueled by them financially. The digital logic of Hyderabad as an IT city and the way the city's people do business, seek education, perform acts of leisure have been significantly transformed by its digital dimension, transformations that are increasingly more visible nearly three years into a global pandemic where most of these activities were rendered through and experienced on digital platforms.

Most people we spoke to as part of the rapid ethnography for this study mentioned the difficulties of crossing the figurative divide between Hyderabad and Cyberabad as part of their everyday lives. People who resided and worked in Cyberabad were keen to point out the lack of necessity to engage with areas of the old city and its quotidian landmarks whereas people from the old city were keen to showcase their capabilities of navigating the digital and thereby minimizing their need to exercise physical mobilities beyond the vicinities of their places of work and residence. Those working in CTC and the traditional commercial centers of Abids and Koti mentioned their need to travel to Cyberabad for business and work but were keen to point out that these trips were now few and far between, as much of what they needed to do could be done online.

It is important to note that areas in the financial district and the new IT corridor are extremely well connected by the city's network of roads and the city's Metro connects to the Cyberabad area at its two extremities (Raidurg and Kukatpally). However, the Metro's connectivity (in its current state) ceases at

---

[5] The Cyberabad area of Hyderabad is also home to leading academic institutions like the University of Hyderabad, The International Institute of Information Technology (IIIT-H), the Indian Institute of Technology, Hyderabad (IIT-H) and the Indian School of Business (ISB) to name a few.

these two points as the network does not traverse Cyberabad and its various areas. The reliance of a network of roads and flyovers in Cyberabad is overwhelmingly apparent as the city's transport machinery has public transport systems (albeit limited) that ferry people and infrastructure to and from specific landmarks in Cyberabad. Dedicated buses that originate and culminate at large corporate complexes ensure that the workforce have means to reach these sites from various sections of the city as well as adhere to the various chronological structures that they function in.

The business that is done in each of these locations is of course different both in scale and nature. The shrinking markets of Koti continue to serve those at the margins of digitality, with their repurposed goods and shortcuts for those who have neither the cultural or financial capital to reach the new malls of Cyberabad, or the tech-savvy to explore the hybrid networks of CTC. Cyberabad, for its part, is an ecosystem in itself, with a subterranean structure that draws on the labour and governance mechanisms of the political centre and a more visible network of high-rises connected to global flows of a skilled workforce and transnational capital. The complex mesh of storefronts and back alleys of CTC represents what we might call the middle layer of the IT economy, enabling digital transformations for various scales of business and a trusted venue for new and existing customers in commercial, leisure, and education markets.

ENDNOTE: THE CITY'S SHIFTING CENTRE(S)

As the map of the city shifts to accommodate the movement of capital, the aggregations of workplace and workforce, the accompanying changes in where people live, how they travel to work (or not), and where they shop, there are secondary level changes that we need to attend to. These are the patterns and modes of governance that urban geographers and sociologists have pointed to, as well as the political motivations that both underlie and emerge from such changes. Sujata Patel (2009) emphasizes that such changes are closely linked to issues of identity politics, with new forms of inequity emerging in global cities. Matheiu Lefevre (2015) notes that global cities, alongside economic growth, also need to focus on issues such as quality of life and the aspirations of those marginalised by the very changes that bring such growth.

For those living in Hyderabad, these nodes of economic activity have also transformed life in other ways. With so much urban development attention focused on creating a smart infrastructure for Cyberabad, there has been less of the city's budget available for other parts of the city. Those who commute to Cyberabad for work must depend on an incomplete and precarious transport network. It seems the Hi-Tech city is built for those with cars or have access to other modes of private transportation. Those who do commerce in CTC must deal with the congestion of the old road networks and lack of parking and other civic amenities. As for the markets in Koti, it quietly awaits an extension of the heritage tag, and the possibility of becoming a relic of old Hyderabad, to be rescued by tourism.

All this is to say that the digital, in all its forms, shapes the everyday, even of those who do not have access to devices, networks, or infrastructures. The digital creates shadows and shines lights, generating growth or prompting atrophy in the city's many parts. There is a demonstrable need to create policy, governance, or programmes that even this out. In the process, one must attend to the nuances of what is happening in all these parts, both at the digital centres and the neglected urban peripheries.

REFERENCES

Banerjee-Guha, S. (2009). Neoliberalising the 'urban': New geographies of power and injustice in Indian cities. Economic and Political Weekly, 95–107.

Britannica, T. Editors of Encyclopaedia (2022). Hyderabad. Encyclopedia Britannica. https://www.britannica.com/place/Hyderabad-India.

Castells, M. (1996). The information age: Economy, society and culture, the rise of the network society. Oxford: Blackwell.

Das, D. (2010). Splintering urbanism in high-tech Hyderabad Department of Geography, National University of Singapore, Singapore

Das, D. (2012). Ordinary lives in extraordinary Cyberabad. The Transforming Asian City: People's Practices and Emergent Spaces. London/New York: Routledge, 112–122.

Das, D. (2015). Hyderabad: visioning, restructuring and the making of a high-tech city. Cities 43: 48–58. https://doi.org/10.1016/j.cities.2014.11.008.

Dayalani, V. (2022). Inside India's $400 Bn Ecommerce Economy. *Inc 42* [Online]. Retrieved from: https://inc42.com/features/inside-india-400-bn-ecommerce-economy/.

Deshbandhu, A. (2020). *Gaming culture(s) in India: Digital Play in Everyday Life*. London, New Delhi: Routledge.

Economic Times (2022). India's ecommerce market to grow by 21.5% in 2022: GlobalData. *Economic Times* [online] Retrieved from: https://economictimes.indiatimes.com/tech/technology/indias-ecommerce-market-to-grow-by-21-5-in-2022-globaldata/articleshow/89038696.cms?utm_source=contentofinterest&utm_medium=text&utm_campaign=cppst.

Eden, G., Sharma, S., Roy, D., Joshi, A., Nocera, J. A., & Rangaswamy, N. (2019, November). Field trip as method: a rapid fieldwork approach. In Proceedings of the 10th Indian Conference on Human-Computer Interaction (pp. 1–7).

Ferrari, E. (2020). Technocracy meets populism: The dominant technological imaginary of Silicon Valley. Communication, Culture & Critique, 13(1), 121–124.

Gordon, J., & Gupta, P. (2005). Understanding India's services revolution. In *India's and China's recent experience with reform and growth* (pp. 229–263). Palgrave Macmillan, London.

Greenspan, A. (2004). *India and the IT Revolution*. New York: Palgrave Macmillan.

Howley, D. (2022). Why you shouldn't expect to get a PlayStation 5 anytime soon. *yahoo! Finance* April 20 [online]Retrieved from: https://finance.yahoo.com/news/why-you-shouldnt-expect-to-get-a-play-station-5-anytime-soon-160137666.html.

Jasanoff, S., & Kim, S.-H. (Eds.) (2015). Dreamscapes of modernity: Sociotechnical imaginaries and the fabrication of power. Chicago, IL: The University of Chicago Press.

Kennedy, L. and Zerah, M. (2009). The shift to city-centric growth strategies: perspectives from Hyderabad and Mumbai. *Economic and Political Weekly*, Vol. 43, No. 39 (Sep. 27–Oct. 3, 2008), pp. 110–117

Knoblauch, H. 2005. "Focused Ethnography."Forum Qualitative Sozialforschung/Forum: Qualitative Social Research, North America, 6 Sep. 2005. Retrieved from: http://www.qualitative-research.net/index.php/fqs/article/view/20.

Lefevre, M. (2015). The mighty metropolis. The World Today, February & March 2015. Retrieved from: https://www.chathamhouse.org/publications/the-world-today/2015-02.

Liang, L. (2006) The other information city. Retrieved from: www.t0.or.at/wio/downloads/india/liang.pdf.

Martin, A. (2022). PS5 shortages set to continue due to global chip shortage, warns Sony. *sky NEWS* February 2 [online] Retrieved from: https://news.sky.com/story/ps5-shortages-set-to-continue-due-to-global-chip-shortage-warns-sony-12530975.

Mirza, I. (2013). The provision of information technology services in a new political economy: a case study from Hyderabad, India. Journal of Contemporary Asia 43 (1): 148–172

Mohan, A. V., Ejnavarzala, H., & Lakshmi, C. N. (2012). University Linkages in Technology Clusters of Emerging Economies-Exploratory Case Studies from Cyberjaya, Malaysia-a Greenfield Development and Cyberabad, India-a Brownfield Development. *World Technopolis Review*, *1*(1), 42–55.

Patel, S. (2009). Doing urban studies in India: the challenges. South African Review of Sociology 40 (1): 31–46.

Pink, S., & Morgan, J. (2013). Short-term ethnography: Intense routes to knowing. *Symbolic Interaction*, *36*(3), 351–361.

Postman, N. (1992). Technopoly: The surrender of culture to technology. Publishers Weekly, New York

Raman, U., Chintakunta, H., and Girigalla, R. (2014). Glittering and grey: the two facets of Hyderabad's IT-enabled growth. Paper presented at the Annual Conference of the International Association for Media & Communication Research (IAMCR), Hyderabad, India, July 15–19, 2014. (Unpublished).

Raman, U. & Komarraju, S. A. (2018). Policing responses to crime against women: unpacking the logic of Cyberabad's SHE Teams. Feminist Media Studies, 18:4, 718–733, DOI: https://doi.org/10.1080/14680777.2018.1447420.

Rangaswamy, N., & Sambasivan, N. (2011). Cutting Chai, Jugaad, and Here Pheri: towards UbiComp for a global community. Personal and Ubiquitous Computing, 15(6), 553–564.

Rediff (1997). Andhra may offer more tax sops to IT companies. *Rediff* October 13 [online] Retrieved from: https://www.rediff.com/computer/oct/13ap.htm.

Sassen, S. (2018). The global city: Strategic site, new frontier. In *Moving Cities–Contested Views on Urban Life* (pp. 11–28). Springer VS, Wiesbaden.

Sassen, S. (2004). The global city: Introducing a concept. *Brown J. World Aff.*, *11*, 27.

Sharma, D. C. (2015). *The outsourcer: The story of India's IT revolution.* MIT Press.

Spivak, G. (2000). Megacity. Grey Room, No. 1 (Autumn, 2000), pp. 8–25.

Venugopal, S. (2022). Hyderabad: Techies told to shift to 'base station.' *Telangana Today* April 7 [online] Retrieved from: https://telanganatoday.com/hyderabad-techies-told-to-shift-to-base-station?.

Williamson, M. (2007). Cyberabad. Engineering & Technology, 2(12), 38–42.

CHAPTER 5

Social Media, Space and Place in South Africa: #egoli (Johannesburg) on Instagram

Tanja Bosch

INTRODUCTION

Social media platforms, particularly those driven by visual imagery such as Instagram, offer users the ability to map their everyday lives online via a curated selection of photographs. The cultural and spatial organisation of urban geographies can thus be reflected in online spaces. This chapter explores visual representations of the city of Johannesburg (known colloquially as Joburg), South Africa, on the photo-sharing app, Instagram. Johannesburg is an interesting choice of case study, as it "shares many realities with other cities in the south. It features luxury as well as slum tourism, gated communities as well as shantytowns, extractive and resource-heavy industry and business, unreliable infrastructure and public transport, mass migration, poorly regulated development, privatisation and neo-colonial investment, youth unemployment and a vast gulf between wealthy elites and an increasingly marginalised poor" (Falkof & Van Staden, 2020, p. 3).

Instagram has become a popular way for users to share their mundane experiences of everyday life in public spaces while simultaneously serving as a platform for visual representations of culture. "Digital media technologies are increasingly playing a role in reconfiguring the spatial order of social life and also affect how we directly experience place" (Bosch, 2021, p. 70) Further, digital technologies might not just represent everyday life, but come to actually transform everyday life as well, since they become part of the fabric of people's

T. Bosch (✉)
University of Cape Town, Cape Town, South Africa
e-mail: tanja.bosch@uct.ac.za

© The Author(s), under exclusive license to Springer Nature
Switzerland AG 2024
H. S. Dunn et al. (eds.), *The Palgrave Handbook of Everyday Digital Life*,
https://doi.org/10.1007/978-3-031-30438-5_5

lives. The act of posting about city-related activities on Instagram becomes embedded in daily social practice.

This chapter draws on a qualitative study of a selection of images from Instagram posts tagged with a Johannesburg city specific hashtag (#egoli), to explore how users curate their visual impressions and representations of the city. The chapter explores online representations of space and identity in the context of offline social and spatial polarisation, as the result of the legacy of apartheid infrastructures of inequality. Johannesburg, also referred to as Jozi, Egoli, the City of Gold, interchangeably, has long held significance as South Africa's largest city and consequently, the heart of global apartheid. It also holds a commanding position in the national social imagination (Harrison et al., 2014). Joburg is a globally linked economic hub and is seen as a linking city within a complex, multimodal network of world cities (Rogerson & Rogerson, 2015). It is an exemplar of urbanity in the global South (Harrison et al., 2014). However, the city is also one of the world's crime capitals with entrenched systems of urban inequality. Falkof and Van Staden (2020) refer to Johannesburg as "a viable template for city life", making it an apt case study, as an exemplar of a global South city.

Through a visual analysis of user posted images, this chapter explores Instagram narratives of the city (Boy & Uitermark, 2017); and how the "materialities and subjectivities of the city are mutually constituted" by social media users (Harrison et al., 2014, p. 20). Contemporary cities are beset with inequalities, where areas or people considered undesirable are rendered invisible, while spaces of upscale consumption are elevated (Boy & Uitermark, 2017). The central research question for this chapter thus asks: How do Instagram users portray Joburg? Following on this, the chapter further attempts to reflect on what these visual portrayals reveal about the fabric and ingredients of everyday life; as well as how users' social media practices themselves transform everyday life. The chapter explores how class, lifestyle and aspiration are visually constructed via Instagram posts, and what social media can reveal about the texture of everyday realities in the city of Joburg. User data from apps such as Instagram add to the methodological toolkit of scholars who study urban dynamics and cities, as such data reflect a curated version of cities, where users selectively represent their everyday lives (Boy & Uitermark, 2016). Boy and Uitermark (2016) further argue that such data can help shed light on segregation, the formation of subcultures, strategies of distinction, and status hierarchies in the city.

Johannesburg, 'City of Gold': The Context

After the discovery of gold there in 1886, Johannesburg became the financial and commercial hub of sub-Saharan Africa (Bremner, 2000). The inner city of Johannesburg has undergone much change over the years, particularly during the post-apartheid period, when it has fallen into a deteriorated state and been considered a 'no-go' zone for middle-class suburbanites. South Africa's pre-apartheid urban policy focused on controlling the black labour force and establishing segregated townships, with the apartheid inner-city a 'whites only' area and black citizens pushed to the periphery. The central and northern areas of Johannesburg were designated for whites while the southern areas were mostly black and working class (Crankshaw, 2008).

After the repeal of the Group Areas Act in 1991, black citizens, as well as African immigrants from countries such as Somalia, Nigeria and the Democratic Republic of the Congo (DRC), moved into the inner city. A consequent exodus of white residents, together with an increase in rent and decline in building maintenance, led to a rapid socioeconomic transformation of the inner city in the 1990s (Bremner, 2000). Johannesburg's inner city has since been perceived as a space of inner decay and criminal activity, though several urban renewal projects have been implemented over the years. The authors in *Anxious Joburg* (Falkof & Van Staden, 2020) trace the city's contradictions from various perspectives, which they argue result in various anxieties, some of which are linked to middle-class fear of crime. Joburg is a gritty urban metropolis "where intense glamour intersects with intense poverty…it is part of the inevitable contradiction of Johannesburg that its parks, museums and coffee shops exist in awkward equilibrium with, not surplus to, its inner-city slums and peripheral informal settlements, its crumbling mines, its failing highways, its car guards, its security companies…" (Falkof & Van Staden, 2020, p. 2).

INSTAGRAM AND CITY SPACES

Globally, Instagram is one of the most popular social media apps, downloaded 3.8 billion times with an audience of more than 1 billion users; and 95 million photos and videos shared everyday (Schaffer, 2022). As of July 2021, there were 6 million Instagram users in South Africa, up from 4.89 million in July 2020 (Statista, 2022). Instagram is the second most downloaded app in the world, with 18–34-year-olds making up the largest user base (Hootsuite, 2022). While the global video application, TikTok (which currently boasts 293 million daily active users worldwide), will most like surpass Instagram in popularity, Instagram remains widely used (Dean, 2022).

Social media users are engaged in ongoing processes of representation, carefully staging and editing images posted on Instagram. Users "selectively and creatively reassemble the city as they mobilize specific places in the city as stages or props in their posts" (Boy & Uitermark, 2017, p. 613). Instagram has become popular amongst users for its visual aspect and ability to add filters to uploaded images. The analysis by Boy and Uitermark (2017) has shown how Instagram representations can "reflect and reinforce processes of gentrification as Instagram users partake in the aestheticization of everyday life and promote places of high-end consumption" (612). Social media plays a role in urban renewal globally, but especially in the Johannesburg inner city, where apps like Instagram have led to physical gatherings of diverse individuals in diverse locations (referred to as InstaMeets) (Hoogendoorn & Gregory, 2016).

Hoogendoorn and Gregory (2016) have argued that Instagrammers contribute to the rebranding of the Johannesburg inner city by helping shift perceptions through their engagement with the inner city. Similarly, Boy and Uitermark (2017) explored how people represent the city of Amsterdam on social media and how these representations feed back into the ways people use the city. Acuti et al. (2018) conducted a content analysis of Instagram images and hashtags to explore the brand image of London and Florence. They argue that user-generated content shapes the brand image of cities, which can help potential residents or visitors form an image of the city. More recently, I probed visual conceptions of space in Cape Town by exploring how Instagram users visualized city space in Cape Town, South Africa (Bosch, 2021), and showing how Instagram reflects a tourist gaze of Cape Town, with the visual culture of the app reflecting the spatialized matrix of the apartheid city. This chapter expands that research and builds on the argument that "The visual storytelling narrative of social media has the capacity to both map and create reality, as a form of collective cultural storytelling" (Bosch, 2021, p. 70). The chapter argues that through engaging with the digital, via Instagram, users not only reflect their experiences of everyday life; but that in turn, this online engagement further holds the potential to transform offline experiences of the city.

Methodology

As Boy and Uitermark (2016) have shown, Instagram can be used as a data source to "shed light on segregation, the formation of subcultures, strategies of distinction, and status hierarchies in the city". Instagram remains a difficult platform for scholars to study as it has not made its API publicly available to researchers. The visual and textual data from the platform thus has to be gathered and analysed manually. For this chapter, images were selected by using a city specific hashtag via a process of elimination as listed below in Table 5.1 and Fig. 5.1. Firstly, a search for all city related hashtags revealed several Johannesburg specific tags, listed below. These were further probed, to reveal the most popular /most used tags as listed below in Fig. 5.1. As previously argued, a limitation of drawing a sample from city-specific hashtags can lead to bias, since tourists also use these hashtags to tag their travel activities (Bosch, 2021). Nonetheless, "exploring the visual narrative of city-related hashtags results in a deep understanding of place, exposing the sometimes-hidden

Table 5.1 General city-specific hashtags

Hashtag	Number of posts
#joburg	866 K
#johannesburg	3.2 m
#jozi	900 k
#egoli	13.6 k

Hashtag			
Number of posts			
#joburg	866k	#johannesburgrestaurants 6k	#jozivibes 66.1k
#joburginyourpocket	4.3k	#johannesburgzoo 4.8k	#igersjozi 145k
#joburgrestaurants	7.2k	#cityofjohannesburg 73k	#jozigrams 58k
#joburgfoodie	32.5k	#johannesburgphotographer 58.4k	#jozimyjozi 4.8k
#joburglife	35.4k		#jozikids 16k
#joburgfashion	24.9k		#jozifashion 14.3k
#joburgcity	19.8k		#jozifood 11.1k
#joburgday	12k		#jozistyle 11.1k
#joburgevents	5.6k		#jozirestaurants 3.4k
#joburgpride	3k		#jozinightlife 1.6k

Fig. 5.1 Expansion of city specific hashtags

narratives and metanarratives (Bosch, 2021, pp. 69–70). Moreover, "location information is a valuable hook for exploring content on Instagram; geographic metadata forms an important basis for much of the initial large-scale analysis of Instagram content (Leaver et al., 2020, p. 86).

Hashtags are a key structural feature of Instagram, and are often used in combination with each other; users often tag uploaded images with several hashtags. The tags serve as "markers for the main subjects, ideas, events, locations, or emotions" featured in the posted images (Highfield & Leaver, 2015, p. 3). Selecting a hashtag for analysis followed an initial process of reviewing all city-related hashtags (listed above in Fig. 5.1) to find a suitable hashtag containing reflective portrayals of the city. Hashtags like #jozifood or #johannesburgrestaurants were found to be too specific, reflecting only food or restaurant-related images. The hashtag #jozi contained predominantly selfies, while #johannesburg was found to contain mostly advertiser and influencer account posts. The hashtag #egoli was selected for this chapter, as an initial preliminary analysis of the tag found that it contained the broadest diversity of images, from a wide range of users. The everyday use of the word Egoli to refer to the city of Johannesburg was popularised by the television soap opera *Egoli: City of Gold*, popular during the early 1990s. The word 'Egoli' means City of Gold in the isiZulu language, as a reference to the discovery of gold as the basis for the city's rapid economic growth.

The visual social semiotic analysis employed in this chapter is based on a dataset of 350 Instagram images tagged with the hashtag #egoli. Hashtags on Instagram serve primarily as captions for accompanying images, as well as locating posts geographically. Of course, as previously argued (Bosch, 2021), tourists also use city-specific hashtags to post their travels, but these posts can still reveal a city's visual identity even if it is only partially constructed by locals. The chapter draws on a small data approach, selecting the first 350 'top posts' using a researcher account and not the author's personal Instagram account. The 'top posts' category on Instagram are selected via the app's algorithm and feature trending posts, though not always from users with the biggest accounts. Instagram does not make its API available to researchers, making this platform typically difficult to study with respect to automating dataset creation. The app's algorithm detects interaction between users to determine which content people most like to see.[1] While we do not know exactly how the Instagram algorithm functions, top posts are 'trending' and 'most engaged with' posts; thus the sample was drawn from these posts to represent not just the visual representations of the city, but also those which were most popular among the app's users. As previously argued (Bosch, 2021), a large dataset of social media images is not necessarily required for a preliminary exploration of Instagram, as reducing the breadth and enhancing the depth and 'thickening' the data (Latzko-Toth et al., 2017) could be a much more useful approach. This small data approach is thus indicative of broader patterns and trends for future research.

Based on an initial review of the images in the dataset, image posts were coded according to the following emergent categories: Arts and culture, city, selfies/people, celebrities, tourism, advertising, food, fashion, sports/fitness, motivational memes or text image posts, outdoor/nature, vehicle and pet/animal. The coding categories were created inductively via a bottom-up process, reviewing all available images to determine dominant patterns and themes to guide the analysis. Several rounds of coding were conducted to refine the themes (Fig. 5.2).

Drawing on the methodology outlined by Jewitt and Oyama (2004), the analysis provides a summary of dominant codes, but also analyses images in terms of the main dimensions including "the form of representation, the setting and the props, the actors' appearance, the composition of each image and the relationship between the represented actors and the viewer (encoded through the use of point of view, distance and contact)" (5).

Arts and culture	Pictures of paintings or tattoos or other artwork, exhibitions
City	Pics of city/buildings/urban landscape
Selfies	Selfies, faces, photos of people
Celebrities	Where you can identify pics of people who are musicians, politicians, celebrities
Tourism	e.g., "10 fun things to do in Joburg"
Advertising	Clear branding in pic or image e.g., Telkom, adverts
Food	Images of food, dishes, meals, wine
Fashion	Highlighting fashion or clothing style, shoes
Sports /fitness	Sporting events, gym pics including selfies, running, cycling etc So don't code these in the selfies category
Memes with text	e.g., motivational memes and texts
Outdoor/nature	Forest, river, nature garden
Vehicle	Cars, motorbikes, planes
Pet/animal	Dog, cat, other animal

Fig. 5.2 Coding categories

[1] https://statusbrew.com/insights/instagram-algorithm/#:~:text=The%20new%20Instagram%20algorithm%202021%20detects%20interaction%20among%20several%20users,creator's%20content%20in%20their%20feed.

Findings and Discussion

The analysis of Instagram posts tagged with the hashtag #egoli revealed a range of city representations, and varied ways in which users curated the city of Johannesburg. The representational work of images serves to reproduce various social imaginaries of the Johannesburg aesthetic of global urbanism. This reproduction of a global aesthetic serves to shape the way the city is imagined and then experienced by Instagram users. The most striking observation from the analysis is that images tagged with the hashtag #egoli tended to reflect a stylized urban imaginary with no evidence of the 'anxious Joburg' reflected by Falkof and Van Staden (2020). The edges of urban city spaces occupied by marginalized groups, the unemployed, low-income groups, or immigrants, are strikingly absent from the dataset. The Joburg imagined by Instagram users via #egoli is an urban landscape of money, power and consumption occupied by economically upwardly mobile individuals. There is no evidence in the dataset of the contradictions and social inequalities of the city. Not a single image in the dataset referenced crime, poverty, homelessness, informal settlements or unemployment.

With reference to the affordances of Instagram, and picture taking, the function of the frame is to exclude (sometimes by virtue of inclusion) and the aesthetic economy of attention is shifted away from the gritty urban realities of everyday Joburg city life, towards glamourous idealized representations. The ways in which Instagram users curate their banal, everyday lives, leaves no visual (or other) space for any person or concept occupying the margins. The Instagram posts analysed for this project reflect the lifestyles of the leisure class, showing people having fun, time off, and engaging in luxurious middle-class lifestyle pursuits.

The majority of images in the sample fell into two main categories, which are discussed in further detail below: (1) Selfies ($n = 121$) and (2) Cityscapes ($n = 108$). The selfies featured showed images of ordinary people in their everyday life contexts, and it is notable that the 'celebrity' category yielded very few posts in the dataset ($n = 3$). Instagram users deployed the hashtag to represent ordinary people's mundane, everyday lives and not for the celebration or recognition of celebrity. Similarly, there were very few posts in the categories of tourism, sports, or fashion. The second most popular set of images covered the areas of arts and culture ($n = 51$), and food ($n = 39$).

Selfies, Race and Gender

Selfies technically refer to images taken by people themselves, typically with a smartphone; though the dataset collected these types of images alongside photographs of people taken by others. Academic research has shown how the selfie has become a powerful means of self-expression, with users sharing intimate moments in a form of creative self-fashioning (Murray, 2015). These often-spontaneous self-portraits have become ubiquitous with modern image-centred social media usage across cultures, alternately seen as expressions of narcissism and explorations of identity. "rather than being narcissistic or frivolous, selfies are important for representation and visibility, promoting personal views and identity, and countering dominant narratives" (Leaver et al., 2020, p. 68).

Selfies comprised the largest proportion of images in the sample with 197 posts, nearly 50% of the total dataset. Of these, the majority featured black South Africans ($n = 157$) with only 24 images featuring white South Africans. These highly stylized and situated self-representations serve to gain attention and position the subject within squarely within the urban cityscape, with the city clearly in the background. As previously stated, the images were not all technically selfies, but all comprised portraits of people; potentially intended to directly engage with the imaginary viewer in a very personalized way. The images were not candid or casual, but rather all were deliberately framed and posed. In terms of gender, most featured people were male, with their images comprising slightly more than half (62%) of the dataset ($n = 122$).

While some images contained pairs or groups of people, most images in this category contained either selfies or images of one person, usually looking directly into the camera lens. Selfies reflect a form of agency, as well as a type of commodity in the marketplace of Instagram images. They position the subject—the person taking the picture and the person in the picture reflect a type of social positionality as a form of reflection about how people fit into the cityscape. Iqani and Schroeder (2016) highlight how common and flexible the vocabulary of the selfie has become, as a "key figure within contemporary visual culture" (409).

The posed representations featured strategic poses, reflecting a particular type of communicative power. Looking directly at the photographer and the viewer, these users make contact with viewers to establish an imaginary relationship with them (Jewitt & Oyama, 2004); but the images were often not closeups but full-length photos, thus still maintaining distance despite attempting connection. The people in these images are all happy and smiling, reflecting the urban city space as a positive place to be. This category of images reflects a 'you could be here with me' style of photograph, in which the viewer is invited to imagine themselves into the frame, creating an intimate "visual co-presence" (Zappavigna, 2016, p. 272).

Images in the dataset were strongly oriented towards heteronormative, heterosexual norms and surprisingly there were no images reflecting non-binary gender identities. This might be the continued association of gay identities with 'whiteness', with gay bars in Joburg originally open to whites only; and black gay people mostly socialising in the townships.

The dominant representations of women were those of young cis-het women in various performances of selfhood. Dunn and Falkoff (2021) argue that Instagram offers young black South African women access to social and cultural capital, in which they construct their identities and idealized selves. "They engage in specific beauty practises, presenting a version of selfhood that is aspirational/inspirational and, at the same time, appears "authentic": genuine, relatable, unvarnished and honest" (Dunn & Falkoff, 2021). These images show young mostly black women in various traditional straight, 'sexy' poses, confidently claiming space and power in their representational strategies.

Images of men showed them also in stylized representation, fashionably or formally dressed, reflecting economic power and privilege. Many portraits were taken in luxury spaces such as expensive looking restaurants or bars, as a form of conspicuous consumption. Photographs were also taken in or outside shopping malls or modern facades of homes. These images reflect a culture of the city that is intrinsically linked to commercial space and consumption. This was a constant conceptual pattern, which as Jewitt and Oyama (2004) argue,

"represent participants in terms of their more generalized, stable or timeless 'essences'. They do not represent them as doing something, but as being something, or meaning something, or belonging to some category, or having certain characteristics or components" (11). In this instance, the people featured in these images are represented as having transcended class barriers associated with race. The images show happy, positive experiences in luxury locations, access to which is via social privilege or economic status.

The predominance of black South Africans—very different to the exploration of Instagram posts in Cape Town (Bosch, 2021)—reflects a sense of belonging and ownership of urban space. While black South Africans are the majority demographic group in the country, social media spaces are not always representative, given the connect between race and class. The demographics of the posted images reflect the growth of the black middle-class in South Africa, despite the fact that inter-racial inequality in South Africa has increased and the working class remains predominantly black (Madlalate, 2017). Race and socio-economic status in South Africa remain closely intertwined.

The physical location and featured backdrops of the photographs also holds significance. As Madlalate (2017) has argued, a certain spatial imaginary and creation of nuanced racialised spaces has been central to forming racial identities and spaces in which beneficial locations are reserved for whiteness and zealously protected (477). Space thus often serves to produce race, with the middle class backgrounds featured in the Instagram posts, usually perceived as white spaces, and sites of poverty and crime as black spaces (Madlalate, 2017). Joburg is a city of stark difference and inequality: "Its privileged economic zones boast all the trappings of a globalised world class city while its marginal spaces eke out an existence in an environment marked by joblessness, stigma and material deprivation" (Madlalate, 2017, p. 485). These nuances are strikingly absent from the curated stream of Instagram posts tagged #egoli. Instead what we see on the social media feed is the phenomenon whereby the "culturally assimilated 'black' middle class" is able to "enjoy the white spatial imaginary along with its traditional beneficiaries while the majority of 'blacks' remain marginalised" (Madlalate, 2017, p. 486). The visual modalities of Instagram, more specifically the selfie, is employed as a claim for space, a demand to be seen and recognized as a citizen. This can be interpreted as a political act—claiming the right to be present physically in city spaces (where previously the rights of black South Africans to space, was curtailed during apartheid). The insertion of black South Africans into the Instagram landscape is a claim to authenticity—as Iqani and Schroeder (2015) point out, the selfie represents a way of saying "look at me," "I exist" (410). Here we see the stark collision of digital imaginary with offline reality. The online assertion of identity and right to space claimed via Instagram, holds political power which is potentially transferred to the offline world. If black people are more visible, in particular ways, in online spaces; it creates the possibility for this way of being to be transferred to the offline. While I have previously argued (Bosch, 2021) that online spaces frequently mirror offline inequalities, in this instance, online assertions hold the power to transform offline reality. The effects of the digital on everyday life come into sharp focus.

Previous academic literature has often considered the black middle class as a homogenous entity, focusing on conspicuous consumption to signal social status. Conversely, the Instagram images collected in this dataset could be read as a deliberate appropriation of space by social media users, signalling citizenship and belonging in urban geographical spaces that were previously out of bounds. However, these public spaces featured remain spaces of power and agency—while they feature on the social media feeds of black Instagram users, the racial inequalities are still starkly and acutely apparent as these spaces still feature predominantly black labour (the wait staff in the restaurants, cleaning staff in hotels etc) and white power. The race based wealth and income gap in South Africa, and on Instagram, still remains firmly in place; once again reminding us how online representations frequently mirror offline inequalities, despite the potential of the online for power claims. The inequality is "not only a material issue, but also affects the way inhabitants understand their own positions in the city" (Falkof & Van Staden, 2020, p. 11). The manifestation of class distinctions on Instagram serves as a mechanism to render the offline economic and social inequalities invisible.

CITYSCAPES, SKYLINES AND MODERN JOBURG

This category of image portrayed images of buildings or city landscapes, often artistically portrayed via black and white pictures; or reflecting stylized images of the city from various views. For example, a range of images framed a colourful landscape filled with blooming jacaranda tree blossoms, while others were framed in such a way as to artistically highlight modern, contemporary-looking tall skyscrapers and urban city lines, images representing finance, power and economic wealth. Gassner (2017) argues for skylines as a "phantasmagoria of capitalist culture: a dazzling image that abstracts from the commodified urban landscape by promoting its further commodification" (754). Urban form, skylines, and the representation thereof can be seen as a promotion of urban finance and wealth. The visual domination of the skyline on Instagram represents an imaginary of financial capitalism, promoting the myth of wealthy Joburg.

Many images showed beautiful sunrise or sunset views of the city framed by the sky. Despite the stark urban landscape of Joburg, many of the images zoomed in on nature, plants and trees, highlighting greenery versus either urban progression or decay.

The cityscapes featured zoom in on a micro view urban city life, and like much of the writing on Joburg, "tends to focus on spaces of crisis or of spectacle but rarely on the ordinary spaces of the city that have their own identities but may attract little fuss" (Harrison et al., 2014, p. 22). The idealized, styled and almost 'glossy' images of the 'good life' of the suburbs with trees and swimming pools feature prominently on Instagram.

There were no images of the suburbs or township life in the dataset, showing users' representations of the city to be a middle-class view from the suburbs. Not a single image in the dataset reflected the ongoing spatial inequality of the city, or any related concerns such as homelessness or informal settlements. There are no images of spaza shops or informal traders but instead the focus is exclusively on urban renewal and gentrification. The disputes over urban space that have arisen out of increasing xenophobic conflict in the city, are also absent from the curated Instagram images. There is no reference to the threat of crime, high fences or gated communities and the security estates, all of which represent social (and sometimes racial) segregation, and which have become pervasive in central Johannesburg.

The images featured on Instagram are all taken in public spaces with no photos of people inside intimate spaces such as their homes or other personalized spaces; or of family life or children and pets. Several images in this category also featured hotels, again highlighting consumption practices and lifestyle aspiration. Instagram is not a surprising space for the presentation of luxury consumption, and the growth of the influencer phenomenon has made it a convenient platform for the visual broadcast of these practices as a public display of social status and economic wealth.

Conclusion

Images place a key role in how people experience being in the world, and also how they shape the world they inhabit, often reflecting people's experiences of everyday life. "The physical city has no meaning without the lives, activities and identities of its residents" (Harrison et al., 2014, p. 20). This exploration of Instagram images tagged with the hashtag #egoli has attempted to show how users co-create a visual identity of the city of Joburg, through their personal posts of their everyday mundane activities. As Instagram users share their co-constructed stories of everyday life via hashtagged posts and the affordances of the app, an aspirational networked narrative is revealed in which users are situated in a particular visual culture of Joburg. Class, lifestyle and aspiration are visually constructed via user posts. Leaver et al. (2020) note how Instagram "highlights the aesthetics of normalization" (45), with users creating a memory archive of the city.

The publicly shared visual representations of the city reflect the contemporary identity of the city and its inhabitants, with the hashtagged posts, a form of collective cultural storytelling The analysis reveals Instagram as a luxurious, elite space where people perform idealized versions of their lives via the technique of the filter. The collectively produced cultural narrative of the city of Joburg is reflected via images of people's banal everyday lives; but the analysis reveals that the representation of the Joburg city space on social media reflects middle class urban black culture as an expression of belonging and cultural citizenship. Young black middle-class urban professionals predominate and frame Joburg as a positive, happy and professional city space, with no reflection on factors such as poverty or crime. In reality, in the offline world, Joburg is city characterized by poverty and an overwhelmingly poor black working class. On Instagram a different version of Joburg is imagined, with the black middle class at the centre of social media imagery. The impact of the sharing of these constructed stories is significant. It results in the perpetuation of social inequalities via the limited social media imaginary of the city.

REFERENCES

Acuti, D., Mazzoli, V., Donvito, R., & Chan, P. (2018). An Instagram content analysis for city branding in London and Florence. *Journal of Global Fashion Marketing*, 9(3), 185–204.

Bosch, T. (2021). *Social media and everyday life in South Africa*. Routledge.

Boy, J. D., & Uitermark, J. (2017). Reassembling the city through Instagram. *Transactions of the Institute of British Geographers*, 42(4), 612–624.

Boy, J. D., & Uitermark, J. (2016). How to study the city on Instagram. *PLoS One*, 11(6), e0158161.

Bremner, L. (2000). Reinventing the Johannesburg inner city. *Cities*, 17(3), 185–193.

Crankshaw, O. (2008). Race, space and the post-Fordist spatial order of Johannesburg. *Urban Studies*, 45(8), 1692–1711.

Dean, B. (2022). Snapchat Demographic Stats: How Many People Use Snapchat in 2022? Available from https://backlinko.com/snapchat-users [Accessed on 7 February 2022]

Dunn, C., and Falkoff, N. (2021). You've got to be real: Authenticity, performativity and micro-celebrity in South Africa. *Frontiers*. https://doi.org/10.3389/fsoc.2021.652485

Falkof, N., & Van Staden, C. (2020). Introduction: Traversing the anxious metropolis. In *Anxious Joburg*. 1–18. Wits University Press, Johannesburg.

Gassner, G. (2017). Wrecking London's skyline? A political critique of how the city is viewed. *City*, 21(6), 754–768.

Harrison, P. et al. (2014). Materialities, subjectivities and spatial transformation in Johannesburg. In Harrison, P., Gotz, G., Todes, A., & Wray, C. (eds.). *Changing Space, Changing City: Johannesburg after apartheid*. Wits University Press: 2–39.

Highfield, T., & Leaver, T. (2015). A methodology for mapping Instagram hashtags. *First Monday*, 20(1), 1–11.

Hoogendoorn, G., & Gregory, J. (2016, December). Instagrammers, urban renewal and the Johannesburg inner city. *Urban Forum*, 27(4), 399–414.

Hootsuite. 2022. 35 Instagram Stats That Matter to Marketers in 2022. Available from https://blog.hootsuite.com/instagram-statistics/#General_Instagram_statistics [Accessed on 06 February 2022].

Iqani, M., and Schroeder, J. E. (2016). # selfie: Digital self-portraits as commodity form and consumption practice. *Consumption Markets & Culture, 19*(5), 405–415.

Jewitt, C. and Oyama, R. (2004). Visual meaning: a social semiotic approach. In Van Leeuwen, T. and Jewitt, C. (eds). *The handbook of visual analysis.* Sage, CA, US.

Latzko-Toth, G., Bonneau, C., & Millette, M. (2017). Small data, thick data: Thickening strategies for trace-based social media research In *The SAGE handbook of social media research methods,* edited by L. Sloan & A. Quan-Haase, 199–214. Sage Publications, London.

Leaver, T. et al. (2020). *Instagram: Visual social media cultures.* Polity Press, UK.

Madlalate, R. (2017). (In)Equality at the intersection of race and space in Johannesburg. *South African Journal on Human Rights, 33*(3), 472–495.

Murray, D. (2015). Notes to self: the visual culture of selfies in the age of social media. *Consumption Markets & Culture, 18*(6), 490–516.

Rogerson, C. & Rogerson, J. (2015). Johannesburg 2030: The economic contours of a "linking global city". *American Behavioral Scientist, 59*(3), 347–368.

Schaffer, N. (2022). The 31 Definitive Instagram Statistics for 2022 You Should Know—And Why. Available from https://nealschaffer.com/instagram-stacatistics/ [Accessed on 06 February 2022].

Statista. (2022). Available from https://www.statista.com/statistics/1029289/instagram-users-south-africa/ [Accessed on 06 February 2022].

Zappavigna, M. (2016). Social media photography: Construing subjectivity in Instagram images. *Visual Communication, 15*(3), 271–292.

CHAPTER 6

Mapping the Digital Fabric of Cities: 'Site Codes' as Spatial Identifiers in Urban China in the COVID-19 Pandemic

Deqiang Ji and Xiaomei Jiang

Introduction—"Codes" as Epidemic Prevention and Control Measures

After the outbreak of the COVID-19 pandemic, the digital codes have played important roles in controlling the flow of people and restoring the order of society. In order to meet the needs of epidemic prevention and movement control in different regions, the digital codes also have evolved into different types. Health Code appeared first, this code mainly uses green, red and yellow colors to represent people's health status, and those who have red or yellow code shall be quarantined, only after their code turn green can they move freely (Fan, 2020; Zixue et al., 2021).

In February 2020, the Health Code was firstly put into application in the city of Hangzhou, where a high level of digital infrastructure maturity is found. And, the Site Code appeared a little later than the Health Code which was used in Beijing and Chengdu at first. At the end of 2021, this technology began to be officially introduced among cities to prepare for the huge turnover during the Chinese Spring Festival.

Site Code, as the name implies, is a special QR code given to a specific place, marking its location, name and other basic information. Individuals who want to enter a certain place have to scan the code and the scanning result must be shown as green for entrance. If abnormal information appears, the data will

---

D. Ji (✉) • X. Jiang
Communication University of China, Beijing, China

© The Author(s), under exclusive license to Springer Nature Switzerland AG 2024
H. S. Dunn et al. (eds.), *The Palgrave Handbook of Everyday Digital Life*, https://doi.org/10.1007/978-3-031-30438-5_6

directly provide feedback to relevant departments and in most cases the person will be quarantined immediately. With these technologies, individuals carry their own digital information everywhere, fully demonstrating the digital form of "Bio-politics Governmentality" (Agamben, 2001, p. 10) and show its high efficiency as well.

It should be noticed that this practice of digital governance was originally developed by the commercial technology magnate Alibaba. The health code was first used within the Group, and later transformed into a public epidemic prevention application at the request of the Yuhang District government of Hangzhou city, then it launched at the "Alipay" platform which belongs to Alibaba.

In only a month, starting from Hangzhou, the health code supported by Alibaba was spread to more than 200 cities in 24 provinces across the whole country. At the same time, another Internet giant Tencent also accelerated the layout of health code based in the city of Shenzhen. It announced that the number of users has exceeded 1.6 billion within one month, covered nearly 900 million people, and the total number of visitors had surpassed 6 billion.

From the perspective of statistics, we see the that epidemic code promotion is rising, but throughout the codes launched all over the country, two characteristics can be obviously found: one is that the codes' standard is not unified because of different epidemic situations and local policies around the country So, data collection and used among different districts is usually separated. On the other hand, both Alibaba and Tencent are researching this epidemic-control measure to help them tap into the huge market behind the digital governance, and strengthen their discourse power by the technology they provided. As a result, even in the same city, there was competition and restraint among different platforms. It was reported that Tencent banned Alibaba's "Dingding" service—an online working application—on "WeChat", which is developed by Tencent and works as the most influential social media platform in China. This action made the health codes inaccessible in 24 provinces, including Alibaba's foundation province of Zhejiang.[1]

In the face of platform competition, the General Office of the State Council of the People's Republic of China quickly instructed stakeholders to establish a national integrated service platform. Alibaba and Tencent were asked to participate in this task. Three years after the outbreak of the pandemic, this national unified system launched simultaneously on Alipay and WeChat and it is very mature now. Unified management of information's input/output has significantly improved cross-regional, cross-tiered and cross-terminal epidemic control, and further enhanced the country's digital governance capacity and efficiency.

The emergence of Site Codes further strengthened personnel flow management. The code sets several nodes for the complex flow track of countless

---

[1] "The health codes for returning to work, how hard it is to use a unified code?" Available at: https://baijiahao.baidu.com/s?id=1662116703989611880&wfr=spider&for=pc.

individuals, and also enables the urban fabric to be expressed in a more concrete way. Within a few seconds, the individual user becomes attached with a deep binding to a specific space, this process is a "double digitization" process for both body and place. We all know that smartphones plus Internet created a greater subversion for re-engineering the city appearance, as platforms, codes, data and algorithms have worked together to construct new organizational forms of people and cities.

Today, governance facilitated by digital platforms is emerging as a new issue for countries around the world, which is also exacerbated by the spread of COVID-19. There are complex relationships between tech platforms, governments, as well as the people involved.

So, this research aims to outline the interaction among the multiple subjects mentioned above, and the Site Code provides an excellent entrance for it. Therefore, firstly, we will focus on the code itself to enter its operational logic and see how it penetrates into people's everyday life.

SITE CODE: RECONSTRUCT THE SENSE OF PLACE BY PROGRAMMING LANGUAGE

In urban sociology, place is always regarded as an implicit language, but the programming technology which turned the place into a QR code is an exact relational language. This new phenomenon enables a literary metaphor "fabric city" to have a tangible, physical image. That is to say, we need to acknowledge the validity of the technology itself at first.

Cosimo (2018/2021, p. 2) described a "programmable future" in which he noted that the code (and its corresponding software) has both philosophical and operational effects, and it's a powerful engine to exert subtle influences on our lives in physical space. Some early researches have paid attention to applications based on space, such as online navigation apps "Amap" and "Google map", or fitness app "Keep" to indicate their extensive guiding functions for human (Tongwen, 2019; Di, 2021). Chinese scholars Wei and Mengying (2021b) directly discuss the codes inside the China's urban landscape, presenting the cities' programming capacity.

Back to our object, the Site Code is to distribute an electronic ID card to each specific location. Behind this square grid QR image, there is a huge network in which crossing data is continuously operating. This technology not only changes the form of space, but also reshapes the relationship among people.

New Identifiability

To identify, as the concept implies, is to recognize and distinguish. Studies on "Identifiability" can be classified into two groups. One is a traditional way focusing on humanities such as architecture, art and urban design. It emphasizes that an object or a place should be distinguished from its surroundings and history by special marks (Coward & Salingaros, 2004). On the other hand, the function of identification operation is considered to be more important. For example, on transportation management, enterprise architecture and library collection, the roles of codes take a key position. Here, identifiability is associated with efficiency, personal information, systematic production and others (Amrou et al., 2019).

The identifiability of cities is generally considered to be included in the former way. Roberts (2015) once used "Archive City" to describe the fact that the material elements inside a city can be regarded as an "archive". He emphasized that all traces of a city like graffiti, monuments, movie theaters and old factories are all readable and recognizable, thus their archaeological significance should not be ignored.

In this sense, a city is built by specific places so it is a junction of past, present and future. Many urban sociologists support this view, as Norberg-Schulz said, the place never just reflects some specific spots. Place is a kind of spirit (1979, p. 6). Tibbalds (1992, p. 71) gives a more specific explanation: places should refer to the context of the time associated with the reality.

However, in today's digital environment, the physical "site" has become the Site Code, and our city has a new name—"QR codes city" (Wei & Mengying, 2021a). The question thus becomes, living in the new spatial form, how can we identify and feel the space?

Obviously, the core of identifiability research includes three aspects: information, exclusivity and the construction of a certain reference relationship. Programmable city is a combination of the digital and humanity. What we need at this moment is a new perspective of ecological philosophy to rediscover it. Murray (2008) comes up with a comprehensive vision: "digitalization is also a kind of aesthetic, as long as we capture the universality of digital technology, we can understand the continuum that reshapes the space and changes the way we experience" (2008, p. 10). After all, this circuit connection has become an irreducible reality. It has deeply and widely embedded in physical landscapes, making it different from spatial configurations to the management of the movement of human bodies.

Gabrys (2016, p. 8), an ecological philosopher of sensing technology, takes it one step further and creatively points out the concept of "becoming environmental of computation". Not only do we humans become part of a new ecology through the "programmability", but the sensors, codes, and machines themselves are also an "experience" as parts of the digital world, through their own, non-human's perception.

Site Code as a technology contains the whole information of a specific space and make it unique through the programming language. At the same time, it achieves an inter-embedded goal, based on a peer-to-peer networks. This tool enables countless scattered bits of information to be gathered up, and it constructs a complete system for "record—test—alarm—isolation", that satisfies the conditions as for new identifiability research.

New Accessibility

Not only does it provide identifiability, by a Site Code is also directly working as a restriction to people's movement. In fact, from ancient states, there are various powerful physical means to archive that: walls, borders and passports, the latter of which is believed to be invented by Henry V of England (1413–1422). All these were for "identifying and managing bodily movement" (Cresswell, 2010, p. 27). However, it does not mean that accessibility was only represented by some physical "things", let us imagine a scene where a beggar wants to enter a luxurious palace, his "awkwardness" could also work as the inaccessibility.

Based on these studies of tools that restrict people's mobility, Mackenzie (2011, p. 86) focuses more on how people's movement has been recreated, especially in an Internet era. He points out, the Internet is a non-human inhabitant in the world and participates in human's traveling, transition and diversion. It is not only as a technical condition, but in a larger sense, as a "state of connectivity" which involves start and stop, as well as disconnection, exposure and re-connection.

In the usage scenarios of Site Codes, our bodies become a series of health, behavior and consumption data. Places also have their electric ID cards, thus the connectivity between the two must go through a new digital license. Through the Internet, the non-human city dweller becomes a "super gate-keeper", and nothing could escape its scrutiny.

The epidemic, which acts like a war or aggression, can quickly change the long-term stability of a city, but not everyone is prepared to accept the legitimacy immediately. In terms of news reports, we saw cases happened in China's Xi'an, Dazhou and other cities where citizens beat staffs for not cooperating with the epidemic prevention work. Through it all, it is the legitimacy of these codes or their privilege that is not yet be fully recognized.

Undoubtedly, in this special period in history of the new power of cultural production, Chinese society is also reshaping urban forms and civic engagements. The relationship between geography and digital technology is both separated and complementary, and the spatial medium intensively display the entanglement in various aspects such as material, practice, and system (Xian, 2021). Take the Site Code as example, we are not entering another virtual world through the codes, we exactly enter an integral world which is composed with "a stone city" and "an ether city" (Remi, 2016). The enhancement of communication networks translates into a redefinition of the city itself, where citizens, devices, networks, databases, servers, and protocols work together to form a "relational space". Here, visible and invisible boundaries both melt away, the where "places matter most" became "relation matters most".

Therefore, the code technology is only a small change that occurs in the overall transformation of the society, but its fundamental and essential roles played in the whole event also need to be emphasized. Only in this perspective can we understand the importance of every tiny prevention measure during the

COVID-19 pandemic. Given that technology has never been an independent force, we have to combine the background and institutional practice to do a further inspection.

Code's Extension? A Holistic Perspective from Political Economy

Observing the system is actually observing how human behavior is constructed in the face of new technologies (Verhoeff, 2012, p. 15). In the past, cyberspace was often considered as detached from the geometry of urban space. But today, media has penetrated into all aspects of the real world and even become inseparable from human culture and social mechanisms. Thus, we should ask: how can we link the microscopic technical issues to the macroscopic structural analysis? What kind of perspective should we adopt to see how technology is subtly integrating into our culture, constituting the social fabric, and changing the system we have established?

To answer this question, political economy analysis provides us with a good perspective. Vincent Mosco (1996, p. 71) points out that political economy is the study of "social relations", especially for the exercise of "power" which is mutually constructed with production, distribution and exchange of resources. In the field of media and communication studies, these resources include dissemination of information and the media technology itself. More specifically, Political Economy is the study of "control" and "survival" in social life (Mosco, 1996, p. 25). The former constitutes relations within the community, and the latter is from the economic dimension, focusing on production and reproduction (Renjie & Jing, 2019). For this study, the great explanatory potential of this perspective can be embodied in the following three aspects:

First of all, it emphasizes a holistic perspective. When analyzing the operation of the dual monitoring of the state and the market, Mosco also reflects on the public dialectically, thinking about the role of each part in the overall operation. As a basic activity, Site Code is the product of data sharing by different subjects, and its application and promotion prove the collaboration of governance. Citizens carry out self-management to avoid risks, enterprises use it to accomplish work and production, grassroots governments accurately manage the cross-regional personnel flows, and senior leaders can make real-time judgments and differentiated prevention and control measures based on the data analysis. All of these subjects should be included in consideration.

Secondly, "spatialization" has always been an inescapable issue of the Political Economy, this research interest connects the critique of urban sociology and the critique of political economy, and could find an important theoretical extension for the discussion above.

The Site Code plays a similar role as the skin of architecture (Venturi, 2005/2009, p. 300), which not only shows how to create new communities through new communication ways, but also exposes how the capital and power achieve all-round domination of spaces. In this sense, studying the production of space is as important as studying the survival of power and capital (Yiqing & Zhiyi, 2020).

Thirdly, it helps us to better recognize and solve the problems in epidemic governance. Half a century ago, the Norwegian sociologist Hernes has pointed out that this is a "media distorted society" (1978). Today, the operation of institutions and capital is increasingly dependent on "media logic" (Hjarvard 2013, p. 16), which is an operational mode of specific media technology, under a specific institution, and with a specific aesthetic (Stromback, 2008). The media logic closely binds the government, tech companies, and the public together, and certainly, makes it more mutable, complicated and inconclusive for digital governance.

In this context, the discussion of multi-agency and its interaction has become the mainstream of digital governance research (Clark & Brudney, 2020; Xin, 2019). Fan (2013) pointed out that there are many approaches from the government to business and citizens, including G2G, G2B, G2C, which emphasized the multi-agent collaboration in the whole system. In other words, the tech companies can act as a force that simply provides a web page connecting the government and the public directly, it can also serve as an intermediary between the government and the public (Xu & Tang, 2020) to promote cooperation between them, in policy review, decision making and policy implementation (Linders, 2012). In addition, Deqiang (2021) proposed the concept of "platformized governance", as a new stage and paradigm of national governance in the digital age.

All the studies above suggest that the holistic perspective is not only a necessary vision to observe the governance issues, but also a crucial way to link the media technology to national governance capacity building.

Nowadays, "intersectionality" has become a hot topic in academic research, but we still lack a specific understanding of how the various powers in the intersection are intertwined. Is there some fixed mechanism? Are there some internal or external forces to maintain the connection? Durkheim (1895/2018, p. 147) said, if we want to explain a complex fact, it can only be done by observing the entire development process in all its social facets. Therefore, in the following part, we will take a holistic perspective to analyze the internal structure of multiple subjects such as government departments, tech platforms, and the public through specific epidemic prevention practices.

Digital Governance Woven by Multiple Subjects during the Epidemic

Emphasizing the holistic vision does not mean formulating a single and ubiquitous model. In China, both the top-level policymaking and the evolutionary model of governance have significant local characteristics. They are often manifested through various institutional changes and deeply cultural biases.

Therefore, against this background, we need to observe the popularization of various epidemic prevention policies, so as to explain the complexity and particularity of China's digital governance.

1. **Platform and government: Depending on and overlapping with each other**

Governance in the digital age includes two forms: one is governance of data, and the other is governance by data. In this study, both are indispensable. For the former, data is an extension of the body and the data is the purpose. From the closure of the Wuhan city to the postponement of resumption of enterprises and schools, the policies are aimed at controlling the virus by restricting the flow of people. This is also why Chinese universities still require students to punch in and fill in their location information every day. Governance by data reflects the government's all-sided control over measures, processes, and efficiency. The vaccination rate of each city, the rapid and accurate investigation required by the policy of "dynamic clearing", and the complete set of data monitoring networks established through codes, all of which reflect the government capacity in responding to an emergent crisis.

At present, China has become the country in which the QR codes are used most widely. China's code applications account for more than 90% of the world, and much of this data come from the need for epidemic control over the past three years. With the maturity of digital technology and the governance system as well, such kind of "governance on code" has more possibilities.

In Shenzhen where Tencent started its business, the application of site codes has been developed to "one bus, one code" since March 1, 2022, that means, each city-operated bus has an independent site code. The policy made the originally fixed concept of site code become more dynamic, and started to get the "connection" between two sites into the scope of supervision, truly building a digital city where nothing could be ignored. According to some news reports, people call it "Electronic Guard" directly.

However, the development and usage of digital tools represented by Health Code and Site Code is not only operated by the government. As users of digital technologies, we are not only a source of political legitimacy, but also for market consumers that commercial platforms compete for even during this public health crisis.

This symbiotic state of mutual depending, entangling and overlapping can be seen from the following case. When the epidemic was recognized as a crucial task, government departments at all levels actively promoted the prevention and control measures, but the result was that official endorsement worked as platforms' advertisement, and the data-based platform became the biggest potential winner. However, when we focus on the competition of technology magnates, we may overlook the fact that more users are included into the government regulation in a quicker way, and the overall security system is rapidly strengthened.

The Site Code can locate suspected cases more accurately, and can quickly establish a network of people's trajectories. This process cannot be separable from platform companies, which provide the technology, code, personnel and the likes. It cannot work without such a huge and well-trained user population provided by the existing platforms either.

Therefore, on the one hand, the Site Code provides a protection model, but in fact, it also secretly buries the harm of a free business model. Compared with the Health Code, the Site Code can grasp people's movement, aggregation and consumption more comprehensively, so platforms can formulate a new set of algorithms. With that, they can push promotional advertisements to people who have been to the same place, or push a kind of fitness product to those who frequently go to the gym, more intuitively.

It can be seen that at the macro level, the government and tech companies work together to weave the Chinese governance ecology. Just as the warp and weft are mutually hidden in the final product, when we look at the complicated governance as a whole, we will find that sometimes we see "public" "guarantee" "welfare" "safety", while sometimes it will reveal "performance" "profit" or "stock market".

The value challenge is an important test where technology is deeply embedded into risk management. According to the opinion of Chinese political scientist Keping (2005, pp. 33–34), good governance has ten indicators, and all the indicators have one common feature, that is, the priority of public interests. Since the application of the Health Code and Site Codes is an emergency measure in an extraordinary time, there are bound to be imperfection in systemization, standardization and power-responsibility balances mechanisms. However, these problems and China's great achievements in controlling the virus are two sides of the same coin. Therefore, we would like to clarify further: what factors provide a steady driving force in the process of "governance on code"? How do they interact with each other with their own internal dynamics in government departments and technology platforms? This analysis will help us examine the exposed problems at the moment and improve the existing systems in the future.

2. Cross-platform and cross-government: The internal driving forces

There are two kinds of forces that affect the formation of urban communities, one is propelling force and the other is pathological force (Rossi, 1966, p. 59). The latter emphasizes the slow and natural adjustment of regions over years. Obviously, the epidemic provides a strong external stimulus belonging to the former, it quickly stirred up the activity of the grassroots governance of China, and made the commercial tech platforms be all set immediately on the track of data collecting and disposing.

In the face of such a terrifying enemy of mankind as the COVID-19 virus, governors must face the huge challenge of finding a balance between rushing for time and taking everyone into consideration, which is difficult to achieve. At the same time, nowadays, social media play an increasingly important role in

China's digital governance, so different voices can be amplified through the media, thereby exposing the deep dilemma in the governance. It prompts researchers and policymakers to catch these warning signs before failures occur so that systems can be optimized in a timely manner.

Except for a few cities like Beijing and Chengdu, most cities in China only rapidly popularized the Site Codes in 2022. Taking Shanghai as an example, it took less than 20 days to popularize more than 18.8 thousand site codes that entered people's living scenes. Only in a small district of Shanghai which called "Putuo", the average daily scanning volume of codes reached 400,000,[2] reflecting the working efficiency of local governments.

In order to ensure safety, the vast majority of the public voluntarily follow the requirements of prevention measures, but there are still some who overtly express their dissatisfaction on social media. An Internet user said: "Now in Shenzhen, we use five different codes in different situations, it is very annoying to switch programs frequently".[3] Another user reported that she has encountered a situation where her healthy code shows green color while her site code shows yellow color at the same time which made her waste time.[4]

Many new problems, such as Complex operations, time-consuming process and changeful standards, have emerged along with the popularization of the codes, and becoming potential crises needed to be paid attention to in many research fields, such as public opinion, digital governance, and emergency management. To some political scientists, this phenomenon is related to China's special institution. Under the pressure system of territorial management, the ultimate responsibility will fall on the grassroots leaders (Taijun & Chengcheng, 2012). At the beginning, we see the health codes between provinces and cities fail to connect with each other (Xuesong & Yunlong, 2021), and then it has evolved into a view of "overlay" of codes. Feizhou (2009), an early "political championship" researcher, pointed out that "overlay" is the basic mechanism in China to promote the work of the grassroots government. This is the most effective institutional feature in China's central-local relations, but also hides the biggest danger.

On the other hand, many scholars believe that different from normalized management, the emergency situation determines that the measures have to be expedient (Xinshui, 2021). The code is a new weapon for modern governance, it is also a double-edged sword and the biggest problem might be that the market takes advantage of its technology and leads to a result of "regulatory capture". (Nechushtai, 2018; Xingdong & Feng, 2020)

---

[2] "The Site Codes in Putuo District: Nearly 20,000 sites got involved, with an average daily scanning volume of nearly 400,000." Available at:
https://baijiahao.baidu.com/s?id=1728238965663561600&wfr=spider&for=pc.

[3] Resource From: https://www.zhihu.com/question/444265780/answer/2370184218. Updated: Mar. 2, 2022.

[4] Resource From: https://m.weibo.cn/5287402649/4746254975763837. Updated: Mar. 12, 2022.

Today, site codes in the majority of cities are still accessed through Alibaba and Tencent. For these two companies, together they have the capital equivalent to a prosperous city in China. The process of implementing site code is actually a process of competing for urban coverage. In this sense, site codes, along with ubiquitous payment codes and shared power bank, will be just one of many sources by which tech giants integrate their vast data sets.

In the industry of internet, the "lock-in effect" proposed by Arthur (1989) is an effective means and important feature of the companies' development, which means whose technology developed first will have the advantage of self-reinforcing. Once users choose a certain system, the conversion cost will be high and "path dependence" will emerge. Subsequently, the continuous strengthening of the lock-in effect helps to maintain the monopoly position of the enterprise.

According to the latest "*Tencent Research and Development Big Data Report*",[5] Tencent's R&D personnel account for 68% of the total, and 2 billion lines of code has been newly produced in 2020. During the year 2020, Tencent participated in the Linux Foundation's new public health program LFPH and became the only founding member unit in China. Even today, Alibaba and Tencent's preemption in public epidemic prevention is still going on. Alibaba directly cooperates with major hospitals, as long as people book test services through the "Alipay", they can get a random discount of 5–20 yuan, which undoubtedly displays the business logic of Internet companies. In this way, we can further understand why there are always negative comments among the public, though both platform and government have put much effort in cooperation to make it so efficient.

3. City dwellers: Surviving in the digital crack

The recipient of the above structural system is people. We cannot obvere the policies or technologies in isolation from the citizen's life. In the paper entitled "*The poetics of augmented space*", Manovich (2006) argues that the city has become a data space, where bodies and behaviors are connected through invisible networks.

For the use of various codes, the most basic difficulty is the physical challenge. The Site Code could be scanned just when the person standing face-to-face with the code, and the data will update in real-time, so a stable Internet connection is required. A respondent in previous studies on health codes pointed out that every time she went to the parking lot, the signal was poor, and she was almost late for several visits. Even though all this infrastructure was working well, once her mobile phone runs out of power, the security guards asked her to show her health code and keep saying: "Without the health code, you won't be able to get in" (Chuncheng, 2021). It is strange that nowadays

---

[5] "The Research and Development Report of Tencent in 2020." Available at: https://xw.qq.com/partner/vivoscreen/TEC2021031800820700?vivoRcdMark=1&vivorcdmark=1.

the confirmation of the green code even surpasses the identification of the human subject itself. There is also a netizen on the Chinese social media platform "Weibo" who said that: "whenever I go to the market or gas station, I need to scan the code, it's too troublesome and I don't want to go out at all."[6] The expression "I don't want to go out at all" embodied a rebellious desire to detach from digital media. It is an apparent moderation in the growing trend of "technological fatigue" (Brennen, 2019), or shows a "push-back activism" to the accelerating information capitalism (Kaun & Trere, 2020).

In fact, new digital phenomena such as site codes have already filled the spaces we live in, accompanying and surrounding us as we move through the cities. Smartphones are increasingly seen as a strong tool of data collection for studying human behaviour (Elevelt, 2021), and we unconsciously become city's data resources, engaging in mapping the digital fabric of cities (Gabrys, 2014), and supporting the ongoing development of the operationalized urban archives (McQuire, 2016, p. 84).

Today, most government departments are not just focusing on the present. As an official said: "as long as the core dataset maintained and all aspects of the data kept connected, these mechanisms and experiences can also be used in somewhere else, such as tracking assets or fugitives."[7] It can be seen that digital governance practices which are based on online-offline integration will become more and more common, and relevant research will inevitably continue to track the growth and variation of this integrated system.

At this technical level, scholars who have done empirical research pointed out that none of the respondents knows how the Health Code works, and their view of the codes is an "algorithmic imaginary" (Bucher, 2017), encompassing both mystical speculation and established stereotype (Chuncheng & Ross, 2021). When the public camouflage is removed, humans will be aware that they have been caught in the process of passively submitting various data to various media platforms.

The problem here is that, as Paul Willis writes in his "*Being Modern in China*" (2020, p. 44), a state of dissociation of sensibility is created. This is extremely microscopic feedback, which almost shows the insignificance and weakness of individuals under the dual design of system and technology: as an actor, we are already involved in the digital life and have to deal with the tension between "living experience" and "digital bodies". As data producers, we are brought into the formation of the platformized governance, so how should we identify and position ourselves when new rules have made a new reality?

In this case, a slightly pessimistic attitude is that "we are just a point of possibilities", just as one of the "digital calculation results" (Byung-Chul,

---

[6] Resource From: https://m.weibo.cn/7058754898/4705945525944677. Updated: Nov. 21, 2021.

[7] "The first line of the health code is in the collection of the National Museum of China, which was created at 20:34 on February 13, 2020." Avilable at: https://baijiahao.baidu.com/s?id=1722886398648491669&wfr=spider&for=pc.

2013/2019, p. 67). But in this chapter, we argue that we should not only emphasize the weight of the social structure, but also emphasize the nuanced differences in life and try to find the breakthroughs. We cannot take it for granted that the post-epidemic era provides us with abundant practical resources and experience resources, "otherwise, when they work together, we will no longer be able to truly understand the evolutionary trajectories of various technologies and the changes in social relations that result from them." (Mumford, 1934, p. 4)

Conclusion

"Codes are modelling the future, and the future is engraved on the codes." (Cosimo, 2018/2021, p. 18) This article takes the "Site Code" as an example, which breaks the boundaries between the digital and the physical. In terms of space production and urban governance, the Site Code reconstructs the identifiability and accessibility of space through programming technology. It injects the algorithmic influence into specific spatial locations, especially the double digitization of spaces and bodies in this process fully reflects the potential power of modernity. At the same time, digital technology has penetrated into the spatial texture of the city naturally, bringing new ritualistic tendencies to residents. People who are immersed in such an environment for a long time will affect the urban production in turn, and give an extension to the power and capital which re-constructed physical places previously.

On the other hand, during the normalized management of the COVID-19 pandemic, the Site Code has played an important role in controlling the flow of people and curbing the spread of the virus accurately and quickly. Here, we see that platform and government are closely intertwined. They are depending on, entangling and overlapping with each other, and actively transform the technological advantages into institutional advantages, which is an inevitable path to enhance the government's resilience (Li, 2022).

We also see that there is an important competitive-cooperative relationship between platforms and government departments, such as "preemption" or "championship", thus forming continuous internal driving forces for the two. It ensures the controllability and stability of epidemic prevention, at the same time, reminds us of the contradictions needed to be solved urgently. Finally, we also see that individuals are spontaneously seeking breakthroughs in various normative requirements, and their demands are worthy of consideration by governors as well.

Government, platform and the public are closely structured in the holistic perspective of political economy, and it is not just an abstract outline. Specifically, this cooperative governance model is composed of the State Council, the experts in epidemic treatment or vaccine development, the enterprises donating various emergency resources and the front-line staff like doctors and nurses. It is the combination of all visible and invisible factors that brought the

COVID-19 epidemic under control quickly and greatly guaranteed the safety of people's lives.

In this view, our purpose is not to demonstrate whether it is perfect in every policy, but to observe every change in the world and prompt the understanding of the complex digital social process. In this article, human subjectivity seems to be placed in a weak position, which is not our original intention, so this research is only half completed and needs to be further advanced. On the one hand, the human factor at the empirical level need to be paid more attention to. Ordinary users, venue operators, grassroots community staffs, and even code engineers are all worthy to be further analyzed.

On the other hand, cities should not only be regarded as the background of digital governance, but also the producers, the promoters and even the deciders of it. Only in this way, we can continue to conceptualize and theorize the relationship between urban space and political communication. Digital governance is not a universal issue, and special consideration should be given to it. In China, the use of technology, the platform privileges and citizen's living preferences all demonstrate significant local characteristics. To understand new social phenomena, we need to know the indigenous identities contained.

REFERENCES

Agamben G. (2001). *Homo Sacer: Sovereignty Power and Bare Life*. Stanford: Sanford University.
Amrou M., Boulmakoul A., Hassan B. (2019). A scalable real-time tracking and monitoring architecture for logistics and transport in RoRo terminals. *Procedia Computer Science*. (151): 218–225.
Coward, L. A., Salingaros, N. A. (2004). The information architecture of cities. *Journal of Information Science*. 30(2): 107–118.
Arthur W. (1989). Competing Technologies, Increasing Return and Lock-in by Historical Events. *Economic Journal*. 99(394): 116–131.
Bucher T. (2017). The algorithmic imaginary: Exploring the ordinary affects of Facebook algorithms. *Information, Communication & Society*. 20(1): 30–44.
Brennen B. (2019). *Opting Out of Digital Media*. New York: Routledge.
Byung-Chul H. (2013/2019). *Im Schwarm: Ansichten des Digitalen*. Translated by Wei C. Beijing: Citic Press Corporation.
Chuncheng L. (2021). Seeing Like a State, Enacting Like an Algorithm: (Re)assembling Contact Tracing and Risk Assessment during the COVID-19 Pandemic. *Science, Technology & Human Values*. (1): 1–28.
Chuncheng L., Ross G. (2021). Making sense of algorithms: Relational perception of contact tracing and risk assessment during COVID-19. *Big Data & Society*. (1–6): 1–32.
Clark B., Brudney S. (2020). Do Advanced Information Technologies Produce Equitable Government Responses in Coproduction: An Examination of 311 Systems in 15 U.S. Cities. *The American Review of Public Administration*, 50(3): 315–327.
Cosimo A. (2018/2021). *In Date Time and Tide: A Surprising Philosophical Guide to our Programmable Future*. (Il mondo dato). Translated by Daokuan H., Beijing: Encyclopedia of China Publishing House.

Cresswell T. (2010). Towards a politics of mobility. *Environment and Planning D: Society and Space.* (28): 17–31.

Deqiang J. (2021). Platformization governance: A new paradigm of State Governance from the Perspective of Communication Political Economy. *News and Writing,* (4): 20–25.

Di X. (2021). Space, Perception and the Embeddedness of Relations: The Mediatization Effect in Digital Space. *Journalism Research.* 186(10): 94–107+120-121.

Durkheim E. (1895/2018). *The Rules of Sociological Method (Les Regles De La Methode Sociologique).* Translated by Yuming D. Beijing: The Commercial Press.

Elevelt A. (2021). Where You at? Using GPS Locations in an Electronic Time Use Diary Study to Derive Functional Locations. *Social Science Computer Review.* 39(4): 509–526.

Fan B. (2013). Achieving Horizontal Integration of municipal E-government in China: Assessment of Managerial Mechanisms. *Information Development,* 29(4): 333–348.

Fan L. (2020). COVID-19 and Health Code: How Digital Platforms Tackle the Pandemic in China. *Social Media + Society,* 6(3): 1–4.

Feizhou Z. (2009). The Tournament System. *Sociological Studies.* (3): 54–77.

Gabrys J. (2014). Programming Environments: Environmentality and Citizen Sensing in the Smart City. *Environment and Planning D: Society and Space.* 32(1): 30–48.

Gabrys J. (2016). *Program Earth: Environmental Sensing Technology and the Making of a Computational Planet.* Minneapolis: University of Minnesota Press.

Hernes M. (1978). "Det mediavridde samfunn" ("The Media-Twisted society"). *Samtiden.* 86(1): 1–14.

Hjarvard S. (2013). *The Mediatization of Culture and Society.* London: Routledge.

Kaun A., Trere E. (2020). Repression, resistance and lifestyle: Charting (dis)connection and activism in times of accelerated capitalism. *Social Movement Studies.* 19(5–6): 697–715.

Keping Y. (2005). *Politics and Political Science.* Beijing: Social Sciences Academic Press.

Li M. (2022). The Logic and Challenges of the Technology Embedding in Significant Risk Management. *Ningxia Social Sciences.* 231(1): 54–62.

Linders D. (2012). From E-Government to We-Government: Defining a Typology for Citizen Coproduction in the Age of Social Media. *Government Information Quarterly.* 29(4): 446–454.

Mackenzie A. (2011). *Wirelessness: Radical Empiricism in Network Cultures.* Cambridge, MA: MIT Press.

Manovich L. (2006). The poetics of Augmented Space. *Visual Communication,* 5(2): 219–240.

McQuire S. (2016). *Geomedia: Networked Cities and the Future of Public Space.* Cambridge, UK: Polity Press.

Mosco V. (1996). *The Political Economy of Communication: Rethinking and Renewal.* London: Sage.

Murray S. (2008). Cybernated aesthetics: Lee Bull and the body transfigured. *Performing Arts Journal.* (30): 38–65.

Mumford L. (1934). *Technics and Civilization.* London: Routledge & Kegan Paul Ltd.

Nechushtai E. (2018). Could digital platforms capture the media through infrastructure? *Journalism.* 19(8): 1043–1058.

Norberg S. (1979). *Genius Loci: Towards a Phenomenology of Architecture.* New York: Rizzoli.

Paul W. (2020). *Being Modern in China.* Cambridge: Polity Press.

Remi M. (2016). Brave New City: The image in the urban data-space. *Visual Communication.* 15(3): 271–391.

Renjie P., Jing W. (2019). Deconstructing the Myth of a Digital Age: An Interview with Prof. Vincent Mosco. *Journalism Bimonthly.* 159(7): 109–119.

Roberts L. (2015). Navigating the "archive city": Digital spatial humanities and archival film practice. *Convergence: The International Journal of Research into New Media Technologies.* 21(1): 100–115.

Rossi A. (1966). *The Architecture of the City.* New York: The MIT Press.

Stromback J. (2008). Four Phases of Mediatization: An Analysis of the Mediatization of Politics. *International Journal of Press/Politics.* 13(3): 228–246.

Taijun J., Chengcheng S. (2012) Government Ecology Management, Core Actors in Local Government and Political Tournament. *Social Sciences in Nanjing.* (6): 65–70.

Tibbalds F. (1992). *Making People-Friendly Towns: Improving the Public Environment in Towns and Cities.* Harlow: Longman.

Tongwen X. (2019). "Medium Characteristics" and "Data Practices": "Running in Campuses" Based on the Locative Media. *Chinese Journal of Journalism & Communication.* (11): 46–69.

Venturi R. (2005/2009). Architecture as Paradox within the Urban Complex. In *Perspective on Architectural Theories: Tongji Architecture Forum.* Beijing: China Architecture & Building Press.

Verhoeff N. (2012). *Mobile Screens: The Visual Regime of Navigation.* Amsterdam: Amsterdam University Press.

Wei S., Mengying L. (2021a). "City of QR Codes": Towards Human-machine Co-poiesis. *Exploration and Free Views.* (08): 121–129.

Wei S., Mengying L. (2021b). Scanning the code: The digital communication capacity of programmable cities. *Journal of Normal University (Philosophy and Social Sciences Edition).* 231(06): 132–143.

Xian H. (2021). Media and communication in digital Geographic studies: The encounter of people and technology. *Shanghai Journalism Review.* 460(6): 15–27.

Xin G. (2019). Towards Interactive Governance: The reformation of "state, market, society relationship" in the innovation of national governance system. *Academic Monthly.* (1), 77–86.

Xinshui X. (2021). The Health Code in Epidemic Management: About Identity and Tension. *E-Government.* 217(1): 2–11.

Xingdong F., Feng Y. (2020). Research on the Challenges of Digital Social Governance Behind the "Health QR Code". *Public Governance.* (8): 78–91.

Xu C., Tang T. (2020). Closing the Gap or Widening the Divide: The Impacts of Technology enabled Cor-production on Equity in Public Service Delivery. *Public Administration Review.* 80(6): 962–975.

Xuesong L., Yunlong D. (2021). Formation Mechanism and Dual Effect of Overlay Use of Health Codes—An Analysis Framework of Institutional Fact. *Journal of Public Management.* (4): 105–115.

Yiqing H., Zhiyi C. (2020). Transcending Tradition and Returning to Media: On Three New Paths of Political Economy of Communication. *Journal of Social Science of Hunan Normal University.* (6): 66–74.

Zixue T., Xiao Y., Bai H. (2021). Locked down through Virtual Disconnect: Navigating Life by Staying on/off the Health QR Code during COVID-19 in China. *Convergence: The International Journal of Research into New Media Technologies.* 27(6): 1648–1662.

PART II

Digital Affordances and Contestations

CHAPTER 7

Hidden Abodes: Digital Lives and Distant Others

Graham Murdock

Our present relations to digital technologies rest on two profound contradictions.

Firstly, the promise of ever-expanding opportunities to live life fully online is increasingly in tension with the role of the dominant commercialized platforms in escalating the threats to individual and collective well-being. These threats are reflected in on-going environmental and health emergencies. The greater the volume of digital traffic, the greater the contradiction.

Communication and Catastrophe: Connectivity, Climate and Corona

Mounting risks from the accelerating climate and environmental emergencies have been joined by the continuing global toll of deaths and disabilities from Covid 19, the latest pandemic caused by a coronavirus. Without substantial changes to current patterns of accumulation it will not be the last and will be accompanied by upsurges in other chronic health conditions. The word catastrophe comes from the Greek 'to overturn'. It originally described the devastating events at the end of classical dramas, the culmination of tensions that had accumulated and intensified over the course of the play. We are currently living with the unfolding catastrophe of capitalist modernity. The central role now played by digital technologies in the organization of everyday life and

G. Murdock (✉)
Loughborough University, Loughborough, UK
e-mail: g.murdock@lboro.ac.uk

© The Author(s), under exclusive license to Springer Nature Switzerland AG 2024
H. S. Dunn et al. (eds.), *The Palgrave Handbook of Everyday Digital Life*,
https://doi.org/10.1007/978-3-031-30438-5_7

contemporary economies directs us to examine how their current modes of organization are contributing to these catastrophes and reproducing the radical inequalities in the risks they pose.

The second contradiction arises from the fact that the enhanced prospects for pleasure, expression and personal agency held out to affluent digital users are predicated on the cumulative dispossession and immiseration of the citizens and indigenous peoples of the global South and the marginalized communities of the North. It is their lands that are seized by the companies extracting the minerals required to build digital devices and the coal, oil and gas they still largely rely on to power them. It is their labour that is exploited to manufacture and deliver devices. And it is their communities that are surrounded by the mountains of hazardous electronic waste formed by successive deposits of discarded machines.

They are also on the front line of the most severe impacts of the climate and pandemic catastrophes. They are more likely to see their livelihoods and ways of living threatened by prolonged droughts and severe flooding and landslips; less likely to possess adequate resources for prevention and mitigation; more likely to be forced to migrate and become permanently displaced; more likely to work in settings that expose them to infection during pandemics and less likely to have ready access to the effective vaccines and anti-viral drugs needed to avoid severe illness and death.

We are faced with a stark choice. We can continue as we are and move into a future shaped by the increasingly destructive impacts of our exploitation of the natural world and the anticipated and unanticipated risks to life they generate, or we can recognize the need for radical change and accept the responsibility to create a future that is socially just and environmentally sustainable.

In the first volume of *Capital*, Marx famously argues that critical analysis in the service of transformation must "leave the noisy sphere" of exchange and consumption "where everything takes place on the surface and in full view of everyone and [enter] the hidden abode of production" (p. 279). As Nancy Fraser reminds us however, we also need to take a further step backwards moving "from the front story of exploitation" in digital chains of production "to the backstory of expropriation" of resources previously held in common (Fraser, 2022, p. 8). Obtaining the resources required to construct digital systems has entailed the appropriation of land, water and mineral deposits and the displacement of indigenous peoples and long-standing communities, and the destruction of natural environments. It has also involved the commercial capture and enclosure of innovations and technologies originally funded from the public purse and their conversion into privatized assets deployed for profit generation.

Embarking on this journey into the hidden abodes of digital exploitation and appropriation immediately confronts us with the multiple ways our digital lives are linked to the lives of distant and unseen others and imposes on us a moral obligation to struggle for changes to the organization of digital systems that sustain environmental integrity, health, and social justice on a global scale.

Carbon Capitalism: Networks and Markets

The industrialised modernity launched at the end of the Nineteenth century has been powered by the energy released by burning the carbon stored in deposits of coal, oil and natural gas. These fossil fuels have generated the majority of the heat, light, and energy that has sustained economic and social activity at every level, from large scale manufacture to car ownership and domestic appliances. This system has been legitimated by a definition of 'progress' that identifies a successful society with ever increasing levels of production and consumption. Pursuing this project has generated cumulative emissions of 'greenhouse' gases, dominated by carbon dioxide, CO_2, that remain in the atmosphere for decades. These emissions have thrown an expanding blanket over the earth's surface, preventing heat from escaping back into the upper atmosphere and causing land and ocean temperatures to steadily rise.

The impact of human activity on the climate "crossed a critical threshold around 1950" with the expansion of mass consumerism in the mature capitalist economies (Owen & Steffen, 2017, p. 58) but "has been most evident "since 1970 (op cit: 55) with the years since 1980 recording the sharpest ever rise in average worldwide temperatures (EPA, 2002).

The legally binding climate agreements brokered in Paris in 2015 commit countries to limiting their emissions to ensure that temperatures do not rise above 1.5 degrees centigrade over pre-early industrial levels. The increase currently stands at 1.1 degrees centigrade which research suggests is already exacerbating the incidence and severity of extreme weather events. Levin, Boehm and Carter note that withering droughts, extreme heat and record floods already threaten the food security and livelihoods of the poorest citizens in low income countries and devastating floods and storms have forced twenty million from their homes each year since 2008. (Levin et al., 2022).

The ten countries with the highest number of UN appeals for humanitarian assistance related to extreme weather events since 2000 account for only 0.13 per cent of global greenhouse gas emissions but have seen the number of their citizens suffering from extreme hunger rise by 123 per cent, from 21.3 million to 47.5 million (Oxfam, 2022) Apart from periodic televised appeals for donations and occasional news reports of famines, they remain largely invisible, casualties of the 77 per cent share of global emissions generated by the leading world economies of the G20. This occurs as the wealth nations pursue a vision of modernity anchored in a renewed emphasis on the central role of markets in organising economic activity.

The 1980's saw countries around the world move away from public ownership and state management and regulation, and reorganize their economies around markets, competition and profit generation. This structural shift to marketisation, was underpinned ideologically by the revival of the liberal emphasis on the primacy of personal rights. This new variant of liberalism, namely neoliberalism, privileged the rights of entrepreneurs to enter every sphere of activity and the right of individuals to search for self-expression and improved quality of life through their consumer choices. This movement occurred for different reasons and to varying extents in different economic zones.

In the Britain and the United States, the heartlands of mature capitalism, it was prompted by the structural crisis of accumulation that gathered momentum from the mid-1970s. Long-standing critics of state intervention were quick to blame the supposed inefficiencies of public ownership and management of core resources and the restrictions on enterprise imposed by public interest regulation. Their militant advocacy of market solutions found enthusiastic political promotion in the governments of Margaret Thatcher in the United Kingdom and Ronald Reagan in the US, establishing a new economic settlement that later Conservative and Democratic administrations left largely unchallenged.

In emerging economies, typified by South Korea, marketisation was imposed as a condition of the 'restructuring' demanded in exchange for international loans. In Russia and across the former Eastern bloc countries, the vacuum created by the collapse of the Soviet system opened the way for buccaneering and often corrupt entrepreneurs. In China the economic reforms introduced after the death of Mao generated opportunities for private investment, competition and profit seeking. With India's turn away from the economic self-sufficiency that had dominated the initial period of nation building, three of the world's major economies which had remained wholly or largely uncoupled from global capitalism for most of the post-war era were incorporated into the new networks of accumulation.

Placing this process of marketisation and its globalization at the center of analysis is an essential first step in understanding how digital media are deepening the climate emergency and creating the conditions for pandemics. Recognizing that the age of digitalization is also the era of marketisation and that the two processes are inextricably tied together, directs us to ask questions about the distribution of power and responsibility. Who controls, which digital innovations will be developed and how they will be designed, manufactured and marketed? Who decides which possible applications will be promoted and which will be suppressed? Who devises the business models that enable digital media to generate profits? And who pays for the negative social and environmental impacts of these various decisions?

The Global Rise of Digital Oligopolies

In capitalist economies, control over the most popular everyday uses of the internet is now concentrated in a handful of companies, all but one, the short video platform TikTok, owned by the Chinese company Byte Dance, are based in the United States. These are: Meta, Alphabet, Microsoft, Apple and Amazon. Their unprecedented control over the organization of public communication is the direct result of marketisation. They have been allowed to appropriate foundational technological innovations developed by publicly-funded research initiatives while returning almost nothing in taxation (Mazzucato, 2018), moving their mega profits to offshore accounts shielded from public scrutiny.

The algorithms they employ to sort and classify user data and target them for promotional appeals are commercially privileged and closed to public scrutiny, making it impossible to challenge the social assumptions that underpin them. Rigorously enforced claims to exclusive rights to data access and use, commodify valuable social information thereby pre-empting its mobilization in support of democratically decided public interventions. The early platforms successfully lobbied to be classified under US law as carriers (like the telephone system) rather than publishers. This has allowed Meta's Facebook and Alphabet's YouTube to avoid the regulatory and editorial controls imposed on traditional media.

In the absence of effective anti-monopoly restraints, the digital majors have been given free range to extend their reach and eradicate competition. Google, launched in 1996, successfully eliminated Netscape and other early rivals to establish itself as the internet's dominant search engine. In August 2022 it commanded a 92 per cent share of global searches (Statcounter Global Stats, 2022). In 2006 it moved into social media acquiring the video sharing site YouTube, building it into a major on-line presence with a global base of 2.46 billion active monthly users in 2022 (op.cit.)

This pattern of aggressive expansion and acquisition is repeated with the other leading internet platform, Facebook. In 2011 the company purchased Beluga appropriating the company's pioneering technology to launch its own highly successful Messenger service. In 2012 it acquired the Instagram photo and video sharing site and in 2014 the WhatsApp mobile messaging service. Taken together these offerings have cemented the company's position as the dominant social media platform outside China. In July 2022 Facebook had 2.934 billion active monthly users worldwide, 36.8 per cent of the planet's population (DataReportal, 2022a) WhatsApp had 2 billion users and Instagram 1.44 billion (DataReportal, 2022b).

The drive to monopolize core functions in established geographical markets has been accompanied by a concerted push to dictate the terms of access in emerging markets. In August 2013 Facebook's CEO, Mark Zuckerberg, launched Internet.org. aimed at enlisting users in low -income economies. His declaration that "connectivity is a human right" (quoted in Mukerjee, 2016, p. 359) was comprehensively undercut by the conditions imposed on access. Users owning a basic mobile phone could view sites selected by Facebook without incurring data charges but access to the full internet packages offered by collaborating service providers was charged at normal rates. The offer was a classic 'loss leader', a marketing ploy designed to install internet use in the everyday lives of first-time users and entice then to upgrade. Rebranded as 'FreeBasics', Facebook's discounted access was limited to sites that joined the initiative, often presented in stripped down versions. While listings on the Bing search engine could be freely accessed, reading search results incurred charges (Solon, 2017). Tim Berners-Lee, the principal architect of the World Wide

Web, the building block of the public internet, observed that "it's not the Internet... Giving people data connectivity to only part of the network deliberately ... is a step backwards" (quoted in Mukerjee, 2016, p. 359).

Facebook's control over the terms of access was a clear violation of the principle of net neutrality specifying that all internet sites, content and platforms should be treated equally without discrimination. In 2016 activists employed this argument to lobby successfully for FreeBasics to be banned in India (Venkatraman and Rangaswamy (2016). By 2017, however, the service was available in sixty countries. They included Kenya, where only one of the sites on offer, a weather forecast, was directly relevant to the central challenges facing the country's rural poor. Such rural communities are at the centre of claims to bringing the internet to previously excluded groups. Reliant on farming and livestock as their primary source of income they are particularly exposed to the impacts of climate change. The comprehensive range of information sources needed to devise practical responses is precisely what FreeBasics withholds (Onyea, 2020).

Anticipating future development, both Facebook and Google have used the profits from their domination of core internet functions to acquire strategic stakes in the emerging technologies at the centre of the next expansion of digital machines. Google owns leading companies in robotics (Boston Dynamics), home automation (Nest Labs), and artificial intelligence (Deep Mind Technologies). Facebook has substantial investments in virtual reality systems through Oculus VR and aims to lead the development of a network of immersive on-line spaces dubbed the Metaverse. Both companies have been renamed and rebranded to reflect their expanding reach, Google as Alphabet and Facebook as Meta.

The digital US majors all now feature in the list of the top corporations in the global economy and their owners are among the richest individuals on the planet. Their only effective global competition comes from the Chinese digital majors developed behind a protective wall. These competitors are designed to replicate core functions, with Baidu offering search, Alibaba providing electronic shopping, and Tencent matching and surpassing Facebook's array of social media options,

In August 2022 four of the world's five biggest corporations, listed by market capitalization (calculated on the total value of their shares), were digital corporations based in the United States with Apple in first place, Microsoft in third, Alphabet in fourth and Amazon in fifth. Meta was in tenth position (Johnston, 2022). The founders of three of the leading digital concerns, Jeff Bezos of Amazon, Bill Gates of Microsoft and Larry Page and Sergey Brin of Alphabet, were listed among the world's ten richest people (Moskowitz, 2022).

Two defining features of the way the major digital companies operate are central to understanding why recent decades have seen both worsening climate and environmental crises and successive corona pandemics: the carbon emissions generated by the manufacture, use and disposal of digital infrastructures and devices, and the saturation product promotion that fills users' screens.

Destructive Devices: Accumulating Carbon Emissions

As we have already noted, the communications devices we use and the networks of wires, satellites and relay stations that connect us are made of metals and other materials. These systems consume energy in their production, transportation and use, and generate accumulating volumes of electronic waste when they are discontinued and discarded. The way these stages in their life cycles are currently organized is generating increasing volumes of harmful carbon dioxide (CO_2).

Digital marketing encourages the possession of multiple machines; laptops, tablets, games consoles and smart phones. Each of these devices involves mining and extraction industries to obtain the metals and materials needed to construct them. Factories are devoted to assembling them, ecologically destructive container ships plough through the oceans to transport them to retail outlets, and at the end of their active life, huge piles of electronic rubbish accumulate. According to Apple's own calculations 77% of the carbon footprint of their devices is generated by the mining and manufacturing processes involved in producing them, before they reach their end users. (Compare and Recycle, 2020).

In addition to multiplying the number of communication devices in use, digitalization has massively increased the volume and diversity of information being transmitted over digital networks. For decades, data generated by companies or routine internet activity were stored on dedicated hard drives or discs owned and controlled by users. It is now increasingly held in 'cloud' computing facilities, vast factory-like complexes owned by the major digital corporations, among others.

Operating these storage installations requires substantial amounts of energy, and water for cooling. Transmitting data to and from end users imposes additional, and sharply increasing demands on energy supplies and rising CO_2 emissions. Changes in personal music consumption provide an instructive illustration. Emissions from the manufacture and use of the successive formats provided by vinyl records, cassette tapes and compact discs, remained more or less constant, varying between 140 and 157 million kilograms. By 2016 streaming services were estimated to be generating more than double that figure, up to 350 million kilograms of emission. (See Devine, 2019). It is also clear that video is significantly more energy hungry and is expanding rapidly with the growth of streaming film and television services, e-sports, and on-line gaming.

Plans to reconstruct the internet as a metaverse, a three-dimensional space which users navigate using virtual reality devices, will further increase carbon emissions. The levels currently generated by advanced video games, which share key features with the proposed metaverse, point to a rapid escalation, coupled with deepening global inequalities. By 2019 gamers in the United States were producing carbon emissions on a par with the overall emissions from a country like Sri Lanka (Vaughan, 2019) and players based in California were consuming more electricity than a number of emerging economies including Ghana, Kenya and El Salvador (Moss, 2019).

Building the Metaverse depends crucially on advances in artificial intelligence. Mark Zuckerberg, who renamed his Facebook company as Meta, signaled his ambition to dominate the development and applications of this new digital domain. He has explained: "we're particularly focused on foundational technologies that can make entirely new things possible. Today, we're going to focus on perhaps the most important foundational technology of our time: artificial intelligence" (quoted in Adebayo, 2022).

The machine learning processes that generate AI applications require systems to be fed raw data to work on. The larger and more diverse the volume of data the more accurate the application and the greater the demands on energy, the more emissions produced and the greater the damage to the planet (Brevini, 2021). "Already… the carbon footprint of the world's computational infrastructure has matched that of the aviation industry at its height, and it is increasing at a faster rate" (Crawford, 2021, p. 42). One estimate predicts that by 2030 communications technologies as a whole will account for 51% of global electricity demand and 23% of total greenhouse gases. (see Andrac & Edler, 2015).

The expanding carbon footprints of the digital devices we use and rely on everyday are essential threads we need to follow in order to understand how digitalization is contributing to the deepening climate crisis A full analysis however also needs to explore the pivotal role they now play in cultivating a culture of hyper consumption that is imposing unsustainable demands on natural resources, creating the conditions for both ecological catastrophe and periodic pandemics of which Covid-19 is the latest example.

Corona Consumption: Fast Foods and Vanishing Forests

The 1970s structural economic crisis in the advanced capitalist societies was in part a crisis of underconsumption. The mass production-mass consumption system that had driven economic growth since the end of World War II hit a wall. People had bought the 'big ticket' household appliances, refrigerators, washing machines, and television sets, that made life more convenient and pleasurable, and increasing numbers had acquired a car. These were all major items of expenditure and people expected to use them for many years. If they broke down there were local trades-people who would replace or repair damaged parts. Addressing the crisis required a new regime of consumption. People had to be persuaded to consume more and replace items on an accelerated basis.

Expanding and intensifying consumption was also central to China's strategies for growth in the post-Mao transition from a state-managed to a market-oriented economy. The rising real incomes of the new middle class fueled a new consumer culture supported by advertising-funded television services and the construction of shopping malls in every town and city. It was a pattern repeated in India and other emerging economies.

The rapid rise of digital media, increasingly organized around smart phones, has played three pivotal roles in generalizing and reinforcing an intensified consumer system.

Firstly, the marketing practices of smart phones have been in the forefront of cultivating the expectation that previous versions of the machines we rely on no longer deliver all the benefits we might wish for and that we urgently need to acquire the latest model. The Apple iPhone is a paradigmatic example of this logic in practice. Each new version promises additions and modifications: improved cameras, finger print security, a new design for the casing, faster speeds. As users, we are encouraged never to be satisfied with the version we have, since the next one will be so much better. The result is a consumer culture based on accelerated disposability that generates increasing pollution and waste.

Secondly, it has become increasingly possible to buy goods by swiping a smart phone across the purchase point or sending an instruction. Normalizing instant, frictionless, payment is the latest stage in an accelerating movement to replace material tokens, coins, notes and plastic credit cards, with non-material electronic transfers. Rendering purchase transactions as invisible and eliminating time for reconsideration are expressly designed to increase consumption.

Thirdly, hyper consumerism is insistently generalized by the ubiquity of product promotion on digital media. Traditionally advertising on terrestrial television channels in the West has been clearly separated from programming, confined to dedicated spaces and subject to strong regulations on the amounts and forms of promotion permitted. Advertising to children has attracted additional restrictions. The limits placed on spot advertising fueled an increasing use of integrated appeals to secure additional space for promotional messages. Sponsorship deals allow corporations to attach their names to popular programmes and the increasing use of product placement inserts branded commodities into the programme's visual field and script. Integrated promotion assumed that the emotional attachments viewers have with admired characters and celebrities and the wish to emulate their life styles would be transferred to the products they are seen using and enjoying.

Social media have expanded with little or no effective regulation, allowing both ubiquitous display advertising and a proliferating array of strategies that incorporate product and brand promotion into informational and entertainment forms. These embedded persuasions have come to play a central role in promoting a culture of hyper consumption. Corporations have increasingly capitalized on the popularity of video gaming to post free 'advergames' featuring their logos and brands and aimed particularly at children.

Recent years have also seen an explosive growth in 'influencers', non-professionals paid by companies to post endorsements on message boards or in short videos. Again, these appeals are aimed particularly at children and young people in the hope that they will identify more readily with presenters who look and act like themselves and be welcomed as virtual friends. In 2020 nine of the ten highest paid influencers on Google's YouTube platform were young people or children. The top position was taken by Ryan Kaji, a nine-year-old living in Texas who earned US$29.5 million from his site promoting toys and his own branded clothing. Other leading influencers demonstrated video games and cosmetics (Berg & Abram, 2020).

Young influencers and advergames are also heavily involved in promoting fast foods such as hamburgers, chicken nuggets and ready-made pizzas. These are often labelled 'junk' food because of their low nutritional value. They illustrate perfectly how the repetitive and addictive appeals of disposable culture have come to colonize everyday life. They are designed not to be fully satisfying, to leave consumers always wanting more. Digital media play a key role in reinforcing these appeals, often using children to promote them. A US based study of the five most watched YouTube channels featuring child influencers (aged between 3 and 14 years) found that promotions for food and drink were viewed one billion times, with McDonalds featuring in over ninety per cent of postings (Airuwaily et al., 2020). Fast foods also appear prominently in advergames with US research recording a million children playing them over the course of a month, with measurable gains in their consumption of junk meals and snacks. (Orcian, 2012).

Diets rich in processed foods are a major contributory cause of overweight and obesity, conditions that account for at least 2.8 million deaths globally a year and significantly increase the risks of contracting diabetes, cancers, and cardiovascular diseases leading to early death (Osayomi & Orhiere, 2017, p. 94). In 2019, an estimated 38.2 million children under the age of 5 years were overweight or obese. Once considered a high-income country problem, overweight and obesity are now on the rise in low- and middle-income countries, particularly in urban settings (World Health Organisation, 2022).

Junk food relies on two basic commodities, processed meat and palm oil. Rising real incomes for an increasing number of households in emerging economies have transformed meat from an occasional addition to diets to a staple contribution. If present trends continue, research conducted under the auspices of the United Nations estimates that global meat consumption is likely to expand by 76 per cent by mid -century (Godfrey et al., 2018). All three major meats: beef, pork and chicken, have carbon footprints considerably higher than either vegetables or grains. Beef, the essential ingredient of burgers, generates the most emissions at 6.61 pounds of CO_2e per serving as against 0.16 for rice and 0.07 for carrots (Centre for Sustainable Systems, 2020). Palm oil, the world's most widely used vegetable oil, is an essential ingredient in the manufacture of a range of fast foods. Its attraction is its versatility. It gives fried products their crispy texture. It is a natural preservative ensuring that bread, cakes and prepared meals have a longer shelf life. It is also a major ingredient in chocolates and spreads.

However, avoiding junk foods does not provide protection against the wider health impacts of rising demands for palm oil and beef. Meeting these demands requires the mass destruction of forests and the conversion of cleared land into pastures and plantations. Between 1978 and 2018 South East Asia, the main center of palm oil production, lost thirty percent of its forest cover (Afelt et al., 2018, p. 2). The world's largest expanse of rain forest, in Brazil's Amazon Basin, has seen accelerated land clearances for logging, mining and most extensively for cattle ranching.

In the year between August 2019 and July 2020 the rate of deforestation increased by almost ten per cent (9.5%) (BBC, 2020). A recent global audit calculated that in 2019 a football pitch sized area of primary rainforest was lost somewhere in the world every six seconds (Weisse & Goldman, 2020). This is an ecological and climate catastrophe. Forests act as 'carbon sinks' reducing warming by absorbing CO_2. Clearances convert them into net emitters of CO_2. They also lead to mass loses in biodiversity, driving multiple insect and plant species that maintain the earth's ecosystem in balance to extinction. In addition, land converted to livestock farming significantly bolsters releases of methane gas from cattle's natural waste discharges, generating a global warming potential that has been estimated to be eighty-six times stronger than fossil fuels (see Jackson et al., 2020).

Deforestation is also a major contributory cause of pandemic disease. Animal species that were previously confined to the self-regulating forest interior are pushed to the edges and into closer contact with humans. All three recent pandemics caused by coronaviruses: SARS, MERS, and Covid-19, are zoonotic infections initially carried by bats and transmitted to humans through intermediary animal hosts. Despite proliferating conspiracy theories claiming that the Covid-19 coronavirus was cultivated in the Wuhan virology laboratory and released either accidently or deliberately, recent research demonstrates with a high degree of certainty that it originated in the city's wet market and was spread by multiple transmission from wild animals on sale there (Jing & Wang, 2022, pp. 925–926).

There are more bats than any other species and they are very adept at adjusting to new habitats. They readily colonize the barns and outbuildings constructed to service the new cattle ranches and find abundant food in the new human settlements. Bats are also able to carry a greater range of pathogens than any other species without harm to themselves.

Bats assemble in huge clusters and their droppings provide nutrients for a range of other species, creating additional routes for disease transmission. Given the estimated number of viruses in wildlife in emerging disease hotspots, future pandemics are inevitable if patterns of land use, agriculture and food production remain unchanged (Daszak, 2020). The brightly lit interiors of Macdonald's and KFC outlets are the last links in a chain connecting fast foods and their ubiquitous promotion on digital platforms to the rapid disappearance of the world's forests, the intensifying climate crisis, and increasingly frequent outbreaks of fatal pandemic diseases.

Confronting Catastrophe: The Conditions of Sustainability

In thinking about the conditions for sustainability, the image of a 'livable' planetary space as doughnut shaped, proposed by the radical political economist, Kate Raworth (2017), offers a useful starting point. The outer edge is defined by the various environmental boundaries that we need to keep within. The inner edge comprises the economic and social conditions that allow everyone to enjoy a life of dignity and opportunity and stop people from falling into the holes created by poverty, discrimination and disrespect.

As this image underlines, the struggle for a sustainable future is a struggle for social justice and respect as well as for ecological stability and a habitable planet. The two are bound together. Marketisation has redistributed income and wealth upwards to the already privileged, creating a widening gap in life chances of the rich and the poor and leaving those at the bottom of the social scale more vulnerable to economic pressures and least well-resourced to cope with environmental and health crises. When devising responses to the current crisis we urgently need to address the often exploitative and damaging conditions of labour involved in digital chains of production.

Securing sustainability, as I have defined it here, involves confronting both contemporary modes of economic organization and the ideologies employed to justify them. We need to stop thinking of 'progress' as a race for economic growth sustained by ever increasing levels of consumption and redefine it as a commitment to secure the conditions that ensure that everyone enjoys a decent quality of life.

This reorientation requires a fundamental shift in our present relationship to the natural word away from viewing natural resources as a free gift to be owned and commercially exploited to the maximum and seeing them instead as an essential life support system that must be preserved and replenished. This ethos of custodianship and care for the natural environment has always informed the cosmologies of indigenous peoples and it is no accident that they have often been on the front line of recent struggles against corporate seizures of land and resources (Murdock, 2017).

As the climate and corona emergencies have demonstrated with brutal clarity our responsibilities for the collective well-being of others reach across the globe. There are no safe places, no escape hatches. But the most severe impacts are felt most acutely among the poorest and least well resourced. Tangible improvements in the quality of their lives and life chances are the ultimate test of movement towards a sustainable future based on social justice and care for the natural world.

In the capitalist West, digital innovation has been comprehensively commandeered by a handful of corporations that have taken advantage of the new arenas of profit generation opened up by marketisation, while transferring the social and environmental costs to workers and users. Critique needs to begin by retrieving the risky lives and restricted life chance of the children digging for cobalt in hazardous open cast mines in the Democratic Republic of Congo (DRC), or scavenging for reusable materials on the great dumps of electronic waste in Ghana. We have to help retrieve the lives of the young migrant women working in assembly plants for wages barely sufficient to live on, the sailors on transporter ships with little or no safety systems, the operatives assembling orders in cavernous dispatch centres working at a pace that opens them to injury and ill health, and the precariously employed van drivers delivering digital devices to shops and homes.

Precisely because media are ubiquitous as both material systems and cultural formations, communication researchers and practitioners have a particular responsibly and opportunity to address both the social and environmental costs of dominant digital chains of production and the ideological narratives that perpetuate them.

This imposes two immediate priorities. Firstly, to move as rapidly as possible towards basing public communication on renewable sources of energy and developing infrastructures and devices that are climate neutral, non-exploitative in their production, and repairable and recyclable. Secondly, to promote resources for change by mobilizing every available expressive form to encourage imaginative and engaging ways of communicating the social, ecological and health costs of the digital technologies we use every day. Continuing warnings of a worsening situation however can all too easily provoke feelings of helplessness and resignation. They need to be counterbalanced by accounts of successful interventions that have made an evident difference to everyday life and well-being in particular communities.

The viability of these initiatives depends in turn on countering corporate annexation and reclaiming digital systems as publicly owned and -administered resources, deployed in the service of social justice and environmental sustainability.

Our quality of life is inextricably bound up with the equitable distribution of shared resources, the maintenance for which we are collectively responsible. Commercial media push this recognition of mutuality and shared fate to one side promoting individual market choices as the primary and privileged spaces of personal satisfaction and social expression, and relentlessly reinforcing an environmentally destructive culture of hyper-consumption.

Past experience teaches us that reintroducing public interest regulation of corporate activity, while absolutely necessary to curb abuses, will not be enough in itself. Concerted political lobbying will secure loopholes and exemptions. We need to provide robust alternatives by reconstituting key communications infrastructures as public utilities and reinventing public service media as indispensable cultural spaces, free from all forms of commercial promotion, that engage audiences and users as citizens rather than consumers and cultivate an ethos of collective care and mutuality (see Fuchs & Unterberger, 2021).

The structural basis for a digital communication system that supports this counter vision already exists. It rests on the progressive digitalization of the collective cultural resources held by public libraries, museums, universities, galleries and archives, coupled with the multiple collaborative on-line initiatives produced by grass-roots involvement. Taken together they hold out the prospect of creating a 'digital commons' that combines the moral economies of pubic goods and the gift relations that sustain voluntary collaborative initiatives (Murdock, 2013, 2018.)

Imagining how this new public communicative space might be organized, ensuring that it is socially inclusive and environmentally sustainable, and devising practical measures to install it at the heart of collective life, is the greatest challenge and the greatest opportunity facing us. It will encounter formidable opposition from the entrenched economic power of the digital majors, from populist deconstruction of mutuality and the public sphere, and from intensifying governmental drives to enlist digital innovation in the service of national narratives and competitive advantage. But it remains absolutely indispensable to any attempt to envision public communications, both materially and imaginatively.

Ignoring or refusing the challenge will ensure the continuation of catastrophe.

References

Adebayo, Kolawole (2022) 'Meta describes how AI will unlock the metaverse' *Venture Beat,* March 2. Available at https://venturebeat.com/2022/03/02/meta-describes-how-ai-will-unlock-the-metaverse/.

Afelt, Aneta, Fruton, Roger and Devaux, Christian (2018) 'Bats, coronaviruses and deforestation:Toward the Emergence of Novel Infectious Diseases?', *Frontiers of Microbiology,* Vol 9, April, Article 702, at https://www.frontiersin.org/articles/10.3389/fmicb.2018.00702/full [accessed December 28 2020].

Airuwaily, Amal et al (2020) 'Child Social Media Influencers and Unhealthy Food Product Placement', *Pediatrics,* Vol 146, No 5 https://doi.org/10.1542/peds.2019-4057.

Andrac, Anders and Edler, Thomas (2015) 'On global electricity usage of communication technology: Towards 2030', *Challenge,* Vol 6 No 1, pp 117–157.

BBC (2020) 'Brazil's Amazon: Deforestation 'Surges to a 12 year high', *BBC News,* 30 November https://www.bbc.co.uk/news/world-latin-america-55130304.

Berg, Madeline and Brown Abram (2020) 'The Highest -Paid YouTube Stars of 2020,' *Forbes,* December 18 https://www.forbes.com/sites/maddieberg/2020/12/18/the-highest-paid-youtube-stars-of-2020/?sh=e43a63e6e508.

Brevini, Benedetta (2021) *Is AI Good for the Planet?* Cambridge. Polity Press

Centre for Sustainable Systems (2020) *Carbon Footprint Factsheet.* University of Michigan Centre for Sustainable Systems css.umich.edu/factsheets/carbon-footprint-factsheet.

Compare and Recycle Blog (2020) iPhone Lifecycle: What is the Carbon Footprint of the iPhone 27 May https://www.compareandrecycle.co.uk/blog/iphone-lifecycle-what-is-the-carbon-footprint-of-an-iphone.

Crawford, Kate (2021) *Atlas of AI: Power, Politics and the Planetary Costs of Artificial Intelligence.* New Haven. Yale University Press.

Daszak, Peter (2020) 'Ignore the conspiracy theories: scientists know Covid-19 wasn't created in a lab', *The Guardian,* June 9, at https://www.theguardian.com/commentisfree/2020/jun/09/conspiracies-covid-19-lab-false-pandemic [accessed December 28 2020].

DataReportal (2022a) Facebook Statistics and Trends. Available at https://datareportal.com/essentail-facebook-stats.

DataReportal (2022b) The world's biggest social media platforms. Available at https://datareportal.com/social-media-users.

Devine, K (2019) *The Political Economy of Music.* Cambridge. Mass. MIT Press.

EPA (2002) *Climate Change Indicators: US and Global Temperatures.* United States Environmental Protection Agency. Available https://www.epa.gov/climate-indicators/climate-change-indicators-us-and-global-temperature.

Fraser, Nancy (2022) *Cannibal Capitalism: How Our System is Devouring Democracy, Care and the Planet-and What We Can Do about it.* London. Verso

Fuchs, C. and Unterberger K. (2021). The Public Service Media and Public Service Internet Manifesto, London, University of Westminster Press.

Godfrey, Charles et al (2018). Meat Consumption, Health and the Environment'. *Science*, Vol 361, Issue 6399, July 20 https://science.sciencemag.org/content/361/6399/eaam5324/tab-pdf.

Jackson, R.B, Saunois M, Bousquet P, Canadell J G, Poulter B, Stavert A, Bergamaschi P, Niwa Y, and Segers A (2020) 'Increasing anthropogenic methane emissions arise equally from agricultural and fossil fuel sources', *Environmental Research Letters,* Vol 15, 15 July, at https://iopscience.iop.org/article/10.1088/1748-9326/ab9ed2 [accessed December 28 2020].

Jing, Xiaowei and Wang, Ruoqi (2022) 'Wildlife trade is likely the source of SARS-CoV 2' *Science*, Vol 377, Issue 6600, 26 August, pp 925–926.

Johnston, Matthew (2022) Biggest Companies in the World by Market Cap, August 22. Available at https://www.investopedia.com/biggest-companies-in-the-world-by-market-cap-5212784.

Levin, Kelly, Boehm Sophie and Carter, Rebecca (2022) *6 Big Findings from the IPCC 2022 Report on Climate Impacts, Adaptations and Vulnerability.* World Resources Institute. 22 February. Available at https://www.wri.org/insights/ipcc-report-2022-climate-impacts-adaptation-vulnerability.

Mazzucato, Mariana (2018) The Entrepreneurial State: Debunking Public vs Private Sector Myths. London, Penguin Books.

Moskowitz, Dan (2022) The 10 Richest People in the World September 06. Available at https://www.investopedia.com/articles/investing/012715/5-richest-people-world.asp.

Moss, Todd (2019) 'Global Energy Inequality Goes Deeper than Bitcoin', *One Zero* 10 September. Available at https://onezero.medium.com/global-energy-inequality-goes-deeper-than-bitcoin-dfd058c31330.

Mukerjee, Subhayan (2016) 'Net neutrality, Facebook, and India's battle to #SaveTheInternet', *Communication and the Public, Vol* 1, No 3, pp. 356–361

Murdock, Graham (2013) 'Communication in Common', *The International Journal of Communication*, 7, pp 154–172.

Murdock, Graham (2017) 'One month in the life of the planet': carbon capitalism and the struggle for the commons' in Benedetta Brevini and Graham Murdock (eds) *Carbon Capitalism and Communication: Confronting Climate Crisis.* London. Palgrave Macmillan, pp. 207–219.

Murdock, Graham (2018) 'Reclaiming Digital Space: From Commercial Enclosure to the Broadcast Commons' in Gregory Ferrrell Lowe, Hilde Van de Bulck and Karen Donders (eds) *Public Service Media in the Networked Society*. Goteborg: Nordicom, pp 41–56.

Onyea, Chisom (2020) 'Internet.org's "Free Basics": Can Free Internet Initiatives Improve the Lives of Kenya's Rural Poor?', *Intersect: The Stanford Journal of Science, Technology and Society*, Vol 14, No 3, pp 1–24.

Orcian, Megan (2012) 'Food company computer games increase junk food consumption' *Yale News*, January 9th.

Osayomi, Tolulope and Orhiere, Maryanne A (2017) Small-area variations in overweight and obesity in an urban area of Nigeria: The role of fast food outlets. In: Biegańska, J. and Szymańska, D. editors, *Bulletin of Geography. Socio-economic Series*, No. 38, Toruń: Nicolaus Copernicus University, pp. 93–108. DOI: https://doi.org/10.1515/bog-2017-0036

Owen, Gaffney and Steffen, Will (2017) 'The Anthropocene Equation', *The Anthropocene Review*, Vol 4, No 1, pp. 53–61

Oxfam International (2022) *Hunger in a Hearting World*. 16 September. Available at https://www.oxfam.org/en/take-action/campaigns/climate-hunger.

Raworth, Kate (2017) *Doughnut Economics: Seven Ways to Think Like a 21st-Century Economist*, London: Random House Business Books.

Solon, O (2017) "It's digital colonialism': how Facebook's free Internet service has failed its users', *The Guardian*, 27 July. Available at https://www.theguardian.com/technology/2017/jul/27/facebook-free-basics-developing-markerts.

StatCounter Global Stats (2022) Search Engine Market Share Worldwide April 2021–2022. Available at https://gs.statcounter.com/search-engine-market-share.

Vaughan, Adam (2019) 'Gaming in the US emits as much carbon dioxide as all of Sri Lanka' *New Scientist*, 12 November. Available at https://www.newscientist.com/article/2223136-gaming-in-the-us-emits-as-much-carbon-dioxide-as-all-of-sri-lanka/.

Venkatraman, Shriram and Rangaswamy, Nimmi (2016) 'Everyday Life in Tamil Nadu. India and its Cost to "Free Basics" '*Ethnographic Praxis in Industry Conference Proceedings*, Volume 1, pp 249–263. Doi. https://doi.org/10.1111/1559-8918.2016.01089

Weisse, Mikaela and Goldman, Liz (2020) 'We lost a football Pitch of Primary Rainforest every 6 seconds in 2019', *Global Forest Watch*, 2 June, at https://blog.globalforestwatch.org/data-and-research/global-tree-cover-loss-data-2019 [accessed December 28 2020].

World Health Organisation (2022) *Obesity and Overweight*. Available at https://who.int/news-room/fact-sheets/detail/obesity-and-overweight.

CHAPTER 8

The Din and Stealth of the Digital Revolution

Renata Włoch

Introduction

The chapter identifies the multiple ways in which the adoption of digital technologies is bringing forth the new digital economy, both directly and indirectly supporting and disrupting its constituent parts, i.e. households and businesses. Focusing on cutting-edge technologies of datafication, it differentiates them from the foundational information and communication technologies, such as the computer, the internet and the mobile phone, and defines them as technologies that allow businesses, public institutions and consumers to make economic, political and social use of the abundant data produced on the web and collected by smart devices. Specifically, technologies of datafication include cloud computing and the Internet of Things, and, most importantly, that group of technologies dubbed artificial intelligence.

Digitalisation spurs business innovation, resulting in the proliferation of new business models (such as platforms) and new products and services. Adoption of digital technologies in workplaces has triggered the destruction of many middle-skill positions due to automation and changes in the human-machine division of work within existing jobs. The transformation of the labour market entails delayed, but nonetheless dramatic changes in other systems, most importantly in education (as new skills are expected of workers) and social security (as jobs are fragmented and stripped of their stability). This in turn affects the way we socialise our children, interact with our significant others, shape our identities and manage our lives.

R. Włoch (✉)
University of Warsaw, Warsaw, Poland
e-mail: r.wloch@uw.edu.pl

© The Author(s), under exclusive license to Springer Nature Switzerland AG 2024
H. S. Dunn et al. (eds.), *The Palgrave Handbook of Everyday Digital Life*,
https://doi.org/10.1007/978-3-031-30438-5_8

The Revolution

In 2022, 6.64 billion people possessed a smartphone, a phone which doubles as a portable computer and whose computing power is more than a thousand times that of the humble computer which, in 1969, helped send a human to the moon. By having a connection to the global Internet at one's fingertips—or, in fact, at the touch of one's favourite finger—we have instant access to a vast archive of knowledge accumulated by humanity, to friends on social networks, and to digital services and various products offered by an array of online platforms. Artificial intelligence using neural networks has learned to beat us at poker, a game that requires not only the skill of deductive thinking, but also intuition—considered a solely human attribute. Those of us who grew up in a world without any internet, smartphones, or artificial intelligence, are experiencing a "future shock", far more severe than that predicted by the coiners of this term, sociologists Alvin and Heidi Toffler (1970).

Scientific and business discourse is overwhelmingly dominated by the opinion that we are currently dealing with the "fourth technological/industrial/social/political revolution" (Schwab, 2016). The numbering of technological revolutions—i.e., sudden economic, social, and political upheavals related to the spread of a new technology—is the result of convention. A division proposed in the 1970s, by American sociologist Daniel Bell (1989), considered the first such revolution to have been brought about by the invention of the steam engine, that the second one came with the advent of electricity, and that the third was then ongoing as a result of automation and computerisation.

The most pronounced feature of the fourth technological revolution is the increasing intensity of the convergence of innovation. The classic approach to technological change, proposed at the beginning of the twentieth century by Austrian economist Joseph Schumpeter (1960), assumed that its first stage was an invention: a new product or process. An invention is of a scientific and technical character and it may never leave the confines of the inventor's laboratory or garage. Innovation, however, is an economic fact that has an impact on the economy, although it may well be of a niche nature. Only diffusion transforms innovation into a socio-economic phenomenon. A newer approach, developed by, among others, Stanford economist W. Brian Arthur in his book *The Nature of Technology* (2009), posits that technology does not arise in a linear way—it is always the result of a combination of various earlier technologies. This mechanism also characterised previous technological revolutions, but it occurred at a much slower pace, partly due to the speed at which knowledge circulated.

Digital devices crown the long and cumulative process of innovation which started more than two centuries ago, when Charles Babbage invented a prototype of a steam-powered computer. The first computers were no more than calculating machines, cherished by the military as their computing power could be used for deciphering codes and estimating the blast range of a nuclear bomb. In 1943, the chairman of IBM, Thomas Watson, opined that "there is a world market for about five computers" (Carr, 2008, par. 1). In 1977, when miniaturisation was already paving the way for the universal use of computers in enterprises, the founder of Digital Equipment Corporation, a then leading computing company, claimed that "there is no reason anyone would want a computer in their home" (Strohmeyer 2008, par. 3). In contrast, the invention and then commercialisation of the internet widened the range of computer functions and its proliferation.

Connected computers gave their users access to new content, and soon enough, to new products and services. This in turn accelerated software development, resulting in more user-friendly interfaces. People using digital devices started to produce reams of data. Data has now become the main "substrate" of a whole range of innovative activities. Hal Varian (2009), Google's chief economist, noted that "the great thing about the current period is that component parts are all bits. That means you never run out of them. You can reproduce them, you can duplicate them, you can spread them around the world, and you can have thousands and tens of thousands of innovators combining or recombining the same component parts to create new innovation. So, there's no shortage". The next breakthrough was the widespread adoption of technologies enabling the effective use of this abundant data, such as cloud technologies and AI. Getting value out of data has since formed the basis of the business and operational models of countless companies.

THE DIN: AI EVERYWHERE

Silicon Valley gurus such as Ray Kurzweil wish to convince us that we are approaching the "singularity", when machine intelligence will transcend that of humans. Yet after almost seven decades of trundling along the bumpy road towards building competent artificial intelligence, most leading experts admit that if it is indeed intelligence, then it is of a rather specialised and narrow kind. What business, public institutions and average citizens and consumers have now at their disposal is a collection of highly-polished statistical tools, rendered operational through immense computing power capable of sifting through unprecedented amounts of data collected by digital devices. The intelligence it applies resembles more that of the "Central Intelligence Agency" than "human intelligence" (Agrawal et al., 2019). Perhaps a proposal by two participants in the famous Dartmouth Conference of 1955 to call the budding area of research "complex information processing" instead of the intuitively hype-laden "artificial intelligence" was in fact closer to the truth (Mims, 2021).

There are many different kinds of artificial intelligence technologies, although all of them operate via algorithms. Some AI algorithms operate using pre-written rules, emulating procedures defined by humans in simple conditional statements (IF a condition, THEN an action). Rule engines (or semantic reasoners) may be used to automate numerous business processes, for example by flagging suspicious payments, suspending subscriptions, running simple chatbots or scoring applications (e.g. loan or even job applications). These applications of AI gain little attention from the media, but are often adopted by companies to automate routine tasks. But most of the din that we hear revolves around algorithms that can perform a feat called *machine learning*.

Some computer systems are able to improve their own performance when applied to vast amounts of data without any human interference. They analyse data by searching for patterns, and then use them to build predictive models. In other words, they "learn" with the use of refined statistical techniques (Russel & Norvig, 2019). Deep learning systems, which may be treated as a subset of machine learning are based on artificial neural networks stacked on one another, with each layer deepening the insight gleaned by sending the information back and forth. Machine learning and deep learning can be *supervised, unsupervised* and *reinforced*. Supervised means that the program operates on data previously labelled by humans or other machines and is given a clearly defined learning aim. Unsupervised means that the program must find patterns in unlabelled data, and reinforced signifies that the program, using a lot of computational power, autonomously tests solutions and chooses the best route to achieve a set goal. Reinforced learning was used in 2016 by Google's DeepMind team to master the ancient Chinese game of Go, widely seen as one of the most complex human games.

Some theoretical accounts relate the notion of artificial intelligence to symbolic, rule-based algorithms, and emphasise the qualitative difference of machine learning as a completely new kind of predictive statistical approach. For example, in 2022, Yann LeCun, Chief AI Scientist at Meta (Facebook's parent company) observed on Twitter that he "never called what [he] was working on AI. AI was supposed to designate "symbolic" methods. Then around 2013, the public and the media became interested in deep learning & 'they' called it AI. We could not explain that AI people didn't view deep learning as AI. Because it made no sense." (LeCun, 2022). This is why a growing number of definitions focus less on what AI is, and more on what AI does. The European Parliament states that AI is "the ability of a machine to display human-like capabilities such as reasoning, learning, planning and creativity" (European Parliament, 2020). Artificial intelligence boils down to algorithms that allow for more efficient, faster and cheaper searching, analysing, matching, recommending and, above all, predicting.

Nowadays "intelligent" algorithms power myriad smartphones and other smart devices in our homes, workplaces and public spaces. The 2022 AI Index Report, prepared by Stanford University, highlights that AI is becoming both more affordable. The cost to train an image classification system, one of the most important applications of AI, decreased by 64% compared with 2018 cost, and is almost twice as effective (Zhang et al., 2022). Private investments in AI doubled in 2021 in comparison to 2020, reaching $93.5 billion, with most investment going to AI companies which specialised in data management, data processing and cloud services, as well as companies developing new products and services in healthcare and the financial sector.

The wide adoption of AI-powered systems and devices will be accelerated by the implementation of a new connection standard, which will become available to citizens, businesses and institutions within just a few years. The 6G standard will provide bandwidth twenty times faster and much more stable than the previous one. Downloading a 21 Tb file will take only 18 seconds, a feat that takes 5 hours through a 5G connection. If need be, it will allow for smooth and reliable connection between billions of devices per square kilometre, instead of mere millions in the case of 5G. Smaller, more mobile and better-connected devices are the backbone of the digital economy: faster connections mean more access and more functions, which attract more users, making internet networks more valuable for future users. 5G and soon 6G will underpin the functioning of a new type of super connected digital device in our homes, workplaces and public places (Holslin, 2021).

These devices will be able to gather, process and even analyse data on the spot. Edge computing, which takes place directly on the device, and its offshoot, fog computing, distributed among nearby devices, will complement or even supplement the transfer of data between local devices and core cloud servers (5G IA, 2021). Our ubiquitous digital devices will sense their surroundings with greater precision and speed and will support even more intense communication between people and machines. Digital networks are becoming thicker and denser as communication is taking place not only between humans, but also between humans and machines, and between machines as well. By 2023, half of all connections will be machine-to-machine (Cisco, 2020). Constant digitisation (turning analogue data into digital, machine-readable data) is saturating networks with more and more data.

Intelligent automation is promoting a reorientation of companies and other kinds of institutions towards business and operation models based on datafication (Śledziewska & Włoch, 2021). Companies are gaining access to abundant data that can be used to increase productivity, optimise business processes, improve management, make more accurate real-time decisions, personalise products, adjust offerings, expand into new markets, and experiment with new ways of building networked relationships and data-driven management (new business models). Data can be bought from technological companies offering information goods and virtual services to consumers. In fact, data is becoming just another commodity one that can be bought and sold in batches, and used for the precise segmentation of customers. Data points are also increasingly created by consumers using a company's own products and services and by machines in factories networked within the Internet of Things (Iansiti & Lakhani, 2020).

Technologies of datafication are turning into general-purpose technologies, with the potential to change the functioning of the economy and society. They are becoming ubiquitous, seamlessly integrated with the connected digital devices in our homes, factories, offices and public spaces. Their impact will not be delivered by humanoid robots governing our collective imagination, but rather through less flashy intelligent systems and agents slowly, but relentlessly, permeating the world of labour.

Stealth: The Changing Labour Market

The spread of datafication technology is changing the way companies operate, and also their business and organisational models, especially in relation to the role of work. In the digital economy, creating value is becoming less and less labour-intensive. This phenomenon is most clearly seen when it comes to technology companies, ranging from Google to Spotify, which are generally "lean"—providing information products to millions of people with just a few employees. The digital transformation is resulting in operational and organisational changes whereby human work has not just become merely one of many other process streams that need to be optimised, but something which has also started to be located on the periphery of a company's operations, not in the centre as it once was.

Task-based work for internal operational processes in 'datafied' companies, that engage in work unbundling. (Mayer-Schönberger & Ramge, 2018) can be outsourced via global platforms, which has led to an unravelling of traditional employment relationships. The digitisation of processes also enables the implementation of artificial intelligence in an increasing number of areas in the average company. These changes are no longer limited to technology companies—they are increasingly affecting companies from traditional sectors.

Yet this does not mean that there will be a massive supplanting of human workers by machines any time soon. Discussions about the digital revolution are, just like conversations about earlier technological revolutions, haunted by the spectre of technological unemployment. One well-known example is the alarmist thesis presented in 2013 by Carl B. Frey and Michael Osborne, who claimed that up to 47% of all jobs may be susceptible to computerisation. It was hailed as visionary by the media, yet the majority of the academic world maintained that changes in the labour market would proceed much more stealthily.

Among economists much respect is accorded to an approach formulated by three economists from MIT: David Autor, Frank Levy and Richard Murnane (2003). Their view is that the risks associated with automation should be assessed not in relation to a given occupation, but in relation to tasks, or bundles of tasks, within a given profession or workplace. Intelligent systems will take over not so much the entire job as those individual, routine, predictable, and often tedious tasks and activities (as seen from the perspective of a human worker). We will see not the replacing of a person by a machine, but the *complementing* of their work with that of a machine, and vice versa.

This thesis regarding the complementarity of human and machine competencies was laid out by Levy and Murnane in a 2004 book entitled *The New Division of Labor: How Computers Are Creating the Next Job Market*. According to it, some activities are done better by people, and others by computers. This assumption should underpin a new division of labour in the economy. In addition, it is important to consider what types of well-paid jobs will be left for humans to do in an increasingly computerised world, and what skills should therefore be developed. This argument was developed by Paul R. Daugherty and H. James Wilson, authors of the book *Human + Machine: Reimagining Work in the Age of AI* (2018), who suggest looking at the integration of human and machine work through the prism of three groups of tasks.

In some tasks, purely human competences will still perform better, especially where it will be necessary to set courses of action, make decisions, and judge, create and empathise. In others, machines will do better—e.g. when performing repetitive tasks or those requiring forecasting. More and more often, though, tasks will be of a hybrid nature, combining and harmoniously complementing the competencies of people and machines. For some activities, people will support and complement machines: this includes training them (e.g. training neural networks), explaining and interpreting their work, and maintaining them. With others, machines will boost humans' potential, enhancing their cognitive, communicative and physical abilities. As a result, people will be relieved of the burden of doing 'dirty, dangerous and dull' work in favour of focusing on truly creative and satisfying tasks.

An unusual aspect of the current phase of AI-driven automation and other datafication technologies is that they affect a group of white-collar workers who have so far escaped other technological advances relatively unscathed. Over the course of the twentieth century, as part of the process of transforming the industrial economy into a service and information-based economy, an ever-increasing portion of the workforce migrated to sectors that dealt with intangible production: operating via ideas and concepts, producing knowledge, processing information, and diligently implementing procedures in the decision-making processes of rational organisations (Castells, 1996). Office-bound work in companies and public institutions has become the foundation of income stability and a major determinant of the identity of a growing middle class.

It was Max Weber who noted that bureaucratic organisation, the cornerstone of the modern state and the modern company, was intrinsically based on routine procedures (Marody & Giza-Poleszczuk, 2004: 249). The rapid spread of PCs in the 1980s, together with the development of office productivity software, paved the way for the automation of these procedures. One could even put forward the cautious thesis that computers gained popularity due to the fact that they made it possible to automate work thanks to subsequent "killer apps," such as spreadsheets. However, operating a computer still required a lot of human input and skill. Overall, though, ICT increased the productivity of the average office worker, and therefore his/her value from an employer's perspective (Ford, 2015).

Currently, robotic process automation (RPA) is becoming more and more widely used in companies that deal with intangible production. RPA is a type of software that harnesses the potential of cloud computing as well as the possibilities of artificial intelligence to automate repetitive tasks previously performed by humans. Usually these are tasks include information retrieval and processing, pattern identification, analysis, and prediction. The deployment of RPA first requires the identification of processes in a given company or institution. This, however, is hampered by various organisational and cultural barriers as well as the silo-like (i.e. fragmented) way in which information is brought together in individual departments of an organisation, something which is especially characteristic of public bureaucracy. Nevertheless, fewer and fewer tasks requiring medium cognitive competencies—searching for information, identifying patterns and trends, data entry and processing, modelling and prediction—are now being performed by humans. Daniel Susskind (2020) proposes that this phenomenon be called *task encroachment*. This does not necessarily mean—especially in the short term—that the number of jobs in the economy will decrease, but there are many indications that there will be less and less of what the International Labour Organization describes as "decent work" (ILO, 2021), work that ensures a stable and satisfactory income and social prestige.

Most people who perform routine mental work are at risk of being moved to less-well-paid positions in the service sector, which will resist automation for longer because it requires, for example, the high dexterity that can only be provided by fingers and hands, or the ability to work directly with the public (Autor & Dorn, 2013). The labour market will become more and more polarised into primary and secondary segments: the former will include highly-paid experts and managers, and the latter will include low-paid service personnel. The income structure associated with positions in the labour market is shifting from a normal distribution to a Pareto distribution, operating on the basis of a continuous probability (Brynjolfsson & McAffee, 2014).

This thesis, about the hollowing out of "average" jobs in the labour market, has been supported by OECD analyses, which for some time have focused on employees with medium competencies. The data laid out in a report entitled *Job polarisation and the middle class* (Salvatori & Manfredi, 2019; see Green, 2019) shows that in OECD countries the number of jobs requiring medium skills is falling. On top of that, professions that require either medium or high levels of skill were less and less likely to ensure a stable income. At the same time, the competencies (i.e. education) of those in the middle class increased. In other words, professions that only really require competencies which so far have been provided by secondary education (e.g. drivers and machine operators, cashiers and secretaries) are taken up more and more often by people with a higher education. A lack of higher education, in turn, went hand in hand with a risk of ending up in a low-paid service or care job.

This tendency was confirmed by subsequent analyses, carried out in 2021 by the OECD (Georgieff & Milanez, 2021), which focused on the question "what has happened to jobs at high risk of automation?". This analysis of data from 21 OECD member states shows that over the decade preceding the survey, all reviewed countries saw an uptick in employment. Moreover, countries identified in 2012 as being threatened by a greater risk of automation saw higher employment growth. However, this increase was significantly lower for occupations at high risk of automation (6% on average) than for occupations with a low risk of automation (18%). Additionally, in occupations with a high risk of automation, the concentration of less-educated employees grew. This data confirmed the thesis that there was a higher risk of automation in the case of less-educated employees and, moreover, highlighted the increasing polarisation of the occupational structure in the world's most economically developed countries.

Datafication technologies are sharpening the information paradigm of work and the workforce that was outlined by Manuel Castells (1996). In his opinion, an economy based on information (and on ICT) is dominated by an antagonistic division into managers operating with information and a "disposable workforce", which "can be automated and/or hired/fired/offshored, depending on market demand and labor costs". In the digital economy, more and more intensive deployment of data technology will simply exhaust the ranks of lower and middle-level managers, taking away some of their tasks involving, for example, supervising the work of subordinates, benchmarking and forecasting, and even decision making (Agrawal et al., 2019). Current technological changes seem to be creating a labour market shaped like a distorted vase: at the top there are disproportionately remunerated "superstars", with competencies so valuable that machines can only supplement their work but not replace them. The number of 'decently' paid middle-class jobs is dwindling, but underpaid jobs in sectors where machines and systems face (so far) insurmountable barriers are proliferating.

Preliminary research on US health care, conducted by a group of researchers from MIT led by David Autor, was presented in a report entitled *The Work of the Future: Building Better Jobs in an Age of Intelligent Machines* (2020) and shows that the impact of digital technologies on employees is also similar in the service and care sectors. These technologies, especially "invisible robots" in the form of software that manages patients' medical data, complement the work of highly qualified workers and are replacing the work of white-collar employees with medium and low-level skills. They are also supplanting the work of highly paid specialists, as long as it is routine and predictable, e.g. that done by x-ray analysts (Couzin-Frankel, 2019). The work of people who take direct care of the infirm, especially physical and care work, will remain difficult to automate for a long time to come, but it will also still be poorly paid.

Intelligent automation resulting in datafication is intensifying the mechanisms of worker exploitation that are typical of capitalism (Couldry & Mejias, 2019; Zuboff, 2019). What is more, new iterations of capitalism seem to be demonstrating an even greater tendency to produce a surfeit of negative side effects for individuals, and societies, than classical incarnations. Regardless of individual effort and structural changes in the education system, there will simply be less and less good-quality, and well-compensated work to be had. Employees who perform relatively uncomplicated, routine tasks, and who lose their jobs to machines, will find new jobs—if they manage to at all—in less technologically dynamic sectors, in professions where human labour will still be more profitable than machine labour. These will especially those involving service and care work, for which there will be growing demand in ageing societies.

As this kind of work will be the only lifeline for people who lose their jobs in sectors subject to the digital transformation, wages will be driven down in line with the eternal laws of supply and demand.

The result will be the increasing precarity of workers and the loosening of employment relations in favour of work being broken down into individual tasks, often mediated by global platforms. We are dealing with a growing polarisation of the labour market, arising, *inter alia*, from increasingly automated intellectual work—first of all that which is routine and predictable, and then also that which hitherto required high-level competencies vouched for by a university degree. The number of jobs that provide a satisfactory salary and relative professional stability is decreasing, and this has led to a disturbance in the social structure, which is based on a middle class with average earnings and average competencies. Researchers delving into the changing labour market agree that capitalism's new trajectories in the digital economy will require novel, far-reaching regulations to protect workers' rights.

The 'platformisation' of work is one of the main reasons for the growing flexibility of various forms of employment, especially within the secondary labour market. A lack of legal and institutional safeguards, as well as exploitation mechanisms inherent in the operation of such platforms, has left those who depend on income obtained through platforms in a highly precarious position (Standing, 2011). Recruiting online meets the needs of employers for short-term workers who will only perform a certain proportion of the activities required to prepare the product or provide the service, thereby reducing the need for full-time employees.

Platforms do not consider themselves employers, but see themselves as intermediaries between the two sides of the market. As a result, people who carry out platform-facilitated work are not connected by the traditional employer-employee relationship with either the owners of the platform or the ordering party (Zysman & Kenney, 2018). During the pandemic, remote work through platforms has encouraged new forms of outsourcing to spring up: companies from highly developed countries can quickly and cheaply avail themselves of the labour resources of less developed countries, without having to move production or establish branches there.

Digital platforms increase the globalisation of work because they enable the outsourcing of specialised tasks. In his book *The Globotics Upheaval: Globalisation, Robotics, and the Future of Work* (2019), Richard Baldwin argues that we are dealing with a situation in which talented foreigners telecommute to workplaces in high income countries, and thus compete directly with local workers. The development of artificial intelligence will reduce language barriers, so that the ranks of 'telemigrants' will be bolstered by competent employees from all around the world. As a result, employee wages in developed countries may draw level with those in the developing world, which in turn may undermine welfare state models in Western countries. Companies from highly developed countries can thus quickly and cheaply avail themselves of the labour resources of less developed countries, without having to move production or establish branches there. The rollout of digital technologies—including enterprise resource planning (ERP) and customer relationship management (CRM) systems and cloud solutions—increasingly involves the demand for employees who can perform specialist tasks more flexibly while working remotely, outside an office. Decreased outsourcing costs have driven further network effects among companies, because smaller companies can also use the services of platforms. This may also reinforce the division into primary and secondary labour markets around the globe: the primary market will prevail in highly developed economies, while the latter will predominate in less developed economies.

The Consequences: A New Social World

Technological revolutions tend to change the character of work, the institutions of employment, and the functioning of the labour market in general (WEF, 2018). What has been called the fourth technological revolution is resulting in intelligent automation, datafication and platformisation. It is specifically intensifying the condition of flexibility in almost every aspect of working life, be it employment, working hours or performance (Gallino, 2006). This is often presented as a positive development, both for organisations and individuals. Victor Mayer-Schönberger and Thomas Ramge (2018) argue that scaling this flexibility will contribute to reinventing capitalism as such. Yet like in a classic piece of existential philosophy, this freedom of choice, underpinned by the "discoverability" brought about by platformisation, may not offset the diminishing sense of security and purpose.

The digital economy is increasingly doing away with the concept of easily identifiable professions that are learned over an extended time at an educational establishment and practised over a whole lifetime until one retires. Fragmented and flexible work may cease to be an important determinant of one's identity. Work is becoming more something you just "do", and less what you "are" (Eriksson & Linde, 2014). To be sure, this is troublesome for sociologists who are accustomed to treating professions as one of the basic elements used when analysing social structure (Huws et al., 2017). But it is much more difficult for people who, until now, have defined themselves to a great extent in terms of whether they are electricians, sociologists or IT specialists. Currently, it is becoming increasingly difficult to define oneself so unambiguously, and reflect the actual scope of one's duties at work, if the tasks are dispersed between different projects, teams and, more and more often, employees.

It will become increasingly difficult to plan a linear and predictable career path. People will have to change their careers many times during their lifetimes. Their acquired skills will become obsolete, forcing them to engage in re-skilling and upskilling. Lifelong learning is often presented as a fulfilling and personally enriching life experience (Weise, 2020). In reality, the task of keeping one's skills relevant to the changing expectations of employers is becoming yet another burdensome duty of the worker. Developments in technology mean that enterprises need to constantly adapt to changing market conditions, especially to the needs of consumers. As a result, the range of competencies required of employees is also changing.

Some of a company's employees are trained as and when required, but more and more staff will be employed for a limited period to perform specific tasks in accordance with their skill profile. Workers are forced to upskill and re-skill, including in their free time, in the evenings and at weekends, something which impinges on their finances, private life and family obligations. Interestingly, the constantly expanding catalogue of skills needed for the future includes not only technological skills, such as programming and other skills necessary for efficient interaction with advanced digital systems, or cognitive skills such as creativity and critical thinking, but also an entire array of emotional skills, which allow one to cope with changes and uncertainty, to facilitate group work and take responsibility. For example, the McKinsey (2021) enumeration of the skills that citizens will need in the future world of work include the virtues of "self-awareness" and "self-management", such as "understanding one's own emotions and triggers", "self-control and regulation", "integrity" and "self-motivation and wellness". The ideal worker should also demonstrate "grit and persistence" and be able to engage in self-development. The dictate of upskilling and re-skilling is becoming another source of the individualisation of risk (Beck, 1992). At the same time, the increasingly flexible conditions of work in the digital economy are exacerbating the processes behind the "corrosion of character", described by Richard Sennet (1998). Workers who are coping with a disappearing sense of purpose, need, simultaneously, to engage in demanding emotional work.

Another important change enabled by datafication and platformisation, and brought about by the Covid 19 pandemic, concerns the role of workplaces in employees' social life. American sociologist Ray Oldenburg treats the workplace as a "second place" (with the home being the "first place", and sites where community life flourishes "third places"). More flexible, fragmented and often remote work mediated through platforms may well diminish the importance of workplaces as the material anchors of sociality among co-workers. Since the first industrial revolution, workplaces—factories and offices—have evolved into comprehensive life-worlds, where face-to-face interactions have helped to create shared understandings and values.

The current discourse—focused on skills for the future—emphasises teamwork, but it also accentuates adaptability and openness to change in recognition of the fact that teams will be dismissed immediately after completing their allotted tasks. Workers will spend less and less time with each other and, consequently, will feel less compelled to invest their time in building long-term social ties and networks conducive to social capital. Additionally, platformisation has been contributing to the geographical dispersion of co-workers, resulting in ephemeral, weak social ties, strictly functional and unhooked from other kinds of social interaction (Wood et al., 2019). Intelligent automation will swell the ranks of human teams with AI agents, again hindering the creation of team-based sociality. During the lockdowns, many types of white-collar tasks were carried out remotely, which contributed to the popularity of distributed workplaces, with some tasks performed at home, some in co-working spaces near home, and only a few activities—conferencing, brainstorming, idea-building—in the office.

This concept may further exacerbate the instability of employment, as employers are already starting to reorganise workflows into geographically dispersed projects carried out by temporary workers. In the digital economy, an increasing number of people will function as portfolio workers, offering their skills on an increasingly flexible labour market. "The 'job' and everything organized around the job—the group of work friends at company, the after-work hangouts, the trade union, even the car pool—lose their social function. They are becoming as 'permanently temporary' as the work itself" (Carnoy, 1999: 33).

The more flexible labour market, together with work increasingly divorced from stable employment, will also change social relations within households. Instability on the macro-level of the labour market easily translates into instability and conflict on the micro-level of human relations within households. Flexible working hours, divergent career trajectories, conflicting claims within restricted timeframes, all may translate into an increase in single-people households. Urlich Beck and Elisabeth Beck-Gernsheim (2002) go as far as to claim that flexibility in the labour market is incompatible with the traditional family, because it sparks conflicts between partners concerning, for example, childcare and other responsibilities.

It will, moreover, be increasingly difficult to plan children within a fluid and non-linear career trajectory. Families with children will also face new demands concerning the socialisation of their children, including skills for the future. Digital skills are now developed very early: children learn them through observation and copying the behaviour of others in the family environment. The key factor is the socio-economic standing of the parents. Parents with low-level digital skills tend to restrict the use of digital devices, and are less skilled in teaching their offspring how to use them to search for information and solve problems (Chaudron et al., 2018). Flexibility and self-governance are also often more common among children from middle-class families than working class ones. Formal education is evolving too slowly to develop skills for the future among children. As a result, children from digitally-excluded and otherwise underprivileged households will have worse opportunities in the skills-based labour market of the digital era. This digital exclusion easily translates to, and underpins, other kinds of social, economic, and political exclusion, resulting in more fragmented and divided societies.

Conclusion

To conclude on a more optimistic note, the onset of the digital economy is hopefully opening up a new phase in the "double movement" construed by Karl Polanyi (2001) in 1944. The double movement is a kind of minuet danced by the market and the state, the main economic and political actors. The market tries to commodify everything, particularly land, labour and money. The political actors create conditions of institutional stability for the market to operate in, in the form of legal rules, but at the same time tries to tame relentless commodification by introducing regulations safeguarding workers' rights.

A more flexible labour market commodifies labour in unprecedented ways, invading the lives of the workers and generating new kinds of economic and social risks. Digital companies, particularly platforms, try to avoid national restrictions, particularly in the area of labour rights. Platforms such as Uber have consistently refused to consider those working through their mediation to be their employees (Parker et al., 2016). This approach was undermined by a British court judgment concerning Aslam and Farrar versus Uber brought in 2016 (Royal Court of Justice, 2018). The court found that, contrary to the claims of the platform, drivers are indeed de facto employees, a state of affairs which was determined based on, among other things, the following conditions: the driver does not know the exact location of the passenger or the passenger's name until they actually get into the car. Therefore, they are entitled to all employee privileges as stipulated by law.

In 2021, the European Commission presented a draft Directive to improve the working conditions of platform workers. Platform workers are to be granted employee status, automated systems used for monitoring and supervising workers' performance are to be made more transparent, and national authorities are to be informed of the platforms' activities when it comes to the work performed by each country's nationals. The time has finally come to re-evaluate outdated, twentieth-century regulations to reflect the changes brought about by the fourth technological revolution, and to safeguard the wellbeing of workers in the twenty-first century.

References

Agrawal, A., Gans, J. S., & Goldfarb, A. (2019). *Artificial Intelligence: The Ambiguous Labor Market Impact of Automating Prediction*. Journal of Economic Perspectives. 33 (2): 31-50. https://www.aeaweb.org/articles?id=10.1257/jep.33.2.31.

Arthur, W.B. (2009). *The nature of technology: What it is and how it evolves.* Free Press.

Autor, D., Levy, F. & Murnane, R. (2003). *The skill content of recent technological change: An empirical investigation.* Quarterly Journal of Economics, 118, 1279–1333. https://economics.mit.edu/files/11574.

Autor, D., & Dorn, D. (2013). *The Growth of Low-Skill Service Jobs and the Polarization of the US Labor Market.* American Economic Review, 103 (5): 1553-97. https://doi.org/10.1257/aer.103.5.1553.

Autor, D., Mindell, D., & Reynolds, E. (2020). *The Work of the Future: Building Better Jobs in an Age of Intelligent Machines.* https://workofthefuture.mit.edu/research-post/the-work-of-the-future-building-better-jobs-in-an-age-of-intelligent-machines/

Baldwin, R. (2019). *The Globotics Upheaval: Globalization, Robotics, and the Future of Work.* Oxford University Press.

Beck, U. (1992). *Risk Society: Towards a New Modernity.* Sage Publications.

Beck, U. & Beck-Gernsheim, E. (2002). *Individualization: Institutionalized Individualism and its Social and Political Consequences.* Sage Publications. https://doi.org/10.1177/000169930204500212.

Bell, D. (1989). *The Third Technological Revolution and Its Possible Socioeconomic Consequences.* Dissent. https://www.dissentmagazine.org/article/the-third-technological-revolution-and-its-possible-socioeconomic-consequences.

Brynjolfsson, E., McAffee, A. (2014). *The Second Machine Age: Work, Progress, and Prosperity in a Time of Brilliant Technologies.* W. W. Norton & Company. https://psycnet.apa.org/record/2014-07087-000.

Carnoy, M. (1999). *Globalization and educational reform: What planners need to know.* UNESCO. http://unesco.amu.edu.pl/pdf/Carnoy.pdf.

Carr, N. (2008). *How many computers does the world need? Fewer than you think.* Guardian. https://www.theguardian.com/technology/2008/feb/21/computing.supercomputers.

Castells, M. (1996). *The Rise of the Network Society.* Wiley. https://onlinelibrary.wiley.com/doi/book/10.1002/9781444319514.

Chaudron, S., Di Gioia, R., & Gemo, M. (2018). *Young Children (0-8) and Digital Technology – A qualitative study across Europe.* EUR 29070 EN, Publications Office of the European Union. Luxembourg. https://publications.jrc.ec.europa.eu/repository/handle/JRC110359.

Cisco. (2020). *Annual Internet Report (2018–2023) White Paper,* https://www.cisco.com/c/en/us/solutions/collateral/executive-perspectives/annual-internet-report/white-paper-c11-741490.html.

Couldry N., Mejias U. (2019). *The Costs of Connection: How Data Is Colonizing Human Life and Appropriating It for Capitalism.* Stanford University Press. https://www.sup.org/books/title/?id=28816.

Couzin-Frankel, J. (2019). *Artificial intelligence could revolutionize medical care. But don't trust it to read your x-ray just yet.* Science. https://www.sciencemag.org/news/2019/06/artificial-intelligence-could-revolutionize-medical-care-don-t-trust-it-read-your-x-ray.

Daugherty, P.R., Wilson, H.J. (2018). *Human + Machine: Reimagining Work in the Age of AI.* Harvard Business Review.

Eriksson, Y.U., Linde, M. (2014). *"Being" or "Doing" a Profession: Work as a Matter of Social Identity,* The International Journal of Interdisciplinary Cultural Studies, 8(1): 33–43, https://doi.org/10.18848/2327-008X/CGP/v08i01/53186.

European Commission. (2021). *Commission proposals to improve the working conditions of people working through digital labour platforms.* European Commission – Press release. https://ec.europa.eu/commission/presscorner/detail/en/ip_21_6605.

European Parliament. (2020). *What is artificial intelligence and how is it used?* https://www.europarl.europa.eu/news/en/headlines/society/20200827STO85804/what-is-artificial-intelligence-and-how-is-it-used.

Ford, M. (2015). *The Rise of the Robots: Technology and the Threat of a Jobless Future.* Basic Books.

Gallino, L. (2006). *Labour flexibility, organisation, workers – A three-dimensional matrix which needs simplification*. Reconciling labour flexibility with social cohesion – Ideas for political action, Trends in social cohesion, No. 16, p. 37–46. https://www.coe.int/t/dg3/socialpolicies/socialcohesiondev/source/Trends/Trends-16_en.pdf.

Georgieff, A., Milanez A. (2021), *What happened to jobs at high risk of automation?* OECD Social, Employment and Migration Working Papers, No. 255. OECD Publishing. https://doi.org/10.1787/10bc97f4-en.

Green, A. (2019). *What is happening to middle skill workers?* OECD Social, Employment and Migration Working Papers, 230. OECD Publishing. https://doi.org/10.1787/a934f8fa-en.

Holslin, P. (2021). *What Is 6G Internet and What Will It Look Like?* HighSpeedInternet.com. https://www.highspeedinternet.com/resources/6g-internet.

Huws, U., Spencer, N. H., & Holts, K. (2017). *Work in the European Gig Economy – Research Results from the UK, Sweden, Germany, Austria, the Netherlands, Switzerland and Italy*. Foundation for European Progressive Studies and UNI Europa. https://uhra.herts.ac.uk/bitstream/handle/2299/19922/Huws_U._Spencer_N.H._Syrdal_D.S._Holt_K._2017_.pdf?sequence=2.

Iansiti, M., Lakhani, K. R. (2020). *Competing in the Age of AI: Strategy and Leadership When Algorithms and Networks Run the World*. Kindle Edition. Harvard Business Review Press. https://hbsp.harvard.edu/product/1054BC-PDF-ENG.

International Labour Organization. (2021). *World Employment and Social Outlook – Trends 2021*. https://www.ilo.org/global/about-the-ilo/newsroom/news/WCMS_794834/lang%2D%2Den/index.html.

LeCun, Y. (2022, March 15). # I never called what I was working on AI (AI was supposed to designate "symbolic" methods). [Tweet]. https://twitter.com/ylecun/status/1503719133506158596.

Levy, F., Murnane, R. (2004). *The New Division of Labor: How Computers Are Creating the Next Job Market*. Princeton University Press.

Marody, M., & Giza-Poleszczuk, A. (2004). *Przemiany więzi społecznych*. Wydawnictwo Naukowe Scholar.

Mayer-Schönberger, V., & Ramge, T. (2018). *Reinventing Capitalism in the Age of Big Data*. John Murray Publishers Ltd.

McKinsey. (2021). *Defining the skills citizens will need in the future world of work*. https://www.mckinsey.com/industries/public-and-social-sector/our-insights/defining-the-skills-citizens-will-need-in-the-future-world-of-work.

Mims, C. (2021). *Why Artificial Intelligence Isn't Intelligent*. https://www.wsj.com/articles/why-artificial-intelligence-isnt-intelligent-11627704050.

Parker, G. G., van Alstyne, M. W., & Choudary, S. P. (2016). *Platform Revolution. How Networked Markets Are Transforming the Economy and How to Make Them Work for You*. W. W. Norton & Company. https://wwnorton.com/books/Platform-Revolution.

Polanyi, K. (2001). *The Great Transformation: The Political and Economic Origins of Our Time* 2nd edition. Beacon Press.

Royal Court of Justice. (2018). Uber B.V. and others versus Aslam and others. *EWCA Civ 2748*. no. A2.2017/3467. https://www.judiciary.uk/wp-content/uploads/2018/12/uber-bv-ors-v-aslam-ors-judgment-19.12.18.pdf.

Russel, S., & Norvig, P. (2019). *Artificial Intelligence – A Modern Approach*. 4th edition. Pearson.

Salvatori, A., & Manfredi, T. (2019). *Job polarisation and the middle class: New evidence on the changing relationship between skill levels and household income levels from 18 OECD countries*. OECD Social, Employment and Migration Working Papers, 232. Paris: OECD Publishing. https://doi.org/10.1787/4bf722db-en.

Schwab, K. (2016). *The Fourth Industrial Revolution*. World Economic Forum. Geneva. https://www.weforum.org/agenda/2016/01/the-fourth-industrial-revolution-what-it-means-and-how-to-respond/.

Schumpeter, J. (1960). *Teoria rozwoju gospodarczego*. PWN.

Sennet, R. (1998). *The Corrosion of Character: The Personal Consequences of Work in the New. Capitalism*. W. W. Norton & Company.

Standing, G. (2011). *The Precariat: The New Dangerous Class (Bloomsbury Revelations)*. Bloomsbury Academic. https://www.hse.ru/data/2013/01/28/1304836059/Standing.%20The_Precariat__The_New_Dangerous_Class__-Bloomsbury_USA(2011).pdf.

Strohmeyer, R. (2008). *The 7 Worst Tech Predictions of All Time*. PCWorld. https://www.pcworld.com/article/532605/worst_tech_predictions.html.

Susskind, D. (2020). *A World without Work: Technology, Automation, and How We Should Respond*. London: Penguin Books.

Śledziewska, K., & Włoch, R. (2021). *The Economics of Digital Transformation*. Routledge.

The 5G IA. The 5G Infrastructure Association, Vision and Societal Challenges Work Group. (2021). *European Vision for the 6G Network Ecosystem*. https://5g-ppp.eu/wp-content/uploads/2021/06/WhitePaper-6G-Europe.pdf.

Toffler, A. (1970). *Future shock*. New York: Random House. https://doi.org/10.1177/019263657005434912.

Weise, M. R. (2020). *Long Life Learning: Preparing for Jobs That Don't Even Exist Yet*. Wiley.

Wood, A., Graham, M., Lehdonvirta, V., Hjorth, I., (2019). Networked but Commodified: The (Dis)Embeddedness of Digital Labour in the Gig Economy. Sociology 1–20, https://doi.org/10.1177/0038038519828906.

WEF. World Economic Forum. (2018). *The Future of Jobs Report 2018*. Insight report Geneva. http://www3.weforum.org/docs/WEF_Future_of_Jobs_2018.pdf.

Varian, H. (2009). *Hal Varian on how the Web challenges managers*, McKinsey & Company High Tech. https://www.mckinsey.com/industries/technology-media-and-telecommunications/our-insights/hal-varian-on-how-the-web-challenges-managers.

Zhang, D., Mishra, S., Brynjolfsson, E., Etchemendy, J., Ganguli, D., Grosz, B., Lyons, T., Manyika, J., Niebles, J. C., Sellitto, M., Shoham, Y., Clark, J., & Perrault, R. (2022). *The AI Index 2022 Annual Report*. AI Index Steering Committee. Stanford Institute for Human-Centered AI. Stanford University. https://doi.org/10.48550/arXiv.2103.06312.

Zuboff, S. (2019). *The Age of Surveillance Capitalism: The Fight for a Human Future at the New Frontier of Power*. Ingram Publisher Services.

Zysman, J. & Kenney M. (2018). *The Next Phase in the Digital Revolution: Intelligent Tools, Platforms, Growth, Employment*. Communications of the ACM, 61(2) p.54–63. https://cacm.acm.org/magazines/2018/2/224635-the-next-phase-in-the-digital-revolution/fulltext.

CHAPTER 9

Contentious Content on Messaging Apps: Actualising Social Affordances for Normative Processes on Telegram

Nathalie Van Raemdonck and Jo Pierson

INTRODUCTION

The physical and digital spaces we spend time in during our everyday life substantially shape our interactions and social norms of behaviour and vice versa. For example, the presence of doors in an office setting can foster a norm where colleagues always leave their door open unless they do not want to be disturbed. This does not mean doors holds an intrinsic social norm not to disturb (Heras-Escribano & de Pinedo, 2016). The office inhabitants themselves have made doors hold this normative significance. So too with platforms. As Bucher and Helmond (2018: 21) state about objections against changing platform features, these features have been attributed a significance beyond their original purpose. Already in 1999 Lawrence Lessig indicated that social norms and architecture are closely tied to each other (Lessig, 1999). They are two of the four forces that regulate individuals, besides the market and the law. This mutual shaping of spaces and norms of social behaviour is also taking place in everyday digital life (Postigo, 2016; Van Dijck, 2013).

N. Van Raemdonck (✉)
imec-SMIT, Vrije Universiteit Brussel (VUB), Brussels, Belgium
e-mail: Nathalie.Van.Raemdonck@vub.be

J. Pierson
imec-SMIT, Vrije Universiteit Brussel (VUB), Brussels, Belgium

School of Social Sciences, Hasselt University, Hasselt, Belgium
e-mail: Jo.Pierson@uhasselt.be

© The Author(s), under exclusive license to Springer Nature Switzerland AG 2024
H. S. Dunn et al. (eds.), *The Palgrave Handbook of Everyday Digital Life*,
https://doi.org/10.1007/978-3-031-30438-5_9

We focus in this chapter on messaging apps as currently a major component of digital life. By 2015 the top messaging apps WhatsApp, Messenger, WeChat, and Viber surpassed the major social networks globally in monthly active use, as reported by Business Insider (2016). According to the PEW research centre, users in the US spent on average 24 minutes per day on messaging apps in 2020 (Auxier & Anderson, 2021), and data from the IMEC digimeter show that 85% of Flemish users in Belgium daily use at least 1 messaging app or form of social media (Sevenhant et al., 2022). These apps are defined as a form of personal media that typically enable de-institutional and de-professional content through symmetrical mediated interaction (Lüders, 2008). They are mainly used for mobile social communication, personalized expression, and information exchange (Levinson, 2018). Within the multitude of messaging apps, we zoom in on the case of Telegram. As one of the fastest growing apps, Telegram topped 1 billion downloads in 2021 and is very popular in countries such as India, Indonesia, Russia and Iran (Singh, 2021). There is some public debate on the way the app organises its digital interactions and the kind of communication and contentious content it does or does not allow, and therefore having a double-edged impact and role in society (Loucaides, 2022).

We look at the mutual shaping of platform architectures and norms through the lens of 'affordances', from an integrated perspective of Media and Communication Studies and Science and Technology Studies (STS). 'Affordances' are emergent relational properties of an individual and its environment. We understand affordances as an opportunity for action. They are generally used to describe what material artifacts, including media technologies, allow individuals to do or not do (boyd, 2011; Bucher & Helmond, 2018; Davis & Chouinard, 2016; Evans et al., 2017; Gaver, 1996; Gibson, 1979; Hutchby, 2001; Norman, 1988; Volkoff & Strong, 2017). Affordances can help us discover the possible complex environmental factors shaping social interaction, avoiding monocausal perspectives of technological determinism and social constructivism (Gaver, 1996; Volkoff & Strong, 2017). Largely missing from existing conceptualisations of affordances is a collective or 'social' perspective on social media.

In particular we wish to investigate which affordances are relevant for normative processes in collectives, by which we mean the establishment, maintenance, and transformation of norms. In this book chapter we first discuss what is meant by 'affordances', pinpointing our interest in 'social affordances' and what we precisely mean by 'normative processes'. We explain the Van Raemdonck and Pierson (2021) affordances taxonomy that we use to identify the relevant affordances for normative processes, which is broadly based on boyd's (2011) structural affordances of the networked publics. We identify these affordances with a walkthrough of Telegram, for which we use the walkthrough method (Light et al., 2018). Following the explanation of this methodology, we position Telegram as a platform, its vision, operating model, and the presumed user base of this messaging app. We then present the findings of the walkthrough method by explicating the relevant affordances for normative processes.

SOCIAL AFFORDANCES AND NORMATIVE PROCESSES

If we understand affordances as an opportunity for action, affordances can emerge from an interaction, which means they are 'actualised'. For example, passing a ball means you have actualised the affordance of 'rolling' of that ball. It is only in the interaction of individuals and artifacts that an affordance can become 'actualised' (Volkoff & Strong, 2017). It is relevant to look at the actualisation of affordances regarding normative processes, as the founding father of the concept James Gibson (1979) himself noted that the richest and most elaborate affordances are provided by other people. Which affordances of (digital) artifacts play a role for behaviour to afford behaviour? We propose to expand on the existing perspective of 'social affordances' in this chapter. Social affordances have been used by sociologists and communication scholars to talk about the ways in which technology affords social practices to individuals and influences everyday life. (Bucher & Helmond, 2018; Hsieh, 2012; Postigo, 2016; Wellman et al., 2003) This perspective considers the social structures in which the relation of individuals and their (technological) environment emerges. Such a social structure can be for instance 'teammates in a football game'.

The social structure we focus on is very broadly 'collectives'. There is already a 'collective affordances' perspective, developed by scholars such as Leonardi (2013) and Weichold & Thonhauser (2019), which proves inadequate for our analysis but is worth noting for its value. From a collective affordances perspective, it is theorized that collectives actualize affordances differently than individuals, since collectives cannot be explained solely as the sum of its individuals. Weichold and Thonhauser (2019) give the example of an orange traffic light that a group of cyclists would not cross in order to stick together, but which an individual cyclist would cross. The orange light makes collectives stop differently than individuals, actualising the 'stopping' affordance of the traffic light differently. We find the perspective of 'collective affordances' useful, but limited, as we do not want to assume that individuals in the collective know that they must stick together purely from their embodied social identity. There is potentially a norm in the group of cyclists that they do not split up, even temporarily, and ways to uphold this norm. In the example of the traffic light, the group of cyclists could for instance agree to use bells to let the head of the group know whether they can or cannot cross the light. The bell is thus an artifact containing a social affordance that is actualised in collectives. Such social affordances contribute to the establishment and maintenance of norms and are complementary to 'collective affordances'.

This perspective provides us with a framework to analyse changing behaviours of collectives in the digital sphere. In particular it can help us to understand the circulation of contentious content such as disinformation, hate speech and extremist propaganda, which is a growing point of concern for Telegram. Telegram has been regularly scrutinised for being the platform of choice of ISIS terrorists, far-right insurgents and conspiracy theorists during the

COVID-19 pandemic (Kaul, 2020; Scollon, 2021; Thomas, 2022). At the same time it is also used as a safe haven for activists in authoritarian countries to coordinate (Akbari & Gabdulhakov, 2019; Urman et al., 2021; Wijermars & Lokot, 2022) and it is increasingly being used for newsgathering in several parts of the world (Lou et al., 2021; Naseri & Zamani, 2019). Indeed, what constitutes contentious content is often up for interpretation of the collective in which it circulates. Content that some might regard as a threat to public safety, might be understood by others as a legitimate form of public contestation (Helberger et al., 2018). Social norms determine for a large part what is acceptable in societies and collectives. There are no clear boundaries to be drawn around such 'collectives' and what constitutes a 'collective' is also complicated in the digital realm. Mizuko Ito (2008) and later danah boyd (2011) talk about 'networked publics', to indicate online publics—in contrast to unmediated publics—that are restructured by networked technologies. Networked publics can consist of many smaller collectives.

Prior research on the governance of online communities has indicated the importance of social norms in regulating harmful behaviour and contentious content (Chandrasekharan et al., 2018; Lampe et al., 2014). This is where the importance of normative processes and affordances comes in. With a very libertarian content moderation policy, Telegram leaves most of its moderation up to its users. We are thus curious how Telegram has created space for normative processes, not only within closed collectives where extremism is the norm, but across the platform. To clarify what we mean by social norms and normative processes, the social science literature broadly defines social norms as informal rules that govern behaviour in groups and societies. According to Talcott Parsons (1951), norms embody a common value system and function as the cement of a society, through which social order and stability are attained. Norms are more dynamic than laws or even traditions. This became evident during the COVID-19 pandemic when citizens all over the world swiftly adapted their norms of interaction, such as not shaking hands, to avoid the spread of the virus, as opposed to adaptations to traditions such as funerals or weddings, where laws were needed to transform them.

Based on a review of the social norms literature, three stages of a norm's lifecycle are identified; norms emerge, they are maintained, and they disappear or transform. (Legros & Cislaghi, 2020) We know that social norms do not emerge out of thin air, as they do not exist outside of a social context. As Wittgenstein posits, an individual cannot establish correctness criteria for another individual, a normative practice is by default shared and established by a collective (Wittgenstein, 1953). Functionalists such as Parsons and later Coleman (1990) theorised that norms emerge to solve collective action problems. Others like Axelrod (1984) see norms merely emerge in repeated encounters among people where they secure a pattern of reciprocity to minimizes the likelihood of misperception. Norms are maintained according to Coleman (1990) for as long as they remain effective to uphold them through social sanctions and social corrections. Such social sanctions and corrections serve to make the norms clear to others who wish to remain part of the collective and adapt their behaviour according to the social norms. They are then passed on through a process of what Parsons (1951) calls 'socialization', where individuals come to learn norms from their social environment and come to internalize them. If social sanctions are no longer effective or ignored and do not appear to be upheld by the collective, the norm could disappear or transform, leading to new norm emergence (Legros & Cislaghi, 2020).

This lifecycle is part of what we call a normative process. How such norms emerge, how they are maintained through sanctions and social corrections, and how they transform, happen primarily through communication. Norms are at their core a communication phenomenon (Rimal & Lapinski, 2015). Norms are perceived, either when people have been explicitly told what the norms are, or when people have observed them in the behaviour of others. These are also called 'descriptive norms' (Cialdini et al. 1990). The presence of descriptive norms is heavily dependent on the actors that communicate these norms. With limited information available, these actors can appear to represent the dominant consensus about norms, but may very well create a 'majority illusion' due to their active presence.

This is especially prevalent in social networks where there is a supremacy of 'superusers'. For example on Twitter, 10% of the users are responsible for 80% of tweets (Wojcik & Hughes, 2019) or on Facebook 3% users are responsible for 52% of interaction in Groups and Page comments (Hindman et al., 2022). Similarly, and of special relevance to this chapter, on Telegram only 7–17% of Group members engage in conversations in Telegram Groups (Hashemi & Zare Chahooki, 2019). These actors can play a strong role in norm emergence, maintenance and transformation and may wrongfully be assumed to represent a majority on these platforms. Descriptive norms form the basis of Rimal and Real's (2005) theory of normative social behaviour (TNSB) where they posit that descriptive norms affect individual behaviour. The recent communications perspective on the TNSB, developed by Geber & Hefner (2019) identifies that people will follow norms when they know that their behaviour is being observed by others, which has become more common and easier in the current (digital) media environment. This is where affordances come in, as they provide an opportunity for action that is visible to others. We are interested in exploring when affordances are actualised, which of them influence these normative processes.

We hypothesize that platform affordances have the potential to influence several elements of normative processes. They can affect how the boundaries of collectives can be articulated thus influencing group identity where norms apply. This gives rise to key issues such as who is part of the 'in-group', how information can flow in and out of collectives and potentially challenge or transform norms, how behaviour can be observed by others, establishing descriptive norms, and which intervention possibilities users must apply social corrections and maintain norms. Van Raemdonck and Pierson (2021) previously identified an overall taxonomy of affordances relevant for group interactions on digital platforms such as social network sites and messaging apps. This taxonomy was broadly informed by boyd's (2011) articulation of structural affordances of networked publics: persistence, replicability, scalability and searchability. The latter were re-categorized under the affordances of **interactability, visibility, ephemerality and interventionability.**[1]

Interactability affordances determine which users can interact with who on a platform and who is ultimately part of a collective. Visibility affordances shape what information travels through the networked publics and enter and exit collectives. Ephemerality affordances influence when users need to be present to be part of the normative process. Lastly, interventionability affordances offer users the possibility to make social corrections to maintain or transform norms, intervening on behaviour they deem acceptable or unacceptable. In this way we see that these social affordances respectively influence the 'who', 'what', 'when' and 'how' of normative processes. The emergence, maintenance and transformation of norms is largely dependent on the people that are in the collective where the social norms apply ('who'), the information that is circulating that influences the social norms ('what'), the time where people in the collective are exposed to the information that influences social norms ('when'), and how they can intervene to enforce the maintenance of social norms ('how').

Methodology

For our research on the everyday digital life of messaging apps and Telegram in particular, we used the walkthrough method (Light et al., 2018). This method lets researchers engage directly with an application to understand how it guides users and shapes their everyday experiences. This walkthrough method, grounded in Actor-Network Theory (Latour, 2005), has its benefits to discover the mutual shaping of Telegram's affordances and its users. It helps us systematically uncover the relevant collective affordances that are mapped in the platform-agnostic taxonomy (Van Raemdonck & Pierson, 2021), and helps us to recognize some of the embedded values of the platform's owners in how the platform is designed. This is especially relevant when we consider the need for cooperative responsibility in governing digital platforms like messaging apps (Helberger et al., 2018). When platforms like Telegram decide on minimal governance and interventions on the platform, it de facto pushes a lot of the governance responsibilities on its users. It therefore matters which affordances allow users to fulfil those responsibilities.

A drawback of this method is that it is explorative and not a data-driven approach that allow us to draw correlations or causations between affordances and behaviour. We cannot make any generalisations of the occurrences we

---

[1] Instead of the original naming of "network interaction" and "intervention" in the taxonomy (Van Raemdonck & Pierson, 2021), we propose to transform this to "interactability" and "interventionability" to emphasize the ability that platforms afford to users to interact with others and intervene on behaviour on the platform.

observed during the walkthrough: we can only hypothesize on potential consequences of observed affordances. However, such hypotheses on the mutual shaping of Telegram's affordances and norm building behaviour in the networked publics on the platform are very valuable. They lay the groundwork for follow-up research to ask more targeted questions and systematise empirical research on the impact of platform affordances on normative processes on platforms like Telegram.

The walkthrough method started with first staking out Telegram's 'environment of expected use', i.e. we investigated the context in which we analyse the technological architecture. This includes enquiring what Telegram's vision, operating model and governance are, which could make clear what the expected user practice is for Telegram. To do the technical walkthrough, we systematically analysed the platform in the period February to April 2022 while situated in Brussels, Belgium. We did this interchangeably on desktop and mobile[2] and cross-checked that there were no big differences between the desktop, Android and iOS versions that would be relevant for the observed affordances.

We first engaged with the platform how we would normally engage with friends and information sources on a new platform to emulate everyday use. We then followed some particular Telegram links shared outside of Telegram's ecosystem to walk through the platform from the perspective of users who would have an interest in particular (contentious) content on the platform. We complemented this with additional desk research on features we would never have access to (for example being the administrator of a large group). Telegram offers many options to customise interactions on the platform, including the creation of customisable bots that administrators can use to automatically intervene in groups (which we will elaborate on when discussing interventionability affordances).

It is impossible to know which of these options are used most. While we also generate some basic understanding from the walkthrough method on the most used options, we only mention which of the options are default. This also provides a glimpse into what Telegram perceives to be the preferable option, contributing to an understanding of Telegram's vision and governance of the platform. We complemented the walkthrough with desk research on comparable empirical research on Telegram. We included research based on digital methods to extract data from Telegram, which allowed us to provide basic statistics on Telegram's use. We made use of the research done by a wide range of scholars, but we recognize potential shortcomings or omissions of existing research.

We validated these findings with third persons who had experience using the platform and with those who had none or limited, generating intercoder reliability. We illustrated some of the affordances with examples that we either encountered during the walkthrough in public Groups and Channels, or that

---

[2] The desktop version was Telegram's app installed on a MacOS version 12, the mobile was the app installed on iOS 14 and Android Galaxy 71.

we created ourselves to increase understanding of how Telegram operates. We will specify whether these screenshots were made on desktop or mobile.

Telegram and Its Users?

Telegram was launched in 2014 by the Russian billionaire Pavel Durov and his brother Nikolai Durov as a private messaging application. Up until 2021, Telegram was fully financed through Durov's personal resources (Durov, 2021a). It recently introduced an ad platform that allows advertisers to display their messages in large Channels (Telegram Ad platform, n.d.). Telegram posits that profit will never be an end-goal for the platform (Telegram FAQ, 2022). Telegram emerged in a context where the Russian Kremlin executed a growing crackdown on civil society and political expression in the country (Wijermars & Lokot, 2022). The platform highlights its support for internet privacy as one of the key tenets of its mission and states that it seeks to protect "your private conversations from snooping third parties, such as officials, employers, etc." and "your personal data from third parties, such as marketers, advertisers" (Telegram FAQ, 2022).

There is a strong conviction that the platform was created to provide users living in authoritarian states with a means of secure communication. (Wijermars & Lokot, 2022) On his own blog, Durov wrote in 2018 that Telegram does not disclose their users' private data to third parties because they *"don't regard Telegram as an organization or an app. For us, Telegram is an idea; it is the idea that everyone on this planet has a right to be free"* (Durov, 2018). It has since been used both by opposition movements in places like Iran, Belarus and Hong Kong, as well as by ISIS terrorists and right-wing extremists globally (Scollon, 2021). The app does not end-to-end encrypt all communication by default, only when 'secret chats' are turned on between two users. So far it does not have the option to encrypt Group communication between more than two users. Telegram's encryption practices are controversial and digital rights activists and tech experts have previously criticised the platform for its misleading security and privacy claims (Greenberg, 2021; Spadafora, 2021; Turton, 2016). Nonetheless, the platform's perception of a freedom-supporting ally and protector of privacy has galvanized its support (Wijermars & Lokot, 2022). The unrest in Belarus in 2020 was even hailed as the 'Telegram revolution' where many Belarusians mobilised their supporters with the use of the messaging app (Litvinova, 2021).

The popularity of Telegram is thus on the rise, being the 5th most downloaded app of 2021 (Blacker, 2021), and even the most downloaded non-gaming application on the Google Play store in January 2021 (Mandavia, 2021). Telegram is likely surfing on the waves of an increasing need for secure modes of communication in the face of expanding authoritarian rule worldwide, as Freedom House writes in its 2022 Freedom in the World report (Repucci & Slipowitz, 2022). As Loucaides (2022) notes and what we will also show under the interactability affordances, Telegram's interesting blend of private Groups and public Channels makes the platform well-suited to activism. Recent popularity can also be attributed to at least three major factors that provide a glimpse on the userbase of the platform: the drop in popularity of Meta's WhatsApp, the deplatforming of users on other platforms, and the increasing use of the app by news organisations and news consumers.

In January 2021 WhatsApp updated its terms of use and privacy policy, which made it impossible for users to opt-out of sharing certain data with Facebook. While this seemed like a far-reaching change, the update merely reflected Facebook's (now Meta Platforms Inc.) existing data sharing practice that has been ongoing since 2016 (Newman, 2021). This policy update brought existing practices and infrastructures to the surface that were otherwise hidden (Pierson, 2021). Users flocked to Telegram and the privacy-friendly messaging app Signal that was created with the same end-to-end encryption protocol as WhatsApp (Deakin, 2021). About 25 million new users flocked to Telegram in 72 hours, which Durov attributed to the fact that "people no longer want to exchange their privacy for free services" (Durov, 2021b). This migration implies that a more privacy-concerned user-base is populating the platform.

The increased January 2021 popularity of Telegram coincided with an important event in the US: the Capitol riot on January 6. This led to a massive crackdown on Twitter and Facebook of prominent far-right and conspiracy figures (Vanian, 2021). Deplatforming has previously been a growth-engine for Telegram. When many prominent far-right internet celebrities were deplatformed in the last few years, many moved to Telegram (Rogers, 2020; Winter, 2019). Besides the perceived privacy and security of Telegram, it's libertarian view on content moderation seems to be one of the reasons for the platform's popularity with these actors. Telegram has repeatedly highlighted that it will not comply with so called "local restrictions on freedom of speech" (Telegram FAQ, 2022). It will however process legal requests to take down illegal **public** content, which Durov claims to only comply with to continue offering the app through the Apple and Google app stores.[3] Telegram however claims not to act against Groups and Channels that are private. As we will show later, these supposedly private activities can still reach thousands and even millions of users and can travel throughout the whole platform.

While Telegram is often spotlighted for its radical user-base or activists in authoritarian countries, there is also a whole ecosystem of users who use the application for daily social use and news gathering. Telegram has become one of the most popular platforms for news in, for example, Singapore (Lou et al., 2021). Mainstreaming the application is actually a goal for Telegram to make the use of the application more acceptable. Telegram argues that their dubious approach on its cloud storage *"allows Telegram to be more widely adopted in broad circles, not just by activists and dissidents, so that the simple fact of using Telegram does not mark users as targets for heightened surveillance in certain*

---

[3] https://twitter.com/durov/status/947208697188581381.

countries" (Telegram FAQ, 2022) Scholars like Lou et al. (2021) found that Telegram's affordances were very attractive for news grazing as the messaging app brings news in a condensed format at several intervals per day. News grazing is a news consumption pattern that prioritises small bits of news, preferably on mobile to gain a general sense of what is going on (Molyneux, 2018; Costera Meijer & Groot Kormelink 2015). Lou et al. (2021) also found that users in Singapore prefer Telegram for news consumption because of its simultaneity to be within a single platform on a single device for multiple media activities. Users can consume news, communicate it with specific contacts and discuss it in specific groups.

Such an affordances-based perspective provides interesting insight into the news dynamics, but in this chapter, we are more concerned with the normative processes that influence the spread of contentious content. We will explicate each of the four affordances identified in the Van Raemdonck and Pierson (2021) taxonomy on collective affordances, informed by boyd's (2011) structural affordances of the networked publics, using the findings of the technical walkthrough. These affordances (interactability, visibility, ephemerality and interventionability) will shed light on the mutual shaping of Telegram's affordances and the normative behaviour of its users.

Findings: Walkthrough Method

Interactability: Who Participates

As pointed out when introducing the Van Raemdonck and Pierson (2021) taxonomy, interactability affordances afford users the ability to interact with other users on the platform. By describing Telegram's interactability affordance we provide a view on (1) which users can interact with each other, (2) who has hierarchical superiority in these interactions and (3) how boundaries can be articulated around these interactions to include or exclude users and form a collective.

Telegram has three types of network interactions on its platform: **one-to-one Chats**, **many-to-many Groups** with up to 200,000 people and **one-to-many Channels** that broadcast to unlimited audiences. These all appear chronologically ranked on the homepage of the app, since Telegram does not have an algorithmically ranked newsfeed.

One-to-one Chat is the interactability feature on Telegram that is most similar to other messaging apps. Users can interact with each other if they have each other's contact details—either a username or phone number, through text, voice and videocalls, as well as exchange media. Chats are important on Telegram since they are the only interaction that can be end-to-end encrypted. We will not devote much attention to them here, as our focus is on social affordances that imply a social dynamic of more than two actors.

Many-to-Many Groups
Who can interact with whom: All users who are part of a Group can interact with each other in the Group.

Who is hierarchically superior: Groups are managed by one or several administrators (up to 50), usually the user who created the Group and possibly members that have been appointed as administrators. These have the hierarchical power to moderate information in the Group and have more access to interventionability affordances, which will be discussed later. Administrators are the de facto guardians of the 'boundary' of the Group, they determine who is part of the collective. Other than these hierarchical powers, administrators and users are equal interaction partners in Groups. Whatever piece of information they share, appears in exactly the same manner in the Group.

How are boundaries articulated:
The Group boundary is articulated through its admission process. Entering a Group can happen in three ways.

1. Users have been invited by an administrator of the Group or by another member, if the administrators allow members to invite.
2. Users have received a URL linking to the Group, which they found inside or outside of Telegram. Members can share this URL if administrators allow them, and the URL can be made accessible for a limited time or limited amount of uses (e.g., after 100 users have clicked the link, it becomes inactivated) by the administrators.
3. Users have found the Group by using Telegram's 'search' function. This is only possible if the Group is public, which is not the default option for Groups.

We understand from the interactability of a Group that anyone who has managed to enter a Group can interact with other members and thus influence the normative process, unless administrators reactively exclude them from the Group.

One-to-Many Channels
Who can interact with whom: When users subscribe to a Channel, they cannot interact with the Channel, nor can they interact with any of the other subscribers of the Channel. Channels function as broadcasts, and subscribers can only receive updates of the Channel on their homepage. This is why Channels fit the 'isolated and directed' description from the Van Raemdonck and Pierson (2021) taxonomy.

As visualised in Fig. 9.1, subscribers are isolated from each other, and the communication is (one-way) directed from Channel administrators to subscribers. This means the collective of subscribers cannot interact with each other on the Channel.

Who is hierarchically superior: Channel administrators are hierarchically superior to all other users subscribed on their Channel. They are the only ones

Fig. 9.1 The interactability in a one-to-many isolated & directed Channel

who can add content to the Channel and are also the only ones who can see the names of subscribers.

How are boundaries articulated: Like Groups, subscribing to a Channel can also happen in three ways:

1. Users have been invited by an administrator. Unlike with Groups, subscribers cannot invite other users.
2. Users have received a URL to the Channel. Like Groups, this URL can be made accessible for a limited time or limited amount of uses. If administrators have made the URL accessible to subscribers, which is the default in case the Channel is public, subscribers can invite other users with the URL.
3. Users have found the Channel in Telegram search. This is only possible if the Channel is public, which—like Groups—is not the default option for Channels.

We understand from the interactability of a Channel that there is no possibility for subscribers to influence the normative process on the Channel itself. Any social correction will need to take place elsewhere on Telegram, which we will explain with the 'interventionability' affordances.

One-to-Many Channels with Discussion Section
Telegram recently introduced Channel discussions, where Channel administrators can allow subscribers to comment on a post. This no longer makes Channels 'isolated and directed' (Telegram, 2020). As visualised in Fig. 9.2, subscribers can both communicate with the channel administrator, and with each other. Administrators cannot simply 'turn on' a discussion section on Telegram. In the platform's architecture logic, the administrator must create a Group and connect it to the Channel for its discussion section.

Fig. 9.2 The interactability in a one-to-many Channel with discussion

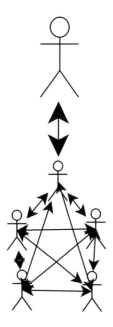

When users interact in the Channel discussion, their comment is cross posted in the Group, and vice versa. Users cannot identify where this comment was originally made. What this means for interactability is that a Group and discussion section of a Channel can have participation of users from separate origins. These comments can also land in a Group without the poster being a member of the group. Those users do not need to pass the boundary of said Group to have their comment land in it. This means users might not be aware of the norms in either space and can influence the normative processes without being part of these collectives. The discussion section transforms the interactability of Channels, but is not a default option on Channels.

We can conclude from this analysis of the interactability of Telegram that collectives on Telegram can be very connected in Groups where all members can participate in the normative process, or very disconnected when Channels are isolated and directed and no member can see engagement of others. Extremism researcher Megan Squire (2020) noted how this blend of private messaging and public Channels is ideal for evangelizing in public and then plotting in secret. We will show later under interventionability why these differences in Telegram's interactability are also significant for normative processes, but for now it is noteworthy who can engage and what superiority they have when able to engage.

Visibility: What Content Influences Normative Processes

The visibility affordances on Telegram can influence how information spreads across the platform when actualised. These affordances influence what information ends up in certain collectives, contributing to normative processes in different places. Visibility affordances can be algorithmic, but this is not the case as we've seen on the walkthrough that content is not algorithmically ranked on Telegram. Content receives visibility beyond the collectives of Channel subscribers and Group members through human amplification. Dissemination thus happens organically through the affordance of 'forwarding'. This brings into perspective how users, Channels and Groups can be influential beyond their collective, potentially influencing normative processes elsewhere.

To understand visibility affordances on Telegram, we need to explain the roles users, Channels and Groups play by demonstrating how they are involved in forwarding relationships. There are three participant nodes in a potential forwarding relationship: (a) the original message provider, (b) the message forwarder and (c) the message receiver.

On our walkthrough we noticed that most often the content shared in Groups and on Channels comes from other Channels. We could discern at least two main types of behaviour for Channels, those that only share their own content as a sort of **content repository**, and Channels that primarily share content from other Channels, serving as a sort of **content aggregator**. The Pushshift Dataset (Baumgartner et al., 2020) seems to confirm that many Channels serve as content aggregators.[4] Previous research also found that most of Telegram's shared content lands in Groups, which have a far higher daily rate of messages published than Channels due to Groups' interactability (Dargahi Nobari et al., 2017). We infer from this that Groups are places where messages land for more fleeting discussion or for further distribution, while Channels are more suitable to be content repositories and network points in Telegram. We hypothesize that Telegram's visibility affordances in the form of this 3-node forwarding relationship allows Channels to spread their content through a network of Channels and Groups, assisted by user activity, serving the evangelising role that Squire (2020) described as previously mentioned.

In our walkthrough of Telegram, we also found several Channels with an explicit **distribution role**, which only post content that directed users to similar Channels and Groups. These serve as directories on the platform and amplify not just content but connect the network in a larger collective. Similarly, Squire (2020) found how many hate Channels would regularly post "follow lists" of other channels, to remedy the low searchability—one can only see 10 results in a search on the platform, which all need to be set to public—and lack of recommendation system on Telegram. Such distribution function also allows users to move around swiftly in the face of deplatforming. Fisher et al. (2019) found that the URL's shared on pro-ISIS channels on Telegram help keep the network connected and keep distributing content despite takedowns on individual

---

[4] Baumgartner et al. (2020) found 346,937 Users, Channels or Groups where forwarded messages originated (the message providers in our forward relationship), and 27,039 Channels where messages were forwarded to (the message receivers).

platforms. Telegram's visibility affordances thus also bring separate collectives together.

One of the reasons why we also highlight Telegram's visibility affordances is that messages can be forwarded from private Groups, Channels and Chats. Unless an administrator has turned off the default setting that allows messages to be forwarded, the content of private Groups and Channels can reach anywhere on the platform and beyond.[5] This decision is important since we noted Telegram has explicitly refused to apply any form of intervention on private Groups and Channels, yet this content does not by default remain in these private places. It can easily spread all over the platform. It also means that comments or content shared in a Group where it is not considered contentious can move beyond this collective and land elsewhere, where its social norms do consider this content contentious. It thus has the power to contest and even transform norms outside of the collective where it originated.

Ephemerality: When Can Users Participate

The ephemerality affordance determines how (un)persistent content can be, and when users need to be present to take part in the normative process. As we previously mentioned, there is nothing algorithmically ranked on Telegram, and according to Durov (2021c) it never will be. This means content is displayed chronologically, in contrast to most (advertising-based) messaging apps. This chronological appearance is what Rajendra-Nicolucci and Zuckerman (2021) describe as "chat logic". Chat logic has a high degree of **perceived ephemerality**, meaning content can seem transient when there is a lot of content shared, while still being retrievable. If users want to engage with a piece of content, thereby contributing to the normative process, they need to regularly check in on the Group. Their real-time and typically high-volume appearance make remarks fade into obscurity quickly. Content will however remain persistent and searchable for existing members on Telegram as it is by default stored in the Group or Channel's history.

This perceived ephemerality also means administrators in Groups must be present at all times to intervene when there is content shared that is not supported by the social norms of the group. The ephemerality has a heavy impact on very active Groups as only those with their eyes regularly on the interactions will be aware of the discourse as well as be able to intervene. This will become even more apparent when we next discuss users' interventionability on Telegram.

---

[5] This also means content from private Groups and Channels—which would not normally be visible outside of Telegram—can be shared outside of Telegram when it is shared on a public Group or Channel.

Interventionability: How Can Users Intervene

Telegram's hands-off decision on content moderation puts a lot of moderation responsibility on to its users. We therefore need to map the interventionability affordances that allow users to moderate on the platform when actualised. Based on our walkthrough we mapped the potential interventionability affordances on Channels and Groups, which can provide users and administrators the opportunity to make social corrections. We have hinted at such interventions in previous sections, but we hereby look at intervention possibilities users and administrators have at their disposal for Channels and Groups.

We already reached the conclusion that there is no interactability for subscribers of **one-to-many Channels** when it is put in its isolated and directed default setting. This also means there is no interventionability for users, as there is no possibility to comment and make a social correction with the Channel. Users can forward this content to Groups where they can discuss this content and make a social correction, or share it on their own Channel and address its contentious nature, thereby potentially amplifying it further. Such a social correction will not automatically reach the other subscribers of the Channel, nor will it reach any of the other message receivers outside where this piece of content is also shared.

What this means is that the collective of subscribers to a Telegram Channel will have very little social norms of acceptable behaviour. Those will be entirely set by the administrator. Social correction on Channel content on Telegram is fragmented and will only be seen by other Channel subscribers if it is made on a Group or Channel that is part of a larger collective in the networked publics. The option to add a comment section to the Channel partially mitigates this problem and allows for centralised social corrections. This however needs to actively be turned on by the Channel administrator who might not be open to such social correction and thus can easily remove such comments.

Not only are there limited interventionability affordances for Channel subscribers, but Channel administrators also have limited interventionability in these networked publics of Telegram. Administrators have no knowledge where their post is being shared, only a view counter that includes the amount views from forwarded copies. The example of a seemingly innocuous European historic Channel that we found on our walkthrough shows how content can be weaponised for different purposes than its initial intentions. We found the European history posts of this Channel on a few Channels and Groups that predominantly posted white supremacist content. We cannot tell whether this Channel is aware and approves of the appropriation of their content, but it would not be the first time that folkloric groups see their content and gatherings co-opted by actors with different motives.

For example, the Swedish Vikings against Racism movement was formed after they saw their folkloric symbols appropriated by neo-Nazis. They set up an organisation to make clear that they do not associate with neo-Nazism and merely care about the folklore and history (Edwards, 2017). There is not much interventionability on Telegram in such an instance. Administrators have limited instruments to steer the interaction on their piece of content being misappropriated on other Channels and cannot continue to set the agenda when their content appears elsewhere on the platform. We found that forwarded posts even remains available after a Channel administrator decides to remove a piece of content. We can conclude that the users interacting with a Channel's content are not managed publics, contrary to how Poell et al. (2018) described the users of Facebook pages. If managed publics afford a certain degree of intervention to the administrators for the interaction with their content, Telegram Channels can be seen as a sort of 'unmanaged publics'.

Many-to-many Groups are thus the place where normative processes are more likely to occur and normative corrections about a piece of content can be made. Interventionability for users in Groups is limited to a textual reply or media reply (video, photo, URL) and an emoji reaction. As we previously saw regarding majority illusions, the users that engage the most are also the most influential in the normative process of a collective. They can be norm leaders and social influencers as Legros and Cislaghi (2020) call them. They can establish, or transform norms, or maintain norms by urging other users to comply with them through their comments. Research by Hashemi and Zare Chahooki (2019) found that between 7 and 17% of Group members engage in conversations on Telegram, meaning a very high number of Telegram users are onlookers. Users who engage on the platform are thus responsible to communicate descriptive norms to a large audience. Users can also support norm enforcement by signalling to the administrator that they should intervene, as administrators have more intervention affordances at their disposal. Users can do this by making a comment or sending a private message to administrators, but there is no built-in option in Telegram to report inappropriate content to the administrators. There is only the option for users to report content to the platform itself for the limited criteria of spam, pornography, violence, copyright, and child abuse.

Administrators can actualise interventionability affordances with a few features: deleting a message or deleting all messages from a specific user, restricting a specific user or all users from interacting for a specific or indeterminate amount of time. 'Restricting' means these users still have access to the Group, but cannot share anything in it, reducing the interactionability affordances for those users. Administrators can finetune this restriction to only include restrictions on sharing links or restrictions on sharing media such as video and pictures. This also means that users are restricted from sharing posts from another Channel that includes links or media, reducing the visibility affordances for those users. Administrators can also ban a user from the Group, in which case they cannot return to the Group, not even on the invitation of another member. When a user is banned, it is by default announced to the Group that the user has been removed by the administrator, which also signals descriptive norms of acceptable behaviour to users.

All these intervention affordances are very user-restriction focused, with very little options to provide an explanation why these interventions were made. Telegram does not provide a dedicated space for administrators to announce a code of conduct in a Group upon which they base their moderation. This would allow users to find descriptive norms about the expectations of behaviour in a Group (Legros & Cislaghi, 2020). In the same vein, Telegram does not offer the possibility to let users comply with rules before joining a Group. The lack of space for descriptive norms makes it difficult for administrators to transparently and moderate, as they cannot clarify against which norm violations they will intervene. Previous research showed how displaying rules in a group influenced how people behaved, especially for newcomers (Matias, 2019). Without visible group rules, compliance with norms hinges upon users being aware of what is permissible from having seen previous interventions. As we mentioned under ephemerality, the perceived ephemerality inherent to chat logic means such interventions are rarely seen by all users, all the time. These barriers for administrators to signal norms are significant to note in terms of the responsibility that Telegram has outsourced to its users. It implies that Telegram does not deem normative influence significant or even welcome for moderating contentious content.

Administrators can choose to **delegate some of their authority** to other users. They can hereby promote certain users to have more access to intervention affordances and moderate interactions in the group. The members of the Group can thus also assist the administrator in its task of enforcing norms. Admins cannot be identified as such by other members and do not visibly have more authority in a Group, unless this is turned on by the Group owner. Administrators can also **outsource moderation to bots**, which significantly increases the potential for administrators to actualise interventionability affordances on Telegram. Telegram encourages administrators to adopt bot accounts to support them in all sorts of tasks, which the platform facilitates by providing access to its bot API. This means users can code tasks that are performed automatically by an artificial account (a 'bot') that a normal user would otherwise have to do manually. Although Telegram encourages the creation and sharing of bots between users, it is also very clear about how third-party bots are not affiliated with Telegram (Telegram FAQ, 2022).

These bots can do a myriad of tasks to support an administrator in its moderation. For example, they can automatically remove any messages mentioning specific words, remove posts shared from specific channels, or ban users who display a certain behaviour. They can also welcome new members with a message stating the rules of the group, making up for the lack of this space in Groups. However, we have not encountered a bot that can force new members to comply with the rules first, and we presume this would require an architectural intervention that bots cannot make. Bots can clean up a group in whichever fashion administrators want, if they can code it to do the work, or find a bot made by someone else. They can also automatically forward content to other Channels or Groups, providing more visibility affordances to administrators.

The use of bots can be seen as what activist Cory Doctorow describes as "adversarial interoperability", where users create a service that plugs into the existing ones without the company's permission (Doctorow, 2019). In the case of Telegram however, there is no adversity from the platform towards the use of bots, its founders even highly encourage users to create them. Such a practice outsources responsibility and in a way grants rights to non-human agents (Makhortykh et al., 2022). It also provides administrators with the opportunity to automate their self-regulation in a manner that is sensitive to the norms of their collectives, contrary to platform-wide automated content moderation on some other platforms like Facebook or Twitter. It does however require administrators to know how to code or employ bots made by others. These accessibility issues can be a big obstacle for less tech-savvy administrators. Not knowing how to employ bots significantly reduces administrators' interventionability on Telegram, meaning Telegram administrators will have a harder time actualising this affordance.

Conclusion

Affordance research has primarily focused on individuals' relationship with their online environment, but rarely on the way affordances guide collectives in establishing norms in their shared environment. We expanded the perspective of social affordances to include 'the collective' as a unit of analysis and explore how it transforms when certain affordances are actualised. Since norms of behaviour in collectives is influenced by perceptions of what others in collectives do and approve of, it is important to identify which affordances guide individuals in influencing what are called descriptive norms. To create a taxonomy of such affordances, we based ourselves on the structural affordances of networked publics that are suggested by boyd (2011).

To illustrate the value of such a taxonomy, we analysed the social affordances of Telegram. We can discern respectively **who** can be part of a normative process by looking at how users can actualise interactability. We therefore examined who they can interact with and is subject to shared social norms; **what** information can travel into collectives by actualising visibility affordances; **when** users can see the information that impacts normative processes when ephemerality on the platform is actualised; and **how** users can influence normative processes by actualising interventionability on Telegram and make clear what they deem certain behaviours acceptable or unacceptable.

Our analysis shows that social corrections on content shared in one-to-many Channels is difficult to achieve. Any attempt subscribers might make at establishing a norm on Channel content needs to take place in parallel spaces like many-to-many Groups or on different Channels. This means social corrections on Channel content is fragmented and will less likely signal descriptive norms to all the subscribers of a Channel. Telegram has recently introduced a comment section to Channels which centralizes such social corrections more, but overall, we consider subscribers to Channels 'unmanaged publics'. This is because subscribers can also wildly contest Channel content all over the platform without the knowledge of the Channel administrator or others in the networked public that encounter this Channel's content.

Another finding is that when users actualise visibility affordances on Telegram, content can travel through a network of Channels of which many serve a role as content aggregators, with Groups serving as potential distribution points. In this way, contentious content can enter collectives, influencing normative processes in many-to-many Groups where new information is constantly introduced, potentially contesting established norms. While social corrections in Groups can be seen by everyone in the Group, the ephemerality in Telegram's chat logic means it is only seen by those present during the interaction. This means an intervention that attempts to enforce a norm can be fleeting and needs to be repeated several times. Telegram's lack of a space for rules that administrators can refer to and base their moderation on, complicates the maintenance of any established norms.

We have seen that Telegram's policy is very hands-off concerning moderation, with even a refusal to intervene on content posted in private Channels and Groups, even if we found that it can still spread outside of those private spaces. This approach outsources a lot of responsibility to users to self-moderate. The lack of affordances to facilitate descriptive norms regarding contentious content implies that the platform has low expectations for normative influence to counter potentially harmful behaviour. The bot API that Telegram has opened up to its community has the potential to afford interventionability to administrators when they do not have their eyeballs on the group at all times. It can facilitate more fine-grained self-regulation that counters the need for blunt platform-wide automated content moderation. It is however not ideal to actualise this affordance, as it requires technical skills for administrators to develop such bots. It also remains ineffective in collectives where the norm is strong approval of contentious content, where individuals challenging such norms have a hard time entering or staying in these collectives.

Overall, Telegram's social affordances provide insight in how the platform affords users the possibilities to influence the normative process in the networked publics. Based on these findings, future research can investigate which affordances are most impactful in the self-moderation of users on the platform.

References

Akbari, A., & Gabdulhakov, R. (2019). Platform Surveillance and Resistance in Iran and Russia: The Case of Telegram. *Surveillance & Society*, 17(1/2), 223–231. https://doi.org/10.24908/ss.v17i1/2.12928

Auxier, B. & Anderson, M. (2021) Social Media Use in 2021. *PEW Research Center*. Last retrieved 13 May 2022 https://www.pewresearch.org/internet/2021/04/07/social-media-use-in-2021/

Axelrod, Robert (1984) *The Evolution of Cooperation*, New York: Basic Books.

Baumgartner, J., Zannettou, S., Squire, M., & Blackburn, J. (2020). The Pushshift Telegram Dataset. *Proceedings of the International AAAI Conference on Web and Social Media*, 14, 840–847.

Blacker, A. (2021). Worldwide and US Download Leaders 2021. *Apptopia*. Last retrieved 19 April 2022 https://blog.apptopia.com/worldwide-and-us-download-leaders-2021

boyd, danah. (2011). Social Network Sites as Networked Publics: Affordances, Dynamics, and Implications. In Z. Papacharissi (Ed.), *A Networked Self: Identity, Community, and Culture on Social Network Sites* (pp. 39–58).

Bucher, T., & Helmond, A. (2018). The Affordances of Social Media Platforms. In J. Burgess, A. Marwick, & T. Poell, *The SAGE Handbook of Social Media* (pp. 233–253). SAGE Publications Ltd. https://doi.org/10.4135/9781473984066.n14

Business Insider (2016) The Messaging Apps Report: Messaging apps are now bigger than social networks. *Business Insider Intelligence*. Last retrieved 13 May 2022 https://www.businessinsider.com/the-messaging-app-report-2015-11

Chandrasekharan, E., Samory, M., Jhaver, S., Charvat, H., Bruckman, A., Lampe, C., Eisenstein, J., & Gilbert, E. (2018). The Internet's Hidden Rules: An Empirical Study of Reddit Norm Violations at Micro, Meso, and Macro Scales. *Proceedings of the ACM on Human-Computer Interaction*, 2(CSCW), 1–25. https://doi.org/10.1145/3274301

Cialdini, R. B., Reno, R. R., & Kallgren, C. A. (1990). A focus theory of normative conduct: Recycling the concept of norms to reduce littering in public places. *Journal of Personality and Social Psychology*, 58, 1015–1026.

Costera Meijer, I., & Groot Kormelink, T. (2015). Checking, Sharing, Clicking and Linking. *Digital Journalism*, 3(5), 664–679. https://doi.org/10.1080/21670811.2014.937149

Coleman, James S. (1990) *Foundations of Social Theory*, Cambridge, MA: Belknap.

Dargahi Nobari, A., Reshadatmand, N., & Neshati, M. (2017). Analysis of Telegram, An Instant Messaging Service. *Proceedings of the 2017 ACM on Conference on Information and Knowledge Management* https://dl.acm.org/doi/10.1145/3132847.3133132

Davis, J. L., & Chouinard, J. B. (2016). Theorizing Affordances: From Request to Refuse. *Bulletin of Science, Technology & Society*, 36(4), 241–248. https://doi.org/10.1177/0270467617714944

Deakin, D. R. (2021). WhatsApp scrambles to stem the flow of users moving to rivals Signal and Telegram as millions protest against controversial privacy policy. *Notebookcheck*. Last retrieved 19 April 2022 https://www.notebookcheck.net/WhatsApp-scrambles-to-stem-the-flow-of-users-moving-to-rivals-Signal-and-Telegram-as-millions-protest-against-controversial-privacy-policy.515474.0.html

Doctorow, C. (2019, October 2). Adversarial Interoperability. *Electronic Frontier Foundation*. https://www.eff.org/deeplinks/2019/10/adversarial-interoperability

Durov, P. (2018) 200,000,000 Monthly Active Users. *Telegram Blog*. Last retrieved 19 April 2022. https://telegram.org/blog/200-million

Durov, P. (2021a) As Telegram approaches 500 million active users, many of you are asking the question—who is going to pay to support this growth? *Telegram*. Last retrieved 19 April 2022 https://t.me/durov/142

Durov, P. (2021b) In the first week of January, Telegram surpassed 500 million monthly active users. *Telegram*. Last retrieved 19 April 2022 https://t.me/durov/147

Durov, P. (2021c) Since my last post, the already massive influx of new users to Telegram has only accelerated. *Telegram*. Last retrieved 19 April 2022. https://t.me/durov/148

Edwards, C. (2017, October 6). 'We can't let racists re-define Viking culture.' *The Local Sweden*. Last retrieved 19 April 2022 https://www.thelocal.se/20171006/we-cant-let-racists-re-define-viking-culture-far-right-runes-swedish/

Evans, S. K., Pearce, K. E., Vitak, J., & Treem, J. W. (2017). Explicating Affordances: A Conceptual Framework for Understanding Affordances in Communication Research. *Journal of Computer-Mediated Communication*, 22(1), 35–52. https://doi.org/10.1111/jcc4.12180

Fisher, A., Prucha, N., & Winterbotham, E. (2019). Mapping the Jihadist Information Ecosystem: Towards the Next Generation of Disruption Capability. *RUSI—Royal United Services Institute for Defence and Security Studies*. https://static.rusi.org/20190716_grntt_paper_06.pdf

Gaver, W. W. (1996). Situating Action II: Affordances for Interaction: The Social Is Material for Design. *Ecological Psychology*, 8(2), 111–129. https://doi.org/10.1207/s15326969eco0802_2

Geber, S., & Hefner, D. (2019). Social norms as communicative phenomena: A communication perspective on the theory of normative social behavior. *SCM Studies in Communication and Media*, 8(1), 6–28. https://doi.org/10.5771/2192-4007-2019-1-6

Gibson, J. J. (1979) *The Ecological Approach to Visual Perception*. Boston: Houghton Mifflin

Greenberg, A. (2021) Fleeing WhatsApp for Better Privacy? Don't Turn to Telegram. Wired. Last retrieved 19 April 2022 https://www.wired.com/story/telegram-encryption-whatsapp-settings/

Hashemi, A., & Zare Chahooki, M. A. (2019). Telegram group quality measurement by user behavior analysis. *Social Network Analysis and Mining*, 9(1), 33. https://doi.org/10.1007/s13278-019-0575-9

Helberger, N., Pierson, J., & Poell, T. (2018). Governing online platforms: From contested to cooperative responsibility. *The Information Society*, 34(1), 1–14. https://doi.org/10.1080/01972243.2017.1391913

Heras-Escribano, M., & de Pinedo, M. (2016). Are affordances normative? *Phenomenology and the Cognitive Sciences*, 15(4), 565–589. https://doi.org/10.1007/s11097-015-9440-0

Hindman, M., Lubin, N., & Davis, T. (2022, February 10). Facebook Has a Superuser-Supremacy Problem. The Atlantic. Last retrieved 19 April 2022. https://www.theatlantic.com/technology/archive/2022/02/facebook-hate-speech-misinformation-superusers/621617/

Hsieh, Y. P. (2012). Online social networking skills: The social affordances approach to digital inequality. *First Monday*. https://doi.org/10.5210/fm.v17i4.3893

Hutchby, I. (2001). Technologies, Texts and Affordances. *Sociology*, 35(2), 441–456. https://doi.org/10.1177/S0038038501000219

Ito, M. (2008). Introduction. In K. Varnelis (Ed.), *Networked Publics* (pp. 1–14). MIT Press. http://networkedpublics.org/book/introduction.html

Kaul, Ayushman. (2020, April 20). Terrorgram: A community built on hate. *DFRLab*. Last retrieved 19 April 2022 https://medium.com/dfrlab/terrorgram-a-community-built-on-hate-e02fd59ee329

Lampe, C., Zube, P., Lee, J., Park, C. H., & Johnston, E. (2014). Crowdsourcing civility: A natural experiment examining the effects of distributed moderation in online forums. *Government Information Quarterly*, 31(2), 317–326. https://doi.org/10.1016/j.giq.2013.11.005

Latour, B. (2005). *Reassembling the social: An introduction to Actor-Network-Theory.* Oxford Univ. Press.

Legros, S., & Cislaghi, B. (2020). Mapping the Social-Norms Literature: An Overview of Reviews. *Perspectives on Psychological Science*, 15(1), 62–80. https://doi.org/10.1177/1745691619866455

Leonardi, P. M. (2013). When Does Technology Use Enable Network Change in Organizations? A Comparative Study of Feature Use and Shared Affordances. *MIS Quarterly*, 37(3), 749–775.

Lessig, L. (1999). *Code and other laws of cyberspace.* Basic Books.

Levinson P (2018) The war of chat apps in US and Europe. TeleMessage, 9 October. Last retrieved 19 April 2022. https://www.telemessage.com/the-war-of-chat-apps-in-us-and-europe-infographic

Light, B., Burgess, J., & Duguay, S. (2018). The walkthrough method: An approach to the study of apps. *New Media & Society*, 20(3), 881–900. https://doi.org/10.1177/1461444816675438

Litvinova, D. (2021, April 20). "Telegram revolution": App helps drive Belarus protests. *AP NEWS.* Last retrieved 19 April 2022 https://apnews.com/article/international-news-technology-business-ap-top-news-europe-823180da2b402f6a1dc9fbd76a6f476b

Lou, C., Tandoc Jr., E. C., Hong, L. X., Pong, X. Y. (Brenda), Lye, W. X. (Rachelle), & Sng, N. G. (Trisha). (2021). When Motivations Meet Affordances: News Consumption on Telegram. *Journalism Studies*, 22(7), 934–952. https://doi.org/10.1080/1461670X.2021.1906299

Loucaides, D. (2022, February 8). How Telegram Became the Anti-Facebook. *Wired.* Last retrieved 19 April 2022 https://www.wired.com/story/how-telegram-became-anti-facebook/

Lüders, M. (2008) Conceptualizing personal media. *New Media & Society* 10(5): 683–702.

Makhortykh, M., Urman, A., Münch, F. V., Heldt, A., Dreyer, S., & Kettemann, M. C. (2022). Not all who are bots are evil: A cross-platform analysis of automated agent governance. *New Media & Society*, 24(4), 964–981. https://doi.org/10.1177/14614448221079035

Mandavia, M. (2021). Telegram becomes the most downloaded app worldwide in January. *The Economic Times.* Last retrieved 19 April 2022 https://economictimes.indiatimes.com/tech/technology/telegram-becomes-the-most-downloaded-app-worldwide-in-january/articleshow/80722399.cms

Matias, J. N. (2019). Preventing harassment and increasing group participation through social norms in 2,190 online science discussions. *Proceedings of the National Academy of Sciences*, 116(20), 9785–9789. https://doi.org/10.1073/pnas.1813486116

Molyneux, L. (2018). Mobile News Consumption. *Digital Journalism*, 6(5), 634–650. https://doi.org/10.1080/21670811.2017.1334567

Naseri, M., & Zamani, H. (2019). Analyzing and Predicting News Popularity in an Instant Messaging Service. *Proceedings of the 42nd International ACM SIGIR Conference on Research and Development in Information Retrieval*, 1053–1056. https://doi.org/10.1145/3331184.3331301

Newman, L. H. (2021). WhatsApp Has Shared Your Data with Facebook for Years, Actually. *Wired.* Last retrieved 19 April 2022 https://www.wired.com/story/whatsapp-facebook-data-share-notification/

Norman, D. A. (1988). *The psychology of everyday things.* Basic Books.

Parsons, Talcott (1951) *The Social System*, New York: Routledge.
Pierson, J. (2021). Digital Platforms as Entangled Infrastructures: Addressing Public Values and Trust in Messaging Apps. *European Journal of Communication.* 36 (4), 349-361
Poell, T., Rajagopalan, S., & Kavada, A. (2018). Publicness on Platforms: Tracing the Mutual Articulation of Platform Architectures and User Practices. In Z. Papacharissi (Ed.), A *Networked Self and Platforms, Stories, Connections,* 43-58 https://doi.org/10.13140/RG.2.2.23091.53283
Postigo, H. (2016). The socio-technical architecture of digital labor: Converting play into YouTube money. *New Media & Society,* 18(2), 332–349. https://doi.org/10.1177/1461444814541527
Rajendra-Nicolucci, E. C., & Zuckerman, E. (2021). Chat Logic: When you want a living room, not a town square. In Rajendra-Nicolucci, E. C., & Zuckerman, E. (eds.) *An Illustrated Field Guide to Social Media.* 74–79. https://knightcolumbia.org/blog/an-illustrated-field-guide-to-social-media
Repucci, S., & Slipowitz, A. (2022). Freedom in the world 2022: The Global Expansion of Authoritarian Rule. *Freedom House.* Last retrieved 19 April 2022 https://freedomhouse.org/report/freedom-world/2022/global-expansion-authoritarian-rule
Rimal, R. N., & Lapinski, M. K. (2015). A Re-Explication of Social Norms, Ten Years Later: Social Norms. *Communication Theory,* 25(4), 393–409. https://doi.org/10.1111/comt.12080
Rimal, R. N., & Real, K. (2005). How Behaviors are Influenced by Perceived Norms: A Test of the Theory of Normative Social Behavior. *Communication Research,* 32(3), 389–414. https://doi.org/10.1177/0093650205275385
Rogers, R. (2020). Deplatforming: Following extreme Internet celebrities to Telegram and alternative social media. *European Journal of Communication,* 35(3), 213–229. https://doi.org/10.1177/0267323120922066
Scollon, M. (2021). The Telegram App Gives Voice to The Oppressed in Belarus and Russia. But Hate Groups Are Using It Too. *Radio Free Europe/Radio Liberty.* Last retrieved 19 April 2022 https://www.rferl.org/a/telegram-messaging-app-russia-belarus-iran-content-concerns/31029359.html
Sevenhant, R.; Stragier R.; De Marez, L. & Schuurman, D. (2022) "IMEC digimeter 2021, Digitale Trends in Vlaanderen" *IMEC.* Last retrieved 13 May 2022 https://www.imec.be/sites/default/files/2022-04/IMEC_Digimeterrapport_2021.pdf
Singh, M. (2021). Telegram surpasses 1 billion downloads. *TechCrunch.* Last retrieved 22 April 2022 https://social.techcrunch.com/2021/08/30/telegram-tops-1-billion-downloads/
Spadafora, A. (2021, July 20). Researchers discover security flaws in Telegram encryption protocol. *TechRadar.* Last retrieved 22 April 2022 https://www.techradar.com/news/researchers-discover-security-flaws-in-telegram-encryption-protocol
Squire, M. (2020). Alt-Tech & the Radical Right, Part 3: Why Do Hate Groups and Terrorists Love Telegram? *Centre for Analysis of the Radical Right.* Last retrieved 22 April 2022 https://www.radicalrightanalysis.com/2020/02/23/alt-tech-the-radical-right-part-3-why-do-hate-groups-and-terrorists-love-telegram/
Telegram FAQ. 2022. Last retrieved 26 March 2022, archived on https://web.archive.org/web/20220326222617/https://telegram.org/faq
Telegram Ad platform. n.d. Last retrieved 19 April 2022 archived on https://web.archive.org/web/20220419150944/https://promote.telegram.org/

Telegram (2020) Search Filters, Anonymous Admins, Channel Comments and More. *Telegram Blog.* Last retrieved 22 April 2022 https://telegram.org/blog/filters-anonymous-admins-comments

Thomas, W. F. (2022). Telegram: The Social Network Where Conspiracies Meet. *Logically AI.* Last retrieved 22 April 2022 https://www.logically.ai/articles/telegram-where-conspiracies-meet

Turton, W. (2016). Why You Should Stop Using Telegram Right Now. *Gizmodo.* Last retrieved 22 April 2022 https://gizmodo.com/why-you-should-stop-using-telegram-right-now-1782557415

Urman, A., Ho, J. C., & Katz, S. (2021). Analyzing protest mobilization on Telegram: The case of 2019 Anti-Extradition Bill movement in Hong Kong. *PLOS ONE*, 16(10), e0256675. https://doi.org/10.1371/journal.pone.0256675

Van Dijck, J. (2013). Disassembling platforms, reassembling sociality. In J. Van Dijck, *The culture of connectivity: A critical history of social media* (pp. 24–44). Oxford University Press.

Van Raemdonck, N., & Pierson, J. (2021). Taxonomy of Social Network Platform Affordances for Group Interactions. *14th CMI International Conference—Critical ICT Infrastructures and Platforms (CMI)*, 1–8. https://doi.org/10.1109/CMI53512.2021.9663773

Vanian, J. (2021). Private messaging apps Signal and Telegram are red hot after the Capitol riots. *Fortune.* Last retrieved 22 April 2022. https://fortune.com/2021/01/13/messaging-apps-signal-telegram-capitol-riots/

Volkoff, O., & Strong, D. M. (2017). Affordance theory and how to use it in IS research. In *The Routledge Companion to Management Information Systems.* Routledge.

Weichold, M., & Thonhauser, G. (2019). Collective Affordances. *Ecological Psychology*, 32(1), 1–24. https://doi.org/10.1080/10407413.2019.1695211

Wellman, B., Quan-Haase, A., Boase, J., Chen, W., Hampton, K., Díaz, I., & Miyata, K. (2003). The Social Affordances of the Internet for Networked Individualism. *Journal of Computer-Mediated Communication*, 8(3), JCMC834. https://doi.org/10.1111/j.1083-6101.2003.tb00216.x

Wijermars, M., & Lokot, T. (2022). Is Telegram a "harbinger of freedom"? The performance, practices, and perception of platforms as political actors in authoritarian states. *Post-Soviet Affairs*, 0(0), 1–21. https://doi.org/10.1080/1060586X.2022.2030645

Winter, A. (2019) Online hate: from the farright to the "alt-right" and from the margins to the mainstream, in Lumsden, K. & Harmer, E. (eds) *Online Othering: Exploring Digital Violence and Discrimination on the Web*, Palgrave Macmillan.

Wittgenstein, L. (1953). *Philosophical investigations.* Oxford-Blackwell.

Wojcik, S., & Hughes, A. (2019). Sizing Up Twitter Users. *Pew Research Center* Last retrieved 13 May 2022. https://www.pewresearch.org/internet/2019/04/24/sizing-up-twitter-users/

CHAPTER 10

Glimpses of the Greek 'Me Too' Movement on Facebook: Tracking Digital Interactivity and the Quest for Equity and Empowerment

Sophia Kaitatzi-Whitlock

> *The oppressor would not be so strong if he did not have accomplices among the oppressed*
> —Simone de Beauvoir

Introduction

We expect our everyday digital exchanges to confer use-value in terms of communication, social interaction, or pleasure. Socially, users anticipate networking, welcoming the thrill of new social bonding occasions. Politically, users pursue activism and 'clicktivism' projects to promote engagement for concrete objectives. Social Media can serve as excellent tools for coordination and meaningful political participation. They have already been instrumental in transactions and, conditionally, could develop further. Irrespective of specific objectives, most users enjoy virtual proximity and seek society or community building. In this light, it is important to explore potential political outcomes and looming options from digital networking.

In this chapter I focus on two rape-cases from the 'Greek-MeToo' movement, as approached and projected digitally by activists and users through Social Media interactions. Through the lens of content analysis, I examine the dynamics and the impact that users obtain on the web, with a focus to options

---

S. Kaitatzi-Whitlock (✉)
Aristotle University of Thessaloniki, Thessaloniki, Greece
e-mail: sophiakw@otenet.gr

© The Author(s), under exclusive license to Springer Nature Switzerland AG 2024
H. S. Dunn et al. (eds.), *The Palgrave Handbook of Everyday Digital Life*,
https://doi.org/10.1007/978-3-031-30438-5_10

for further development of digital social bonding. I monitor the transactions and the contents of posts of some Facebook users, with the analysis focusing particularly on interactions prompted by two notorious 'MeToo' incidents in Greece. The aim is to explore the extent to which lasting and effective forms of sociality and of *activist engagement* can accrue on digital-virtual spaces and be successfully achievable.

What are the limits and under what circumstances is the virtual virtuous, socio-politically? How can the virtual become concretely rewarding? I complete the study with a broad perspective, contrasting highly mediatized ongoing cases, with the masses of less visible instances of trafficking. So, I distinguish macro-plan trends, from cases acutely present 'here and now'. I deem to be crucial the relationship between two types of material: notorious, close to heart, 'here and now' cases *versus* the masses of 'unnoticed' or unnoticeable cases of gender-violence, undertaken over digital platforms. In conclusion, I pose the question of whether, on balance, the empowering and positive aspects of digitality and Social Media uses outweigh the disempowering ones.

Greek 'Me Too' Rapes in Interactions of Facebook Users

Two rape-cases shook Greece and were catalytic in several ways. In terms of public discourse, a reverse intermedia agenda setting took place. This remarkable effect originated from Social Media, generated by ordinary members of society, thereby imposing new themes for traditional media discourses. This ambushed the agenda of the *ancien media regime* intensely and explicitly for the first time. The outbreak of a series of activist events provoked a long overdue 'social concussion', inducing what seemed like a redeeming effect on society.

It led to the bursting out of the long persisting *omerta* and secretive practices that kept sex abuse crimes, such as rapes, pederasty and femicides, covered up. It sparked multi-level popular reactions. Since the first denouncing personality, Sophia Mpekatorou, is a national star, she could not be sidelined and so, the entire nation got involved with the 'MeToo' movement through this affair. People got vocal, spoke out, and the outcry in masses of Social Media posts, including criminal evidence, gave rise to a social and institutional awakening in the country.

Actual political and legal changes, such as reviewing of legislation, even if not quite satisfactory, occurred. Rapists and sex-abusers got arrested after admitting crimes and litigations were set in motion. All this sociopolitical convulsive turmoil effected a reorientation of *national attention* on a huge scale, triggering multiple cycles of public debates. The hashtag #metooGR was established on 16 January 2021, and instantly started attracting enormous attention (Akrivos, 2021). It kept capsizing and reshuffling positions among influential public sphere speakers and reorienting the media agenda.

Professionally assembled and AI-treated big data are supplied by firms, such as Brandwatch, for industrial purposes, confirming the dynamics of information traffic and trading processes.¹ Activist communicative manifestations accelerated the cycles of Social Media exchanges. Digital engagement grew, coordinated largely through Social Media in many ways.

The first victim to go public, Sophia Mpekatorou, is a psychologist, former athlete and Olympic champion in sailing, who denounced her rape by her coach. In the period of two months following Mpekatorou's rape denouncement, more than 122,000 twitter messages under the '#MeToo' hashtag were uploaded in the country.² Thus, Social Media traffic amassed a valuable and diverse user exchange material, readily available also for exploration and research (Lupton, 2015). Significantly, all these interactions occurred during the COVID-19 pandemic crisis, the managing protocols of which intensified virtual interactions still more, turning Social Media into a *sui generis* surrogate of the absent social proximity and an antidote to social distancing. This *rape* disclosure also sparked reactions and controversial events which triggered, first, more denunciations and, secondly, an enormous rise in Social Media interactions. This outcome turned them into key *objects* for content analysis of related Facebook interactions.

The second case concerns Georgia Mpika who denounced her rape to the police on the first day of the year 2022.³ These two 'MeToo' rapes determined the monitoring periods, the first starting on 14 January 2021, while the second on 14 January 2022. More to the point, on the 14 January 2021, at a conference, Sophia Mpekatorou disclosed that she had been raped by her coach, in her youth.⁴ The second disclosure, related to Georgia Mpika got publicly known only on January 14, 2022, through an Instagram video by Elias Gionis, a supporter of the victim, subsequently concurred by Mpika's own interview (19 January 2022).⁵ It is noteworthy, that although she filed formal complaint with Police on 1st January 2022 against her rapists, Greek citizens learned about it all of two weeks later and, first, from Social Media.⁶

According to the victim, Mpika, this was a group rape involving at least two men, after she was drugged unconscious during a New Year's party.⁷ Circumstantial evidence suggests that her rape may be linked to organized sex trafficking, which is under detective and legal investigation. In an Instagram

---

¹ The British platform Brandwatch employs advanced AI software in its packages of big data. https://www.brandwatch.com/

² Brandwatch 'Key Insights' tables depict a rally of #MeToo posts with recorded increases up to 240% (Retounioti, 2022).

³ Academic research analyses relating to the 'Greek MeToo' movement were conducted while others are underway.

⁴ Her denouncement confers crucial political, social, moral, and activist value. But it cannot be tried, as the case is legally forgone.

⁵ This is half an hour's interview of G. Mpika to Makis Triantafilopoulos. https://www.youtube.com/watch?v=iONvrOCSjrk

⁶ This is remarkable as Greek TV news bulletins devote large chunks of time on police and legal reportage.

⁷ See: https://www.reader.gr/koinonia/399448/biasmos-24hronis-sti-thessaloniki-kataggelies-gkioni-gia-10-atoma-poy-dialegoyn.

post, one of the accused admitted that 'sex took place, but consensually'. Apart from suspected trafficking through 'parties supplying women for sex', the accused are belong to Athenian high society, which may explain why an instantly, officially reported rape case was hidden from the public, who learned about it only two weeks later, after it 'went viral' on Social Media platforms. The victim, an eloquent young lady, detailed the sequence of events, as experienced, in her interview, which made a huge impression and also became viral, on the internet.[8]

FACEBOOK AS 'SOCIAL SPACE' AND AS TOOL FOR CONTENT ANALYSIS

Many Social Media users, notably subscribers of Facebook, are preoccupied with the *self*, through the 'selfie-tool' and industry. Self-exposure, visibility and promotion projects prevail. "Facebook friends are presenting the best possible picture of their lives" (Schwartz, 2016, p. 195) aiming to appear appealing and likable by preferred others. In short, Social Media projects are determined, largely, by an urge for recognition and the desire to be noticed. Strategically minded users aim higher, at being distinguished as influencers,[9] for economic power or fame. The social platform of Facebook boasts some 3.5 billion accounts, of which 2.9 million were active in 2021. Its comparative advantage is that it welcomes multimedia posts, setting no strict upper limits on message volumes. Longer reasoning or argumentative texts fit well into such a framework. Conversely, Twitter originally limited the number of characters in posts, while Instagram specializes in videos and photos. So, Facebook gained popularity with users who wanted to exploit it for daily routine uses or for trivial responses to others. However, "The banality of most people's Facebook pages should not blind us to the larger implications" (Wu, 2010, p. 298), as they result also in the mounting phenomenon of what I have called 'infoflation' (Kaitatzi-Whitlock, 2015). Besides, posting phatic messages suits the "I am the product" conception of platforms and serves established power relations.[10] Statistical accounts indicate that most Facebook users belong to '*follower*' types (Nielsen, 2006). Users 'prosume' likable, flattering, pleasing or anodyne PR-type messages[11] which cultivate largely shallow social ties, while conserving the status quo. Yet, exceptions to the rule obtain.

Although many users deal merely in banal or predictable posts, and even if they remain silent, they can still see, listen and *read* an unprecedented volume

---

[8] See: https://www.youtube.com/watch?v=iONvrOCSjrk, https://www.youtube.com/watch?v=qD3s1ird0To.

[9] A large literature exists already on influencers of all kinds, notably, specializing in marketing. https://greenleafbookgroup.com/learning-center/book-marketing/how-to-connect-with-influencers-to-market-your-book

[10] See also Olsson (2014).

[11] Comprising, typically, name-day, birthday, health wishes and numerous types of congratulations.

of posts, originating from genuinely diverse sources. Compared to the largely monolithic commercial TV-output, this is qualitatively a crucial difference. They are amenable to positive influence by a huge diversity of 'prosumers' and may interact further, face to face. This implies that even silent Social Media users are dynamic and cannot be underestimated, especially, concerning the future prospects of *horizontality*. Socio-gramme patterns of Social Media networks, suggest that the dynamics of power relations, inertias and inequalities operating in real life also operate digitally. Yet, the very *structure of horizontality*, in tandem with the condition of constant flux, hold potentialities for changes, including shifts of conduct.

Surprises, towards initiative-taking, should not be excluded, because *horizontality* advances, structurally, the ethos of participation and activation (Kaitatzi-Whitlock, 2013, 2021). Over time, it is a transformative and balancing factor in social relations. Social Media platforms do offer opportunities to capable,[12] goal-oriented, determined individuals, granting them tools, visibility, horizon vistas and recognition.

Sampling 'Friends' for Analysis

The criteria for selecting the 20 friends to be analyzed evolved from their personality and Facebook profiles. I looked for young extrovert Facebook friends who expressed a distinct sensitivity to human rights issues, demonstrating concern particularly for gender equity and respect of human rights of all people. Quality of extroversion and dynamism were important for including them in the group for analysis, as well as indications that they were manifestly socially minded individuals. They were analyzed on issue-specific contents in their timelines, namely, posts and topics relating to the Greek 'Me Too' movement, rape cases and gender violence. The Facebook friends analyzed are real persons.[13] They are female and male in equal proportion. Their age spanned early twenties and early thirties. They were vetted individually, but also considered as groups. Most had completed undergraduate or graduate studies at the leading School of Journalism and Communication, pursuing careers or holding responsible positions. Many were in search of networking opportunities and open to identity-negotiating, for constructing and developing their personalities and dealing with professional challenges, in a crisis-stricken, fluid and uncertain world.[14]

---

[12] Diligent digital communicators gain privileged rewards and distinction accompanied with fame, thereby sustaining the tendencies of '*aptocracy*' (Lupton 2015). See also Ragnedda (2017).

[13] The researcher's fear is risking to monitor *personas* behind whom might hide botts, or pseudonymous infiltrators aiming at damaging or disruption. Such fears question the veracity of findings of web research.

[14] Indicatively, some are members of PHYLIS, a new Aristotle University feminist organization, established in the wake of the 'Greek MeToo' revelations, in 2021. https://www.facebook.com/phylis.auth/, https://www.instagram.com/phylis.auth/?hl=el

Such profiles set them apart as a category, among general users, as they transcend roles, combining both ordinary 'prosumer' features and professional 'media-worker' functions, a particularity reflected on their Facebook outputs. However, journalism is facing a severe economic decline, causing precariousness in this job-market. It is fraught with demands for cheap labour, a desire for conformity or subject to controlled information and 'fake news'. Not surprisingly, the most dynamic professionals are trying to forge novel media careers 'outside the system'. Overall, they are well-educated graduates. They belong among the best placed youth in the country, aiming to achieve a decent life, in a fairer world with equal gender-relations in an improved Greek society.

These features suggest that socio-politically they are bold, radical and outspoken. Two-thirds of those selected were mutual Facebook friends, while some interacted offline in political collectivities, to stop violence against women and other vulnerable individuals. Extrovert dynamic users, favouring the *general public good* are in focus here.[15] I shall call the twenty analyzed participants: 'intra-group friends' or just 'friends'. Responses are divided as coming from two friend-tanks: 'all one's friends', and from 'intra-group friends'. I am here concerned primarily with the second category.

DELVING INTO INTERACTIONS AND CONTENT

This *content analysis* is of an explorative nature, unlike f.ex. cases of normative checking about adhering or not, to journalistic editorial principles. It explores contents and interactions of twenty young people, as generated digitally, while communicating and pursuing their goals. Depicted contents follow the standard Facebook entry-counts of 'likes *et cetera*'[16] but include also some additional aspects. Core entry categories examined include: (i) posting own, genuine 'MeToo' or 'gender-specific' content or reposting of such material by 'friends' or feminist collectivities. (ii) receiving feedback reactions on such posts. (iii) offering reactions to others' posts, (reverse feedback) notably, the intra-group friends. (iv) receiving essential (non-trivial) comments and conversely, posting such material on the pages of others. (v) further sharing of

---

[15] THE ANALYZING researcher friend: I joined Facebook in 2016, accidentally on purpose, to connect with a specialist team, already established as a closed-FB-group for internal coordination. I launch posts on social and political issues. I am friends with all-twenty 'friends' analyzed. I know these 'FB friends' personally, since most have been past students at Aristotle University (AUTH). Between us, we react, comment, exchange views and agree or disagree on current affairs issues. We exchange posts on policies or platform premises. We share broader political orientations or overlap socio-politically. Namely, we react to, or exchange posts on topics of civic equality, freedom of expression, gender equality, feminist movements, violence against women, feminicides. The tragic outcomes of sharply increasing femicides in Greece, the rise of the 'MeToo' movement which revived feminism are central topics in my FB-page. In this capacity, I am automatically placed also as an interactive 'participant observer', like FB-friends can normally be.

[16] The term 'likes etcetera' refers to the standard cues, as set by FB algorithms including a. "likes", b. "cares", c. "amazed", d. "cry-sorry", e. "angry". I should add that running 'stories' as posts not publicly visible, are not considered here.

posts by intra-group friends. (vi) pursuing and sparking dialogue or advanced discourse.

Two Rapes: Overall, posts instigated by Sophia Mpekatorou's rape denouncement were massive and diverse. They expressed indignation but also feelings of redemption. Exclamations of an "at last" nature. Friends' posts attacked all those who continued 'blaming the victim' or asking, "why now?". Numerous critical posts disapproved of views tolerating misogynist society taboos, notably, the practice of silencing and secretiveness. Other posts criticized tendencies to ridicule or trivialize such issues of deep trauma and of craving for human decency. Many more congratulated the victim for her bravery. Some of the examined friends are feminist activists or belong to political parties, involved with gender equality issues and communicating them in the public arena. Disapproving and indignant posts were regular along with reposts of related anti-rape moves, by feminist organizations, following Mpekatorou's rape denouncing.

The Georgia Mpika's case triggered enormous public empathy, anger and engagement through soaring Social Media posts. Manifestations such as mass rallies erupted in support of her, throughout the country. Social Media posts inundated platforms. However, Georgia Mpika is a Thessaloniki-victim, intra-group friends posted and interacted less intensely, comparing with Mpekatorou's case. However, many took to the streets to protest with fervour against her rape. In addition, many dramatic live events occurred, which were concurrently covered in friends' Facebook activity. Several friends were more preoccupied with, and posted more, on the high number of 21 atrocious femicides in the country during 2021, which overshadowed her rape case. Due also to the pandemic's effects, intra-group posting activity scored comparatively lower on this second case.

(i). *Posted contents* covered all possible kinds of expressions. Texts, lyrics, pictures, videos, cartoons, graphs, news clips, music clips, interviews, webinar announcements, articles, commentary, critique on missing policies. Some posts astonished with originality of design and ingenuity. Many were informative, eye-catching, even eye-opening. Re-posts of personal story tales exposed feelings of pain, depression, fear, empathy, compassion and defiance. A connecting red thread that emerged was the topic of bitterness against the corrupt society. Defiance and attacks were directed against commercial TV-channels which ceaselessly promoted models of 'consumable pathetic women', notably through ongoing 'reality shows'. The media were blamed for cultivating suspicions against both rape and femicide victims, as well as against everyday liberated women. Such an ongoing discursive social battle was fought by Social Media users, including our twenty 'friends', against all those who were misconstruing female victimhood, those who denied it, misrecognized its nature or underestimated its dimensions.[17]

Posts attacked those who propound stereotypical notions like 'women go asking for it'. Many activist 'friends' posts called directly for people to speak out, to report assaults and to turn to available facilities to get help, and be rescued from violence, fear of violence and fear of fear. Several posts dealt with the issue of female feelings of guilt. Longer discursive posts elaborated on values or definitions of key notions such as 'patriarchy'. They explained gender stereotypes, or argued against 'disapproved conducts' for women. Text-posts rationalized or argued against tolerating sexist practices. Thus, such posts enlightened the more ambivalent or ignorant friends, and encouraged them. Certain females emerged as more enthusiastic and diligent posters than others, and got rewarded.

(ii). *Harvesting 'Likes Etcetera'*: Overall, reactions received were few, certainly less than anticipated. Disappointingly fewer than female 'friends', even in the face of some brilliantly inventive posts. This numerically disappointing outcome, on such a prominent issue, is perplexing, as most female friends rarely exceed the ceiling of 50–100 'likes etcetera'. Yet, of those receiving poor feedback, most insisted on carrying on posting and uploading material, even in the face of very scant feedback.[18] In terms of positioning, for the most part, responses concurred with rather than challenged posts. Not surprisingly, reactions received in the form of 'likes etcetera' were meagre also in the numerous closed feminist sub-groups. This was probably due to dispersion of forces and the multiplicity of operating feminist collectivities. Interestingly, most male friends scored comparatively higher in reactions than females, on their 'feminist' contents. So, 'gender attention' inequality was manifest here also. As the focus of this study is essentially qualitative, the proportional estimates are tentative or summarized in nature.

The study revealed the need for an exhaustive quantitative monitoring of Facebook friends' pages. Such a study, which is not within the scope of this indicative chapter, would consider, *inter alia*: (a) total number of friends of each friend, correlating it with fractions of received 'reactions'; (b) percentage of posts addressed to the broader public *versus* those addressed to circles of 'own friends' or to narrower, closed sub-groups; (c) sketches of the two circles of those examined, who are mutual friends, as opposed to those who are not;

---

[17] A multiplicity of webinars dealt with such engaging topics. Indicatively: https://www.dinfo.gr/%cf%84%ce%bf-%cf%83%cf%85%ce%b3%ce%ba%ce%b9%ce%bd%ce%b7%cf%84%ce%b9%ce%ba%cf%8c-%ce%b2%ce%af%ce%bd%cf%84%ce%b5%ce%bf-%cf%84%ce%bf%cf%85-%ce%bd%ce%b7%cf%80%ce%b9%ce%b1%ce%b3%cf%89%ce%b3%ce%b5%ce%af/

[18] Signs of some tiredness and diminishing of efforts emerged, but no total retreat was recorded.

(d) attempts at closer interpretative and numerical analysis of users' identifiable aims and targets of their posts directed towards the variety of Facebook 'publics'; (e) total individual scores of received reactions in comparison to the estimated average of 'the twenty'; (f) determining a calibrated 'critical mass', for the advancement of the movement. These data could help in concretizing parameters of tracing 'lasting digital bonding' and organization. Such objectives can be pursued in a comprehensive future study.

(iii). *Reverse outward reactions*: How do intra-group friends react to peers in terms of 'likes etcetera'? When examining reactions to peers' posts in terms of the typical list of 'likes-etcetera', results confirm mutuality regarding approvals or disapprovals. Certainly, reactions in terms of 'likes etcetera' were delivered broadly and repeatedly. Findings on this count are randomly confirmed. This is partly due to variable categories of posts, including: (a) for the general Facebook public, (b) for all one's friends, and (c) exclusively for closed sub-groups friends. Moreover, estimates here derive partly from what has been described as a hybrid participant observation practice (Lupton, 2015).

(iv). *Reception of Comments*: Comments do appear but only occasionally. Content-wise, comments concerned points of clarification, requests of specification through examples, or expressions of explicit agreement or approval. Such comments then, were instrumental in reassuring each other, and in creating trust and mutuality. Essential, non-trivial comments, especially of the kind that might launch a rich or liberating dialogue were rare. Reciprocity and overlapping of views and attitudes emerged clearly in the intra-group. Questionings, ironic comments, and other challenges appeared often, but from others, of the secondary, wider circle of friends. So, there emerged a visible index of reinforcement of the intra-group-coherence.

(v). *Sharing and Reciprocating*: Sharing took place among most, if not all intra-group friends. Generally, it is a popular practice. Whenever this practice is mutually reciprocal, it provides foundations of bonding. Many regularly reposted relevant news, or striking controversial opinions. Significantly, some male friends uploaded posts by females and vice versa, an activity indicating maturity, freedom from prejudices, while promoting a sense of cohesion around commonly shared humanist principles. The more systematically engaged and engaging friends, almost always, belonged to some organized collectivity, such as the feminist groups: 'Phylis', 'Feminist network', 'Rosa', 'Purple' (Mauve) or to political parties.

(vi). *Developing dialogue*: As regards capacity to induce dialogue, attempts at such practices did occur, especially among the more diligent, engaged or agitative friends. Yet, it was only at the beginners' stage. Interestingly, initiatives that could raise advanced discussions, received applause and signals of gratification. Nevertheless, not much further ensued in the way of essential responses. Rarely do comments concern essential controversies. Nor do they venture to settle ongoing legal contestations. Did any of the intra-group friends publish posts provoking any significant effects, thereby acting as Social Media influencers or even as agents of intermedia agenda-setting[19]? Scarcely. Whenever such ambitious posts did appear, they failed to get due feedback. This quest relates to the capacity to advance serious e.g. policy related discourse. However, such outcome depended on collective capabilities. Nevertheless, this 'count' required attention, because our 'friends' are journalism graduates or practicing journalists.

Yet, no such signs exist. Lack of experience and an *ethos* of declining dialogue could explain this. A lively public debate was ongoing, concurrently, on whether to officially adopt the term '*femicide*'. There were re-posts about it, but no adequate posts from among the friends' group. Occasional, opinions in singled out manifesto-posts appeared concerning feminist ideological and political issues. These indicated that advancing gender equality could be promoted through constitutional civic equality measures, by launching explicit *equity* and 'positive discrimination' actions.

Gender Differences: An observable difference is that females generally posted more frequently than males. Some friends posted every day and some even several times per day. More often than not, posts derived from lived or testified experiences of *victimhood* and gender-violence;[20] or they elaborated on the causes of sex-related violence and victimhood, in conjunction with the sharp rise of femicide cases. Suggestions about practical self-help measures and group-solidarity information flowed abundantly. They contained tips about sheltering options and legal aid provisions.

Comparisons appear between national and global trends, but also between cultural differences and diverse religious approaches. Conversely, male friends challenged social conventions and tended to focus on matters of human rights, 'theoretically' or in principle rather than linking them to concrete incidents. They criticized taboos and oppressive conduct conventions and rejected stereotypes and prejudices. Thus, observed counter-distinctions between females' and males' interactions were informative and surprising.

Personalities: For movements to secure solid organization, progress and continuity they require leadership. Without such life-infusing power, movements wither away. So, were there any leaders emerging through this Greek 'MeToo' movement segment? Among the intra-group friends, signs of nascent

---

[19] This may seem so, but it is not excessive to expect from Social Media users, considering that G. Mpika's affair got known only thanks to the post by activist Elias Gionis on Instagram, who revealed the case and defended her valiantly.

[20] Such instances are correlated with higher unemployment, dependency and powerlessness among younger women.

leadership surfaced. Indications of leadership tendencies emerged from some posts. Although forging gender equality is often seen as primarily a female task and the terrain for social battles, both male and female 'friends' demonstrated beneficial yet distinguishable posting profiles. Given the peculiarity and the specificity of the 'Me Too' movement, this outcome is interesting.

Estimates of potential leadership were based on traits of boldness, dynamism and quality of launched discourses. Leadership shines through capacity for advanced analysis and comprehensive persuasive power; qualities which supersede digital platform performance. It can be reflected in or derived from popularity in terms of 'likes etcetera' and appeals fetched in reactions on Social Media. This is a test of digital attraction power exerted on friends of both sexes. Leading personalities belong to a rare breed, conditional on extraordinary charisma, which is neither generously afforded, nor evenly distributed. They can elucidate obscure and complicated matters and argue convincingly about them. They advance affirmative action vigorously, postulating on conflicts and contestable issues. They can introduce dialogue and raise participation through posts, responses and shares, but especially through inspiring and mobilizing engagement.

This is a contestable terrain of vital rights and identity claims, largely misrecognized in women. Many among the 'left democratic forces' do not recognize yet, that women are the harshest hit and the new underclass of digital capitalism. Even if interlinked concurrently with major other social conflicts or battles, the subjugation of women must be addressed *per se*.

Group Cohesion: A commitment to posting feminist and gender related materials was confirmed. Posts were demonstrable during the core periods, with the exception of the observed comparative 'slump' in Mpika's case. Overall traffic amounts concerning anti-gender-violence and 'MeToo' posts kept growing. Advances were made in terms of frequency, diversity and in intra-group feedback. Group cohesion and ties were increasing, thereby strengthening the 'MeToo' movement and its discourses. Indeed, the total volume of contents exchanged amounted to an impressive diversity of posts provoked by the multiplicity of tragic incidents. Quite a few posts confronted opponents of the 'MeToo' movement, such as conservative or misogynist commentators, thereby reinforcing cohesion.

Such group cohesion positions members in a typical "*us versus them*" opposition.[21] Intra-group re-posts, especially when repeated, work as a reinforcing ligament and a bridge eliciting mutual support, approval and *digital social bonding*. These links portray an 'imagined identity' of interests, which could help to propel the movement into the future. Taking into consideration the trend of younger Facebook users abandoning it, to migrate to newer upbeat platforms, it was commendable that this specific group stayed put with tenacity. They used the platform actively and affirmatively, trusting that, as a digital

---

[21] This is a group assembled and created 'arbitrarily' for my research purposes. Nonetheless, metonymically, it stands for the local 'MeToo movement'.

platform, it produces results. Combining this with belonging to both a 'real' and an 'imagined community can intensify the impact of the movement considerably. Such combined impact empowers individuals expressively; it advances solidarity, validates emulation and encourages public interventions. Conversely, those less willing to team up and to join groups such as this one, stay loose.

Some male and female 'intra-group' friends are affiliated to LGBTQ collectivities, or are sympathetic with LGBTQ communities which, consistently, denounce sex-violence crimes. The common ground among them all is the defense of human and individual rights. All empathize with victims and project the 'MeToo' movement as a common cause. Heterosexual male feminists also emerged in the intra-group of friends, and act strongly in support of the 'MeToo' movement.

In summing, female intra-group friends received positive ratings on the three (out of five standard) primary considerations. The same applies for all but two of the males. Overall. internal differences and fluctuations, observable more clearly among female friends, lead to a four-level taxonomy:

- Firstly, those mindful of equality and fair gender relations, but who did not express this often or publish on the topic.
- Secondly, those who care about feminist values, but who fit in along with many other post-types, prioritizing individual projects. They make a weaker '*type A group*'.
- Thirdly, those posting regularly on gender equality and feminist issues, identifying the regime of *patriarchy* as a core political challenge. They belong to a medium '*type B group*'.
- Fourthly, those who are 'proper' activists; highly conscious of underlying political economy conflicts and controversies and who are particularly diligent activists. They act as consistent and creative agents in such ongoing controversies, committed strategically to the objectives of the 'cause' of gender equality. They form an advanced '*type C group*'.

These sub-groups were roughly equal in numbers within the 'friends' group, and their gradations defined levels of activity and commitment to the cause of gender equality or 'the movement', charting a weaker-to-stronger engagement scale. The most vocal and brilliant, even inspired posts emanated from the third 'type C group' which is strongly represented. Respectively, most male friends were positioned between type A and B groups, with the exception of two males who emerged as strong and active feminists. There exist then many communicationally and persuasively advanced activists. The question is whether their numbers and equivalents can attain the indispensable *critical public mass* to make a major difference in the struggle against gender-violence.

Discussing Findings

During the second decade of the twenty-first century, the digitally borne 'MeToo' movement became globally prominent. Indeed, it spread across several "countries and continents" (Starkey et al., 2019, p. 437). Eventually, it arrived in Greece, intensely preoccupying people's attention. Digital social exchanges about it generated a remarkable 'digital emotional proximity', promising opportunities for forging new terrains to negotiate social and gender equality.

The Covid-19 pandemic effected locked-downs and living conditions which augmented domestic violence and femicides in Greece and elsewhere. These in turn propelled the eruption of the 'MeToo' movement, which, in Greece, was triggered originally by Mpekatorou's notorious rape-case. Posts, discursive elaborations and projections by the twenty young friends whose on-line posts were reviewed, are regarded as informative in a number of ways. Although content-monitoring extended only over two months, nonetheless, this case-study offers some indicative findings. Posts reviewed gave glimpses of *interactions* among friends and provided the stock for assessments. Certainly, the total output resulted from the *interplay* between these prosumers and the internet's systemic algorithms (Noortje, 2017, p. 64 & 74).

This underlines the importance of correlating *functional* and *structural* parts. So, the question arises as to what extent do friends achieve positive outcomes, such as *influence*? Most intra-group friends received poor feedback and achieved few Facebook followers. This pessimistic assessment concerns females more. Since Social Media users strive for recognition, also in terms of the 'right to be heard', reactions and any kind of feedback to their posts was critical. For the dynamic, ambitious graduates, such limited responses were disenchanting, obliging them to realize that Social Media popularity and influence are hard to get, requiring consistent, but perhaps also more intuitive 'prosumer work'. To fulfill their goals, they need to keep trying: to reach out, interact and connect. Especially, since they are linked with communication sectors and are obliged to carry on communicating smartly.

The harsh social controversies about sexism and gender violence are nowadays preoccupying people in the public sphere of Greece. Feminist friends enjoin those capable of doing so to dare *speak out* on these controversial issues. Many established public speakers raise gender-equality to the fore, trying to keep it high on the agenda. Writers publish reasoned articles elucidating the intricate and contestable problems that result in femicides. However, most of our young intra-group friends rarely broke through with striking posts on these centrally contestable issues, to elicit discussion. Such outcomes reveal possible timidity and powerlessness; conversely, also indifference and passivity of the targeted online segment of society to the cause.

Expressions of formerly suppressed feelings now figure regularly. They are overshadowed by sadness or despair. Overcoming that guilt and fear must be the prevailing response even among younger Greek women. The long-persisting ethos of 'silence' operating through multi-layered 'spirals of silence' (Noelle-Neumann, 1984) curbed many women's urge to 'cry freedom'. Fear to speak out in public, on controversial issues, results in a self-censoring, which was evident on Facebook. Yet, the sense prevails among 'friends' that personality stifling and limitations of freedom[22] cannot be tolerated.

Female predicaments and 'specificity' suggest that women should empathize and mobilize themselves. The other side of the coin, 'male specificity' implies that since it is arguably only men who can rape, they often emerge as the enemies. The logical fallacy is the syndrome of treating the fraction (of rapists), as if they were the totality (of men). Indeed, proportionately, a considerable number of males speak out loudly on *feminist-humanist* claims, in argumentative, challenging ways, including on cases of rape and femicides.[23]

Whenever sympathetic responses come from male friends, they are welcomed as positive blessings, elevated to the category of affirmative humanist stances. Today, many more men realize that *gender equality* is a precondition for social peace; for the 'general humanist interest' and that this is the only way to rescue human relations and advance humanity. A strong need, then arises, for more male feminists! To the extent that such reinforcing intra-group interactions are reflective of a more global pattern, hope exits.

One research quest relates to *activist influencers*, as needed by the movement. As regards opportunities exploited for public discourse, it is remarkable that only a few among intra-group friends, opted for benefiting from the tremendous opportunities of '*isegoria*' supplied by Social Media, even if conditionally to deploy their own claims discursively. Few users, and fewer women, post propositions strategically. That is, explicitly aiming at influencing, or stirring others. Even fewer post critical statements. Evidently, criticism itself causes fear and is treated as a taboo, particularly concerning contestable, thorny issues. One young woman in the friends group defied such tendencies and stood out as a potential leader. She is intellectually powerful, expresses vision, tenacity of conviction, critical views, readiness for confrontation to pursuit of goals. Others strive, with feeble results. Facebook sociograms do not reward them, suggesting a deeply rooted misogyny, even among women, as part of 'the power regime'. It would appear that even outstandingly competent women could remain discursively and literally suppressed.

Given the interest in questions of *gender equality* among the intra-group friends, one could anticipate more ardent reciprocity in cross-postings and cross-transferals of positions. This happened to some extent, yet, not frequently enough to mark 'the difference'. Interactions which foster fear, defensiveness

---

[22] This tendency ties in with trends in classroom dialogue, where a minority of female students claim the floor to speak. Conversely, male students speak publicly regularly. This 'pathology' is reflected largely among Facebook friends.

[23] https://www.theguardian.com/global-development/2021/nov/09/greek-campaign-domestic-violence-femicides

or which hurt people can result in accruing *solidarity*. They might create the bases for the future dynamic movements of the twenty-first century. However, it seems, some fundamental parameters are still missing. Friendly cross-postings and more systematic liaisons for the sake of the 'cause' occurred, but never took off strongly. Despite the study's limitations, such findings suggest that digital options for associating firmly may remain modest. Feeble or elusive outcomes counteract efforts and objectives to further engage more effectively for a 'common cause'. They confer a passing, volatile progress, irrespective of high levels of rhetorical and communicative activity invested. Obviously, the structural foundations of the internet, that is, of addressing users individually, at a distance, thereby fragmenting and weakening 'publics' (Kaitatzi-Whitlock, 2013, 2021; Olsson, 2014) matter, and need constantly to be taken into consideration. Customized services split people, undermining common causes. While touted as benefits of a new individualized media, audience atomization can also be powerful and its corrosive traits cannot be underestimated.

Much of this dialogue on the values inherent in emerging technologies should be taking place within and outside of universities, as intellectual venues and enlightening discursive spaces, including for liberation movements. Students, as an online active part of such institutions, often live in precarious conditions, struggling to forge decent lives and careers. This necessity implies that there may lurk present or potential conflicts between pressing personal needs and radical ambitions which need to be negotiated, balanced out and decided individually. Moreover, perennial hurdles often arise to thwart individual and collective goals, causing some to stumble into difficulties in becoming active or building trust on virtual digital platforms, despite anonymity (Miller, 1996; Kaitatzi-Whitlock, 2021).

Nevertheless, in our study, intra-group friends published their own, strong 'MeToo' posts, thereby belonging to a proactive or reactive category of graduate users. Normally social interactions of this nature construct and strengthen connections and may progressively result in bonding of a lasting nature. To what extent could this sustained bonding hold true for our Social Media friends? This remains still an open question.

Conclusion

As both physical and online (digitally-assisted) sex violence crimes are soaring by all accounts, including such official reports as that done by the Internet Organised Crime Threat Assessment (IOCTA, 2020), this study has explored how online platforms can provide tools for an active defense against them. This 'MeToo' content analysis revolved around three objectives. It aimed to chart concrete utilizations of the Facebook platform by a group of twenty young graduates and to assess their interactions through their posts and results. It also sought to monitor the flow of such activity, under the impact of concurrently ongoing crises: the Covid-19 pandemic and the femicides-crisis in Greece. The study also explored options for sustainable forms of sociability and of fostering novel types of digital solidarity and bonding.

In monitoring Facebook interactions and posts among these 20 users, as sparked by two pivotal 'MeToo' rape cases, I compared and assessed respective posted content relating to gender violence and society. The students' Facebook posts enabled us to assess the online reactions to these cases and crises, and to classify them in terms of their symbolic impacts and potential benefits as influencers in the struggle for gender equity in Greek society. We were able to correlate the essence of these limited Social Media experiences with the wider realities of Greek society, interrogating whether there could be a lasting and effective digital sociability and sociality.

The original rape denunciation by local media personality Sophia Mpekatorou, that triggered a social and a political quake in Greece, formed our analytical point of departure. It alerted many lethargic state institutions and citizens about the tragic harm that was being inflicted on women in the society. Yet, its immediate impact was not sustained and seemed to have taken place as a random act of outrage in Greece. Consequently, derived individual benefits were seemingly not tangible and the accompanying online outrage appeared limited in scope. Similarly, the wider social outcomes as reflected in online responses within our target group, was disappointing, and may suggest restricted foreseeable outcomes and goals.

It appears difficult, therefore, for future advocates to secure planned practical gains, or to establish concrete advances against the *status quo* on the central issues of concern, which were intended to protect and secure the public interest. Nevertheless, we can conclude that social media and its everyday digital tools played an important initial role in exposing this and other atrocities against women in Greece, as globally. These digital tools in the hands of determined gender advocates and their allies, remain powerful instruments, if used by a critical mass in the cause of equity and social transformation.

References

Akrivos, D. (2021). *'Old-fashioned alpha males' against 'professional homosexuals': media justice and discriminatory reporting in the wake of the Greek# MeToo movement*. The International Forum for Responsible Media (INFORRM).

IOCTA. (2019/2020). Internet Organized Crime Threat Assessment, Europol, EU Agency for Law Enforcement Cooperation, Brussels. Retrieved October 14, 2020, from www.europol.europa.eu.

Kaitatzi-Whitlock, S. (2013). Changing media ontology and the polity, in Pierre-François Docquir and Muriel Hanot, *Nouveaux écrans, nouvelle régulation?*, 25–54. Louvain, Larcier.

Kaitatzi-Whitlock, S. (2015). E-waste, human waste, infoflation, in Richard Maxwell, Jon Raundalen and Nina Vestberg (eds) *Media and the ecological crisis*, 69–88. Routledge Research in Cultural and Media Studies Series, New York and Oxford, Routledge.

Kaitatzi-Whitlock, S. (2021). Towards a digital civil society: Digital ethics through communication education, *Journal of Information, Communication & Ethics in Society (JICES)*, 19/ 2, 187–206.

Lupton, D. (2015), Digital sociology, London, Routledge.

Miller, S. (1996). Civilizing cyberspace: Policy, power and the information superhighway, ACM Press Books

Nielsen, J. (2006). The 90-9-1 rule for participation inequality in social media and online communities. Retrieved April 09, 2020, from www.nngroup.com/articles/participation-inequality/

Noelle-Neumann, E. (1984), The spiral of silence. Public opinion—our social skin. Chicago University Press.

Noortje, M. (2017). Digital sociology, Cambridge, Polity Press.

Olsson T. (2014). In a community, or becoming commodity? critical reflections on «social» in social media, In Media practice and everyday agency in Europe, Bremen, Kramp L. et al. (eds) Editions Lumière.

Ragnedda, M. (2017), The third digital divide: A Weberian approach to digital inequalities, Routledge, London.

Retounioti, Y. (2022). *Agenda setting and the role of Twitter: The case of #MeTooGR*, MA Dissertation, School of Journalism and Communication, Aristotle University of Thessaloniki (in Greek).

Schwartz, B. (2016), The paradox of choice: Why more is less, New York, Harper Collins.

Starkey, J. C., Koerber, A., Sternadori, M., & Pitchford, B. (2019). # MeToo goes global: Media framing of silence breakers in four national settings. Journal of Communication Inquiry, 43(4), 437–461.

Wu, T. (2010). The master switch, London, Atlantic Books.

CHAPTER 11

Non-Consensual Intimate Image Sharing on the Internet: Regulating Betrayal in Jamaica and India

Allison J. Brown

Introduction

Digital communication technologies such as the smartphone, the internet, and social media have diversified the channels, quickened the pace, and amplified the reach of everyday communications. Such transformations restructure and redefine everyday communication practices in interpersonal relationships. Among these are the everyday practices that take place in intimate relationships, including the more harmful and abusive ones. Non-consensual dissemination of intimate images (NCII), commonly referred to as revenge porn, is one such practice that is on the rise due to the rapid growth of digital tools and the internet. While the practice of sharing images of individuals without their consent is not new, online channels can be particularly potent tools for the dissemination of NCII messages that are often intended to humiliate, shame, punish, and control NCII targets. NCII over the internet introduces into the everyday a new mechanism for abuse and control of individuals, especially women and other vulnerable persons. The growing practice elicits new types of privacy concerns in the everyday performance of intimacy. The impact on the everyday lives of victims in many cases is profound, and governments globally have been responding to this harmful practice in the online environment.

NCII involves the sharing of sexually graphic images or videos of someone without their consent. NCII is growing in its incidence and therefore

A. J. Brown (✉)
Indiana University Bloomington, Bloomington, IN, USA

© The Author(s), under exclusive license to Springer Nature Switzerland AG 2024
H. S. Dunn et al. (eds.), *The Palgrave Handbook of Everyday Digital Life*,
https://doi.org/10.1007/978-3-031-30438-5_11

becoming an everyday concern for individuals (Bates, 2017, p. 2; Snaychuk & O'Neill, 2020, p. 984), and its regulation has been a concern for governments worldwide. The rise in smartphone use is one reason for the growth of NCII occurrence, since smartphones enable individuals to easily capture, store, and transmit digital photos with minimal barriers. NCII is not unique to the internet or social media. For example, early cases have been documented in the magazine *Hustler* that published nude photos of women that were often submitted by their spurned lovers (Poole, 2015, p. 186). However, given the speed and ever-growing reach of the internet, it makes the objectionable images shared non-consensually more accessible and there is the possibility to do more harm to victims. In addition, since more individuals have access to the tools relevant to the creation and dissemination of intimate images, NCII over the internet is becoming more of an everyday occurrence globally.

Several governments have noted NCII over the internet as a legal and policy issue to be addressed. Some governments have sought to address this problem through various laws and policies, meanwhile others have bills under review, and other governments have not addressed this problem through law or policy at all. This chapter considers how NCII laws have been enforced in Jamaica and India by analyzing two legal cases of NCII, the Donovan Powell case in Jamaica (Powell v. R, 2021) and the Animesh Boxi case in India (State of West Bengal v. Boxi, 2018), to discuss the issues and challenges that remain unresolved on the matter of NCII. Both cases demonstrate the way that digital tools can be engaged to enact intimate partner abuse. They also demonstrate the way NCII can impact on the everyday life of victims. Through the analysis of legal documents, along with news and media items, the chapter will identify areas of challenge and key considerations for NCII-relevant policy making and regulation. The objective of this analysis is to make the everyday impacts of NCII more legible and to elucidate prevailing challenges with its regulation.

New Everyday Terms

With the upsurge of NCII cases in everyday romantic relationships, new terms have entered the everyday vocabulary that are specifically relevant to this harmful content practice. In addition, there are ongoing debates on the appropriate naming of the practice of NCII that will likely shape the everyday language that will be used to name it in the future. Policy scholars and advocates are concerned with how this practice is named (as detailed in Maddocks, 2019) since the naming of the practice can influence perceptions of NCII, perceptions of NCII victims, and the way the practice is regulated. 'Revenge porn' is a commonly used term for NCII. However, it is now widely considered to be a misnomer among legal and policy scholars because revenge is not the only motive for the non-consensual sharing of intimate images (Henry et al., 2017, p. 3). Further, Citron and Franks (2014) argue that the term 'revenge' implies that the perpetrator is somehow justified for acting after being wronged in some way. Consequently, 'revenge porn' is a term likely to encourage victim blaming, casting the responsibility for NCII on the victim while failing to recognize that NCII was a violation embarked on by the offender.

While scholars later began using the term "non-consensual pornography" (e.g., Citron & Franks, 2014) for the practice being discussed, the term pornography has been considered to have the connotation that the content was created and/or shared with the consent of the participants for entertainment (Henry et al., 2017, p. 3). In addition, the sharing of sexual images of a person can be deemed a sexual act that requires consent. This has led to the introduction of other terms for this practice that emphasize the 'consent' aspect, or the lack thereof, including terms such as NCII, 'image-based sexual abuse', and 'cyber rape') (see Maddocks, 2018). More recently scholars have begun to emphasize that this practice is entangled with patterns of intimate partner violence, thus introducing another term, 'technology-facilitated sexual violence' (see Henry & Powell, 2018).

The introduction of new terms such as revenge porn and NCII into everyday conversations as well as the ongoing debate on the naming of NCII demonstrate the continuation of the transformation of our environments and interactions with the introduction of digital tools. Revenge porn and NCII are now new terms entering everyday discourse, and increasingly, these practices are experienced by ordinary citizens as they perform everyday romantic interactions. As noted, NCII is not a practice that was introduced with the internet. But terms such as NCII and revenge porn are usually associated with the online environment since this is the venue where these infractions have often been carried out. Further developments are anticipated with the prospect of new emerging manifestations of NCII and similar practices, which will continue to shape everyday discourse and debates and require regulation by governments as appropriate.

Defining NCII

For this chapter, I will use the term non-consensual dissemination of intimate images or NCII which is a term that is increasing in use among internet policy scholars that I consider to be an appropriate description of the range of practices under consideration in this chapter. Notwithstanding my settlement here on the term non-consensual dissemination of intimate images or NCII, the definition for non-consensual pornography has been adapted here to define NCII. Citron and Franks define non-consensual pornography as, "the distribution of sexually graphic images of individuals without their consent. This includes images originally obtained without consent … as well as images originally obtained with consent, usually within the context of a private or confidential relationship" (2014, p. 346). The elements of this definition will constitute my definition of the term NCII as follows:

1. the image(s) must be 'distributed' or shared with at least one other person (other than the offender and the victim),

2. consent has not been given (by the person who is photographed or video-recorded) for the distribution of the image(s),
3. The image(s) must be sexually graphic,
4. The image(s) may have been originally shared to the distributor within the context of a 'private or confidential' relationship, however this is not always the case.

There are several possible permutations that NCII might take in everyday life. Intimate images of victims sometimes originate as images that have been shared with romantic partners (such as in the case of sexting), but later shared without the knowledge and/or permission of the victim. In some cases, victims are unaware that the intimate images even exist, such as wherever the images have been captured by the perpetrator in secret. Otherwise, intimate images captured consensually during sexual encounters are later shared, or the intimate images of sexual encounters can be acquired without the permission of the victim and then later shared. Although the situations described here are not necessarily unique to romantic relationships, they are among the most frequently cited permutations noted in the NCII cases in romantic relationships. Although NCII is an issue that emerges regularly in everyday romantic relationships, it is not only committed by current or former romantic partners. It is also committed by persons with some other vendetta of some type, and sometimes even strangers. As digital technology continues to advance, more new ways of enacting NCII may make its way into everyday practice and introduce new challenges to keeping track of and controlling the problem.

Everyday Impacts of NCII

NCII is a significant and far-reaching practice in the information society that affects the everyday lives of individual victims. Hundreds of revenge porn websites exist and social media apps such as Facebook and WhatsApp often act as conduits for NCII (Haynes, 2018, p. 405). Globally the prevalence of NCII victimization has been measured from a range of one per cent in Spain (Gámez-Guadix et al., 2015, p. 149), to two per cent in the US (Lenhart et al., 2016, p. 4), to about 20 per cent in a three-country study of the United Kingdom, New Zealand, and Australia (Powell et al., 2020, p. 3). Women, persons under 30 and persons identifying as LGBTQ are more likely to experience NCII (Snaychuk & O'Neill, 2020, p. 984, Lenhart et al., 2016, p. 16; Powell et al., 2020, p. 4).

One reason for the continuous growth of NCII is sexting, which has become an everyday communication practice within the context of intimate relationships enabled by digital technology. Sexting is "the sharing of personal, sexually suggestive text messages, or nude or nearly nude photographs or videos via electronic devices" (Mori et al., 2020, p. 1103). In the US, 21% of adults reported sending sext messages, while 28% reported receiving sexts (Garcia et al., 2016, p. 428). Meanwhile a global study found that over half the respondents reported engaging in sexting (about 58%) (Gesselman et al., 2020, p. 8). The practice is increasingly becoming a normal, everyday component of romantic relationships (Drouin et al., 2017, p. 754). As a result, individuals are increasingly engaging in the practices that make them susceptible to NCII. Sext messages, such as intimate photos and videos which are commonly shared among romantic partners, can potentially be the material that emerges in NCII cases if the intimate images are shared non-consensually.

For victims, numerous negative impacts can affect their everyday lives. With access to intimate images, ill-intentioned individuals may attempt to extort NCII targets. This practice, which is commonly known as sextortion, has become an everyday consideration for individuals online as the population of the information society continues to grow. Sextortion is "the act of threatening to expose a nude or sexually explicit image to get a person to do something such as share more nude or sexually explicit images, pay someone money, or perform sexual acts" (Cyber Civil Rights Initiative, 2022a). While NCII may include sextortion, "sextortion is essentially the *threat* to expose a sexual image to coerce the victim into doing something, even if exposure of the image never actually occurs" (emphasis in original, Wolak et al., 2018, p. 73). Online sextortion (the threat to release images) often precedes the actual unauthorized sharing of intimate images on the internet and so it can be a component of the practice of NCII. While sextortion may have parallels in the non-digital world, digital tools allow those who commit sextortion to reach out to their targets more easily, allow them the potential to share the images more widely and offer a greater speed of transmitting the harmful content. Given the wide reach of the internet, such threats may be very potent in achieving the purpose of extortion and the threats themselves could cause emotional harm to the sextortion target.

NCII can lead to depression, humiliation, and reputational harm (Bates, 2017). Some NCII victims face termination of employment, cessation of schooling, social withdrawal, and ostracism (Bates, 2017). In different cases, victims have also committed suicide (see Baker, 2016; Berger, 2013; The Local, 2019). Further, the practice and control of NCII is interrelated with individual rights to privacy (Maddocks, 2018, p. 349) and rights to sexual autonomy (Patton, 2015, p. 411). NCII is an affront to the victim's right to choose. In many cases offenders are menacing the victim to shame, humiliate them, and control the victim's actions and choices. The practice of NCII is therefore one that can disrupt the everyday lives of those targeted in significant ways as digital technologies extend the abilities of ill-intentioned individuals to abuse and violate the rights of victims. Digital communication technologies are increasingly being used as the new conduits to perform such violations.

Romantic relationships are often mediated by digital communication technology not only in benign situations but also in abusive ones. In some cases, NCII allows the internet to form a channel through which intimate partner violence can take place (Eaton et al., 2021, p. 5). NCII is often a strategy for coercion and control, intended to violate and invade personal space thereby inhibiting the autonomy of victims. This includes the autonomy to leave their current romantic relationship or to move on to a new one (Bloom, 2014, p. 237). As the everyday performance of romantic relationships is enabled through digital communication technologies, so too is the everyday performance of abuse and control that sometimes exist therein. This includes the enactment of NCII through digital channels.

Vulnerable persons are more likely to experience NCII's most harmful effects which can impact how victims participate in the online environment. NCII is more often experienced by women (Snaychuk & O'Neill, 2020, p. 984) and women are more likely to be featured on non-consensual pornographic websites (Uhl et al., 2018, p. 50). Because of the persistence of victim blaming, women are more likely to suffer negative mental health effects after being targeted for NCII (Bates, 2017, p. 22) and they often suffer reputational harm due to patriarchally informed associations made between a woman's sexual activities and her character. NCII victims in non-heterosexual relationships are also more susceptible to emotional harm (and even possibly physical harm). This is important context for understanding the way that the information society is developing. As more vulnerable and marginalized persons find themselves exposed to NCII, this could have a silencing effect where such individuals withdraw from participation in the information society. For Langlois and Slane, NCII is a type of networked violence that "deeply and perhaps irreparably, shapes and short-circuits the victim's capacity to define [themself] online" (2017, p. 11) and can result in a loss of online subjectivity as the non-consensually shared images come to 'stand in' for the victim's online self. This can result in an 'internet exile' where victims limit their interaction with the online world, ultimately limiting the victim's everyday participation in the online environment, and thereby reducing victims' opportunities for self-expression and reducing victims' access to benefits of online participation.

Global Regulation of NCII

Given the wide reach of NCII and the burgeoning negative impacts, internet policy makers have enacted laws and policies that serve to regulate everyday instances of NCII. Several jurisdictions have regulations. Neris et al.'s study (2015, pp. 9–10) of 27 countries revealed that the majority of countries surveyed regulate NCII through non-specific laws, meaning laws that do not directly address NCII. Some governments have enacted specific laws to address NCII, such as the Philippines, Israel, Japan, and the United Kingdom. Others have bills for NCII-specific laws pending. Forty-eight US States, Washington DC and two US territories have laws regulating NCII (Cyber Civil Rights Initiative, 2022b). No federal law exists in the US; however, two bills have been proposed in Congress: The Intimate Privacy Protection Act and the Protecting the Rights of Individuals Against Technological Exploitation Act. Both Jamaica and India regulate NCII through non-specific laws, the Cyber Crime Act of 2015 in the case of Jamaica and in India the Indian Penal Code of 1890 (2013 Amendment) and the Information Technology Act of 2000 (2008 Amendment).

NCII is a serious problem that enacts sexual violence and harms women and vulnerable groups disproportionately. It is one of the mechanisms where abusive activities are enacted in the online world. The control of this everyday practice is becoming very important for governments since NCII is potentially limiting to the rights of those who experience it. For the remainder of this chapter, I turn to cases from Jamaica and India where there exist laws that address NCII, with a view to understanding what challenges persist in the regulation of this practice and the ways to offer further protection for targets of NCII as they carry out their everyday lives using digital tools on the internet.

The Jamaican Case

Background

Jamaica is a parliamentary democracy and constitutional monarchy. It is a Commonwealth realm of the United Kingdom. Jamaica is a sovereign state that retains the UK monarch as its Head of State. It is an upper-middle income country (World Bank, 2020) with a population of 2,697,983 in 2011 (Statistical Institute of Jamaica, 2014).

NCII is a practice that affects the everyday lives of some Jamaicans. Intimate images are often disseminated non-consensually via WhatsApp or Facebook. Common motives are "separation of partners and instances of distrust and disloyalty, including cheating" (Haynes, 2018, p. 405). Law enforcement officers in Jamaica note that NCII instances are underreported, particularly among male victims. It is also underreported because it is not widely known among Jamaicans that NCII can be a criminal offense (Haynes, 2018, p. 405). Jamaica regulates NCII through a non-specific law, the Cybercrime Act of 2015, which criminalizes NCII. No specific laws have been incorporated in Jamaica to govern the practice of NCII. The Donovan Powell case demonstrates how NCII can be enacted in the course of an intimate partnership, how the practice can impact on the everyday life of the victim, and how regulatory mechanisms were engaged to address the case.

The Donovan Powell Case

Donovan Powell is a Jamaican man who was in a romantic relationship with Darieth Chisolm, an American news anchor. While they were together Powell took photos of Chisolm including nude photos that he took of her without her knowledge while she was sleeping. When the relationship ended Powell threatened that she would be "shot, stabbed, ruined, or destroyed" (*Powell v. R*, p. 2) if she did not return to the relationship. In her TED Talk, she described months of cyber-harassment meted out by Powell to have her return to Jamaica and resume their relationship (Chisolm, 2018).

In March 2017, Powell sent Chisolm a text message telling her to look at a website where he had posted her nude photos and he threatened to make the website public. The court documents note that he threatened to kill her if she did not rekindle the relationship (*Powell v. R*, p. 7). Powell later published the website and sent the website to some of Chisolm's professional and other contacts. Chisolm first learned that the website had gone public when she received a phone call from her ex-husband who directed her to the website. In her own words:

> My manipulative, jealous, stalker ex-boyfriend did exactly what he said he would do: he put up a website with my name on it and posted ... several explicit photos that he had taken of me while I was asleep, living with him in Jamaica. (Chisolm, 2018)

Chisolm was faced with extreme distress and the court documents note that:

> She explained that this was the worse time of her life, as his actions made her feel ashamed, humiliated, and reduced her ability to gain employment as a television show host and speaker. She further explained that she was affected emotionally and mentally. (*Powell v. R*, p. 7)

In 2019, Donovan Powell pled guilty to two charges of using a computer to send obscene data to Chisolm "with the intention to cause harm or to harass" her (p. 5). He also pled guilty to one charge of sending obscene data to the victim and "persons unknown" via a website (p. 5). These are criminal charges in the category of malicious communication under the Jamaica Cybercrimes Act of 2015. Powell was sentenced to one year in prison and a fine of J$1,000,000 (about US$6500) for two counts of malicious communication and was also sentenced to serve four months in prison concurrently for a third count. Later, on appeal his sentence was reduced to six months and the fine was reduced to J$500,000 (about US$3250) after an examination of the mitigating and aggravating factors.

The law that was applied was the Cybercrimes Act of 2015, which had been in effect for four years at the time of the conviction. The Act, which replaced an older 2010 version, included a new section that criminalized malicious communication using a computer:

> 9.--{1) A person commits an offence if that person- (a) uses a computer to send to another person any data (whether in the form of a message or otherwise) that is obscene, constitutes a threat, or is menacing in nature; and (b) intends to cause, or is reckless as to whether the sending of the data causes, annoyance, inconvenience, distress, or anxiety, to that person or any other person.

Following the sentencing of Powell, Chisolm posted on social media:

> Yes! Yes .... finally victory in my case!!! I've fought for over two years to win my international case of revenge porn and cyber harassment and now, with the help of U.S. Homeland Security Investigations Special Agents, The Jamaican Constabulary Force and The Office of the Director of Public Prosecution in Jamaica, it's over. (Chisolm, 2019)

While this was a victory for Chisolm, the judge in the Jamaican Appeals Court noted an inadequacy while making the final assessment of the appeal:

> We are compelled to comment on the fact that the fine, which can be viewed as the lesser punishment, was imposed for the most egregious act of creating the website ... the imposition of this sentence seemed not to fully reflect the serious nature of this offence when compared with the first two. (*Powell v. R*, p. 19)

The judge's comments note that the building of the website which exposed Chisolm to the greatest measure of humiliation and potential harm, did not receive a harsh enough punishment. This suggests that revision of the punishment for building a website could add further protections for NCII victims.

THE INDIAN CASE

Background

India is a parliamentary democracy and federal republic. It consists of 28 states and eight union territories. Like Jamaica, India is a former colony of the United Kingdom and is a member of the Commonwealth of Nations. It is a lower-middle income country (World Bank, 2020) with a population of 1,210,854,977 in 2011 (Census, 2011).

India regulates NCII through non-specific laws, specifically through the Indian Penal Code of 1890 (2013 Amendment) and the Information Technology Act of 2000 (2008 Amendment), although specific laws have not been enacted in India to govern the practice of NCII. In spite of the existing regulation, NCII continues to affect the everyday lives of Indians. Deb notes that "the lack of awareness, training, care, and resources to help enforce and protect" needs to be addressed alongside the current legislation (2020, p. 19). Underreporting is common, prompted by the shame that stems from cultural notions of feminine propriety, since victims are more commonly women. While female NCII victims in India can request a female police officer at the time of reporting the crime, as a way of mitigating the shame associated with making such reports, this information is not widely known (Dasgupta, 2017). Similar to the Powell case in Jamaica, the Animesh Boxi case is one that demonstrates the everyday impact of NCII and its regulation in India.

The Animesh Boxi Case

In December 2018, a 23 year-old Indian man, Animesh Boxi, was convicted for NCII in India (State of West Bengal v. Boxi, 2018). Boxi was a mechanical engineering student at the Budge Budge Institute of Technology. He was in a relationship with the victim for three years. While in the relationship Boxi had requested nude photos from the victim, however the victim declined to send any photos. Eventually, the relationship ended. But even so, Boxi demanded his ex-girlfriend to go with him to Digha which is a resort town on India's coastline. When she refused to go with him, he threatened he would share explicit nude photos and video clips of her. The images were never sent to him by the victim but acquired by hacking into the victim's cell phone. During the relationship the victim had allowed him to see her phone and he also knew where she had her passwords written down. Following the victim's persistent refusals to go to Digha with him, Boxi eventually made good on his threats and posted the nude photos and videos to several websites including the Pornhub website.

According to court documents, the victim became aware that the explicit images of her were online when contacted by her "khurtuto" cousin (her father's younger brother's son), who came across the images while searching online for their shared family name. With this knowledge the victim involved her parents. She and her father reported the case to the Panskura Police Station in West Bengal. In the video itself, the victim could not be identified. But Boxi added her name and the name of her father to ensure her identifiability. However, the names of the victim and her father were not disclosed in the court case. The victim suffered extreme emotional distress as her mother was reported as saying that "her daughter was broken" in the court documents (State of West Bengal v. Boxi, 2018, p. 22). Even at the time of the trial the video was still available online. In the victim's own words: "Today my personal nude photos are spreading everywhere in this world and it is now impossible for me to live in this world" (p. 47).

Boxi was charged under several statutes and was found guilty of all charges. He was found to be guilty of the following offenses:

- Under the Indian Penal Code, he was found guilty of outraging the modesty of a woman; defamation; and intrusion of a woman's privacy.
- Under India's Information Technology Act, he was found guilty of transmitting a person's private parts without their consent; and transmitting obscene or lascivious material electronically.

Animesh Boxi's penalty was a sentence of five years in prison, and he was fined Rs. 9000 (about US$120). Boxi also was required to compensate the victim as a rape survivor under the Victim Compensation Scheme (India Today, 2018).

Challenges and Considerations

These cases describe situations where everyday romantic relationships fizzled and later became the venues for the enactment of NCII over the internet. New circumstances brought about by digital transformation have motivated the introduction of new laws that address the different possible permutations of inflicting harm on the internet. These cases give the opportunity to examine the situations in the two countries where these NCII cases were prosecuted. Comparison is possible because the cases bear some similarities. Both cases originated in a romantic relationship that had ended before the offences. These were both adult cases and the objectionable images were received by the perpetrator without the permission of the victim. The intention behind the NCII acts was to revive a relationship that had previously ended. Both cases resulted in criminal convictions. This section discusses the challenges and considerations that emerge from the analysis of these cases, specifically, the irreparable nature of harm from NCII; the need for prevention through legislation and public education; and the need to re-assess sentencing recommendations.

NCII Inflicts Irreparable Harm

The NCII events in these cases had profoundly negative impacts on the victim's everyday lives. The cases illustrate irreparable harm experienced by the victims. The Indian victim speaks to not being able to "live in this world." She is described by her mother as "broken." Chisolm spoke in her TED talk about the shame and humiliation of the NCII experience. The act of NCII cannot be undone. Victims will always be plagued with the possibility of the intimate images re-emerging in their everyday lives.

It is not likely that victims will be able to escape future encounters with the NCII violation that they experienced. Let us consider here that in each case the court documents anonymized the victim. While Chisolm has come forward and made it clear that she is the complainant in the Jamaican case, the victim of the Indian case remains anonymous. It could be argued that the choice to remain anonymous is not available to the victim in the Indian case. Details in the court documents on the name of the perpetrator, where he attended school, his phone number, the duration of the relationship with the victim, geographic locations, and other specifics make the victim identifiable. Such details invalidate any attempts to keep the victim anonymous in court documents. Indeed, if Chisolm did not reveal that she was the victim it could also be possible to identify her. The challenge here is not that the victims could be identified, but that the harm done by the offenders cannot be easily erased by anonymizing court documents. The harm done is long-standing and will likely continue to affect victims for several years (maybe for their whole lives). Once the decision is taken to maliciously release compromising images, it can never be undone. Given the potential for irreparable damage, there should be a greater focus on the prevention of NCII in everyday situations.

Emphasize Prevention and Deterrence

The analysis of cases reveals that revenge porn has the potential for long-lasting effects on victims' everyday lives, which in many cases cannot be undone by criminal prosecution and monetary compensation. While penalties can be imposed, there must also be an emphasis on prevention. Haynes speaks to legislative intervention as having a "symbolic and educative function" (Haynes, 2018, p. 426). He argues that the enactment of specific laws to address NCII would identify for the public that this behavior is prosecutable and would "clearly [reinforce] the 'wrongfulness' of revenge porn" (p. 426). As such the intervention of specific laws could act as a deterrent more so than the non-specific laws that now exist in these countries. Such interventions would provide greater control of NCII in everyday online communication.

Public education may render a useful solution to the problem of NCII. Would-be offenders could be informed that they may face criminal prosecution since the law stands behind persons who have experienced this offence. Such public education could reduce the instances of NCII and stem the growth of this practice online. On the societal level, public education is needed to broaden the understanding of NCII beyond the trite impression that it is caused by revenge and retaliation, including implications that victims have done something to deserve the offence. In the cases presented here, the offenders used extortionary measures for the purpose of controlling the victims' choice to leave the relationship. Threats to commit NCII and the execution of it often coexist with other forms of online and offline intimate partner violence. Increased public awareness of this connection is needed. Such public education may mitigate the negative impacts that victims of NCII experience in their everyday lives.

The everyday understanding of consent in relationships and sexual circumstances needs to be defined with consideration of the new types of interactions enabled by digital communication technologies and this should be clarified for ordinary citizens. Citizens should be made aware of the boundaries of sexual consent in online contexts and the consequences of overstepping such consent. Consent to take an intimate image of an individual should not be understood as the same as consent to share those images over the internet. In the Powell case, the victim allowed the offender to see her naked while they were together. This is not to be understood to extend to consent to taking photos of her without her knowledge and later uploading them online. For Boxi, the consent to view the victim's phone did not extend to acquiring the nude images of her that she kept there and later uploading them online. Public education should note the seriousness of these matters for lay citizens while also building awareness that there are legal consequences for overreaching the limits of consent.

Law enforcement officers, judicial officers and other professionals who encounter victims should be further sensitized to the violation and invasion that is experienced by NCII victims. The sharing of sexual images is becoming an everyday practice within the context of the digital environment. It is a common belief that the victim who ends up being the target of NCII did something wrong. Such beliefs can potentially hinder the victim's access to the recourse that is available to him or her. NCII over the internet and social media is a new type of infraction that violates and exploits individuals, but it mirrors everyday intimate partner violence practices from offline contexts that preexisted the internet. This larger picture should be a part of the education offered to these officials. Such training should note the difficulty of coming forward and identify ways to facilitate reporting and the pursuit of offenders. Also, officials who engage with NCII victims should be trained to understand the ill effects of victim blaming and strategies to avoid it.

The after-effects of NCII are pervasive and inescapable. While NCII should have criminal penalties which are enforced systematically, I argue that preventative measures are equally necessary. Public education should target all members of society, including school children, parents, the elderly, law enforcement officials and all other persons who might come into contact with NCII victims.

Re-Assessing Sentencing Recommendations

Both Powell and Boxi were convicted of criminal offences and their NCII infractions will be on their criminal records. But there is a vast difference at the level of sentencing. The Jamaican offender will spend six months in jail, while the Indian offender will spend ten times that. This seems dissonant as both offenders were convicted of seemingly similar offences. Additional protections for women that have been written into the Indian laws may account for the difference in sentencing. Also, as the Jamaican appeals judge admits, the most "egregious" offense by Powell attracted the lightest penalty. This suggests that further examination of maximum and minimum sentencing times could be useful for policy makers working on NCII legislation. Such examinations would take account of global patterns in sentencing in tandem with national imperatives and priorities.

Conclusion

Digital tools and channels have transformed communication patterns in romantic relationships, giving rise to new types of interactions. Such tools and channels have been adapted for the execution of abusive and controlling practices in intimate partnerships, such as NCII over the internet. In this chapter, I illustrated two cases where NCII was enacted in intimate relationships, I demonstrated the impact of these NCII events on the everyday lives of the victims, and I discussed the challenges and considerations raised by these cases. National governments continue to work through ways to create and enforce the rules that govern this behavior and limit its impact on the everyday lives of victims. There is no true remedy to the infraction of NCII. The released images can follow victims for the rest of their lives. Policymakers who wish to control NCII will focus on its prevention and deterrence through legislation. Increased public education on the consequences of NCII (including the possibility of prosecution where applicable) is also a preventative measure. Public education can emphasize the harm of NCII to victims, the relevance of intimate partner violence to NCII, the ill-effects of victim-blaming and the boundaries of consent. Such measures would begin to minimize the number of incidents and make it easier for victims to seek justice. Policy makers should also review maximum and minimum sentencing timelines in line with other countries while still considering national priorities.

Acknowledgements This paper builds on my Dissertation Prospectus which was guided by my Dissertation Advisor Stephanie Deboer. I am also grateful to Pragya Paramita Ghosh who made clarifications on the Indian context.

References

Baker, N. (2016, September 15). Revenge Porn Suicide: Mortified woman commits suicide after she suffered barrage of online abuse when her ex leaked sex tape of her with new man. The Sun, UK Edition. https://www.thesun.co.uk/news/1787316/tiziana-cantone-sex-tape-leak-leads-her-to-commit-suicide-after-she-suffered-barrage-of-online-abuse/.

Bates, S. (2017). Revenge porn and mental health: A qualitative analysis of the mental health effects of revenge porn on female survivors. *Feminist Criminology, 12*(1), 22–42.

Berger, M. (2013, November 20). Brazilian 17-Year-Old Commits Suicide After Revenge Porn Posted Online. *BuzzFeed News*. https://www.buzzfeednews.com/article/miriamberger/brazilian-17-year-old-commits-suicide-after-revenge-porn-pos.

Bloom, S. (2014). No vengeance for revenge porn victims: Unraveling why this latest female-centric, intimate-partner offense is still legal, and why we should criminalize it. *Fordham Urb. LJ, 42*, 233–290.

Census. (2011). Population Census 2011. https://www.census2011.co.in.

Chisolm, D. (2018). How Revenge porn turns lives upside down TEDx. https://www.ted.com/talks/darieth_chisolm_how_revenge_porn_turns_lives_upside_down#t-148718.

Chisolm, D. (2019, July 22). Instagram Post. https://www.instagram.com/p/B0PNPLUlLRd/.

Citron, D. K., & Franks, M. A. (2014). Criminalizing revenge porn. *Wake Forest L. Rev., 49*, 345-392.

Cyber Civil Rights Initiative. (2022a). Definitions. https://cybercivilrights.org/definitions/#

Cyber Civil Rights Initiative. (2022b). Nonconsensual pornography laws. https://cybercivilrights.org/nonconsensual-pornagraphy-laws/

Dasgupta, P. (2017, July 13). What Can Victims Of Revenge Porn In India Do To Get The Criminals Punished? *Huffiington Post*. https://www.huffpost.com/archive/in/entry/what-can-victims-of-revenge-porn-in-india-do-to-punish-the-perpe_a_23027563.

Deb, A. (2020). The Case for a New Statutory Regime Addressing Revenge Porn in India: Exploring the Disputed Terrain From a Feminist Perspective. https://papers.ssrn.com/sol3/papers.cfm?abstract_id=3884351.

Drouin, M., Coupe, M., & Temple, J. R. (2017). Is sexting good for your relationship? It depends.... *Computers in Human Behavior*, 75, 749–756.

Eaton, A. A., Noori, S., Bonomi, A., Stephens, D. P., & Gillum, T. L. (2021). Nonconsensual porn as a form of intimate partner violence: Using the power and control wheel to understand nonconsensual porn perpetration in intimate relationships. *Trauma, Violence, & Abuse*, 22(5), 1140–1154.

Gámez-Guadix, M., Almendros, C., Borrajo, E., & Calvete, E. (2015). Prevalence and association of sexting and online sexual victimization among Spanish adults. *Sexuality Research and Social Policy*, 12(2), 145–154.

Garcia, J. R., Gesselman, A. N., Siliman, S. A., Perry, B. L., Coe, K., & Fisher, H. E. (2016). Sexting among singles in the USA: Prevalence of sending, receiving, and sharing sexual messages and images. *Sexual Health*, 13(5), 428–435.

Gesselman, A. N., Druet, A., & Vitzthum, V. J. (2020). Mobile sex-tech apps: How use differs across global areas of high and low gender equality. *PloS one*, 15(9), e0238501.

Haynes, J. (2018). Judicial approaches to combating 'revenge porn': a multi-jurisdictional perspective. *Commonwealth Law Bulletin*, 44(3), 400–428.

Henry, N., & Powell, A. (2018). Technology-facilitated sexual violence: A literature review of empirical research. *Trauma, violence, & abuse*, 19(2), 195–208.

Henry, N., Powell, A., & Flynn, A. (2017). Not just 'revenge pornography': Australians' experiences of image-based abuse. A summary report. Melbourne: RMIT University.

India Today. (2018, March 12). Revenge Porn: In a first, 5-year jail for Indian man who shared nude video of ex-girlfriend. https://www.indiatoday.in/technology/news/story/revenge-porn-in-a-first-5-year-jail-for-indian-man-who-shared-nude-video-of-ex-girlfriend-1187451-2018-03-12.

India's Information Technology Act.

Indian Penal Code.

Langlois, G., & Slane, A. (2017). Economies of reputation: The case of revenge porn. *Communication and Critical/Cultural Studies*, 14(2), 120–138.

Lenhart, A., Ybarra, M., & Price-Feeney, M. (2016). Nonconsensual image sharing: one in 25 Americans has been a victim of "revenge porn".

Maddocks, S. (2018). From non-consensual pornography to image-based sexual abuse: Charting the course of a problem with many names. *Australian Feminist Studies*, 33(97), 345–361.

Maddocks, S. (2019, January 16). "Revenge Porn": 5 Important Reasons Why We Should Not Call It By That Name. GenderIT.org. https://www.genderit.org/articles/5-important-reasons-why-we-should-not-call-it-revenge-porn.

Mori, C., Cooke, J. E., Temple, J. R., Ly, A., Lu, Y., Anderson, N., ... & Madigan, S. (2020). The prevalence of sexting behaviors among emerging adults: A meta-analysis. *Archives of sexual behavior*, 49(4), 1103–1119.

Neris, N., Pacetta Ruiz, J., & Valente, M. (2015). Fighting the dissemination of non-consensual intimate images: a comparative analysis. InternetLab.org. https://www.internetlab.org.br/wp-content/uploads/2018/11/Fighting_the_Dissemination_of_Non.pdf.

Patton, R. B. (2015). Taking the sting out of revenge porn: Using criminal statutes to safeguard sexual autonomy in the digital age. *Geo. J. Gender & L.*, 16, 407–434.

Poole, E. (2015). Fighting back against non-consensual pornography. *USFL Rev.*, 49, 181–214.

Powell v. R. (2021). Jamaica Court of Appeal. https://www.courtofappeal.gov.jm/sites/default/files/judgments/Reissued%20Judgment%20-%20Powell%20v%20R%20%28Donovan%29%20v%20R.pdf.

Powell, A., Scott, A., Flynn, A., & Henry, N. (2020). *Image Based Sexual Abuse: An international study of victims and perpetrators.* RMIT University.

Snaychuk, L. A., & O'Neill, M. L. (2020). Technology-facilitated sexual violence: Prevalence, risk, and resiliency in undergraduate students. *Journal of Aggression, Maltreatment & Trauma*, 29(8), 984–999.

State of West Bengal v. Boxi, GR: 1587/17 (2018). https://globalfreedomofexpression.columbia.edu/cases/state-of-west-bengal-v-boxi/.

Statistical Institute of Jamaica. (2014). Press Release. Population and Housing Census 2011 Findings. https://statinja.gov.jm/PressReleases/pressreleasecensus.aspx.

The Local. (2019, May 29). Police investigate suicide of woman after 'revenge porn' sex tape. https://www.thelocal.es/20190529/police-investigate-suicide-of-woman-after-revenge-porn-sex-tape/.

Uhl, C. A., Rhyner, K. J., Terrance, C. A., & Lugo, N. R. (2018). An examination of nonconsensual pornography websites. Feminism & Psychology, 28(1), 50–68.

Wolak, J., Finkelhor, D., Walsh, W., & Treitman, L. (2018). Sextortion of minors: Characteristics and dynamics. *Journal of Adolescent Health*, 62(1), 72–79.

World Bank. (2020). World Bank Country and Lending Groups. 2020. https://datahelpdesk.worldbank.org/knowledgebase/articles/906519-world-bank-country-and-lending-groups.

PART III

Digital Divides and Inclusion Strategies

CHAPTER 12

Indigenizing a Developing Country's Digitization Agenda: Re-visioning ICTs in Ghana

Kwaku O. Antwi and William Asante

INTRODUCTION

There is no doubt that stronger societies are made possible when all citizens are accounted for and empowered to fully participate in the world economy. Technology is key in this venture. It is against this backdrop that digitization has gained traction in recent times. Digitization although viewed variously, may refer to the spread and the use of digital technologies like the Internet, mobile phones, and other tools and processes to collect, store, analyze, and exchange information digitally (Klapper et al., 2019; Bloomberg, 2018). In simple terms, it may consist of the various activities and processes of transforming data on paper records into digital data, which we can identify, search, access, retrieve, update, and archive electronically (Kimura, 2015). Globally, countries have been very receptive to digitization. As a result, various digital policy initiatives have been developed to lead this trajectory, outcomes of which have seen investments in infrastructure, expansion of markets, increased tax revenues and reforms that are disrupting systems of work, domestic lives, access to media, language, customs and methods of communicating every day.

K. O. Antwi (✉)
Ghana Institute of Management and Public Administration, Accra, Ghana

W. Asante
Ghana Institute of Management and Public Administration, Accra, Ghana

Simon Diedong Dombo University of Business and Integrated Development Studies, Wa, Ghana

© The Author(s), under exclusive license to Springer Nature Switzerland AG 2024
H. S. Dunn et al. (eds.), *The Palgrave Handbook of Everyday Digital Life*,
https://doi.org/10.1007/978-3-031-30438-5_12

The way we live today has emphasized the notion of change being the only permanent or constant value in everyday life (Matthess & Kunkel, 2020; Johansson, et al., 2019). While we continue to experience the effects of climate change, innovators of information and communication technologies (ICTs) are constantly bombarding us with advancements in technology that are now not only physically present for use but can be virtually experienced and embedded in our very beings (Gangadharbatla, 2020; Juma, 2016). Digitization and its associated concept of digitalization have created new challenges for the development of society, questioning the perspective of human quality of life (Issa, & Isaias, 2022; Juma, 2019). Negative aspects of the impact of digitization on quality of life are levelled out in societies that attach great importance to education and training, culture, civic activities, health, and equal development opportunities (Kryzhanovskij et al., 2021).

We truly live in a global village (McLuhan, 1964) whereby at the touch of a button or click of a finger we reach across the globe through the internet. Today we live in a technologically pervasive world that has people connecting using powerful Internet technologies. The International Telecommunication Union (ITU) reveals that currently 4.1 billion people are active online still leaving out a whopping 2.9 billion people that are offline. It is observed that the majority of the connected people live in advanced countries (ITU, 2021a, 2021b, 2022). It must be mentioned that for decades, ICTs have driven profound changes in the way in which individuals, organizations and governments interact everyday (BC, 2021; A4AI, 2022). Digital transformation is disrupting traditional systems of work, domestic lives, access to media, language, customs and methods of communication. Particularly, the internet has been very crucial in the development of a more globalized knowledge-based economy impacting everyday digital life. Digital inclusion initiatives have been brought to the fore because social inequalities are not only replicated but also amplified in the digital sphere (Ragnedda, 2020). The aim of digital inclusion is about creating an informed society by including the digitally excluded as we proceed on the road of development, where accessing technology is imperative to the whole process of bridging the digital divide and fomenting cohesion.

The literature suggests a digital divide between the haves and the have-nots as far as access to Internet connection is concerned (Alamelu, 2013). However this first level divide (access gap) initially debated by various authors (Attewell, 2001; Hargittai, 2002) fails to acknowledge the multifaceted nature of the dichotomous problem, further discussions show how a second level divide (Van Deursen & Van Dijk, 2019; Helsper, 2017) of digital skills, usage differences and quality of digital experience. More recently other scholars have also introduced the third level divide of useful life outcomes (Heeks, 2022; Ragnedda, 2017). As such, a digitization agenda must capture the various levels of the digital divide for both the traditional communications technologies such as the Internet, mobile phones and interactive digital television, and support new ways of working, managing information, improving the delivery of public services and ensuring personal development in a digital inclusive manner for everyday digital life.

The ITU Connect 2030, the African Union Agenda 2063 and the Africa Continental Free Trade Area (AfCFTA), are major driving forces for the digital economy which seek to synthesize the aspirations of the people. Most countries in Africa have achieved close to 100 percent mobile voice penetration with mobile Internet following a similar trajectory (AU, 2020). Significant gaps, therefore, remain in the continent's household Internet access and digital data literacy. Additionally, the situation has been made worse by the impacts of Covid-19 on people's lives (ITU, 2021a, b; UNCTAD, 2021). However, for the above efforts in digitizing Africa to bear many fruits, they must be accompanied by an enabling policy and regulatory environment. While digital technologies continue to transform peoples' well-being through the convergence of information communications technologies (ICTs) and reorganization of various sectors of the economy, serious gaps and questions remain in the areas of indigenous innovation and ownership, and collaborative approach to tackle the challenges of access, affordability, knowledge and capacity. Additionally, Dunn (2021) has also noted that most countries in the Global South have often been recipients of external innovation, and are subject to the marketing thrusts of big conglomerates. They assimilate most of their policy ideas from outside as reflected in his popular phrase "Globalization from Above". The historical absence of indigenous ownership in the sector (technology) has harmed how receptive and committed people have been toward technology-related initiatives and the accomplishments of their ultimate objectives.

With digital transformation disrupting traditional systems of work, domestic lives, access to media, language customs and methods of communicating we argue for a more humanitarian and participatory approach in rolling out digitization initiatives highlighting deficiencies in the top-down implementation approach often associated with many developing countries government policies that relegate inclusion to the background and make way for more exclusion of the have-nots.

This chapter attempts to critically assess the Ghanaian government's digitization efforts against global digital inclusion best practices. Specific questions that the chapter seeks to address include, what strategies have the government adopted to ensure digitization and digital inclusion? To what extent do these digitization strategies reflect digital inclusion best practices? The rest of the chapter is organized as follows—conceptual and literature review on digital inclusion, Ghana's digitization efforts or strategies, Ghana's strategies of digitization versus digital inclusion best practices, conclusion and policy implications.

Digital Inclusion: A Conceptual and Literature Review

Broadly, the notion of digital inclusion may be said to have emerged from the discourse on social inclusion and exclusion. Domain scholars have not been unanimous in explaining the meaning of social inclusion and exclusion. However, some earlier writers have observed that social inclusion for instance is more readily identified through its counterpart, *social exclusion* (Hayes et al., 2008; Gidley et al., 2010). It is said that the terms began to gain popularity in public policy analysis and practice in the 1990s, especially in Europe and in the work of international organizations such as the International Labour Organization (ILO), and the United Nations (UN) among others. Also in the UK, it was reflected in the activities of Tony Blair's Government's Social Exclusion Unit which ensured that their social agendas are built around such concepts (MacPherson, 1997; Porter, 2000; Davies, 2005; Mascareño & Carvajal, 2015).

Again, some analysts have argued that both inclusion and exclusion are inseparable sides of the same coin. Given that, social exclusion has been defined as the process through which individuals or groups are wholly or partially excluded from full participation in the society within which they live (Gidley et al., 2010). Inclusion on the other hand becomes the opposite of the above definition. Some key areas that individuals may be excluded or included consist of socio-economic status, culture, religion, geography, gender and sexual orientation, age, physical and mental disabilities, and unemployment, among others (Gidley et al., 2010; Mascareño & Carvajal, 2015). Digital systems are significantly associated with inequality, and that association has traditionally been understood in terms of the digital divide or related terminologies whose core conceptualization is the exclusion of some groups from the benefits of ICTs (Heeks, 2022; Grošelj, 2021). Therefore the digital divide, a multidimensional phenomenon, which mostly reflects on one's race, gender, socioeconomic status or geographical location, stands in the way of progress. It has become the gap between individuals, households, businesses and geographic areas of different socio-economical levels with regard both to their opportunities to access information and communication technologies and to their use of the Internet for a wide variety of activities (Hilbert, 2011; OECD, 2001; Ragnedda, 2020; Mutsvairo & Ragnedda, 2019).

It is observed that various authors have expanded the literature on digital inequities, inequalities, and divides to the extent of even linking it with Weber's social stratification work to explain differences in online engagements (Blank & Groselj, 2015; Ragnedda & Muschert, 2015; Wessels, 2015). However, with these important contributions, there is less focus on what works to alleviate these inequalities and divides in a variety of cultural contexts. Digital inclusion can be defined as the activities necessary to ensure that all individuals and communities, including the most disadvantaged, have access to and use of Information and Communication Technologies, this requires intentional strategies and investments to reduce and eliminate historical, institutional and structural barriers to access and use technology (NDIA, 2017). Digital inclusion has become a core topic for policymakers across the globe. The issue of digital inclusion as a core component of social inclusion has come to the forefront (Reisdorf & Rhinesmith, 2020).

Drawing from the above discussion on social inclusion and exclusion, digital inequality captures the complex layers that must work together to produce digital inclusion. The above-identified areas of inclusion/exclusion perfectly tie in with areas of the digital divide as well. It is evident how rapidly digital inequalities are becoming implicit in every field of human endeavor and more importantly, leaving those without resources ever further behind in the digital ecosystem (Heeks, 2022; Robinson et al., 2020b). Furthermore, the digital divide debate has mostly centered on access, use, and outcomes. Access may refer to physical access to computers and the Internet. This tends to look at the digital divide in largely technical terms about the haves and have-not access to necessary hardware, but it has been argued that the divide consists of first level (access), second level (skills and use) and third level in outcomes of Internet use (Robinson et al., 2020a; Ragnedda, 2017; Helsper, 2017). With regards to usage, the mere fact that people have access does not necessarily mean they are equally successful in the use of the internet. This aspect of the discussion takes the issue further by examining the question of who makes effective use of digital technologies. Here, emphasis is placed on inequalities in participation based on digital skills, particularly how the Internet is used, as well as demographic predictors (Ragnedda, 2020; Robinson et al., 2020a; Ragnedda, & Gladkova, 2020; Van Deursen & Van Dijk, 2019).

However, it could be argued forcefully that access, skills, and use also turn out not to be sufficient to characterize Internet use; they are inputs, and what we care about are outcomes of the meaningful experiences by persons utilising the technologies in everyday life. So after gaining technology access and usage skills, people should be able to apply their digital capabilities by being able to apply for a passport online or sell homemade plantain chips on a Facebook page, receiving payment through a mobile money wallet. This is where the focus is shifted to impact on learning, information-seeking, productivity and most importantly income generation. The general observation has therefore been that people from more privileged backgrounds tend to engage in more capital-enhancing activities whereas their counterparts the have-nots may focus on the entertainment aspect (Elahi, 2020; Correa et al., 2020). It is observed that much of the contemporary discussions on ICTs have shifted to how to support new ways of working, managing information, improving the delivery of public services or enabling personal development through electronic gaming (Alamelu, 2013; Robinson et al., 2020a, 2020b; Lamberti et al., 2021). Today it is normal to share pictures on social media app status to update friends and followers, but digital life is more rewarding when people can share creative content videos or pictures that not only trends on Tik Tok or Youtube platforms for good or bad reasons but gives opportunity to monetize views by selling products, sponsorship endorsements (Toresson, 2022).

The aim of digital inclusion is about creating an informed society by including the digitally excluded as we proceed on the road of development. Accessing technology is imperative to the whole process of bridging the digital divide and fomenting a digital cohesion that secures opportunity through the internet, mobile services and computerization of processes, bringing in a new era of a connected nation and using technology better on behalf of citizens and communities. It must be highlighted that digital inclusion is not just a matter of being connected to technology. It is also not a question of being connected or disconnected. Alamelu (2013) argues for addressing digital inclusion issues through digital empowerment which entails enabling people to tailor technology to meet their needs and aspirations, to innovate and participate in planning and design decisions, digital opportunity comprising access to ICTs and the ability to influence their design, and digital equity which seeks inclusion for all residents, small business and community based non-profit organizations. Technology then becomes a central tool for education, economic development, and social well-being. This will in turn enable people to be digital participants, as their everyday life is digitized.

Therefore, it must be rehashed that the element of empowerment is crucial to digital inclusion and may consist of the ability to use the wealth of resources in computing and the Internet to learn, communicate, innovate, and enhance wealth—to move from being a digital novice to a digital professional or innovator. An effective Digital Inclusion strategy provides a path to full participation in a digital society. The authors agree with Alamelu's (2013) suggestion that inclusion could be viewed as a hierarchical framework of progress just like the popular Maslow's hierarchy of needs, with the different levels representing stages of progression (Maslow, 1943; Aruma & Hanachor, 2017). Starting from Level 1 which centers on the provision of infrastructure to provide access to ICT and then to Level 2 which focuses on digital awareness programmes and campaigns to increase awareness of what is available. This is also followed by Level 3 which dwells on the development of know-how with basic IT skills training for citizens. Level 4 touches on digital opportunity i.e. access to ICTs and the ability to influence their design and then finally Level 5 becomes the digital empowerment stage where people are capable of tailoring technology to meet their needs and aspirations, innovate, participate in planning and design decisions (see Fig. 12.1). Figure 12.1 will provide the analytical framework with which Ghana's digitization effort would be assessed.

Ghana's Digitization Efforts

The digital transformation for Ghana's development can be viewed as a journey to a promised land, even though such journeys are often tortuous and require persistence and commitment. For Ghana to capture its share of growth in the burgeoning global digital economy, several government initiatives are being rolled out. These initiatives are supported by many policies consisting of the National Telecommunication Policy (NTP) 2005 and the Information Communication Technology for Accelerated Development (ICT4AD) 2003. In line with the above policies, an array of laws have been passed for the development of Ghana's ICT industry and digitalization of the economy including, the National Communications Authority (NCA) Act 769 of 2008, National Information Technology Agency (NITA) Act 771 of 2008, Electronic Transactions (ET) Act 772 of 2008, Electronic Communications (ECA) Act

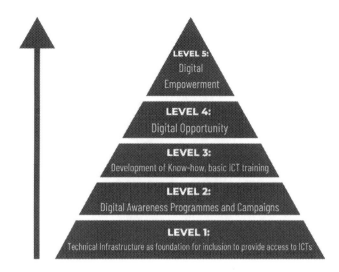

Fig. 12.1 Digital inclusion pyramid. (Source: Author construct from the literature)

775 of 2008, Data Protection (DPA) Act 843 of 2012, Payment Systems and Services (PSS) Act 987 of 2019 and Cyber Security (CSA) Act 2020. Also, Ghana currently has four (4) mobile network operators (MNO) namely MTN Ghana, Vodafone Ghana, Glo Mobile and AirtelTigo, providing services such as text messaging, Internet and mobile money services except for Glo Mobile. Ghana has shown remarkable achievement in mobile telephone penetration, internet diffusion, television and radio stations among other pervasive technologies (NCA, 2020, 2021).

Aside from this, some of the crucial digitization efforts Ghana's government has rolled out include but are not limited to the following; *Ghana National Identification (GNI), Paperless Port Operations (PPO), Ministry of Communications and Digitalization Girls in Information Communication Technology Programme (GICTP), Ghana Interbank Payment and Settlement Systems (GhIPSS), The Driver and Vehicle Licensing Authority (DVLA), Motor Insurance Database(MID), Registrar-General's Department (RGD), Social Security and National Insurance Trust (SSNIT), Scholarship Secretariat Applications(SSA), Ghana.Gov Platform, Digitization of the Passport Office, and Integrated Tax Application and Preparation System* (Business and Financial Times, 2021).

The introduction of the above digital policy interventions to improve livelihoods and onboarding digitization is a step in the right direction. These digital inclusion initiatives influence how we live and work in the digital society which has implications for the everyday life of citizens. Digital transformation is disrupting traditional systems of work, domestic lives, access to media, language, customs and methods of communication. For instance the introduction of the GNI brings the citizenry into a new dimension of digital life, unpacking its intended uses and application to life gives us a glimpse beyond its embedded security and digital address features. Today the GNI, not only serves as a default ID of choice but a digital document that seeks to bring together national ID datasets of the National Health Insurance Scheme (NHIS), Social Security and National Insurance Trust (SSNIT), and the Driver and Vehicle Licensing Authority (DVLA) ID cards. Also, with the ongoing re-registration of all mobile devices subscriber identity module (SIM) cards with the GNI as directed by the Ministry of Communications and Digitalization (MOC), and instructions by the Central Bank, the GNI card has become the only acceptable means of identification for all banks transactions. In addition, the GNI card serves as an Economic Community of West African States (ECOWAS) ID document. Currently, immigration officials in collaboration with major airlines allow passengers entry into the country on the GNI. The utility of GNI is in the ability of authorized service providers to access its database details to verify identities promptly, but some of the experiences so far have been found wanting in many instances. Downtime of Internet service at banking halls for example leaves customers unable to access transaction funds and the banks themselves inability to connect to database servers to verify customers' details. Where there are complications with the ID details, holders have to go back to the offices of the National Identification Authority (NIA) to rectify discrepancies.

These digital platforms created for the services, need some degree of digital capabilities for one to be able to navigate and utilize these services making virtual interactivity a feature of everyday life. Citizenry now navigates portals such as the Ghana.gov website to access public services like tax payments and passport application among others where hitherto they could just walk to a service point, this interaction with digital systems have also become a cause for cybersecurity concern given low-level awareness. An application for a passport for instance requires citizens to be able to log on to the website whether, through an access point of a computer or mobile phone, or payment options through electronic money platforms but today persons who do not have the wherewithal (finances, computers, knowledge) have to rely on or seek assistance for instance from non-official sources such as Internet cafes/documentation centres where they have to incur financial as well as data protection costs.

Here, the service has to be paid for, and if not careful, the personal details used in the completion of activity when not protected can be used by unscrupulous persons for illegal activities. Some financial institutions have increased banking hall computers for use by customers and virtual banking assistants for self-service. The NHIS insurance renewals have been linked to mobile money wallets for ease of payments, while this initiative is convenient, inability to navigate the platform for payments and reliance on acquaintances has seen unsuspecting owners' funds being syphoned by unscrupulous persons. Accessing pensions for scheme beneficiaries with conveniently networked computing systems, now poses a problem for the senior citizens who will have to upgrade their digital skills, often when there are technology challenges, seniors have to go back to the SSNIT offices to get them resolved. This mostly causes delays in disbursements of pension benefits.

With climate change disrupting weather seasons, the Ghana Metrological Agency (GMET) and National Disaster Management Organization (NADMO) have adopted social media channels with official handles to share information to the citizenry. People are able to access weather updates on mobile phone apps created by these agencies (GMET, 2022; NADMO, 2022). However, those without smartphones and knowledge about these apps are not benefitting from these daily updates. Similar situation pertains in the area of transportation, where citizens who are technology savvy are taking advantage of apps like Uber, Bolt, Yango, etc. aided by digital interactive maps such as google maps to navigate terrains, and locations with ease, thereby facilitating movements of goods and services. Also, general communications have improved with access to digital content at the fingertips. Public, private and socio-cultural institutions are daily devising ways to engage the citizenry for information sharing. Today the security agencies, including the Police Service have very interactive social media pages that have been found to help inform and react to viral content that often leads to arrests and also rewards for the citizenry (Myjoyonline, 2021; Daily Guide Network, 2022; Ghanaweb, 2022). The Ministry of Information has also established briefing sessions carried on traditional media (television, radio, print), which are shared on the websites of ministries, agencies and social media platforms with content-friendly sharing capacity. These transformations in digital technologies are disrupting traditional systems of work, domestic lives, access to media, language, customs and methods of communication and have been further exacerbated by the post-pandemic recovery efforts which seek to operationalize virtual and hybrid (virtual and physical) activities also known as the new normal.

Ghana's Digitization Efforts versus Digital Inclusion Best Practices

The digital inclusion literature reveals that at the basic level, any digital inclusion agenda should commence with infrastructure that will provide access to ICTs. Infrastructure here should encapsulate connectivity to the Internet, hardware and software in addition to tools for people with disabilities, and then most significantly access to technical support (Grošelj, 2021; Robinson et al., 2020a, 2020b; Lyons et al., 2020; Ragnedda, 2019; Chohan & Hu, 2022. Alamelu, 2013). A cursory glance at the above-enumerated digitization efforts by the Ghanaian government suggests that major inroads are being made as far as digitization on the part of government is concerned. From national identification down to the integrated tax application and preparation system, it could be seen that basic ICT infrastructure is available. However, this is not widespread in the entire population. Inequalities as far as infrastructure and access are concerned are pronounced. Infrastructure is at its basic level, with rural areas being more deprived. Again, it is taken for granted that citizens' capacities are the same. Most of the above digitization efforts do not take into consideration the plight of people with disabilities. As far as level 1 of the digital inclusion pyramid is concerned, Ghana is yet to have a full infrastructure in place to make ICTs accessible to the various sections of the populace, rural-urban, able-disable and rich-poor(Van Deursen et al., 2021; Alhassan & Adam, 2021; Sieck et al. 2021; Lyons et al., 2020). There are still places in the country where access to a communication network is problematic. These places are automatically cut out from the benefits that digitization presents, for example rural cocoa farmers accessing agricultural data on their mobile phones for extension services, harvesting and sales (Quayson et al., 2020). It is observed that those who are excluded from the digital realm end up missing out on being able to enhance their everyday life meaningfully. Highlighted by the three-level digital divides, social and digital inclusion/exclusion are intertwined concepts because the absence of digital participation is an amplification of underlying social inequality issues.

Subsequently, the second level of digital inclusion focuses on digital awareness programmes and campaigns to increase awareness of what is available and to improve take up or participation. Citizens are unlikely to realize the positive impact of digitization if they are ignorant about its availability (Kryzhanovskij et al., 2021; Alamelu, 2013). In the Ghanaian case, for instance, the vice president (HE Dr. Mahamadu Bawumia) has taken a leadership role in creating awareness about available digitization programmes. A recent one of these awareness creation efforts by the vice president was a lecture he delivered at the Ashesi University in Ghana on November 2, 2021, on the theme "Transforming An Economy through Digitalization—The Ghana Story". The vice president used the occasion to enumerate most of the digitization efforts by the government (Frimpong, 2021). The deficiency however is that state institutions such as the National Commission for Civic Education (NCCE), the various Metropolitan, Municipal and District Assemblies as well as the institutions that are witnessing the changes in their operations have not made any significant contribution as far as awareness creation is concerned. As a result, most of the populace is unaware of most of these digitization efforts. Once people are unaware of what is available, then it becomes difficult for them to access and participate. The inequality gap then widens as the few with the information take advantage of it and leave the majority of the others without information behind (Robinson et al., 2020a, 2020b).

Furthermore, the third level in the sequence, as far as digital inclusion is concerned focuses on the development of 'know how", understanding of the technology usage through basic IT skills training for citizens (Alamelu, 2013; Alhassan & Adam, 2021). Here, the digital divide is very wide, because skills training is not readily available. Incremental progress is being made by the government through the community ICT programmes, but this is woefully inadequate. Also, the Girls in ICT programme spearheaded by the Ministry of Communication and Digitalization is expected to help in this aspect, but it is only in the pilot stage. This programme could be very beneficial if it is fully rolled out as it will help mentor, motivate and expose young girls to the opportunities that exist in the ICT sector and also bridge the gender gap in the sector which is considered to be dominated by men. In the meantime, those citizens who have the financial capacity to afford ICT training are doing so to enhance their digital inclusion (Dunn, 2021; Dunn et al. 2021; Robinson et al., 2020a, 2020b).

Not only the above but also the fourth and fifth levels are very crucial for attaining digital inclusion. For instance, Level 4 focuses on digital opportunity, that is, access to ICTs and the ability to influence their design. It is expected that before arriving at this level, the other three levels should have been achieved by a country. However in the Ghanaian case, the first three levels have only witnessed incremental progress, and so attaining the fourth becomes a myth rather than reality. Significantly, the Ghanaian case shows that the fourth level is slowly being worked at, particularly access to ICTs. However, this is still dependent on the financial capability of the individual citizens. The other leg of level 4 which is the ability to influence ICT design has not seen government efforts. Also, the fifth level centers on digital empowerment, that is, enabling people to tailor technology to meet their needs and aspirations, to innovate and participate in planning and design decisions (Dunn, 2021; Alamelu, 2013; Alhassan & Adam, 2021). It must be emphasized that this is yet to receive the needed response from the government. It is important to restate that the different levels identified above are incremental stages enabling progression from Level 1 provision of access to infrastructure for connecting to the Internet, through to Level 5 where people are empowered to influence the design and shaping of digital technologies. Ghana's case demonstrates that grassroots engagement, as well as leadership from government and major corporations, will be key to the successful delivery of digital inclusion at all levels.

Conclusion and Policy Implications

The discussion above has clearly shown that the government has initiated a number of digitization strategies to encourage digital inclusion. The aim of digital inclusion is about creating an informed society by including the digitally excluded as we proceed on the road of development. Examples of these include GNI initiative, Paperless Port Operations, GhIPSS, the DVLA, and Motor Insurance Database, among others. It could be deduced that the numerous digitization initiatives by the government are aimed at improving governance generally. More specifically, it is purposed to make citizens access and obtain government services in an efficient and timely manner, encourage more participation in governance, generate more revenue through taxation and improved service delivery, demand more accountability from politicians and public officials, and then make governance more transparent.

The above clearly shows that Ghana as a country has made major inroads as far as digitization and digitalization of the economy and other aspects of the country are concerned. Information or data has been obtained, and processes have been computerized, however, getting the data or information is one thing and making it work is another. It is expected that efforts would be put in place to ensure that the data becomes useful and meet the objectives with which it was collected. In light of all this, the integration of databases is key. The key to building a data based economy is not only in generating data but even more importantly the usage of it. Ghana, however, has the opportunity to learn from others who have taken the lead in this venture and make efforts to integrate the databases that have been generated from the ongoing digitization process.

In this regard, the integration of the databases will bring transparency, discipline and efficiency into the country's economy, and also help law enforcement track down criminals. With proper protection of privacy as provided by the Data Protection Act 2012, employers would be able to do an online background check on prospective employees. It will also be much more difficult for people to avoid paying tax as the GRA will have a broad overview of transactions across a broad spectrum of activities. Police can easily tell a fake vehicle registration, driver's license or insurance.

Furthermore, a careful examination of the government of Ghana's digitization strategies in connection with digital inclusion best practices suggests that although incremental progress is being made as far as the first three levels are concerned, a lot more efforts and political will are needed to reach the level of digital empowerment. In the meantime, while working at it, it is expected that efforts should be made to ensure that policy-making and regulation in the ICT sector of the country be informed by global best practices but adapted to the specific needs and context of Ghana. It is expected that this will lead to expanding affordable access to, and effective use of, ICTs as tools for broad-based development and poverty reduction.

Subsequently, Ghana and other developing countries can take a cue from the strategic approach of 'Globalization from Within', by transforming individual ideas and local innovations into global-level enterprises. This is expected to garner indigenous ownership and impact rather than the numerous top-down digitization processes that are borrowed elsewhere and are localized without much success. Governments and enterprises in developing countries, through private-public partnerships, deliberate product promotions, subsidies and South-South trade, must empower local businesses within their jurisdictions to enable them to become more globally competitive. By helping their start-ups innovate locally and grow globally, such countries can contribute to expanding wealth creation and digital productivity, led by visionary individuals and adaptive enterprises originating within their borders.

Citizen engagement should be a key element in this venture. This is because citizens play a critical role in advocating and helping to make public institutions more transparent, accountable, and effective, and contributing innovative solutions to complex development challenges. Engaging citizens is particularly important in ventures like digitization. Informing and receiving feedback from citizens in real-time can provide insights into how challenges associated with the rolling out of digitization initiatives are affecting communities. This enables real-time course correction to find solutions in fast-evolving situations. Additionally, in order to enhance citizen awareness, literacy and digital productivity, ICT should be prioritized and digital access effectively managed.

Fundamentally, securing our gains through digital security should be a national priority as well. As we digitize, we also ensure that stakeholders are protected from unscrupulous digital criminals. The Cyber Security Act 2020 mandates the Cyber Security Authority to regulate cybersecurity activities and promote the development of cybersecurity in the country by making efforts to assist all businesses to invest in some baseline cybersecurity measures. Additionally, the cyberspace also requires that our national Authority collaborates with international bodies such as the World Economic Forum, which has a set of internationally-accepted standard guidelines. Awareness creation and capacity building in the public and private sectors is a priority. The more educated the society is about cybersecurity issues, the better it can ensure a robust digital ecosystem.

In conclusion, digital technologies are gradually permeating all spheres of life in developing countries like Ghana. It is however anticipated that the transformation that these ICTs bring will continue to disrupt everyday life, causing some to be excluded and others included. The latter is expected to set us on the path of development, which should be the ultimate goal. This is because in a digitally inclusive society, where majority of the people are informed and skilled to participate in all facets of a technology-driven society, meaningful progress is expected to be realized particularly in the area of political governance.

References

Africa Union (AU). (2020). Draft digital transformation strategy for Africa (2020–2030). https://au.int/sites/default/files/documents/38507-doc-dts-english.pdf

Alamelu, K. (2013). Digital Inclusion—A conceptual framework. *International Journal of Advanced Research in Management and Social Sciences.* 2(12), 228–248.

Alhassan, M. D., & Adam, I. O. (2021). The effects of digital inclusion and ICT access on the quality of life: A global perspective. *Technology in Society, 64,* 101511.

Alliance For Affordable Internet (A4AI). (2022). Advancing meaningful connectivity: Towards active & participatory digital societies. https://1e8q3q16vyc81g8l3h3md6q5f5e-wpengine.netdna-ssl.com/wp-content/uploads/2022/02/FullreportFINAL.pdf.

Aruma, E. O. & Hanachor, M. E. (2017). Abraham maslow's hierarchy of needs and assessment of needs in community development. *International Journal of Development and Economic Sustainability.* 5(7), 15–27.

Attewell, P. (2001). Comment: The first and second digital divides. *Sociology of Education, 74*(3), 252–259.

Blank, G. & Groselj, D. (2015) Examining internet use through a Weberian lens. *International Journal of Communication,* 9, 2763–2783.

Bloomberg, J. (2018). Digitization, digitalization and digital transformation: Confuse them at your peril. https://www.forbes.com/sites/jasonbloomberg/2018/04/29/

digitization-digitalization-and-digital-transformation-confuse-them-at-your-peril/?sh=1b34672f2c7f

Broadband Commission for Sustainable Development (BC). (2021). *State of broadband report 2021: People centred approaches for universal broadband*. International Telecommunication Union and United Nations Educational, Scientific and Cultural Organization, Geneva. https://broadbandcommission.org/publication/state-of-broadband-2021/

Business & Financial Times. (2021). Tax evasion & digitization of the Ghanaian economy. https://thebftonline.com/2021/11/09/tax-evasion-digitization-of-the-ghanaian-economy/

Chohan, S. R., & Hu, G. (2022). Strengthening digital inclusion through e-government: Cohesive ICT training programs to intensify digital competency. *Information Technology for Development*, 28(1), 16–38.

Correa, T., Pavez, I., & Contreras, J. (2020). Digital inclusion through mobile phones?: A comparison between mobile-only and computer users in internet access, skills and use. *Information, Communication & Society*, 23(7), 1074–1091.

Daily Guide Network. (2022). *Sword wielding Lebanese arrested over death threats*. https://dailyguidenetwork.com/sword-wielding-lebanese-arrested-over-death-threats/

Davies, J. S. (2005). The social exclusion debate: Strategies, controversies and dilemmas. *Policy Studies*, 26(1), 3–27.

Dunn, H.S. (2021). Globalization from within: Enhancing digital productivity and technology transformation in the South. In *Re-Imagining Communication in Africa and the Caribbean*, (33–52). Cham: Palgrave Macmillan.

Dunn, H.S., Moyo, D., Lesitaokana, W.O., & Barnabas, S.B. (2021). Re-imagining communication in Africa and the Caribbean: Releasing the psychic inheritance. In *Re-Imagining Communication in Africa and the Caribbean* (1–15). Cham: Palgrave Macmillan.

Elahi, F. (2020). Digital inclusion: Bridging divides. https://www.cumberlandlodge.ac.uk/sites/default/files/cumberland_lodge_digital_inclusion_-_bridging_divides_august_2020_for_web_0.pdf

Frimpong, E. D. (2021). Bawumia on digitalisation of Ghana's economy [LIVE VIDEO]. https://www.graphic.com.gh/news/general-news/bawumia-on-digitizing-ghana-s-economy.html

Gangadharbatla, H. (2020). Biohacking: An exploratory study to understand the factors influencing the adoption of embedded technologies within the human body. *Heliyon*, 6(5),1–9.

Ghana Meteorological Agency (GMET). (2022). https://www.meteo.gov.gh/gmet/regional-weather/

Ghanaweb. (2022). How market woman rewarded taxi driver who returned her GH 8400. https://www.ghanaweb.com/GhanaHomePage/NewsArchive/How-market-woman-rewarded-Taxi-driver-who-returned-her-GH-8-400-1538153

Gidley, J. M., Hampson, G. P., Wheeler, L., & Bereded-Samuel, E. (2010). From access to success: An integrated approach to quality higher education informed by social inclusion theory and practice. *Higher Education Policy*, 23(1), 123–147.

Grošelj, D. (2021). Re-domestication of internet technologies: Digital exclusion or digital choice?. *Journal of Computer-Mediated Communication*, 26(6), 422–440.

Hargittai, E. (2002). Second-level digital divide: Differences in people's online skills. *First Monday*, 7(4). http://firstmonday.org/issues/issue7_4/hargittai/index.html

Hayes, A., Gray, M., & Edwards, B. (2008). Social inclusion: Origin, concepts and key themes. Paper prepared by the Australian Institute of Family Studies. *Canberra: Commonwealth of Australia*. https://www.researchgate.net/publication/322160853_Social_Inclusion_Origins_concepts_and_key_themes.

Heeks, R. (2022). Digital inequality beyond the digital divide: conceptualizing adverse digital incorporation in the global South. *Information Technology for Development*, 1–17. https://doi.org/10.1080/02681102.2022.2068492

Helsper, E. J. (2017). The social relativity of digital exclusion: Applying relative deprivation theory to digital inequalities. *Communication Theory*, 27(3), 223–242.

Hilbert, M. (2011). The end justifies the definition: The manifold outlooks on the digital divide and their practical usefulness for policy-making. *Telecommunications Policy*, 35(8), 715–736.

International Telecommunications Union (ITU). (2021a). The affordability of ICT services 2021. Policy Brief. https://www.itu.int/en/ITU-D/Statistics/Documents/publications/prices2021/ITU_A4AI_Price_Brief_2021.pdf

International Telecommunications Union (ITU). (2021b). Measuring digital development: Facts and figures 2021. https://www.itu.int/en/ITU-D/Statistics/Documents/facts/FactsFigures2021.pdf.

International Telecommunication Union (ITU). (2022). Partner2Connect action framework report. https://www.itu.int/itu-d/reports/partner2connect-action-framework/wp-content/uploads/sites/7/2022/03/Partner2Connect-Action-Framework-Report.pdf

Issa, T., & Isaias, P. (2022). Innovative technologies: Applications in the present and considerations for the future. In *Sustainable design* (pp. 193–215). London: Springer. https://doi.org/10.1007/978-1-4471-7513-1_8

Johansson, E., Sutinen, K., Lassila, J., Lang, V., Martikainen, M, & Lehner, O. M. (2019). Regtech-a necessary tool to keep up with compliance and regulatory changes. *ACRN Journal of Finance and Risk Perspectives, Special Issue Digital Accounting*, 8, 71–85.

Juma, C. (2016). *Innovation and its enemies: Why people resist new technologies*. Oxford: Oxford University Press.

Juma, C. (2019). Digital services and industrial inclusion: Growing Africa's technological complexity. In M. Graham (Ed.). *Digital Economies at Global Margins*. Boston: MIT Press.

Kimura, K. (2015). What does digitization mean for Ghana? https://www.weforum.org/agenda/2015/04/what-does-digitisation-mean-for-ghana/

Klapper, L., Miller, M., & Hess, J. (2019). *Leveraging digital financial solutions to promote formal business participation*. Washington DC: World Bank. https://openknowledge.worldbank.org/handle/10986/31654

Kryzhanovskij, O. A., Baburina, N. A., & Ljovkina, A. O. (2021). How to make digitalization better serve an increasing quality of life? *Sustainability*, 13(2), 611.

Lamberti, G., Lopez-Sintas, J., & Sukphan, J. (2021). The social process of internet appropriation: Living in a digitally advanced country benefits less well-educated Europeans. *Telecommunications Policy*, 45(1), 102055. https://doi.org/10.1016/j.telpol.2020.102055

Lyons, A., Kass-Hanna, J., & Greenlee, A. (2020). Impacts of financial and digital inclusion on poverty in South Asia and Sub-Saharan Africa. https://doi.org/10.2139/ssrn.3684265

MacPherson, S. (1997). Social exclusion. *Journal of Social Policy*, 26(4), 533–541.

Mascareño, A. and Carvajal, F. (2015). The different faces of inclusion and exclusion. *Cepal Review*, 116, 127–141.

Maslow, A. H. (1943). A theory of human motivation. *Psychological Review*, 50(4), 370–96.

Matthess, M., & Kunkel, S. (2020). Structural change and digitalization in developing countries: Conceptually linking the two transformations. *Technology in society*, 63, 1–13.

McLuhan, M. (1964). *Understanding media: The extensions of man*. Cambridge, MA: MIT Press.

Mutsvairo B. & Ragnedda, M. (2019). Comprehending the digital disparities in Africa In B. Mutsvairo & M. Ragnedda (Eds)., *Mapping the digital divide in Africa. A mediated Analysis* (pp. 13–26). Amsterdam: Amsterdam University Press.

Myjoyonline. (2021). Police arrest man driving dangerously in viral video. https://www.myjoyonline.com/police-arrest-man-driving-dangerously-in-viral-video/

National Communications Authority (NCA). (2020). Communications industry statistics. https://nca.org.gh/assets/COMMUNICATIONS-INDUSTRY-STATISTICS-MD-Q1.pdf

National Communications Authority (NCA). (2021). Quarterly statistical bulletin on communications: Fourth quarter. https://nca.org.gh/wp-content/uploads/2022/07/Q4-2021-statistical-Bulletin.pdf

National Digital Inclusion Alliance (NDIA). (2017). Definitions. https://www.digitalinclusion.org/definitions

National Disaster Management Organisation (NADMO). (2022). http://www.nadmo.gov.gh/

Organisation for Economic Co-operation and Development (OECD). (2001). Understanding the digital divide. *OECD Digital Economy Papers*, 201(5). OECD. http://www.oecd.org/dataoecd/38/57/1888451.pdf

Porter, F. (2000). Social exclusion: What's in a name? *Development in Practice*, 10(1), 76–81.

Quayson, M., Bai, C., & Osei, V. (2020). Digital inclusion for resilient post-COVID-19 supply chains: smallholder farmer perspectives. *IEEE Engineering Management Review*, 48(3), 104–110.

Ragnedda, M. (2017). The third digital divide: A Weberian approach to digital inequalities. In M. Ragnedda & G. W. Muschert (Eds.) *Theorizing digital divides* (pp. 63–74). New York: Routledge.

Ragnedda, M. (2019). Reconceptualising the digital divide. In B.Mutsvairo & M. Ragnedda (eds)., *Mapping the digital divide in Africa. A mediated Analysis* (pp. 27–43). Amsterdam: Amsterdam University Press.

Ragnedda, M. (2020). *Enhancing digital equity: Connecting the digital underclass*. Cham: Palgrave Macmillan.

Ragnedda, M., & Gladkova, A. (2020). Understanding digital inequalities in the global south. In *Digital Inequalities in the Global South* (pp. 17–30). London: Palgrave Macmillan.

Ragnedda, M. & Muschert, G. (2015) Max Weber and Digital divide studies: Introduction. *International Journal of Communication*, 9, 2757–2762.

Reisdorf, B., & Rhinesmith, C. (2020). Digital inclusion as a core component of social inclusion. *Social Inclusion*, 8(2), 132–137.

Robinson, L., Schulz, J., Blank, G., Ragnedda, M., Ono, H., Hogan, B.,..., & Khilnani, A. (2020a). Digital inequalities 2.0: Legacy inequalities in the information age. *First Monday*, *25*(7). https://doi.org/10.5210/fm.v25i7.10842

Robinson, L., Schulz, J., Khilnani, A., Ono, H., Cotten, S., Mcclain, N., ... & Tolentino, N. (2020b). Digital inequalities in time of pandemic: COVID-19 exposure risk profiles and new forms of vulnerability. *First Monday*, *25*(7). https://doi.org/10.5210/fm.v25i7.10845

Sieck, C. J., Sheon, A., Ancker, J. S., Castek, J., Callahan, B., & Siefer, A. (2021). Digital inclusion as a social determinant of health. *NPJ Digital Medicine*, *4*(1), 1–3.

Toresson, G. L. (2022). Khaby Lame on how he won Tiktok and his plan for the oscars. https://www.forbes.com/sites/gustavlundbergtoresson/2022/03/12/khaby-lame-on-how-he-won-tiktok-and-his-plan-for-the-oscars/?sh=7e96c8595c4f

United Nations Conference on Trade and Development (UNCTAD). (2021). *Digital economy report 2021 on Cross-border data flows and development: For whom the data flow*. New York: United Nations Publications. Retrieved from https://unctad.org/system/files/official-document/der2021_en.pdf

Van Deursen, A.J., Van der Zeeuw, A., De Boer, P., Jansen, G. & van Rompay, T. (2021). Digital inequalities in the internet of things: Differences in attitudes, material access, skills, and usage, *Information, Communication & Society*, *24*(2), 258–276.

Van Deursen, A. J., & Van Dijk, J. A. (2019). The first-level digital divide shifts from inequalities in physical access to inequalities in material access. *New Media & society*, *21*(2), 354–375.

Wessels, B. (2015) Authentication, status, and power in a digitally organized society. *International Journal of Communication*, 9, 2801–2818.

CHAPTER 13

Nurturing the Transformative Agency and Activism of Children Through Digital Technology

Netta Iivari and Marianne Kinnula

Introduction

In contemporary society, digital technology has entered all spheres of our everyday life; it is embedded in and shaping the everyday practices of people from babies to the elderly. Particularly, digitalization will be shaping the lives of the young generation: they will certainly be living their adult life embedded with and completely intertwined with digital means and tools. Hence, the young generation needs to be educated to be able to manage and master their digital futures and to prevent digital divides and exclusions (Iivari et al., 2018a). They will not only need to have access to digital technology and be able to use it and integrate it into meaningful practices to gain full benefits from it, but they should also be able and encouraged to take part in making and shaping of it (e.g. Iivari et al., 2018a, 2020). The literature maintains that the young generation should be invited into the design, development and innovation of digital technology (Iivari et al., 2018a; Iversen et al., 2017), which implies that children's technology education needs to be reconsidered (e.g. Chu et al., 2017; Iversen et al., 2018; Dindler et al., 2020).

There have been some developments along these lines: for example, there has recently been great interest in integrating programming or digital fabrication and making into children's basic education (e.g. Szabo et al., 2019).

N. Iivari (✉) • M. Kinnula
University of Oulu, Oulu, Finland
e-mail: Netta.Iivari@oulu.fi; Marianne.Kinnula@oulu.fi

© The Author(s), under exclusive license to Springer Nature Switzerland AG 2024
H. S. Dunn et al. (eds.), *The Palgrave Handbook of Everyday Digital Life*,
https://doi.org/10.1007/978-3-031-30438-5_13

However, there are many limitations in the current approaches, those being, e.g., too technology and engineering-oriented. We maintain that engaging children in the development of digital technology is in itself not enough, but rather digital technology should be approached as a tool for serving other kinds of goals and purposes in our life and society; the focus should be on where, how, and why digital technology is developed and used. These types of considerations should be integrated into children's basic education, and children's agency in shaping our digital future as active citizens should be nurtured. There is a separate literature base advocating activism education for children (e.g. Kirshner, 2007; Torres-Harding et al., 2018; Westheimer & Kahne, 2004), while so far, these two streams of education—activism and technology education—have not been utilized to cross-fertilize each other. We see a lot of potential in this endeavor.

This chapter is set to explore "how to nurture children's agency and activism in and through digital technology design and development?" We address this question by examining several projects entailing digital technology design and development, in which we have in collaboration with children ideated, designed, developed and evaluated digital technology for various kinds of purposes. We inquire about the projects from the perspective of children's agency and activism in and through digital technology development, showing variety in the projects.

The chapter is structured as follows. Section "Theoretical Background" introduces the theoretical basis for this work, particularly theories on children's agency and activism as well as Child Computer Interaction (CCI) literature on engaging children in the design, development and innovation of digital technology. Section "Research Design" introduces the methodology involved in this study, including the projects under examination. Section "Summary of the Results" presents our findings from the projects while Section "Towards a Framework for Nurturing Children's Digital Technology Development Agency and Activism" proposes a framework for nurturing children's agency and activism in and through digital technology development. Section "Conclusion" concludes the chapter with a summary of the results, their implications for research and practice, their limitations and paths for future work.

THEORETICAL BACKGROUND

This section introduces the theoretical basis of this study from the viewpoint of central concepts and related research.

Approaching Children's Agency

In this chapter, the focus is on nurturing the agency of children. There are many interpretations, disciplines, and traditions associated with the concept of agency (e.g. Emirbayer & Mische, 1998), while we acknowledge agency is always historical and contextual, social and relational as well as inventive and reflective (Emirbayer & Mische, 1998). We approach it particularly through the concept of transformative agency, relying on the work of Kajamaa and Kumpulainen (2019) and others (e.g. Rajala et al., 2013; Rainio, 2010), who discuss the concept in relation to children and the context of school and advocate a socio-cultural and cultural-historical perspective. Kajamaa and Kumpulainen (2019, p. 267) view transformative agency as a collective process, a "continuous, non-linear and tension-laden process, always related to the socio-material context and practical actions" that entails breaking away or transforming the given, taken for granted practices, involving initiative and commitment of children to influence and transform the world. Important is to learn to see the world as changeable, as "imagining alternative futures is at the heart of agency" (Rajala et al., 2013, p. 119, citing Emirbayer & Mische, 1998; Rainio, 2010). According to Kajamaa and Kumpulainen (2019, p. 268), transformative agency can also be connected with "a transformative activist stance", in which the actor, instead of adapting, makes an effort to transform the existing practices, for the purpose of serving personal or collective ends, such a process potentially leading also to identity implications on children.

In the projects we have organized, we have aimed at nurturing the transformational agency of children in different ways and to various extents. Our projects have engaged children in collaborative long-term processes that have encouraged children to take initiative; break away from the existing, taken-for-granted practices; transform their practices; the projects overall serving various kinds of personal or collective ends, potentially having also identity implications on children. Next, we discuss the concept of activism, to enrich the discussion on the transformative activist stance introduced by Kajamaa and Kumpulainen (2019).

Research on Children's Activism

This chapter is inspired by the literature on children's and youth activism, which is viewed from the perspective of Freirean Pedagogy of the Oppressed as social action entailing collective action taking and problem solving for the purpose of combatting societal or community oppression or injustice (see Aubrey, 2004; Freire, 2017; Torres-Harding et al., 2018). Youth activism can be generally considered as aiming at "influencing political change toward socially just ends", oftentimes taking place outside of education in the community and leisure time contexts (Kirshner, 2007, p. 367). We address activism in the context of school and children's education (in line with, e.g., Kirshner, 2007; Torres-Harding et al., 2018), in which context, activism has been seen to contribute to student's educational success and their development as "socially responsible, healthy, and civically engaged individuals" (Torres-Harding et al., 2018, p. 4). Concerning these goals, three conceptions of being a good citizen can be advocated: being a personally responsible citizen, being a participatory citizen and being a justice-oriented citizen (Westheimer & Kahne, 2004). Personally responsible citizen obeys the laws and acts responsibly in one's community, participatory citizen actively participates in civic matters, communities and organizations, is knowledgeable of civic matters and ways of civic engagement as well as takes actions on civic matters, while justice-oriented citizen is sensitive towards social justice in the sense of critically analyzing and taking action towards it as well as knowledgeable of strategies for achieving it (Westheimer & Kahne, 2004). Youth activism, as defined in this chapter, most closely links with the last conception, while all of them are relevant. It is important also to realize that these conceptions of being a good citizen can be intertwined but that there can also be contradictions between them (Torres-Harding et al., 2018).

Three aspects are argued to characterize youth activism learning-wise: collective problem solving, positive youth-adult relationships, development of identities as powerful civic actors, and bridging young people with mainstream institutions (Kirshner, 2007). Hence, young people are to be invited to collectively tackle problems deemed societally significant, to collaborate also with involved adults and institutions and to develop their identities in relation to civic matters and activism. Along these lines, their engagement in goal-setting, action-taking, and critical reflection is to be supported (Torres-Harding et al., 2018).

Research on Children's Participation in the Design, Development and Innovation of Digital Technology

Our projects have been heavily geared towards digital technology: we have supported children to adopt an activist stance towards digital technology development and to utilize it as a means when adopting an activist stance towards societal matters. In this endeavor, we have been inspired by CCI literature that has for long enabled children to take part in the design, development and innovation of digital technology. A central value for CCI researchers has been to give children a voice in the development of digital technology children themselves use.

Adults have invited children into the technology development process in various roles: as informants (Scaife et al., 1997), evaluators (Salian et al., 2013), and design partners (Druin, 2002), who participate in ideating, designing, developing and evaluating digital technology for themselves and for other children. The role of the design partner has been particularly prominent in CCI research. It entails adults and children working together towards a shared goal, and stresses listening to children's voices and supporting children in making their thoughts and opinions visible (Druin, 2002), i.e., it aims for giving children agency in the process. CCI researchers have developed several methods for children's participation in the development of digital technology over the years, covering the entire technology development process that entails (1) brainstorming, envisioning and ideating novel technologies, (2) designing technology in the sense of specifying its behavior, contents, and look-and-feel, (3) implementing technology e.g. through programming, digital fabrication and making, and (4) evaluating it (in the CCI literature see e.g. Hourcade, 2008, in the Human Computer Interaction literature more generally, see e.g. Sharp et al., 2019).

Recently, CCI researchers have advocated for this wider scale of digital technology development skills to be integrated into children's basic education curricula, instead of teaching only programming skills, which has been emphasized a lot in some countries (e.g. Szabo et al., 2019). In this discourse, these skills are seen as 'twenty-first century skills' (ECDG, 2019), useful and even necessary for all future citizens to make and shape their increasingly digital futures. Recently, the notion of a technology 'design protagonist' has been brought up, entailing children having not only skills in digital technology development, but also the ability to critically reflect on the role of technology in their own everyday life as well as in the society, and even capability and agency for driving technology development, and changing the world through that (Iversen et al., 2017, see also Iivari & Kinnula, 2018). In relation to the design protagonist notion, innovation education has also been brought up (e.g. Hartikainen et al., 2021; Unterfrauner et al., 2021), combining digital technology development skills and business understanding, both listed as twenty-first century skills (ECDG, 2019).

Overall, as is obvious, various kinds of goals, skills and competences can be associated with children's digital technology education, ranging from ideation, design, implementation, and evaluation of digital technology to adopting a critical approach towards it and combining business considerations with it. What is currently lacking, however, is an explicit attempt to nurture children's agency and activism to make in these endeavours a change in the world for a better future. So far, children's activism education has stayed separate from children's technology education. We will propose ways how to combine those, to different extents.

Research Design

We have organized several digital technology development projects with children (e.g. Iivari & Kinnula, 2016, 2018; Iivari et al., 2018a, 2018b, Kinnula et al., 2017, 2022; Molin-Juustila et al., 2015; Ventä-Olkkonen et al., 2021, Ventä-Olkkonen et al., 2021). The projects have been conducted within our research group during different years and with different collaborators, purposes, and motives. We selected five projects (see Table 13.1) for this chapter to illustrate the variety involved in our work, related to digital technology design and development and aiming at children's increased agency through those. They offer the basis for us to develop the framework of agency and activism in and through digital technology development. Three projects are about the design and development of games: one addresses increasing the reading interest of children through games; one experiments with genuine participation of children in game design; and one enables the participation of children in the design and making of an interactive board game. Two projects address

Table 13.1 Presentation of the analyzed projects

Project goal	Data	Publications
Increasing children's reading interest through game design and development	Multimodal data from the workshops with children, game and game editor development-related data, project management data, results reports, email correspondence, field notes of researchers, questionnaires from children, and interviews of children and their teacher.	Iivari and Kinnula (2016), Iivari et al. (2018a), Kinnula et al. (2017)
Offering children design, programming, and making experiences of an interactive board game	Multimodal data from the workshops with children, game development-related data, project management data, results reports, email correspondence, field notes of researchers, questionnaires from children, interviews of children	Iivari and Kinnula (2018), Iivari et al. (2018a)
Offering children genuine experiences in game design	Multimodal data from the workshops with children, game development-related data, project management data, results reports, email correspondence, field notes of researchers, interviews of children, interviews of junior researchers	Iivari et al. (2018a), Molin-Juustila et al. (2015)
Offering children experiences in artificial intelligence and its application in sustainable development	Multimodal data from the workshops with children, teaching material, children's business plans and presentations of those, questionnaires and reflections from children, interviews of children	Kinnula et al. (2022)
Tackling bullying at school through digital technology	Multimodal data from the workshops with children and adults, data of the development of digital tools against bullying, project management data, results reports, email correspondence, field notes of researchers, interviews of children, interviews of teachers	Sharma et al. (2022), Ventä-Olkkonen et al. (2021), (2022)

broader societal concerns: one addresses bullying at school and another one artificial intelligence and sustainable development, through digital means. The empirical studies carried out in relation to the projects have all been qualitative and participatory. The empirical data has been gathered through different methods, mostly through interviews, observation, questionnaires, and the collection of created documentation (see Table 13.1).

The data analysis carried out for this chapter included use of the theories on agency and activism and the literature on design and development of digital technology as sensitizing devices. The analysis examined each project from these perspectives, considering what was aimed at and accomplished. In every phase of analysis, the authors collaboratively discussed the findings and refined the shared understanding of how agency and activism are pictured in the project arrangements.

Agency and Activism in Digital Technology Development Projects

This section analyzes and discusses five example projects we have conducted in collaboration with children, showing variation in the ways agency and activism have been addressed in these digital technology development projects.

Project Raising Children's Interest in Reading Through Game Design

Aims of the project. The project aimed at understanding and strengthening children's multiliteracies and arousing their interest in reading through game design and development.

Organization of the project. The project included a group of senior and junior researchers responsible for conducting the research as well as a steering group of representatives from educational sciences and from an open-source software development project that offered a game engine as a basis of the work. The senior researchers supervised the work of the junior researchers, who were a group of university students. One school with one class of pupils (7th graders, 13–14 years) and their class teacher were involved.

Activities of the project. The project included five phases: first, the children were familiarized with an adventure game previously developed, utilizing the game engine of the open source project involved, to spark their ideation of the game they would like to develop (1). Next, they took part in an ideation workshop (2) in which they in groups envisioned how the existing game could be developed or modified. They identified new themes for the game, new puzzles that would be solved within, and new spaces and objects that would be available. Thereafter, the children took part in a game design workshop (3) in which they in groups specified a new space for the game with new puzzles, new objects, new storyline and associated textual elements. At the end of the session, the children voted on which idea would be further developed. In the next session, the children evaluated a game editor developed to modify the existing game (4). The children were asked to modify the spaces and objects available in the game with the editor and the editor was later developed to support the children even better. The last phase included again use of the game editor to modify the game (5) combined with exploring and evaluating other games.

Addressing Agency with Digital Technology

Envisioning digital technology. The project invited children to imagining future games based on an existing game that had been developed with a particular kind of game engine. The children were given freedom to decide (to ideate and vote) the theme of the future game.

Designing digital technology. The project invited children to concretize their game ideas into design solutions, for which they specified a storyline, puzzles, space, objects and textual elements.

Developing digital technology. The project invited, although to a limited extent, the children to actually modify the existing game with a game editor developed by the junior researchers for the purpose of allowing the children to actually develop the game.

Evaluating digital technology. The project included evaluation of digital tools during different events: the children evaluated the game editor during two occasions as well as other games during the last phase. However, they did not evaluate the game they had been developing.

Addressing Activism

Conceptions of being a good citizen. In the project, these conceptions were not addressed.

Learning goals of activism education. We maintain two of the learning goals pictured in this project (cf. Kirshner, 2007). Collective problem solving was central for the project: the children as a class and in their groups were involved in collective problem solving around the game and its development related to strengthening their reading interest and multiliteracies. Positive youth-adult relationships were fostered as the teacher and the researchers emphasized children's participation and influence in the game design a lot, starting from children being able to specify the theme of the game developed. The junior researchers worked closely with the children, trying to realize children's participation in game design and development.

Activities of activism education. We argue the project included two of the three central activities (Torres-Harding et al., 2018): goal-setting and action-taking. The children were invited to define the theme of the game to be developed and to take part in the development process. However, these activities are related only to children's agency to shape digital technology, not to societal problems in any broader sense.

Project Offering Children Design, Programming, and Making Experiences of an Interactive Board Game

Aims of the project. The project aimed at offering children experiences in design, programming and making through building an interactive physical board game, using digital fabrication and programming tools as resources.

Organization of the project. The project included a group of senior and junior researchers responsible for conducting the research. The senior researchers supervised the work of the junior researchers, who were a group of university students. One school with two classes of pupils (5th and 6th graders, 11–13 years) and their math teacher were involved.

Activities of the project. The project had four phases. In the first phase (1), the children were sensitized to the topics of gaming, programming and digital technology and familiarized with the concept of Fab Lab (including digital fabrication machinery). The researchers also presented the children with the overall design and development process and the idea of an interactive board game. In the design phase (2), the children were assigned into groups and they ideated their game spots, including the theme of the spot and the problem to be solved within. The children created sketches, storyboards and textual descriptions describing their game spot. They were also familiarized with various kinds of digital fabrication and programming tools with which to add interactivity to their game spots. The third phase involved making activities (3): the groups decided on art and craft materials and digital fabrication and programming tools to add interactivity to their game spot. They also visited the university Fab Lab for modelling and to create some physical objects needed for the game spots. Fourth, the pupils assembled and finalized the game spots in the school crafts facilities (4). The phase also included playing the game and evaluating it. The game was set on the school library floor: it was a playable version with all the game spots connected with 'tracks' leading to the next game spot. The children evaluated all the game spots and gave constructive feedback and improvement ideas for each game spot. They also were interviewed either in pairs or in groups of three pupils.

Addressing Agency with Digital Technology

Envisioning digital technology. The project invited children to imagine interactive future game spots that could be built with art and craft material and different kinds of digital fabrication and programming tools. The children were given the freedom to decide the theme of their game spot.

Designing digital technology. The project invited children to concretize their ideas into design solutions, for which they specified the theme, the problem to be solved and player interaction with the game.

Developing digital technology. The project invited, although to a limited extent, the children to add interactivity into the game spots with different kinds of digital fabrication and programming tools. The children were allowed to decide on the tools they would like to use.

Evaluating digital technology. The project included an evaluation of the game spots after playing the game: the children were asked to give constructive feedback and improvement ideas for all the game spots.

Addressing Activism

Learning goals of activism education. We maintain two of the learning goals pictured in this project (cf. Kirshner, 2007). Collective problem-solving was central to the project. The children as a class and in their groups were involved in collective problem-solving around the game and its development, related to strengthening their design, programming and making skills. Positive youth-adult relationships were also fostered: the researchers emphasized children's participation in the game design, allowing children to decide on the details of the game spots they developed. The junior researchers worked closely with the children, trying to realize children's participation in game design and development.

Activities of activism education. We argue the project included two of the three central activities (Torres-Harding et al., 2018): goal-setting and action-taking. The children were invited to define the theme of the game spots to be developed and to take part in their realization. However, these activities are related only to children's agency to shape digital technology, not to societal problems in any broader sense.

Project Offering Children Genuine Experiences in Game Design

Aims of the project. The project aimed at offering children genuine experiences in game design through children working in a team with adults, adults treating them as equal team members as much as possible. The project focused on ideating, designing, and testing a learning game for ~7–10-year-old children.

Organization of the project. The project included two senior researchers responsible for conducting the research and supervising the work of five junior researchers, who were university students and worked as a team with two 12–13-year-old children.

Activities of the project. The work simulated a real-life game development project. It consisted of requirements specification, design, implementation, and testing phases. Emphasis was paid to participating children's genuine contribution to the final outcome of the project, the game prototype, as well as children's participation in decision-making during the project. From the children's perspective the project started with collaborative face-to-face design workshops for the purposes of requirements specification for the game (1), the children and junior researchers working together and ideating and making decisions regarding the game requirements. Next, they worked together with the game graphics and user interface design (2), once again ideating and making decisions as a team, children having equal authority and decision-making power with adults. The adults implemented the game prototype (3) but the children participated once again in testing and evaluating it (4), this time doing the work online. In the end of the project the junior researchers and the children were interviewed.

Addressing Agency with Digital Technology

Envisioning digital technology. The project invited children to imagining a game for learning purposes. The children worked as equal team members with adults and made decisions together with adults.

Designing digital technology. The project invited children to concretize their ideas into design solutions such as game features, user interface design, and graphics for the game, working and making decisions equally with adults.

Developing digital technology. The children did not participate in the implementation of the game.

Evaluating digital technology. The children participated in testing the game prototype to search for faults in the software as well as in the evaluation of the design decisions in the prototype.

Addressing Activism

Conceptions of being a good citizen. These conceptions were not addressed in the project.

Learning goals of activism education. Collective problem solving and positive youth-adult relationships (cf. Kirshner, 2007) were central in this project. The children and adults worked as a team to solve a shared problem—how to create an engaging learning game—and the adults were specifically guided to treat children respectfully, listening to them, and giving them equal decision-making power to adults.

Activities of activism education. The project included all three central activities (Torres-Harding et al., 2018) to some extent: goal setting, action taking, and critical reflection. The children were invited to ideate and design a learning game for children younger than themselves; they took action for that purpose; and they reflected on the working process afterwards in interviews. However, these activities related only to children's agency to shape digital technology, not to societal problems in any broader sense.

Project Offering Experiences in Artificial Intelligence and its Application in Sustainable Development

Aims of the project. The project aimed at offering children increased understanding on artificial intelligence (AI) and its application through working with machine learning, robotics, and sustainable business ideating.

Organization of the project. A large multidisciplinary group of researchers planned and implemented a one-week project (5 days, 6 hours/day) where the 21 participants were 14–15-year-old children.

Activities of the project. The project included five phases. First, the children reflected on how they understand artificial intelligence (1). After that, they assembled a robot hand using given parts and instructions and, using natural language programming, programmed the hand to do certain tasks, training at the same time an AI application (2). After that, they were familiarized with history and basics of AI and machine learning, sustainable social innovations, and business idea development (3). In the next phase, they ideated a sustainable business idea that utilizes AI with an intention of 'making the world a better place' (4), working with a modified lean business model canvas (Maurya, 2022). Finally they presented their idea to a review board who gave them feedback (5). They also visited the university Fab Lab and did a small digital fabrication project there. Towards the end of the week they were interviewed and they were also asked to reconsider their understanding of what is AI. All work was done collaboratively in groups of 2–4 children.

Addressing Agency with Digital Technology

Envisioning digital technology. The project invited the children to imagine sustainable future AI technologies with a business case in mind.

Designing digital technology. Some of the children sketched preliminary designs of the AI technologies out of their own interest but it was not part of their task.

Developing digital technology. The project invited the children to assemble hardware (a robot), program software to control the hardware, train the related AI application, and use digital fabrication and programming for creating a small object, following given instructions when doing all these tasks.

Evaluating digital technology. The children presented other children their business ideas that used sustainable future AI technologies, and gave feedback to each other; this can be considered as evaluation of digital technology ideas.

Addressing Activism

Conceptions of being a good citizen. These conceptions were not addressed in the project.

Learning goals of activism education. Collective problem solving, development of identities of children and bridging with mainstream institutions (cf. Kirshner, 2007) can be seen to picture in the project. The children solved technical problems in teams when assembling the robot and doing the related programming tasks. They also addressed in their teams the problem of "how to make the world a better place" with the use of digital technology and new business, and gave feedback to other teams on their solutions. Development of identities of children was present to much smaller extent: the children were placed in a position where they imagined how the world would change through their own actions and many of them discussed whether that was realistic or not, but they were not specifically asked to reflect on their own identity as an actor in the process. Bridging with mainstream institutions (Kirshner, 2007) can be also seen to happen in some sense, as the children needed to consider what kind of structures 'in the adult world' (companies, funding organizations, technology developers) they would need to collaborate with to make their vision come true.

Activities of activism education. The project included all three central activities (Torres-Harding et al., 2018) to some extent: goal setting, action taking, and critical reflection. The children were asked to imagine how they could make the world a better place through their own actions (sustainable business idea that uses AI) and thus they needed to envision a goal they wanted to reach. They also needed to consider, to some extent, what actions would be needed to reach that goal, i.e., what kind of partners and funding they would need for their business and what kind of technology could potentially be used to solve the problem and how. They received feedback and critique from their peers as well as from adults and had a possibility to make changes in their business idea based on that feedback, i.e., they needed to do critical reflection of their own plans to some extent. So, they addressed societal problems from their own agency perspective but in a relatively mild form.

Project Tackling Bullying at School Through Digital Technology

Aims of the project. The project aimed at exploring the potential of critical design and critical making with children to tackle the problem of bullying at school.

Organization of the project. The project included a group of researchers responsible for conducting the research as well as a steering group with representatives from the educational administration of the City of Oulu and a youth research expert. Three schools with one class of pupils (2nd graders, 8–9 years or 6th graders, 12–13 years) and their class teachers were involved. After the work with the pupils, a group of university students continued developing the solutions further in collaboration with the children, supervised by the researchers.

Activities of the project. The project had nine phases for the participating children: the children were sensitized with the topic of bullying (1) and with their relationship with digital technology (2) through different kinds of reflective and creative activities and interviews. Afterwards, the children were invited in groups to ideate various kind of digital tools to tackle the problem of bullying at school through brainstorming and therapy inspired methods (3) as well as to critically reflect on their ideas through discussion of their underlying assumptions, laddering interviews and best and worst case scenario building (4). Thereafter, the child groups engaged in design, specifying their selected design solutions (5) and demonstrating their ideas with prototypes, starting with low-fidelity prototypes, continuing with interactive ones, using digital fabrication and programming tools (6). After this phase, the children engaged in drama: they ideated drama scenes through which they could showcase the value of their design solutions to their local school community and afterwards engaged in drama performances, in which other children and teachers acted as audiences (7). Thereafter, the children reflected on the work done: they presented their prototypes to their classmates, gave feedback to each other and were interviewed on their experiences (8). After these activities, a group of university students analyzed the children's prototypes and drama scenes, created video presentations of those and invited the children to vote on the idea most suitable for further development and to further refine the selected idea (9). Afterwards, the junior researchers developed more advanced prototypes based on the results of the children's work.

Addressing Agency with Digital Technology

Envisioning digital technology. The project invited children to imagining futures with digital tools that can be used for preventing or reducing bullying. Different kinds of brainstorming and reflection arousing methods were used for the purpose. However, the children were not allowed to specify the purposes of the digital tools to begin with, but instead their ideation was bounded by the bullying focus.

Designing digital technology. The project invited children to concretize their ideas into design solutions, for which they specified who would be using the design solution, where, when, and how as well as how the solution would look like and behave.

Developing digital technology. The project invited, although to a limited extent, children to actually deliver digital solutions: they were invited to use programming and digital fabrication tools to create interactive prototypes of their design solutions. However, the development of these digital tools was limited among children: they did not engage in programming or building of these solutions in any serious sense.

Evaluating digital technology. The project included evaluation of the digital tools during different phases. The children critically reflected on their own ideas during the early phases and they prototypes were placed under public scrutiny during the drama performances, even if this was not a formal evaluation event for the prototypes. In the next phase, the children were invited to comment on each others' ideas. The university students later on asked children to vote on their ideas using particular criteria. Hence, evaluation was accomplished in versatile ways in the project.

Addressing Activism

Conceptions of being a good citizen. In the project, we argue all these conceptions were addressed. The project aimed at tackling bullying at school, which can be connected with being a personally responsible citizen: entailing responsible behavior within one's community and which can also be seen to connect with obeying the law and following the school rules and principles (cf. Westheimer & Kahne, 2004). Moreover, the project invited children to take action in their school to address bullying that can be considered to be a civic matter and the children were familiarized with ways on civic engagement through the project and particularly the drama phase (cf. Westheimer & Kahne, 2004). The children were also invited to act as justice-oriented citizens, as social justice is heavily connected with tackling bullying and the children were engaged in critically analyzing the situation and in taking action towards increased social justice (cf. Westheimer & Kahne, 2004).

Learning goals of activism education. We maintain three out of the four learning goals pictured in this project (cf. Kirshner, 2007). Collective problem solving was central for the project: the children as a class and in their groups were involved in collective problem solving around the topic of bullying. The children's collaboration with the university students entailed development of new relationships with adult actors: the university students analyzed children's ideas and invited them to decide which idea to develop further which the university students did. The children were also later informed of the further developments. Another quite essential element was development of identities of children: both in the beginning of the project and in the end, children were invited to reflect on their own stance and activities related to being digital technology user, designer, maker and activist, trying to influence important societal matters. This, together with the project activities, aimed to strengthen children's identity considerations around these important topics. However, the project did not address bridging young people with mainstream institutions (Kirshner, 2007): on the topic of bullying, this could have been attempted as there are many institutions involved in the anti-bullying interventions in society, while this was not considered as part of this particular project.

Activities of activism education. We argue the project included two of the three central activities (Torres-Harding et al., 2018): the children were involved in action taking and critical reflection on their activities. However, they were not invited to define the goals of the project on a higher level, even if they were able to define the goals of their groupwork on a lower level: they were able to define within the framing of bullying what exactly they wish to advocate and address.

Summary of the Results

Table 13.2. summarizes our findings of the projects in terms of whether they were nurturing agency and activism in and through digital technology development.

Towards a Framework for Nurturing Children's Digital Technology Development Agency and Activism

Based on the insights gained through (1) combining literature on agency and activism of children with CCI literature on children's engagement in the development of digital technology and (2) analysis of a set of digital technology design and development projects with children, geared towards nurturing children's agency in different senses, we propose a framework (Fig. 13.1) for categorizing and mapping projects aiming at nurturing children's agency and activism in and through digital technology development. Figure 13.1 presents the framework as well as maps the projects analyzed in this chapter in order to concretize it.

As for the framrwork, the concept of transformative agency guides us to focus on the initiative and commitment of children to influence and transform

Table 13.2 Summary of the results

	Reading interest game	Interactive board game	Learning game with genuine participation	AI and sustainable development	Digital tools against bullying
Activities in digital technology development					
Digital technology envisioning	yes	yes	yes	yes	yes
Digital technology design	yes	yes	yes	no	yes
Digital technology implementation	yes	yes	no	yes	yes
Digital technology evaluation	somewhat	yes	yes	yes	yes
Activities in activism education					
Goal setting	somewhat	no	yes	no	no
Action taking	somewhat	somewhat	yes	yes	yes
Critical reflection	somewhat	somewhat	somewhat	somewhat	yes
Conceptions of being a good citizen advocated					
Responsible citizen	no	no	no	yes	yes
Participatory citizen	no	no	no	somewhat	yes
Justice oriented citizen	no	no	no	no	yes
Learning goals of activism education					
Collective problem solving	yes	yes	yes	yes	yes
Positive adult-child relationships	yes	yes	yes	no	yes
Bridges to mainstream institutions	no	no	no	yes	no
Activist identity development	no	no	no	somewhat	yes

the world, which entails seeing the world as changeable and imagining of alternative futures (Kajamaa & Kumpulainen, 2019; Rajala et al., 2013, citing Emirbayer & Mische, 1998; Rainio, 2010). The framework maintains that there are two dimensions relating to transformative agency along which to approach the projects: *digital technology development agency*, i.e. whether they make visible to children that digital technology is changeable and invite children to make a difference as regards it, and *societal agency*, i.e. whether they make visible to children that societal and civic matters are changeable and invite

Fig. 13.1 Framework for mapping projects on children's agency and activism through digital technology development. (Source: Figure generated by the authors)

children to make a difference as regards them. Overall, transformative agency entails going beyond adapting to breaking away or transforming the current practices (Kajamaa & Kumpulainen, 2019).

Figure 13.1 includes a mapping of our five example projects, which illustrate that it is possible to combine activism education with digital technology education in various ways and to various extents in the quest of nurturing the transformative agency of children. All five projects showcase how transformative agency regarding digital technology can be nurtured, entailing envisioning, designing, implementing, and/or evaluating (future) digital technologies. Of our five projects, three also showcase how children's transformative agency regarding societal and civic matters can be nurtured: they advocate tackling bullying or sustainable development through digital means or equal treatment of adults and children in collaborative projects, these projects also encourage children to collaboratively take action with peers as well as potentially with adult participants as well as to critically reflect on the process and the outcomes. We showcase how various conceptions of being a good citizen can also be integrated into the work.

However, we do acknowledge that there is room for improvement in terms of activism education. Our background is strong in children's digital technology education, particularly in one that encourages children to take part in the development of digital technology, not only to use it as it is. For activism, some projects illustrate interesting developments, while a lot more could be done. We wish to point out that transformative agency includes children questioning the current practices and breaking away from them, which could be accomplished in the projects in a much stronger sense than is the case with the current projects. Projects aiming at nurturing children's transformative agency could entail children inventing or transforming the existing digital technology development, digital technology education, activism, and activism education practices. This has not been nurtured in our projects, for which reason we see room for improvement along both dimensions in Fig. 13.1.

Our study has interesting implications for activism and digital technology education research and practice. We show it is possible to combine them in meaningful ways. We maintain that research and practice on activism education (e.g. Kirshner, 2007; Torres-Harding et al., 2018; Westheimer & Kahne, 2004) benefit from this study by being now better equipped to address digitalization and digital means in supporting the activism of children. Their activism and agency can and should be supported *in* digital technology development but even more importantly *through* digital technology development, i.e. such that is geared towards addressing important societal concerns. Children's digital technology education research and practice (e.g. Chu et al., 2017; Dindler et al., 2020; Iivari et al., 2018a, 2020; Iversen et al., 2017; Iversen et al. 2018) gain through this study important insights on how to integrate societal matters into digital technology education. Digital technology as such is not important but how and for what purpose it is used: children should be invited to critically reflect on that and to utilize digital technology for making the world a better place. We showcase how this is doable.

Table 13.3 presents some guidelines for researchers and practitioners interested in combining digital technology education with activism education. We propose guidelines for (1) basic projects entailing mere digital technology development, (2) advanced ones combining elements of activism education to the project, as well as (3) transformative ones that are specifically geared towards nurturing of transformative agency of children.

Conclusion

Our aim with this study was to explore how to nurture children's agency and activism in and through digital technology design and development. For that purpose, we analysed literature addressing agency, activism and children's participation in the development of digital technology as well as five digital technology design and development projects we have conducted with children. Our specific interest was to combine understanding from CCI research with agency and activism research to gain an increased understanding of how children's digital technology education can be advanced towards a more activism-oriented direction, which we consider valuable for researchers and practitioners engaged in activism as well as in digital technology education. For activism education, we showcase examples of how digital technology education can serve as a vehicle for increasing children's agency and activism competences, whereas for CCI research we give directions for where future research regarding child design protagonists could go.

This study has several limitations to consider. Our background is strong in CCI, not in activism education or in educational sciences. Therefore, aspects of activism education likely can be integrated into the projects in more versatile and stronger senses. Our projects have all been conducted in Finland, with a

Table 13.3 Guidelines for projects aiming at nurturing children's agency and activism in and through digital technology development

Project type	Project characteristics and learning goals
BASIC PROJECT—technology as a useful tool in everyday life: Digital technology development project showing digital technology as changeable—one can make a difference regarding it	• Increased agency in relation to digital technology: Children invited to envisioning, designing, implementing and evaluating (future) digital technologies
ADVANCED PROJECT—technology as a tool for solving a problem: Digital technology development project showing digital technology and societal and civic matters as changeable—one can make a difference regarding them	• Increased agency in relation to digital technology: Children invited to envisioning, designing, implementing and evaluating (future) digital technologies • Increased agency in relation to civic matters: Children encouraged to act as responsible, participatory and justice-oriented citizens • Increased agency in relation to activism: Children invited to collaborative problem solving with peers, adults, and mainstream institutions of relevance, building an activist identity
TRANSFORMATIVE PROJECT—technology as a component in transforming the world: Digital technology development project showing digital technology, societal and civic matters, and digital technology development and activism as changeable—one can make a difference regarding them	• Increased agency in relation to digital technology: Children invited to envisioning, designing, implementing and evaluating (future) digital technologies • Increased agency in relation to civic matters: Children encouraged to act as responsible, participatory and justice-oriented citizens • Increased agency in relation to activism: Children invited to collaborative problem solving with peers, adults, and mainstream institutions of relevance, building an activist identity • Increased transformative agency: Children invited to set the project goals, to specify how to take action and to do so, and to critically reflect on the project and its outcomes

particular educational system and cultural context. Projects in other contexts should be carried out to generate more generalizable insights. Also children's age needs to be considered as well as the influence of varied adults involved in the projects. As to the paths for future work, we particularly propose researchers and practitioners to try-out transformative projects with children, to understand in more detail what kind of challenges can be encountered and how children should be scaffolded in such projects.

References

Aubrey, J. (2004). The roots and process of social action. *Groupwork*, 14(2), 6–23.

Chu, S. L., Angello, G., Saenz, M., & Quek, F. (2017). Fun in Making: Understanding the experience of fun and learning through curriculum-based Making in the elementary school classroom. *Entertainment Computing*, 18, 31–40.

Dindler, C., Smith, R., & Iversen, O. S. (2020). Computational empowerment: participatory design in education. *CoDesign*, 16(1), 66–80.

Druin, A. (2002). The role of children in the design of new technology. *Behaviour and information technology*, 21(1), 1–25.

ECDG. (2019). *European Commission, Directorate-General for Education, Youth, Sport and Culture: Key competences for lifelong learning.* Publications Office. https://data.europa.eu/doi/10.2766/291008

Emirbayer, M., & Mische, A. (1998). What is agency?. *American Journal of Sociology*, 103(4), 962–1023.

Freire, P. (2017) *Pedagogy of the oppressed*. Penguin Random House, London.

Hartikainen, H., Venta-Olkkonen, L., Kinnula, M. & Iivari, N. (2021). Entrepreneurship education meets FabLab: Lessons learned with teenagers. *Proceedings of the FabLearn Europe/MakeEd 2021—An International Conference on Computing, Design and Making in Education (FabLearn Europe/MakeEd 2021)*. Association for Computing Machinery, New York, NY, USA, Article 2, 1–9.

Hourcade, J. (2008). Interaction design and children. *Foundations and Trends in Human-Computer Interaction* 1(4), 277–392.

Iivari, N., & Kinnula, M. (2016). Inclusive or inflexible: A critical analysis of the school context in supporting children's genuine participation. In *Proceedings of the 9th Nordic Conference on Human-Computer Interaction,* Association for Computing Machinery, New York, NY, USA, 1–10.

Iivari, N., & Kinnula, M. (2018). Empowering children through design and making: towards protagonist role adoption. In *Proceedings of the 15th Participatory Design Conference: Full Papers-Volume 1,* Association for Computing Machinery, New York, NY, USA, 1–12.

Iivari, N., Kinnula, M., & Molin-Juustila, T. (2018a). You have to start somewhere: initial meanings making in a design and making project. In *Proceedings of the 17th ACM Conference on Interaction Design and Children*, Association for Computing Machinery, New York, NY, USA, 80–92.

Iivari, N., Kinnula, M., Molin-Juustila, T., & Kuure, L. (2018b). Exclusions in social inclusion projects: Struggles in involving children in digital technology development. *Information Systems Journal*, 28(6), 1020–1048.

Iivari, N., Sharma, S., & Venta-Olkkonen, L. (2020). Digital transformation of everyday life–How COVID-19 pandemic transformed the basic education of the young generation and why information management research should care? *International Journal of Information Management*, 55, 102183.

Iversen, O. S., Smith, R. C., & Dindler, C. (2017). Child as protagonist: Expanding the role of children in participatory design. In *Proceedings of the 2017 conference on interaction design and children*, Association for Computing Machinery, New York, NY, USA, 27–37.

Iversen, O. S., Smith, R. C., & Dindler, C. (2018). From computational thinking to computational empowerment: a 21st century PD agenda. In *Proceedings of the 15th Participatory Design Conference: Full Papers-Volume 1*, Association for Computing Machinery, New York, NY, USA, 1–11.

Kajamaa, A., & Kumpulainen, K. (2019). Agency in the making: Analyzing students' transformative agency in a school-based makerspace. *Mind, Culture, and Activity*, 26(3), 266–281.

Kinnula, M., Durall, E., & Haukipuro, L. (2022). Imagining better futures for everybody–Sustainable entrepreneurship education for future design protagonists. In *6th FabLearn Europe/MakeEd Conference 2022*, Association for Computing Machinery, New York, NY, USA, 1–8.

Kinnula, M., Iivari, N., Molin-Juustila, T., Keskitalo, E., Leinonen, T., Mansikkamäki, E., Käkelä, T. & Similä, M. (2017). Cooperation, combat, or competence building–what do we mean when we are 'empowering children' in and through digital technology design? In *Proceedings of International Conference on Information Systems 2017*, Association for Information Systems.

Kirshner, B. (2007). Introduction: Youth activism as a context for learning and development. *American Behavioral Scientist*, 51(3), 367–379.

Maurya, A. (2022). *Running lean*. O'Reilly Media, Inc.

Molin-Juustila, T., Kinnula, M., Iivari, N., Kuure, L., & Halkola, E. (2015). Multiple voices in ICT design with children–a nexus analytical enquiry. *Behaviour & Information Technology*, 34(11), 1079–1091.

Rainio, A. P. (2010). *Lionhearts of the playworld: An ethnographic case study of the development of agency in play pedagogy*, 233. University of Helsinki, Institute of Behavioural Sciences, Studies in Educational Sciences.

Rajala, A., Hilppö, J., Lipponen, L., & Kumpulainen, K. (2013). Expanding the chronotopes of schooling for the promotion of students' agency. *Identity, community, and learning lives in the digital age*, 107–125. Cambridge University Press.

Salian, K., Sim, G., & Read, J. (2013). Can children perform a heuristic evaluation? In *Proceedings of the 11th Asia Pacific Conference on Computer Human Interaction, APCHI'13*, Association for Computing Machinery, New York, NY, USA, 137–141.

Scaife, M., Rogers, Y., Aldrich, F. & Davies, M. (1997). Designing for or designing with? Informant design for interactive learning environments. In *Proceedings of the ACM SIGCHI Conference on Human Factors in Computing Systems, CHI '97*, Association for Computing Machinery, New York, NY, USA, 343–350.

Sharma, S., Hartikainen, H., Ventä-Olkkonen, L., Eden, G., Iivari, N., Kinnunen, E., Holappa, J. Kinnula, M., Molin-Juustila, T., Okkonen, J., Iversen, O., Kotilainen, S. and Fatas, R. (2022). In Pursuit of Inclusive and Diverse Digital Futures: Exploring the potential of design fiction in education of children. *Interaction Design and Architecture(s) Journal* 51, 219–248.

Sharp, H., Preece, J. and Rogers, Y. (2019). *Interaction Design. Beyond human-computer interaction*. John Wiley & Sons, Indianapolis, Indiana, USA.

Szabo, C., Sheard, J., Luxton-Reilly, A., Becker, B. A., & Ott, L. (2019). Fifteen years of introductory programming in schools: a global overview of K-12 initiatives. In

Proceedings of the 19th Koli Calling International Conference on Computing Education Research, 1–9.

Torres-Harding, S., Baber, A., Hilvers, J., Hobbs, N., & Maly, M. (2018). Children as agents of social and community change: Enhancing youth empowerment through participation in a school-based social activism project. *Education, Citizenship and Social Justice*, 13(1), 3–18.

Unterfrauner, E., Voigt, C. & Hofer, M. (2021). The effect of maker and entrepreneurial education on self-efficacy and creativity. *Entrepreneurship Education* 4(4), 403–424.

Ventä-Olkkonen, L., Iivari, N., Sharma, S., Molin-Juustila, T., Kuutti, K., Juustila-Cevirel, N., Kinnunen, E. & Holappa, J. (2021). Nowhere to now-here: Empowering children to reimagine bully prevention at schools using critical design fiction. In *Designing Interactive Systems Conference 2021,* Association for Computing Machinery, New York, NY, USA, 734–748.

Westheimer, J., & Kahne, J. (2004). What kind of citizen? The politics of educating for democracy. *American Educational Research Journal*, 41(2), 237–269.

CHAPTER 14

The Challenges of Gamification in Brazil's Educational Delivery During Covid 19

Julia Stateri

Introduction

After almost 2 years of the COVID-19 pandemic, I am seeking to critically address the scope of the application of gamification in the remote work environment. I intend to discern the methodology of gamification from the concept that sells the idea of its application as a solution for increasing employee productivity in a way that, unfortunately, does not pay attention to their well-being.

In previous work, I spoke about the distrust, discouragement, unfamiliarity with technology, and constant distractions that are just some of the challenges that students mentioned to teachers when emergency remote education was proposed at the beginning of the lockdown period. Teachers, in turn, were forced to adapt urgently, often without the provision of resources for the task. Their new workday mixed asynchronous content preparation and the routine of synchronously teaching classes.

In this scenario, the idea of 'gamification' was being sold as a magic solution to the problems of student engagement, supposedly guaranteeing a light and dynamic teaching-learning process. However, to comprehend the reality of things, it is necessary to analyze the application of gamification under a broad perspective of economic limitation imposed on social minorities. These constraints directly impacted their access to information and to the collaborative construction of knowledge.

J. Stateri (✉)
Instituto de Tecnologia e Liderança - Inteli, São Paulo, Brazil

© The Author(s), under exclusive license to Springer Nature Switzerland AG 2024
H. S. Dunn et al. (eds.), *The Palgrave Handbook of Everyday Digital Life*,
https://doi.org/10.1007/978-3-031-30438-5_14

Gamification

Although it has gained greater visibility in Brazil over the last decade, gamification (locally called "gamificação") appeared in 2002. Its creation was attributed to Nick Pelling, a game designer and programmer in an attempt to establish a consultancy to create interfaces similar to those found in video games, transposing them to other devices. Pelling used elements, hitherto found only in electronic games, in interfaces of ATMs, cell phones, among others.

In its first 20 years of existence, gamification has gained attention in the world, beyond the global north, especially from 2010 onwards, due to the popularization of consultancies that use its premises mainly in the areas of marketing and sales. Sometimes its application is fundamentally based on the so-called PBL triad (*Points, Badges, Leaderboards*), but gamification is far from limited to these resources.

From the universe of existing definitions, for this consideration, I select the one presented by Dan Hunter and Kevin Werbach (2012, p. 26) in the book *For the Win: How Game Thinking Can Revolutionize your Business*. The authors define gamification as "the use of game elements and game-design techniques in non-game contexts." We can scrutinize this definition in the understanding that gamification, as a methodology, aims to use elements found in games—such as real-time feedback, learning by doing, and many of the motivation and engagement resources used in these specific products—in systems proposed in a non-game environment. These systems can be more or less pleasant, with relaxed or synthetic and functionalist language. It is important to know that the main change is the reversal of the priority of the fun factor, which must be present, but which—unlike the game—is not set as the main objective.

The COVID-19 Pandemic and Gamification in Brazil

The introduction of the social isolation policies as a strategy to contain the new Coronavirus in Brazil began to be established in March 2020. We saw, in different reaction times, companies and educational institutions, from basic to higher education, suspending their face-to-face activities. Quite quickly, depending on the type of tasks to be performed, the work environment began migrating to the home office, and classes began to take place in the virtual environment. Regarding remote teaching, there was a reaction of initial resistance by most parents and students, as well as anxiety among some teachers who were helpless in the adoption of technologies for connectivity that until then were not part of their daily lives.

In the specific case of the resistance of parents to remote classes from elementary to high school, one of the difficulties encountered was to establish a routine in which parents could work at home with their children attending and having classes in the same environment. Depending on income of the family, there were difficulties such as separating work and study environments. The availability of sufficient computers and internet with adequate bandwidth to

14 THE CHALLENGES OF GAMIFICATION IN BRAZIL'S EDUCATIONAL DELIVERY... 247

support multiple devices and video calls simultaneously, were some of the factors that contributed to the adaptation process becoming even harder.

Still in relation to emergency remote teaching, after the adaptation phase, it became increasingly noticeable that classes taught in the digital environment could not be the mere repetition of tiring explanatory classes, a model whose use is questionable even during face-to-face meetings. The lack of student engagement and the difficulty of promoting the motivation of both parties involved in the teaching-learning process stood out as the main reasons for the search for new teaching methodologies in the virtual or hybrid environments.

A simple way to measure the growing interest in gamification in Brazil can be done using the Google Trends tool. According to Statcounter data from February 2022 (Statcounter, 2022), Google is the search tool preferred by 98.15% of the Brazilian online population. Thus, even though Google Trends offers a segment of this population that has access to the internet, loaded by the possible biases of a proprietary tool, it provides an interesting overview that is relevant to the topic that we will discuss here.

As demonstrated in Fig. 14.1 below, use of 'search term' and 'subject' on Google Trends tool, generated a comparative graph (see Fig. 14.1) that shows us the increase in the demand for information on gamification in 2019 (in blue), through 2020 (red) to in 2021 (yellow).

It indicates that, in 2019, searches remained reasonably constant, given the common and expected variations. In 2020, the first peak of searches can be found in the month of May, the third month of the suspension of face-to-face activities in the country. From then on, the intensity of searches only increases, demonstrating that as the tension of isolation increases and it becomes more difficult to maintain engagement in remote activities, gamification became a more and more attractive and promising methodology.

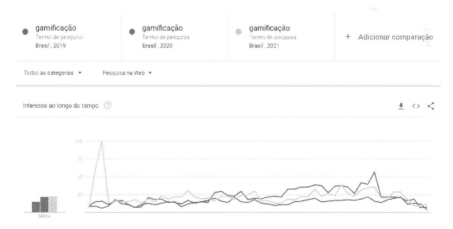

Fig. 14.1 Increased interest in gamification in Brazil. (Source: Figure generated using Google Trends (2022))

Fig. 14.2 Regional section of searches. (Source: Figure generated using Google Trends (2022))

In January 2021, we have the sharpest peak of the comparative chart, at a time when the population was more acquainted with the practice of remote teaching and learning activities. However, the difficulty of staying active and productive in these times became an even greater challenge.

If we consider the regional sections (Fig. 14.2), we can see that, in 2020, most searches took place in the Southern regions, part of the Midwest region, and in the North of the country. In 2021, searches also intensified in the Southeast and Northeast regions.

It is interesting to note that every year searches related to the term gamification have also changed. In 2019 (Fig. 14.3), related searches indicated interests in understanding what gamification would be in education and in companies.

In 2020 (Fig. 14.4), searchers started forming more pragmatic questions, focused on the educational themes that we can assume are related to the challenges of teaching students through remote learning, while maintaining attention. Teaching plans for early childhood education are sought. The Active Methodology is associated with gamification, and the PDF file extension is placed. The user was probably hoping to find a more complete guide or a book that could explain the step-by-step use of the gamified methodology in education.

Fig. 14.3 Related searches in 2019. (Source: Figure generated using Google Trends (2022))

Fig. 14.4 Related Searches in 2020. (Source: Figure generated using Google Trends (2022))

Finally, in 2021 (Fig. 14.5), searches on tools and solutions (Kahoot[1] and Brainly[2]) were associated, and, at the same time, searches on gamification in companies reappeared.

In a survey with similar terms, in the related queries in 2019, both the term 'gamification' and the subject 'ludification' had the bulk of their searches triggered by associations in the following order: "gamification meaning", "what is gamification", "what is gamification", "gamification", "gamification in education", and even "gameficação" (sic). It should also be noted that "gamification in companies" appears among the main related queries. In 2020, the main research related to the search for the term 'gamification' featured "gamification in education", "gamification what is it", "gamification in early childhood

---

[1] Kahoot is a free game-based learning platform that uses multiple choices trivia that can be accessed by a browser—https://kahoot.it/.

[2] Brainly is a knowledge-sharing community between students and experts whose focus is to help with homework—https://brainly.com.br/.

Fig. 14.5 Related searches in 2021. (Source: Figure generated using Google Trends (2022))

education" and "gamification in education". Regarding searches related to the subject of 'gamification', the main related searches were: "gamification", "gamificação," and "gamification in education".

Based on this unpretentious investigation, we can venture to say that gamification is being considered, throughout the analyzed period, as an increasingly attractive alternative for education. We may also conclude that there is a direction of this interest in Brazil associated with early childhood education. The watchful eyes on gamification in companies before the pandemic, once again considered it as an interesting alternative for the engagement of their employees. This was the case even as we are experiencing the beginning of a resumption of the face-to-face work regime, given the advance of mass vaccination in the country at the end of 2021 and beginning of 2022. But is gamification the answer to the problems accentuated by the pandemic? Before we directly address the gamification of work, we need to understand what we are referring to when we talk about digital work and remote work.

Digital Work and Remote Work

There is a lot of speculation about the formation of a globalized economy, especially considering that the demands of employability in different parts of the world are quite similar. These range from the need for constant up-skilling to the adoption of proprietary technologies. In some instances, the ethical stance of the corporations owning these software products are not always aligned to the interests or safety of their users. Ursula Huws affirms that:

> With the terms of employability of an ever-increasing share of the world's population determined directly or indirectly by these same corporations, the conditions would apparently finally be in place for the fulfillment of Karl Marx's injunction found at the end of the *Communist Manifesto*: 'Workers of the world, unite.' However, are there in fact signs of the emergence of a global proletariat with a common conscience? (Huws, 2009, p. 37)

Even today, the likely answer will be "no." The author explains that human activities are at both ends of the production and consumption processes. The situation combines the inexorable industrialization of the globe, structured on the production of goods, the process of capital accumulation and the expansion of consumer dependence on the products necessary for survival. We can mention consumables like food, medicine and fuel, but there are also technologies that we have become dependent on in order to work, share information and even build personal relationships.

Ruy Braga (2009, p. 60) says that amid the existing changes in contemporary work, there is a certain optimism regarding the use of technology. For Braga, the possibilities that emerge from the connection and organization in a network would bring "the unique opportunity to rescue work from the bureaucratic domination imposed by the capitalist company." Informational work, as the author designates it, would have the potential to solve the issue of the division of labor between those who design products and those who actually perform their production. Braga then turns to the work *of* Manuel Castells (1999), in the observation of the new complexities that arise with the establishment of this new scenario of the world of work:

> [...] Castells presents the desolation picture of a "new social fracture" polarized by skilled workers included and unskilled workers excluded by the network. Under the impact of information flows, the network welcomes winners and abandons losers. At the same time, the Catalan sociologist describes informationism as a necessary and positive historical overcoming of industrialism. (Braga, 2009, p. 62)

Theorists of the 1990s such as those by Castells (1999) and Lojkine (1995), despite presenting reflections relevant to the understanding of the 'informationalization' of work, carry a technological optimism that remains evident among scholars in the area. It is possible, however, to find counterpoints, as in the work of Jamie Woodcock (2020, p. 146), who says:

> Marx describes two ways in which surplus-value can be generated. The first is by increasing the exploitation of 'relative surplus-value', which means reducing the total amount of labor time needed to produce the equivalent of the wages of workers—or making them produce more while working. This may involve new machines or technologies or finding more efficient ways to organize the workspace. The second way is by increasing 'absolute surplus-value', which involves increasing productive time at work—making people work longer.

The author addresses the precariousness of the work of professionals in the gaming area, in which many believe they will find the 'dream job', especially an entire generation that grew up playing video games. However, far from enjoying more time to perform creative activities, with more autonomy in making decisions that involve product development, workers in the game industry are often subjected to crunch time—strenuous workdays and without enough time to rest because they must meet absurd delivery deadlines.

Our expectations of a technological world in which heavy or repetitive work would be taken over by machines so that humanity could become free to live and create in harmony, were quickly relegated to the realm of science fiction. Today, we know very well that the adoption of new technologies and increased productivity are not always linked to an improvement in the worker's quality of life and work.

The same can be said for remote work. Although this modality brings indisputable advantages such as the reduction of fuel expenses and long, stressful commutes, new problems are generated, such as the difficulty of managers in understanding the existing limits between the time dedicated by the employee to their private lives and that dedicated to their working day. Working from home does not mean that the worker's time should be dedicated 24 hours a day, 7 days a week to meet the demands of their employers.

In Brazil, according to a survey published in July 2021 by the Instituto de Pesquisa Econômica Aplicada [Institute for Applied Economic Research] (IPEA), 11% of employed people who were not on leave were performing their tasks remotely throughout 2020. The research brings results from a Covid 19 survey called the Pesquisa Nacional sobre Amostra de Domicílios [National Survey on Household Sample] (PNAD) COVID-19, conducted from May to November 2020. It was observed that most remote workers had completed higher education and worked with the private sector, with strong participation of education professionals.

Of the 8.2 million people working remotely in Brazil during the COVID-19 pandemic, 56.1% were women, 65.6% were white, 74.6% had completed higher education, 31.8% were aged between 30 and 39 years, and 63.9% were employed in the private sector. Of this last slice, 14.5% of the people surveyed were in service activities, 10.3% in the education area, 7.7% in the communication area, 5.5% in the financial sector, and 3.6% in the health area. In the public sector, 14.4% were municipal workers, 13.9% worked in the state public sector, and 7.8% in the federal sector.

The research presents an interesting perspective when comparing the percentage of people in remote activity by sector, for example in the area of private sector education, where 51% of professionals worked remotely during the period. In the financial area, 38.8% of Brazilian professionals worked remotely, and 34.7% worked in the communication area.

Regionally, most of the people surveyed were in the Southeast region: 58.2%, from a base of 4.7 million people. The region with the lowest ranking was the North, with 3.3% of people working remotely.

Based on these research results, we were able to observe that the possibility of remote work—even in a critical moment like the pandemic—was a privilege reserved for a specific part of society. It has a regional, racial and class differentiation. This reality cannot be ignored when we think about the future of 'informationalized' and remote work in our society.

Working in a Connected Brazil

When we observe the positive changes from the advent of information technology and, above all, network connections, it is quite often mentioned that there is an increase in the dissemination of publicly accessible information. This is usually associated with a whole imaginary linked to the democratization of access to information and, therefore, to education. It is also linked with the transfer of responsibility for learning to the one who would be the protagonist in the process: the student. In a simplistic view, it may seem that information is available to anyone who wants to make use of it. Were that so, we would all be information curators and self-taught learners through the internet. But how much truth is there in that original statement? While the scope of this chapter does not extend to a broad analysis of the myth of universal information access, we will consider here the infrastructure issues that enable audience connectivity, something easier to measure based on surveys performed by third parties.

To talk about the ubiquity of connectivity, we can look at access data for the technologies currently used. In terms of education, for example, an article published by UN News in April 2020, established that half of the students who were out of school due to the COVID-19 pandemic did not have a computer at home. Considering that there were about 826 million students out of school at that time, worldwide, a UNESCO study (apud UN News, 2020) showed that almost 706 million of them did not even have internet connection in their homes. In the Global South, the situation was even worse, as in the case of Sub-Saharan Africa, where 89% of students did not have computers at home, and 82% did not have access to the internet at the time of the study. There were about 56 million students without access to mobile phone networks—one of the main access alternatives that was and continues to be used for communication. The phone would usually be used to send notices and extra materials to students for study and even for daily message exchanges between teachers and students, mainly in this remote emergency teaching period.

Our local example within Brazil reaffirms the difficulties presented even before the pandemic period. At a June 2020 press conference held by TIC Educação (ICT Education) on the results of a 2019 survey, it was disclosed that: 98% of students from urban schools access the internet by smartphone, 40% of rural schools had at least one computer with internet access, and 9% of rural schools had access to the network through other devices. Among teachers, 33% claimed to have participated in a continuing education course on computers and the internet. These data may be viewed in the light of another survey conducted by Comscore (2020) about the impact of COVID-19 on the media and internet sector in Latin America. This showed that 71% of the Brazilian population had used the internet, with some 97% of the population gaining access via mobile devices. The profile of the Brazilian student who accesses emergency remote education is one who accesses the internet via smartphone, often using a network with low connectivity to receive and transmit data.

Although it is not the intention of this chapter to delve deeply into the specific issues of gender, it should be noted that most of the people surveyed about the removal from face-to-face work and the adoption of the home offices were women. In this sense, it is fair to mention that the impact of the pandemic on the productivity of women was felt greatest among female teachers, black women, with or without children, and white women with children. This outcome was a confirmation of the inequalities faced mainly in the distribution of domestic tasks that consume time and energy during the work day and with remote studies by their children (UFRGS, 2020).

According to the Pesquisa Nacional por Amostra de Domicílios Contínua [Continuous National Household Sample Survey] carried out by the Instituto Brasileiro de Geografia e Estatística—IBGE [Brazilian Institute of Geography and Statistics] and published in May 2020, women dedicated an average of 21 hours per week to housework and care for family members, while men performed these activities for an average of 11 hours per week only. In the case of female research professors, the result can be seen in low productivity during the pandemic period, compared to their male peers (Parent in Science, 2020). This situation contributes to accentuating the vulnerability of women arising from the gender/race intersectionality and economic fragility.

Gamification of Work: Vulnerabilities Before and During the Pandemic

In the previous section, we discussed the reduction in professional productivity by gender, race and social class. In these scenarios, gamification emerged as a promise of engagement and of increased productivity in both the educational and corporate environments. But what does that really mean? Does gamification emerge as a tool for the better organization of work by those who perform it or as an instrument of oppression by the employer?

In May 2011, Ian Bogost, a US-based Professor and Director of the Program in Film & Media Studies and Professor of Computer Science & Engineering at Washington University in St. Louis, published on the website Gamasutra (current Game Developer) the text: "Persuasive Games: Exploitationware." In this text, Bogost explores the rhetoric of serious games and gamification and ponders on the popularity of the latter term.

Bogost explained that the idea of games being used beyond entertainment, in fields of application such as business, health, education and even the military field is something built thanks to the power of attraction they have. Games attract and captivate us to perform repetitive activities, make us spend money on things that don't physically exist, like clothing and equipment for avatars and, more recently, NFTs,[3] for example. This power of attraction, of engagement with the media, is what makes even those who don't study or work pro-

---

[3] NFT stands for Non-Fungible Token. It represents a cryptographic token that is unique and data stored in a form of digital ledger called 'blockchain'.

fessionally in the field of game development feel tempted to use games for their own purposes. Bogost affirms:

> "Serious games" has a specific rhetorical purpose. It is a phrase devised to earn the support of high-level governmental and corporate officials, individuals for whom "game" implies the terror just described; something trite and powerful, something that trivializes things, even if that trivialization is precisely part of its power. (Bogost, 2011a)

According to this author, gamification would also have its own rhetoric. The suffix "-ification" would imply that the application of game elements in any media and tasks would become easy and automatic. The details of solving the problems identified in the gamified products or services would be left aside, due to this facility, this glaze, and therein lies the problem, as pointed out by the author. Would gamification be applied to solve the root problems identified in educational and professional structures or would it just transpose operational mechanics that make games work to generate a sense of enjoyment in a problematic process?

> When you -ify something, you put it in a particular state, or you fill it with a particular quality. We can purify water by running it through a filter. We can clarify a confusing topic through explanation. We can amplify a signal by boosting its oscillation rate. We can beautify a city by planting trees or removing litter. We can falsify a report by interweaving lies with truth. We can humidify a dry bedroom by introducing water vapor into the air. We can magnify an image by placing it behind an optical instrument. We can terrify a child by jumping out unseen from behind an obstruction. (Bogost, 2011a)

Bogost then uses the term "exploitationware" to refer to the process proposed by the defenders of gamification, arguing that the process supported by the concept would replace real result incentives with fictional ones. Such rhetorical benefits would be dissociated from the practice of playing, because, while games would exist for the purpose of entertainment without the burden of commitments of the world outside the game, gamification or "exploitationware" would connect the user to mandatory actions that do not solve the problems and only encourage the practice of repetition. Gamification, he argues, would lead to more gamification, not increased knowledge production or creative work. Superficial and repetitive actions would encourage the mechanization that we have already seen in other work models, such as the Fordist model. In short, for Bogost (2011b), gamification is a marketing term for making businesses more attractive, as categorically expressed in his text as follows:

> More specifically, gamification is marketing bullshit, invented by consultants as a means to capture the wild, coveted beast that is videogames and to domesticate it for use in the grey, hopeless wasteland of big business, where bullshit already reigns anyway. (Bogost, 2011b)

The revolt expressed by the author is understandable if the marketing perspective is taken as the only true outcome of gamification. It would replace important decisions on productivity issues at work tied to employee needs based on the enjoyment of an interface that encourages empty repetition of tasks. Rewards such as a prominent position in the system for the "employee of the month" in lieu of a real bonus or financial stability may be offered. Upgrading your user level with an increase in the number of tasks performed instead of offering a healthy environment of work or more free time outside the company may also be proffered. These represent just some of the examples of pitfalls the use of gamification can instill in employees already exposed to exhausting working hours, with rights undermined by political and economic crises that only seem to multiply in current times. Let us evaluate, then, if there are other directions for gamification and its application.

To Gamify Or Not: That Is the Question

Against the background of the preceding analysis, the short answer would be: "Individually, no." There are two problems that can be identified in the attempt to associate gamification as a possible solution to the difficulties of engagement, both in the field of teaching and in the field of work. The first one, as pointed out by Bogost (2011a, 2011b), regards the application of elements found in games in the proposition of systems that do not solve problems found in the structural base of the institution or moreso in the society in which the user is inserted. This is whether this user is a student at a school undergoing a remote emergency teaching stage or an employee working via home office during the pandemic. If this user's access to the system is limited by issues such as low internet connectivity, for example, there is little to discuss about how the gamified system itself can solve this problem or facilitate improved work or study.

In the case of educational institutions during the pandemic, ways were often sought to overcome infrastructure barriers, such as Unicamp (2020), which loaned equipment and provided internet access to its undergraduate and graduate students. Other possible solutions were indicated by the director-general of UNESCO, Audrey Azoulay, in an interview with ONU News [UN News] (2020), including the use of community radio and television broadcasts as tools for remote education.

On the other hand, in a specific scenario where the infrastructure in educational institutions is taken for granted, gamification can be one of the many methodologies that can help engage the students in the learning process. A tool that must be handled by prepared teachers, due to planning with clear metrics and objectives, supported by the institution.

Now, regarding companies, especially those of a private nature, it was noticeable that employees unable to adapt to the new demands of work in a short time would be replaced by others with better adaptability or resources to perform their functions. These structures are not limited to technological issues, as we see in an excerpt from a report by Nádia Silva to the BBC.

> "Sometimes I would wake up at 4 am to finish my work before the baby woke up. I also did all the housework," she tells BBC News Brasil. "Two months later, I asked the company for a new arrangement and a raise, so I could pay for a babysitter. I think they thought I wasn't worth all that. Their generosity was to fire me, which at least gave me compensation." (Idoeta, 2020)

It must be seen that, even if the issue of access to technology and information is resolved, it is possible that the user is not in a position to sufficiently master the gamified environment to be self-actualized, due to the lack of minimum conditions that meet their livelihood needs. A quick reference to the Theory of Human Motivation, published in 1943 by Abraham Maslow, can help us understand that, for the subject to feel willing to create and seek fulfillment, it is necessary that they have their basic needs satisfied.

Maslow (1943) explains that motivation linked to physiological needs overrides any others. A person who is in need of food, security, esteem and self-actualization will look for a way to satisfy their hunger before even considering their own safety—let alone start engaging in the activities proposed by a gamified system for task management. The reality of unemployment and the deprivations resulting from it are accentuated in the context of the pandemic, which makes it even more difficult to address the problem of remote education and work in a democratic and egalitarian way.

The second problem to be addressed is the erroneous assumption that gamification is something unique to the digital environment only. If we go back to Hunter and Werbach's (2012, p. 26) definition that "gamification is the use of game elements and game design techniques in a context other than the game itself," we can think about games, whether they are digital or not, as products composed of smaller parts, as a system. Rules, analog and digital resources such as board, cards, dice, or electronic visual interface, and programmatic code, must present themselves in harmony to provide the integrated experience of the game.

One of the main characteristics of games, transposed to gamified systems, is real-time feedback. If we think of the example of a shooting video game, when the character controlled by the player is hit, it receives information that says something is happening: the joystick can vibrate, the avatar makes some sound and the wound is usually represented through some kind of visual effect. What matters here is to understand that if something to be avoided happens during the game with your character, the real-time feedback causes the player to correct their action or strategy while continuing the previous shooting game, perhaps looking for a wall to hide and avoid getting hit again.

If, in the traditional teaching environment, the teacher usually transmits information in an explanatory way to the students and then demands in some way that this content be learned. The same occurs in the corporate environment with the tasks to be performed, whether they are parts of larger projects or related to sales targets that the employee will need to achieve. In both cases, this charge usually takes place through periodic monthly, bimonthly, half-yearly, or even annual reports or balance sheets. There is a long time-span between the transmission of demands, the execution of the task and the identification of results or execution difficulties.

Considering the possibility of breaking an assessment into smaller challenges, gradually more complex as the tasks are solved, it would be possible to apply the characteristic of fast (if not real-time) feedback that can be translated into a gamified system counting on points and extra activities, with the distribution of personal attributes to the profile of each user, etc. While none of this need to take place exclusively in a digital environment, it is far more practical to do so in a digital environment where tracking methods and assertive metrics to follow up the progress of the student are already available in the gamified platform.

Games have very specific objectives to be achieved, which facilitates the understanding of basic tasks, minimizing errors and sectioning problems that are too big to be solved at once or by a single person. A gamified system with a clear objective can be outlined by the gamification methodology, establishing an action plan that can be present in the digital environment or outside it. In order for user participation to be stimulated, it is necessary to understand their motivations to provide the desired engagement.

Ideally, when creating a gamified system, users are expected to participate and feel engaged without the promise of rewards external to the system such as gifts or the like. The same engagement found in the game for pleasure is sought—the motivation to move forward and surpass new challenges to overcome limits and develop new skills.

Therefore, it can be said that gamification is also a form of 'motivational design', especially for providing a means by which system users can choose to develop new behaviors. Hunter and Werbach (2012) use the idea of 'intrinsic motivation' to characterize this motivation that arises from the user's own interest in developing through the system, in contrast to the other motivation that comes from rewards external to the systems, called 'extrinsic.'

Understanding what motivates users of a given gamified system, working on the elements extracted from games to stimulate engagement and making behavioral changes naturally pleasant are not simple tasks. However, it is essential to understand that these aspects do not represent a work that is restricted to the digital environment. Pre-configured online tools can make the process more practical for those who are embarking on this world, but their technical mastery hardly solves the whole scenario, as we have seen so far.

To draw a conclusion based on all the information that has been presented in this chapter, we can summarize the following: gamification is not a magic solution to all engagement and motivation problems. Even before applying it, we need to look more broadly at the entire scenario composed of elements that range from the socioeconomic context of users to the prospect of adequate tools for implementation and access by all people involved.

Conclusion

Gamifying education or the corporate environment does not depend on the most advanced technological resources or complex digital interfaces. It depends much more on understanding the structural problems that involve the user's context and corresponding with the creation of systems that are really at their disposal, facilitating their workflow, making processes clearer, avoiding errors, with increased productivity as a consequence. The same can be said about other technologies and the supposed neutrality regarding them. That is precisely the reason why it is of the utmost importance that we discuss the context regarding the use of digital media and the same reason why I approach this theme specifically in this handbook chapter. What happens in the digital doesn't only have an impact in the virtual environment, but also in the offline world.

The reflection of the increase in the aforementioned productivity, for instance, needs to be punctuated by clear and real benefits reaped by these employees: more free and quality time, decent payment, and recognition of their personal needs in a humanized way. If we think of a post-COVID-19 future where face-to-face or hybrid education and work (with resources for accessing knowledge that does not solely depend on the internet) finally break away from traditional models of exploration, gamification can be one of the tools that will help us make the relationship between teaching and learning, as well as working, more horizontal, natural and pleasurable, as is the process of discovering new worlds and new skills that the game experience gives us. However, for this to happen, gamification needs to be put at the service of the user, not the administrator.

References

Agência IBGE Notícias. (2020). *Em média, mulheres dedicam 10,4 horas por semana a mais que os homens aos afazeres domésticos ou ao cuidado de pessoas.* https://agenciadenoticias.ibge.gov.br/agencia-sala-de-imprensa/2013-agencia-de-noticias/releases/27877-em-media-mulheres-dedicam-10-4-horas-por-semana-a-mais-que-os-homens-aos-afazeres-domesticos-ou-ao-cuidado-de-pessoas.

Bogost, I. (2011a). *Persuasive Games: Exploitationware.* https://www.gamedeveloper.com/design/persuasive-games-exploitationware.

Bogost, I. (2011b). *Gamification is bullshit: My position statement at the Wharton Gamification Symposium.* http://bogost.com/writing/blog/gamification_is_bullshit/.

Braga, R. (2009). A vingança de Braverman: o infotaylorismo como contratempo. In R. Braga & R. Antunes (Eds.), *Infoproletários: degradação real do trabalho virtual* (pp. 59–88). São Paulo: Boitempo.

Castells, M. (1999). *A sociedade em rede.* Rio de Janeiro: Paz e Terra.

Comscore. (2020). *Impacto do Covid-19 no setor de mídia e internet.* https://www.comscore.com/por/Insights/Apresentacoes-e-documentos/2020/Impacto-do-Covid-19-no-setor-de-midia-e-internet.
Google Trends. (2022). *Google Trends.* Retrieved from https://trends.google.com.br.
Hunter, D., & Werbach, K. (2012). *For the Win: How Game Thinking Can Revolutionize Your Business.* Pennsylvania: Wharton School Press.
Huws, U. (2009). A construção de um cibertariado? Trabalho virtual num mundo real. In R. Braga & R. Antunes (Eds.), *Inforproletários: degradação real do trabalho virtual* (pp. 37–58). São Paulo: Boitempo.
IBGE. (n.d.) *Instituto Brasileiro de Geografia e Estatística.* https://www.ibge.gov.br/pt/inicio.html.
Idoeta, P. (2020). *As mães demitidas durante a pandemia: "Tentei conciliar trabalho com meu bebê, mas perdi o emprego".* https://www.bbc.com/portuguese/brasil-54329694.
Lojkine, J. (1995). *A revolução informacional.* São Paulo: Cortez.
Maslow, A. H. (1943). *A Theory of Human Motivation.* https://psychclassics.yorku.ca/Maslow/motivation.htm#r21.
Parent in Science. (2020). *Produtividade acadêmica durante a pandemia: Efeitos de gênero, raça e parentalidade.* https://327b604e-5cf4-492b-910b-e35e2bc67511.filesusr.com/ugd/0b341b_81cd8390d0f94bfd8fcd17ee6f29bc0e.pdf?index=true.
Statcounter Global Stats. (2022). Search Engine Market Share Brazil. https://gs.statcounter.com/search-engine-market-share/all/brazil.
UN News. (2020). *Metade dos alunos fora da escola não tem computador em casa.* https://news.un.org/pt/story/2020/04/1711192.
Universidade Federal do Rio Grande do Sul. (2020). *Pesquisa da UFRGS revela impacto das desigualdades de gênero e raça no mundo acadêmico durante a pandemia.* https://www.ufrgs.br/coronavirus/base/pesquisa-da-ufrgs-revela-impacto-das-desigualdades-de-genero-e-raca-no-mundo-academico-durante-a-pandemia/.
Woodcock, J. (2020). *Marx no fliperama: Videogame e luta de classes.* São Paulo: Editora Autonomia Literária.

CHAPTER 15

Re-thinking Critical Digital Literacies in the Context of Compulsory Education

Anastasia Gouseti, Liisa Ilomäki, and Minna Lakkala

INTRODUCTION

As other chapters in this Handbook demonstrate, digital transformation and disruption have become prevalent in most aspects of our everyday lives and have led to changes in traditional systems of work, education, governance and other areas of private and public life. Within an educational context, digital technology use has become deeply embedded in schools and various technology-mediated practices have been adopted to facilitate teaching, learning, communication and collaboration, whilst there has also been a rapid take-up of digital technology in the lives of children and young people.

In light of this, it appears to be more timely than ever to consider teachers and students' critical digital literacies and develop relevant understandings within the context of compulsory education. As others have highlighted "digital literacy has now entered common parlance in education research, policy and practice" (Nichols & Stornaiuolo, 2019, p. 14) and rapid changes to economic, social and technological environments pose significant challenges for understanding what it means to be digitally literate today (Bulfin & McGraw, 2015). Although the importance of developing digital competences is well recognised by policy-makers and a range of relevant frameworks are available, these often

---

A. Gouseti (✉)
University of Hull, Hull, UK
e-mail: A.Gouseti@hull.ac.uk

L. Ilomäki • M. Lakkala
University of Helsinki, Helsinki, Finland
e-mail: liisa.ilomaki@helsinki.fi; minna.lakkala@helsinki.fi

© The Author(s), under exclusive license to Springer Nature Switzerland AG 2024
H. S. Dunn et al. (eds.), *The Palgrave Handbook of Everyday Digital Life*,
https://doi.org/10.1007/978-3-031-30438-5_15

tend to focus predominantly on basic technical skills and a few key issues like e-safety or information literacy, and do not capture the complexity and multi-dimensionality of teachers and students' current digital practices. In addition, because of rapid digital developments, existing frameworks quickly become out-dated and, therefore, constant re-evaluation and modification is needed.

In this chapter we argue that critical digital literacies (CDL) need to be framed within the range of social, economic and political factors that underpin digital engagement in the twenty-first century and we present a new CDL framework created as an original output of an EU-funded, international research collaboration (Developing Teachers' Critical Digital Literacies—DETECT[1]). Whilst our account of CDL builds on previous work that explores the intersections between 'digital' and 'literacy', it is novel as it introduces a more open-ended approach towards capturing the different dimensions that can be associated with CDL practices within and outside classrooms. In particular, we argue that this new CDL framework is more responsive to current digital contexts and practices and is informed by a range of emerging phenomena, which we suggest, are key to reconceptualising CDL.

Furthermore, the Covid-19 pandemic forced teachers and students to switch to emergency remote education practically overnight, and there has been much heterogeneity in the teaching and learning methods implemented during school closures (Greenhow et al., 2021; Palau et al., 2021). The move to emergency remote education also highlighted the variation regarding teachers and students' critical digital literacies when facilitating remote teaching or engaging with remote learning. In particular, research suggested that didactic modes of teaching prevailed with virtual learning platforms largely been used as repositories for sharing educational resources, and students were offered limited opportunities for online collaborative and creative practices (Brink et al., 2020; Gouseti, 2021). Furthermore, while the lack of digital access was reported to be a fundamental barrier to digital participation and engagement during remote education (Andrew et al., 2020), digital skills were also a key factor in determining whether teachers and students could translate digital technology use into real benefits. For instance, those with lower skills faced greater risk of being left behind compared to those with more advanced digital competences who could reap more benefits during the move to remote education (ibid.).

Given the focus of this book on Everyday Digital Life, we are interested in exploring the critical digital literacies, which are particularly pertinent for teachers and students navigating digital worlds within and outside the context of compulsory education. We achieve this through three phases of discussion. First, we present an expanded conceptualisation of critical digital literacies drawing on the DETECT CDL framework. Here we focus our discussion on particular dimensions, which we identify as predominantly relevant for addressing recent and/or overlooked aspects of digital engagement. Second, we consider the uncongenial rhetoric of transformation manifested in global

[1] https://www.detectproject.eu/.

policy making and reflect on its impact regarding how CDL is operationalized in classrooms. We end this chapter by considering the implications that re-thinking critical digital literacies in light of this new framework has for research, teaching and policy making globally.

An Overview of Critical Digital Literacies

Approaches to critical digital literacies vary considerably and multiple definitions and interpretations of digital literacy can be found in academic literature since the term was first coined by Gilster (1997). Furthermore, various conceptual digital literacy or competence frameworks have been developed over the past decades by international organisations and institutions (see European Union, 2021; OECD, 2019; UNESCO, 2018). Still, despite these continuing and ongoing developments, the field of critical digital literacies is largely characterised by complexity, uncertainty and tensions concerning conceptual clarity (Erstad et al., 2021; Spires, 2019).

In the face of constant and wide-ranging socio-political, environmental, cultural and other changes brought about by digital technology use, we argue that critical digital literacies should be perceived less as a finite and tightly bounded concept and more as an assemblage of meanings and practices (Nichols & Stornaiuolo, 2019). We adopt the plural form 'critical digital literacies' rather than 'literacy' in order to depart from one-dimensional understandings of the term and emphasise instead its diverse, nuanced and dynamic nature shaped by social, political, cultural and other contexts. In particular, we see engagement in contemporary digital practices as requiring 'a complex amalgam of linguistic, technological, contextual, and critical skills, knowledge, and understandings' (Tour et al., 2021, p. 2). At the same time, emphasis is placed on conceptualising digital literacies through the lens of criticality. Indeed, as Pötzsch (2019, p. 226) reasons 'awareness for and knowledge about the practices and logics of exploitation, commodification, and profit maximisation underlying contemporary techno-capitalism constitute crucial aspects of literacies, competencies, and skills relevant for the current era'.

Against this background, we now go on to look at how critical digital literacies have been conceptualised within the context of the Erasmus+ DETECT project. As we have already highlighted, we do not perceive critical digital literacies as a tightly focused field but rather as an assemblage of meanings and practices, and for this reason we do not aim to provide a precise—albeit elusive—definition, which will become quickly out dated. Instead, we view critical digital literacies as encompassing eight main dimensions, which in turn accommodate a range of sub-dimensions. More specifically, we draw on a new critical digital literacies framework which has been the result of collaborative work across the nine DETECT project partners and has been informed by a range of research and other activities. These included: (1) a systematic literature review in the area of critical digital literacies (see Ilomäki et al., in press); (2) empirical research conducted across the project's four primary and secondary EU school partners (see Gouseti et al., 2021b); and (3) expert panel meetings at various stages that helped to refine and finalise the framework (see Gouseti et al., 2021a).

The main dimensions of critical digital literacies identified in the framework are the following: *Technology Use, Data Literacies, Information Literacies, Digital Knowledge Creation, Digital Communication and Collaboration, Digital Well-being and Safety, Digital Citizenship* and *Digital Teaching and Learning* (see Fig. 15.1).

Furthermore, an overview of the different sub-dimensions that have been identified as pertinent to each main dimension of critical digital literacies can be found in Fig. 15.2 and these are discussed in detail in a relevant project report (see Gouseti et al., 2021a).

We use this framework as the basis of our discussion but it should be pointed out that the structure of the sub-dimensions is innately somewhat artificial. We acknowledge that there can be potential overlap since some of the sub-dimensions could easily fall under two different dimensions and we also recognise the fuzzy boundaries across some of the dimensions and sub-dimensions. For this reason, these should not be seen as necessarily 'distinctive' but instead as an assemblage of meanings, understandings and practices which aim to capture the complexity of digital teaching, learning and engagement in the twenty-first century.

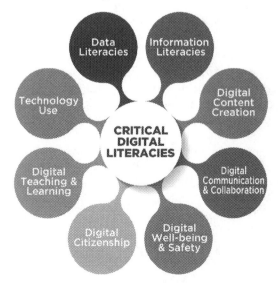

Fig. 15.1 Critical digital literacies framework—Biblioteca UOC. (Figure generated by the authors)

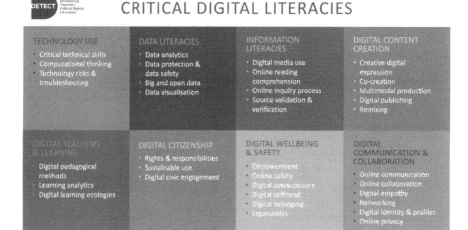

Fig. 15.2 Critical digital literacies (DETECT Project). (Figure generated by the authors)

As such, although our conceptualisation of critical digital literacies builds on previous work that explores the intersections between 'digital' and 'literacy', it is original as it proposes a more fluid approach towards explicating the various dimensions that can be associated with CDL practices within and outside classrooms. Although we recognise all dimensions of critical digital literacies as relevant in the context of compulsory education, we acknowledge that their appropriateness will vary based on the age and educational level of the students. For the purposes of this chapter we will now go on to discuss in more detail in the next sections particular dimensions and sub-dimensions which have received less attention by policy making agendas or feature less in current educational practices despite their pronounced relevance for teachers and students' digital engagement.

Data Literacies

The digitisation of modern life and educational systems and practices has resulted in great levels of what scholars have named 'datafication'. This refers to 'the process in which actions and behaviours are translated into data that can be recorded, sorted or indeed commodified by governments and private companies' (Pangrazio & Sefton-Green, 2022, p. n.p.). The past decade has seen academic research increasingly focusing on issues relating to data literacy and data justice as schools are becoming more and more 'data-driven'. A range of data is now routinely collected by schools via various technologies with the intention of enhancing organisational efficiency, making pedagogical interventions and gauging students' learning experience and capabilities. On one hand, as Selwyn et al. (2022) argue this 'data turn' is often perceived positively in educational spheres since the use of digital data is seen as a basis for improving and reforming the school system. For instance, learning analytics and educational data mining have the potential to advance our understanding of the learning process and provide insights into educational practice (Gašević et al., 2015).

Social media tools and apps are also often used by educators for professional learning and as a part of teaching and learning activities often with little awareness of data privacy policies (Marín et al., 2020). Similarly, students' everyday digital engagement generates a range of personal data. This can include data that users might give voluntarily to devices and systems (e.g. self-tracking information, social media data, emails and videos); data that devices and systems extract from users involuntarily (e.g., online searches); and data that devices and systems process on behalf of users (e.g. dashboards, analytics pages) (Pangrazio & Selwyn, 2018).

As, such the increased datafication of schooling as well as of our everyday lives has a range of implications. From concerns regarding privacy of personal data and the dataveillance of children and the implication this has for their rights (Lupton & Williamson, 2017) to dystopian visions of data as instrument of surveillance capitalism and totalitarianism (Zuboff, 2019) datafication remains a contested and conflicted area.

In light of the above, we argue that the dimension of data literacies is key to any critical digital literacies framework. However, it is largely overlooked in current policy making agendas and national curricula with the emphasis being predominantly on good practices around GDPR or focus only on one aspect of critical data education. For instance, the UNESCO (2018) global framework of reference on digital literacy identifies 'information and data literacy' as a key competence relating to the ability to browse, search, filter, evaluate and manage data while the Children's Commissioner for England recommends that 'schools should teach children about how their data are collected and used, and what they can do to take control of their data footprints' (The Children's Commissioner for England, 2018, p. 22).

However, data literacies are more complex than this and relate to an intertwined set of skills and understandings around data analytics, data protection and data safety, big and open data usage, and data visualisation. This includes knowledge and understandings not only of the 'techniques to process data but also the ability to analyse data as a social and cultural phenomenon with implications for our personal lives' (Gouseti et al., 2021a, p. 11). More specifically, it is imperative to go beyond students' understandings and practices relating to the production of personal data. A critical perspective around data encompasses differentiated areas of practice which include but are not limited to the following: considering the favourable potential of data on democracy and social innovation when shared as open, public knowledge; being able to critically interpret and evaluate graphs and other types of data visualisation; understanding how the sharing and extraction of personal data can be used to feed algorithms supporting intelligent systems and how greater sense of agency regarding our data and its use can be developed (ibid.).

Digital Content Creation

One dimension of digitality that provides us with new types of possibilities is *digital content creation*. For example, in creative digital expression and digital art production, digital applications are not just tools for producing pieces of art, but they enable the creation of artefacts in forms that are different from anything before, such as augmented or virtual reality systems (Lin & Wang, 2021; Yilmaz & Goktas, 2017). A digital tool might also be an active agent in the creation process, like in poetry writing based on artificial intelligence (Kangasharju et al., 2022). Engaging students in creative digital activities supports their empowerment and promotes taking the role of producer instead of consumer in digital spaces, forums and services (García-Ruiz et al., 2014; O'Byrne, 2014). Producing new digital artefacts (music, videos, pictures, etc.) through remixing existing products is also a new phenomenon associated with digital tool engagement, but it also involves an obligation to be aware of and respect copyright (Burwell, 2013).

Co-creational practices are central in today's world of work, and competences for productive team working are required and expected in various professions (Paavola & Hakkarainen, 2014). Web-based digital tools and cloud services, such as online writing applications, have vitally changed the nature of co-production, because they facilitate the working with digital content collaboratively in ways that have not been possible before. To this end, school education should provide students with possibilities to practice these kinds of co-creational ways of working that require skills for social interaction, coordination of activities, and shared modification of products digitally. Instead, our teacher interview study (Gouseti et al., 2021b) suggested rather the opposite with teachers barely mentioning creative digital practices, especially co-creation, in their discussions about aspects of CDL relevant to take into account in schools. This poses the question of whether teachers themselves can use digital tools creatively or have sufficient knowledge and skills to guide students' digital creativity.

Engaging in co-creational activities also requires understanding and mastering the principles and practices of digital participation and communication. For instance, findings among Finnish adolescents showed the importance of socio-emotional skills in promoting students' academic well-being and emphasised how it was especially important to better support students who were at risk of burnout during the pandemic (Salmela-Aro et al., 2021). As such, we should seriously consider what kind of challenges and opportunities digitalization creates, e.g., for interaction, empathy, sense of belonging, or inclusion, and how school education could strengthen students' various social and emotional skills especially in digital environments.

Sustainable Use

Tackling climate change and environmental degradation lies in the heart of various policy making agendas (OECD, 2021) and education is seen as a key instrument to achieve Sustainable Development Goals (UNESCO, 2017) and address the environmental crisis. Still, recent findings from a review of National Curriculum Frameworks on 100 countries suggest that only 53% of these curricula make an explicit reference to climate change and even when the topic is mentioned, this is varied and often superficial (UNESCO 2021). One means of addressing the current climate crisis is supporting students with developing climate literacy (Harker-Schuch & Watson, 2019) so that not only can they have relevant knowledge and understanding of environmental issues but they can also develop an awareness around issues of climate injustice and they can become change-makers who are actively involved in the fight against these issues (Halstead et al., 2021).

Discussions around the climate crisis, however, tend to largely focus on issues such as global temperature rises or biodiversity loss and the impact of digital technology use on the planet is largely overlooked. Notwithstanding the gravity of these climate issues, it is also important to consider the environmental impact of the ever-increasing consumption and use of digital technologies around the world. More specifically, the impact of digital technology use on the planet can take a range of shapes and forms and can span across different areas. For instance, digital hardware production relies on the extraction, smelting, processing and mixing of non-renewable minerals and rare metals often shipped around the world to be assembled with all these stages involving the production and disposal of toxic waste products (Selwyn, 2021).

Similarly, data processing and data storage is also seen to pose great ecological hazards on the environment since this does not happen 'on the cloud' but in data centres and server farms which require substantial physical infrastructure and electricity consumption to run and account for significant greenhouse emissions and environmental pollution (Gregg, 2015; Thylstrup, 2019). Furthermore, it is also important to consider the short shelf-lives of digital technologies and the environmental impact of these in terms of the 'e-waste' produced leading to increased levels of contamination and pollution in some of the poorest areas of the world (Maxwell & Miller, 2020).

For these reasons, we view 'sustainable' use as a central sub-dimension of critical digital literacies and particularly relevant to 'climate literacy'. According to the DETECT CDL framework, developing critical digital literacies around sustainable use refers to 'developing awareness and understanding of how digital technology use impacts the natural environment and how it contributes to digital pollution' (Gouseti et al., 2021a, p. 26). This includes making sense of how digital technology use contributes to energy consumption and greenhouse gas emissions and understanding how the inappropriate disposal of digital devices causes environmental contamination and pollution. This will empower teachers and students to consider not only how educational technology use can be made more sustainable within the school but also at personal level.

This emphasis on developing awareness around sustainable use of digital technologies ties in with efforts to promote climate literacy in the curriculum and supporting students with understanding the materialities of digital technologies and creating appropriate attitudes around their use and care. As Houston and Jackson (2016) argue establishing cultures of 'ethics of care for materials' and the 'right to repair' among schools and student communities is particularly relevant in light of the ongoing climate crisis.

Digital Civic Engagement

The internet has created a forum for digital participation and has the potential to facilitate different opportunities and modes of online engagement. As early as 2005 Livingstone et al. reported how young people used the internet for various participation activities, such as communicating, peer-to-peer connection, interactivity, digital content creation and visiting civic or political websites depending on a range of demographic factors (2005). Over the years, the opportunities for online participatory activities and the different types of digital engagement have increased. Such opportunities can emerge from social media use and out-of-school activities, but also these can constitute formal educational activities, such as taking part in online collaborative projects with other schools.

An essential and relatively new type of digital participation is digital civic participation, or else known as digital activism, which can consist of active production of online content, participating in digital social platforms, moderating groups, engaging in polling, boycotts, buycotts, protest movements, and political campaigns (Vassallo, 2020). Although these types of participation might be more pertinent to older students and adults in general, and less relevant for younger children, there are studies, which suggest that, online civic activism should also be taken into account at school, as a way of facilitating participation in the democratic society. According to Vassalo (ibid.), digital activism is a relevant example of political involvement, especially among younger individuals, while it is also relevant for compulsory education students.

Gleason and von Gillern (2018) investigated high school students' participation in informal and formal learning spaces and the development of digital citizenship. They suggested that in-school, traditional citizenship education and out-of-school activities aimed at civic engagement can be integrated through a social media-facilitated curriculum. As Castellví et al. (2020) emphasised this of course raises questions about teachers' competence to teach societal issues related to digitality for democratic participation and how these can be taught through citizenship education. To this end, digital civic participation is something which needs to be introduced to learners at all levels, with schools stipulating effective environments within which to teach responsible physical and digital citizenship.

Digital Wellbeing and Digital Identity

Digital well-being is an emerging issue as the daily life of all people is so profoundly connected to digital technology use and this can have implications for one's physical and mental welfare. Gui et al. (2017, p. 163) defined digital well-being skills 'as a set of skills needed to manage the side effects of digital communication overabundance' and instead achieve strategic attention and avoid the stress that the overwhelming flow of information can cause. For instance, for children and young people this can relate to mitigating the risks associated with social media engagement or regulating the time used for gaming. It appears that digital well-being in children's and teenagers' life is often investigated from a negative point of view, such as not becoming bullied (Liau et al., 2017) or by increasing e-safety also digital well-being increases (Vanderhoven et al., 2016).

During the recent pandemic, for instance, the well-being of children and teenagers has been often presented through a negative lens, such as focusing on the isolation of peers, lack of teacher support and too demanding independent learning (see Salmela-Aro et al., 2021). Digitality is, however, such a major part of children's and teenagers' life that well-being should be thought also from a positive perspective, such as empowering individuals to seek and create connections and friendships online, participate in collaborative gaming, having others to talk with about difficult issues (e.g., about sexual minorities), and learning digital skills and competencies. For instance, research conducted with young people around the world reported that active digital participation and online engagement are critical to realizing one's own rights in the contemporary world (Third & Moody, 2021).

Similarly, other case studies have reported on digital practices that have supported students' digital well-being. One such example relates to facilitating the empowerment of teenage girls who during summer camps had various activities with digital technology. Their technology literacy skills improved but, moreover, they investigated digital identities through their own production of digital outcomes (England & Cannella, 2018). Also various examples of students as producers have reported positive results such as making videos, writing lifestyle blogs, and engaging in online role-playing games (Kupiainen, 2013) or creating games collaboratively (Mouws & Bleumers, 2015). As such, while enhancing students' understandings regarding online safety and how to mitigate online risks remains relevant, it is also important to foreground and address their needs around agency and empowerment so that they can also reap the positive benefits of online participation and engagement.

Last, the increasing digitisation and platformisation of schools can reconfigure the work of teachers and impact their well-being negatively since the time and place that 'work' takes place have shifted and the boundaries between online and offline have become more blurred. For instance, research in this field has shown how the extension of work outside school due to digital technology use can lead to digital overload and the expectation for an 'always-on' mode of working without setting boundaries between work and home, and this can have serious implications for one's health and well-being (Heffernan & Selwyn, 2021). As such, it is important for educators to take appropriate steps to ensure that they manage their digital workload effectively and maintain a healthy and positive work/life balance.

Digital Empathy

The concept of digital empathy is multifaceted and can be conceptualised in a plethora of ways. Within the CDL framework digital empathy is, firstly, associated with a teachers or students' ability to recognise and respect the feelings of other participants within an online environment. For instance, as Andrejevic and Volcic (2020) emphasise the utilization of digital media can raise concerns regarding increasing polarization and extremism and the internet can give voice to dangerous forms of anti-empathy. Therefore, there is no doubt that teachers and students alike need to be aware of how private and public online actions can have a significant negative impact on the wellbeing of others. It is important for both students and teachers to understand that empathy, including acting empathetically in digital spaces, can and should be learnt and taught—empathy is a skill, not a personal disposition (Friesem, 2016). Some methods have been suggested in research literature to promote students' digital empathy, like video production activities (Friesem, 2016; Jiang & Gao, 2020), or computer games targeting empathic learning (Wu et al., 2020) but there definitely is a need for more examples and guidelines about practical and easy, yet proven, methods to teach digital empathy as part of school education.

At the same time we offer an alternative interpretation of empathy by looking at it through the lens of digital inequalities. There is a wealth of research that reports on students' experiences of long standing digital inequalities, such as the so-called 'homework gap' (Anderson & Perrin, 2018). Others have also emphasized the importance of 'digital capital', which refers not only to externalised resources (such as digital access) but also to internalised digital competences (Ragnedda & Ruiu, 2020). More recently, the move to emergency remote education has demonstrated that 'digital inequalities are as entrenched and important an issue as ever' (Selwyn & Jandrić, 2020, p. 992) and empirical findings have suggested that digital inequalities have been exacerbated during the pandemic particularly for children from low-income families (Andrew et al., 2020; Bayrakdar & Guveli, 2020).

To this end, digital empathy is seen 'as having a deep awareness and consideration in relation to one's access to digital infrastructure, internet connectivity and digital competences' (Gouseti et al., 2021a, p. 21). More specifically, within a compulsory education context this means that teachers are attuned and alert to students' needs relating to digital technology use. They acknowledge that students may have diverse online experiences and varied levels of digital access and competences and they are able to address these experiences and needs accordingly. Furthermore, they are aware of potential accessibility issues when planning their lessons and homework tasks and they ensure that all students have access to the digital resources, virtual learning environments etc. used for teaching and learning.

In light of the above, schools have a very important role to play with regard to extenuating digital inequalities instead of reproducing or exacerbating these. Although schools alone might not be able to address issues relating to home access and infrastructure, they can instead serve as an important space in which teachers develop digital empathy and students are provided with opportunities to enhance their digital literacies. Recent research findings highlight how the school environment can have a compensatory effect since both the frequency and quality of use of ICT at home are more affected by school ICT integration than by a student's socio-economic-status (González-Betancor et al., 2021). As such, schools need to explore ways to address digital inequalities by creating more opportunities for students to develop critical digital literacies, establishing relevant support systems for teachers and families, and considering whether a post-pandemic over reliance on online educational practices might widen further the so-called 'homework gap'.

The Uncongenial Rhetoric of Transformation in Policy-making

As highlighted earlier in this chapter, the ongoing digitisation of societies and the impact this has had for the everyday lives of those who live within them is seen to be shaping policy making and has resulted in the development of a range of frameworks and strategic plans in the areas of digital literacies or digital competences and capabilities. These at large aim to monitor, assess and further enhance citizens' digital literacies with the ultimate aim often associated with building employment capacity and upskilling the future workforce to meet the needs of the modern economy. For instance, according to UNESCO (2018) digital literacy is defined as 'the ability to access, manage, understand, integrate, communicate, evaluate and create information safely and appropriately through digital technologies for employment, decent jobs and entrepreneurship' (p. 6). Similarly, the new Digital Education Action plan developed by the EU (2021) sets out two priority areas that focus on the development of a high-performing digital education ecosystem, and the enhancement of digital skills and competences for digital transformation. More specifically, digital skills identified as relevant include basic technical competences, computing, 'digital literacy, including tackling disinformation', 'good knowledge and understanding of data-intensive technologies, such as artificial intelligence (AI)' and 'advanced digital skills, which produce more digital specialists' (ibid., n.p.).

Notwithstanding the relevance and importance of supporting people of all ages with developing such digital capabilities in order to access and participate in increasingly digitised societies, it is equally important to acknowledge the pertinence of other soft skills or competences (Schulz, 2008) such as critical thinking, creativity, collaboration and problem-solving and consider how these are particularly relevant for technology-mediated social practices not only for employment but for individuals in their daily life. Some of these competences do feature on recent frameworks, for instance the DigitCompEdu framework includes areas such as fostering learners creative engagement, deep thinking and problem solving or developing their awareness of the environmental impact of digital technology use (see Redecker, 2017). Still this example is the exception rather than the rule and policy making agendas continue at large to be driven and shaped by the uncongenial rhetoric of digital transformation and are underpinned by the disputable notion that education needs to cater to the needs of the global networked society (Biesta, 2013). This is particularly contested since it is based on 'a utilitarian approach of education, that takes a global competitive economy as an unquestioned frame of reference' (Volman et al., 2020, p. 651).

Another viewpoint that is missing from the policy-driven digital strategies and frameworks is the absolute value of individuals to feel empowered through digital means: be creative, express themselves, feel competent and self-confident, and have experiences of belonging and contacts with other people relevant for oneself. All these have a significant influence on well-being. When emphasizing instrumental values, human aspects are often overlooked, and this is accentuated in the discussions about digitization and digital competence. It is important to also highlight those aspects of digitalisation which emphasise amongst others freedom of expression, opportunities for life-long learning, or being literate as essential elements of human rights (Koren 2021).

As discussed in the previous section, the area of critical digital literacies should be perceived as a complex assemblage of meanings, understandings, skills and practices which should not be shaped merely by neo-liberal agendas but instead by social, political, cultural and other contexts. We need to remain mindful that, for teachers and students alike, engagement with technology does not inevitably have to be associated with performativity and digital transformation, and with acquiring competences suited to fit the future knowledge economy as political agendas appear to dictate. Quite the contrary, in light of the increasing platformisation, datafication and automation of educational institutions, there is a pressing need to support teachers and students with developing 'a critical disposition in a context in which technical proficiency is prioritised' (Pangrazio, 2016, p. 163). This is particularly relevant since the various dimensions of critical digital literacies are also transferable across digital contexts and, therefore more relevant to the fast-paced realities of their everyday digital practices (ibid.). As Livingstone et al. (2020, p. 197) point out:

> Even when children develop the operational skills necessary for functional internet use, challenges remain in ensuring they have the critical, informational and creative skills for uses that bring tangible outcomes of value in their everyday lives.

Despite the shift in academic literature from prescriptive skill-based taxonomies of digital literacies to looser conceptualisations of the term that aim to capture people's social practices with digital technologies and emphasise the importance of criticality, policy and curricula documents continue to prioritise digital upskilling and transformation (Nichols & Stornaiuolo, 2019). This is particularly problematic for two reasons. First, teachers' practices are at large shaped by curricula imperatives, assessment regimes and other educational policies rather than their own perceptions and experiences of critical digital literacies. In other words, even if teachers acknowledge the relevance of supporting their students with developing often overlooked dimensions of critical digital literacies, their practices will instead by shaped by national curriculum aims and assessment regimes (Gouseti et al., 2023). Similarly, Oudeweetering and Voogt's (2018) study also highlighted that the dimensions of digital competencies that were less integrated into teachers' practice were those who had not been integrated into education policy.

The second reason why the prioritisation of digital skills for future employability and upskilling is problematic relates to Initial Teacher Education (ITE) programmes and teachers' continuing professional development (CPD). Since ITE programmes and formal CPD activities are largely shaped by national educational policies and curricula, it is only natural that they will also focus on equipping teachers with '21st century skills' and overlook other relevant dimensions of critical digital literacies. For example, research has highlighted the pressing need to re-imagine prevailing forms of cybersafety education in schools 'to complement more critical and agentic forms of digital learning' (Pangrazio & Selwyn, 2020, p. 14) and enhance teachers' critical perceptions of data literacy (Marín et al., 2020). In the same vein, Nagle (2018) emphasises the relevance of supporting preservice teachers with developing critical social media literacy and reasons that critical conversations around this area are lacking in teacher education.

Some Implications of Re-thinking Critical Digital Literacies for Compulsory Education

Digital technology use has the potential to provide a range of new opportunities for teaching and learning as well as for other areas of life, and as our CDL framework demonstrates, a range of new dimensions of critical digital literacies are now required for teachers and students alike. Children and young people are quick to adopt and experiment with new possibilities, but they should not be left alone in this or rely only on the influence of peers or the supervision of parents and homes. Teachers and schools need to stay on track with the developments and take responsibility for how the new trends—both possibilities and challenges—are taken into account in the education of children and young people. Digitality is also a phenomenon which stretches to various domains and topics of curricula. For this reason, teaching new digital competencies in schools cannot be a responsibility of an individual teacher, but a collaborative activity of teachers and all members in the school community.

At national and international level, these new digital possibilities present a continuous challenge. Teachers and schools need resources, training and guidelines on how to provide educational opportunities related to digitality equally for all, but also to balance the opportunities with students' well-being and find meaningful pedagogical practices which should be based on visions of digitality in the future. To this end, countries need to consider whether their current national curriculum addresses the increasingly more complex range of critical digital literacies required for teaching, learning and living in a digital world. For example, while research acknowledges that young people's digital experiences are diverse and they need not only operational skills but also critical, informational and creative skills in order to reach tangible outcomes of value in their everyday lives (Livingstone et al., 2020), this is not often followed through when national curricula are developed or redesigned.

Some countries have responded to this challenge and Godhe (2019), for example, highlights how the conceptualisations of digital competences in Nordic curricula share an emphasis on societal issues and a critical and ethical approach. Similarly, Olofsson et al. (2021) report that within a Nordic policy making context there has been a shift from a focus on technological competence to a more stretched out interpretation of digital competences that includes dimensions that acknowledge citizens' role in the digitalised society. However, these are examples from a Nordic context and more systematic approaches are needed in order to address the discrepancy between the complexity of students' digital experiences and how these are operationalized as digital literacies or digital competences in national curricula, teacher training programmes and policy making agendas all over the world.

A recent review of the literature on critical digital literacies revealed that especially the research articles (compared to policy documents) too often emphasised negative consequences or dangers and problems associated with digital technology use, and at large focused on adults' point of views (Ilomäki et al., in press). Whilst our work on critical digital literacies joins an emergent body of research that aims to identify the complexity of capturing the multi-dimensionality of critical digital literacies, more research is needed to explore some of these rather overlooked sub-dimensions discussed in this chapter. In addition, research should give voice also to children and young people and capture their understandings and experiences in relation to these complex issues.

Conclusion

All the above point towards the need for re-conceptualising critical digital literacies and acknowledging the complexity of supporting teachers and students with developing not only technical skills but a critical understanding of how to navigate digital environments and participate in a digitised world safely, responsibly and ethically. Suffice to say, developing critical digital literacies is not something that should be 'done' to educators and students but instead they should play active roles in deciding how this multifaceted terrain of critical digital literacies can be operationalized in the context of education.

As discussed in this chapter, policy making agendas tend to overlook the multidimensionality of critical digital literacies and instead promote a competence-oriented approach seen as suitable for supporting students with developing '21st century skills' pertinent for their future employability. However, supporting teachers and students' with developing diverse, complex, multimodal critical digital literacies essential for teaching, learning and living in a digital world requires the development of relevant international and national policies, curricula documents and teacher training opportunities. This is certainly an ambitious ask as it would involve a reorientation of policy agendas away from the logics of education seen as having to cater to the needs of the global networked society (Biesta, 2013).

At the same time, policy making efforts to support children and young people with participating in an increasingly interconnected and digitalised world predominantly focus on minimising risks and 'harm'. Relevant efforts instead should also be focused on facilitating the conditions needed for their empowerment and enabling them to express themselves creatively, become autonomous, active and critical digital citizens and develop awareness about their digital rights but also the responsibilities that come with self-expression.

In conclusion, we perceive the DETECT CDL framework as a timely and novel response to teachers and students' current needs in relation to critical digital literacies and as a useful tool for informing the redesign of national curricula and policy making agendas. Still, our understanding of this area should continue to evolve and be shaped by future developments in this field as well as by teacher and students' voices around their digital experiences and critical digital literacies needs.

References

Anderson, M., & Perrin, A. (2018). *Nearly one-in-five teens can't always finish their homework because of the digital divide*. Pew Research Center. https://www.pewresearch.org/fact-tank/2018/10/26/nearly-one-in-five-teens-cant-always-finish-their-homework-because-of-the-digital-divide/.

Andrejevic, M., & Volcic, Z. (2020). Virtual empathy. *Communication, Culture and Critique, 13*(3), 295–310. https://doi.org/10.1093/ccc/tcz035.

Andrew, A., Cattan, S., Dias, M. C., Farquharson, C., Kraftman, L., Krutikova, S., Phimister, A., & Sevilla, A. (2020). *Inequalities in children's experiences of home learning during the COVID-19 lockdown in England*. Institute for Fiscal Studies. https://www.ifs.org.uk/publications/14975

Bayrakdar, S., & Guveli, A. (2020). *Inequalities in home learning and schools' provision of distance teaching during school closure of COVID-19 lockdown in the UK*. Institute for Social & Economic Research. https://www.iser.essex.ac.uk/research/publications/working-papers/iser/2020-09.

Biesta, G. (2013). Responsive or responsible? Democratic education for the global networked society. *Policy Futures in Education*, *11*(6), 733–744. https://doi.org/10.2304/pfie.2013.11.6.733.
Brink, R., Ozolins, K., & Jenavs, E. (2020). *Report 1: How have schools coped with Covid-19? Findings from the Edurio Covid-19 Impact Review, summer term 2020*. Edurio. https://home.edurio.com/covid-19-impact-report1.
Bulfin, S., & McGraw, K. (2015). Digital literacy in theory, policy and practice: Old concerns, new opportunities. In M. Henderson & G. Romeo (Eds.), *Teaching and Digital Technologies: Big Issues and Critical Questions*. Cambridge University Press.
Burwell, C. (2013). The Pedagogical potential of video remix: Critical conversations about culture, creativity, and copyright. *Journal of Adolescent & Adult Literacy*, *57*(3), 205–213. https://doi.org/10.1002/JAAL.205.
Castellví, J., Díez-Bedmar, M.-C., & Santisteban, A. (2020). Pre-service teachers' critical digital literacy skills and attitudes to address social problems. *Social Sciences*, *9*(8), 134. https://doi.org/10.3390/socsci9080134.
England, J., & Cannella, R. (2018). Tweens as technofeminists: Exploring girlhood identity in technology camp. *Girlhood Studies*, *11*(1), 75–91. https://doi.org/10.3167/ghs.2018.110107.
Erstad, O., Kjällander, S., & Järvelä, S. (2021). Facing the challenges of 'digital competence'. *Nordic Journal of Digital Literacy*, *16*(02), 77–87. https://doi.org/10.18261/issn.1891-943x-2021-02-04.
European Union. (2021). *Digital Education Action Plan 2021–2027, resetting education and training for the digital age*. Education and Training – European Commission. https://ec.europa.eu/education/education-in-the-eu/digital-education-action-plan_en.
Friesem, Y. (2016). Empathy for the digital age: Using video production to enhance social, emotional, and cognitive skills. In S. Y. Tettegah & D. L. Espelage (Eds.), *Emotions, Technology, and Behaviors* (pp. 21–45). Academic. https://doi.org/10.1016/B978-0-12-801873-6.00002-9.
García-Ruiz, R., Ramírez-García, A., & Rodríguez-Rosell, M.-M. (2014). Media literacy education for a new prosumer citizenship. *Comunicar, Media Education Research Journal*, *22*(43), 15–23. https://doi.org/10.3916/C43-2014-01.
Gašević, D., Dawson, S., & Siemens, G. (2015). Let's not forget: Learning analytics are about learning. *TechTrends*, *59*(1), 64–71. https://doi.org/10.1007/s11528-014-0822-x.
Gilster, P. (1997). *Digital literacy*. John Wiley.
Gleason, B., & Gillern, S. von. (2018). Digital citizenship with social media: Participatory practices of teaching and learning in secondary education. *Undefined*. https://www.semanticscholar.org/paper/Digital-Citizenship-with-Social-Media%3A-Practices-of-Gleason-Gillern/a5a4cf4df2cac98e4200284f512da5972505f524.
Godhe, A.-L. (2019). Digital literacies or digital competence: Conceptualizations in Nordic curricula. *Media and Communication*, *7*(2), 25–35. https://doi.org/10.17645/mac.v7i2.1888.
González-Betancor, S. M., López-Puig, A. J., & Cardenal, M. E. (2021). Digital inequality at home. The school as compensatory agent. *Computers & Education*, *168*, 104195. https://doi.org/10.1016/j.compedu.2021.104195.
Gouseti, A. (2021). 'We'd never had to set up a virtual school before': Opportunities and challenges for primary and secondary teachers during emergency remote education. *Review of Education*, *9*(3), e3305. https://doi.org/10.1002/rev3.3305.

Gouseti, A., Bruni, I., Ilomäki, L., Lakkala, M., Mundy, D., Raffaghelli, J. E., Ranieri, M., Roffi, A., Romero, M., & Romeu, T. (2021a). *Critical Digital Literacies framework for educators – DETECT project report 1.* https://doi.org/10.5281/zenodo.5070329.

Gouseti, A., Bruni, I., Ilomäki, L., Lakkala, M., Mundy, D., Raffaghelli, J. E., Ranieri, M., Roffi, A., Romero, M., & Romeu, T. (2021b). *Schools' perceptions and experiences of critical digital literacies across four European countries – DETECT project report 2.* https://doi.org/10.5281/zenodo.5070394.

Gouseti, A., Lakkala, M., Raffaghelli, J., Ranieri, M., Roffi, A., & Ilomäki, L. (2023). Exploring teachers' perceptions of critical digital literacies and how these are manifested in their teaching practices'. *Educational Review.* https://doi.org/10.1080/00131911.2022.2159933

Greenhow, C., Lewin, C., & Staudt Willet, K. B. (2021). The educational response to Covid-19 across two countries: A critical examination of initial digital pedagogy adoption. *Technology, Pedagogy and Education, 30*(1), 7–25. https://doi.org/10.1080/1475939X.2020.1866654.

Gregg, M. (2015). Inside the data spectacle. *Television & New Media, 16*(1), 37–51. https://doi.org/10.1177/1527476414547774.

Gui, M., Fasoli, M., Carradore, R., & Carradore, R. (2017). "Digital well-Being". Developing a new theoretical tool for media literacy research. *Italian Journal of Sociology of Education, 9*(1), 155–173. https://doi.org/10.14658/pupj-ijse-2017-1-8.

Halstead, F., Parsons, K., & Jones, L. (2021). *How students can use storytelling to bring the dangers of climate change to life.* The Conversation. http://theconversation.com/how-students-can-use-storytelling-to-bring-the-dangers-of-climate-change-to-life-166693.

Harker-Schuch, I., & Watson, M. (2019). Developing a climate literacy framework for upper secondary students. In W. Leal Filho & S. L. Hemstock (Eds.), *Climate Change and the Role of Education* (pp. 291–318). Springer International Publishing. https://doi.org/10.1007/978-3-030-32898-6_17.

Heffernan, A., & Selwyn, N. (2021). Mixed Messages: The enduring significance of email in school principals' work. *The Australian Educational Researcher.* https://doi.org/10.1007/s13384-021-00486-0.

Houston, L., & Jackson, S. J. (2016). Caring for the 'next billion' mobile handsets: Opening proprietary closures through the work of repair. *Proceedings of the Eighth International Conference on Information and Communication Technologies and Development,* 1–11. https://doi.org/10.1145/2909609.2909658.

Ilomäki, L., Lakkala, M., Kalunki, V., Romeu, T., Romero, M., Mundy, D., & Gouseti, A. (in press). Critical digital literacies at school level: A systematic review. *Review of Education.*

Jiang, L., & Gao, J. (2020). Fostering EFL learners' digital empathy through multimodal composing. *RELC Journal, 51*(1), 70–85. https://doi.org/10.1177/0033688219898565.

Kangasharju, A., Ilomäki, L., Lakkala, M., & Toom, A. (2022). Lower secondary students' poetry writing with the AI-based Poetry Machine. *Computers and Education: Artificial Intelligence, 3,* 100048. https://doi.org/10.1016/j.caeai.2022.100048.

Koren, M. (2021). Serving the child: A human rights approach to literacy and learning. In *IASL Annual Conference Proceedings: The Multiple Faces of Literacy: Reading,*

Knowing, Doing. The International Association of School Librarianship. https://doi.org/10.29173/iasl7922

Kupiainen, R. (2013). Young people's creative online practices in the context of school community. *Cyberpsychology: Journal of Psychosocial Research on Cyberspace, 7*(1), Article 1. https://doi.org/10.5817/CP2013-1-8.

Liau, A. K., Park, Y., Gentile, D. A., Katna, D. P., Tan, C. H. A., & Khoo, A. (2017). iZ HERO adventure: Evaluating the effectiveness of a peer-mentoring and transmedia cyberwellness program for children. *Psychology of Popular Media Culture, 6*(4), 326–337.

Lin, Y. J., & Wang, H. (2021). Using virtual reality to facilitate learners' creative self-efficacy and intrinsic motivation in an EFL classroom. *Education and Information Technologies, 26*(4), 4487–4505. https://doi.org/10.1007/s10639-021-10472-9.

Livingstone, S., Bober, M., & Helsper, E. J. (2005). Active participation or just more information? *Information, Communication & Society, 8*(3), 287–314. https://doi.org/10.1080/13691180500259103.

Livingstone, S., Burton, P., Cabello, P., Helsper, E., Kanchev, P., Kardefelt-Winther, D., Perovic, J., Stoilova, M., & Ssu-Han, Y. (2020). Media and information literacy among children on three continents: Insights into the measurement and mediation of well-being. In J. M. Pérez Tornero, G. Orozco, & E. Hamburger (Eds.), *Media and information literacy in critical times: Re-imagining learning and information environments* (No. 2018/2019; Issue 2018/2019, pp. 191–206). United Nations Educational, Scientific and Cultural Organization (UNESCO). https://en.unesco.org/themes/media-and-information-literacy/milidnetwork/milidyearbook.

Lupton, D., & Williamson, B. (2017). The datafied child: The dataveillance of children and implications for their rights. *New Media & Society, 19*(5), 780–794. https://doi.org/10.1177/1461444816686328.

Marín, V. I., Carpenter, J. P., & Tur, G. (2020). Pre-service teachers' perceptions of social media data privacy policies. *British Journal of Educational Technology, n/a*(n/a), e13035. https://doi.org/10.1111/bjet.13035.

Maxwell, R., & Miller, T. (2020). *How green is your smartphone?* Polity.

Mouws, K., & Bleumers, L. (2015). Co-creating games with children: A case study. *International Journal of Gaming and Computer-Mediated Simulations (IJGCMS), 7*(3), 22–43. https://doi.org/10.4018/IJGCMS.2015070102.

Nagle, J. (2018). Twitter, cyber-violence, and the need for a critical social media literacy in teacher education: A review of the literature. *Teaching and Teacher Education, 76*, 86–94. https://doi.org/10.1016/j.tate.2018.08.014.

Nichols, T. P., & Stornaiuolo, A. (2019). Assembling "Digital Literacies": Contingent pasts, possible Futures. *Media and Communication, 7*(2), 14–24. https://doi.org/10.17645/mac.v7i2.1946.

O'Byrne, W. I. (2014). Empowering learners in the reader/writer nature of the digital informational space. *Journal of Adolescent & Adult Literacy, 58*(2), 102–104. https://doi.org/10.1002/jaal.337.

OECD. (2019). *The future of education and skills: Education 2030.* Organisation for Economic Co-operation and Development. https://www.oecd.org/education/2030-project/teaching-and-learning/learning/core-foundations/Core_Foundations_for_2030_concept_note.pdf.

OECD. (2021). *Think green: Education and climate change* (No. 24; Trends Shaping Education Spotlights). OECD Publishing. https://doi.org/10.1787/2a9a1cdd-en.

Olofsson, A. D., Lindberg, J. O., Young Pedersen, A., Arstorp, A.-T., Dalsgaard, C., Einum, E., Caviglia, F., Ilomäki, L., Veermans, M., Häkkinen, P., & Willermark, S. (2021). Digital competence across boundaries – Beyond a common Nordic model of the digitalisation of K-12 schools? *Education Inquiry*, *12*(4), 317–328. https://doi.org/10.1080/20004508.2021.1976454.

Oudeweetering, K. van de, & Voogt, J. (2018). Teachers' conceptualization and enactment of twenty-first century competences: Exploring dimensions for new curricula. *The Curriculum Journal*, *29*(1), 116–133. https://doi.org/10.1080/09585176.2017.1369136.

Paavola, S., & Hakkarainen, K. (2014). Trialogical approach for knowledge creation. In S. Tan, H. So, & J. Yeo (Eds.), *Knowledge Creation in Education* (pp. 53–73). Springer.

Palau, R., Fuentes, M., Mogas, J., & Cebrián, G. (2021). Analysis of the implementation of teaching and learning processes at Catalan schools during the Covid-19 lockdown. *Technology, Pedagogy and Education*, *30*(1), 183–199. https://doi.org/10.1080/1475939X.2020.1863855.

Pangrazio, L. (2016). Reconceptualising critical digital literacy. *Discourse: Studies in the Cultural Politics of Education*, *37*(2), 163–174. https://doi.org/10.1080/01596306.2014.942836.

Pangrazio, L., & Sefton-Green, J. (2022). *Learning to Live with Datafication: Educational Case Studies and Initiatives from Across the World*. Routledge.

Pangrazio, L., & Selwyn, N. (2018). 'Personal data literacies': A critical literacies approach to enhancing understandings of personal digital data. *New Media & Society*, 1461444818799523. https://doi.org/10.1177/1461444818799523.

Pangrazio, L., & Selwyn, N. (2020). Towards a school-based 'critical data education'. *Pedagogy, Culture & Society*, *0*(0), 1–18. https://doi.org/10.1080/14681366.2020.1747527.

Pötzsch, H. (2019). Critical digital literacy: Technology in education beyond issues of user competence and labour-market qualifications. *TripleC: Communication, Capitalism & Critique. Open Access Journal for a Global Sustainable Information Society*, *17*(2), 221–240. https://doi.org/10.31269/triplec.v17i2.1093.

Ragnedda, M., & Ruiu, M. L. (2020). *Digital capital: A Bourdieusian perspective on the digital divide*. Emerald Group Publishing.

Redecker, C. (2017). *European framework for the digital competence of educators: DigCOmpEdu*. EUR 28775 EN. Publications Office of the European Union.

Salmela-Aro, K., Upadyaya, K., Vinni-Laakso, J., & Hietajärvi, L. (2021). Adolescents' longitudinal school engagement and burnout before and during COVID-19—The role of socio-emotional skills. *Journal of Research on Adolescence*, *31*(3), 796–807. https://doi.org/10.1111/jora.12654.

Schulz, B. (2008). The importance of soft skills: Education beyond academic knowledge. *Journal of Language and Communication*, *2*(1), 146–154.

Selwyn, N. (2021). Ed-Tech Within Limits: Anticipating educational technology in times of environmental crisis. *E-Learning and Digital Media*, 20427530211022950. https://doi.org/10.1177/20427530211022951.

Selwyn, N., Cumbo, B., & Pangrazio, L. (2022). Data classes: An investigation of the people that 'do data' in schools. In L. Pangrazio & J. Sefton-Green (Eds.), *Learning to Live with Datafication: Educational Case Studies and Initiatives from Across the World*. Routledge.

Selwyn, N., & Jandrić, P. (2020). Postdigital living in the age of covid-19: Unsettling what we see as possible. *Postdigital Science and Education, 2*(3), 989–1005. https://doi.org/10.1007/s42438-020-00166-9.

Spires, H. A. (2019). Critical perspectives on digital literacies: Creating a path forward. *Media and Communication, 7*(2), 1–3. https://doi.org/10.17645/mac.v7i2.2209.

The Children's Commissioner for England. (2018). *Who knows what about me? A Children's Commissioner report into the collection and sharing of children's data*. https://www.childrenscom missioner.gov.uk/publication/who-knows-what-about-me/.

Third, A., & Moody, L. (2021). *Our rights in the digital world: A report on the children's consultations to inform UNCRC General Comment 25*. 5Rights Foundation and Western Sydney University.

Thylstrup, N. B. (2019). Data out of place: Toxic traces and the politics of recycling. *Big Data & Society, 6*(2), 2053951719875479. https://doi.org/10.1177/2053951719875479.

Tour, E., Creely, E., & Waterhouse, P. (2021). "It's a Black Hole …": Exploring teachers' narratives and practices for digital literacies in the adult EAL context. *Adult Education Quarterly*, 0741713621991516. https://doi.org/10.1177/0741713621991516.

UNESCO. (2017). *Education for sustainable development goals—Learning objectives*. UNESCO. https://en.unesco.org/themes/education/sdgs/material.

UNESCO. (2018). *A global framework of reference on digital literacy skills for indicator 4.4.2*. UNESCO. http://uis.unesco.org/sites/default/files/documents/ip51-global-framework-reference-digital-literacy-skills-2018-en.pdf.

UNESCO. (2021). Getting every school climate-ready: How countries are integrating climate change issues in education. UNESCO. https://unesdoc.unesco.org/ark:/48223/pf0000379591

Vanderhoven, E., Schellens, T., & Valcke, M. (2016). Decreasing risky behavior on social network sites: The impact of parental involvement in secondary education interventions. *The Journal of Primary Prevention, 37*(3), 247–261. https://doi.org/10.1007/s10935-016-0420-0.

Vassallo, F. (2020). Teaching comparative political behavior in the era of digital activism. *Journal of Political Science Education, 16*(3), 399–402. https://doi.org/10.1080/15512169.2019.1683454.

Volman, M., Karssen, M., Emmelot, Y., & Heemskerk, I. (2020). The focus of schools on twenty-first–century competencies and students' experience of these competencies. *The Curriculum Journal, 31*(4), 648–665. https://doi.org/10.1002/curj.57.

Wu, L., Kim, M., & Markauskaite, L. (2020). Developing young children's empathic perception through digitally mediated interpersonal experience: Principles for a hybrid design of empathy games. *British Journal of Educational Technology, 51*(4), 1168–1187. https://doi.org/10.1111/bjet.12918.

Yilmaz, R. M., & Goktas, Y. (2017). Using augmented reality technology in storytelling activities: Examining elementary students' narrative skill and creativity. *Virtual Reality, 21*(2), 75–89. https://doi.org/10.1007/s10055-016-0300-1.

Zuboff, S. (2019). *The Age of Surveillance Capitalism*. Profile Books.

CHAPTER 16

Universal Design and Assistive Digital Technologies: Enhancing Inclusion of Persons with Disabilities

Floyd Morris

INTRODUCTION

Since the turn of the new millennium in 2000, modern technologies have been evolving at a rapid pace. The speed of this expansion is contributing to a transformation of the world and its people (Munroe, 2002; Dunn, 2012). All citizens, including marginalized groups such as persons with disabilities have been impacted (Lafayette, 2018). According to the Global Report on Assistive Technology there are approximately 2.5 billion individuals who are benefitting from one or more assistive technology. Futuristically, the report is projecting 3.5 billion individuals benefitting from assistive technology based on the aging population and chronic diseases by 2050 (WHO & UNICEF, 2022).

Notwithstanding the massive improvements in modern technologies for persons with disabilities, a significant portion of this population has not been able to access developments in their societies due to the high cost of such technologies (Kayange, 2021). The 2022 study on assistive technologies for persons with disabilities has shown that 85% of persons with disabilities in developed countries have access to modern assistive technologies, whereas only approximately 10% in developing countries have similar access (WHO & UNICEF, 2022). The 2011 World Report on Persons with Disabilities by the WHO revealed that there are over one billion individuals across the world living with a disability, of which 85% are living in the global south. Therefore, the

F. Morris (✉)
The University of the West Indies, Mona, Jamaica

vast majority of persons with disabilities across the world are not benefiting from the development of these modern assistive technologies.

Through universally designed products and assistive digital technologies, persons with disabilities are being presented with opportunities to assist in eliminating some of the barriers that contribute to their exclusion, isolation and discrimination in society (Kayange, 2021; Morris, 2021; Waller, 2018).

In this chapter, the author examines the issue of universal design and assistive digital technologies and how they are paving the way for the participation, inclusion and non-discrimination of persons with disabilities in a growingly digitized world. Through the lens of a phenomenological and autoethnographic study, the author chronicles how the world is being transformed to allow for the participation and inclusion of persons with disabilities in everyday activities. The fundamental question the paper addresses is to what extent is universal design and assistive digital technologies assisting the everyday participation, inclusion and non-discrimination of persons with disabilities in a digitized world?

In answering this question, the chapter documents some available literature on the subject of study; outlines the theoretical framework underpinning the arguments; the methodological approach to the study and results from personal experiences of the author who has a visual disability for over 30 years. The chapter concludes with some recommendations for actions that would ensure that persons with disabilities gain greater access to technological devices that would facilitate their everyday inclusion in society on an equal basis with others.

Participation, Inclusion and Non-Discrimination

For justice to be done to this chapter, it is prudent for one to understand what the concepts of participation, inclusion and non-discrimination mean in the context of everyday activities for persons with disabilities. In 2001, the WHO in its framework for the International Classification of Functioning, Disability and Health, introduced a definition for participation. It defines participation as "involvement in a life situation" or "the lived experience" of people in the actual context in which they live (WHO, 2001).

The definition posited by the WHO suggests that where participation and persons with disabilities are concerned, these individuals must be 'involved' or the 'experience' must be factored in. But the experience might be such that these individuals are isolated from the mainstream of society. Therefore, when we speak of participation, we must deal with the active involvement and lived experiences of persons with disabilities on an everyday basis. For this active involvement to take place, universally designed and modern assistive technology must play a quintessential role. These are needed for constant interaction with individuals without a disability on an everyday basis.

Inclusion in the context of this chapter speaks to the process of improving the ability, opportunity and dignity of people, disadvantaged based on their identity, to take part in society. The definition proffered by the World Bank (2013) was largely within the context of social inclusion. Nevertheless, it is a fittingly appropriate definition for this chapter. Undoubtedly, the identity of persons with disabilities has been used for centuries to isolate them from participating in society on an everyday basis. Modern assistive technologies are tools that have been developed to improve the ability, opportunity and dignity of persons with disabilities in society on an everyday basis (WHO/UNICEF, 2022). These modern assistive technologies have enhanced the capabilities of persons with disabilities to participate and be included in schools, workplaces, churches, sports and other such activities.

The Convention on the Rights of Persons with Disabilities (CRPD) articulated a definition for discrimination based on disability. It stated that "discrimination based on disability means that any distinction, exclusion or restriction on the basis of disability which has the purpose or effect of impairing or nullifying the recognition, enjoyment or exercise, on an equal basis with others, of all human rights and fundamental freedoms in the political, economic, social, cultural, civil or any other field" (United Nations, 2006, p. 3). The CRPD definition of what constitutes disability discrimination is quite lucid. Therefore, non-discrimination in the context of disability must be seen as 'no' distinction, exclusion or restriction on the basis of disability which has the purpose or effect of impairing or nullifying the recognition, enjoyment or exercise, on an equal basis with others, of all human rights and fundamental freedoms in the political, economic, social, cultural, civil or any other field". Persons with disabilities must therefore be allowed to participate and be included in the political, economic, social, civil and other fields of society on an everyday basis. This is the quintessence of non-discrimination. Modern assistive technology has to be one of the driving forces behind this means of non-discrimination. For example, it is a modern assistive technology that has to lead the everyday connection to the Internet for persons with disabilities to interact with others in society (Lafayette, 2018).

Universal Design and Assistive Digital Technology

Since the fall of the Berlin wall in 1989 which saw the end of communism, the world has been experiencing an acceleration in modern technologies. These modern technologies have transformed the way individuals in societies think and act (Giddens, 1991; Dunn, 1995). Persons with disabilities have been benefiting from this seismic shift taking place where modern technologies are concerned (Kayange, 2021; King, 1999; Morris, 2021).

For persons with disabilities to be meaningfully included in society on an equal basis with others, mechanisms must be put in place to facilitate this (WHO & UNICEF, 2022). Technologies are the tools that aid in bridging the gap between persons with disabilities and the various social organisms (Oliver, 1990). It significantly enhances the capacity of persons with disabilities to relate with individuals in society on an everyday basis. This is why the issue of accessibility is a foundational tenet of the Convention on the Rights of Persons with Disabilities (CRPD).

The Committee on the CRPD, in its General Comments on Accessibility (CRPD Article 9) indicates the following:

> The International Covenant on Civil and Political Rights and the International Convention on the Elimination of All Forms of Racial Discrimination clearly establish the right of access as part of international human rights law. Accessibility should be viewed as a disability-specific reaffirmation of the social aspect of the right of access. The Convention on the Rights of Persons with Disabilities includes accessibility as one of its key underlying principles — a vital precondition for the effective and equal enjoyment of civil, political, economic, social and cultural rights by persons with disabilities. Accessibility should be viewed not only in the context of equality and non-discrimination, but also as a way of investing in society and as an integral part of the sustainable development agenda. (Committee on the CRPD, 2014, p. 2)

Since the establishment of the CRPD in 2006, greater emphasis has been placed on the accessibility of modern technologies for members of this marginalized community. It is recognition by the United Nations and its States Parties, that for persons with disabilities to be meaningfully included in a rapidly digitized world and allowed to participate on an everyday basis, access to modern technologies for persons with disabilities is paramount. Modern technologies enables persons with disabilities to communicate more efficaciously with others on an everyday basis; it improves navigability for persons with disabilities; it enhances social life for persons with disabilities and it improves productivity of persons with disabilities, among other things (WHO & UNICEF, 2022; King, 1999; Mosar, 2006). It is what is regarded as 'glabilitization', a new word introduced in 2021. 'Glabilitization' is the process by which globalization through the introduction of modern technologies have been significantly enhancing the abilities of persons with disabilities and facilitating their inclusion in mainstream society. The word is a conflation of globalization and disability (Morris, 2021, p. 5). In this process, the concepts of universal design and assistive digital technology have been preeminent.

The CRPD in Article 2 defines what constitutes universal design. It states: "Universal design" means the design of products, environments, programmes and services to be usable by all people, to the greatest extent possible, without the need for adaptation or specialized design. "Universal design" shall not exclude assistive devices for particular groups of persons with disabilities where this is needed (United Nations, 2006, p. 3).

Since the publication of the 1991 Institute of Medicin (IOM) report Disability in America, the world of assistive technology has changed significantly in several areas. Perhaps the most dramatic advances involve the expanded communication options that have accompanied the improvement and widespread adoption of personal computers for use in homes, schools, and workplaces. Spurred in part by United States federal policy incentives and requirements, the industry has developed a range of software and hardware options that make it easier for people with vision, hearing, speech, and other impairments to communicate and, more generally, take advantage of electronic and information technologies. In many cases, these options have moved into the realm of general use and availability (Institute of Medicin, 2007). For example, people who do not have vision or hearing loss may find technologies like voice recognition software valuable for business or personal applications. Prosthetics technology is another area of remarkable innovation, with research on the neurological control of devices resulting in, for example, prosthetic arms that people can move by thinking about what they want to do.

The Assistive Technology Act of the United States (1998) defines assistive technology as: "Any item, piece of equipment, or product system, whether acquired commercially, modified or customized, that is used to increase, maintain or improve the functional capabilities of individuals with disabilities." These devices increase the communication and information interaction between persons with disabilities and their environment (Raja, 2016). For example, a hearing-aid assists a hard-of-hearing person to hear more clearly what is taking place around him or her.

Most importantly, assistive digital devices enable persons with disabilities to function efficaciously in education and employment activities. Research has shown the quintessence of education to the employment of persons with disabilities (Rieser, 2008; Gayle-Geddes, 2015; Morris, 2021; WHO & UNICEF, 2022). For persons with disabilities to perform at their optimum, they must have the technological support that will enable them to relate to their teachers or lecturers in the educational institution. This is why it is pivotal for persons with disabilities to have some form of assistive digital technology to use whilst attending an educational institution (King, 1999; Rieser, 2008).

Similarly, persons with disabilities must have the assistive digital technology to utilize once they are employed. For persons with disabilities to be productive at the workplace, there must be assistive digital technology to give support. This is particularly important because the employee with a disability must interact with individuals without a disability on an everyday basis (Lafayette, 2018; WHO & UNICEF, 2022).

The Internet is the major means of accessing information in modern societies (Dahlgren, 2005). But not all individuals have access to this vital source of information. One such group of individuals who are unable to consistently access the Internet is persons with disabilities. Their restrictive access is caused by a plethora of factors. Chief among these is the unavailability of assistive digital technology to facilitate persons with disabilities use of the Internet (WHO & UNICEF, 2022; Kayange, 2021; Petrick, 2015).

Not all persons with disabilities can access the Internet via the use of a regular computer. For an individual who is blind to read what is on the Internet, he or she must have assistive software that would enable him or her to navigate the Internet independently. The only way this could be accommodated for a person who is blind without assistive software is if the computer is universally designed with an in-built speech programme such as the I-pad (Lafayette, 2018). However, long before the concept of universal design came into existence, persons with disabilities were using assistive digital software to gain access to the Internet. Persons who are blind for example, have been using the Job Access with Speech (JAWS) to assist in accessing the information on the Internet (Morris, 2021). It is therefore incumbent for these assistive digital technology to become accessible and beneficial to persons with disabilities (Holt, 2018).

But the development of these devices has not been cheap and readily available to persons with disabilities (Kayange, 2021). Assistive digital devices are specialized equipment designed for particular disability groups. They do not emerge in mass production as that of ordinary goods which will allow for economies of scale. In other words, they do not have a major market where a producer can mass produce and therefore get the particular assistive digital device at a cheaper cost.

Most persons with disabilities are very poor individuals (World Bank, 2016). Additionally, these individuals are largely unemployed due to the stigma and stereotypical images relating to their disability (World Health Organization-WHO, 2011; United Nations, 2018; Morris, 2021). Therefore, they are unable to stimulate the kind of global demand for assistive digital devices that would encourage a producer to engage in mass production which will result in cheaper costs (Maskery, 2007).

The fix to this is for the production of universally designed devices that would benefit both persons with disabilities and those without a disability (Kayange, 2021). In the application of universal designs, companies would be able to mass produce for their regular clientele. However, they would incorporate features for persons with distinct disabilities to utilize their devices on an everyday basis.

Policy Advocacy for Technology Inclusion

But, for this to happen, persons with disabilities will have to engage with serious political actions. The community of persons with disabilities will have to organize themselves in a powerful advocacy group to pressure governments to cater to their needs (Oliver, 1983). Politics is a numbers game and governments do pay attention to pressure groups that are likely to influence the balance of power. The World Health Organization 2011 World Report on Persons with Disabilities postulated that between 15 and 17 per cent of a country's population constitute persons with disabilities. Whenever this estimate is conflated with the family members of persons with disabilities, the potential pressure group mushrooms into a mighty political force that can shake the foundations of any government. Thus, persons with disabilities and their families must coalesce around some core issues, including that of gaining access to assistive digital technology, and getting governments to cater to the needs of this marginalized group.

Notwithstanding the multiplicity of research on the issue of universal design and assistive technology for persons with disabilities (WHO & UNICEF, 2022; Kayange, 2021; Lafayette, 2018; McDonald & Clayton, 2013; Maskery, 2007; Mosar, 2006; King, 1999; Petrick, 2015), there is a lack of research showing persons with disabilities in their everyday use of these modern assistive devices. The experiences of persons with disabilities with universal design and assistive technology are foundational to understanding the participation, inclusion and non-discrimination of these individuals in society on an everyday basis. Indeed, this is a fulfillment of the global mantra for persons with disabilities: "nothing about us, without us" (Crowther, 2007). The content of this chapter is a response to such lacuna.

The Theoretical Framework

The theoretical framework of this chapter is anchored in both social constructionism and human rights. These frameworks capture the quintessence of the arguments being presented in this chapter. In social constructionism, it is postulated that meanings and understandings are shaped and developed in society. Berger and Luckmann (1966) opine that meanings are fashioned in society due to a repetitive process that becomes deeply entrenched over time. This process they regard as 'habitualization'.

Meanings and understandings of persons with disabilities have been habitualized in societies and become a preeminent feature of everyday life. Such meanings and understandings have contributed to the isolation, exclusion and discrimination of persons with disabilities on an everyday basis. Ultimately, this has contributed to between 15 and 17 per cent of the world's population being marginalized and categorized among the poorest on an everyday basis (WHO, 2011).

The work of Berger and Luckmann, undoubtedly influence Mike Oliver who developed the social model of disability. In this model of disability, Oliver (1990) posits that it is social organizations that create barriers against individuals with impairments, thus restricting their participation in society. These barriers Oliver cites as social, economic, environmental, technological and attitudinal. For persons with impairments to be included in this growingly digitized world, these barriers have to be removed. This is where the human rights framework becomes relevant and applicable to this chapter.

The human rights theory places emphasis on the fundamental rights and freedoms that are foundational to every human being. These rights and freedoms are universal, indivisible and inalienable (Degener, 2017). Some of these rights include: the right to life; right to vote; the right to education; the right to health care; the right to work and employment, freedom of expression and the right to information. All of these rights are entrenched in diverse international treaties (United Nations, 1948).

In the context of this chapter, the Convention on the Rights of Persons with Disabilities (CRPD), adopted by the United Nations in 2006 is preeminent (United Nations, 2006). It must be noted that the rights entrenched in the CRPD are not new rights. They are merely a reaffirmation of rights prescribed in other established treaties (Degener, 2017).

The CRPD is the irrefutable gold standard of the human rights model of disability. The Committee on the CRPD (2018) in its General Comments on Equality and Non-discrimination noted the following:

> The human rights model of disability recognizes that disability is a social construct and impairments must not be taken as a legitimate ground for the denial or restriction of human rights. It acknowledges that disability is one of several layers of identity. Hence, disability laws and policies must take the diversity of persons with disabilities into account. It also recognizes that human rights are interdependent, interrelated and indivisible. (CRPD, 2018, p. 2)

Here we see the Committee on the CRPD recognizing that disability is a social construct. This synchronizes with the arguments postulated by Oliver (1990). There is thus an intimate link between the social model of disability and that of the human rights model.

But, as the CRPD is implemented in States Parties that have signed and ratified this global treaty, there is a conspicuous tension emerging with the new approach and that of the older models of disability. For example, in the Caribbean, the established models of disability that have shaped public policy are the charity and medical models (Gayle-Geddes, 2015). These models have posited the view that persons with disabilities are unable to make any meaningful contribution to society unless they are cured of the disease that contributes to their impairment. Consequently, these individuals should be confined to their homes and depend on the State, their families or church for support (Grech, 2009). In other words, persons with disabilities are construed as objects of charity.

Now that the human rights model of disability is being enforced and persons with disabilities are seen as rights holders, there are growing tension in Caribbean societies. Persons with disabilities are pushing for greater self-actualization, embolden by the new human rights paradigm. As these individuals make this push, they are encountering more challenges in their society.

A classic example of this tension is manifested in how Articles 5 and 9 of the CRPD make provision for reasonable accommodation and access to information respectively. Yet, persons with disabilities in the Caribbean have been struggling to get reasonable accommodations with information in an accessible format to them. Persons with visual disabilities and those with hearing impairments have been experiencing considerable challenges in accessing information in a form that is compatible with their disability and this is restricting the participation and inclusion of these individuals in their society on an everyday basis (ECLAC, 2017). One of the fixes to this is the availability of universal design and modern assistive technology that make it easier for these individuals to access information on an equal basis with others.

According to the Global Report on Assistive Technology: "Assistive technology enables and promotes the participation, inclusion and engagement of persons with disabilities, aging populations, and people living with chronic conditions in the family, community and all areas of society, including the political, economic and social spheres" (WHO & UNICEF, 2022, p. 11). This is why access to modern assistive technology is treated as a human right for persons with disabilities. The said Global Report on Assistive Technology states: "Access to assistive technology is a human right and a pre-requisite for equal participation and opportunities. Member States and their institutions are responsible for ensuring that their citizens have access to safe, effective and affordable assistive technology" (p. 5).

The arguments presented in this chapter can be summarized using the theories under consideration. On an everyday basis, persons with disabilities are being isolated, excluded and discriminated against in the growingly digitized world due to multiple barriers imposed by society. These barriers are socially constructed and violate the fundamental rights of these marginalized individuals. Persons with disabilities are human beings and are thus subject to all the fundamental rights and freedoms nestled in diverse international treaties. Modern technologies, through universal designs and assistive digital devices, offer significant hope for the inclusion, participation and non-discrimination against persons with disabilities on an everyday basis. The experiences proffered in this chapter are perfect testimony to this.

Methodology

A phenomenological study was conducted on the situation of universal design and assistive technology. A phenomenological approach is utilized because it seeks to create meaning and understanding of an activity or event based on one's feelings and perceptions (Patton, 2015). The formation of the concept of universal design is indeed a modern phenomenon as it seeks to create a level playing field for persons with disabilities. With this phenomenon, technologies are designed and developed for all users to utilize efficaciously. For example, the I-Pad is a modern device that was designed and developed so that individuals with or without a disability can use it. More persons with disabilities are now able to use these technologies on an everyday basis through the principle of universal design.

Similarly, assistive digital technology have been developed to bridge the socio-economic divide between persons with disabilities and those without disabilities. Assistive digital technology thus constitute a phenomenological development because it has a transformational effect on the lives of individuals in society. It is aiding persons with disabilities to participate and be included in everyday activities that prior to 2000 were unfathomable.

In conducting this phenomenological study, an auto ethnographic approach is also used to assist with the analysis. The author has a visual disability and as such; has been using assistive digital technologies and universally designed equipment to aid in his work on an everyday basis.

An autoethnographic study is a qualitative research technique that allows a researcher to write about a topic of great personal relevance in which his or her experiences are situated in the social context. Poulos (2021) states that "*Autoethnography* is an autobiographical genre of academic writing that draws on and analyzes or interprets the lived experience of the author and connects researcher insights to self-identity, cultural rules and resources, communication practices, traditions, premises, symbols, rules, shared meanings, emotions, values, and larger social, cultural, and political issues" (4).

Autoethnography thus requires deep reflection on both one's unique experiences and the universal within oneself. The important thing is for the researcher to document the facts of the phenomenon in order to ensure descriptive and interpretive validity. Thus, the researcher has to be quite accurate in stating the facts of the phenomenon in order to enhance the credibility of the research.

Adams et al. (2015) explained that "autoethnography is a qualitative research method that: (1) uses a researcher's personal experience to describe and critique cultural beliefs, practices, and experiences; (2) acknowledges and values a researcher's relationships with others; (3) uses deep and careful self-reflection—typically referred to as "reflexivity"—to name and interrogate the intersections between self and society, the particular and the general, the personal and the political; (4) Shows people in the process of figuring out what to do, how to live, and the meaning of their struggles; (5) balances intellectual and methodological rigor, emotion, and creativity; and (6) strives for social justice and to make life better." (Adams et al., 2015, p. 2)

Recognizing the importance of autoethnography as a valid qualitative research approach, it is deemed appropriate for this study. The author has been a strong advocate for persons with disabilities (social justice) over the past 30 years in his capacity as a person who is blind, policy maker, researcher and parliamentarian. The author has been using the software called Job Access With Speech (JAWS), along with an I-Pad and an I-Phone to execute his everyday tasks for research, parliamentary duties, political activities, regional and international responsibilities and personal matters. All of these have been efficaciously executed and contributed to varied successes of the author as a blind person. These universally designed devices and assistive digital technologies will be the subject of analysis in this chapter. Resultantly, emphasis will be placed on the Kurtzweil Reading Machine, laptop and JAWS as assistive digital technology, along with the I-Pad and the I-Phone as universally designed devices.

The author outlines the use of these assistive technology and universally designed devices and expresses how each assists persons with disabilities in their everyday activities. Importantly, the author links the phenomena of modern technologies to his personal life experiences and shows how these have contributed to the varied successes that he has experienced in a growingly digitized world. Recommendations are then made on how to make these technologies more readily available to persons with disabilities so that the sphere of success can be enlarged.

The Development of Modern Assistive Technology

Technological intervention for persons with disabilities has a long history. It had its genesis from the funding of assistive technology in 1967 by Education for the Handicapped Act in the United States. The Individual with Disabilities Education Act (IDEA) mandates schools to provide assistive technology services and equipment for a student with a disability to ensure a "free and appropriate" public education. The reauthorization of IDEA (1997) mandates assistive technology to be included in the Individual Education Program (IEP). Since 2001, with passage of the No Child Left Behind (NCLB) Act, the US Department of Education has been embracing technology research in order to improve the effectiveness of educational intervention and in turn, academic achievement. A plethora of assistive digital technology and universally designed devices have emerged subsequently and are contributing to a phenomelogical transformation of the lives of persons with disabilities (Weikle & Hadadian, 2001; WHO & UNICEF, 2022).

The development of digital clocks and watches to tell the time to blind persons; the development of Job Access with Speech (JAWS) to convert print to speech; along with the development of the I-Pad and the I-Phone with built in speech and sign language features for the blind and deaf; are all phenomena that have been positively impacting on the everyday participation and inclusion of persons with disabilities in an increasingly digitized world. The author is a perfect testimony to this burgeoning situation of access to modern assistive technology that has allowed for equal participation and inclusion in my everyday activity in Jamaica.

Personal Experiences

In 1989, one of the most traumatic experiences to affect an individual happened to this author. I became totally blind due to the onset of glaucoma. This occurred six years after the eye disease was first detected during my high school years in 1983. The rapid deterioration of my eyesight contributed to me graduating from high school without a single academic subject.

At the time, there were no available assistive digital technology or universally designed equipment to facilitate my learning experience in school on an everyday basis. Resultantly, I sojourned through high school without getting the opportunity to successfully complete my academic courses.

In my society, developing a disability is equivalent to a life sentence in poverty (Gayle-Geddes, 2015). There are deeply entrenched negative attitudes and stigma that Oliver (1990) speaks about, that serves to restrict the participation of persons with disabilities in society on an everyday basis. Such restrictions are largely due to the compendia of social, economic, environmental, attitudinal and technological barriers that are constructed by human hands: becoming blind in a society with such humongous impediments seemed indeed, daunting.

Nevertheless, I was strengthened with the resolve that come what may, I was going to challenge the system and become whatever I wanted to be. It was never easy because I had to leave the confines of my home in a rural community, to travel to the city of Kingston where rehabilitation services were available for a person who is freshly disabled. At the Jamaica Society for the Blind (JSB), I was exposed to a new approach to life. I had to develop survival skills that would allow for me to participate effectively in society on an equal and everyday basis with others. Thus, I had to learn to read and write braille, basic typing skills, mobility training and other everyday living skills. My learning to read and write braille was the first experience with assistive technology for a person with a disability. This I did through the use of a braille machine. It was by no means 'digital' and would make sufficient noise to disturb an entire community.

The braille machine is a piece of equipment that allows a person who is blind to braille information. It has seven keys, inclusive of a space bar. The person who is blind has to juggle the different key combinations to form letters and when they are put together, produce words from a system of raised dots and these allows the person who is blind to read by feeling. The juggling of the keys on the metallic equipment contributes to the noise level produced.

Notwithstanding the noise level, braille was an essential skill that equipped me in re-entering the education system to redo my academic subjects.

1991 was a critical juncture in my life, as it was the year that I re-entered the education system. I had to redo my academic courses in order to get qualified for university. Being at the JSB was added motivation as I met and saw other persons with disabilities who were attending university and I realized that it was not a pipe dream. Thus, I quickly registered in an inclusive education institution where both individuals with and without disabilities attended (UNESCO, 1994). Here I did five General Certificate Examinations (GCE) and two Advance Level GCE subjects.

Doing these academic courses meant that I had to do tremendous reading. This was a challenge for me as a person who is blind. There were volunteers who gave considerable support to students with disabilities who visited the organization. However, there was a sophisticated piece of assistive technology known as the Kurtzweil Reading Machine that assisted in my reading engagements and facilitated some independence.

The Kurtzweil Reading Machine is a device that scans and converts printed text into voice and reads back the scanned information to a person who is blind. The assistive digital device capacitates persons who are blind to read large volumes of printed text that would not be otherwise available to them. It must be noted that the vast majority of books are in print and therefore not in an accessible format to persons who are blind. Alternate means therefore have to be found to ensure that printed text are converted to voice for these individuals.

But whilst the Kurtzweil was a welcome addition to my reading arsenal, it was not readily available to my use at home. It was an expensive piece of equipment that was donated to the JSB. As expressed by WHO & UNICEF (2022) and Kayange (2021), the ordinary person who is blind could not find US$5000.00 to purchase such assistive digital technology.

By 1993, I had successfully completed my academic courses at the evening college and these allowed me to meet the matriculation requirement for the University of the West Indies, the premier academic institution in the Caribbean. My braille machine was all the assistive technology that I had to assist me at this level of the education system. Measures had to be put in place to ensure that at this level, I was producing on par with my non-disabled students. The UWI was in its infancy in establishing systems to support students with disabilities.

Two years prior to my entrance, the institution had established a special committee to give support to students with disabilities. Included in this support mechanism was the procurement of assistive digital technology for students with disabilities. A similar Kurtzweil machine was secured and placed in the Main Library for use. This meant that I had to leave the confines of my accommodation on the hall of residence that I was residing, to visit the library at odd hours to use this piece of assistive digital equipment that was nestled in a special room to prevent disturbing other students.

I was accepted to read for a Bachelor of Arts (BA) in Media and Communication. Again, this required extensive reading and this seemed daunting for a person who is blind. However, I had embraced the philosophy that education is the key to social transformation and upward mobility (Mandela, 1994) and so I was committed to the task at hand.

I secured an additional piece of equipment that was a small tape recorder, to record all my classes. This would enable me to play back and listen to lecturers at my own convenience. There was also a cadre of student volunteers who would read for me from time to time. Additionally, whenever the reading materials got extensive, I would go to the library to use the Kurtzweil Reading Machine.

For three years, this was the routine for my undergraduate degree. I was not exposed to the most efficacious assistive digital technology for a person with a disability for everyday use. However, I made the best use of what was available. Resultantly, I completed my Bachelor of Arts in Media and Communication with upper second-class honours in 1996: finishing just one point outside of the designated score for first-class honours. One can therefore ask the presumptive question, what would be the outcome if I had all modern assistive digital technology for a person with a disability?

The success at the undergraduate level dilated my appetite for further education. This is the 'self-efficacy' that Bandura (1986) speaks about in Social

Cognitive Theory. My personal experiences in completing the first degree had bolstered my confidence to pursue further academic work. Thus, I applied for and was accepted to pursue a Master of Philosophy (M.Phil.) in Government at the said UWI.

I had received two scholarships based on my performance at the undergraduate level and this gave me sufficient funds to pay for my tuition and purchase additional assistive technology. Pursuing and completing an undergraduate degree is one thing. Doing so for a research-based post-graduate degree is a whole different ball-game. It requires dedication and discipline, since one is not required to be in the classroom on an everyday basis. Instead, one is on his or her own and is guided by an academic supervisor. The bulk of the work has to be done by the individual pursuing the degree and this requires prodigious efforts.

Yet, I was equal to the task. I was exuding with confidence after completing my first degree. And, with my new found assistive digital technology, a Braille and Speak machine, I felt as if I could conquer the world.

The Braille and Speak is a digitized version of the Braille machine. It carries the said seven keys, inclusive of a space bar. However, it is a less noisy, digitize device that allows for the person who is blind to braille the information and it is converted to voice, so that individuals can hear what is being brailed. Furthermore, it gives the person who is blind the option of whether to convert the information into braille via a Braille Embosser or to send to a regular printer for printing so that sighted individuals can observe the work that has been done. I was particularly excited about the latter option. Because, I had to consistently interact with my academic supervisor and this kind of assistive digital technology was needed to assist with my everyday work. Additionally, the prospects for employment were now real as I could easily interact with employer and employees in a work environment.

POLICY ADVOCACY FOR ASSISTIVE TECHNOLOGY AT THE NATIONAL LEVEL

For the first time, in 1998, a person with a visual disability was appointed to the Senate of Jamaica. I gladly accepted the appointment, because, for the first time, there was going to be a voice of a strong advocate for persons with disabilities in the highest decision making institution of the country-the Parliament. My appointment was never for persons with disabilities. Rather, it was an appointment as a member of the Government team but I chose to speak on issues relating to persons with disabilities.

My experiences as a blind person, coupled with interactions with ordinary blind persons at the Jamaica Society for the Blind (JSB), on my entrance into Kingston in 1991, had given me tremendous insights as to the plight of these marginalized individuals. They needed a voice in the Parliament to speak about their living conditions. The abject poverty in which they live (ECLAC, 2017;

World Bank, 2016); the inaccessible environment in the country (Morris, 2020); the inequalities in education and employment affecting them on a daily basis (Gayle-Geddes, 2015; MLSS, 2015; Anderson, 2014) and the negative attitude towards these individuals in society (UNICEF, 2018) were all issues to postulate in the Parliament on behalf of these marginalized citizens, estimated to be 15 per cent of the population (WHO, 2011).

My appointment to the Senate was not to be accomplished without concerns. There were individuals in the society who wondered how as a person with a visual disability, I was going to function in the Senate that is the review chamber of the Parliament. Here is where the laws that are passed in the House of Representative must come to this upper chamber of the highest decision making body for review. Again, it required members to review voluminous documents and these have to be cross-referenced with the Constitution- the supreme law of the land. How then would a person who is blind be able to execute this awesome responsibility some asked?

But, these questions are not abnormal for persons with disabilities who have broken the glass-ceiling. It is not the normal thing for persons with disabilities to be successful in societies where restrictions through barriers continue to impede the effective participation of these individuals with impairments on an everyday basis (Oliver, 1990). Furthermore, political participation and involvement in public life are ablest domains (Campbell, 2021) as persons with disabilities are never conceived to be active political participants. This is why the Convention on the Rights of Persons with Disabilities (CRPD) in Article 29 has reinforced the right to political participation and public life (United Nations, 2006).

The concerns expressed by members of the public reflect the tensions that emerge between the medical and charity models of disability and that of the social and human rights models. For centuries, the Jamaican society have practiced the charity and medical models of disability, reflecting its colonial experience with Britain (Grech, 2009). Under such models, it is inconceivable for a person with a disability to assume such a significant role in the Jamaican society that requires active participation on an everyday basis. Being appointed to the Senate is an embrace of the human rights and social models of disability and this cuts against the existing practice in the Jamaican society.

My response to the public concerns was just to attend the Senate and do the work that is mandated in the Constitution for me. By then, I had secured additional assistive digital technology that would radically improve my efficacy. I now had a regular laptop and secured the revolutionizing software for persons who are blind, the Job Access with Speech (JAWS). JAWS is a software that was developed by Ted Henter, to convert printed text into voice. All documents, once they are not pictures, can be easily read by a person who is blind via use of this software.

I could now go on the Internet all by myself and conduct research without assistance from anyone. I could send and receive e-mails without having to call someone to read them for me. My dignity was elevated and I felt liberated with the addition of this new assistive digital technology JAWS.

JAWS contributed exponentially to my productivity both at school where I was doing post-graduate studies and in the Parliament where I had to review and present on varied legislation. So impressive was my participation and contribution to the Senate that by 2001, I was promoted to the position of Minister of State in the Ministry of Labour and Social Security: an administrative arm of the Government of Jamaica. During that said year, I successfully completed the M.Phil. in Government at the UWI.

Being involved with the government at this level means that one will see and handle a lot of confidential documents. A mechanism must be in place to preserve this high level of confidentiality. When I was interviewed for the job as Minister of State, I had to explain to then Prime Minister Patterson how assistive digital technology capacitated me in my everyday tasks. Obviously, he was satisfied with my response and during the seven years that I served as a Minister of State, there was never an issue or complaint about my work.

The development of the JAWS software is indeed a revolutionary assistive digital technology that bridges the gap between a person who is blind and his or her sighted counterparts. It is a technology that all persons who are blind should have to use at work, school or in their social interactions. But, the cost of such software is extremely prohibitive (WHO & UNICEF, 2022). It cost approximately US$1400.00 and the average person who is blind cannot find such funds to purchase this enabling tool. Most persons with disabilities are unemployed and those who are employed, barely earn salaries above the minimum wage (United Nations, 2018; WHO, 2011). The minimum wage in Jamaica for example; is approximately JA$9000.00 or US$60 per week.

This is why in my capacity as a Senator and Minister of State in the Parliament of Jamaica, I consistently argued for mechanisms to be put in place to ensure that such technologies, along with the requisite training for usage, be made available to persons with disabilities. The advocacy yielded some results as in 1999, the Government of Jamaica introduced the Information and Communication Technology Training Programme for Persons with Disabilities. Persons with disabilities were exposed to the use of the JAWS software and trained to use the computer. Over 500 persons with disabilities were trained under this initiative. This is the kind of governmental initiative that Lazar et al. (2015) articulate as needed to ensure digital accessibility for persons with disabilities.

Additionally, as a member of the Senate, I argued for legislation to include persons with disabilities in access to the Internet infrastructure that was being built in the country. Legislation is cited as one of the tools that are quintessential for the improvement in accessibility for persons with disabilities (Committee on the CRPD, 2014). Resultantly, The Telecommunications Amendment Act (2012) included persons with disabilities and their organizations as groups that could apply for and benefit from the Universal Service Fund (USF).

The USF is a special funding mechanism that was created by the Government of Jamaica (GOJ) post-liberalization of the telecommunications industry, to widen access to the Internet in communities across the island. It is funded by a charge levied on overseas calls terminating in Jamaica. The funds are collected by the GOJ and used to improve the access to the Internet in marginalized communities and persons with disabilities have benefitted from this endeavour. For example, between 2015 and 2019, over 200 students attending tertiary institutions and persons with disabilities who are employed, benefitted from a grant project that was funded by the USF to provide: laptops, JAWS software, Dragon Naturally Speaking and other such assistive technologies for persons with disabilities.

Policy Advocacy at the Global Level

My efforts to have persons with disabilities benefit from the technological revolution that was taking place were never confined to the hallowed walls of the Jamaican Senate. I had the distinct opportunity of negotiating the Convention on the Rights of Persons with Disabilities at the United Nations between 2002 and 2006. Consistently, as head of the Jamaican delegation, I emphasized the need for access to modern technologies for persons with disabilities. Specifically, Articles 9 and 32, which deals with accessibility and international cooperation respectively, were highlighted (United Nations, 2006). In the context of international cooperation, the argument was strongly advanced that for persons with disabilities in developing countries to have greater access to modern technologies at a cheaper cost, international cooperation will have to take place and greater emphasis on universal design.

Earlier in this chapter I spoke about universal design and how it is contributing to the technological revolution and transformation taking place in the everyday activities of persons with disabilities. Indeed, it has been one of the positive responses to making modern assistive digital technologies available to persons with disabilities. Smart phones and tablets have been designed with accessibility features that allow diverse disability groups to use on an everyday basis (Lafayette, 2018). These continue to grow, especially since the CRPD was established in 2006.

Modern Assistive Technologies as a Preeminent Enabler to Work and Study

In my work and study, I continue to benefit from these technological advancements. In 2010 I commenced the pursuit of a Doctor of Philosophy (PhD) in Government at the UWI. Similarly, in 2013 I was promoted to the top position in the Senate as the President of that noble institution. Both roles required extensive reading and writing. For my PhD I had to consult over 150 different books and journal articles and all of these were printed materials. Thankfully, I now had an I-Pad among the assistive devices to use in my work. The I-Pad is universally designed and has built in voice activated features for a person who is blind. Additionally, I could use the I-Pad to access books that were electronically formatted so that I could read with relative ease. All of these devices, the I-Pad and my laptop with JAWS, made the work to complete a PhD in 2017 possible, some 31 years after graduating from high school without a single academic subject.

In my role as President of the Senate, I continued to benefit from my laptop with the JAWS software and therefore some of the issues relating to confidentiality never arose. Additionally, I had a scanning machine with a Kurtzweil software installed to my laptop and this enabled me to scan and convert parliamentary documents into an accessible version of Microsoft Word. This capacitated me significantly in reviewing and approving over 100 pieces of legislation during my tenure as President. This included the Disabilities Act that was approved by the Parliament in 2014 (MLSS, 2014).

The Kurzweil software is an evolution from the Kurtzweil Reading Machine that was discussed earlier in this chapter. Due to the design of modern laptops with Optical Character Recognition (OCR), it was now possible to have documents scanned and read via the laptop, once the Kurzweil software is available. The software operated similar to that of the reading machine, save and except that the laptop was now the machine that was scanning the information and storing it.

A universally designed talking watch was another important tool in the compendia of assistive digital technology that I was using to conduct my work in academia and politics. I had secured this digital talking watch, with braille inscriptions for a blind person to read. The watch had the capacity to speak to me so that I could track the time of the day. This was preeminent for my work, as timing was vital for the execution of my varied tasks. For example, in the Senate, each Senator is given 30 minutes to make their presentation on a Bill or motion that is being debated. The digital talking watch aided me significantly in tracking the time of each participant in the debates and this gave me added independence and dignity.

Conclusion

For centuries, persons with disabilities have been isolated and marginalized from the mainstream of society. Through no fault of their own, these individuals have not been allowed to participate and included in education, healthcare, labour market, public transportation and other such everyday activities. This has contributed to between 15–17 per cent of the global population being among the poorest in the world (World Bank, 2016).

The consistent marginalization of persons with disabilities in a digitized world constitutes a blatant violation of their fundamental rights and freedoms (Committee on the CRPD, 2018). The establishment of the CRPD by the United Nations in 2006 is a cogent response to correcting these human rights violation (United Nations, 2006). The CRPD re-affirmed certain fundamental rights to persons with disabilities and included in this is the right to information and information communication technologies.

As indicated in the Global Report on Assistive Technology, modern technologies have emerged to deal with some of the social barriers and restrictions that have contributed to the marginality of persons with disabilities (WHO & UNICEF, 2022). Through the development of universally designed and assistive digital technology, persons with disabilities have been participating efficaciously in society on an everyday basis.

The Global Report on Assistive Technology has shown that approximately 85% of the population of persons with disabilities in developed countries have access to some form of assistive technology. Similar reports have shown up to 50% of persons with disabilities in developed countries having access to gainful employment (WHO, 2011; United Nations 2018). Conversely, the said Global Report on Assistive Technology has shown a mere 10% of persons with disabilities in developing countries having access to modern assistive technology. Research data is also showing very low employment levels in developing countries of up to 90% (WHO, 2011; ECLAC, 2017; United Nations, 2018). Research data is thus suggesting a strong connection between modern assistive technology and the employment of persons with disabilities.

The autoethnographic study shared in this chapter whilst focusing on the life of one person with a disability who shares similar experiences of most persons with visual disabilities across the world; has strongly suggested the enormous potential of universal design and assistive digital technology in contributing to the inclusion, participation and non-discrimination of persons with disabilities in society on an everyday basis. The evidence shows irrefutably that persons with disabilities can make a meaningful contribution to their society if they are provided with the requisite technological tools and training to do so. But, some preeminent issues must be addressed in order to unlock the abundance of talent that exists among this group of citizens.

One such issue that must be addressed is the high cost for universal design and assistive digital technology that need to be more affordable for persons with disabilities. As postulated by Kayange (2021), the very high costs of these devices have restricted the effective participation of persons with disabilities in everyday life. Governments across the world, along with multi-national corporations must play a greater role in reducing the cost of these devices and make persons with disabilities have greater access to them (Lazar et al., 2015). A human right is not a right if it is not exercisable and the denial of persons with disabilities to universal design and assistive digital technology severely limits these marginalized individuals to exercise their rights in other basic areas such as access to health, education, information and employment.

Recommendations

Consistent with the provisions of the CRPD to promote the right of persons with disabilities to modern technologies globally, the following are some recommendations to make this a reality:

1. For the United Nations to press for States Parties to engage with global technology companies to increase production and distribution of cost-effective universally designed and assistive digital technologies to benefit the estimated 15% of persons with disabilities globally.
2. These States Parties should accelerate the enactment of legislation and allocate budget resources that would allow persons with disabilities to have greater access to modern assistive digital technologies.
3. States Parties should remove the import duties on universally designed and assistive digital technologies for persons with disabilities to make them more affordable.
4. States Parties should stimulate the demand for universally designed and assistive digital technologies for persons with disabilities by mandating the employment of persons with disabilities and registration in inclusive education institutions for persons with disabilities and that modern technology must be provided for their inclusion and participation in society on an everyday basis.
5. States Parties should establish special funding mechanisms to provide persons with disabilities access to universally designed and assistive digital technologies that would facilitate their equal participation in everyday life and a growingly digitized world, with dignity and independence.

References

Adams, T., Holman Jones, S. & Ellis, C. (2015). Autoethnography. Oxford University Press.

Anderson, S. (2014). Climbing every mountain: Barriers, opportunities, and experiences of Jamaican students with disabilities in their pursuit of personal excellence. Kingston, Jamaica: Arawak publications.

Assistive Technology Act of the United States (1998). Assistive Technology Act of 1998. Retrieved from https://www.govinfo.gov/app/details/PLAW-105publ394/summary

Bandura, A. (1986). Social foundations of thought and action: A social cognitive theory. Englewood Cliffs, N.J.: Prentice-Hall.

Berger, P. & Luckmann, T. (1966). The social construction of reality. Penguin Books.

Campbell, F.K. (2021). The concept of ableism: Challenges to deep thinking and critique. Keynote prepared for the ALTER (European Society for Disability Research) 2021 Conference.

Crowther, N. (2007). Nothing Without Us or Nothing About Us? *Disability and Society*, 22(7), 791–794.

Committee on the Rights of Persons with Disabilities. (2018). Article 5: equality and non-discrimination. General Comments No. 6. http://www.ohchr.org.
Committee on the Rights of Persons with Disabilities. (2014). Article 9: Accessibility. General Comments No. 2. http://www.ohchr.org.
Dahlgren, P. (2005). The Internet, public spheres and political communication: Dispersion and deliberation. *Political Communication*, 22(2), 147–162.
Degener, T. (2017). A new human rights model of disability. in V. Della Fina, R. Cera & G. Palmisano (eds.), *The United Nations convention on the rights of persons with disabilities: A commentary*, 41–60, Springer, Cham, Switzerland.
Dunn, H. (Ed) (1995). Globalisation, communication and Caribbean identity. St. Martin's Press, New York and Ian Randle Publishers, Kingston.
Dunn, H. (Ed.). (2012). *Ringtones of opportunity: Policy, technology and access in Caribbean communications.* Kingston, Jamaica: Ian Randle.
ECLAC. (2017). Disability, human rights and public policy. Port of Spain, Trinidad and Tobago: United Nations.
Gayle-Geddes, A. (2015). *Disability and inequality: Socioeconomic imperatives and public policy in Jamaica.* New York: Palgrave Macmillan.
Giddens, A. (1991). *The consequences of modernity.* Cambridge, UK: Polity Press.
Grech, S. (2009). Disability, poverty and development: critical reflections on the majority world debate. Disability and Society, 24(6). 771–784.
Holt, R. (2018). Making computers accessible: disability rights and digital technology: Making computers accessible: disability rights and digital technology, by Elizabeth R. Petrick, Baltimore, MD, John Hopkins University Press.
Individuals with Disabilities Education Act of the United States. (1997). Individuals with Disabilities Education Act (IDEA). Retrieved from https://sites.ed.gov/idea/about-idea/
Institute of Medicin. (2007). Seven Assistive and Mainstream Technologies for People with Disabilities. The Future of Disability in America. The national Academies Press, Washington DC.
Kayange, G.M. (2021). Analysis of the impact of accessible digital technologies on public libraries: A case of organizations of persons with disabilities in Botswana. Academia Letters.
King, T. W. (1999). Assistive technology: Essential human factors. Allyn and Bacon: Boston.
Lafayette, P. (2018). Apple devices: The perfect tool for the blind." In Transforming and Empowering Persons with Disabilities through Modern Technologies: A Myth or Reality, edited by F. Morris, pp. 4–9. Kingston: UWI Centre for Disability Studies.
Lazar, J., Goldstein, D.F. & Taylor, A. (2015). Ensuring digital accessibility through process and policy. Waltham, MA: Morgan Kaughmann.
Mandela, N. (1994). Long walk to freedom: the autobiography of Nelson Mandela. Boston: Little, Brown.
Maskery, H. (2007). Crossing the digital divide- possibilities for influencing the private-sector business case. Information Society. 23(3). 187–191.
McDonald, S.J. & Clayton, J. (2013). Back to the future, disability and the digital divide. Disability and Society. 28(5). 702–718.
Ministry of Labour and Social Security. (2015). Socio-economic study of persons with disabilities in Jamaica. Unpublished.

Ministry of Labour and Social Security (2014). The Disabilities Act 2014. Retrieved from https://japarliament.gov.jm/attachments/341_The%20Disabilities%20bill%202014%20No.13.pdf.

Morris, F. (2021). Prospects for the employment of persons with disabilities in the post-COVID-19 era in developing countries. Disability and Society. https://doi.org/10.1080/09687599.2021.1932757.

Morris, F. (2020). Accessible and inclusive city: Can Kingston Jamaica measure up? Disability Studies Quarterly. 40(2). https://doi.org/10.18061/dsq.v40i2.6682.

Mosar, I. (2006). Disability and the promises of technology: technology, subjectivity and embodiment within an order of the normal. Information, Communication and Society. 9(3). 373–395.

Munroe, T. (2002). An introduction to politics. Jamaica: Canoe Press

Oliver, M. (1990). *The politics of disablement*. London: Macmillan Press Ltd.

Oliver, M. (1983). The politics of disability. Paper Presented at Annual General Meeting of Disability Alliance April 15, 1983.

Patton, M. Q. (2015). Qualitative research & evaluation methods (4th ed.). Thousand Oaks, CA: Sage Publications.

Poulos, C.N. (2021). Essentials of autoethnography. American Psychological Association. https://doi.org/10.1037/0000222-001.

Petrick, E.R. (2015). Making computers accessible: Disability rights and digital technology. Making Computers Accessible: Disability Rights and Digital Technology (pp. 1–196). Johns Hopkins University Press. https://doi.org/10.1080/09687599.2017.1401325

Rieser, R. (2008). Implementing inclusive education: A Commonwealth guide to implementing article 24 of the UN convention on the rights of persons with disabilities. Commonwealth Secretariat, London.

Raja, D. S. (2016). Bridging the disability divide through digital technologies. World Development Report, 1–37. Retrieved from http://www.worldbank.org/en/publication/wdr2016 and http://pubdocs.worldbank.org/pubdocs/publicdoc/2016/4/123481461249337484/WDR16-BP-Bridging-the-Disability-Divide-through-Digital-Technology-RAJA.pdf.

The Telecommunications Amendment Act. (2012). The Telecommunications Amendment Act. Retrieved from https://www.informatica-juridica.com/ley/telecommunications-amendment-act-2012/

UNICEF. (2018). Report on the situational analysis of children with disabilities in Jamaica 2018. Retrieved from www.unicef.org.

United Nations Educational, Scientific, and Cultural Organization. (1994). *The Salamanca statement and framework for action on special needs education*. Salamanca, Spain: World Conference on Special Needs Education. www.unesco.org.

United Nations. (2018). Disability and development report- Realizing the sustainable development goals by, for and with persons with disabilities. Retrieved from https://www.un.org/development/desa/disabilities/wp-content/uploads/sites/15/2018/12/UN-Flagship-Report-Disability.pdf.

United Nations. (2006). Convention on the rights of persons with disabilities. Retrieved from www.un.org.

United Nations. (1948). Universal declaration of human rights. United Nations. https://www.un.org/en/universal-declaration-human-rights/.

Waller, L. (2018). Envisioning democracy: the role and potential of information technologies for the visually impaired. Ian Randle Publishers. Kingston.

Weikle, B., & Hadadian, A. (2001). Can assistive technology help us to not leave any child behind? *Preventing School Failure*, 47(4): 181–185.

World Bank. (2016). Disability overview (online data). Retrieved from http://www.worldbank.org.

World Health Organization and the United Nations Children Fund. (2022). Global report on assistive technologies. Retrieved from www.who.org.

World Health Organization/World Bank. (2011). World Report on Disability, Geneva: World Health Organization.

World Health Organization. (2001). International classification of functioning, disability and health. Geneva, Switzerland.

CHAPTER 17

Digital Divides and Policy Interventions in a Pandemic World: Issues of Social Inclusion in Argentina

Bernadette Califano

INTRODUCTION

The coronavirus disease (COVID-19) pandemic has revealed in a stark way the inequalities and exclusions that exist in terms of access to connectivity services, in a context where more and more events of daily life have moved online. Faced with a growing demand for activities that relied on telecommunication networks—including various forms of telework, distance education, telehealth, electronic commerce, digital entertainment and virtual social interactions—the pandemic has shed light on the fact that major segments of the population in several countries of the Global South have insufficient access to the Internet.

In Latin America, only 66.7% of the region's inhabitants had an Internet connection in 2019, while the remaining third had limited or no access to digital technologies due to their economic and social conditions. The percentage of households without connectivity ranged from 60% to 85%, compared to around 30% in the countries with the highest connection rates. The Economic Commission for Latin America and the Caribbean estimated that teleworking was feasible for roughly 21.3% of employed persons and that 46% of the children lived in households without an Internet connection (ECLAC, 2020b).

This chapter aims to analyze the public actions and interventions to address the digital inequalities that emerged and became a central issue on the public

---

B. Califano (✉)
National Scientific and Technical Research Council (CONICET), National University of Quilmes (UNQ), University of Buenos Aires (UBA), Buenos Aires, Argentina

© The Author(s), under exclusive license to Springer Nature Switzerland AG 2024
H. S. Dunn et al. (eds.), *The Palgrave Handbook of Everyday Digital Life*,
https://doi.org/10.1007/978-3-031-30438-5_17

agenda during the pandemic in Argentina. Specifically, this analysis has a threefold objective: (a) to give an overview of the status of connectivity services in the country, in the broader context of Latin America; (b) to consider public initiatives taken between March 2020 and December 2021 in terms of connectivity services and internet access; (c) to provide insights regarding public policies implemented in a pandemic context, taking into account how digital transformations have disrupted traditional systems of work, education, domestic lives, and methods of communicating, and to what extent the public actions have helped to cope with the online activities of everyday life.

The period under review begins in March 2020, when COVID-19 started to spread in the country. As measures for mandatory preventive isolation and social distancing were introduced, access to ICT services became extraordinarily relevant, given that most of the population had to stay at home to do their work, educational and cultural activities, and to access information, entertainment and social interaction. In this context, the government implemented a series of public policy initiatives, which included, from the start, the prohibition of discontinuing fixed and mobile telephony, internet and cable television services for low-income users due to non-payment. The period of analysis covers until December 2021, to address not only the phase of the emergence of the problem and how it made its way to the institutional agenda but also the phase of formulation and implementation, that is, the execution of the necessary actions to achieve the objectives that had been formulated, as well as the hurdles encountered in said process.

The study draws on statistics on ICT access and usage in the country and the region, the analysis of the set of regulations and policy initiatives introduced in the field of telecommunications, and official documents prepared by the public and private sectors.

After this first introductory section, the conceptual approach is explained. The third section offers an overview of Argentina in terms of access to information and communication technology (ICT) services, emphasizing the digital inequalities that are identified between its different regions. The fourth section deals with the public actions implemented by the government in terms of connectivity and Internet access during the pandemic (March 2020–December 2021). Finally, some insights on public policies are provided, evaluating to what extent they have helped to cope with the digital activities of everyday life and which are the challenges for social inclusion that emerge in a country of the Global South.

Conceptual Framework

Public policies consist of a set of actions and decisions in specific fields of public administration (economic, labor, social, cultural, communications, telecommunications, etc.), which undergo a social process with interactions and negotiations between several actors (Califano, 2015; Oszlak & O'Donnell, 1984; Vilas, 2011).

All public policy begins with a phase in which emerging problems are identified, and set on the agenda as the first step to find a solution. The agenda comprises the overall set of issues that will be considered within the range of concerns that deserve the attention of politicians (Cobb & Elder, 1971), so agenda-building represents a key phase in the broader process of public policy-making. From there, policies go through different phases from their formulation to their implementation—i.e., the execution of the necessary actions to achieve the objectives that were set out, together with the monitoring, evaluation and, eventually, the reformulation of the initial objectives.

As Van Cuilenburg and McQuail (2003) have pointed out, the main elements of media and telecommunications policy, leaving aside differences between contexts, consist of the goals or objectives to be pursued; the criteria by which these goals are recognized; the various content and communication services to which policies apply; the unequal distribution of services; and finally, the appropriate policy measures and means of implementation.

Telecommunications policies as a field has been thoroughly studied in Latin America, mainly focused on the political dynamics of market-oriented reforms in the late twentieth century (Andrés et al., 2007; Murillo, 2009). The process of liberalization of the telecommunications sector, which began in the late 1980s and continued throughout the 1990s in the region, had a series of positive impacts, mainly in terms of service coverage and a higher penetration rate of fixed telephony, which came with an increase in fees. According to Andrés et al. (2007), the involvement of the private sector evolved from practically none at all in 1990 to a share of more than 86% in telephone connection infrastructure in 2004.

In the Argentine case, in the early 1990s, the National Telecommunications Company (ENTel) was transferred to two consortiums led by transnational companies Telefónica de Argentina S.A. and Telecom Argentina S.A. Thus, the once-monopolistic provision of the basic telephone service was split into two zones, the north and the south of the country, each operated by one consortium that accessed the distribution of the long-distance service with exclusivity in its respective zone, while value-added services were open to competition (see Abeles, 1999; Azpiazu, 2002; Azpiazu & Basualdo, 2004; Gerchunoff, 1992; among others). In 2000, after ten years of service provision under the exclusivity regime, the basic telephone service and international services became deregulated (Califano, 2017). However, the market structure that had been formed during the years of exclusivity played a key role in preventing the entry of new bidders when the sector was liberalized (Azpiazu, 2003).

The digital revolution that took place in the following decades in the region gradually disrupted traditional systems of work, communications, education, and social and domestic lives. Therefore, the implementation of public policies on connectivity became increasingly paramount. Initially, these public actions were designed to narrow the first level of the digital divide, related to material access to connectivity networks and computer equipment. According to Van Dijk (1999), the notion of access to ICTs can be made more complex at other levels, taking into account motivational access, i.e., having interest, experience and a certain predisposition for the use of technologies; access to the necessary skills, abilities and knowledge; and access to the concrete opportunities for using ICTs. In general, when the problems of material and motivational access have been totally or partially solved, difficulties in terms of competencies and structurally dissimilar uses are revealed.

Moreover, digital and communicational divides cannot be approached in isolation, without considering the structural inequality of societies that contain them. Latin America is the most unequal region in the world, where the gap between the richest and the poorest is the greatest. Throughout the nineties, inequality would have increased in Argentina, hand in hand with globalization and neoliberal reforms, becoming a severe structural condition (Kessler, 2011).

As a legacy of the reforms of the 1990s, there are currently significant imbalances in access to telecommunications services and the deployment of infrastructure, both at the regional level and within Latin American countries, with important sectors of the population having no access to affordable and quality connectivity services. This situation can be attributed partly to the fact that private sector investments in recent decades have been concentrated mainly in the urban areas with higher incomes, and partly to the failure to implement actions aimed at mitigating these effects: mainly, the incumbent operators' obligations for the buildout of networks and the limited impact of funds allocated to ensure universal service (see Galperin et al., 2013, 2021).

Towards the end of the first decade of the twenty-first century, several governments in the region began to implement national broadband plans for the buildout of connectivity infrastructure, realizing that Internet access is a relevant driver of development and social inclusion. In 2010, Argentina introduced the National Telecommunications Plan "Argentina Conectada", comprising various complementary initiatives designed to provide conditions of equal access to information and communication technologies for all inhabitants (Decree No. 1552/2010). A core element of the Plan was the deployment of a Federal Fiber Optic Network, whose operation was entrusted to AR-SAT, the Argentine satellite company that had been established in 2006, to solve regional imbalances in terms of access to networks with high transmission capacity.

Although the Cristina Fernández de Kirchner administration (2007–2011 and 2011–2015) did not comply with the schedule and goals that the broadband "Argentina Conectada" Plan proposed to achieve by 2015, within five years 95% of the backbone network was built, 25% was illuminated, and 500 new locations were reached. The change in the role of State intervention in telecommunications and the media was drastic starting in December 2015, when Mauricio Macri took office as President of the Nation (Becerra & Mastrini, 2021; Califano, 2020). Several state-run programs on connectivity—including the One Laptop Per Child "Conectar Igualdad" Plan and the development of Digital Terrestrial Television—were downsized or defunded. The buildout of broadband infrastructure—renamed the Federal Internet Plan in

2016—was one of the few initiatives that had continuity. However, it received minimal state funding, and its partial progress fell short of the goals set by the new administration, as it failed to reach even half of the promised 1200 locations with broadband in a two-year period, and there were no price reductions for the connectivity services paid by end users (Krakowiak, 2018).

More than a decade after the inception of these public policy initiatives, it has not been possible to close the digital divide in terms of internet access, mainly for low-income sectors. Furthermore, digital inequalities have emerged among people from different regions and backgrounds, in the way the Internet is incorporated into their lives, their digital skills and usages differ, and in how the life outcomes associated with these differences vary (Hargittai, 2021; Ragnedda & Gladkova, 2020).

In the context of the COVID-19 pandemic, public policies for material access to ICTs and connectivity services were placed at the center of the public agenda, leading to the implementation of a series of urgent actions and initiatives by the Argentine government, which aimed to cope with everyday digital needs and activities of the population. However, the vulnerability of public services has been revealed as they cannot guarantee coverage and rights for the most vulnerable sectors, and new digital inequalities have emerged between those who have access to broadband Internet and those who do not.

Overview of Connectivity Services in Argentina

With an estimated population of 46 million inhabitants,[1] Argentina is the southernmost country on the American continent, and the second largest nation in South America territory-wise, after Brazil, making it the world's largest Spanish-speaking country. The nation is organized as a decentralized federal State, made up of 24 jurisdictions: the Autonomous City of Buenos Aires (CABA)—the federal capital—and 23 self-governed provinces.

In 2020, when the COVID-19 pandemic broke out in the region, 85.5% of the Argentine population was an internet user. This percentage grew gradually throughout the first two decades of the twenty-first century, with a considerable surge of 90% between 2010 and 2020. However, to date, an increasingly noticeable gap persists between the exponential growth of internet users and the low level of expansion and penetration of broadband (see Fig. 17.1).

The low level of fixed broadband penetration nationwide became worrisome in the context of the pandemic, when people needed connectivity services to remotely carry out all kinds of work, educational and social activities, and to access information and healthcare services. When the lockdown was ordered in March 2020, 35.79% of Argentine households did not have fixed internet access. The situation was even more severe in several provinces: while the fixed

---

[1] The estimated population as of July 1, 2022 is 46,234,830 million inhabitants, according to the National Institute of Statistics and Census of Argentina. Source: https://www.indec.gob.ar/ Consulted: 02/15/2022.

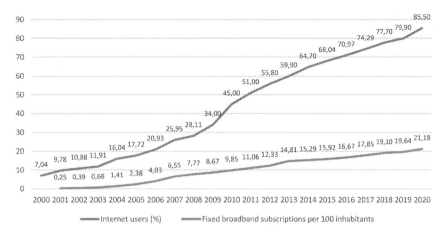

Fig. 17.1 Individuals using the internet and fixed broadband subscriptions per 100 inhabitants in Argentina (2000–2010). Source: Own analysis with data from ITU Database, 2021

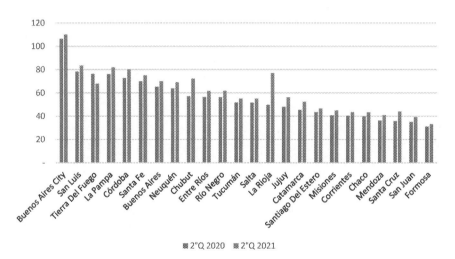

Fig. 17.2 Fixed internet penetration rates per 100 households by province (2°Q 2020–2°Q 2021). Source: Own analysis, with data from ENACOM

internet penetration rate exceeded 106% in Buenos Aires City, more than 60% of households had no access to this type of connectivity in provinces such as Formosa, San Juan, Santa Cruz, Mendoza and Chaco (see Fig. 17.2).

Interestingly, a comparison can be made between the fixed internet penetration rates at the onset of the pandemic and the same rates after the first year of the pandemic. In general terms, it shows that the fixed internet penetration rate hardly increased in all provinces by an average 5.6%—with the exception of Tierra del Fuego, where it decreased by 8.5%—and grew particularly in La

Rioja (27%) and in Chubut (15%). In any case, more than 50% of households continue not having fixed connectivity services in eight Argentine provinces, as of the second quarter of 2021.

This situation was utterly serious in popular and low-income neighborhoods, affecting day-to-day activities, especially in terms of education and access to information. During the pandemic, a long period of mandatory social isolation was established and people had to stay in their homes, while schools were closed. Consequently, students of different educational levels (primary, secondary, university) had to continue with learning activities through their computers, for which they needed quality internet access, ICT equipment, skills, and a certain predisposition, besides from a quiet social environment.

A survey on access to technology and the necessary materials to study in vulnerable neighborhoods of the City of Buenos Aires, carried out in June 2020 by the Barrios de Pie movement, revealed that 70% of students did not have a computer at home and that 82.5% did not have Internet access. According to the City Government itself, 3525 secondary school students and more than 1600 primary schoolchildren have stopped having contact with their schools since preventive and mandatory isolation was decreed (*Tiempo Argentino*, 08/23/2020). Therefore, new inequalities gaps in educational terms were created, in one of the richest districts of the country, between those who were able to continue studying during this period—since they had access to quality connectivity services and skills to use them—, and those who were unable to do so due to lack of computer equipment and broadband access.

By the end of 2020, only 63.8% of urban households had access to a computer at the national level (INDEC, 2020). The technologies through which the population connects to broadband internet also show disparity throughout the country. Of the almost ten million active accesses in the second quarter of 2021, there is a clear predominance of connectivity through coaxial cable (57.2%), followed by ADSL technology (20.47%) and, to a lesser extent, fiber optics (14.93%).

These numbers reveal that the national penetration of fiber optic technology, which enables better data transmission speeds, is very low. Out of 100 households, only ten connected to the internet via fiber optics in the second half of 2021, and these connections were mainly concentrated in four provinces: Buenos Aires, Córdoba, Santa Fe and Tucumán. The penetration of fiber optic connections nationwide is also low compared to other countries in the region: Uruguay has 78%, Brazil 56% and Chile 49% of fiber optic connections out of the total broadband connections, compared to the aforementioned 14.93% in Argentina (CABASE, 2021). These circumstances reinforced the digital inequalities between regions and inhabitants throughout the pandemic, since people living in households with low data transmission speed Internet connections could not cope with online activities of daily life, such as telecommuting, e-learning, social and entertainment pastimes.

Furthermore, an analysis of data download speed places Argentina 82nd in the worldwide ranking of fixed broadband, with an average speed of 38.47

Mbps, and 84th in terms of mobile broadband, with an average of 20.07 Mbps. These speeds are well below the world average (59.84 Mbps for fixed broadband and 29.62 Mbps for mobile broadband), a situation similar to that experienced by several Latin American countries (see Califano & Becerra, 2021), with the partial exception of Chile, Panama, Brazil and Uruguay.

As ECLAC (2020a) points out, low connection speeds consolidate situations of exclusion, preventing the development of certain everyday online activities, such as teleworking and distance education. The situation worsens when one considers the disparity in internet access speeds across the different regions of the country: during the second half of 2020, 42% of total national access did not reach a data download speed of 10Mbps.

In terms of mobile telephony, Argentina has a high penetration rate, reaching 119.47% in the second quarter of 2021. In other words, there are more active lines (54,685,210) than inhabitants in the country. However, if we disaggregate these numbers, pronounced inequalities surface: of the total active accesses, 90.12% are through prepaid plans. The prepaid plan is one in which the user pays in advance for telecommunications services before using them, it is usually the option chosen by lower-income sectors and, paradoxically, the most expensive service for mobile communications and data usage. During the pandemic, several low-income families used their mobile data plans to have their children take classes online via mobile phones, as they did not have access to broadband Internet or computers (*Tiempo Argentino*, 08/23/2020). Consequently, they spent high sums on connectivity via 3G through the most expensive telecommunications plans.

In summary, there are significant inequalities and digital divides in Argentina not only in terms of the material access to connectivity services but also in the manner in which the Internet is accessed among the connected population, as well as connection speeds, connectivity technologies and devices used for connecting throughout the country. The Covid-19 pandemic crisis contributed to reinforcing previous social structural inequalities and created new digital gaps among the population, even within the wealthiest districts of the country, in terms of access to information, media, education, teleworking and social activities.

Public Actions Regarding ICT Services During the Pandemic

As soon as the pandemic began, a series of measures were adopted to ensure the continuity of access to ICT services and to sustain the networks in the face of growing traffic and data consumption demand. These initiatives included the establishment of minimum connectivity commitments, the prohibition of discontinuing services due to non-payment, the freezing of prices during the period of mandatory social isolation, and agreements with over-the-top (OTT) content providers to lower the quality of streaming audiovisual services.

Following the enactment of mandatory social distancing measures, the government ordered the prohibition of cancelling or discontinuing the services of fixed or mobile telephony, Internet and cable TV, by radio-electric or satellite link, due to non-payment, which included up to seven consecutive or alternate invoices (Decree No. 311/2020). This measure was implemented for users of disadvantaged sectors (recipients of social assistance, retirees and pensioners, low-income workers, and beneficiaries of unemployment insurance, among others), and for small and medium-sized companies, labor cooperatives, healthcare institutions and certain public welfare entities, until December 31, 2020. Telecommunication providers were also required to offer a reduced service that guaranteed connectivity for users with a prepaid mobile phone or Internet service system, without paying a surcharge to enable consumption.

In addition, price increases for mobile and fixed telephony, Internet and pay television services were barred until December 31, 2020 (Decree No. 690/2020). However, as of January 2021, partial increases were authorized in fees for mobile telephony and ICT services, which reached a 30% increase within a year.

So-called "inclusive plans" were introduced for fixed and mobile telephony and internet services, in both postpaid and prepaid modalities, for a fixed price agreed with the companies. The main objective was to enable people facing economic hardship during the pandemic to have the possibility of changing their plan and accessing a connectivity service at an affordable price (ENaCom, 2020b). This measure represented economic aid for low-income social sectors (recipients of social assistance, retirees and pensioners, and beneficiaries of unemployment insurance, among others), which allowed them to have a minimum level of access to connectivity services to carry out their daily activities of communication and access to information—the first level of digital divide according to Van Dijk (1999). However, it turned out to be insufficient to deal with the everyday requirements imposed by the pandemic. Several people, afflicted by a critical economic situation (unsatisfied basic needs, informal employment or unemployment, among other factors), did not have the skills, motivations or abilities to suddenly turn their lives and daily activities online. Moreover, the connectivity speeds of the "inclusive plans" were low, so they did not allow long video calls, nor continue the education and learning activities of children remotely through mobile devices and limited data plans.

An increase in internet traffic occurred in all countries after people were asked to stay at home, following social distancing measures. Although the rising trend in fact preceded the pandemic in Argentina, some more pronounced peaks and variations have been observed since March 2020. There was a 35% growth in traffic during March and April, after the start of the lockdown on March 20, compared to the average traffic in February. However, a comparison of April 2020 data against the same month of 2019 reveals an increase of 65% (CABASE, 2020). State-run company AR-SAT, which manages the largest fiber optic backbone in the country, reported that wholesale traffic increased by 40% during the first months of the sanitary emergency. Although growth slowed throughout the following months of the pandemic, it maintained a monthly growth rate of 15%. In October 2021, traffic had increased by 52% compared to the same month of the previous year (CABASE, 2021).

To help cope with increased traffic and ensure an efficient use of telecom networks, agreements with over-the-top (OTT) content providers to lower the quality of streaming audiovisual services were implemented. These arrangements followed the experience of the European Union, which had asked companies such as Netflix, Amazon Prime Video and YouTube to reduce transmission quality on their platforms. In Argentina, Netflix reduced transmission bitrates for a period of 30 days, in order to decrease the bandwidth used by 25%, without compromising the resolution included in the plans hired by users. The initiative was followed by YouTube, which temporarily reduced the image quality of its videos worldwide to standard definition, to lessen the burden on internet traffic.

In addition to the reduction in video quality, several pay TV operators in the region opted to release certain content on demand and some "premium" signals at no additional cost to their customers. This strategy was adopted by Telecom-Cablevisión in Argentina.

Once again, while these agreements helped preserve networks from data traffic overload, they were designed considering only people who already had access to quality Internet before the pandemic, but not residents who were disconnected or who had limited access due to low connection speeds.

A policy that was replicated by several countries all over the world was the establishment of zero-rating agreements with telecommunication carriers, enabling citizens to access official information and educational sites from mobile apps, without this being counted as consumption of data in their subscription plans. In Argentina, an agreement was reached with the mobile phone carriers to provide free access to use the Cuid.ar health app and the platform "Seguimos educando" of the Ministry of Education, after primary and secondary schools were closed for face-to-face classes. In April the agreement was extended to facilitate access for university students to the platforms of 57 national universities (ENaCom, 2020a).

Unlike previous actions, the zero-rating agreements were among the most inclusive decisions taken in this initial pandemic period. These measures aimed to level the population's access to official information online and to public educational portals, without being counted as consumption of data. As developed in "Overview of Connectivity Services in Argentina" section of this chapter, the penetration rate of mobile telephony in the country is high, so this measure might have influenced on people's daily digital activities related to access to public information.

However, the widespread use of proprietary applications and platforms throughout the educational system in Argentina has hindered the delivery of virtual classes for students and teachers in low-income sectors. A large number of students had to follow the virtual classes through proprietary applications on their cell phones, out of the scope of the aforementioned zero-rating agreements.

In October 2020, the "Connectivity Access Program for Public Institutions" was presented with the aim of guaranteeing Internet access for all higher education centers through financing from the Universal Service Trust Fund (ENaCom, 2020c). The educational authorities and the regulatory body agreed on a technical plan to implement the project. One year later, they announced the progress of the program that would allow Wi-Fi 6 to be deployed within national universities and to incorporate blended learning modalities in order to transfer certain activities and learning processes outside the classroom (ENaCom, 2021).[2]

Since most educational institutions were not prepared for the transition to remote education, the abovementioned public actions were complemented by others, such as free distance education courses for teachers, the increase in server infrastructure capacity to host virtual campuses and classrooms, and the distribution of netbooks and tablets to students from vulnerable areas.

In connection with telecommunications infrastructure, a cooperation and reciprocal support agreement was signed in terms of network capacity by the regulator, the state-owned telecommunications company AR-SAT, and the four wholesale incumbent companies in the country (Telecom, Telefónica, América Móvil and Silica Networks). The agreement was aimed at leveraging the existing infrastructure of the main providers nationwide, which is linked with local connectivity service operators (SMEs and cooperatives) throughout the country for the deployment of last-mile networks.

Moreover, a new "General Regulation of Universal Service" was promulgated in June 2020, specifying the contributions, in the form of investments, that ICT service providers must make on a monthly basis (1% of total net income from the provision of ICT services), as well as the guidelines that programs and projects in this area should observe in order to reduce the digital divide.

In consideration of the agreements and commitments signed between the governments and the telecommunication companies, the latter received some benefits and compensations. Therefore, the regulatory agency suspended a series of administrative procedures, and extended, on an exceptional basis, the term of validity for permits, authorizations, registrations, filings and licenses with expiration dates from March 16 to September 17, 2020 (Resolution No. 326/2020, extended by Res. No. 771/2020).

With a longer-term vision, the government tried to regulate some of the ICT services as public services in August 2020, which caused a strong dispute with the main telecommunications carriers operating in the country. Despite this antagonism, which led to several implementation problems, the policy's

---

[2] This last announcement had not yet been implemented at the time of closing of this chapter, so its impact could be evaluated in future investigations.

goal was paramount in terms of equal rights and digital inclusion, and revealed the importance that digital technologies had acquired in everyday lives.

The Declaration of ICT Services as Essential Public Services

With a measure that was surprising for both the business sector and the government areas involved, the President of the Nation, Alberto Fernández, decreed that Information and Communication Technology (ICT) services be considered essential and strategic public services in competition (Decree No. 690/2020). The measure granted the rank of public service to mobile telephony, a feature that fixed telephony already had in the country. Likewise, it established greater regulatory powers for the State in terms of tariff and price controls and introduced the obligation for providers to offer basic services under equal conditions. This last provision, called "universal basic service", was intended to achieve inclusion targets and help close digital divides as a result of previous structural inequalities, in a context in which it became indisputable that the population without connectivity or with precarious ICT access had little or no chance of accessing information services, education, entertainment and forms of teleworking.

The measure was presumably motivated by the rise in the prices of ICT services, which had increased by 10% above the record inflation of 55.8% reported in 2019, had increased again in March 2020, and were expected to increase once more in September of that year, between 13 and 19% (Genoud, 2020).

The reaction of telcos and business chambers was immediate, with joint statements against the decree. Their main arguments pointed out that the measure represented a change of rules without prior consultation, which would have a negative impact on investments and employment in the sector; and that the classification of ICT services as "public services" was allegedly a regulation that entails limitations, which would not ensure expanding the level of connectivity of the population.[3]

In early September 2020, the National Senate endorsed the presidential decree. From then on, the regulatory body began a series of meetings with the stakeholders interested in the regulation of this measure, which gathered ICT chambers, SMEs and cooperatives from all over the country, as well as user and consumer associations, and later on, the main private companies in the sector.

However, the decree never became fully regulated. Several companies filed lawsuits against the State to prevent its application, and obtained favorable

---

[3] This was expressed by companies Claro, Telefónica, Telecom, Telecentro, DirectTV, AmCham (United States Chamber of Commerce), CCAC (Argentine-Canadian Chamber of Commerce), Argentine-Finnish Chamber of Commerce, Italian Chamber of Commerce, CICOMRA, GSMA, ASIET, ATVC, CACPY (Argentine Chamber of SME Cable Operators), Huawei, Express, Red Intercable and SION, in a joint advertorial published in the main newspapers of national circulation in Argentina, in August 2020.

precautionary measures that stopped its implementation and allowed them to continue unilaterally increasing the prices of their services.[4]

A year later, in an act for the launch of the second stage of the "Argentina Programa" plan, an initiative designed to train young people in programming and encourage them to advance in their studies with subsidies to acquire computers and connectivity cards, President Fernández once again announced that the government was willing to regulate internet access as a public service. Thus, the issue was again placed at the center of the public agenda, after a few months in which the discussion had calmed down, and a senator for the official party presented a bill in National Congress that proposed replicating the provisions of Decree No. 690/2020, to give this measure greater legitimacy.

Towards the end of 2021, the Commission on Systems, Media and Freedom of Expression of the Senate of the Nation promoted the debate on a series of bills that proposed to regulate ICT services as essential and strategic public services in competition. These were six legislative bills submitted between 2020 and 2021, both by pro-government and opposition senators, which shared certain similar proposals regarding the consideration of internet access as a human right but differed regarding the terms of the regulation. The meeting of the commission to discuss the issue was attended by specialists, government officials and user associations in late September,[5] but the bills did not thrive in their legislative procedure in the Congress of the Nation.

Basic ICT Services for Low-Income Sectors

One area that was initially expected to achieve progress was the implementation of the so-called universal basic service (*"prestación básica universal"*, PBU) provided for by the aforementioned Decree No. 690/2020. In December 2020, the regulatory agency specified under what conditions telcos were required to offer basic plans of fixed and mobile telephony services, Internet and cable television, at affordable prices set by the government (Resolution No. 1467/2020). These basic services were destined for more than ten million people from low-income sectors, including beneficiaries of social plans, allowances and unemployment insurance, low-income workers registered under the simplified tax regime, and public welfare entities, among others.

The procedure to access these basic ICT services was complex and the companies did not comply with the obligation to widely publicize the PBU.[6] To qualify for the benefits, low-income users had to prove their status by down-

---

[4] At the time of writing this chapter (March 2022), these lawsuits continue with their judicial process.

[5] The meeting of the Commission on Systems, Media and Freedom of Expression of the Senate of the Nation, held on 09/29/2021, is available at the following link: https://www.youtube.com/watch?v=LeW3uWxxboo.

[6] Resolution No. 1467/2020 sets forth, in article 11, that the terms and prices of the Universal and Mandatory Basic Service must "be communicated to the users by the incumbent operators through invoices, their institutional websites and on all the social media and channels through which they communicate with their customers and/or advertise their services," something that was not fulfilled immediately.

loading an affidavit from the website of the regulatory body. It was necessary to print said affidavit, complete it, certify the user's eligibility for the benefit, and present it to the desired telephone, internet access or cable television service provider. In the event of noncompliance or refusal by the company to provide the service, the user had the possibility of filling out another form to notify the ENACOM of the irregularity. This procedure was far from being an agile and simple system for low-income people to obtain the promised basic benefits, as they were mostly mobile phone users without access to computer equipment at home.

According to the research carried out for this work, based on a request for access to public information filed with the regulatory body, in August 2021—eight months after the launch of the plan—the companies reported that, through the PBU mechanism, they had provided 5,047 fixed telephony services, 353,214 mobile telephony services, 5,871 Internet access services, and 2,024 paid television services. In other words, 94.5% of the requests asked for mobile plans. Nevertheless, these numbers make up a tiny 3.7% of the more than ten million people that the government had announced would be reached by the initiative. As for the claims of users before the regulatory entity, until May 2022, 307 complaints had been submitted with rejected requests for basic service plans.

No less important is the fact that ICT service companies continued to primarily advertise their own contracting plans. After several complaints, some enterprises were required to send a text message to their users advertising the universal basic plan and communicating it on their websites. But faced with telephone inquiries from several users, the response of the private operators has generally been to offer another business promotion or discount, subject to future increases, which ended up convincing the user that it was neither convenient nor beneficial to start the cumbersome PBU application process.

To sum up, throughout almost two years of the pandemic crisis, digital technologies turn out to be paramount in most activities of daily life, and public actions and official announcements tending to regulate ICT services as "public services" demonstrated this capital importance in the political arena. However, the government failed to carry out effective measures to implement this policy in order to reduce digital inequalities and to underpin digital inclusion.

Discussions and Conclusions: Insights on Digital Policies in a Pandemic Context

The public actions implemented in the field of connectivity services and Internet access in Argentina during the first two years of the COVID-19 pandemic can be broken down into two stages.

The first stage begins in March 2020 and runs until August 2020. This first period is characterized by the recognition of the relevance of digital technologies in everyday life activities, in the context of the pressing conditions imposed by the pandemic, and by the implementation of palliative public actions and emergency interventions. The second stage begins in late August 2020, with the acknowledgement that digital inequalities tend to increase due to differences in access to connectivity services and, consequently, the usages, skills, and the exercise of economic, social, cultural and education rights among the population differ. From there on, the government expresses its intention to introduce long-term public policies by declaring ICT services as essential public services. This second stage lasts until December 2021, with the lessening of public interventions to broaden access to the Internet for lower-income sectors, and the lifting of restrictions on social circulation, together with the decrease of COVID-19 cases in the summer of the southern hemisphere.

In the first stage (March–August 2020), public actions and policies regarding ICT services were reactive in nature, rapidly rolled out in response to the challenges posed to everyday digital activities by the pandemic, and mostly based on agreements with the private sector. Throughout the first six months during which COVID-19 spread, the government focused primarily on implementing measures to ensure the continued operation of networks and to guarantee a minimum level of services in the face of growing traffic and data consumption demand. These initiatives included the establishment of minimum connectivity commitments, the prohibition of discontinuing services due to non-payment, the freezing of prices during the period of mandatory social isolation, the implementation of "inclusive plans" to help people facing economic hardship to access connectivity services at an affordable price, several zero-rating agreements with telecommunication carriers to enable citizens to access official information and educational sites, and agreements with over-the-top content providers to lower the quality of streaming audiovisual services, among others. However, the digital divides that persisted from previous structural inequalities lessened the impact of the actions implemented during the pandemic emergence. Likewise, these actions revealed that inequalities tend to increase, as a digitally underserved segment of the population becomes deprived of access to education, health information, entertainment, and work-from-home services in their various forms in this context. In this first period, initiatives aimed at implementing long-term infrastructure plans were not a priority.

In the second stage (August 2020–December 2021), the government tried to implement public policies with a more medium- and long-term view. The actions taken in this period recognized the importance of digital technologies in everyday life and their role in accessing knowledge, education, information and entertainment, along with the different digital divides and inequalities faced by the population.

In this regard, efforts were made to regulate ICT services as essential and strategic public services pursuing the goal of digital inclusion, and to establish greater tariff controls in a country in which inflation rates exceed 50% per year. But these measures, which were enacted without the agreement of the private sector—unlike the first stage—gave way to an immediate confrontation with the main companies in the ICT sector, which brought legal actions against the

State in order to prevent their implementation and continue with price increases. This confrontation made the effective regulation of ICT services as public services unfeasible. Likewise, it revealed the historical dependence on the private sector that persists as a legacy in the telecom regulatory field since the privatizations of the 1990s. Although timid progress was made on the implementation of basic connectivity plans for low-income sectors, the outcomes of this initiative were meager compared to initial expectations and did not bring significant improvements in correcting structural inequalities with regard to access to ICT services.

On a positive note, it should be highlighted that throughout both stages and supported by some commendable regulatory intentions, the discussion about Internet access as a human right and as an essential condition to guarantee the exercise of economic, social and cultural rights—notably, education, work, healthcare and access to information—was reintroduced on the public agenda. In the same way, the debate was reopened about the role that the State should assume to encourage and ensure broad access to connectivity services, in particular for the most vulnerable sectors, and to guarantee that no one is left behind in the development of daily activities that increasingly require digital technologies. This has also led to the presentation of various bills in the National Congress with the goal to regulate this subject, although their parliamentary process did not thrive.

Nevertheless, the policy actions implemented were insufficient to narrow the deep digital divides that still persist in terms of connectivity and Internet access in the country. For both socioeconomic and geographic reasons, major social sectors remain excluded from coverage or affordability of basic connectivity services. As discussed in this chapter, more than 30% of Argentine households do not have access to fixed Internet connections, and there are great disparities in terms of access to devices. Furthermore, the penetration rate of fiber optic technology is low at the national level compared to other countries in the region, and the same goes for connection speeds.

Two years after the onset of the pandemic, public policies to promote access to ICT services and the deployment of telecommunications infrastructure have gained new relevance, requiring dialogue and consensus between the State, ICT service companies, user associations and the population at large, with the goal to achieve comprehensive, well-articulated long-term policies to stop digital divides and social inequalities from deepening.

References

Abeles, M. (1999). El proceso de privatizaciones en la Argentina de los noventa. ¿Reforma estructural o consolidación hegemónica? *Época*, *1*(1), 95–114.

Andrés, L., Diop, M., & Guasch, J. (2007). Un balance de las privatizaciones en el sector infraestructura. *Nueva Sociedad*, (207), 113–129.

Azpiazu, D. (2002). *Privatizaciones y poder económico*. Buenos Aires: FLACSO - Universidad Nacional de Quilmes - IDEP.

Azpiazu, D. (2003). *Las privatizaciones en la Argentina. Diagnósticos y propuestas para una mayor competitividad y equidad social*. Buenos Aires: Miño y Dávila - Fundación OSDE/CIEPP.

Azpiazu, D., & Basualdo, E. (2004). Las privatizaciones en Argentina. Génesis, desarrollo y principales impactos estructurales. Buenos Aires: Facultad Latinoamericana de Ciencias Sociales, Sede Argentina.

Becerra, M., & Mastrini, G. (Comp.) (2021). *Restauración y cambio. Las políticas de comunicación de Macri (2015-2019)*. Buenos Aires: SiPreBA - ICEP.

CABASE. (2020). *CABASE Internet Index. Primer semestre 2020*. Buenos Aires.

CABASE. (2021). Internet Index. Primer semestre 2021. Buenos Aires: Cámara Argentina de Internet.

Califano, B. (2015). Perspectivas conceptuales para el análisis del Estado y las políticas de comunicación. *Austral Comunicación*, 4(2), 283–318.

Califano, B. (2017). En nombre de la convergencia: cambios en la política de regulación de las TIC en Argentina. *Estudos Em Comunicação – Communication Studies*, (24), 1–25. https://doi.org/10.20287/ec.n24.a01

Califano, B. (2020). Urgencias públicas e intereses privados: la regulación de medios en la agenda del gobierno argentino (2015–2019). *Ensambles*, 6(11), 72–90.

Califano, B., & Becerra, M. (2021). Public policies of connectivity in Latin America in the context of COVID-19. *Journal of Digital Media & Policy*, 12(1), 117–136.

Cobb, R. W., & Elder, C. D. (1971). The Politics of Agenda-Building : An Alternative Perspective for Modern Democratic Theory. *The Journal of Politics*, 33(4), 892–915.

ECLAC. (2020a). COVID-19 Latin America and the Caribbean and the COVID-19 pandemic. Economic and social effects. *Special Report*, (1), 1–14.

ECLAC. (2020b). Universalizing access to digital technologies to address the consequences of COVID-19. *Special Report*, (7), 1–25.

ENaCom. (2020a, April 8). ENACOM y el Ministerio de Educación gestionan datos libres para las Universidades. Retrieved 20 August 2020, from https://www.enacom.gob.ar/institucional/enacom-y-el-ministerio-de-educacion-gestionan-datos-libres-para-las-universidades_n2282

ENaCom. (2020b, May 18). El gobierno Nacional congela los precios de telefonía fija y móvil, internet y de la tv paga. Retrieved 20 August 2020 from https://www.enacom.gob.ar/institucional/el-gobierno-nacional-congela-las-tarifas-de-telefonia-fija-y-movil%2D%2Dinternet-y-de-la-tv-paga_n2365

ENaCom. (2020c, October 20). Reunión virtual con representantes de universidades nacionales. Retrieved 11 March 2022, from https://www.enacom.gob.ar/institucional/reunion-virtual-con-representantes-de-universidades-nacionales_n2801%0AReunión

ENaCom. (2021, October 15). Se conectará con Internet de última generación a 58 universidades nacionales de la Argentina. Retrieved 11 March 2022, from https://www.enacom.gob.ar/institucional/se-invierten-1-000-millones-para-garantizar-la-conectividad-en-los-centros-universitarios_n3485%0ASe

Galperin, H., Mariscal, J., & Viecens, M. F. (2013). *Análisis de los planes nacionales de banda ancha en América Latina* (No. 11). *Documento de Trabajo Nº 11*. Buenos Aires.

Galperin, H., Mariscal, J., & Viecens, M. F. (2021). *Las primeras reacciones de América Latina ante la pandemia COVID-19: conectividad y digitalización* (Policy Report: TIC en tiempos de Covid-19 No. 2).

Genoud, D. (2020, August 26). Los Fernández, las telcos y el riesgo de actuar al margen de la crisis. *El Canciller*.

Gerchunoff, P. (1992). *Las privatizaciones en Argentina. Primera etapa*. Buenos Aires: Instituto Torcuato Di Tella.

Hargittai, E. (2021). Introduction to the Handbook of Digital Inequality. In E. Hargittai (Ed.), *Handbook of Digital Inequality* (pp. 1–7). Cheltenham, UK: Edward Elgar Publishing.

INDEC. (2020). Acceso y uso de tecnologías de la información y la comunicación. EPH. Cuarto trimestre de 2020. *Informes Técnicos*, 5(1), 89.

Kessler, G. (2011). Exclusión social y desigualdad ¿nociones útiles para pensar la estructura social argentina? *Lavboratorio. Revista de Estudios Sobre Cambio Estructural y Desigualdad Social.*, (24), 4–18.

Krakowiak, F. (2018, May 1). El plan de internet que logró saltar la grieta, aunque camina lento. *Letra P*.

Murillo, M. V. (2009). *Political Competition, Partisanship, and Policy Making in Latin American Public Utilities*. Cambridge: Cambridge University Press.

Oszlak, O., & O'Donnell, G. (1984). Estado y políticas estatales en América Latina: hacia una estrategia de investigación. In G. Flores & J. Nef (Eds.), *Administración pública. Perspectivas críticas*. San José de Costa Rica: ICAP.

Ragnedda, M., & Gladkova, A. (Ed.) (2020). *Digital Inequalities in the Global South*. Cham, Switzerland: Palgrave Macmillan.

van Cuilenburg, J., & McQuail, D. (2003). Media Policy Paradigm Shifts. Towards a New Communications Policy Paradigm. *European Journal of Communication*, 18(2), 181–207.

van Dijk, J. A. (1999). *The network society. Social aspects of new media*. Thousand Oaks, California: Sage.

Vilas, C. M. (2011). Política y políticas públicas. In *Después del neoliberalismo. Estado y procesos políticos en América Latina* (pp. 74–98). Universidad Nacional de Lanús.

PART IV

Work, Culture and Digital Consumption

CHAPTER 18

The Changing Nature of Work in Digital Everyday Life

Jessica S. Dunn and Hopeton S. Dunn

INTRODUCTION

Throughout history, technology and innovation have reliably demonstrated their power to enhance human capability and efficiency. Regarded as more of a work companion than a tool, digital technology occupies an integral space in global everyday life and human experience.

While a steady and predictable increase in the reliance on technology was already apparent prior to the COVID-19 pandemic, as it unfolded, the strategic and practical importance of technology to economic survival was profoundly reinforced.

This chapter examines how digital technology has been leveraged to support increased organisational efficiency, but also highlights how technological change has impacted on the quality of work engagement in other respects. Budget cuts, downsizing, automation, office closures, dispersed teams and gig work are a few common strategies adopted by organisations to manage economic shocks.

The chapter discusses the increasing integration of digital technology in everyday work life. Recommendations for strategic reforms in education and industry are proposed, alongside a discussion on the future of work. Together, the chapter underscores the relevance of these issues and the need for them to feature more readily in organisational planning, in work design initiatives,

---

J. S. Dunn (✉)
Nottingham Trent University, Nottingham, UK

H. S. Dunn
University of Botswana, Gaborone, Botswana

© The Author(s), under exclusive license to Springer Nature
Switzerland AG 2024
H. S. Dunn et al. (eds.), *The Palgrave Handbook of Everyday Digital Life*,
https://doi.org/10.1007/978-3-031-30438-5_18

education and in technology policy development in intra and post-pandemic global contexts.

THE CHANGING NATURE OF WORK IN DIGITAL EVERYDAY LIFE

Contemporary digital technology in all its forms occupies an integral space in everyday life experiences, operating as both a disruptive and a stabilising force. Disruptive, for its track record of driving change; while its stabilising effect is arguably marked by the efficiency, convenience and productive capability it confers to the world of work. In 2020, the International Telecommunications Union (ITU) correctly surmised that the increasing reliance on information and communication technologies (ICTs) signalled the coming a post-pandemic era in which, "the ability to leverage digital technologies will be vital to the future resilience and prosperity of nations, communities and individuals." (ITU Academy, 2020, p. iii)

In this context, it is important to note the fundamental ways in which 'everyday' work life has changed, particularly during the COVID-19 pandemic dispensation of the digital age. With a focus on the ways in which these changes have affected people at work, organisations are challenged to determine whether their strategic priorities and policy frameworks are future-ready and to define how they will navigate the interplay between people and technology at work for the foreseeable future.

As tools that provide access to information through telecommunications, digital technologies are assimilated into all aspects of the global political economy (Dunn H., 2009, 2012). ICTs, encompassing smartphones, the internet, and the worldwide web, and have added value in the ever-expanding suite of social media and other innovations for both interpersonal communication and work execution. These technologies facilitate the progression of workflows; provide monitoring and surveillance of worker productivity; and enable the simultaneous meeting of multiple occupational objectives and quick access to information with the click of a button. In the world of work, ICTs facilitate cross-team collaboration, including the provision of real-time virtual communications across local and global domains.

The emergence of office-based computing and the internet over the last four decades and the rapid shift towards digitalisation have transformed what 21st Century everyday work-life represents. The worldwide web has emerged as an enabling mechanism for individuals and for businesses, providing a myriad of advantages in the creative use of digital data, virtual interactions and instant communication, including for cost-saving and revenue generation. The rise of social media and its centrality to personal, entrepreneurial and organisational communication and marketing, stands as a major departure from traditional work-life practices. The practical utility of digital technologies beckons users to interminable routines of investment in newer and more advanced models, promising better and more efficient performance. The cultivation and predictability of consumer appetite for 'the newer, faster and better' help to generate the continuum of supply and demand and drive the political economy underpinning the notion of Industry 5.0 in manufacturing.

INDUSTRY 5.0 AND INDUSTRIAL 'UP-CYCLING'

Industry 5.0 encompasses new ways for more efficient manufacturing and waste management as well as improved interaction between people, the environment and fast-changing productivity technologies. The term Industry 5.0 is among numerous attempts to classify the various stages of human and machine development, from the early tool-making efforts of primitive humans to the latest high-end cyber-physical technologies of robots, self-driving cars, 'internet of things' and their motive forces of machine learning, algorithms and artificial intelligence. This idea of rapid technology reform of manufacturing arises in the context of the 'Fourth Industrial Revolution' (4IR) (Schwab 2016) in which new and so-called 'intelligent' technologies are said to be transforming work and society at an extraordinary pace by their human and machine interactions. While 4IR speaks to a broad scope of technology-led changes affecting all aspects of human society globally, the concept of 'Industry 5.0' is more narrowly focused on efficient manufacturing processes through better interaction of humans and artificial intelligence technologies, while limiting waste and protecting the environment.

Industry 5.0 was initially developed under the name 'Industry Up-cycling' by a Czech waste-management and logistics expert, Michael Rada, in 2015. Its origin also emphasised efficient electricity usage and custom-built products over mass-produced items. Its implementation is said to revolve around the practices of (a) reducing (b) reusing and (c) recycling, in a conjoined 'up-cycling' process. (Rada: Ecoamet.com 2022). It seeks to empower the workforce while building awareness of the business opportunities and benefits of protecting the Anthropocene.

Industry 5.0 is itself a take-off from a group of German government policies known as 'Industrie 4.0', designed in 2011 to develop that country's competitiveness by promoting the use of smart factories, a clean environment, economic growth through greater manufacturing productivity, improvements in the human work environments and effective technology use.

According to the European Union, "Industry 5.0 provides a vision of industry that aims beyond efficiency and productivity as the sole goals, and reinforces the role and contribution of industry to society. It places the well-being of the worker at the centre of the production process and uses new technologies to provide prosperity beyond jobs and growth, while respecting the production limits of the planet" (European Commission 2022).

According to Akundi et al, an analysis of various themes and research trends indicate that "the term Industry 5.0 is observed to have various views of how it is defined and what constitutes the reconciliation between humans and machines." (Akundi et al. 2022, np). Their data-mining study identified five major themes in the concepts and technologies associated with Industry 5.0.

These include supply chain evaluation and optimization; enterprise innovation and digitalization; smart and sustainable manufacturing; transformation driven by the internet of things (IoT), AI and Big Data; and human-machine connectivity (Akundi et al. 2022). This concept holds significance as a roadmap for how one of the world's traditionally most labour-intensive sectors, manufacturing, is transforming itself to greater efficiency and productivity.

The Future of Work Is Actually the Present

It is in the context of the fore-going that we may argue here that the future of work is actually in the present. Yet, forecasting persists. The mechanics underpinning future forecasting include an array of both empirical and speculative approaches (O'Neill, 2023; Furnham, 2005; Katzell, 1979; Kerr & Rosnow, 1979). Forecasting is regarded by some as error-prone and "fraught with danger given that quite unexpected and novel occurrences (inventions, wars, economic crises), with substantial wide-ranging effects, [they] upset reasonable, rational forecasts" (Furnham, 2005). Counted among some contemporary methods used by prognosticators is case study observation of new, cutting-edge operational models being tested by organisations in the present. These models adopt new applications of technology and artificial intelligence, new roles, new approaches to problem-solving and decision making, and other initiatives that break the status quo. These models get attention, and ultimately influence changing trends in the world of work. The use of this type of information for forecasting signifies that, in some ways, the 'future of work' as it is understood, is actually more about what is happening in the present, as the precise future is likely unknowable.

Importantly, two major trends have underpinned global discourse surrounding the future of work (ILO, 2021; Balliester & Elsheikhi, 2018; SAP, 2022). The first, is the changing physical distribution of the workforce and the rise in remote and hybrid workforce models. These models inform where and how work is done. The reliance on video conferencing platforms for communication, the use of automated enterprise content management systems and other work-based software facilitate these new ways of working. Some can be seamlessly integrated with other applications and digital platforms that make work more efficient. The second trend, as we have seen, is the increasing integration of artificial intelligence (AI), machine learning, and robotics in organisational operations.

Business process automation has been visible in a wide cross-section of industries and organisations over many years—including in public sector organisations, private industry, non-profit organisations and beyond. Automation absorbs systematic, process-driven and repetitive work tasks. Automated systems range from simple digital workflows that carry out tasks such as billing and processing payments to more complex solutions that cover entire business operations, including managing enterprise content, organisational data, reporting, analytics and a range of other operational tasks.

In light of these advancing technological developments, there has been recognition of the fact that jobs done by human beings now often require rethinking and redesign, involving fewer manual and repetitive forms of work and necessitating more knowledge and insight-oriented work. This raises questions and concerns, as if knowledge and insight are the future of work, it is uncertain where this leaves individuals geared towards more manual, mechanical and repetitive jobs? Implicated here are the key questions of training and preparedness to embrace new roles involving digital technologies and automated systems (Dunn, 2012). While the costs to build and implement automated systems are more heavily foregrounded by businesses, the key corollaries of employee training and re-skilling may be neglected in the process. There is evidence of an increasing focus on learning, training and reskilling in human factors research, across various sectors and industries, as a wider cross-section of work tasks demand more digital literacy. Organisational agility in responding to this changing trend is more apparent in industrialised Global North societies relative to those of the Global South (Loebbecke & Picot, 2015; Branca et al., 2020; Cirillo et al., 2021). The expectation is that the technology overheads will reduce overtime, eliminate certain labour costs and yield rich financial benefits. But new human skills are always required and this reality partly explains why many organisations that draw on these technological innovations to grow their business still encounter productivity challenges.

Table 18.1 provides some examples of changes to the nature of jobs and services brought about by digital automation and artificial intelligence since the start of the twenty-first century.

Technological innovation is constantly evolving as scientists, technologists, futurists, programmers, engineers and other-related disciplines thrive on the business potential of new types of work.

It is also important to recognize that workers, organisations and countries around the world often contend with the realities of the digital divide. Inequalities of access, differences in economic scale and levels of industrialisation from country to country mean that there is uncertainty regarding the pace of change. There will be widely differing scenarios and future expectations of digital automation, use of AI, algorithms and robotics. The rate of adoption will vary, depending on internet access, skills training, advanced knowledge levels, and abilities to deploy and market these innovations. (Dunn H., 2020).

REFLECTIONS ON PANDEMIC CHALLENGES AND THE ROLE OF ICTS

The year 2020 and its sequel 2021 were sad milestones for the history books. In these years hundreds of thousands of lives around the world were lost to a global pandemic stemming from the rapid spread of the severe acute respiratory syndrome-related coronavirus (SARSr-CoV2) commonly referred to as COVID-19. The seriousness of the pandemic led to worldwide lockdowns that

Table 18.1 Illustrative examples of changing jobs, work processes and services derived from digital automation and artificial intelligence

Industry or sector	Jobs & roles: past and present	Jobs & roles: today and of the future
Manufacturing	Heavy mechanical tools and manual processes in manufacturing with limited automation.	Robotics in manufacturing. Production plants using machine learning and other AI applications.
Construction and building maintenance	Manual building facilities management and dense staffing.	Hybrid manual and robotic facilities management, 'just in time' building supplies and digital systems design.
Transport and logistics	Manual vehicle repairs and logistics services, analogue inventories and labour-intensive systems.	Hybrid manual and robotic logistics. Automated warehouse packaging and delivery. Digital monitoring.
Waste management	Manual household garbage collection and disposal in municipal dumps. Limited re-cycling and inattention to harmful wastes.	Domestic and industrial recycling and automated waste disposal. Recovery of useful residues. Privatised and digital management of landfills.
Retail and food services	In-store retail and heavy staffing, Restaurant reservation and drive by fast food services.	Online shopping, including order and delivery. Customised food preparation and home delivery.
Hospitality and entertainment	Primarily human-driven hospitality services. Venue based live entertainment and in-cinema screenings.	Hybrid manual and robotic hospitality services and facilities. App-based reservations management systems. Online streaming platforms for portable and home viewing and live digital event screenings.
Engineering	Manual design and mechanical engineering by hand and factory assembly. Limited digital automation.	AI-led engineering and designs reliant on programming and robotic technology (e.g. robotic welders).
Agriculture	Conventional farming methods. Mechanical tractors and reapers. Manual and electronic-based irrigation system. Physical sales and media advertising-based product marketing.	Automated irrigation and harvesting systems. Internet-based marketing, online disease-protection advice and digitally-enabled shipping and other distribution systems.
Library services	On-site Librarians and lending services. Hard copy books and printed journals.	Digitised information services and decentralisation of databases. Internet search engines. E-books and electronic journals.
Media and communication	Mechanical press operators, paste-up artists, AM radio technicians, analogue broadcast system operators.	Digital production, internet and social media sources, mobile phone connectivity, digital broadcast systems.

Table by co-authors Dunn J. S. and Dunn H. S.

required persons to isolate at home to 'stay safe'. Governments around the world introduced country-wide lockdowns for months, closing airports and banning travel. These measures eventually sent economies into a downward spiral without the certainty of recovery or when it would all come to an end. The pandemic left a devastating impact on economies, communities and households, claiming hundreds of thousands of lives, displacing people in vast numbers, creating mental disorders and costing nations billions in damage.

It is worth noting that for a number of countries COVID-19 happened alongside other calamitous events (Centre for Disaster Philantrophy, 2020; Aon, 2020; Dyer and Shepherd, 2021). Some examples include natural disasters from the 2020 Monsoon season in various countries in Asia; a more active hurricane season than usual in the Atlantic region; the forest fires in the US and elsewhere (Nijhuis, 2020); the major earthquake in Puerto Rico; Cyclone Fani in India and Cyclone Idai in Southern Africa; famine in parts of northeastern Africa; the numerous raging armed conflicts around the world extending from 2019 into 2020 and beyond (Comolli, 2020) and the humanitarian crises in Yemen, Venezuela, Rohingya and along the southern border of the United States. The year 2020 also saw various rounds of political and civil unrest in the United States—including the growth of the Black Lives Matter Movement following the police killing of George Floyd in July—an event which quickly mushroomed into a mass protest that grew to international proportions. The US election in November 2020 and the announcement of the results that followed was also met with civil unrest.

It is worth noting that in the midst of these cases of extreme societal chaos and lockdown, humans have managed to remain informed, educated, entertained and perhaps most importantly, connected, through ICTs. The international news media, social media and the internet recorded unprecedented increases in usage, and have played a significant role in global life during the height of the pandemic. Forbes magazine reported, for example, a surge in internet use of up to 70 percent in the first month of the pandemic (Beech, 2020). At the same time, the pandemic and other catastrophic events impacted adversely on the civic freedoms, gender relations and occupational prospects of people all over the world.

Notwithstanding these challenges and the physical distance, it necessitated, the COVID-19 pandemic experience underscores the interconnectedness and resilience of humanity around the world and depicts the crucial role that ICTs play in keeping people connected in the best and worst of times.

WORKPLACE TRANSFORMATION, AI AND HYBRID WORKING

During the last two decades, there has been growing interest in digital workplace transformation through innovative and more flexible hybrid work models. The COVID-19 pandemic accelerated those trends, fundamentally changing how we look at the workplace of the future. The adoption of AI in the workplace continues to be a growing trend (Parker & Grote, 2020). A

2020 survey conducted by Deloitte (Bayiates et al., 2020) reported that 71% of executives had intentions to spend more on AI in the subsequent year. Another conducted by Price Waterhouse Cooper (PWC) reports that 86% of executives surveyed expected to see AI becoming a mainstream technology in their businesses going forward (PWC, 2021). The growing popularity of the gig economy is also noteworthy. An ADP Research Institute report (Yildirmaz et al., 2020) indicates that there was an expansion by over 15% in this type of informal work since 2010.

The world of work has undergone continuous evolution, with particularly noteworthy changes in the twenty-first Century. The rise of the digital workplace in the wake of rapidly evolving technology, demands change at many levels. It shapes not only how and where we work, but also the nature of the roles and skills that are in demand within the dynamic landscape of the global labour market.

'The Great Resignation', Covid 19 and Emerging Occupational Trends

As the world of work continues to evolve in the Digital Age, business leaders have been pushed to become more comfortable with the regularity of change and the demand for innovative solutions. However, employees also now increasingly understand the flexibility and opportunity that they can enjoy in this new digital work domain. The phenomenon in the United States, known as "the great resignation" started to occur in late 2020. According to Phipps (2022) "the 'Great Resignation' is a term that describes the trend of the mass voluntary exit of employees from their employment obligations." While it is often associated with the COVID-19 pandemic, Phipps points out that the trend predated Covid and that "the pandemic may have simply exacerbated an already occurring, if not yet overwhelmingly pervasive problem." (Phipps, 2022, np). This assessment was corroborated by Fuller and Kerr (2022), who indicate that "the Great Resignation really started before the pandemic, as employees were increasingly resigning at least ten years prior (Fuller and Kerr 2022).

A Pew Research Centre survey reported by Parker and Horowitz (2022), indicated that low pay, a lack of opportunities for advancement and feeling disrespected at work were among the top reasons for quitting jobs in the US in 2021. However, Farrell (2021) reflecting on the fore-going period, suggested that strong demand for workers in a burgeoning digitally-driven pre-Covid economy, enabled many quitters to seek their fortunes in more lucrative and greener pastures. (Farrell 2021). While the trend had been most markedly evident in the United States, Phipps asserts that the pattern is "definitely not an American phenomenon". Citing instances in Europe, Latin America, the Caribbean and parts of Asia, she indicated that, "the great resignation or some version of it, has disrupted industries and markets, and impacted all stakeholders, including employers, employees and the community" (Phipps, 2022, np). Many employees left their jobs to start new digital or retail businesses, to migrate or take more flexible work arrangements elsewhere that would allow greater involvement in family life.

This phenomenon, driven at least in part by the affordances of digital technology, underline the opportunities that can be created by more flexible working arrangements that typify work in the gig economy and emerging digital occupational niches. The quality of corporate leadership in this dynamic and transitional period will be very important to facilitate the healthy advancement of employees who choose to remain in mass workplaces of the present and future. At the same time, former employees or enterprising individuals who start own-accounts or enter into freelance or flexible work arrangements can use the evolving digital technologies of everyday life to create lucrative careers and to meet evolving customer needs and expectations.

THE DISPERSED WORKFORCE AND VIRTUAL TEAMS: CHANGES TO HOW AND WHERE WE WORK

Virtual teams utilise digital media to communicate and coordinate their work with typically at least one member of the team working in a different time zone or location (Krumm et al., 2013; DeFilippis et al, 2020; Dyer & Shepherd 2021).

In the past, a mobile device was simply a phone—but today, smartphones are used by workers as portals for increasingly sophisticated software and data management tools. In a recent study, 87% of companies were dependent upon employees having access to mobile business apps from their devices. When portable devices such as laptops, tablets and mobiles are augmented with AI and connected to advanced digital systems, employees become untethered from the cubicle (Shields, 2022). They are freed up to work wherever they are—and to focus their minds more on solutions and innovation, and less on repetitive tasks and a static work environment. Parkes (2021) asserts the necessity of emotionally intelligent leadership in supporting productivity and wellbeing among disbursed teams.

THE EVOLVING NOT SO 'NEW NORMAL'

It is worth reiterating here that a steady and predictable increase in the reliance on digital technologies was apparent prior to the COVID-19 pandemic. But as we have seen, the spread of the disease around the world disclosed the practical and socio-economic importance of digital technologies. Government-mandated lockdowns forced businesses to operate remotely, leaving many to regroup to determine how they would maintain operations and, particularly in the case of small businesses, how they would survive. This reality ushered in a new paradigm of work, as well as commercial and personal activity that drew on new approaches to reaching consumers through purely digital means. As a result, we have witnessed the relationship between people and machines intensify exponentially in a short time span (Press, 2020; Balliester & Elsheikhi, 2021).

As a response, we saw a quick expansion of remote and hybrid teamwork in organisations. In traditionally client-facing operations (such as public services and financial institutions), we saw a wide range of client services being made accessible online. In other settings, as conventional forms of income generation (such as in-store product sales and face-to-face conference meetings) became impracticable, alternatives were introduced. Companies restructured staffing arrangements to accommodate fewer staff doing repetitive tasks such as switchboard management that could be handled by automated systems. Walk-in customers were invited to place and process their own orders using touch screens in some places. In some societies, making such a hi-tech transition would have been less economically practicable. However, all around the world alternatives were being put in place to protect health and safety and to enable productivity. Physical distancing among customers, pre-packaging goods, the increased use of hand sanitisers and frequent handwashing are classic examples of what enterprises implemented to conform to new protocols of disease prevention while maintaining business operations.

The use of business process automation software has become quite common within a wide cross-section of organisations during the pandemic. Teaching the learning institutions across the full spectrum of education systems worldwide introduced online and hybrid course delivery through a variety of virtual learning environments (Hayle & Dunn, J., 2021; Holt & Murray, 2021; Tadesse & Muluye, 2020). Online shopping and contactless payment methods, digital signatures, and the expansion of business logistics to include at-home and curb-side delivery options all demonstrated what can be achieved when the solutions to human problems are assisted by technology, guided by the human capacity for fluid thinking and intelligence (Cattell, 1963). What we have been observing since 2020 is not solely a matter of the advancing capability of machines, but the importance of the human user and creator guiding technological development and being centrally involved in the deliberate design and adaptation of technology to suit the evolving needs of human everyday life.

In the process, some adaptations will inevitably become the norm as people may not return to some of the pre-pandemic legacy technologies and interpersonal practices. An alternative viewpoint proposes that having been deprived of interpersonal contact and opportunities for public and private gathering during the imposed Covid-related restrictions, certain pre-pandemic practices may re-emerge that are, quite intentionally, humanist and detached from automation. This matter has been extensively discussed with respect to sectors such as education, hospitality and entertainment (Neuwirth et al., 2021); Itani & Hollebeek, 2021; Nhamo et al., 2020; El-Said & Aziz, 2022).

It is important to note that discourses surrounding the future of work in fields such as business, psychology, sociology and industrial relations have expanded beyond a focus on demographic developments (such as the ageing population, changing gender roles and embracing diversity). Such conversations now also include the central role of ICTs and artificial intelligence. They also entail analyses on the changing nature of work design and the associated risks and implications (including in areas such as the regulation of gig work). Given ongoing technology advances and the pandemic-induced state of the world economy, there is a high expectation of continued reliance on ICTs to manage our present and future challenges.

Leveraging Digital Technologies: Exploring Benefits and Occupational and Health Challenges

As we have seen, digital technology applications that are in wide everyday use within organisations confer many benefits including enhancing operational efficiency and profitability. But many of these technologies are not without their occupational risks and health challenges. Among these are human or machine errors in design and functionality; cyberbullying and cyber-security problems that can adversely affect the mental health of employees, compromise productivity and impair product or service integrity. There are also challenges of physical harm through the use of workstations or tools with poor ergonomics, inappropriate lighting, absence of facilities for persons with disabilities; overuse and addiction to technology; loss of privacy, inadequate data protection and an absence of ethics, institutional policy and decision-making in the use of technology. These continue to be central issues under discussion in the contemporary landscape of work-life (Aagaard, 2021; Dunn H, 2020; DeFilippis et al, 2020; Dunn H, 2012; Turel et al., 2011).

There are also issues of geographical disparities and differential levels of access and support systems. Dunn H. (2020) provides a cogent account of some key differences in the experiences of Global North and Global South societies in engaging with digital and communication technologies, refuting the notion that these societies operate on a level playing field where access to policies of net neutrality and technological integration are enjoyed by all. In like manner, we argue here in favour of more affordable internet access for underserved societies, more systematic innovation training across underdeveloped regions and a greater emphasis on the training of both girls and boys in such technical skillsets as coding and data analytics (Dunn H. 2020).

While on the subject of degrees of difference, it is worth noting that the experience of the pandemic in Asia, where countries' behavioural responses to COVID-19 were generally more rapid and effective in controlling the spread of the virus, stands in contrast to that of Western countries where countless changes to consumer and organisational behaviour emerged as a response to the crisis (Lund et al., 2021).

Spagnoli et al. (2020) affirm that the COVID-19 pandemic necessitated sudden changes to working circumstances for many. They coin the term 'technostress' to refer to the adverse outcome of an abrupt occupational life change. Technostress includes a range of physiological, cognitive, and psycho-emotional effects following extended periods of engagement with digital technology. It is a classic example of how the quality of life can diminish in the absence of balance between an understandably regular interface with the digital on the one hand, and the purely human, non-digital, aspects of everyday life on the other. Arguably, what is critical is striking the balance between the necessary use of technology and the inherent need to 'switch off' and to experience social connection, including in person.

The onset of COVID-19 saw many healthcare systems around the world adopting rapid-response organisational change interventions, using technology, to cope with the highly complex nature of the situation. The provision of face-to-face primary care delivery in some contexts shifted to the greater use of telemedicine and other remote and hybrid modalities to help to contain the virus by protecting both patients and healthcare workers from exposure. Maintaining in-person accident and emergency services alongside the mounting numbers of critical COVID-19 cases at the time put a strain on national healthcare systems all around the world. Primary care General Practitioner (GP) medical services also experienced necessary shifts in their available services and, in some cases, significant appointment backlogs resulted (BBC, 2022). The adoption of telephone and virtual appointments aided by video conferencing software applications were implemented in some settings as a response. Using remote means of communication with patients however meant the prolonged absence of provision of medical diagnoses and treatment through in-person physical examination, and in turn, a heavier reliance on patients' abilities to describe their symptoms and to precisely follow GP instructions to facilitate the desired outcomes. This type of scenario introduced risk and challenge at many levels and illustrated, the important role and function of the human, and indeed, the 'human touch' in health care services. .

Contrastingly, Hughes (2020) reports that Boston Dynamics—the US-based technology company behind 'Spot the Robot Dog' - published their application designs on GitHub in 2020 making them open source and vendor-neutral (therefore compatible with other robotics platforms) for the purpose of helping healthcare staff reduce exposure to infection, enabling them to perform essential high-risk services. This technology allowed clinicians to talk to patients suspected of infection with coronavirus, accurately check their vital signs, and transport supplies (Karabegović et al, 2023). This stands as an example of how technological innovation can be leveraged to assist in solving human problems, including in crises, as well as how organisations within the ICT sector can be innovative and prudent, demonstrating social responsibility.

Stress and IAD

Despite these innovations, many people have experienced heightened adverse reactions and outcomes. Internet Addiction Disorder (IAD) is a disorder that has been discussed for over two decades. It is described by Goldberg in 1996 as "a maladaptive pattern of internet use leading to significant impairment or distress". Diagnostic criteria are proposed which explore factors associated with the patient's tolerance, withdrawal and intention. Persons affected display addictive behaviours marked by an inability to exercise restraint in their use of the Internet (Goldberg, 1996)

IAD has been associated with other psychiatric disorders such as social anxiety, depression, attention deficit hyperactivity disorder and substance use, among others. While not yet listed as a disorder in the Diagnostic and Statistical Manual of Mental Disorders (American Psychiatric Association, 2013) support groups exist and, not surprisingly, it continues to be actively discussed in the literature (Lozano-Blasco et al., 2022; Young, 2017; Weinstein et al., 2014; Ko et al., 2012). Gaming Addiction Disorder on the other hand has been identified and referenced in the DSM-5 as a condition of interest, warranting more clinical research (APA, 2013).

Claims of significant risks posed by sustained radiation exposure from mobile phones and cell towers are still widely contested, in denial of any appreciable or potential carcinogenic impact on users. The risks, however remote, and the rise of dysfunctionalities deemed to be generated by excessive use of digital technologies, require continued investigation as externalities of the digital age. This situation is particularly worrying in relation to children and the prospect of overexposure to radiation, impairing their cognitive and social development.

There have been discussions among futurists about digital everyday life reaching a state of artificial general intelligence where machines and humans are deemed to have equivalent capacities across all disciplines (the earlier example of changes to the practice of general medicine included) and about the risk, ethics and policy mechanisms that would necessarily underpin this development (Baum, 2017; Goertzel, 2014; Goertzel, 2007). They predict that the next phase is where 'super-intelligent' machines are able to carry out unprompted interventions and ask sophisticated questions (Al-Imam et al., 2020). While these phenomena, often called the 'singularity' are, not yet to be realised, they may not be too far on the digital horizon.

JOB DISPLACEMENT AND THE DIGITAL WORKPLACE

With the increasing use of AI in the workplace, there has been a greater demand for roles that are primarily knowledge-based and cognitive. This has come with concerns about job security and whether large numbers of humans will be pushed out of the workforce by AI and robotic technology (Akhtar & Moor, 2016). However, some analysts and researchers continue to argue that displaced jobs will be substituted by new ones and that the future of work is brighter than many may think (O'Neill, 2023). A 2018 World Economic Forum report indicate that while disrupting certain more traditional roles, the trend of digitalization of the workforce has been shown to be on track to create over a hundred million new work roles by 2022, including in novel areas that are forecasted to reach up to a third of the total employee base of large firms around the world (WEF, 2018). However, these forecasts were pre-pandemic, and may well not be realised.

As the digital workplace reduces the need for an on-site workforce, there is also an increasing need for knowledge-intensive tasks. The German software corporation, SAP (2022) reports that from 2000 to 2019, the proportion of employees with graduate-level qualifications among large global organisations rose from 24% to 42%. SAP further reports a nearly 20% rise in the past 10 years in jobs calling for evidence of complex problem-solving and innovative thinking (SAP, 2022). It is clear that a sophisticated level of ICT and software literacy currently is and will continue to be essential for the global workforce. Central to this, as we will now, discuss, is the need for systematic industry training in the context of what has been described as Industry 5.0. This term describes a modern industrial work context that integrates people and digital technologies in a manner that maximizes human agency and protects the global environment. Notions of virtual reality, the metaverse, avatars, and digital gaming, are examples of what can be seen as essential elements of the new work environment. Fun as they may seem, they are no joke. While there are potential psychological implications of their uncontrolled use at an individual level, they have vast economic, employment and entertainment potentials that are still not yet fully understood.

Occupational Training and Educational Reform for Industry 5.0

Whether we call it 'Industry 5.0', or use the wider frame of the Fourth Industrial Revolution, the present era demands new and innovative ways of working and of delivering education and training appropriate to global and local human productivity demands. The process of preparing for this new industrial environment must begin with new visions of the educational system. To become effective contributors to this process of industry innovation, students should be exposed at an early age to the value of indigenous innovation, critical thinking, analytical reading and effective human communication.

The conventional practice early in the secondary school system in many global regions, of streaming students separately into 'arts' and 'sciences', must give way to what is more appropriately called a 'convergent education'. This is where knowledge in both the arts and sciences can be deployed by students in the selection of new careers that often require this such dual educational exposure. Running one's own business in this era requires diverse skillsets. Many companies and government departments are also looking for employees with multiple skills and new competencies.

Regrettably, some educational institutions are out of step with these aspirations and will need to engage in more thorough-going institutional reforms. This would include rethinking the structure of their discreet 'silos' called Faculties and Departments that promote education in often narrow disciplinary frameworks that rarely converge or interact. While society will still need subject specialists, it is appropriate in this era to train a wide range of multi-skilled professionals in a manner that will improve their social value, industrial relevance, human sensibilities and digital competencies. Curricula will need to deliver more rounded courses in such emerging fields as the digital humanities, data analytics, data science, digital design strategy, software management and robotics, among others.

Greater budgetary allocations to education by governments would be one key response to creating these new career paths that are becoming part of the everyday needs of industry and society. Such reform interventions would also need to be accompanied by investment resources to create the decent jobs into which these educated professionals would graduate.

Despite the emphasis of Industry 5.0 on large-scale manufacturing, a majority of graduates will enter the services sector and some will start their own businesses. Whatever route they choose to pursue, they will need a dynamic, multi-disciplinary education. Educational institutions should be re-structuring and integrating their departments and preparing lecturers, teachers and trainers to meet these changing needs.

Another area of importance is the increasing availability of short digital skills-based technical certifications, as national and corporations seek to fill the digital skills gap. These short-term certifications are important vectors of technical knowledge that can be quickly acquired and assimilated in dynamic ways for personal, career or corporate development. The ITU Academy urges special attention to new skills development under accelerated conditions:

> This accelerated speed towards digitization in the corporate sector goes hand in hand with a growing demand for employees with specialized digital skills who need to install, maintain and secure information and communication systems and provide technical support to the workforce. In addition, the pandemic spurred innovation in digital tools and platforms and increased digitization of business processes, products and services. As the pandemic continues, there is growing focus on the use of digital technologies. (ITU Academy, 2020, p. 1)

At the same time, students who can gain entry to higher education institutions should not pass up this opportunity in favour of technical 'certifications' and short courses. Instead, they should be seeking the more expansive 'education' mostly offered by universities, while securing their software certifications or short-term digital training in summer programmes or other part-time exposures.

In many parts of the world, government-funded educational institutions may not be equipped with adequate resources to provide the new kind of education that is required under Industry 5.0. New labs, digital work tools, re-tooled educators, and better staff training resources are often among the pressing unmet needs of such institutions. At the same time, the responsibility of preparing students, employees and the national workforce for dynamic new careers whether in manufacturing or service delivery does not reside solely with universities, colleges or other educational institutions. Industry, whether as manufacturing or service delivery, has a big role to play in providing scholarships, paid internships, job rotations, and organized mentoring of students, graduates, new recruits and retraining of long-standing employees. It is acknowledged that many good corporate citizens are already performing some of these roles.

At the same time, some companies are reluctant to support staff members going for further educational qualifications or up-skilling, for fear of losing them to better-paying competitors or to migration. However, industry research has long suggested that the key factors that engender a corporate environment that promotes loyalty are decent wages, environmental protection, wellbeing and personal growth (Furnham, 2005). In such contexts, an employer who invests in the training and remuneration of capable employees and provides a secure future for them, will retain most of them because of a shared commitment to the corporate goals.

Conclusion

The current experience with work-life is one that combines transience with enduring practices. It relies on the ability of people to demonstrate agility as well as resilience. The notion of 'everyday' connotes the expectation of a common and predictable way of life, something that COVID 19 quickly up-ended. What will go on to pass as 'everyday' is uncertain in a dynamic and fast-changing world where the goalposts of innovation and consumer demand are always shifting. ICTs and their home-based use in the present era of the information age is so all-embracing, that often the lines between work and the rest of life, can feel artificial. While technological advancements and digital ways of working will accelerate, these developments need to be managed to protect psychological health and resilience, and to promote human-centredness, industrial agility and scientific integrity.

This fundamental and often contradictory sense of human and machine integration will be increasingly felt as we discover and explore alternative domains of identity through the emerging virtual worlds. These trends will have profound implications for education, work, governance, leisure and new occupational pursuits in both the present and future.

References

Aagaard, J. (2021). Beyond the rhetoric of tech addiction: why we should be discussing tech habits instead (and how). *Phenomenology and the Cognitive Sciences*, 20(3), 559–572.

Akhtar, P & Moor, P. (2016). The psychosocial impacts of technological change in contemporary workplaces and trade union responses. *International Journal of Labour Research*, 8(1/2), 101–131.

Akundi, A., Euresti, D., Luna S., Akobiah, W., Lopes, A. and Edinbarough, I (2022). State of Industry 5.0 – Analysis and Identification of Current Research Trends, in *Applied System Innovation*, 5 (1):27.

Al-Imam, A., Motyka, M. A., & Jędrzejko, M. Z. (2020). Conflicting opinions in connection with digital superintelligence. *IAES International Journal of Artificial Intelligence*, 9(2), 336.

American Psychiatric Association. (2013). *Diagnostic and statistical manual of mental disorders* (5th ed.).

American Psychiatric Association, D. S. M. T. F., & American Psychiatric Association. (2013). *Diagnostic and statistical manual of mental disorders: DSM-5* (Vol. 5, No. 5). Washington, DC: American psychiatric association.

Aon (September, 2020). Global Catastrophy Recap, September 2020. URL: http://thoughtleadership.aon.com/documents/20200810_analytics-if-september-global-recap.pdf#:~:text=Global%20Catastrophe%20Recap%3A%20September%20 2020%205%20After%20bringing,least%20eight%20fatalities%20and%20several%20 injuries%20were%20reported

Balliester, T., & Elsheikhi, A. (2018). The future of work: a literature review. ILO Research Department Working Paper, 29, 1–54.

Baum, S. (2017). A survey of artificial general intelligence projects for ethics, risk, and policy. *Global Catastrophic Risk Institute Working Paper*, 17-1.

Bayiates, A; Weiss, D; Downey, E.; Ranjan, R. & Bhat, R.(Eds.). (2020). *Becoming and AI-Fuelled Organization: Deloitte's State of AI in the Enterprise*. 4th Edition. Deloitte AI Institute and Deloitte Centre for Integrated Research.

BBC (May 7, 2022). Nearly 100,000 People faced delayed GP appointments. URL: https://www.bbc.co.uk/news/uk-england-gloucestershire-61318916

Beech, M. (2020). COVID-19 Pushes up Internet Use 70% and Streaming more than 12%, First Figures Reveal. Forbes. March 25, 2020. URL:https://www.forbes.com/sites/markbeech/2020/03/25/covid-19-pushes-up-internet-use-70-streaming-more-than-12-first-figures-reveal/

Branca TA, Fornai B, Colla V, Murri MM, Streppa E, Schröder AJ. The Challenge of Digitalization in the Steel Sector. *Metals*. 2020; 10(2):288.https://doi.org/10.3390/met10020288

Cattell, R. B. (1963). Theory of fluid and crystallized intelligence: A critical experiment. *Journal of Educational Psychology*, 54: 1–22. https://doi.org/10.1037/h0046743

Centre for Disaster Philanthropy. (December, 2020). 2020 Monsoon Floods, *Disaster Philantrophy*, December 17, 2020. URL: https://disasterphilanthropy.org/disasters/2020-monsoon-floods/ (archived at https://perma.cc/D8GL-5GAN)

Cirillo, V., Evangelista, R., Guarascio, D., & Sostero, M. (2021). Digitalization, routineness and employment: An exploration on Italian task-based data. *Research Policy*, 50(7), 104079.

Comolli, V. (2020). Armed Conflict Survey, Editor's Introduction, *IISS*, May 27, 2020. URL:https://www.iiss.org/publications/armed-conflict-survey/2020/armed-conflict-survey-2020

DeFilippis, E., Impink, S. M., Singell, M., Polzer, J. T., & Sadun, R. (2020). *Collaborating during coronavirus: The impact of COVID-19 on the nature of work* (No. w27612). National Bureau of Economic Research.

Dunn, H.S. (2009). Teleworking the Mobile Caribbean: Enabling Remote Work Among the Marginalized in Jamaica and Trinidad and Tobago. *Information Technologies and International Development*, 5(2): 52–66.

Dunn, H.S. (Ed.) (2012). *Ringtones of Opportunity: Policy, Technology and Access in Caribbean Communications*. Kingston: Ian Randle.

Dunn, H.S. (2020). Creative resilience and globalization from within: evolving constructs for analysing culture, innovation, and enterprise in the global south, *Annals of the International Communication Association*, 44:1, 4–18, DOI: https://doi.org/10.1080/23808985.2018.1547121

Dyer, C. & Shepherd, K. (2021). *Remote Work: Redesign Processes, Practices and Strategies to Engage a Remote Workforce*. London: Kogan Page.

Ecoamet 2022. Michael Rada - Industry 5.0 & Industrial Upcycling. URL: https://ecoametsolutions.com/industry-5-0/#

El-Said, O., & Aziz, H. (2022). Virtual tours a means to an end: An analysis of virtual tours' role in tourism recovery post COVID-19. *Journal of Travel Research*, 61(3), 528–548.

European Commission (2022). Industry 5.0: What this approach is focused on, how it will be achieved and how it is already being implemented. URL: https://ec.europa.eu/info/research-and-innovation/research-area/industrial-research-and-innovation/industry-50_en

Farrell, C. (2021, July 23). *Older workers and 'the big quit.'* Forbes. URL:https://www.forbes.com/sites/nextavenue/2021/07/23/older-workers-and-the-big-quit/?sh=4b88b9933e47

Fuller, J., & Kerr, W. (2022, March 23). *The great resignation didn't start with the pandemic*. Harvard Business Review. URL: https://hbr.org/2022/03/the-great-resignation-didnt-start-with-the-pandemic

Furnham, A. (2005). The Psychology of Behaviour at Work: The Individual and the Organisation. Hove: Psychology Press.

Goertzel, B. (2007). *Artificial general intelligence* (Vol. 2). C. Pennachin (Ed.). New York: Springer.

Goertzel, B. (2014). Artificial general intelligence: concept, state of the art, and future prospects. *Journal of Artificial General Intelligence*, 5(1), 1.

Goldberg, I. (1996). Internet addiction disorder. URL: https://view.officeapps.live.com/op/view.aspx?src=https%3A%2F%2Feps.ulpgc.es%2FJR%2FDocumentos%2Fciberadictos.doc&wdOrigin=BROWSELINK

Hayle, C and Dunn, J.S. (2021). Role of the UCJ in supporting continuous quality improvement in higher education institutions. In S.I. Gift (Ed.) *Caribbean Quality Culture: Persistent Commitment to Improving Higher Education* (pp.329–341). Mona: UWI Press.

Holt, L. & Murray, L. (2021). Children and COVID-19 in the UK. *Children's Geographies*, 1–8.

International Labour Organization. (2021). The role of digital labour platforms in transforming the world of work [Full report] [Report]. International Labour Organization. http://www.ilo.org/global/research/global-reports/weso/2021/WCMS_771749/lang–en/index.htm

Itani, O. S., & Hollebeek, L. D. (2021). Light at the end of the tunnel: Visitors' virtual reality (versus in-person) attraction site tour-related behavioral intentions during and post-COVID-19. *Tourism Management*, 84, 104290.

ITU Academy (2020). Digital Skills Insight 2020, International Telecommunications Union, Geneva. URL: https://academy.itu.int/sites/default/files/media2/file/Digital%20Skills%20Insights%202020.pdf

Karabegović, I., Banjanović-Mehmedović, L., Husak, E., & Omerčić, M. (2023). Trend of implementing service robots in medical institutions during the COVID-19 pandemic: A review. *Medical and Healthcare Robotics*, 237–262.

Katzell, R. (1979). Changing attitudes to work. In C. Kerr & J. Rosnow (Eds.). Work in America: The decade ahead (pp.35–57). New York: Van Norstrand.

Kerr, C. & Rosnow, J (Eds). (1979). Work in America: The decade ahead. New York: Van Norstrand.

Ko, C. H., Yen, J. Y., Yen, C. F., Chen, C. S., & Chen, C. C. (2012). The association between Internet addiction and psychiatric disorder: a review of the literature. *European Psychiatry*, 27(1), 1–8.

Krumm, S., Terwiel, K. & Hertel, G. (2013). Challenges in Norm Formation and Adherence: The Knowledge, Skills and Ability Requirements of Virtual and Traditional Cross-Cultural Teams. *Journal of Personnel Psychology*, 12(1): 33–44. DOI:https://doi.org/10.1027/1866-5888/a000077

Loebbecke, C., & Picot, A. (2015). Reflections on societal and business model transformation arising from digitization and big data analytics: A research agenda. *The Journal of Strategic Information Systems*, 24(3), 149–157.

Lozano-Blasco, R., Robres, A. Q., & Sánchez, A. S. (2022). Internet addiction in young adults: A meta-analysis and systematic review. *Computers in Human Behavior*, 107201.

Lund, S., Madgavkar, A., Mischke, J., & Remes, J. (2021). What's next for consumers, workers, and companies in the post-COVID-19 recovery. *McKinsey & Company*.

Neuwirth, L.S.; Jovic, S. & Mukherji, B.R. (2021). Reimagining higher education during and post-COVID-19: Opportunities and challenges. *Journal of Adult and Continuing Education*, 27(2): 141–156.

Nhamo, G., Dube, K., & Chikodzi, D. (2020). Implications of COVID-19 on gaming, leisure and entertainment industry. In *Counting the Cost of COVID-19 on the Global Tourism Industry* (pp. 273–295). Springer, Cham.

Nijhuis, M. (October 2020). The Westcoast wildfires are apocalypse, again, *The New Yorker*, October 20, 2020. URL: https://www.newyorker.com/news/annals-of-a-warming-planet/the-west-coast-wildfires-are-apocalypse-again

O'Neill, M. (2023). Future Hackers. Cheltenham, Gloucestershire: The History Press/Flint Publishing.

Parker, K. & Horowitz, J. M. (2022, March 9). *Majority of workers who quit a job in 2021 cite low pay, no opportunities for advancement, feeling disrespected*. Pew Research Center. URL: https://www.pewresearch.org/fact-tank/2022/03/09/majority-of-workers-who-quit-a-job-in-2021-cite-low-pay-no-opportunities-for-advancement-feeling-disrespected/

Parker, S.K. & Grote, G. (2020). Automation, algorithms and beyond: Why work design matters more than ever in a digital world. *Applied Psychology: An International Review*, 1–45.

Parkes, M. (2021). *Leading Remotely: Achieving Success in a Globally Connected World*. London: Bloomsbury Business.

Phipps, S. (2022). What exactly is "The Great Resignation?", Blog April 21, 2022. Middle Georgia State University, USA. URL: https://www.mga.edu/news/2022/04/what-is-the-great-resignation.php

Press, G. (2020). The Future of Work Post-COVID-19. Forbes. July 15, 2020. URL:https://www.forbes.com/sites/gilpress/2020/07/15/the-future-of-work-post-covid-19/

Price Waterhouse Coopers (PWC). (2021). *AI Predictions 2021*. PWC. URL: https://www.pwc.com/us/en/tech-effect/ai-analytics/ai-predictions.html

SAP (2022). What is the future of work? URL: https://www.sap.com/insights/what-is-future-of-work.html#:~:text=The%20future%20of%20work%20is%20defined%20by%20two,rise%20in%20remote%20employees%20and%20gig%20workers.%20

Schwab K. (2016). The Fourth Industrial Revolution - World Economic Forum, Portfolio Penguin.

Shields, C. (2022). Bring Your Own Device Policy Tips and Best Practices for 2022. URL: https://www.ntiva.com/blog/bring-your-own-device-byod-policy

Spagnoli, P., Molino, M., Molinaro, D., Giancaspro, M. L., Manuti, A., & Ghislieri, C. (2020). Workaholism and technostress during the COVID-19 emergency: The crucial role of the leaders on remote working. *Frontiers in Psychology*, 11, 620310.

Tadesse, S. & Muluye, W. (2020). The Impact of COVID-19 Pandemic on Education System in Developing Countries: A Review. Open Journal of Social Sciences 8: 159–170. DOI: https://doi.org/10.4236/jss.2020.810011.

Turel, O., Serenko, A., & Giles, P. (2011). Integrating technology addiction and use: An empirical investigation of online auction users. *MIS Quarterly*, 1043–1061.

Weinstein, A., Feder, L. C., Rosenberg, K. P., & Dannon, P. (2014). Internet addiction disorder: Overview and controversies. *Behavioral addictions*, 99–117.

World Economic Forum (2018). *The Future of Jobs Report 2018*. World Economic Forum. URL: https://www3.weforum.org/docs/WEF_Future_of_Jobs_2018.pdf

Yildirmaz, A., Goldar, M. & Klein, S. (2020). *Illuminating the Shadow Workforce: Insights into the Gig Workforce in Businesses*. ADP Research Institute. URL: https://www.adp.com/-/media/adp/resourcehub/pdf/adpri/illuminating-the-shadow-workforce-by-adp-research-institute.ashx

Young, K. (2017). The evolution of internet addiction disorder. *Internet addiction*, 3–18.

CHAPTER 19

Indigenous People and Digital Misinformation in the Brazilian Amazon

Cristian Berrío-Zapata, Monica Tenaglia, and Sheyla Gabriela Alves Ribeiro

Introduction

Digital transformation disrupted indigenous communities, increasing the complexity of their relationships with the global world. Globalization maintains a strong white-patriarchal-Christian-industrial-capitalist perspective. Thus, governments continue to treat indigenous communities as an obstacle to "development and civilization." This has affected indigenous communities' access to, and appropriation of, digital technology, which remains limited by complex and unexpected forms of technological exclusion and abuse. The COVID-19 pandemic revealed some of these complexities in Brazil, as disinformation spreading though digital social media platforms, such as WhatsApp, affected vaccination campaigns and aid to indigenous communities and compromised their survival.

Between 2020 and 2021, the Brazilian BBC and other local media reported on situations of violence and distress produced in indigenous communities by disinformation. Health missions were attacked, ineffective COVID-19 treatments were accepted, vaccine rejection—based on conspiracy and mystique

---

C. Berrío-Zapata (✉) • M. Tenaglia
Federal University of Pará (UFPA), Belém, Brazil
e-mail: berriozapata@ufpa.br; monicatenaglia@ufpa.br

S. G. A. Ribeiro
Federal Rural University of the Amazon (UFRA), Belém, Brazil
e-mail: gabriela.ribeiro@ufra.edu.br

© The Author(s), under exclusive license to Springer Nature
Switzerland AG 2024
H. S. Dunn et al. (eds.), *The Palgrave Handbook of Everyday Digital Life*,
https://doi.org/10.1007/978-3-031-30438-5_19

theories—skyrocketed, and plots to eliminate indigenous people, who were blamed for COVID-19 outbreaks, were exposed. Indigenous communities in Brazil have been trapped into heavy use of encrypted social media platforms, like WhatsApp, which comes "free of charge" following zero-rating practices from carriers. Encryption, along with lack of alternative sources of information due to zero-rating, and geographical isolation make these communities easy prey for disinformation. However, few studies have been conducted regarding this issue.

To contribute toward the filling of this research gap, this chapter describes how disinformation affected indigenous communities in Brazil during the pandemic between 2020 and 2021. In order to establish context, this paper reviews the situation of digital media and skills in Brazil and then describes the situations produced by disinformation spread via WhatsApp, based on a systematic collection made on media news during the period. Finally, the authors had a dialog with a chief member of an indigenous community to gain perspective on these events and have his perception on the problem. This study offers a postcolonial approach to technology access and appropriation, implicating systematic online and offline exclusions as an articulated form of digital capital destruction, and alternative means of ethnic violence that imperil the survival of these communities.

Digital Media and Skills in Brazil

Brazil is the sixth most populous country in the world (Worldometer, 2022), but only 75 percent of its citizens have any internet access, while leading countries surpass 90 percent (World Bank, 2022). For those who do have access, network quality and reliability may be a problem, as the country ranks 68th in the world for broadband quality (Cable.co.uk, 2022). Brazil's high rate of economic inequality, along with the costs associated with internet access, also affects the ability of its population to gain access to the internet. This is reflected in the country's 79th place ranking with respect to the relative cost for broadband access (Numbeo, 2022).

Moreover, the situation may worsen in certain of Brazil's five regions. In terms of economic performance, gross regional income in the North Region (the Amazon), where most of the nation's indigenous people live, is only one-ninth of that in developed regions like the Southeast and South, which include São Paulo and Rio de Janeiro (IBGE, 2021). The poorest areas, in terms of income and infrastructure, are the North (the Amazon and Maranhão), part of the Central-West Region (Mato Grosso, including Cerrado and Pantanal), and the semi-arid Caatinga area of the Northeast Region. All these are relatively-wild and digitally-excluded territories with significant indigenous populations.

Digital exclusion is also determined by the differences between rural and urban development. Capital cities in the poorest regions have significant internet coverage, while the opposite counts for rural areas in developed regions. For example, North Amazonic capitals like Belém and Manaus have

86.5 percent coverage, not bad compared with capital cities in the South which enjoy 88.9 percent coverage (Azevedo & IBGE, 2019). However, rural areas lag behind urban areas in all regions, i.e., in the South they reach 67.2 percent coverage, while only 38.4 percent in the North, where the largest concentration of indigenous communities in Brazil is located.

Infrastructure improvement in the nation's regions depends on market prospective, thus sparsely populated areas like the Amazon have little chance of improved internet access. Only 4.70 inhabitants per square kilometer make their home in the Amazonic North Region, compared with 51.38 inhabitants per square kilometer in the South and 94.63 inhabitants per square kilometer in Southeast (IBGE & Educamaisbrasil, 2019). Hence, the Amazon is far from being an attractive market in which to invest for telecommunication companies. As a result, rural indigenous communities suffer an endemic digital exclusion, along with other rural minorities who share this huge territory with them: the *quilombolas*, descendants from runaway enslaved Africans; the *extrativistas*, typically fishermen or peasants, some of them descendants from workers held captive in rubber Fazendas during the "rubber fever" of the early the twentieth century. Indigenous people, *quilombolas*, and *extrativistas* all share ethnic, ethical, and economic commonalities that tend to be incompatible with globalization and capitalism.

Due to limited access to computers and/or wired internet, Brazilians have turned to mobile telephones to engage with the digital ecosystem. The country is ranked fifth in the world in terms of smartphone usage (WPR, 2022), but ranks 65th with respect to computer access (EON, 2005). Internet mobile penetration reached 95 percent in 2020 (BID & gov.br, 2020), however such access cannot compensate for lack of broadband or cable, because its lower quality and relative higher cost. On the other hand, mobile-only internauts develop fewer digital skills than those using both computers and smartphones (de Araujo & Reinhard, 2019), so many people may have access to digital space but lack the conditions to master it.

Cheap mobile data-packs offer limited connectivity and are often associated with zero-rating practices, which offer customers "free" unlimited access to digital social media such as, WhatsApp and Facebook, but encage users by limiting surfing time on other platforms or services. Brazil is the world's second largest WhatsApp market, with an estimated 108 million users in 2021—almost half the nation's population; only India surpasses Brazil (Backlinko, 2021). In terms of Facebook, Brazil is the global fourth largest market, with 116 million individual users, or more than 50 percent of the population (Statista, 2022a). The country is among the world's three largest markets for both Instagram and TikTok, as well (Datareportal, 2022; Statista, 2022b). Thus, Brazil's digital social media culture exerts tremendous influence, this effect is replicated within indigenous communities in terms of communication.

The combination of high mobile phone penetration and massive digital social media use has created a paradise for carriers who employ zero-rating practices. Carriers offer "sponsored" data packs for mobile communication with "no charge," in exchange limiting data to certain other Apps and browsers, or, potentially, to simply induce users to use their limited data on targeted digital social media platforms. Such practices lure Brazilian mobile users into heavy use of WhatsApp, Facebook, TikTok and the like, so accessing alternative sources may seem useless, or a waste of valuable data packs because other services are not given "for free." Users may, therefore, decline to cross-check information when someone on WhatsApp has already given them the answer. Worse still, there is no external data checking or source reliability analysis among information sharing communities, as corporate entities that operate the platforms claim to be unable to track fake news or hate speech because messages are encrypted to protect users' privacy. In this manner, zero-rating has contributed to the evolution of disinformation in Brazil (Lorenzon, 2021).

Although Brazil is a major world player in digital social media markets, national policies on digital transformation are scarce. Only 40 percent of the states have implemented public policies toward developing digital capacities in citizens and preparing them to face challenges such as fake news, digital online life, e-commerce, and cybersecurity. Only 20 percent of Brazilian states have conducted studies on the benefits of digital transformation in public services or developed digital policies based on such studies (BID et al., 2020; BID & gov. br, 2020). Brazil is not developing digital literacy and ranks below the world's average for digital skills proficiency (3.20 over a note of 5.00 vs. 4.20), with a negative growth of -5.79 percent since 2017 (World Bank, 2019).

Digital Social Media: Coloniality and Weaponizing of Information

Endemic digital divides, lack of digital transformation policies and low e-literacy levels in Brazil produced the conditions for a perfect storm of disinformation that had the most impact on indigenous communities when the COVID-19 pandemic began. The rise of digital disinformation campaigns originated during the 2018 presidential campaign transformed disinformation into a business model and political strategy. Disinformation, e-bullying, and defamation campaigns were successful in winning elections, helping to elect radical authoritarian politicians, some of whom espouse the view that indigenous communities are obstacles to "progress and civilization." Disinformation evolved into a style of governance and a type of public administration 'policy' in itself, while Facebook and WhatsApp became permanent instruments of this 'policy' of weaponizing information (Newman et al., 2020).

Conservative right-wing political and religious movements in Brazil found in social digital media the key to consolidating power under democratic rules, replicating colonial discourses. Their narratives sought to naturalize white supremacism, misogyny, religious exclusivism, and an indiscriminate profit-centered perspective. Coloniality penetrated the cognitive-affective structures of the digital world, in antithesis to modern rationality. Such messaging was integrated into massive communication outputs from populist leaders, which were supported by market-driven incentives for continuous deceptive engagement in online environments (Udupa, 2020).

In modern, democratic, and globalized Brazil, coloniality took the form of religious intolerance, mainly toward Afro-Brazilian and indigenous communities (Barreto, 2021) and white supremacist capitalism, that sought to expand to indigenous territories and ecological reserves in a crusade for 'economical productivity' and "civilization." In this context, indigenous communities face an epistemological and economical struggle (Brighenti, 2015). Under radical authoritarian politicians elected in 2018, coloniality was transformed into a permanent agenda of systematic disinformation, accompanied by legal erosion of the rights protecting "undesired" communities. Within this latter group, indigenous communities were regarded as a major inconvenience.

The elected government's support-base consisted of conservative evangelical movements, as well as radical right-wing sectors of the army and agribusiness (Pacheco & DW, 2021; Vinícius Lemos & BBC, 2021). Preservation of the "unproductive" Amazon rain forests reserves guarded by indigenous communities implied a serious threat to these groups, especially those related to agribusiness. Agribusiness in Brazil has invested significant marketing resources into positioning itself as the economic locomotive of the country for regional sustainable development. In reality, though, this sector tends toward a white-industrialist perspective that is spatially selective, socially excluding, economically concentrating, environmentally destructive, and culturally devastating (Elias, 2021).

With respect to religion, urban Afro-Brazilian minorities who retain African cults, like Candomblé and Umbanda, have been harassed, and indigenous communities have been besieged by missionaries. Massive conversions in indigenous communities, promoted by fundamentalist groups, have not only imperiled native traditions but have induced religious intolerance and conflict between converted and non-converted groups (Moraes, 2014).

Brazilian Indigenous Communities and Environmental Racism

The current situation for indigenous communities in Brazil is complex and threatening. With lobbying from dominant economic groups like agribusiness and cooptation from the elected right-wing government, opposition in Congress to dismantling protections and aid to indigenous communities was reduced to 16 percent of congress members (Congresso em Foco, 2022). It is a context of environmental racism against indigenous communities that includes removing the demarcation of indigenous conservation units, and convincing them to develop or accept industrial-scale extractive activities in their lands, such as mining and agribusiness. Meanwhile in international fora, the government tries to disguise cultural assimilation as indigenous inclusion, while internally, there is a systematic dismantling of ecological and indigenous protection agencies (Fellet & BBC, 2020).

At the United Nations General Assembly in 2019, the Brazilian President claimed that "[…] it is necessary to understand that our native people are human beings, exactly like any one of us. They want and deserve to enjoy the same rights as all of us [, but…] NGOs insist on treating and maintaining our indigenous people as true cave men." (gov.br & Bolsonaro, 2019). The President insists in opening up these reserves to large-scale extractive activities, as he stated "Indians cannot continue being poor on top of rich land" (Brasil & MRE, 2019).

In the internal front, demarcation of indigenous conservation units was frozen claiming that it preserved "too much land for few Indians" (Estadão Conteúdo, 2019). Statistics showed that Brazil is below the world's average for protected indigenous territories (15 percent), while 41 percent of land is held by agribusiness concerns (ISA, 2021; OBIND, 2021). Most of indigenous land is located in the Amazon and Mato Grosso. Fortunately, the government's interference and downsize of ecological and indigenous protection agencies was slowed down by fierce protests among indigenous movements, and the opposition from the Federal Supreme Court, who reversed some of these actions.

Such narratives ignore the ecological and spiritual bond between indigenous culture and preservation, and attempt to replace them with a white capitalistic perspective in disregard of the ecological and sociocultural impacts such views may cause (ISA et al., 2021). Although it tries to present itself as a humanitarian cause, still it adheres to a colonial view. Under this political context, Brazil's current government reinforced disinformation strategies and narratives that support environmental racism against indigenous communities. This has worsened economic inequality, lack of educational quality and infrastructure abandonment for these communities, so digital exclusion, lack of e-skills and the consumption of disinformation continues to grow, acting as an effective tool for acculturation and gradual elimination of indigenous communities occupying "remote geographies" (Holifield, 2001).

Symbolic violence characterizing the informational relationship between indigenous communities and the outside world, has been enhanced by mobile access to internet without sufficient digital skills. Coloniality has evolved into sophisticated forms of exclusion, but also of wicked inclusion, mainly through digital social media, becoming a potential threat to indigenous communities who are limited in both digital skills and internet access.

Indigenous Communities from "Remote Geographies" in the Digital Realm

Brazil's North Region, the Amazon, holds a population of approximately 305,873 indigenous people as per IBGE, or about 37.4 percent of the country's total indigenous population. Eighty percent of them are located in rural areas (those who live in cities are frequently considered "not real indigenous people") (IBGE, 2012). As a nation, Brazil's digital inclusion and skills are lacking, and the Amazon lags far behind the rest of the country (dos Santos et al., 2020). Among the few studies available in the region, the Agricultural Family Schools survey found that mobile internet usage is dominant with 85 percent, and that skills for finding, accessing, organizing, critically evaluating, and sharing information electronically, were only mastered by 34 percent of the students. In contrast, 77.2 percent mastered texting and meme exchanging (Torres et al., 2020). A second study from the Federal University of Pará (UFPA), with a large sample of approximately 9000 students and professors, showed that 88 percent of students accessed the internet via smartphones and 45 percent of them rejected online education. The use of online platforms among professors was 12 percent (UFPA et al., 2020).

In conclusion, the Amazon, and other "remote geographies" suffer overlapping multiple exclusions, making the creation of digital capital (Ragnedda, 2018) a very difficult mission. Environmental racism worsens the situation for indigenous communities, some of which possess extensive rich lands desired by powerful external actors. Digital technology can be a tool to contain this, but exclusion, abandonment and harassment weakens indigenous communities' use of technology for autonomy and self-management of their territories. Access to technology without digital skills made them victims of interference in their believes and cultural heritages (da Costa Oliveira, 2008). The combination of zero-rating, digital social media encryption policies, disinformation, COVID-19, isolation and absent healthcare, resulted in a "hidden genocide" during the pandemic (Oliveira, 2021).

Misinformation and COVID-19 Affecting Indigenous Communities

During the COVID-19 pandemic in Brazil, there was increasing concern in regard to the effects of the virus on indigenous populations. Reports warned that due vaccination refusal and increasing distrust in medical services, fatalities skyrocketed in these communities, with mortality rates three to five times higher than in the white population (Modelli, 2020). Elders were more affected by the virus, so tribal memories and heritage were weakened. As the epicenter of this situation, the government's policies and omissions, combined with disinformation campaigns about the vaccine on digital social media, created a lethal discourse of confusion, distrust, and even violence.

Jamamadi and the "Beast in the Microchip"

The Jamamadi tribe at Labrea, in Southern Amazon, are Christian converts with a close attachment to Pentecostal missionaries. One of these missionaries, who lived since childhood with the Jamamadi, was expelled from the territory by FUNAI (National Indigenous Foundation) as he illegally entered the neighboring Hi-merimã territory to evangelize, in violation of their lawful isolation rights (Brasil, 1973). Due to their unconditional support to this missionary, the Jamamadi became involved in a conflict in which digital social media served as an amplifier, feeding religious hate-speech and paranoid fantasies that induced violence.

Messages within Jamamadi WhatsApp groups alleged that COVID-19 was an invention of white men, that the community was used as guinea pigs, vaccines were to implant demonic chips with the "number of the beast" into their bodies, and that the serum was made of fetal cells containing HIV virus (Merlino, 2021). Jamamadi's WhatsApp groups also circulated fake news indicating that 900 Xingu people had died upon receiving the vaccine. As a result, in February 2021, the Jamamadi attacked a military helicopter bringing vaccine doses, forcing it to withdraw. After negotiation, the Jamamadi chief agreed to receive the health mission but most of the 399 members of the community refused vaccination (Gragnani, 2021; Gragnani & BBC, 2021).

Historical Distrust at Rio Tapajós

At Rio Tapajós, in the state of Pará, indigenous communities rejected vaccination as their mistrust in "white medicine" was exacerbated by disinformation and false cures circulating via WhatsApp. Digital rumors affirmed that the vaccine would kill them within 15 days after the shot, that the Chinese had included chips into the serum to monitor them, or that they may turn into alligators. This last idea was taken from an ironic comment made by the President during a public discourse, suggesting that the vaccine might turn people into alligator as side effect, but as that was a free choice of those taking the shot, he would not object (AFP, 2020). Narratives such as these, in combination with recommendations of ineffective treatments by high government officers, increased the number of infections and the spread of the disease within these communities (Giovanaz, 2021).

The Avá-Guaraní and the Military Dictatorship Legacy

In Guaíra, Paraná, the Avá-Guaraní communities expressed their deep apprehension toward vaccination. Some of them remembered stories from the time of the Brazilian military dictatorship (1964–1985), when a number of their ancestors died due to contaminated vaccines supplied by the military government, who had intended to decimate them. This historical legacy served as fertile soil for conspiracy theories on WhatsApp, especially those about indigenous people being used as "guinea pigs" to test vaccines that would cause cancer and alter DNA (Carignano, 2021).

Disinformation Takes the Last Tupi Kagwahiva Chief Warrior

Disinformation via digital social media, and declarations from prominent government representatives, took a heavy toll on renowned indigenous leaders. Chief Aruká, from the Juma Tupi Kagwahiva died at 86 years old in February 2021 in Porto Velho, Rondonia, after being infected with COVID-19. During January, Aruká was treated in a hospital at the south of the Amazon with the so-called "early treatment." This was a proven ineffective drug cocktail, including chloroquine, sponsored by government officers on presidential order. He was one of the last chief-warriors of the indigenous resistance in Brazil and a survivor of the 1964 Assuã River massacre, which was perpetrated by traders who invaded the Juma Kagwahiva territory to crop chestnut. Aruká organized the resistance and achieved legal recognition for the Juma territories in 2004 (Kaxinawá, 2021).

Plotting Against the Xavante and Bororo Tribes

Disinformation via digital social media also fueled violence between white settlers and indigenous communities. In Mato Grosso, lack of adequate health assistance, poverty, and malnutrition caused indigenous communities to experience double the risk COVID-19 infection than the white population (Drague Ramos & OPAN, 2020). In the municipality of General Carneiro, white farmers assumed that the Xavante and Bororo tribes were the cause of the COVID-19 outbreak in the area, so they used digital social media to plot the elimination of these communities. Offensive messages and hate speech circulated freely in WhatsApp groups within the city and progressively transformed into suggestions for violent action. Some of these messages and audios were downloaded by members of the Xavante and Bororo communities and delivered to authorities with pleas for protection. Legal action was taken, and some of the instigators were arrested (Lemos & BBC, 2020).

CONCLUSION: CONVERSATIONS WITH CHIEF URUMA FROM THE KAMBEBA

This case review showed how the circumstances in which Brazilian indigenous communities live can produce a toxic effect in their relation with digital technology, different to that seen in western urban environments. Geographical and/or social isolation, economic harshness, educational limitations, and systematic disinformation, combined with intensive consumption of digital social media, zero-rating unawareness, encryption issues, limited information sources, and fragile digital skills, all combined, are an invitation to disaster.

The colonial history and context of rejection and depredation affecting these groups, gained renewed force and acceptance with the election of radical right-wing politicians, who obstructed all measures to provide infrastructure and education to enhance the digital capital of these communities. Radical religious groups looking to convert them, corporations lobbying to gain access to exploit their territories, and myriads of poachers searching for timber, minerals, or exotic animals, complete the ongoing siege of external forces that indigenous communities face in Brazil. From a postcolonial perspective, the global information society, and its digital information regime, produced by former colonial powers and following colonial representations and interests, created a paradox for indigenous communities: digital technology may empower them, but only if they had similar cultural and socioeconomic circumstances to western white groups, which they do not have or do not want to have.

To conclude this study, the authors joined Chief Uruma from the Kambeba, near Manaus, State of Amazon, to have his perspective on these matters. The Kambeba are located 47 kilometers from the city of Manaus and are considered an urban indigenous community. Their access to internet is mainly through mobile as well as through a shared cable that the chief describes as difficult and slow. This cable connection costs up to R$400 (Brazilian reais) per month, that account for one-third of the minimum monthly salary in Brazil (approximately R$1200 or US$233). Thus, the community receives a low-quality connection at a high price and shares it via Wi-Fi from the settlement's school. As it can be imagined, Chief Uruma answered our interviewed via WhatsApp. He explained,

> *We need computers for our school and a good Internet. Although, we have access to basic education in our mother tongue, with a teacher which is from the community. The municipality pays for it. Here we have two Internet points, and we share them with anyone that has a cell phone in the community, splitting the cost. We call it shared internet.*

The Community uses "*zap*" (WhatsApp), Facebook, and Instagram, as almost all Brazil does. When asked how they use these apps, the Chief answers that it is more work, with the understanding that in an indigenous community, "work" implies connecting the daily activities of the extended family and not necessarily professional office telework. Videoconference meetings are useful to coordinate activities in the community and decision making, so digital social media lies at the heart of the community's routine.

When sked about zero rating and encryption, the Chief's answer was negative: There is no awareness of the problem or how it affects the community. The Kambeba do not have access to sophisticated mobile telephones with extensive capacities, a situation which reinforces their reliance on WhatsApp, but the Chief senses no limitations to alternative internet resources. This is a general perception in Brazil, as zero-rating is so widely practiced that it became naturalized, and there are no plans for a social internet that would expand web surfing alternatives for deprived communities.

When asked about disinformation and how fake news are filtered, Chief Uruma emphasized that they take care to avoid criminal schemes but acknowledged they do not have any training in the area of fake news and disinformation. The effect of this lack of skill is visible when he talks about ineffective cures administered to his people:

> *Ribeirinhos* [people who live on the riverside] *and indigenous people have little access to true information. In the case of COVID19 ineffective cures, no one really knew the truth, that whoever took it would die.*

The vulnerability of Amazon communities due to lack of information competence and digital skills is worrying, given their situation. In their environment, information can mean the difference between life and death, as they are isolated, with no nearby hospitals or police stations. The COVID-19 pandemic made this very clear, turning disinformation into lost lives.

Asked about aid or education given to the community to enhance digital access and skills, the Chief said that basic health and education were covered by the municipality, but information and digital skills were totally abandoned. The interview ended and left the impression that, once again, aid given to indigenous communities responds to a colonial perspective of patronage, and not respect to the civil rights of fellow Brazilian citizens. Ignoring their needs for infrastructure, education, and digital skills is an attack their self-determination and defense capacity of their homeland, a capacity that could be empowered by technology.

Mobile internet created a revolution in access, but such revolution is driven by profit and consumption. Without access to computers and broadband internet, complemented by quality education and digital skills, connectivity serves consumerism and power concentration but not citizenry or ethnic groups. In a global ecosystem where disinformation became an industry, digital skills are a must. Further, in a system that inherited coloniality, the historical limitations imposed upon indigenous communities in economic, symbolic, social, and personal capital compromise the production of digital capital. Not only do they have been disarticulated from opportunities, but they have become easy prey within the global digital ecosystem.

Technology is a representation of the world and the actions we applied to it (Ellul, 1978), hence, it implies culture, ideology, and power relations. For outsiders in the global-capitalist-white society, technology is an alien utility produced and controlled outside their context, forcing them into them foreign languages, and cultures. However, technology also holds the access to basic public and private services, so refusal or exclusion will have a direct effect on civil rights. As WhatsApp has become so central to life in Brazil's indigenous communities, its multiple benefits also carry the potential for significant damage, as the reports collected in this chapter have shown.

No research on the perils of intensive digital social media use in isolated communities, such as the indigenous populations of Brazil, yet exists. This study offers an initial glimpse into this problem, yet without the necessary empirical base to clarify how indigenous populations maybe ensnared by digital social media and how to measure this peril. Advancements in 5G may fix certain problems with respect to lack of broadband in the Amazon. Yet, digital networks will not be a fully-liberating technology until we fully understand this entrapment and how to solve it in terms of digital infrastructure, education, and skills to support the autonomous administration of their lives and territories. It is hoped that this study will be a call for research and action in Brazil and across the world.

References

AFP. (2020, dezembro 18). Bolsonaro sobre vacina da Pfizer: "Se você virar um jacaré, é problema seu". *ISTOÉ Independente*. https://istoe.com.br/bolsonaro-sobre-vacina-de-pfizer-se-voce-virar-um-jacare-e-problema-de-voce/

Azevedo, A. L. M. dos S. & IBGE. (2019). *IBGE Educa*. IBGE Educa Jovens. https://educa.ibge.gov.br/jovens/materias-especiais/20787-uso-de-internet-televisao-e-celular-no-brasil.html

Backlinko. (2021, março 2). *WhatsApp 2022 User Statistics: How Many People Use WhatsApp?* Backlinko. https://backlinko.com/whatsapp-users

Barreto, R. C. (2021). Racism and Religious Intolerance: A Critical Analysis of the Coloniality of Brazilian Christianity. *Mission Studies*, *38*(3), 398–423. https://doi.org/10.1163/15733831-12341811

BID & gov.br. (2020). *Índice de Oferta de Serviços Digitais ABEP-TIC*. Jornal Abeptic. https://www.jornaldaabep.com.br/indice-de-oferta-de-servicos

BID, Lafuente, M., Leite, R., Porrúa, M., & Valenti, P. (2020). *Tendências na transformação digital em governos estaduais e no Distrito Federal do Brasil*. Inter-American Development Bank. https://publications.iadb.org/publications/portuguese/document/Transformacao-digital-dos-governos-brasileiros-Tendencias-na-transformacao-digital-em-governos-estaduais-e-no-Distrito-Federal-do-Brasil.pdf

Brasil. (1973). *Lei Nº 6.001, de19 de dezembro de 1973, Estatuto do Índio*. Presidência da República, Casa Civil, Subchefia para Assuntos Jurídicos. http://www.planalto.gov.br/ccivil_03/leis/l6001.htm

Brasil & MRE. (2019). Speech by Brazil's President Jair Bolsonaro at the opening of the 74th United Nations General Assembly – New York, September 24, 2019. Ministério Das Relações Exteriores. https://www.gov.br/mre/en/content-centers/speeches-articles-and-interviews/president-of-the-federative-republic-of-brazil/speeches/speech-by-brazil-s-president-jair-bolsonaro-at-the-opening-of-the-74th-united-nations-general-assembly-new-york-september-24-2019-photo-alan-santos-pr

Brighenti, C. A. (2015). Colonialidade do poder e a violência contra os povos indígenas. *PerCursos*, *16*(32), 103–120. https://doi.org/10.5965/1984724616322015103

Cable.co.uk. (2022). *Worldwide Broadband Research 2020*. Cable.Co.Uk. https://www.cable.co.uk/broadband/pricing/worldwide-comparison/

Carignano, J. C. (2021). Informações falsas fazem indígenas temerem vacinação contra COVID-19 no Paraná. *Brasil de Fato*. https://www.brasildefato.com.

br/2021/01/27/informacoes-falsas-fazem-indigenas-temerem-vacinacao-contra-COVID-19-no-parana

Congresso em Foco. (2022). *Radar do Congresso*. Radar do Congresso. https://radar.congressoemfoco.com.br/governismo/camara

da Costa Oliveira, A. (2008). LUCIANO, Gersem dos Santos. O índio brasileiro: O que você precisa saber sobre os povos indígenas no Brasil de hoje. Brasília: MEC/SECAD; LACED/Museu Nacional, 2006. 233p.(Coleção Educação Para Todos. Série Vias dos Saberes n. 1). *Espaço Ameríndio, 2*(2), 186.

Datareportal. (2022). *The Latest TikTok Stats: Everything You Need to Know*. DataReportal—Global Digital Insights. https://datareportal.com/essential-tiktok-stats

de Araujo, M. H., & Reinhard, N. (2019). Substituting Computers for Mobile Phones? An Analysis of the Effect of Device Divide on Digital Skills in Brazil. Em P. Panagiotopoulos, N. Edelmann, O. Glassey, G. Misuraca, P. Parycek, T. Lampoltshammer, & B. Re (Orgs.), *Electronic Participation* (Vol. 11686, p. 142–154). Springer International Publishing. https://doi.org/10.1007/978-3-030-27397-2_12

dos Santos, R. P., Bülbül, M. Ş., & Lemes, I. L. (2020). Evidence from Google Trends of a Widening Second-level Digital Divide in Brazil. Even Worse with the COVID-19. *Acta Scientiae, 22*(4), 121–154.

Drague Ramos, & OPAN. (2020, agosto 31). *Indígenas de Mato Grosso têm mais que o dobro de chances de morrer por COVID-19*. OPERAÇÃO AMAZÔNIA NATIVA. https://amazonianativa.org.br/2020/08/31/indigenas-de-mato-grosso-tem-mais-que-o-dobro-de-chances-de-morrer-por-COVID-19/

Elias, D. (2021). Mitos e nós do agronegócio no Brasil. *GEOUSP, 25*. http://www.scielo.br/j/geo/a/RbJHXNzykF8jP9Tn8BbQqBv/

Ellul, J. (1978). Symbolic function, technology and society. *Journal of Social and Biological Structures, 1*(3), 207–218.

EON. (2005). *Personal computers (per 100 people)—Other—Education Statistics, Country Comparison, Nations Statistics*. Encyclopedia of the Nations. https://www.nationsencyclopedia.com/WorldStats/Edu-other-personal-computers.html

Estadão Conteúdo. (2019, agosto 30). *É muita terra para pouco índio, diz Bolsonaro*. Exame. https://exame.com/brasil/e-muita-terra-para-pouco-indio-diz-bolsonaro/

Fellet, J., & BBC. (2020). Os 5 principais pontos de conflito entre governo Bolsonaro e indígenas. *BBC News Brasil*. https://www.bbc.com/portuguese/brasil-51229884

Giovanaz, D. (2021). Fake news se espalham entre indígenas e dificultam vacinação: "Medo de virar jacaré". *Brasil de Fato*. https://www.brasildefato.com.br/2021/02/18/fake-news-se-espalham-entre-indigenas-e-dificultam-vacinacao-medo-de-virar-jacare

gov.br, & Bolsonaro, J. M. (2019). *Speech by Brazil's President Jair Bolsonaro at the opening of the 74th United Nations General Assembly – New York, September 24, 2019 (photo: Alan Santos/PR)*. Ministério Das Relações Exteriores. https://www.gov.br/mre/en/content-centers/speeches-articles-and-interviews/president-of-the-federative-republic-of-brazil/speeches/speech-by-brazil-s-president-jair-bolsonaro-at-the-opening-of-the-74th-united-nations-general-assembly-new-york-september-24-2019-photo-alan-santos-pr

Gragnani, J. (2021). Epidemia de fake news ameaça vacinação em terras indígenas. *BBC News Brasil*. https://www.bbc.com/portuguese/brasil-56433811

Gragnani, J., & BBC. (2021, maio 8). The misinformation bubble threatening Brazil's indigenous people. *BBC News.* https://www.bbc.com/news/blogs-trending-56919424

Holifield, R. (2001). Defining environmental justice and environmental racism. *Urban Geography,* 22(1), 78–90. https://doi.org/10.2747/0272-3638.22.1.78

IBGE. (2012). *Os indígenas no Censo Demográfico 2010: Primeiras considerações com base no quesito cor ou raça* (Censo Demográfico 2010, p. 31). Instituto Brasileiro de Geografia e Estatistica. https://www.ibge.gov.br/indigenas/indigena_censo2010.pdf

IBGE. (2021). *Produto Interno Bruto—PIB.* https://www.ibge.gov.br/explica/pib.php

IBGE & Educamaisbrasil. (2019). *IBGE Educa.* Educa+ Brasil. https://www.educamaisbrasil.com.br/enem/geografia/densidade-demografica

ISA. (2021). *#MarcoTemporalNão: Entenda por que não tem "muita terra para pouco índio" no Brasil.* ISA - Instituto Socioambiental. https://www.socioambiental.org/pt-br/noticias-socioambientais/marcotemporalnao-entenda-por-que-nao-tem-muita-terra-para-pouco-indio-no-brasil

ISA, de Paula Batista, J., Oviedo, A., & Moreira dos Santos, T. (2021, agosto 21). *Recurso Extraórdinário N.º 1.017.365.* https://www.socioambiental.org/sites/blog.socioambiental.org/files/arquivos/memoriais_-_isa_-_re_1017365_-_marco_temporal_-_25.08.21.pdf

Kaxinawá, L. (2021). *Morre de COVID-19 o guerreiro Aruká, o último homem do povo Juma.* Brasil de Fato. https://www.brasildefato.com.br/2021/02/18/morre-de-COVID-19-o-guerreiro-aruka-o-ultimo-homem-do-povo-juma

Lemos, V., & BBC. (2020). *"Isso não é gente": Os áudios com ataques a indígenas na pandemia que se tornaram alvos do MPF.* https://noticias.uol.com.br/ultimas-noticias/bbc/2020/07/27/isso-nao-e-gente-os-audios-com-ataques-a-indigenas-na-pandemia-que-se-tornaram-alvos-do-mpf.htm

Lorenzon, L. (2021, dezembro 9). *The High Cost of "Free" Data: Zero-Rating and its Impacts on Disinformation in Brazil.* Data-Pop Alliance. https://datapopalliance.org/the-high-cost-of-free-data-zero-rating-and-its-impacts-on-disinformation-in-brazil/

Merlino, T. (2021, fevereiro 25). *Indígenas recusam vacinas da COVID-19a flechadas e exigem presença de missionário.* Repórter Brasil. https://reporterbrasil.org.br/2021/02/indigenas-recusam-vacinas-da-COVID-a-flechadas-e-exigem-presenca-de-missionario/

Modelli, L. (2020). Comunidades indígenas na bacia amazônica são cinco vezes mais atingidas pela COVID-19 que o resto do Brasil, alerta Opas. *G1.* https://g1.globo.com/bemestar/coronavirus/noticia/2020/07/14/comunidades-indigenas-na-bacia-amazonica-sao-cinco-vezes-mais-atingidas-pela-COVID-19-que-o-resto-do-brasil-alerta-opas.ghtml

Moraes, J. A. S. (2014). O pentecostalismo entre os índios da reserva indígena de dourados, da década de 1980 aos dias atuais. *Democracias e ditaduras no mundo contemporâneo: XII Encontro da Associação Nacional de História.,* 15. http://www.encontro2014.ms.anpuh.org/resources/anais/38/1412825204_ARQUIVO_comunicacao-anpuhms-2014_jose-augusto-santos-moraes.pdf

Newman, N., Fletcher, R., Schulz, A., Andı, S., & Kleis Nielsen, R. (2020). *Reuters Institute Digital News Report 2020* (p. 112). Reuters & University of Oxford.

Numbeo. (2022). *Price Rankings by Country of Internet (60 Mbps or More, Unlimited Data, (Cable/ADSL, Utilities (Monthly).* Numbeo Costo of Living. https://www.numbeo.com/cost-of-living/country_price_rankings?itemId=33

OBIND. (2021, agosto 31). ISA: #MarcoTemporalNão: entenda por que não tem 'muita terra para pouco índio' no Brasil. *Observatório dos direitos e políticas indígenas*. http://obind.eco.br/2021/08/31/isa-marcotemporalnao-entenda-por-que-nao-tem-muita-terra-para-pouco-indio-no-brasil/

Oliveira, J. (2021, julho 3). *Los indígenas de Brasil denuncian a Bolsonaro en La Haya por genocidio y ecocidio*. El País. https://elpais.com/internacional/2021-07-03/los-indigenas-de-brasil-denuncian-a-bolsonaro-en-la-haya-por-genocidio-y-ecocidio.html

Pacheco, R., & DW. (2021, fevereiro 21). *"Barões evangélicos são parceiros de projeto de Bolsonaro", diz pastor*. Poder360. https://www.poder360.com.br/brasil/baroes-evangelicos-sao-parceiros-de-projeto-de-bolsonaro-diz-pastor-dw/

Ragnedda, M. (2018). Conceptualizing digital capital. *Telematics and Informatics*, 35(8), 2366–2375.

Statista. (2022a). *Facebook users by country 2021*. Statista. https://www.statista.com/statistics/268136/top-15-countries-based-on-number-of-facebook-users/

Statista. (2022b). *Instagram: Users by country*. Statista. https://www.statista.com/statistics/578364/countries-with-most-instagram-users/

Torres, T. Z., Souza, M. I. F., Cunha, L. M. S., de Carvalho, J. R. P., Daltio, J., & Mangabeira, J. A. C. (2020). Mediatic, Informational and Digital Skills and Competencies in Students from Agricultural Family Schools and Rural Family Home, in the Amazon Biome, Brazil. *Creative Education*, 11(08), 1469–1496. https://doi.org/10.4236/ce.2020.118107

Udupa, S. (2020). Decoloniality and Extreme Speech. *65th E-Seminar, Media Anthropology Network, European Association of Social Anthropologists*, 24.

UFPA, Morbach, J., & Berrío-Zapata, C. (2020). *Uso de Tecnologias Digitais de Informação e Comunicação (TDICS) por docentes e discentes da UFPA, em tempos de COVID-19* (p. 25). UFPA.

Vinícius Lemos & BBC. (2021). Como líderes evangélicos usam redes para apoiar ato pró-Bolsonaro. *BBC News Brasil*. https://www.bbc.com/portuguese/brasil-58442769

World Bank. (2019). *TCdata360: GCI 4.0: Digital skills among population*. TCdata360. https://tcdata360.worldbank.org/indicators/h945a9708?country=BRA&indicator=41400&countries=IND,RUS,CHN&viz=line_chart&years=2017,2019

World Bank. (2022). *Individuals using the Internet (percent of population)*. World Bank Data. https://data.worldbank.org/indicator/IT.NET.USER.ZS?end=2020&start=2020&view=map

Worldometer. (2022). *Population by Country (2022)*. Worldometer. https://www.worldometers.info/world-population/population-by-country/

WPR. (2022). *Cell Phones by Country 2022*. World Population Review. https://worldpopulationreview.com/country-rankings/cell-phones-by-country

CHAPTER 20

Regenerating African Languages and Cultures Through Information Technology Strategies

Thapelo J. Otlogetswe

INTRODUCTION

The prevailing linguistic situation in African countries is a consequence of biased linguistic choices by African states at independence. Alidou (2004) has argued that in post-colonial Africa, to avoid ethnic wars, African governments ironically retained colonial languages which were viewed as neutral means of communication. She also argues that governments felt that in the interest of national unity, it was crucial that a country rallied behind a single flag, a single constitution, and a single local language. This choice contributed to the exclusions of hundreds of African languages from use and development by governments.

Most African languages lack an official status. The majority of those with an official status in their countries, are yet to be intellectualized. An intellectualized language is one "which can be used for educating a person in any field of knowledge from kindergarten" (Sibayan 1999, p. 229). They are instead used in very restricted domains largely as oral languages or used in the writing of creative pieces such as novels, plays and poetry. Most are excluded from formal domains such as law (except for customary courts), medicine, engineering, as mediums of instruction etc. Specialized terminologies in the domains of science, engineering, health, construction, computing, and law remain underdeveloped in African languages since African languages are excluded from such domains of language usage. Many are therefore not adequately embedded in

T. J. Otlogetswe (✉)
University of Botswana, Gaborone, Botswana
e-mail: OTLOGETS@ub.ac.bw

© The Author(s), under exclusive license to Springer Nature Switzerland AG 2024
H. S. Dunn et al. (eds.), *The Palgrave Handbook of Everyday Digital Life*,
https://doi.org/10.1007/978-3-031-30438-5_20

scientific data bases, in technical online forums and in other domains of digital everyday life.

What exacerbates the challenges confronting African languages is that many of them are cross-border, or their speakers are spread over a wide geographical area. This leads to neighbouring countries with the same language pursuing different developmental policies and strategies towards the same language. In certain cases, the consequence of such a situation is different orthographies of the same language and parallel terminology developments. Standardized orthographies are essential for the development of literacy skills, and for the production of literature.

Setswana: Data Resource

In the development of this chapter, we source most of our examples from Setswana—a member of a Sotho subgroup (also known as Sotho languages) of closely related Bantu languages found in southern Africa (Chebanne 2008, p. 96). Setswana is spoken by about 10 million speakers in four southern African countries of Botswana, South Africa, Namibia and Zimbabwe. In Botswana, Setswana is a national language and not considered an official language (Onibere et al., 2001, p. 503). In Zimbabwe Setswana is an official language while in Namibia is one of the minority languages. In South Africa, Setswana is one of the 11 official languages. The difference in status of Setswana in these four countries can be explained by the difference in constitutional dispensation regarding languages (cf. Finlayson and Madiba, 2002; Andersson and Janson, 1997) where Setswana's official status is provided for in the South African and Zimbabwean constitutions and left out in the Botswana and Namibian constitutions.

A country's constitution determines to a large extent the language policies and functionality of languages (Janson and Tsonope, 1991 and Webb, 2004). Setswana is Botswana's dominant language spoken by the majority of the citizens as a mother tongue (Andersson and Janson, 1997, p. 21). It is also widely spoken as a second language and widely used as a national lingua franca. It is taught in Botswana, Namibian and South African schools and used widely in the government and private radio stations in Botswana and South Africa. It is one of the languages that have been selected for development and promotion by the African Academy of Languages (ACALAN), an arm of the Social Affairs Commission of the African Union. ACALAN believes that African languages that have wide geographical spread and are used across borders must be strengthened to improve communication, enhance trade, and facilitate enjoyment of cultural ties (Otlogetswe and Chebanne, 2018). Although like many African languages, Setswana has faced numerous challenges, it has benefitted from modest ICT development and has a limited digital print on the web.

A noticeable digital footprint is essential to a healthy and vibrant language. For a language to have a digital footprint it must have an orthography, something which many African languages lack. An orthography is a precursor to a grammatical sketch, story transcription and dictionary compilation. At the same time, having accessible on a digital platform presents advantages over and above its availability in traditional formats such as print. The digital domain can also carry interactive audio-visual content. With a smart phone, audio visual material can be recorded and made available on the digital domain and be shared among language speakers. However, if the relevant linguistic communities are not online, the effort at linguistic digitalization can be counterproductive. It will be useful at this juncture, therefore, to examine internet penetration in Africa which is essential for the digital development of African languages. While specific penetration statistics with vary over time, our interest here is the trends conveyed by the penetration figures, and what they portend for the future.

THE ICT INFLUENCE IN AFRICA

Advances in information technology present an excellent opportunity for the development and preservation of African languages. With the rapid spread of mobile telephony and an increasingly widening access to the internet, ICT should, and can, be harnessed by Africa researchers and scholars to preserve African languages and cultures.

The 2021 GSM Association reports that at the end of 2020, 303 million people across Sub-Saharan Africa were connected to the mobile internet, equivalent to 28% of the population. Several operators in Sub-Saharan Africa have implemented initiatives to improve digital inclusion for women. By 2025, more than 170 million people across the region will have started using mobile internet for the first time, taking the penetration rate to just under 40% of the population by then.

Internet World Stats reports different statistics from those of GSM 2021. Table 20.1 shows that about 66% of the world's population had access to the internet which facilitates communication and sharing textual and audio-visual data. Most of this population (53%) was found in Asia while Africa's internet access constituted 11.5% of the world population. The continent statistics reveal that North America had the largest number of internet users at 93.4% while internet penetration in Africa was estimated at around 43%. This low level of internet connectivity has grave implications for what can be achieved through the use ICTs in the development and preservation of African languages.

LANGUAGES ON THE INTERNET

For a while now, it has been generally known that there is a disproportionate representation of languages on the internet. English continues to dominate (Fletcher, 2007). The Inktomi and Cyveillance study (Moore and Murray, 2000) has concluded that most online webpages are in English. This has been supported by Grefenstette and Nioche (2000) who have demonstrated the dominance of European languages on the web. Their study focused on the size

Table 20.1 World Internet Statistics

World internet usage and population statistics

2022 year-Q1 estimates

World regions	Internet users 31-Dec-21	Penetration Rate (% Pop.)	Growth 2000–2022 (%)	Internet World (%)
North America	347,916,694	93.40	222	6.6
Europe	743,602,636	88.40	608	14.2
Latin America / Carib.	533,171,730	80.40	2851	10.1
Middle East	205,019,130	76.40	6141	3.9
Oceania / Australia	30,549,185	70.10	301	0.6
Asia	2,790,150,527	64.10	2341	53.10
Africa	601,327,461	43.10	13,220	11.50
World total	5,251,737,363	66.20	1355	100.00

Source: www.internetworldstats.com, 2022

of the web presence, reflected in the number of words on a website. They have showed that on the basis of number of words, English, German, French, Spanish and Italian dominate the web. *The Fifth Study of Language and the Internet* (Agence de la Francophonie, 2001) documents has reported a growth among the non-English languages in the proportion of webpages relative to English and observes that the number of webpages in the Romance languages and German was roughly proportional to the population of Web users with those languages as native tongue.

Historically Anglophone users and content have overshadowed other languages on the Net, but the trend toward diversity is clear and growing (O'Neill et al., 2003). Statistics compiled by Global Reach illustrate this long-term development trend. In 1996, four-fifths of the 50 million Internet users were native speakers of English. By September 2004, Anglophones constituted only 35% of the world's estimated online population of 801 million users. The Language Observatory Project and its Cyber Census Survey aim to raise awareness of this digital divide among languages and writing systems and to track the distribution of languages online (Mikami et al., 2005). UNESCO is also actively promoting linguistic and cultural diversity on the Web. The phenomenal growth in the non-Anglophone segment of the Web is spurring expansion of online resources in other tongues, particularly the smaller non-Western ones, to the benefit of those who investigate, teach and learn these languages.

While in general, as we have shown, there is low internet penetration in Africa, this phenomenon is not characteristic of all African countries. Countries such as Kenya (85%), Libya (84%), Nigeria (73%), Mauritius (72%) and Seychelles (72%) have an internet penetration of over 70% each. Table 20.2 presents an assessment of the 21 countries with the highest internet access and demonstrate that internet penetration in parts of Africa has exploded in the last 20 years. Access to mobile phone devices has resulted in many young Africans

Table 20.2 African countries—internet access 2022

Africa 2021 population and internet users statistics

Africa	Population (2021 Est.)	Internet Users 31-Dec-20	Penetration (% population)	Internet Growth (%) 2000–2021	Facebook Subscribers 31-Dec-20
Kenya	54,985,698	46,870,422	85.2	23,335	10,444,000
Libya	6,958,532	5,857,000	84.2	58,470	5,857,000
Nigeria	211,400,708	154,301,195	73	101,484	31,860,000
Mauritius	1,273,433	919,000	72.2	956	919,000
Seychelles	98,908	71,300	72.1	1088	71,300
Morocco	37,344,795	25,589,581	68.5	25,489	21,730,000
Tunisia	11,935,766	8,170,000	68.4	8070	8,170,000
Reunion (FR)	901,686	608,000	67.4	367	608,000
Cabo Verde	561,898	352,120	62.7	4302	287,000
Gabon	2,278,825	1,367,641	60	9017	830,000
Mali	20,855,735	12,480,176	59.8	66,284	2,033,300
South Africa	60,041,994	34,545,165	57.5	1339	24,600,000
Algeria	44,616,624	25,428,159	57	50,756	25,140,000
Eswatini	1,172,362	665,245	56.7	6552	339,900
Senegal	17,196,301	9,749,527	56.7	24,273	3,802,000
Zimbabwe	15,092,171	8,400,000	55.7	16,700	1,303,000
Djibouti	1,002,187	548,832	54.8	39,102	258,100
Egypt	104,258,327	54,741,493	52.5	12,064	48,830,000
Zambia	18,920,651	9,870,427	52.2	49,252	2,543,000
Namibia	2,587,344	1,347,418	52.1	4391	792,000
Botswana	2,397,241	1,139,000	47.5	7493	1,139,000

Source: Internet World Stats, 2022

accessing the internet via social media platforms, such as Facebook, Twitter and WhatsApp for chatting, general information sharing and collaboration.

Crowdsourcing Content in the Digital Domain

Rundell (2016) has argued that the Web and social media platforms have created conditions which have overturned the older, top-down media model, where a restricted number of information providers delivered expertly edited content to language users and producers globally. In such a model, language users were largely passive consumers of lexical or audio-visual content. In the new paradigm, the general public are seen to participate as content contributors and distributors and are increasingly expected to do so. (Rundell, 2016) This state of affairs has created opportunities for African languages to crowdsource linguistic and cultural content from speech communities to build linguistic and cultural repositories. Crowdsourcing proper is "a distributed working method in which a large, centrally-managed task is completed with the help of hundreds, even thousands, of volunteers, each of whom makes a small contribution" (Rundell, 2016, p. 4).

While the word crowdsourcing was coined relatively recently (Howe, 2006), the practice of enlisting large numbers of volunteers to contribute content in the execution and completion of a substantial task is much older. A well-known lexicographic example is the collection of words and their meanings from newspaper and book readers to compile a new historical English dictionary in the UK that would later be known as the Oxford English Dictionary by the Philological Society from 1857 (Winchester, 2002). In this project, thousands of book and news readers supplied words and examples of word usage from material they read. Their submissions were used by a team of dictionary editors to compile entries for the ambitious dictionary project.

The crowdsourcing approach was preferred in this project since the task was so massive that doing it conventionally would be financially unsustainable and unachievable. Crowdsourcing content is therefore an attractive approach for the compilation of African language content from speakers who, though widely dispersed geographically, are linked digitally on the web or social media. Crowdsourcing material is particularly attractive for content that cannot be automated but can be generated by non-expert individuals. While content generators may not be experts, crowdsourcing content is better managed by experts who can edit the crowdsourced data to filter out errors and inaccuracies. Therefore, there must be a system of quality control in place to optimize the benefits of user participation and minimize the amount of "noise" that dictionary editors must deal with. Thus, an army of volunteers complements the work of subject specialists in doing the heavy lifting while the experts manage, edit, and refine submitted content. Crowdsourcing content in the digital domain can be an effective mechanism of uniting and engaging a speech community in completing a large project.

To a degree, this depends on the type of volunteers engaged, and Rundell (2016) has identified broadly two types of volunteers that could be used in a lexical and cultural crowdsourcing. The first group comprises lay people with no special expertise but who are linguistically fluent speakers of a language being described. The second group is subject-specialists, such as language experts, lawyers, doctors, journalists, and various professionals, who can make an informed contribution to the description of domain-specific vocabulary. The second group is particularly important in the compilation or translation of specialized terminologies such as a dictionary of medical terms or the translation of ICT terminology into a local language.

It must be emphasized that any crowdsourcing activity must develop strategies of encouraging potential contributors to participate in submitting content consistently over a long period. They must remain engaged and see the broader value in their engagement and contribution. There is therefore a need for a sustainable system of constant engagement of speakers of a language, the language experts and the technical persons who are not necessarily linguists. Such engagement must include cross-border speakers of a language for data elicitation, capture, processing, and distribution to a large population of users. Popular platforms such as Facebook, WhatsApp, Twitter and various applications may be used.

A Challenge to Develop Terms

A central element in the development of a language for broad use in different domains is the development of terms that could be used in the different functional domains. The challenge to terminology development, including ICT terminologies, remains the use of African languages in specialized domains. It is commonly wrongly assumed that African languages are absent from specialized domains such as science and technology because they lack specialized terminologies. The real challenge is that African languages lack terminologies because they are systematically excluded from such specialized domains of language use which are maintained as the preserve of three colonial languages: English, Portuguese and French, in Africa.

Terminology development in African languages is therefore needed, including in different technical domains, to equip such languages to become functional languages that express the day-to-day experiences of their speakers. Terminography is a subdivision of lexicography that deals with the documentation of the terminology of different subject fields, such as technical and scientific terms (Alberts, 2001). The terminology of any subject field (physics, mathematics, biology, chemistry, etc.) or domain (sport, music, etc.) can be documented in terminographical dictionaries, called "technical dictionaries" or "specialized dictionaries".

Terminologists are highly dependent on the input and collaboration of subject-field specialists and experts of various occupational domains. In Africa much is yet to be achieved in this field systematically. The specialist must liaise with various subject committees and linguists while doing research on terminology, and need to systematically document terminological information. For instance, the 2010 translation of the Google Search into Setswana necessitated the involvement of Computer Science experts to deal with terms such as *website, webpage, password, cache* etc. In the 1980s, the South Africa Department of Education and Training was producing large collections of terms which were developed by government-established committees. The collections are still available in print, but the terms never caught on (Department of Education, 1988). Largely, this was because of a failure of usage. This is where conventional media and online presence come in.

Every language speaker must participate in the creation of terms for themselves. Developed terms, whether developed online or offline, must not stay in books somewhere away from potential users. They must be kept online for easy access by students, writers, and other users. They must be promoted and used widely in such everyday media as radio, television, and print, including social media such as Facebook and Twitter, as well as in publications such as schoolbooks, specialized literature, and dictionaries. It is important however, that dictionaries document language as used by speakers and not function as legitimizing tools for terminology development. Use is not only key: it is king.

We wish to propose five different ways in which African linguistic communities can use ICTs to preserve, develop, and promote African languages. They include are the development of dictionaries and spellcheckers, localizing software tools, developing lemmatizers and POS taggers using social media platforms such as Facebook and developing online repositories.

Digitally Compiled Dictionaries and Spellcheckers

It is now possible to create high quality dictionaries for African languages leveraging ICT and social media. Freely available software packages such as the Summer Institute of Linguistics *Fieldworks Language Explorer* (Flex) (Rogers, 2010; Baines, 2009; Butler & Van Volkinburg, 2007) enable teams of compilers to work remotely on a project to create high-quality dictionaries. It has an inbuilt ingenious crowdsourcing which can be used by non-experts to produce new dictionaries. Flex has been used in the compilation of hundreds of dictionaries around the world. For instance, it was used in a dictionary project for Buli, a language of northern Ghana, in which 30 or so enthusiastic local volunteers, collected the core vocabulary of Buli (over 10,000 words) in just two weeks. These data were quickly processed into the first-ever Buli dictionary (see Higby, 2013). It was also used in the compilation of the first Siswati monolingual dictionary from Eswatini, *Umphandza: sichazamagama sesiSwati* (Hlophe et al., 2015).

Linguists and lexicographers working with poor communities usually cannot afford expensive software and usually possess basic computer skills. They can use open source software applications, such as *WeSay* (Albright and Hatton, 2008; Perlin, 2012; Hatton, 2011), designed to involve language communities in the description and documentation of their languages. *WeSay* has a simplified interface which facilitates the involvement of community members with limited computational skills. Word gathering tasks use semantic domains, wordlists or patterns of likely words to build up a dictionary.

Some of my own experiences in crowdsourcing dictionary compilation have used primarily university students as research assistants and have resulted in the following publications: *Poeletso-medumo ya Setswana: the Setswana Rhyming dictionary* (Otlogetswe, 2010), *Tlhalosi ya Medi ya Setswana* (Otlogetswe, 2012), *Dipoeletso-ditumamodumo tsa Setswana: A dictionary of Setswana alliteration and Consonance* (Otlogetswe, 2015), and *Setswana Oxford Living Dictionary* (Otlogetswe, 2016)—an Oxford University Press online dictionary.

Otlogetswe and Scannell (2015) have also developed the Setswana Firefox OS predictive text software and the Setswana Firefox spellchecker. LibreOffice is a free Office suit similar to Microsoft Office. The Setswana Open-Office spellchecker was also developed by Scannell and Otlogetswe (2004) and is widely available online. It is critical that dictionary making technologies are available online and on mobile applications and that they can be accessible even without internet connectivity. Dictionary applications should facilitate learning and language production even when one is offline.

Localisation of Technology

Localizing ICTs is essential to making them more accessible to local communities. Localization "includes the translation and cultural adaptation of user interfaces and software applications, as well as the creation of internet content in diverse languages and the translation of content from other languages" (Osborn, 2010, p. 1). Localising ICTs can domesticate technology and make innovation a part of a local experience. It demystifies technology applications and uncloaks them from the perceptions or reality of 'foreignness', making them relevant to a local community (Osborn, 2006). Locally adapted technologies open new opportunities for advancing digital and all-round human development. There is therefore a need to localize, through indigenous languages, the everyday technologies used by people in Africa and other contexts, especially technologies such as used on Facebook and in Google Search. Some of that work has started in languages such as Setswana. For instance, The Setswana Google Search (Otlogetswe, 2009/2010) makes it possible for those searching text through Google Search to use a Setswana interface.

African institutions such as banks, universities and companies should also localize their websites and offer options for users to access them in any of the local languages. An example of such an attempt is at the North West University of South Africa, where information is available in English, Setswana and Afrikaans. Such linguistic choices create ownership of technologies amongst users and elevate African languages to a similar status of English, French and Portuguese. They also affirm linguistic pluralism as an important characteristic feature of African everyday life.

Development of Lemmatizers and Parts of Speech Taggers

To gain a better understanding of a language, two of the important technologies are lemmatizers and parts of speech taggers. Lemmatisers are modules that find the linguistic normalised form of a word (Eiselen and Puttkammer, 2014; Plisson et al., 2004). Such computational work requires sophisticated computing that draws on a good knowledge of a language's morphology (Bosch et al., 2006). Parts of Speech taggers assign each word in a corpus (text) to a grammatical category based on use and definition. Taggers are essential to computational analysis since they are often used to characterise the context in which a word is used in text or speech. POS tagging can also help determine authorship—who authored a certain document.

Many African languages lack lemmatizers and POS taggers which creates challenges in their analysis using large corpora (Groenewald, 2009). There is therefore a need for computational linguists to develop lemmatizers and POS taggers for most African languages, to facilitate deep level corpus analysis. The South African Centre for Digital Language Resources (SADiLaR), which runs the digitization programme of the eleven official languages of that country, and supports research and development of language technologies such as lemmatizers and part of speech taggers, has brought hope to the development of African languages (Bosch et al., 2021). Their work needs to be replicated across the continent if African languages are to be successfully computerized and revitalized.

Facebook Pages and Other Social Platforms

Opportunities exist in the use of social media platforms to contribute to the development and preservation of African languages (Zourou, 2012). Such platforms are ubiquitous and can be harnessed to connect members of a linguistic community from various countries and regions to their languages online in a relaxed and natural manner (Harran & Olamijulo, 2014). They can bring together and engage young people, who are critical to language revitalization efforts (Liu, 2010). Speakers of an African language can organize themselves into groups based on usage or interested in aspects of a specific language such as idioms and proverbs. Such groups can encourage an exclusive use of a specific language daily.

Social media platforms can also be used by researchers to collect specialized information such as names of animals, plants, or insects in the language. Grammatical information about the language can also be shared to increase competence in the language use. Evidence of this development is already available in the development of the Setswana language. There are multiple Facebook pages on Setswana such as *Lekgotla la Setswana, Puo Letlotlo,* and *Setswana se se kwenneng* which exist to promote the language.

There are also Setswana blogs such as *Puo ya rona* and Setswana pages at www.setswana.info which introduces one to the Setswana language. There is also evidence that there is Setswana use on Twitter, where the number of tweets written in a specific indigenous language can be recorded. Indigenous Tweets is a website that records minority language Twitter messages to help indigenous speakers find each other and follow each other on Twitter (Scannell, 2022). For instance, http://indigenoustweets/tn/ collates tweets which have been made in Setswana. This is particularly attractive since the interface is in Setswana. Indigenous tweets are the result of smart computing by Kevin Scannell of St Louis University (Bhroin, 2015; Trye et al., 2022). It is a demonstration of what can be achieved with computing to bring together speakers of a specific language.

Cultural Repositories

African countries are rich in cultural heritage. Such cultural elements include music and musical instruments; methods of food production, preparation, and preservation; knowledge of plants, their cultivation and uses; knowledge of animals and insects, their rearing, management and uses; a rich knowledge of medicinal plants: where they are harvested, the disease they treat, how they are prepared and administered, as well as other cultural heritage which have been handed down from one generation to another. Much of this cultural knowledge is vanishing every year as its holders die and it is not handed over to a succeeding generation. One way to redress this is to digitize cultural heritage and keep it in online repositories for use by researchers and the public (Malekani & Kavishe, 2018; Balogun & Kalusopa, 2021). This is an attractive route to take in cultural preservation because the digitization equipment is largely low-cost and the web is popular and widely accessible (Patel et al., 2004).

Cultural elements can be photographed, explained, and uploaded onto online repositories. Written documents held in libraries and by individual can be scanned and uploaded; digital audio and video recordings can also be uploaded to online repositories enriched with much commentary (Abd Manaf, 2008). Advanced technological tools such as 3D scans and models of physical artefacts can also be used. (Nishanbaev, 2020). All of these will prove useful in teaching, research, cultural preservation and rejuvenation. Such collections must, however, not remain obscure and available just to the academic few, because that would equate them to the position of journal articles (Mukwevho, 2017). The public must be engaged through crowdsourcing in putting such repositories together and social media platforms must be exploited in making such collections live, fascinating, and useful to communities.

Conclusion

Africa with her rich multilingualism can leverage ICTs to develop and preserve her languages and cultures. Much of that work will be achieved through crowd-sourcing and broad cooperation between members of a speech community. As more people every year acquire internet access, mobile telephones and join social media platforms, there will be growing opportunities for such devices and platforms to be used on an everyday basis in the preservation of Africa's linguistic and cultural heritage.

Institutions and research centres must explore crowdsourcing opportunities to systematically document Africa's linguistic and cultural wealth and preserve it from possible extinction or external appropriation. Unexplored possibilities of online radio stations, local newspaper, and magazines are exciting platforms through which individual and community creativity could find expression. Community music, poetry, paintings, craft have potential to have a wider reach and influence through the appropriation of digital technologies. Developments in social media platforms such as Facebook and Twitter have also put pressure on African countries to adapt, adopt, and modernize their democracies and consultation processes.

In countries such as Botswana, political and ethnic leaders are forced to consider the use of such platforms to consult the public. Social media platforms have become the de facto *makgotla* (public meeting places) extending communicative access to the wider digital public. African communities must adopt various technologies if they are to effectively rejuvenate their languages and cultures. Such technologies are essential and critical if African communities are to participate and thrive in the what has been called the Fourth Industrial Revolution (Schwab, 2016).

The future of African languages and cultures is not all gloom and doom. Some work has gone into translating Google search into various African languages. To date, Google Translate is in over 80 African languages (https://africa.googleblog.com/) while there are Wikipedia pages in over 250 African languages (van Pinxteren, 2017). Microsoft has also released the *Microsoft Office Language Interface Pack 2010* in multiple Africa languages such as Setswana. African knowledge exists in African languages and such knowledge must be in African-held databases. Having much of the world's knowledge in English and other European languages such as French, Portuguese and German sends a false message that knowledge is synonymous with such cultures.

While there is an increasing volume of content online from Africa, most of it is uncoordinated. There is therefore a need to create cross-border groups which could produce and publish material online for the benefit of African speaking communities wherever they are. There is an encouraging use of African languages on social media such as Facebook and Twitter which must be supported and promoted. There is a need to coordinate corpora compilations for African languages and make them freely available to researchers and speech communities. On a technical level, there is a need to develop taggers and parsers for African languages corpora so that they can be exploited more efficiently.

The digitization of African languages and content will be essential to the broader interest of intellectualizing African languages for use in scientific and theoretical developments which reflect the rigor of objective thinking (Havránek, 1932; Prah, 2017; Khumalo and Nkomo, 2022). African languages must be available in digital format to facilitate more consistent everyday use in expressing African knowledge and experience, drawing on online repositories and digital platforms.

References

Abd Manaf, Z. (2008). Establishing the national digital cultural heritage repository in Malaysia. *Library Review*.

Agence de la Francophonie (2001). The Fifth Study on Languages and the Internet. Retrieved 18 October 2021 from the World Wide Web: http://funredes.org/LC/english/L5/L5contents.html

Alberts, M (2001) Lexicography versus terminography. *Lexikos*. 11. 71–84.

Albright, E., & Hatton, J. (2008). WeSay: A tool for engaging native speakers in dictionary building. *Documenting and revitalizing Austronesian languages*, *1*, 189.
Alidou, H. (2004). *Medium of instruction in post-colonial Africa*. Mahwah, NJ: Lawrence Erlbaum Associates.
Andersson, L-G, and Janson, T. (1997). *Languages in Botswana; language ecology in Southern Africa*. Gaborone: Longman Botswana.
Baines, D. (2009). FieldWorks Language Explorer (FLEx). *eLEX2009*, 27.
Balogun, T., & Kalusopa, T. (2021). A framework for digital preservation of Indigenous knowledge system (IKS) in repositories in South Africa. *Records Management Journal*. 31(2), 176–196.
Bhroin, N. N. (2015). Social media-innovation: The case of indigenous tweets. *The Journal of Media Innovations*, 2(1), 89–106.
Bosch, S., Fellbaum, C., Griesel, M., Rademaker, A., & Vossen, P. (2021). South African Centre for Digital Language Resources (SADiLaR) Potchefstroom, South Africa.
Bosch, S., Jones, J., Pretorius, L. & Anderson, W. (2006). Resource development for South African Bantu languages: computational morphological analysers and machine-readable lexicons. In Proceedings on the Workshop on Networking the Development of Language Resources for African Languages. 5th International Conference on Language Resources and Evaluation. pp. 38–43.
Butler, L., & Van Volkinburg, H. (2007). Review of Fieldworks Language Explorer (FLEx). *Language Documentation & Conservation*, 1(1), 100–106.
Chebanne, A. (2008). A sociolinguistic perspective of the indigenous communities of Botswana. African Studies Monographs 29(3): 93–118.
Department of Education. (1988). Setswana Terminology and Orthography No 4. Pretoria: Government Printers.
Eiselen, R., & Puttkammer, M. (2014). Developing text resources for ten South African languages. In *Proceedings of the Ninth International Conference on Language Resources and Evaluation (LREC'14)*. 3698–3703.
Finlayson, R and M. Madiba. (2002). *The Intellectualisation of the Indigenous Languages of South Africa: Challenges and Prospects*. Current Issues in Language Planning. 3(1): 40–61.
Fletcher, W. H. (2007). Concordancing the web: promise and problems, tools and techniques. In *Corpus linguistics and the web* (25–45). Brill.
Grefenstette, Gregory & Julien Nioche. (2000) Estimation of English and non-English Language Use on the WWW. RIAO 2000, Paris, 12–14 April 2000. Retrieved 12 October 2001: http://www.xrce.xerox.com/research/mltt/publications/Documents/P19137/content/RIAO2000gref.pdf
Groenewald, H. J. (2009, March). Using technology transfer to advance automatic lemmatisation for Setswana. In *Proceedings of the First Workshop on Language Technologies for African Languages* (32–37).
Harran, M., & Olamijulo, C. (2014). Social media communication spaces to develop literacies in a higher education language classroom context. *South African Journal of Higher Education*, 28(2), 410–435.
Hatton, J. (2011). Software for Remote Dictionary Collaboration. *International Journal of Lexicography*, 24(4), 420–431.
Havránek, B. 1932. The Functions of Literary Language and its Cultivation. Hávranek, B. and M. Weingart (Eds.). A Prague School Reader on Esthetics, Literary Structure and Style: 32–84. Prague: Melantrich

Higby, D. (2013). tapping the brain for words. Macmillan Dictionary Blog, August 27, 2013. http://www.macmillandictionaryblog.com/tapping-the-brain-for-words

Hlophe, C., Mgabhi, T.E., Dlamini-Nkomo, B. and Tsabedze, D.S. (2015). *Umphandza: sichazamagama sesiSwati* CASAS: Cape Town

Howe, J. (2006). The rise of crowdsourcing. *Wired magazine, 14*(6), 1–4.

Internet World Stats. (2022). Internet world stats: usage and population statistics. https://www.internetworldstats.com/

Janson, T and Tsonope, J. (1991). *The Birth of a National Language.* Gaborone: Heinemann.

Khumalo, L., & Nkomo, D. (2022). The Intellectualization of African Languages through Terminology and Lexicography: Methodological Reflections with Special Reference to Lexicographic Products of the University of KwaZulu-Natal. *Lexikos, 32*(2), 133–157.

Liu, Y. (2010). Social media tools as a learning resource. *Journal of Educational Technology Development and Exchange (JETDE), 3*(1), 8.

Malekani, A. W., & Kavishe, G. (2018). The role of Institutional Repositories in making lost or hidden cultures accessible, a study across four African University Libraries.

Mikami, Y., Zavarsky, P., Rozan, M. Z. A., Suzuki, I., Takahashi, M., Maki, T., Ayob, I. N., Boldi, P., Santini, M., & Vigna, S. (2005). The language observatory project (LOP). In *Special interest tracks and posters of the 14th international conference on World Wide Web* (pp. 990–991).

Moore, A. & Murray, B.H. (2000). Sizing the Internet. July 10, 2000. Arlington, VA: Cyveillance, Inc. Retrieved: 8 February 2022 from the World Wide Web: http://www.cyveillance.com/resources/7921S_Sizing_the_Internet.pdf

Mukwevho, N. J. (2017). *Enhancing visibility and accessibility of public archives repositories in South Africa* (Doctoral dissertation).

Nishanbaev, I. (2020). A web repository for geo-located 3D digital cultural heritage models. *Digital Applications in Archaeology and Cultural Heritage, 16*, e00139.

O'Neill, E. T., Lavoie, B. F., Bennett, R., Staples, T., Wayland, R., Payette, S., ... & Rudner, L. M. (2003). Trends in the Evolution of the Public Web, 1998–2002; The Fedora Project: An Open-source Digital Object Repository Management System; State of the Dublin Core Metadata Initiative, April 2003; Preservation Metadata; How Many People Search the ERIC Database Each Day? *D-Lib Magazine, 9*(4), n4.

Onibere, E. Morgan, A.S., Busang, E.M. and Mpoeleng, D. (2001). Human-computer interfaces design issues for a multi-lingual English-speaking country - Botswana. *Interacting with Computers* 13:497–512.

Osborn, D. (2010). *African languages in a digital age: Challenges and opportunities for indigenous computing.* Human Science Research Council Press: Cape Town

Osborn, D. Z. (2006). African languages and information and communication technologies: Literacy, access, and the future. In *Selected proceedings of the 35th annual conference on African linguistics* (86–93). Summerville: Cascadilla Proceedings Project.

Otlogetswe, T., & Chebanne, A. (2018). Setswana. In *The Social and Political History of Southern Africa's Languages* (187–221). Palgrave Macmillan, London.

Otlogetswe, T. J. (2009/2010). The Setswana Google Search. The translated version is available at www.google.co.bw and www.google.co.za

Otlogetswe, T. J. (2010). Re-thinking the position of Setswana at university. *LONAKA: Journal of Learning and Teaching*, 1–8.

Otlogetswe, T. J. (2012). *Tlhalosi ya Medi ya Setswana* (Setswana monolingual Dictionary). Medi Publishing, Gaborone.

Otlogetswe, T. J. (2015). *Dipoeletso-ditumamodumo tsa Setswana: A dictionary of Setswana alliteration and Consonance.* CASAS Book Series No. 116. Centre for Advanced Studies of African Society: Cape Town.

Otlogetswe, T. J. (2016). *Setswana Oxford Living Dictionary.* Oxford University Press: Oxford: https://tn.oxforddictionaries.com.

Otlogetswe, T. J. and Scannell, K. 2015. The Setswana Firefox spellchecker. https://addons.mozilla.org/en-US/firefox/addon/tswana-spell-checker/.

Patel, M., Walczak, K., Giorgini, F., & White, M. (2004). A Cultural Heritage Repository as Source for Learning Materials. In *VAST* (213–222).

Perlin, R. (2012). Review of WeSay, A Tool for Collaborating on Dictionaries with Non-Linguists. *Language Documentation & Conservation*, 6, 181–186.

Plisson, J., Lavrac, N., & Mladenic, D. (2004). A rule based approach to word lemmatization. In *Proceedings of IS. 3*, 83–86.

Prah, K. 2017. The intellectualization of African languages for higher education. *Alternation* 24(2), 215–225.

Rogers, C. (2010). Review of fieldworks language explorer (flex) 3.0. *Language Documentation & Conservation*, 4, 78–84.

Rundell, M. (2016). Dictionaries and crowdsourcing, wikis and user-generated content. *International handbook of modern lexis and lexicography*, 1–16.

Scannell, K. P. (2022). Managing Data from Social Media: The Indigenous Tweets Project. *The Open Handbook of Linguistic Data Management*, 481.

Scannell, K., & Otlogetswe, T. J. (2004). The Setswana Open-Office spellchecker Freely available here: http://pkgs.org/opensuse-11.4/opensuse-oss-x86_64/aspell-tn-1.0.1-24.1.x86_64.rpm.html

Schwab, K. (2016). The Fourth Industrial Revolution. Penguin and the World Economic Forum (WEF), United Kingdom.

Sibayan, B.P. (1999). The Intellectualization of Filipino and other Essays on Education and Sociolinguistics. Manila: The Linguistic Society of the Philippines. De La Salle University Press.

Trye, D., Keegan, T. T., Mato, P., & Apperley, M. (2022). Harnessing Indigenous Tweets: The Reo Māori Twitter corpus. *Language resources and evaluation*, 1–40.

van Pinxteren, B. (2017). African Languages in Wikipedia–A Glass Half Full or Half Empty? *Available at SSRN 2939146.*

Webb, V. 2004. Language policy in post-apartheid South Africa in J.W. Tollefson and A.B.M. Tsui. *Medium of instruction policies: Which agenda? Whose agenda?* London: Lawrence Erlbaum Associates Publishers.

Winchester, S. (2002). *The surgeon of Crowthorne: a tale of murder, madness and the Oxford English Dictionary.* Penguin UK.

Zourou, K. (2012). On the attractiveness of social media for language learning: A look at the state of the art. *Alsic. Apprentissage des langues et systèmes d'information et de communication*, 15(1).

CHAPTER 21

Dancing in the Digital Domain: Mas, Media and Covid 19 in Caribbean Carnival

Alpha Obika

The ability or inability of societies to master technology, and particularly technologies that are strategically decisive in each historical period, largely shapes their destiny.
—Castells (1996, p. 7)

Introduction

This chapter discusses how Carnival 2021 in Trinidad and Tobago resorted to the use of digital technology tools of everyday life, in the face of challenges posed to its much-anticipated physical events by Covid 19, and a declaration by the country's Prime Minister that the event was to be cancelled. Several artistes and leaders of the Carnival movement opposed the idea of cancelling Carnival, with one declaring:

> Tell them, tell them keep it virtual
> No don't stop the Carnival. (Yearwood, 2020)

In the end, while street parades, competitions and mas were not performed in the usual 'in person' format, numerous virtual representations of the event took place. The chapter examines the everyday digital tools that came into play, to enable a version of Carnival 2021 to be staged, through what this chapter describes as 'dancing in the digital domain'.

A. Obika (✉)
The University of the West Indies, Kingston, Jamaica

THE RESISTANCE

In October 2020 on the eve of Trinidad and Tobago's 2021 Carnival season, Soca artiste Olatunji Yearwood released a song titled "Don't Stop Carnival":

> Local regional into global,
> No don't stop the Carnival
> Corona shell down Carnival,
> No don't stop the Carnival. (Yearwood, 2020)

The song's chorus speaks to the impact of the covid-19 pandemic on plans to stage the annual carnival celebrations. A prominent feature of the song is a direct appeal to the government that carnival not be stopped as a result of the pandemic which threatened to 'shell' and ultimately shelve plans to stage the festivities in 2021. On September 28, 2020, Trinidad and Tobago's Prime Minister, Keith Rowley, announced:

> I see no future for Carnival in Trinidad and Tobago in the months ahead and today I could put everybody on notice that unless there's some dramatic wind that will blow across us whereby Christmas the pandemic would be a thing of the past Carnival in T&T in 2021 is not on. (Trinidad and Tobago Guardian, September 28, 2020)

The announcement by Prime Minister Rowley was widely criticized by 'carnivalists' who argued that the government lacked an understanding of the vital role carnival plays in the cultural and economic development of the twin-island state. In the words of artiste and actor Muhammad Muwakil, "Is over 400 years this thing [carnival] survived under all kinda pressure and strain. Genetically speaking, I'm saying: it is impossible to cancel carnival" (Muwakil, 2020). Using poetic verse and dressed like a Pierrot Grenade,[1] Muwakil's message was released via his Facebook page one day after the Prime Minister's announcement. Valmiki Maharaj, a masquerade band leader, echoed similar sentiments about the threat to cancel carnival 2021: "You cannot cancel what can't be cancelled. It is within us. None of us in the industry were surprised by the announcement but when it came it was still hard to digest" (Haseley, 2020). Maharaj views the situation as a crisis and as an opportunity to innovate and spark an evolution in the way carnival is produced and experienced. While expressing skepticism about the efficacy of a 'virtual' carnival, he agrees that technology and media will be paramount to the transformation. All three carnival artists (Yearwood, Muwakil and Maharaj) highlight a cultural resilience

---

[1] The Pierrot Grenade is a "a finely dressed masquerader and deeply learned scholar" who "delights in displaying his knowledge and ability to spell any word". The character is dressed in a costume made with "multicoloured pieces of cloth" (National Carnival Commission of Trinidad and Tobago, 2020).

necessary to allow the festival to evolve beyond the physical limits imposed by the pandemic, as it has weathered challenging periods throughout its history.

Yearwood's song *Don't Stop Carnival* shows an understanding of the dire circumstances that could prevent the physical festival from taking place, while providing a solution to "keep the carnival virtual":

> No don't stop the Carnival
> Tell them, tell them keep it virtual
> No don't stop the Carnival. (Yearwood, 2020)

The artiste views technology as an alternative modality that had escaped policymakers and government officials, who appear uncertain of the way forward for the festival during the pandemic. While the government was steadfast in its decision not to invest any funds in the staging of Carnival 2021, a virtual carnival of sorts did indeed take place. According to Dowrich-Phillips (2021) "There may be no parades or actual fetes happening in Trinidad and Tobago for Carnival 2021 but the annual festival will be celebrated in the virtual space thanks to Covid-19". This virtual and alternative initiative was driven by many of the artistes, event promoters, private sector sponsors, technology providers and media houses. "From fetes to concerts, private events … [were staged] in 2021 across various virtual platforms" (Dowrich-Phillips, 2021).

This chapter focuses, therefore, on the staging of virtual carnival celebrations in Trinidad in 2021. Data were obtained from an examination of flyers and posters placed online for the carnival activities held during that season. The recorded live streams for those events that were circulated via social media (YouTube, Instagram, Facebook) were examined, and other digital platforms were also observed. The streaming approaches were mapped to assess the impact of technology on the staging of Trinidad Carnival 2021 and the potential for such digital innovations to continue in the future. It would appear that with or without Covid 19, sections of the Carnival movement had embarked on a process of deploying digital tools that would be used in their everyday life towards alternative or parallel celebrations online.

To gain a deeper understanding of the tools that were used in the virtual Carnival 2021, content analyses of the online flyers, digital posters, websites and online platforms were conducted, guided by the following research questions: Which online platforms were used to stage the event? Which organizations staged virtual events? Was any fee charged for access to the event? Who were the sponsors listed on the promotional material? Were any traditional media houses involved in the staging, sponsorship or broadcast of the event? Ultimately this chapter will seek to identify the technologies used in Carnival 2021 and to discuss future impacts of technology on the staging of the Trinidad and Tobago Carnival.

Carnival and Cultural Resilience

The Oxford Dictionary defines resilience as the "ability to recover quickly after something unpleasant such as shock" or the process of "returning to its original shape after being bent, stretched, or pressed" (Oxford University Press, 2022). Building on this concept, cultural resilience can be viewed as "The capability of a cultural system (consisting of cultural processes in relevant communities) to absorb adversity, deal with change and continue to develop" (Holtorf, 2018, p. 639). Culture itself, being both tangible and intangible, encompasses the full gamut of human experience when shock or pressure is applied to it. Certainly, the Covid-19 pandemic can be categorized as a global shock that caused physical, socio-economic, political, social, psychological and cultural trauma. The reverberations from the pandemic were especially felt by volatile economies in Small Island Developing States (SIDS), where key sectors like tourism and entertainment suffered devastating losses.

According to the United Nations Conference on Trade and Development (UNCTAD):

> In the wake of the COVID-19 pandemic, SIDS suffered an estimated 70% drop in travel receipts in 2020. The UN World Tourism Organization estimates that it could take up to four years for international tourism, an essential source of jobs and livelihoods, to recover to levels observed in 2019. (2021)

One can imagine that in some SIDS the decline has been greater than 70%, negatively affecting lives and livelihoods in the process. Against this backdrop of decline must be viewed attempts to stage Trinidad Carnival 2021. Festival tourism and entertainment are particularly important as significant contributors to the overall economies of countries in the Caribbean. Nurse (2007, p. 235) observes that "In many territories the peak in tourist arrivals coincides with some event, particularly a musical or carnival festival." Trinidad and Tobago is one of the Caribbean territories singled out for having a viable festival tourism product that attracted an estimated 32,000 visitors in 1998, spending an approximately USD$14.08 million (Nurse, 2001). On the eve of the pandemic hitting Trinidad in 2020, Lopez (2021a & 2021b) reported that the Trinidad and Tobago carnival welcomed an estimated 38,000 international visitors, spending approximately USD$68 million. It is anticipated that with the proposed cancellation of the physical carnival in 2021, most if not all this income would be lost. The idea of counting on its resilience as a means of recouping some losses and continuing a revered tradition loomed large in the minds of those who wanted to "keep it virtual". But what is the background and historical context that gave rise to this Carnival in the first place? From all accounts, it is a carnival that was born out of adversity and trauma. A brief look into its history tells a story of cultural resilience that makes its evolution and as well as a digital and physical resurgence seemingly inevitable outcomes.

Carnival—Origins and Challenges

After over 300 years of chattel slavery in the Caribbean, Emancipation in 1834 marked an opportunity for the formerly enslaved Africans to express themselves as free human beings. According to the National Carnival Commission (NCC) "Africans started to participate in the festivities from 1833 after the Emancipation Bill was passed" (NCC, 2020). In fact, Carnival during pre-emancipation reflected the hierarchical and inhumane system of slavery, where the white planter class dominated celebrations and "Africans and coloureds (persons of mixed race) were forbidden by law to participate in street festivities" (NALIS, 2022). Despite this barrier, the Africans found creative ways to participate in their own version of the celebrations. Cultural resilience was further exhibited where Trinidad and Tobago Carnival survived cancellations due to the Water Riots of 1903,[2] World War I and World War II and a postponement as a result of the 1972 polio outbreak.[3] Even the Ebola virus "which ravaged several countries in West Africa" in 2014 and caused panic globally did not stop the celebration of the festival in 2015 (NCC, 2020). The government boldly launched Carnival 2015 and took the following position: "We have taken an active role and will work alongside our partners to spare no effort in ensuring that Ebola does not reach our shores or that if it does, it is contained" (NCC, 2020).

And then came the Covid-19[4] pandemic. Although Carnival 2020 was not directly affected by Covid-19, the virus spread rapidly across the planet and by January 2020, the Director-General of the World Health Organization (WHO) "declared the novel coronavirus outbreak a public health emergency of international concern (PHEIC), WHO's highest level of alarm" (WHO, 2022b). More than two years later in March 2022, the WHO Health Emergency Dashboard is reporting that the world has experienced "446,511,318 confirmed cases of covid-19, including 6,004,421 deaths" (WHO, 2022c). The collapse of health care systems also mirrors a socio-economic catastrophe for small and vulnerable nations, particularly Small Island Developing States (SIDS). A June 2021 report from the United Nations Conference on Trade and Development (UNCTAD) summarized that "SIDS face an uphill battle as

---

[2] The Water Riots of 1903 was "a protest against the imposition of an increased water rate upon the residents of Port-of-Spain". In the immediate aftermath of the tragic event "16 people were killed on the spot or died of their wounds through the use of 'authorised firing' and 43 others treated at hospital for injuries received" (The National Archives, n.d.).

[3] The polio outbreak of 1972 caused the festivities to be shifted to May of that year (The National Trust of Trinidad and Tobago, 2021).

[4] According to the World Health Organization (WHO), covid-19, also known as coronavirus, "Is an infectious disease caused by the SARS-CoV-2 virus" (2022a). "The virus can spread from an infected person's mouth or nose in small liquid particles when they cough, sneeze, speak, sing or breathe" (WHO, 2022a).

they strive to recover from the impact of the COVID-19 crisis amid vulnerabilities worsened by the pandemic"[5] (UNCTAD, 2021).

Despite the mounting health, economic and social crisis faced by Trinidad and Tobago, Carnival 2021 was staged virtually, with many events utilizing the digital technologies for the first time, reaching audiences at home and abroad. It is important to note that the government was not directly involved in the 'unofficial' staging of the 2021 virtual Carnival in Trinidad, as seen from a statement by the Chairman of the National Carnival Commission (NCC), Mr. Winston 'Gypsy' Peters: "We [The NCC] are not planning any virtual events the way that the private promoters or whoever are planning" (Doughty, 2020). The former Minister of Arts and Multiculturalism (Peters) was also quoted as saying Trinidad and Tobago "Can't have a virtual Carnival, as that was an oxymoron" (Doughty, 2020). 'Carnivalists' and private sector stakeholders proceeded to stage a broad range of virtual events utilizing various combinations of digital everyday technology and traditional media to broadcast and commercialize the activities. In so doing, they made clear that decisions on culture were not the exclusive preserve of government, but that citizens and available technologies can provide alternative routes to meeting certain needs in the country's cultural life.

Trinidad and Tobago would not be the only Caribbean country to stage virtual carnival celebrations in 2021. Cayman Islands, St. Kitts and Nevis and St. Lucia staged official 'virtual carnivals', whilst some of the other traditional destinations staged unofficial 'virtual' carnival celebrations: Crop Over (in Barbados), Vincy Mas (in St. Vincent and the Grenadines) and Spice Mas (in Grenada). In the midst of a Covid-19 pandemic, the cultural resilience displayed by these and other SIDS in the Caribbean, must be acknowledged. It is important that the role of digital technology be critically examined in relation to the festival tourism and the changing process of event management. The innovations utilized out of necessity could possibly be the key to unlocking new global audiences in the increasingly interconnected digital world.

KEEP IT VIRTUAL—TECHNOLOGY AND THE EVOLUTION OF TRINIDAD AND TOBAGO CARNIVAL

While there is no concrete data on the number of virtual events staged during Trinidad Carnival 2021, an unofficial survey of entertainment websites, such as visitTrinidad.com, CaribbeanEntertainmentHub.com and TriniJungleJuice.com, online daily newspapers, such as Newsday, Guardian and Trinidad Express, revealed that approximately 27 soca events took place from January 1 to February 28, 2021. All the events were planned and executed by a mixture of corporate entities, schools, cultural organizations, media houses and artistes. While the Trinidad and Tobago government clearly outlined a policy of

---

[5] The UNCTAD Report indicated that 'shocks' were felt in the areas of trade, the economy, environment, health and the population (UNCTAD, 2021).

non-involvement in carnival festivities, the Ministry of Tourism, Culture and the Arts sponsored three of the events.[6] Highlighting these events are significant as an indication of the historical relationship that the government has had with events aligned to the protection of cultural heritage. Twenty-two of the other events can be categorized as commercial endeavours, namely fetes and concerts. The final two events are a calypso tent[7] and audiovisual theatrical production with music and carnival elements.[8] All 27 events under study here were staged with virtual components, reaching local and international audiences. It must be stated that there are possibly other carnival events that were staged but may have been missed by the researcher due to their lack of online visibility and promotion. Additionally, there were possibly other virtual soca events that took place outside of Trinidad during the January to February 2021 period that were not included in this population. The study also focused exclusively on Trinidad and did not include any events that may have taken place in Tobago.

Carnival as a cultural product was tested for its resilience and ability to adapt to the circumstances of the global covid-19 pandemic. Whilst carnival lovers and aficionados could not experience the festival in its traditional in-person sense, the 2021 season saw the introduction of multiple variations and combinations of strategies to stage events. Common among all events was the utilization of online streaming either via websites, social media sites or media house simulcasts. In some cases, events utilized all digital options to reach audiences locally and internationally. Of the 27 events surveyed, 13 utilized YouTube, while 9 used Facebook and 6 employed Instagram for streaming. Social media has been one of the driving forces of global digitization and the reliance on these platforms made sense for widespread delivery and access to streamed content. In all instances where social media platforms were used, the events were free to the public. This meant that access to the streaming technology and internet were the only requirements for enjoying the carnival event. Many of the social media sites were driven to users via cell phones. It essentially meant that the carnival experience was accessed in the palm of cellphone users.

The country of Trinidad and Tobago has been one of the Caribbean front runners with its digital infrastructure and access to technology. In 2020 the twin-island state reportedly had a cellphone penetration rate of 136% (Kepios, 2020), while "In June 2021, mobile phones made up 46.25% of the web traffic" (Statista, 2022). The use of social media by event organizers to stream events served to democratize access, eliminating barriers of cost usually associated with participating in soca fetes during carnival. The use of social media is

---

[6] The three events are the Chutney Soca Monarch, The International Soca Monarch and Pan Trinbago's Pan Is Spirit.
[7] A Calypso Tent is a physical location where calypsonians perform primarily calypsoes, mainly during the annual Carnival celebrations in Trinidad and Tobago.
[8] This event is titled *Lavway: Our Story*. It is a film that tells the story of carnival in Trinidad and Tobago.

also significant due to the ability of users to experience events wherever they are and communicate using the chat feature.

This ability to communicate digitally engenders an imagined community, based on what could be considered digital 'citizenship'. Two of the pillars in Benedict Anderson's 'imagined community' (1991) are "production and productive relations (capitalism)" and, "technology of communications (print)" (p. 43). The virtual staging of Trinidad carnival brings together cultural production and technology, albeit digital technology. Netizens were able to link with carnivalists at home and in the diaspora, forming a virtual carnival network.

While the national borders of Trinidad and Tobago remained closed to international air traffic during the season, carnival chasers[9] were still able to dance in the digital domain, linking with friends, relatives and strangers to enjoy a new virtual experience. The boundary between technology user and carnival participant became blurred with a synergy creating a new experience and carnival netizens. While Anderson (1991) describes a community that is 'imagined' because "The members of even the smallest nation will never know most of their fellow members, meet them, or even hear them" (p. 6), the virtual diasporic carnival community fostered 'real' communication. Far from imagined, some event organizers combined social media with other online platforms and apps to deliver the production to carnival netizens.

In addition to YouTube, Facebook and Instagram, four events utilized the D'Music app by telecommunication company Digicel. This app has many benefits, including access to a "catalogue of over 45 million local and international songs", access to live concerts in the app and use of the app without data (Google, 2022). While the innovation certainly has capitalist motives, access to live carnival concerts by customers without data on their devices ushers in a new level of digital democracy thereby empowering the netizen. Events such as *Black 2 Blue: Backyard Jam*, *Patrice Roberts: Strength of a Woman* and *CHANCE: The Origins* were accessible to anyone in the world with the D'Music app.

The marketing exposure to the artistes featured in the aforementioned concerts would be felt primarily across the Caribbean and Central America where the app is available. 'Carnival in the palm of your hands' must be part of the digital future of the festival. Digicel has taken the initiative to innovate, albeit with commercial imperatives. Policy makers and government officials must recognize the opportunity to integrate everyday digital technology with the traditional carnival experience to increase the footprint in the Caribbean diaspora and beyond.

In Trinidad Carnival 2021 some of the event planners chose to utilize the websites of host institutions to stream live. Two such events were the *Flight of the Virtual Phoenix* by Holy Name Convent Port of Spain and *Iz WE Carnival Week* by Kes the Band. The use of websites allowed for the extensive promotion of the brand beyond the event itself. In the case of Holy Name Convent, the

---

[9] Carnival chasers are persons who travel to multiple carnivals around the world.

secondary school capitalized on the opportunity to solicit donations on their website from persons viewing the event. This was not the only secondary school to get involved in the virtual carnival. Events by Fatima College (*Fatima STRIVE ON*) and Trinity College (*Soca In Moka: Uploaded*) were staged to raise funds for the schools while *Xperience Fete* was staged to support the San Fernando Boys' Roman Catholic School Past Students' Association. It is possible that other educational institutions staged virtual carnival events or benefited from the proceeds of these events. The virtual carnival presented a unique opportunity to unite current students with the alumni association and carnival lovers worldwide. A follow-up study could investigate the financial viability of the virtual events but is outside of the scope of this research undertaking.

Kes the Band's website was used in conjunction with their extensive social media following globally to promote a series of concerts staged during the carnival season. The band's Instagram page has 320,000 followers while the Facebook page has 285,000 followers, as at April 1, 2022. The followers' information is being captured more than 1 year later but highlights the capacity for an integrated digital marketing approach to virtual events that can be lucrative and successful. *Iz WE Carnival Week* included a combination of free and paid events which also utilized traditional media, in CNC3 television. Interestingly, many of the events during the virtual carnival strategically combined traditional media and digital streaming, in a process which Dunn (2013, p. 3), in another context, describes as "conjoint approaches" to media output and exposure.

Rise of Traditional Media?

With the rise of digital technology and internet infrastructure proliferating in the global market, small island developing states (SIDS) like Trinidad and Tobago have also benefitted. Citizens are now more connected locally and internationally. Traditional media has had to adapt to the technological changes and greater audience demands for digital content. In *The slow death of legacy media*, Desjardins (2016) made the following observation:

> Over the last five to ten years, people have been talking about how the newspaper, magazine, or radio station would become all but obsolete. And while certainly things have changed in all of these industries, it's clear that there has not been a full paradigm shift yet. (2016)

In the middle of a global pandemic in 2021, traditional media continued to make its presence felt ensuring its relevance as audiences navigate the digital landscape with increased technical prowess. The survey of the indicated 27 virtual carnival events in Trinidad in 2021 revealed that 16 utilized traditional media to live stream and broadcast their events. Twelve of the virtual events used a television station and 7 streamed via radio. CNC3 Television was involved in 8 of the 12 events, making it the most visible and digitally engaged television station of Trinidad Carnival 2021. CNC3 Television is part of the Guardian Media Limited[10] conglomerate owned by locally based corporate giant ANSA McAL.[11] The television station has a mandate to be "dominant on digital platforms and social media, through its own website (cnc3.co.tt)" and also has an app available in the Google Play Store (CNC3 Television, 2018–2019). CNC3 Television has integrated digital technology and software to adapt to the needs of the tech savvy citizens being served. Joining CNC3 Television were Trinidad and Tobago Television (popularly referred to as TTT), TV6 and Synergy TV.

WACK 90.1FM was heavily involved in the 2021 carnival season streaming 4 of the 7 events covered by stations. In fact, in 2 of the 4 events WACK 90.1FM was also the promoter, planning and implementing the cultural activities. The mandate of the radio station is to play music indigenous to Trinidad and Tobago. In addition to the broadcasts on the FM band, the station offers free and pay-per-view streaming services. In many instances, the broadcasts and streams operate simultaneously making WACK 90.1FM a critical component of the local radio landscape reaching local audiences as well as the 'Trinbagonian' diaspora in North America and beyond.

Some of the events streamed during the 2021 carnival season includes a steelpan concert,[12] a traditional calypso tent[13] and a soca dance music concert. While calypso and steelpan are considered less commercial in the context of Trinidad Carnival, WACK 90.1FM is playing a critical role in showcasing and promoting local music and culture through diverse outlets. The data provided on WACK 90.1FM scratches the surface of the full-scale and full-time involvement of the station in Trinidad and Tobago's culture beyond carnival. Significant in the operation of the radio station is the infusion of digital technology and online streaming in every aspect of the service delivery. The station is notably dedicated to the promotion of indigenous content. The digital innovations adopted will help to sustain the relevance and viability of the radio station in a fiercely competitive field. It is significant that Trinidad and Tobago, with a population of 1.3 million people, has 36 radio stations on the FM band (Telecommunications Authority of Trinidad and Tobago, 2014). With the rise of digital and online radio, it is expected that digital technological innovation and multicasting could be among the factors that allow these stations to thrive.

---

[10] Guardian Media Limited owns the Trinidad and Tobago Guardian (print), CNC3 Television (television), the TBC Network (consisting of seven radio stations) and The Big Board Company (electronic billboards).

[11] ANSA McAL is a "Conglomerate in the Caribbean region with seventy-three companies spanning seven sectors in over eight territories" (ANSA McAL, 2017).

[12] *Pan Is Spirit Concert Series* by Pan Trinbago (the organizing body for steelpan in Trinidad and Tobago).

[13] *Kaiso House Tent* by the Trinbago Unified Calypsonian Organization (TUCO). TUCO is organizing body for calypsonians.

Soca in Moka: Virtual Reality Meets Trinidad Carnival

With the innovations of Carnival 2021 as a point of departure, it has also become evident that many other digital media innovations are underway in the country. One such is an event called 'Soca in Moka'. On January 17, 2021, The Trinity College Soka in Moka Foundation staged the '*Soka in Moka: Uploaded*' virtual event. This event stands out as a trailblazing venture which wholeheartedly embraced the mantra of digital innovation. Trinidad Carnival 2021 saw event promoters using various combinations: from virtual only events; to blended events using limited live, in-person, audiences and streaming via social media and digital platforms; to blended simulcast events utilizing live audiences and streaming simultaneously across multiple traditional and social media platform. Thus far we have covered an array of events utilizing multiple everyday digital media combined with traditional outlets. *Soka in Moka: Uploaded* stands out because it introduced virtual reality (VR) to the traditional fete experience in Trinidad Carnival. According to the Virtual Reality Society (2017), virtual reality is:

> A three-dimensional, computer-generated environment which can be explored and interacted with by a person. That person becomes part of this virtual world or is immersed within this environment and whilst there, is able to manipulate objects or perform a series of actions.

The 'reality' created is generated by computer software and technology, enabling event planners to conceptualize and orchestrate the experience of the participant. Partnering with online streaming company YellarTV.com, the event allowed patrons to "watch the show on their devices, as well as using their mouse to move around to different parts of the virtual venue" (Lindo, 2021). With the use of virtual reality googles, patrons could get a more immersive experience. While the event had some difficulties with levels of security and internet connectivity that eventually led to the organizers issuing a formal apology and full re-broadcast, *Soka in Moka: Uploaded* attracted approximately 300 patrons, each paying USD$15 (Dowrich-Phillips, 2021). The shortcomings of the first virtual reality carnival event are dwarfed by the daring attempt to innovate and bring interactive technology and digital culture into one mold.

Postman (1992) suggested that "technologies create the ways in which people perceive reality" (p. 21). Virtual reality has the potential to allow netizens to experience almost anything the mind can conceive. For the creative industries and the carnival sector in particular, the impact of digital technology can be transformative allowing netizens to travel to Rio de Janeiro for Brazil Carnival, New Orleans for Mardi Gras and Port of Spain for Trinidad Carnival, without leaving the comfort of their homes, or rather the comfort of their devices. This is a virtual process that we may call 'travel without traveling'. With sustained investment in an improved internet infrastructure, increased digital literacy among netizens and event promoters willing to take risk, the

Carnival experience beyond the Covid-19 pandemic will never be the same. However, lessons must be learned from event organizers, government and participants alike. *Soka in Moka: Uploaded* has produced an opportunity that must be exploited and strongly considered when seeking to transform the carnival experience using digital technology.

What Market Failure? The Private Sector Steps-Up

The question of whether the country's population, as the paying patrons of Carnival events would have been ready to patronize a market of virtual carnival events arises as part of this discussion. It was perhaps a fear of 'market failure' that propelled the government to attempt to cancel Carnival 2021 under Covid 19 pandemic conditions. Market failure "is a situation defined by an inefficient distribution of goods and services in the free market" (Investopedia, 2023). Situations of market failure usually encourage governments to get involved to correct the imbalances and inequities to ensure social and economic cohesion. Applied to the cultural and creative industries, governments have typically had to subsidize artforms that were not supported commercially by corporate entities or patrons.

In Trinidad and Tobago, cultural policy around carnival has been managed primarily through the National Carnival Commission (NCC). NCC is the governing body responsible for the planning, implementation and sustainable development of Carnival. Specific stakeholders[14] receive annual subventions from the NCC for their operations, generally because most of the events and activities that are more traditional and less commercial tend to obtain insufficient financial support from the private sector. However, when in 2021 the government took the decision not to stage carnival, the private sector stepped in and sponsored 21 of the 27 events under investigation in this study. Through the Ministry of Tourism, Culture and the Arts, 4 events were eventually sponsored by the government, 3 of which had historically been the recipients of funding.[15] The 4 government sponsored events also received sponsorship from the private sector., and all the events enjoyed audience support and patronage where required.

The role of traditional media houses cannot be overstated when examining the substantial support provided to the carnival events as organizers, media outlets, sponsors and marketers. Digital platforms and social media were the driving forces disseminating the carnival experience to device users. Traditional media houses connected the creative industry to the sponsors, serving as a legitimizing force for many of the carnival events that were aired and streamed

---

[14] Some of the institutions receiving the largest subventions are Pan Trinbago (for steelpan), the Trinbago Unified Calypsonians Organisation (for calypso) and the Trinidad and Tobago Carnival Bands Association (for mas and the masquerade).

[15] *The International Soca Monarch, Chutney Soca Monarch, Pan Is Spirit Concert Series* and *Soca in White: Artistes for Artistes.*

live, many for the first time. In fact, media houses like WACK 90.1FM and CNC3 Television conducted simulcasts while also driving live streams to their social media accounts, to increase the digital footprint.

In Trinidad Carnival 2021, the media showed up in a big way, which augers well for the future of the virtual cultural product and the stakeholders who depend on it. For many international 'carnivalists' who could not make the annual pilgrimage to Trinidad for the festival, Carnival 2021 via online tools and personal devices, was a breath of fresh air, a digital experience that made them feel connected. Carnival as it is traditionally celebrated may have been cancelled in 2021, but the festival lived on in the virtual space.

Several of the carnival event hosts relied on a business model that involved both corporate sponsorship and a paywall, with stipulated costs of access for participants. Of the 27 events surveyed, 18 were free events to participants. The cost of access was therefore absorbed by the organizers through the acquisition of sponsorship both from the public and private sectors. For the events that did have an access fee, some were charged in US dollars whilst others were charged in local currency, the Trinidad and Tobago (TT) dollar. The prices in USD ranged from $15 to $45, while events charged in TT dollars ranged from $200 to $500. One consistent feature of the events charged in US dollars was that they tended to be fully virtual events, whilst the TT dollar events had a limited live audience in addition to a virtual stream which was sometimes pay-per-view. Seven of the 27 events setup mechanisms for participants to donate or contribute funds via text message or dedicated online platforms. Events like Fatima College's *Fatima STRIVE ON* and Holy Name Convent Port of Spain's *Flight of the Virtual Phoenix* facilitated donations to the school via their institutional webpages, while other events used Fundmetnt.com and text messaging providers Bmobile and Digicel for contributions. Future studies on this topic could examine the viability of online and text messaging platforms for subscriptions, contributions and donations.

Conclusion: Carnival's Digital Present and Future

Trinidad Carnival 2021 was not a perfect affair and did suffer from challenges including Covid 19 related obstacles. However, valuable lessons were demonstrated from the pioneering effort of the many virtual service providers, including the organizers of *Soka in Moka: Uploaded*. The challenges of the Trinity College Soka in Moka Foundation were also reflective of national issues with cyber security, internet bandwidth and digital literacy. The proliferation of cellphone technology is a positive step for digital inclusion but such statistics do not highlight national inefficiencies and service gaps that need to be addressed. Despite these challenges, the digital space is what came to the rescue of Carnival 2021 in Trinidad. While the government had a vision of Carnival limited to crowded in person events at physical event sites, an alternative vision by the artistes, innovators and business enterprises showed that digital everyday tools and even more advanced technologies such as VR, can be deployed in circumstances prohibiting large physical gatherings. The experience of Carnival 2021 also showed the possibility of 'conjoint' events integrating the physical with the virtual in the delivery of entertainment.

Event promoters and carnival stakeholders need to continue to be bold and to incorporate digital technology to transform the carnival experience. Dunn and Minto-Coy (2012) suggest that "In the Caribbean's quest for a new developmental strategy, a number of opportunities have presented themselves", particularly as it pertains to digital innovations and the creative industries (p. 33). It is precisely these opportunities for digital transformation and ultimately economic diversification that will make the integration of culture and technology a winning formula for developing countries like Trinidad and Tobago.

However, the lack of investment by the government at a time when the biggest opportunity for digital innovation presents itself, is part of the conundrum of mis-governance in the Caribbean. The government's position to 'cancel' carnival is symptomatic of a lack of knowledge and understanding of the value of the creative industries to boost the national economy while also promoting brand Trinidad and Tobago to the world.

Another dilemma highlighted by the government's decision to not invest in the virtual carnival is an inherent ignorance of the opportunity to bolster the national digital infrastructure and increase access and digital literacy among citizens. This public private partnership in a government supported virtual Carnival would have yielded even more positive results, contributing to sustained growth based on national needs rather than focusing solely on the commercial viability of events and activities.

In this regard, Dunn (2005) is correct in suggesting that the strategic use of technology by Caribbean countries can unlock sustainable development in the region:

> Cultures of the world, including those in the Caribbean, stand a better chance of withstanding the technological and information flows if they seek both to modify the global technologies and create their own products and services for economic, social and cultural development. (Dunn, 2005, p. 358)

In the globalized twenty-first century, technology must become synchronous with society and culture in the way that Castells (1996) recommends. The mastery of technology and its deliberate use to make sense of an increasingly digital and global existence requires that countries and sectors like the creative industries in Trinidad and Tobago be more integrated with new and emerging technological trends of virtual reality, artificial intelligence, 5G technology, blockchain, NFTs[16] and visibility in the metaverse.

Popularized by Facebook's bold move to rebrand as Meta, the metaverse can be described as "(a) combination of multiple elements of technology,

---

[16] NFT stand for Non-Fungible Token, which is A "digital asset that represents real-world objects like art, music, in-game items and videos" (Conti & Schmidt, 2022).

including virtual reality, augmented reality and video where users "live" within a digital universe" (Snider & Molina, 2021). Where Trinidad Carnival is concerned this presents an opportunity for stakeholders and policymakers to capitalize on this new virtual world. Conventional thinking will always prioritize the traditional face-to-face experience, which is arguably irreplaceable. The question is therefore not about technology replacing traditional culture, but how cultural expressions can be enhanced by digital technology, and transmitting it to a much wider audience than would be possible with the traditional experience.

With the emergence of an ever-increasing array of digital tools that are becoming part of people's everyday life, it is argued here that the future of digitally enhanced carnival is bright. Trinidad Carnival 2021 has long ended but the technological lessons and possibilities must not be forgotten as new paths and trajectories are plotted for cultural sustenance.

Carnival netizens must be allowed to 'travel without traveling', bridging barriers of distance and space to experience the wonders of the local culture via digital and online technology. 'Dancing in the digital domain' and 'meeting in the metaverse' must become part of the new cultural experience that will happen when stakeholders continue to experiment and innovate, while enhancing their own capacity and mastery of the emerging digital universe.

References

Anderson, B. (1991). *Imagined Communities: Reflections on the Origin and Spread of Nationalism*. London, New York: Verso.

ANSA McAL. (2017). *About Us*. Retrieved on March 31, 2022 from https://www.ansamcal.com/about-us/vision-mission/.

Castells, M. (1996). *The rise of the network society*. Massachusetts: Blackwell.

CNC3 Television. (2018–2019). *About*. Retrieved from https://www.cnc3.co.tt/about/.

Conti, R., & Schmidt, J. (2022, April 8). "What Is An NFT? Non-Fungible Tokens Explained". *Forbes*. Retrieved from https://www.forbes.com/advisor/investing/cryptocurrency/nft-non-fungible-token/.

Desjardins, J. (2016, October 10). "The slow death of legacy media". *Business Insider*. Retrieved from https://www.businessinsider.com/the-slow-death-of-legacy-media-2016-10.

Doughty, M. (2020, December 20). "No virtual NCC events for Carnival 2021". *Newsday*. Retrieved from https://newsday.co.tt/2020/12/29/no-virtual-ncc-events-for-carnival-2021/.

Dowrich-Phillips, L. (2021, January 18). "Soka in Moka Foundation promises full rebroadcast of event". *Loop (Digicel)*. Retrieved from https://tt.loopnews.com/content/soka-moka-foundation-promises-full-rebroadcast-event#:~:text=Soka%20in%20Moka%20Uploaded%20was,300%20people%20on%20the%20Livestream.

Dunn, H.S. (2005). "Globalisation from below: Caribbean cultures, global technologies and the WTO". In C. Ho & K. Nurse (Eds.), *Globalization, diaspora and Caribbean popular culture* (pp. 341–360). Kingston: Ian Randle.

Dunn, H.S. (2013). "Something Old, Something New ...": WikiLeaks and the Collaborating Newspapers—Exploring the Limits of Conjoint Approaches to Political Exposure. In B. Brevini, A. Hintz, & P. McCurdy (eds) *Beyond WikiLeaks*. Palgrave Macmillan, London. https://doi.org/10.1057/9781137275745_6.

Dunn, H.S., & Minto-Coy, I. D. (2012). "Caribbean ICT's: Strategic issues, challenges and opportunities". In H. Dunn (Ed.), *Ringtones of opportunity: Policy, technology and access in Caribbean communications* (pp. 19–39). Kingston: Ian Randle.

Google. (2022). "D'Music". *Google Play*. Retrieved on March 31, 2022 from https://play.google.com/store/apps/details?id=com.kuackmedia.digicel&hl=en&gl=US.

Haseley, M. (2020, October 6). "The Lost Tribe: 'Carnival cannot be cancelled'". *Newsday*. Retrieved from https://newsday.co.tt/2020/10/06/the-lost-tribe-carnvial-cannot-be-cancelled/.

Holtorf, C. (2018). "Embracing change: How cultural resilience is increased through cultural heritage". *World Archaeology*, 50(4), 639–650. https://doi.org/10.1080/00438243.2018.1510340.

Investopedia (2023, May 25). *"Market Failure: What It Is in Economics, Common Types, and Causes"*. Retrieved from https://www.investopedia.com/terms/m/marketfailure.asp.

Kepios. (2020, February 18). "Digital 2020: Trinidad and Tobago". *Datareportal*. Retrieved from https://datareportal.com/reports/digital-2020-trinidad-and-tobago#:~:text=The%20number%20of%20mobile%20connections%20in%20Trinidad%20and%20Tobago%20in,136%25%20of%20the%20total%20population.

Lindo, P. (2021, January 15). "Soka in Moka Uploaded on Sunday". *Trinidad and Tobago Newsday*. Retrieved from https://newsday.co.tt/2021/01/15/soka-in-moka-uploaded-on-sunday/.

Lopez, A. (2021a). "Inbound tourism volume during Trinidad & Tobago Carnival 2013-2020". *Statista*. Retrieved on March 21, 2022 from https://www.statista.com/statistics/789521/trinidad-tobago-carnival-number-tourist-arrivals/.

Lopez, A. (2021b). "Visitor spending at Trinidad and Tobago Carnival 2013–2020". *Statista*. Retrieved on September 22, 2021 from https://www.statista.com/statistics/814358/trinidad-tobago-carnival-visitor-spending/.

Muwakil, M. (2020, September 29). "Cancel Carnival?!." *Facebook*. Retrieved on April 1, 2022 from https://www.facebook.com/521305121/videos/10164595131980122/.

NALIS. (2022). *Carnival*. Retrieved on March 8, 2022 from https://www.nalis.gov.tt/Resources/Subject-Guide/Carnival.

National Carnival Commission of Trinidad and Tobago. (2020). *RE: Ebola Virus and Carnival 2015*. Retrieved from http://ncctt.org/new/index.php/news/223-re-ebola-virus-and-carnival-2015.html.

NCC. (2020). *History of Carnival and Its Elements*. Retrieved on March 7, 2022 from http://www.ncctt.org/new/index.php/carnival-history/history-of-carnival.html.

Nurse, K. (2001). *Festival Tourism in the Caribbean: An Economic Impact Assessment*. Washington, DC: Inter-American Development Bank.

Nurse, K. (2007). "Festival Tourism: The Case of Trinidad Carnival". In C. Jayawardena (Ed.), *Caribbean Tourism: More than Sun, Sand & Sea* (pp. 234–249). Jamaica: Ian Randle Publishers.

Oxford University Press. (2022). *Resilient*. Retrieved on March 21, 2022 from https://www.oxfordlearnersdictionaries.com/definition/english/resilient.

Postman, N. (1992). *Technopoly: The surrender of culture to technology*. New York: Vintage Books.

Snider, M., & Molina, B. (2021, November 10). "Everyone wants to own the metaverse including Facebook and Microsoft. But what exactly is it?". *USA Today*. Retrieved on March 12 from https://www.usatoday.com/story/tech/2021/11/10/metaverse-what-is-it-explained-facebook-microsoft-meta-vr/6337635001/.

Statista. (2022). *Share of web traffic in Trinidad and Tobago in June 2021, by device*. Retrieved on March 11, 2022 from https://www.statista.com/statistics/934678/trinidad-tobago-web-traffic-share-device/#statisticContainer.

Telecommunications Authority of Trinidad and Tobago. (2014). *FM Radio Broadcasting Services*. Retrieved from https://tatt.org.tt/RadioandTV/ListofRadioBroadcasters.aspx.

The National Archives. (n.d.). *The Trinidad Water Riots of 1903*. Retrieved on March 8, 2022 from http://blog.nationalarchives.gov.uk/the-trinidad-water-riots-of-1903/?fbclid=IwAR3-BVWabaGejM0vY2CHbMKcSHWZXHAzBl0-Ce9Clqn8ukjoJa3a37W4HVU#return-note-8269-3.

The National Trust of Trinidad and Tobago. (2021). *When Carnival Was Cancelled*. Retrieved on March 8, 2022 from https://nationaltrust.tt/cancelled-carnival/.

Trinidad and Tobago Guardian. (2020, September 28). *PM: Carnival 2021 is NOT on*. Retrieved on March 28, 2022 from https://www.guardian.co.tt/news/pm-carnival-2021-is-not-on-6.2.1223567.4df75c5443.

UNCTAD. (2021). *Small island developing states face uphill battle in COVID-19 recovery*. Retrieved on March 8, 2022 from https://unctad.org/news/small-island-developing-states-face-uphill-battle-covid-19-recovery.

Virtual Reality Society. (2017). *What is Virtual Reality?* Retrieved on April 8 from https://www.vrs.org.uk/virtual-reality/what-is-virtual-reality.html.

World Health Organization. (2022a). *Coronavirus disease (COVID-19)*. Retrieved on March 8, 2022 from https://www.who.int/health-topics/coronavirus#tab=tab_1.

World Health Organization. (2022b). *Timeline: WHO's COVID-19 response*. Retrieved on March 8, 2022 from https://www.who.int/emergencies/diseases/novel-coronavirus-2019/interactive-timeline.

World Health Organization. (2022c). *WHO Coronavirus (COVID-19) Dashboard*. Retrieved on March 8, 2022 from https://covid19.who.int/.

Discography

Yearwood, O., & System32. (2020). "Don't Stop Carnival". *Don't Stop Carnival*. Fox Fuse. Retrieved on March 7, 2022 from https://www.youtube.com/watch?v=qDEBYQFZpo8.

CHAPTER 22

Digital Transformation in Development Settings: Remote Volunteering and Digital Humanitarianism

Bianca Fadel and Thiago Elert Soares

Introduction

This chapter will analyse experiences of digital transformation in humanitarian and development settings, with a particular emphasis on the use of digital technologies in response to crises and disasters, as well as in the engagement of remote volunteers. Our understanding of humanitarian and development work goes beyond life-saving activities and emergency response to encompass also wider forms of community engagement aimed at the promotion of sustainable development in the longer term.

The review of existing academic and policy literature reveals that the relationships between technology and humanitarian and development spaces have been part of long-lasting discussions (Stephenson & Anderson, 1997). Nevertheless, the unprecedented levels of connectivity, availability, and speed of data, alongside the general digitalisation of many aspects of our lives have recently elevated this original connection to new grounds. The Covid-19 pandemic and its impacts on restricting social interactions within and between countries have also accelerated the process of digital transformation, hereby understood as "the ongoing process of significant changes and effects on everyday life in the economy and in society

B. Fadel (✉)
Northumbria University, Newcastle upon Tyne, UK
e-mail: bianca.l.fadel@northumbria.ac.uk

T. Elert Soares
Newcastle upon Tyne, UK

through the use of digital technologies" (Perold et al., 2020, p. 17). From improved communications to increased concerns about privacy and personal data, the extensive use of digital technologies has led to unparalleled developments that are intertwined into the fabric of our day-to-day lives. This tendency is also no longer restricted to populations from global North countries (i.e., mostly in Europe and North America). With increased rapidity, individuals and communities in the global South have been seizing spaces in a global technology and telecommunications community, including in countries and territories affected by active conflict and political instability (Sandvik et al., 2014).

The last years of pandemic have thus seen different humanitarian and development organisations, their staff, and volunteers progressively adapting to a new reality of work governed by limited mobility, especially across borders, if not strict lockdowns. Nonetheless, the definition of virtual volunteering as "volunteer tasks completed, in whole or in part, via the Internet and a home or work computer or hand-held communications tool" (Cravens, 2000) dates back to the late 1990s and early 2000s, when the practice started to gain prominence amongst non-profit organisations, particularly in the global North. We recognise that volunteering can hold distinct and context-specific meanings but, for the purposes of this chapter, it is understood as an individual or group activity performed willingly, not primarily envisaging material compensation, and to the benefit of others, beyond volunteers' familial circles (Fadel, 2020).

Considering this background, this conceptual chapter analyses secondary data from selected peer-reviewed academic sources as well as policy reports to situate digital transformation processes in humanitarian and development work and provoke critical questions aiming to move these debates forward. We identified relevant literature in view of our experience as academics and practitioners working in this sector for the past decade. As much as we have sought to engage with a wide range of academic and policy scholarship, this analysis was restricted to materials published mainly in English due to time and resource constraints. Consequently, we recognise a predominance of published work from authors and organisations from the global North. Our effort to address this limitation involved analysing these materials from a critical standpoint, recognising the divergences and complexity of this area of study and practice.

This chapter is organised into three main sections. We start by reviewing existing literature in this field, particularly in terms of the use of digital tools for responding to crises and disasters, as well as engaging volunteers remotely. Considering the identified need of discussing digital divides and inequalities in the sector, the following two sections build upon the work of Ragnedda (2017) and Roberts and Hernandez (2017, 2019) to situate distinct dimensions of the digital divide in relation to experiences of digital humanitarianism and remote volunteering. First, we explore how humanitarian digital transformation processes are intertwined in multiple layers of inequalities and exclusions affecting both staff and volunteers, and the communities they work with. Finally, we conclude this critical analysis by foregrounding key aspects and critical questions for conceptualising sustainable digital ecosystems as a forward-thinking agenda for advancing debates on digital transformation in humanitarian and development work.

DIGITAL TRANSFORMATION IN HUMANITARIAN AND DEVELOPMENT SETTINGS: LITERATURE SNAPSHOT

In this section, we examine key academic and policy literatures situating our analysis in relation to the existing body of knowledge on digital transformation, both in terms of the broader use of digital technologies in the humanitarian and development sector, as well as the multiple forms of remote engagement for volunteers. This will help contextualise our critique about the different levels of digital divides experienced within humanitarian and development work. Our contribution aims to provide nuance to the ways this digital transformation is understood not only in relation to the benefits of accuracy and agility in response to humanitarian and development needs but also vis-à-vis the types of dependencies and inequalities that it can create or reproduce in such spaces.

THE USE OF DIGITAL TECHNOLOGIES IN RESPONSE TO HUMANITARIAN AND DEVELOPMENT NEEDS

The growing complexity of humanitarian crises continues to threaten hard-earned socioeconomic advances and pathways towards peace and sustainable development. In 2022 alone, estimates indicate that 274 million people will need humanitarian assistance and protection, a major surge from 235 million individuals the year before (UN OCHA, 2021). The health and economic impacts of Covid-19 and the drastically unequal distribution of vaccines worldwide have only aggravated the situation. In many countries in the global South, the pandemic is still exerting severe pressure on national health systems, limiting access to even the most basic medical care and services. Fuelled by the impacts of climate change, environmental hazards, ongoing conflicts, and political instability, humanitarian emergencies currently impact the largest number of people compared to any point in documented history (Kohrt et al., 2019).

Given this context, delivering effective and timely assistance to affected populations in terms of safety, shelter, food security or cash assistance has become increasingly challenging (European Parliamentary Research Service, 2019). As crises grow to be more intricate and enduring, responding to the needs of communities while reducing risks and vulnerabilities has also required transforming traditional structures and practices in humanitarian action and development work. As such, humanitarian and development actors have been relying on innovative ways to tackle vulnerabilities and poverty levels, safeguard the rights of individuals, and foster peace. Organisations are increasingly exploring ways in which digital technologies and practices can improve their access, response, and recovery efforts (Belliveau, 2016; Burns, 2014). From blockchain solutions (Hunt et al., 2022) to the use of unmanned aerial vehicles (Estrada & Ndoma, 2019), big data and open-source platforms (Gazi & Gazis, 2020), and artificial intelligence (Baryannis et al., 2018), a large body of academic and popular literatures have emphasised the benefits of emerging technologies for more agile and fit for purpose humanitarian and development initiatives.

For instance, many scholars and practitioners consider the response to the 2010 earthquakes in Haiti a milestone in the use of novel humanitarian technologies (Sandvik et al., 2014). At that moment, mobile phone messaging, crowdsourced work, and collaborative maps were pioneered to assess damage and identify survivors of the large-scale disaster in the country (Ergun et al., 2014), also highlighting the possibility of using real-time data to inform emergency operations (Read et al., 2016). Different organisations and individuals self-organised to respond to requests for help or resources generated through a dedicated SMS number, while others were involved in georeferencing and mapping important events on the ground (Burns, 2015).

Blockchain is another nascent technology that has been increasingly utilised in humanitarian and development settings to improve transparency and accountability as a decentralised database that stores digital information and records of assets across a peer-to-peer network (Hunt et al., 2022). Originally conceived as the sustaining technology of the Bitcoin cryptocurrency, blockchain offers the possibility of facilitation interagency coordination, distribution and authentication of cash assistance, and supply chain management, among others in a crisis situation (Zwitter & Boisse-Despiaux, 2018). International organisations such as the UN World Food Programme (WFP), the UN Children's Fund (UNICEF), UN Women and other cooperating actors have been piloting different solutions leveraging blockchain capabilities to improve their operations.

This process has been facilitated by the widespread use of the Internet worldwide. Although gender, age, geography and literacy divides remain acute in the digital world, Internet access increased by 23 per cent in Africa and 24 per cent in the Asia Pacific region between 2019 and 2021, which coincides with the Covid-19 pandemic—and is likely to have considerably pushed this rise. In the UN-called 'least-developed countries', the number of Internet users has expanded by 20 per cent over the same period (ITU, 2021). Furthermore, mobile Internet users, as well as both data consumption and traffic are steadily growing as a share of the world population. By the end of 2020, for the first time, more than half of the world's population was using the mobile Internet (Delaporte & Bahia, 2021). While various humanitarian technologies had already been available before 2019, the pandemic forced numerous sectors to step up its adoption and implementation (Soto-Acosta, 2020) in ways that cannot be compared to previous crises (Nagel, 2020). For many, the use of remote working tools and digital applications was the only way to access information, conduct work, and earn an income. In the activities of humanitarian and development workers, aid organisations also had to adapt their ways of working to a new reality in which direct contact with affected populations was rather limited. Some of them, such as the International Organisation for Migration (IOM), Save the Children, and the UN High Commissioner for Refugees (UNHCR) switched to remote ways of data collection by relying almost exclusively on the use of digital tools to conduct telephone and online surveys, remote key informant interviews and secondary data analysis (Gazi & Gazis, 2020). In addition, Covid-19 increased the need for digital skills and training for humanitarian staff and frontline workers themselves, who were bound to use new devices and programmes to perform their work effectively during crises (Hamilton, 2021). Nonetheless, the different levels of digital divides and exclusions arising from this process of digital transformation remain an area requiring further attention, as we will discuss later in this chapter.

In terms of volunteer management in humanitarian and development activities, data systems have also been increasingly adopted by organisations for the recruitment and coordination of the volunteer workforce, facilitating training and volunteer motivation strategies, as well as monitoring and reporting of tasks (Schonbock et al., 2016). The Red Cross and Red Crescent Movement, for instance, have been notably improving their learning platforms for mobile access (IFRC, 2022). In addition, they have been conducting studies and actively engaging with volunteer managers across their global humanitarian network to support the dimension of data management systems for strengthening evidence-based decision-making (Spanish Red Cross, 2022). Over the years, we have also seen the emergence of digital volunteer networks and innovations in collective citizen engagement in response to crises and disasters (Park & Johnston, 2017; Spear et al., 2020). Hence, the surge of 'remote volunteers' is also a key area of attention in this analysis due to the (often forgotten) roles of volunteers in humanitarian response and development work, and how their types of engagement have been evolving alongside the increased use of digital technologies that can facilitate multiple ways of voluntary action—both online *and* offline.

REMOTE FORMS OF VOLUNTEERING

Although Covid-19 might have accelerated the digitalisation of processes and decision-making in various areas, remote ways of working in humanitarian and development settings certainly precede the Covid-19 pandemic. This broader digital transformation in the sector has taken many forms over the past decades, and the current section will focus particularly on experiences of remote volunteering. The practice of remote volunteering is also commonly referred to as digital, virtual or online volunteering, as well as e-volunteering—terms that are here used interchangeably. Since the early 2000s, studies analysing the phenomenon of remote volunteering have examined pro-social behaviour and the use of the internet for the promotion of social change (Amichai-Hamburger, 2008; Wright & Li, 2012). This also relates to the previous discussion about the potential of digital tools for service-delivery in the face of increasing demands perceived in humanitarian and development spaces. In this regard, Table 22.1 provides a non-exhaustive overview of key tasks most often performed by remote volunteers in different areas of work.

As seen in Table 22.1, the scope of remote volunteering activities is broad, ranging from direct person-to-person support (e.g. mentoring or counselling) to indirect forms of engagement and advocacy notably scaled up by social media, such as through crowdsourcing funds and/or information, fact-checking or informing media coverage during crises. Studies have explored how offline and online volunteering can often be connected, suggesting that the latter complements the former, rather than substituting it (Ihm, 2017). Others have also questioned how the mediatory roles of our digital lives during Covid-19 might have led to a redefinition of boundaries "of what it means to care, and be cared for" (Woods & Ying, 2021, p. 52). In this context, the pandemic has driven debates on the redefinition not only of discursive boundaries in volunteering but also geographical borders affecting placements of volunteers involved with international development and humanitarian organisations.

The presence of international volunteers, notably from Northern countries temporarily working in the global South for specific volunteer assignments, has been widely explored in volunteer and development literatures. It has also been increasingly questioned in relation to the (re)production of colonial

Table 22.1 Overview of different types of remote volunteering engagement

Area of volunteer work	Examples of key remote activities
Psychosocial support & mentorship	Listening to and/or counselling people via audio or video-calls; sharing technical expertise or skills with others via remote trainings and peer-to-peer sessions; tutoring or mentoring others
Online mobilisation & social media advocacy	Promoting causes, online petitions, fundraising; recruitment of volunteers for online and/or offline work; moderating online discussion groups
Humanitarian crowdsourcing	Adding information to collective maps during disasters; informing media coverage on relief needs and existing efforts; making sense of 'big data' as 'digital humanitarians' in crisis response
Fact-checking	Verifying reliability of information and news shared online, notably through social media
Web design & visual materials	Designing web pages, databases, graphics, print publications; producing or editing videos and podcasts; cataloguing photos and files; offering feedback or suggestions to websites, graphic design, event materials, etc
Research, writing & management	Conducting research for non-profit organisations or 'citizen science'; writing or editing proposals, press releases, articles, etc.; developing materials for curriculum, classes, and trainings; managing other volunteers
Language support & translation	Translating documents and publications; providing simultaneous interpretation for online activities

Source: Authors' own work with information from Cravens (2014), Meier (2015) and Cox et al. (2018)

relationships privileging Northern knowledge and mobility in detriment of local agency (Laurie & Baillie Smith, 2018; McLennan, 2014). Humanitarian and development organisations—which for decades had relied on the physical presence of international volunteers in their programmes—were forced by Covid-19 to repatriate their volunteers and re-think the uses of digital technologies to redefine their ways of working (Perold et al., 2020). In this regard, online volunteering has been identified as an alternative form of involvement allowing such organisations to maintain an international presence in partner countries and foster volunteer collaborations, although not without its challenges, particularly in terms of the digital divide and limited access to technologies in the various contexts (Perold et al., 2021). Moreover, recent evidence also suggests that the types of belonging and identity among online volunteers complicate the traditional organisation-volunteer relationships by widening their scope of communication, as well as affecting the ways volunteers identify with their organisation(s) and the broader social causes (Ihm & Shumate, 2022). For example, when considering the recognition of volunteers' efforts, the expression of gratitude has been identified as a key aspect affecting online volunteers' experiences of building relatedness with organisations and beneficiaries—with higher motivations identified when appreciation is more clearly expressed by recipients of their support (Naqshbandi et al., 2020). From the perspective of volunteer managers from the Iranian Red Crescent Society, although many advantages of online volunteering have been identified during the Covid-19 response, different local challenges included the lack of accountability, cultural issues, infrastructure, reimbursement, and particular needs for volunteer management (Seddighi et al., 2020).

Finally, while emergency response volunteering is characterised by the on-site presence of volunteers in affected locations, research has also been undertaken on the value of smartphone-based applications for the pre-registration and coordination of volunteers in 'technology-aided systems' that can support volunteer responses (Horstmann et al., 2018). An example of such application was seen in practice in the UK during the Covid-19 volunteer response led by the national government which mobilised over 750,000 volunteers in the country (NHS, 2020). The government's flagship programme 'NHS Volunteer Responders' was set up by the UK National Health Service (NHS) in collaboration with the organisation Royal Voluntary Service to develop an app-based scheme connecting people in isolation due to the pandemic with pre-registered volunteers available for micro-volunteering tasks (i.e., one-off or short-term volunteer activities such as helping with groceries shopping or pharmacy prescriptions). In two years, from April 2020 to April 2022, the app-based service estimated the completion of more than 2.2 million tasks across the country (NHS, 2022) and was positively evaluated by volunteers and service-users (Dolan et al., 2021). Beyond government-led programmes, the Covid-19 pandemic has also seen the emergence of similar online platforms for mobilisation of so-called informal or spontaneous volunteers in different countries and contexts, channelling the types of support in relation to existing needs, as well as fulfilling information gaps during a crisis (Trautwein et al., 2020).

As shown by this review, digital technologies have gained an increasingly important role in facilitating humanitarian and development activities in multifaceted ways, particularly in the context of crises such as the current pandemic. Notwithstanding its significance, there remains further scope for analysing the inequalities and exclusions emerging from—or being reproduced through—this digital transformation in the sector. The next sections of the chapter will turn to this critical area, notably in relation to the different dimensions of the digital divide in humanitarian and development settings.

Unpacking Humanitarian and Development Digital Divides and Exclusions

There is growing evidence on the use of digital technologies for different purposes in the humanitarian and development work performed by staff and volunteers across the globe, particularly affecting the types of activities, scale of action and relationships that can be built with(in) communities. Considering the literatures explored so far, as well as our own lived experience as practitioners navigating these spaces, we will critically discuss the impacts and pitfalls of this digital transformation to humanitarian systems and volunteering practices. We will do that by building upon Ragnedda (2017)'s three-dimensional conceptualisation of the digital divide, as well as Roberts and Hernandez (2017, 2019)'s work on digital technologies and citizenship to argue that although remote volunteering and digital tools can provide flexibility and expand humanitarian and development outreach, they are not a panacea for the sector.

The digital transformation is indeed marked by inequalities and exclusions at different levels. Socio-political and economic factors are key to unravel the complexity of the digital divide in the humanitarian and development sectors. The notion of 'digital divide' refers here to the division between individuals and communities who have access to and use information and communications technologies and those who do not (van Dijk, 2020). The UN has previously stated that "the debate has moved from 'a' digital divide to 'multiple digital divides', which are not only a global challenge but also local contextualised problems in terms of availability of content, bandwidth, and skills, among other issues" (UN DESA, 2018, p. 34). Here, we analyse the socio-political and economic factors mentioned earlier in relation to three levels of digital divide experienced in humanitarian and development work. This follows Ragnedda's conceptualisation not only of the first and second levels of digital divide—related to people's access to the Internet and how they use it, respectively—but also the third level of the divide affecting individuals in terms of "what social benefit and tangible outcomes they obtain from this use" (Ragnedda, 2017, p. 91).

In our analysis, we also refer to Roberts and Hernandez scholarly work which highlights five key 'A's impacting technology access in citizen participation in the Philippines: "Availability: to whom is the technology (un)available?; Affordability: to whom is the technology (un)affordable?; Awareness: who is (un)aware of the technology?; Abilities: who has digital literacies to use the technology?; and Agency: who has the self-efficacy to make use of the technology?" (Roberts & Hernandez, 2019, p. 4). We argue that *availability* and *affordability* constitute helpful lenses to unpack the first divide of who can effectively access digital humanitarianism tools, as well as remote volunteering opportunities. Then, *awareness* and *abilities* help explain the second level of digital divide in terms of how the degree of digital literacy affects the scope of the humanitarian digital transformation. Finally, *agency* is key to understand how the third level of digital divide is perceived by those affected by humanitarian and development work in their own communities, and how these digital tools can 'translate' (or not) into social benefits, particularly among marginalised groups. In this third level of digital divide, we also identify the importance of considering *community resilience* not as a condition, but a construct emerging from both online and offline forms of citizens' engagement and therefore also affecting the digital transformation processes.

As a starting point to discuss the first level of digital divide, we recognise that (the lack of) connectivity remains particularly relevant to the context of humanitarian and development work in so-called developing countries, where live 96% of the 2.9 billion people who remain offline in current days (ITU, 2021). This is despite an overall increase in Internet usage mentioned earlier in Africa and the Asia Pacific region, particularly during the Covid-19 pandemic. We thus need more than dualistic discourses to understand digital access in humanitarian spaces beyond a yes/no connectivity question. Building upon Roberts and Hernandez's framework (2019, pp. 3–4), *availability* here encompasses not only the provision of Internet connection, but also the existence of accessible and inclusive humanitarian tools for the provision of services in ways that are adequate to each context (e.g., various languages, adaptive technologies for people with disabilities, user-friendly platforms). In addition, unlike the usual commercial processes, the development of digital solutions for humanitarian and development contexts requires following a different set of principles and guidelines (Baharmand et al., 2021). This requires, for example, thorough consideration of time-constraints, volatile and fast-changing environments, power-dynamics, as well as the need of coordinating the roles of different humanitarian and development actors during crisis operations to avoid duplicated work.

In this first level of divide, the awareness about *availability* is combined with an expanded understanding of *affordability* not only in relation to the cost of accessing the Internet per se, but also the hidden charges of mobility and maintenance of mobile devices for remaining connected, particularly in remote and rural settings. These are crucial aspects to determine the viability of remote volunteering activities vis-à-vis the costs associated with being 'connected' both to those providing and/or receiving support via such means. One of the main concerns related to the application of digital solutions in emergency situations is that oftentimes innovative technologies are not yet matured or more affordable than conventional tools, requiring extensive piloting and testing before been able to be scaled up (European Parliamentary Research Service, 2019).

Moving on to the second level of digital divide, we highlight the usability of digital tools and the required skills for humanitarian and development staff and volunteers. Although assessing the level of digital literacy has been increasingly part of non-governmental organisations priorities (NCVO, 2021) this issue remains one to be further addressed for achieving the full potential of remote volunteering. In the voluntary sector in the UK, despite an important increase in the level of digital engagement required by staff and volunteers driven by the needs arising from the Covid-19 pandemic, "organisations identified the skills of staff, volunteers and service users as well as cost of equipment or software as the main barriers they faced in trying to increase or improve the use of digital technology in organisational operations" (CPWOP, 2021, p. 9). On an international scale, this is also particularly visible in terms of the different levels of online capabilities from volunteer-involving organisations present in the global North in relation to their counterparts in the global South, as well as gender norms affecting the level of online engagement among women, especially in rural settings in Africa (ITU, 2021, p. 3). Therefore, digital *awareness* and *abilities* have a direct impact on the scope and inclusivity of the humanitarian digital transformation. This refers not only to *if* but also *how* people can benefit from remote tools during a cash-based intervention in response to a disaster or more long-term access to remote psychosocial support delivered by volunteers, for example.

Finally, we need to consider the implications of the 'third digital divide' (Ragnedda, 2017) in digital humanitarianism and online volunteering activities in terms of the returning benefits of using the Internet and remote tools in social life. This echoes wider critiques to digital humanitarianism that have previously asked "whether connectivity is helping reproduce stagnation, inequality and external control rather than ameliorate such conditions" (Duffield, 2016, p. 148). Humanitarian digital technologies are often credited with the potential for quicker and more efficient service-delivery for the promotion of life-saving support. However, this third level of the digital divide is part of an overdue discussion in the sector about the types of dependencies that can be inadvertently reinforced in this digital transformation process deemed emancipatory. This is where it becomes central to discuss the third divide in relation to individuals' *agency*, which we understand as "the power people have to think for themselves and act in ways that shape their experiences and life trajectories, individually or collectively" (Cole, 2019). Moreover, we also connect this debate to the notion of *community resilience*, conceptualised as a "transformative process allowing communities to adapt and respond to the pressures of uncertainty and make the required changes to ensure their members survive and thrive" (Chadwick & Fadel, 2020, p. 6).

In this respect, alongside socioeconomic benefits, the application of digital technologies in humanitarian and development settings stimulates new forms of power and control in social life. A crucial matter relates to the involvement of private companies and businesses in different phases of the development and operation of innovative solutions to support affected populations. While technology companies frequently play an important role in providing the necessary resources and infrastructure for operating information and communications technologies in crisis scenarios, they also perpetuate a notion of development deeply rooted in existing frameworks that do not foster the structural changes needed for economic growth (Mann, 2018). Furthermore, the heightened vulnerability of individuals in emergency situations can make them susceptible to handle their private data to service companies' interests without proper informed consent or acknowledgement (Sandvik et al., 2014). Lastly, without thorough consideration for the humanitarian principles of humanity, neutrality, impartiality, and independence, partnerships between private companies and local governments for the collection and registration of personal information through data collection devices can strengthen unlawful government surveillance systems (Hosein & Nyst, 2013). While we recognise the positive contributions that these technologies have generated to different areas of humanitarian and development work—such as cash-based transactions, funding and information crowdsourcing, and virtual engagement of volunteers—a more nuanced approach sheds light onto the forms of power and control that accompany socioeconomic benefits. As highlighted by the examples above, some forms of online engagement might ultimately limit individuals' agency and liberties, particularly when their involvement is associated with market dominance and surveillance mechanisms. These are key questions for consideration for advancing debates on sustainable digital ecosystems in humanitarian and development work.

Towards Sustainable Digital Ecosystems in Humanitarian and Development Work

In light of the context and complexity of the digital transformation in humanitarian and development spaces discussed so far, we suggest the notion of *sustainable digital ecosystems* as part of a forward-thinking agenda to strengthen the participation and ownership of staff and volunteers in relation to the use of digital technologies in their work. The UN has been one of the lead actors developing an open platform for sharing humanitarian data (i.e. information on context, affected populations, needs and response) across crises and organisations (UN OCHA, n.d.), as well as collaborating with the Red Cross and Red Crescent Movement and other stakeholders to advance the protection and responsible use of humanitarian data (Centre for Humanitarian Data, 2020).

However, here we move beyond data management processes to argue that sustainable digital ecosystems must account not only for the ways of sharing and processing information digitally, but also how to overcome divides in the forms of access, usability and social implications of such tools and systems to humanitarian and development staff and volunteers, and the communities they work with.

The notions of 'humanitarian data ecosystem' (Haak et al., 2018) and 'sustainable digital ecosystems' for humanitarian assistance (Baah & Hamilton, 2021) have emerged recently as part of ever more needed debates on how to avoid siloed approaches to the use of digital technologies in the sector. Moreover, at the core of the concept of sustainability is the importance of social equity, while also accounting for its economic and environmental dimensions. Rather than suggesting a *one-size-fits-all* solution to the disconnections and exclusions that have persisted at different levels, our discussion of sustainable digital ecosystems aims at raising critical questions on the three levels of digital divide discussed earlier.

As seen in Table 22.2, our critical questions are mapped against the different interconnected levels of the digital divide that need to be considered in a holistic manner if we are to advocate for truly sustainable digital ecosystems in the sector. We draw attention to the importance of interrogating which stakeholders are driving the digital agendas in the first place, and for which purposes. This becomes central in the face of persistent top-down structures in

Table 22.2 Critical questions towards sustainable digital ecosystems in humanitarian and development work

Digital divide level	Key concerns	Critical questions towards sustainable digital ecosystems
First digital divide (access)	Availability Affordability	• Who is able to access the humanitarian digital technologies and at what cost? • To what extent are the risks of accessing digital tools and remote activities mitigated?
Second digital divide (usability)	Awareness Abilities	• How is the digital literacy level of *givers* and *receivers* affecting the types of humanitarian and development support given/received? • How are digital technologies appropriate to different groups according to specific needs? (e.g. age, gender, ethnicity, disabilities).
Third digital divide (online engagement in relation to offline social outcomes)	Agency Community resilience	• How are technologies contributing to strengthening existing systems, capacities and coping strategies of individuals and communities rather than replacing them? • Who is driving the humanitarian and development digital agendas and for which purposes?

Source: Authors' own work building upon conceptual work from Ragnedda (2017) and Roberts and Hernandez (2017, 2019)

humanitarian and development work. In practice, such structures remain driven, or largely shaped, by the interests of external donors and stakeholders, who often hold a position of power in relation to affected communities. We highlight the risk of extractive uses of digital tools in humanitarian and development contexts in ways that are not necessarily converted into social benefits to the respective communities. Therefore, the types of digital systems and the ways they are employed can determine what types of social benefits derive from them and to whom.

We also call attention to the political uses of remote volunteering as a form of 'replacement' to international volunteer assignments that were halted by the Covid-19 pandemic. Here, we highlight the importance of virtual volunteering being driven by the needs of those affected by crises rather than dictated by donor agendas—some of whom have already identified the risk of online volunteering contradicting the principle of reciprocity (Perold et al., 2021, p. 6). To build sustainable digital ecosystems for the involvement of online volunteers, the sector needs to, first, consider how to make the best use of digital technologies in terms of strengthening existing capacities rather than perpetuating top-down relationships.

Echoing Veron (2022), we emphasise the roles of digital technologies as *enablers* instead of *solutions*; it is thus key to make the most of its capabilities while simultaneously minimising the threats that arise from its application for humanitarian and development purposes. Other scholars have also highlighted the absence of ethical standards in this process, since volunteer-involving organisations often lack appropriate standards or internationally agreed ethical norms in the use of digital technologies, particularly when it comes to working with marginalised groups (Akhmatova & Akhmatova, 2020). This highlights the importance of ethics in building sustainable digital ecosystems for humanitarian and development workers to engage with communities over time, and not only during emergency response to disasters.

Beyond the dilemmas of applying digital technologies into the ways of working of humanitarian and development staff and volunteers, the critical questions raised in Table 22.2 expand the debate by underlining the need of accounting for the asymmetrical relationships of power and vested interests that characterise such environments. Accordingly, the path towards sustainable digital ecosystems in humanitarian and development work can only be fully achieved if these ethical questions and responsibilities at the three levels of the digital divide are not only acknowledged but also appropriately addressed by the relevant stakeholders in close coordination with the communities they work with.

Conclusion

In this chapter, we have critically analysed the impact of digital transformation and the use of innovative technologies in humanitarian and development activities, especially considering experiences of digital humanitarianism and remote volunteering. We have shown how advancements in digital technologies have not only transformed the way in which organisations, their staff, and volunteers engage in humanitarian and development action, but also how this process is affecting individuals' everyday lives. Furthermore, our review emphasised the importance of conceptualising the different levels of digital divide in humanitarian and development spaces in this digital transformation process. Although the increasing use of digital tools in the sector precedes the emergence of Covid-19, we recognise that it was largely impacted and, in many ways, accelerated by the effects of the pandemic on the work and personal experiences of staff and volunteers. This process is entangled in multiple layers of inequalities and exclusions that need to be better understood—and acted upon—if we are to move towards a more egalitarian future in the use of digital technologies for responding to crises and facilitating the long-term development of communities across the globe.

Overall, while understanding the continuous advancements of digital technologies, we need to challenge assumptions of their use as ultimate tools to empower and liberate individuals from their humanitarian and development needs. By accounting for the three dimensions of the digital divide, we call for policy-makers, donors, humanitarian and development scholars and practitioners advocating for new forms of digital technologies to recognise, understand, and mitigate—to the best of their capacities—risks to individuals' own agency. Addressing such critical questions is paramount for the sector to advance research and debates about sustainable digital ecosystems that can effectively enhance individuals' freedoms and social benefits in an increasingly interconnected world.

References

Akhmatova, D.-M., & Akhmatova, M.-S. (2020). Promoting digital humanitarian action in protecting human rights: hope or hype. *Journal of International Humanitarian Action*, 5(6), 1–7. https://doi.org/10.1186/S41018-020-00076-2.

Amichai-Hamburger, Y. (2008). Potential and promise of online volunteering. *Computers in Human Behavior*, 24, 544–562. https://doi.org/10.1016/J.CHB.2007.02.004.

Baah, B., & Hamilton, Z. (2021). Building and strengthening digital ecosystems in humanitarian contexts. In *GSMA Reports*. https://www.gsma.com/mobilefordevelopment/wp-content/uploads/2021/07/Building-and-strengthening-digital-ecosystems-in-humanitarian-contexts.pdf.

Baharmand, H., Saeed, N., Comes, T., & Lauras, M. (2021). Developing a framework for designing humanitarian blockchain projects. *Computers in Industry*, 131. https://doi.org/10.1016/j.compind.2021.103487.

Baryannis, G., Validi, S., Dani, S., & Antoniou, G. (2018). Supply chain risk management and artificial intelligence: state of the art and future research directions. *International Journal of Production Research*, 57(7), 2179–2202. https://doi.org/10.1080/00207543.2018.1530476.

Belliveau, J. (2016). Humanitarian Access and Technology: Opportunities and Applications. *Procedia Engineering*, *159*, 300–306. https://doi.org/10.1016/j.proeng.2016.08.182.

Burns, R. (2014). Moments of closure in the knowledge politics of digital humanitarianism. *Geoforum*, *53*, 51–62. https://doi.org/10.1016/j.geoforum.2014.02.002.

Burns, R. (2015). Rethinking big data in digital humanitarianism: practices, epistemologies, and social relations. *GeoJournal*, *80*(4), 477–490. https://doi.org/10.1007/s10708-014-9599-x.

Centre for Humanitarian Data. (2020). *Introducing the Humanitarian Data and Trust Initiative*. https://centre.humdata.org/introducing-the-humanitarian-data-and-trust-initiative/.

Chadwick, A., & Fadel, B. (2020). *Volunteerism and Community Resilience: Locally Owned Solutions Delivering Impact* (Volunteering Together to Enable Change and Create a Better World Context Papers). https://www.iave.org/iavewp/wp-content/uploads/2020/07/Volunteerism-and-Community-Resilience-Locally-Owned-Solutions-Delivering-Impact.pdf.

Cole, N. L. (2019, January 22). How Sociologists Define Human Agency. *ThoughtCo*. https://www.thoughtco.com/agency-definition-3026036.

Cox, J., Oh, E. Y., Simmons, B., Graham, G., Greenhill, A., Lintott, C., Masters, K., & Woodcock, J. (2018). Doing Good Online: The Changing Relationships Between Motivations, Activity, and Retention Among Online Volunteers. *Nonprofit and Voluntary Sector Quarterly*, *47*(5), 1031–1056. https://doi.org/10.1177/0899764018783066.

CPWOP—Centre of People; Work and Organisational Practice at Nottingham Business School. (2021). *Respond, recover, reset: the voluntary sector and COVID-19*. http://cpwop.org.uk/wp-content/uploads/sites/3/2021/08/RRR-August-21-Report.pdf.

Cravens, J. (2000). *Virtual Volunteering Project*. Charles A. Dana Center, University of Texas at Austin. http://www.coyotecommunications.com/vv/.

Cravens, J. (2014). *Internet-mediated volunteering in the EU. Its history, prevalence, and approaches and how it relates to employability and social inclusion* (J. Stewart (ed.)). Publications Office of the European Union. https://publications.jrc.ec.europa.eu/repository/handle/JRC85755.

Delaporte, A., & Bahia, K. (2021). The State of Mobile Internet Connectivity 2021. In *GSMA Reports*. https://www.gsma.com/r/wp-content/uploads/2021/09/The-State-of-Mobile-Internet-Connectivity-Report-2021.pdf.

Dolan, P., Krekel, C., Shreedhar, G., Lee, H., Marshall, C., & Smith, A. (2021). *Happy to help: The welfare effects of a nationwide micro-volunteering programme*. http://cep.lse.ac.uk/pubs/download/dp1772.pdf.

Duffield, M. (2016). The resilience of the ruins: towards a critique of digital humanitarianism. *Resilience: International Policies, Practices and Discourses*, *4*(3), 147–165. https://doi.org/10.1080/21693293.2016.1153772.

Ergun, Ö., Gui, L., Heier Stamm, J. L., Keskinocak, P., & Swann, J. (2014). Improving Humanitarian Operations through Technology-Enabled Collaboration. *Production and Operations Management*, *23*(6), 1002–1014. https://doi.org/10.1111/poms.12107.

Estrada, M. A. R., & Ndoma, A. (2019). The uses of unmanned aerial vehicles -UAV's- (or drones) in social logistic: Natural disasters response and humanitarian relief aid.

Procedia Computer Science, *149*, 375–383. https://doi.org/10.1016/j.procs.2019.01.151.

European Parliamentary Research Service. (2019). *Technological innovation for humanitarian aid and assistance*. https://doi.org/10.2861/545957.

Fadel, B. (2020). Volunteering: Connecting the Global Agenda on Sustainability to the Community Level. In W. Leal Filho, A. M. Azul, L. Brandli, A. L. Salvia, & T. Wall (Eds.), *Partnerships for the Goals. Encyclopaedia of the UN Sustainable Development Goals*. Springer, Cham. https://doi.org/10.1007/978-3-319-71067-9_64-1.

Gazi, T., & Gazis, A. (2020). Humanitarian aid in the age of COVID-19: A review of big data crisis analytics and the General Data Protection Regulation. *International Review of the Red Cross*, *102*(913), 75–94. https://doi.org/10.1017/S1816383121000084.

Haak, E., Ubacht, J., Van Den Homberg, M., Cunningham, S., & Van Den Walle, B. (2018). A Framework for Strengthening Data Ecosystems to Serve Humanitarian Purposes. In A. Zuiderwijk & C. C. Hinnant (Eds.), *Proceedings of 19th Annual International Conference on Digital Government Research (dg.o'18)*. ACM. https://doi.org/10.1145/3209281.3209326.

Hamilton, Z. (2021). COVID-19 and Digital Humanitarian Action: Trends, risks and the path forward. In *GSMA Reports*. https://www.gsma.com/mobilefordevelopment/wp-content/uploads/2021/02/M4H_COVID-19-Report.pdf.

Horstmann, A. C., Winter, S., Rösner, L., & Krämer, N. C. (2018). S.O.S. on my phone: An analysis of motives and incentives for participation in smartphone-based volunteering. *J Contingencies and Crisis Management*, *26*, 193–199. https://doi.org/10.1111/1468-5973.12174.

Hosein, G., & Nyst, C. (2013). Aiding Surveillance: An Exploration of How Development and Humanitarian Aid Initiatives are Enabling Surveillance in Developing Countries. *SSRN Electronic Journal*. https://doi.org/10.2139/ssrn.2326229.

Hunt, K., Narayanan, A., & Zhuang, J. (2022). Blockchain in humanitarian operations management: A review of research and practice. *Socio-Economic Planning Sciences*, *80*. https://doi.org/10.1016/j.seps.2021.101175.

IFRC—International Federation of Red Cross and Red Crescent Societies. (2022, April). *IFRC Learning Platform—Mobile Learning App Guide*. https://ifrc.csod.com/clientimg/ifrc/LiveFeed/14ae506b-fce9-4934-bdc9-238d58a58d6b_Your_mobile_learning_app_guide_IFRC_Learning_Platform_April_2022.pdf.

Ihm, J. (2017). Classifying and Relating Different Types of Online and Offline Volunteering. *Voluntas: International Journal of Voluntary and Nonprofit Organizations*, *28*, 400–419. https://doi.org/10.1007/S11266-016-9826-9.

Ihm, J., & Shumate, M. (2022). How Volunteer Commitment Differs in Online and Offline Environments. *Management Communication Quarterly*. https://doi.org/10.1177/08933189211073460.

ITU—International Telecommunication Union. (2021). Measuring digital development: Facts and figures 2021. In *ITU Publications*. https://www.itu.int/en/ITU-D/Statistics/Documents/facts/FactsFigures2021.pdf.

Kohrt, B. A., Mistry, A. S., Anand, N., Beecroft, B., & Nuwayhid, I. (2019). Health research in humanitarian crises: an urgent global imperative. *BMJ Global Health*, *4*(6), e001870. https://doi.org/10.1136/bmjgh-2019-001870.

Laurie, N., & Baillie Smith, M. (2018). Unsettling geographies of volunteering and development. *Transactions of the Institute of British Geographers*, *43*(1), 95–109. https://doi.org/10.1111/tran.12205.

Mann, L. (2018). Left to Other Peoples' Devices? A Political Economy Perspective on the Big Data Revolution in Development. *Development and Change*, *49*(1), 3–36. https://doi.org/10.1111/dech.12347.

McLennan, S. (2014). Medical voluntourism in Honduras: "Helping" the poor? *Progress in Development Studies*, *14*(2), 163–179. https://doi.org/10.1177/1464993413517789.

Meier, P. (2015). *Digital Humanitarians: How Big Data Is Changing the Face of Humanitarian Response* (1st ed.). Routledge.

Nagel, L. (2020). The influence of the COVID-19 pandemic on the digital transformation of work. *International Journal of Sociology and Social Policy*, *40*(9/10), 861–875. https://doi.org/10.1108/IJSSP-07-2020-0323.

Naqshbandi, K. Z., Liu, C., Taylor, S., Lim, R., Ahmadpour, N., & Calvo, R. (2020). "I Am Most Grateful." Using Gratitude to Improve the Sense of Relatedness and Motivation for Online Volunteerism. *International Journal of Human–Computer Interaction*, *36*(14), 1325–1341. https://doi.org/10.1080/10447318.2020.1746061.

NCVO—UK National Council for Voluntary Organisations. (2021, March 2). *How to carry out a digital skills survey*. https://beta.ncvo.org.uk/help-and-guidance/digital-technology/digital-leadership-people-skills-and-strategy/how-carry-out-digital-skills-survey/.

NHS—National Health Service UK. (2020, April 7). *NHS army of volunteers to start protecting vulnerable from coronavirus in England*. https://www.england.nhs.uk/2020/04/nhs-volunteer-army-now-ready-to-support-even-more-people/.

NHS—National Health Service UK. (2022). *NHS Volunteer Responders*. https://nhs-volunteerresponders.org.uk/.

Park, C. H., & Johnston, E. W. (2017). A framework for analyzing digital volunteer contributions in emergent crisis response efforts. *New Media & Society*, *19*(8), 1308–1327. https://doi.org/10.1177/1461444817706877.

Perold, H., Haas, B., & Goodrow, T. (2020). *Volunteering and the Digital World: Extending the Power of Volunteering through New Technologies* (Volunteering Together to Enable Change and Create a Better World Context Papers). https://www.iave.org/iavewp/wp-content/uploads/2020/09/Volunteering-and-the-Digital-World-Extending-the-Power-of-Volunteering-through-New-Technologies.pdf.

Perold, H., Mati, J. M., Allum, C., & Lough, B. J. (2021). *COVID-19 and the Future of Volunteering for Development*. https://forum-ids.org/covid-19-and-the-future-of-volunteering-for-development-research-report/.

Ragnedda, M. (2017). *The Third Digital Divide: A Weberian Approach to Digital Inequalities* (1st ed.). Routledge. https://doi.org/10.4324/9781315606002.

Read, R., Taithe, B., & Mac Ginty, R. (2016). Data hubris? Humanitarian information systems and the mirage of technology. *Third World Quarterly*, *37*(8), 1314–1331. https://doi.org/10.1080/01436597.2015.1136208.

Roberts, T., & Hernandez, K. (2017). *The techno-centric gaze: incorporating citizen participation technologies into participatory governance processes in the Philippines*. https://opendocs.ids.ac.uk/opendocs/handle/20.500.12413/13344.

Roberts, T., & Hernandez, K. (2019). Digital Access is not Binary: The 5'A's of Technology Access in The Philippines. *E J Info Sys Dev Countries*, *85*, 1–14. https://doi.org/10.1002/isd2.12084.

Sandvik, K. B., Gabrielsen Jumbert, M., Karlsrud, J., & Kaufmann, M. (2014). Humanitarian technology: a critical research agenda. *International Review of the Red Cross*, *96*(893), 219–242. https://doi.org/10.1017/S1816383114000344.

Schonbock, J., Raab, M., Altmann, J., Kapsammer, E., Kusel, A., Proll, B., Retschitzegger, W., & Schwinger, W. (2016). A survey on volunteer management systems. *2016 49th Hawaii International Conference on System Sciences (HICSS)*, 767–776. https://doi.org/10.1109/HICSS.2016.100.

Seddighi, H., Salmani, I., Basheva, O., & Shari Sedeh, M. (2020). *The Challenges and Opportunities of Online Volunteering for COVID-19 Response in Iran: A Qualitative Study*. 1–14. https://doi.org/10.21203/rs.3.rs-48770/v1.

Soto-Acosta, P. (2020). COVID-19 Pandemic: Shifting Digital Transformation to a High-Speed Gear. *Information Systems Management*, *37*(4), 260–266. https://doi.org/10.1080/10580530.2020.1814461.

Spanish Red Cross. (2022). *Volunteering data management in National societies*. https://www2.cruzroja.es/volunteerdatamanagement.

Spear, R., Erdi, G., Parker, M. A., & Anastasiadis, M. (2020). Innovations in Citizen Response to Crises: Volunteerism & Social Mobilization During COVID-19. *Interface*, *12*(1), 383–391. http://citeres.univ-tours.fr/actu/actu512/covid.pdf.

Stephenson, R., & Anderson, P. S. (1997). Disasters and the Information Technology Revolution. *Disasters*, *21*(4), 305–334. https://doi.org/10.1111/1467-7717.00065.

Trautwein, S., Liberatore, F., Lindenmeier, J., & von Schnurbein, G. (2020). Satisfaction With Informal Volunteering During the COVID-19 Crisis: An Empirical Study Considering a Swiss Online Volunteering Platform. *Nonprofit and Voluntary Sector Quarterly*, *49*(6), 1142–1151. https://doi.org/10.1177/0899764020964595.

UN DESA—United Nations Department of Economic and Social Affairs. (2018). *United Nations e-Government survey 2018: Gearing e-Government to support transformation towards sustainable and resilient societies*. https://www.unescap.org/sites/default/files/E-GovernmentSurvey2018_FINAL.pdf.

UN OCHA—United Nations Office for the Coordination of Humanitarian Affairs. (n.d.). *Humanitarian Data Exchange*. Retrieved April 9, 2022, from https://data.humdata.org/.

UN OCHA—United Nations Office for the Coordination of Humanitarian Affairs. (2021). Global Humanitarian Overview 2022. In *Global Humanitarian Overview*. United Nations. https://doi.org/10.18356/9789210012423.

van Dijk, J. (2020). *The Digital Divide* (1st ed.). Polity Press.

Veron, P. (2022). *Digitalisation in humanitarian aid: opportunities and challenges in forgotten crises*. https://reliefweb.int/sites/reliefweb.int/files/resources/Digitalisation-humanitarian-aid-ECDPM-Briefing-note-143-2022.pdf.

Woods, O., & Ying, S. S. (2021). The digital void of voluntourism: Here, there and new currencies of care. *Geoforum*, *124*, 46–53. https://doi.org/10.1016/j.geoforum.2021.05.016.

Wright, M. F., & Li, Y. (2012). Prosocial behaviors in the cyber context. In Z. Yan (Ed.), *Encyclopedia of Cyber Behavior* (Vol. 1, pp. 328–341). IGI Global. https://doi.org/10.4018/978-1-4666-0315-8.CH028.

Zwitter, A., & Boisse-Despiaux, M. (2018). Blockchain for humanitarian action and development aid. *Journal of International Humanitarian Action*, *3*(16). https://doi.org/10.1186/S41018-018-0044-5.

PART V

New Media and Digital Journalism

CHAPTER 23

Digital Journalism: The State of Play in Russia and in Global Academia

Elena Vartanova, Anna Gladkova, and Denis Dunas

INTRODUCTION

The rise of networks, de-institutionalization and de-professionalization, increased participation and personal agency, the growth of platform power and platform convergence has led to re-conceptualization of journalism as a professional field and as a social domain. Digital journalism has been in this vein in the spotlight of academic attention in recent years, with scholars suggesting definitions for the term 'digital journalism', problematizing research developments and discussing implications for future research (Eldridge et al., 2019). However, while Digital Journalism Studies have been increasingly explored in regard to its premises, principles, actors, methods, technologies and platforms (Zelizer, 2019; Duffy & Ang, 2019; Ekström & Westlund, 2019; Napoli, 2021), there are quite different approaches to understanding what digital journalism and Digital Journalism Studies mean, and how they can be defined. Furthermore, as Steensen and Westlund (2021) suggest, Digital Journalism Studies constitute a cross-disciplinary field that does not focus on journalism solely from the traditions of journalism studies but is open to research from and conversations with related fields.

This work is supported by the Russian Science Foundation, Project Number 22-18-00225

E. Vartanova (✉) • A. Gladkova • D. Dunas
Lomonosov Moscow State University, Moscow, Russia
e-mail: dunas.denis@smi.msu.ru

This chapter first shows a vast majority of approaches to digital journalism as a field, together with several terms used by scholars in discussing digital journalism: online journalism, cyber journalism, multimedia journalism, and many others. We argue that while 'digital journalism' term seems to be commonly and widely used today in discussing journalistic practices closely associated with the use of ICTs and digital platforms, there is no universally accepted definition or approach to digital journalism in academia. A closer look at different academic traditions in approaching digital journalism enables us to reveal differences based on cultural, professional, and national contexts: something we discuss in the first section of this chapter and further on, examining how digital journalism is presented in Russian scholarly works.

Putting this study in a broader theoretical and societal context, we argue that overall lack of common understanding of digital journalism as a theoretical and practical/professional journalistic field calls for more detailed examinations of digital journalism in different regions of the world. From a professional side, earlier research shows that journalists are gradually adapting to the new digital reality and start following the new rules it sets—when it comes to both the Global North and Global South regions of the world (Carlson, 2003; Deuze, 2001, 2004; Jamil, 2020; Ragnedda & Gladkova, 2020). Although in some newsrooms ICTs are still not being fully used due to the remaining digital divide in access or skills, lack of motivation from journalists, or other reasons (Mutsvairo & Ragnedda, 2019; Gladkova & Mkrtycheva, 2021), a gradual implementation of digital technologies in daily journalistic work is currently becoming more widespread around the world. Specific attention in this vein has been given to the use of digital journalism practices in newsrooms, showing that while some digital journalism tools, such for example social media tools and messengers for collecting and sharing data are being used more actively by journalists, others, including data and statistics websites, data visualization tools, image and audio editing tools are used less frequently (ibid).

In a broader context of digital life and the benefits of digitalization practices, we think the positive implications of ICTs for journalists' work should be certainly mentioned. Among them are opportunities to make news production and distribution processes easier and quicker. In this context, mobile journalism, news websites and news applications are certainly helpful. Mobile phones and other devices play an important role too, allowing journalists to gather, produce and distribute news, as well as to communicate with the audience quicker and more efficiently.

From a theoretical side, closer attention to digital journalism as a theoretical area—apart from professional practices and benefits for journalistic work it brings—is very important too. Here questions about scholarly understanding of digital journalism and its changing practices worldwide are being raised. In particular, there has been an ongoing discussion about 'diversifying diversity in Digital Journalism Studies', namely diversifying our attention to diversity by referring not only to gender and race, but also to different geopolitical, methodological, and theoretical representations, as well as arguing that discourses on and about diversity should not only highlight problems but also include solutions (Tandoc et al., 2020; Boczkowski, 2004, 2005, 2010).

This chapter fully acknowledges the first—professional/journalistic based—part of the digital journalism phenomenon but focuses mostly on the second, theoretical one. We start therefore this chapter by systematizing earlier research on digital journalism and Digital Journalism Studies, showing a multitude of approaches and understandings of these concepts. Then we proceed to discuss how digital journalism as a theoretical and educational area, given its complex multi-layer nature signalled in the first section, is represented in Russian higher education and journalism programs. Further on, we cover a previously under-explored topic, which is digital journalism in Russian academia. Here we discuss the results of a meta-analytical study we conducted to analyze the place and discourse of Digital Journalism Studies in the Russian academic field. By analyzing titles, keywords and citations across leading academic journals in media and communication fields published in Russia (44 publications in total), we will identify main themes, degrees of diversity and interdisciplinary, as well as biases and blind spots. All in all, we expect the chapter therefore to contribute to a broad academic discussion about digital journalism and Digital Journalism Studies and to explore the concept regarding Russian academic and professional context.

Digital Journalism and Digital Journalism Studies as Theoretical Areas

Digital journalism is a changing and multifaceted concept, which has triggered academic attention since the very beginning of its development. The most frequently used terms in this vein are 'digital journalism', 'cyber journalism', 'online journalism', 'multimedia journalism' and etc. There are some terms such as 'mobile journalism' ('mojo') which appeared with the proliferation of a new devices, for example, smartphones.

In the profusion of definitions, 'digital journalism' is the most widespread term in most countries. In 2003, Kawamoto gave such a definition to 'Digital journalism': 'the use of digital technologies to research, produce and deliver (or make accessible) news and information to an increasingly computer-literate audience'. The use of the other terms is occasionally associated with local preferences and subtle differences between the expressions. In Spanish- and Portuguese-speaking countries academics prefer 'cyber journalism' ('cyberperiodismo' in Spanish and 'cyberjornalismo' in Portuguese) to 'digital journalism'. The difference is subtle but significant: 'cyber journalism' is a more specific and narrower term than 'digital journalism'. It refers to journalism carried out 'on' digital networks while digital journalism, a broad term, is carried out 'with' digital technologies and includes all forms of journalism: not only Internet resources and mobile networks but also digital radio and digital television.

Among English- and German-speaking countries 'online journalism' ('online journalismus' in German) is more commonly used. We have mentioned that digital journalism is a wide definition while others have specific significance. However, it seems that online journalism is closer in its meaning to digital journalism than others. Carlson in his paper *The history of online journalism* in some cases replaces 'online journalism' with 'digital journalism'. Salaverría (2015, 2019) puts 'multimedia journalism' at the same level as 'digital journalism' or 'online journalism'. However, some scholars write that 'multimedia journalism' is researched 'in online journalism'. Deuze in his paper *What is multimedia journalism* gave two ways of defining multimedia in journalism: as 'a presentation of a news story package on a website using two or more media formats' and as an 'integrated presentation of a news story package through different media'.

Digital journalism was born with the appearance of the first online media in the mid 1990s. However, journalism's encounter with computing dates back to 1950s when some media started to use computers in media coverage. The most representative case is the use of a primitive computer, the gigantic *Univac*, by CBS on the occasion of the US presidential elections in 1952. Further, until 1990s media and digital technologies had been approaching especially in the cases of handling information. In the 1970s, precision journalism, which has a connection with data-driven journalism, was formed. Until the late 1980s there had appeared theoretical treatises and empirical research on the adoption of new technologies in journalism, technological changes focused on TV, a smaller number of studies published on the use of computers and databases in journalistic information.

With the appearance of the first news publication of a newspaper *Palo Alto Weekly* (San Francisco, the USA) in the World Wide Web in 1994 and the foundation of online media all over the world the history of online media and digital journalism began. The proliferation of online media caused the sudden interest of researchers. In 2019, the research communities celebrated the 25th anniversary of digital journalism which is why the discussion on the main essentials of the concept and subtotals is possible.

One of the most crucial issues is the models of digital journalism. There are many indicators of how we can divide digital publications: general and specialized publications, free and paid publications, global and national, local publications, and publications adopted for several different devices or for a special one (solely for computer, tablet or smartphone). However, it is customary to divide digital publications in online media into two types: digital outlets linked to traditional journalism brands and native digital media outlets.

The first publishing model consisted of the reproduction of the content confirming a transition between what exists and what is in the process of being born and also confirms Scolari's idea: 'each new media that appears fills its space with content from other media' (Scolari, 2013). The model, 'online media based on traditional media', was popular in the 1990s and in the early 2000s when media reproduced on the Internet the content that was created for other platforms. The second model is based on the production of the original content for the Internet. Salaverría and Cores named the evolution of digital media in four stages: repetition, enrichment, renovation and innovation. Nowadays after more than 25 digital media are on the fourth stage.

The appearance of user generated content is a phenomenon of the 2000s. It caused a new divide and an issue for research: professional journalism—user-published content. The scholars started to research modalities and consequences of user-generated content, journalists' assimilation of it into their daily professional routines. Over the years different points of view have been presented. Earlier research criticized traditional media and claimed that they would not be able to adapt to the new context. Such predictions made twenty years ago have not been fulfilled as well as the predictions about the death of radio, TV and newspapers. While some researches shaped the theoretical bases of citizen journalism critically, other academics were carrying out empirical research and concluded that participatory journalism is not a substitute, but a complement to the media.

Gradually, native digital media have become an independent subject of studies. In the early 2000s, Manovich studied new media and identified the features of the language of this field. In the book *The Language of New Media*, he not only presented the theory of new media but also noted: despite the novelty, new media inherited the narrative conventions of old media. Manovich used the term 'language' as an umbrella term that referred to 'emergent conventions, recurrent design patterns and key forms of new media' (Manovich, 2002).

However, soon online media slowed down the process of being inspired by traditional media formats and genres and started to exhibit independent ones based on their own characteristics. Although the term 'language' (Manovich, 2002) for the full description of the conventions and structure of new media remained widely used. In the paper *Digital journalism: Emerging media and the changing horizons of journalism* Kawomoto defined typical characteristics of digital journalism such as hypertextuality, interactivity, nonlinearity, multimedia, convergence, customization and personification. Today scholars focus only on three traits: hypertextuality, interactivity and multimedia.

Digital journalism and Digital Journalism Studies were developing in parallel. Digital Journalism Studies is also an elusive and changing field. It has emerged from journalism studies, which in turn can be included in the larger discipline of communication (Carlson et al., 2018). Since the appearance of the first online media in 1994 and the publication of the first studies, Digital Journalism Studies have started to develop. It is a cross-disciplinary field which focuses on journalism not only in terms of the traditions of journalism studies, but also in relation to other fields: economy, technology, sociology, culture, language, psychology, and philosophy of journalism.

Digital Journalism Studies explore and examine digital journalism, and disruption results in paradigmatic and tectonic shifts in scholarly concerns. Therefore, there is a necessity to reconsider research methods, theoretical analyses and responses to changes in 'a moment of mind-blowing uncertainty'.

Boczkowski wrote in this vein that there was a strong need to shift 'the stance of theoretical work from tributary to primary' in studies focusing on journalism in digital times. Today, researchers define Digital Journalism Studies as a new field that is based not only on communication, political communication, sociology, and economics but also on fields more focused on 'digital' aspects, such as computer science and information science. A lot of attention is being paid also to how self-identifying digital journalists define the field, their identity, mission and much more.

As Digital Journalism Studies is an elusive and multifaceted field, scholars tried to develop some analytical frameworks which help to explain the development of digital journalism in relation to Digital Journalism Studies. This framework encompasses three dimensions: society, sector and scholarship. The first one refers to the peculiarities of the changes at a global, national, and local level, including but not limited to political, economic, social, and technological factors. The second one encompasses journalism as a 'phenomenon and institution, as a market and industry, as well as a profession, practice, service, and products' (Steensen & Westlund, 2021). The last dimension tries to explain what to do with the epistemologies with which scholars produce knowledge. It helps to highlight the interrelationship between the journalism sector and scholarship on Digital Journalism Studies: whether the journalism sector and Digital Journalism Studies scholars have focused on similar or dissimilar questions.

In 2019, Eldridge II, Hess, Tandoc Jr., & Westlund introduced the Digital Journalism Studies Compass, reassessing the field of Digital Journalism Studies and mapping a future editorial agenda for *Digital Journalism*, premier academic journal in the field of digital journalism and Digital Journalism Studies. The article defined Digital Journalism Studies as a field which should strive to critically explore, document, and explain the interplay of digital and journalism, continuity and change, and further focus, conceptualize, and theorize tensions, configurations, power imbalances, and the debates these continue to raise for digital journalism and its futures. It also presented a new heuristic device—the Digital Journalism Studies Compass—anchored around digital and journalism, and continuity and change, as a guide for discussing the direction of the growing field and this journal.

Digital Journalism Studies is a cross-disciplinary field, which means scholars rely on a multitude of theories. Today, there is a noticeable tendency: sociological perspectives are most common in Digital Journalism Studies followed by technological and political science perspectives. Digital Journalism Studies do not differ strongly from journalism studies in its fundamental aspects but sociological and political science perspectives incorporate emphatic technology aspect.

Sociological perspectives consider digital journalism as a kind of social system with certain roles and practices. The articles draw on different theories: Bourdieu's field theory, new institutionalism that mediates 'the impact of macro-level forces on micro-level actions' (Steensen & Westlund, 2021), organizational theory, news values, gatekeeping theory, the hierarchy of influence theory, practice theory and the theory of media logic and etc.

Digital journalism as a socio-technical practice considers with following theories: technological determinism, the social construction of technology (SCOT), affordance theory, actor-network theory (ANT) and such similar to ANT network theories like homophily, resource dependence, and social influence theory.

Digital journalism as a democratic force. Having this research interest, scholars use political science as a common disciplinary framework in Digital Journalism Studies: the four theories of the press, procedural or competitive democracy theories, participatory and deliberative democracy theories, agenda-setting theory, second-level agenda setting and inter-media agenda setting.

Digital journalism as a post-industrial business endeavor. In a time of economic distress digital journalism has become interesting for scholars as business with its organizational structures and economic sustainability. Economic theories like rational choice theory, path dependency theory, uses and gratification theory, organizational development theory, diffusion of innovation theory, business model canvas are the most applicable ones.

In Digital Journalism Studies, traditional methods such as content analysis, comparative research interviews, text analyses and others can be combined with new research methods: data analytics and computational methods (Karlsson & Sjøvaag, 2016). New methods are becoming common in practices of digital journalism. However, today there is a strong challenge. New methods are sometimes perceived with a fascination and digital journalism scholars should remain skeptical in relation to new methods. Researchers should ask themselves why this method is necessary, what it can achieve that other one cannot and whether the new method can provide new knowledge.

Research on digital journalism has been achieved a lot since its appearance. Not so long ago, digital journalism was in the shadow of more classical areas of media research, today it is the most dynamic area of research on journalism. Digital journalism implements its own native publications, formats and genres as Digital Journalism Studies came up with the concepts, methods and continues adapting pre-existing theories and tools to examine what is digital journalism effectively and profoundly (Franklin & Canter, 2019). Digital journalism has broadened the essential elements of journalism—the who, what, where, when, why, and how news is reported, and those fundamental elements should be reconsidered and revised today (Waisbord, 2019).

Despite the prosperity, there are still some challenges, some aspects which need a profound reconsideration or complementation: the promotion of advanced native digital research, research that goes beyond comparative studies with other platforms and focuses on studying digital media, the usage of the advanced research technology, preference for innovation-oriented research, strengthening the analysis of phenomena with actual methods and topics and areas that are not received enough.

Being a wide field, Digital Journalism Studies, according to Boczkowski and Mitchelstein, is marked solely by two limitations: 'the ability to connect empirical findings from Digital Journalism Studies across other domains of digital culture, and a lack of conceptual exchanges with other fields and disciplines' (Steensen & Westlund, 2021). The scholars argue that it would be beneficial if Digital Journalism Studies included more perspectives from the humanities, and not only methodological perspectives but also theoretical ones from information science and computer science.

Lastly, a lot of attention today is being paid to digital journalism practices in specific national and cultural contexts, including for example recent study by Ganter and Paulino (2021) on digital journalism in Brazil explored under challenging political and economic environment, as well as earlier works by Bosch (2010), who looked at emerging trends and theories in the South African context, focusing on the public sphere created by bloggers, the citizen journalism and journalists' engagement with online social media. At the same time, digital journalism in Russian context seems to be understudied, with few works approaching it mostly as a professional journalistic field (Dovbysh et al., 2022), and not talking that much about how digital journalism is understood by Russian academia, or how it is represented as an educational field, in other words how digital journalists are prepared in Russia. The following sections will aim at exploring these currently underrepresented topics as well as drawing some suggestions for further research.

DIGITAL JOURNALISM IN EDUCATIONAL PROCESS: THE CASE OF RUSSIA

As we have shown in the previous section, digital journalism and Digital Journalism Studies are complex multi-faceted and multi-layer concepts that have gained a lot of attention in media, communication and journalism fields. At the same time, we feel there is a need to 'diversify Digital Journalism Studies' as Tandoc et al. (2020) suggest, and focus attention on two areas that have not really been in spotlight of academic attention that much yet, namely teaching digital journalism at higher education institutions, and researching digital journalism and Digital Journalism Studies in Russian academia.

In this context, we carried out analysis of the leading Russian journalism universities according to several Russian rankings,[1,2,3] which showed that the number of Digital Journalism educational programs is substantially limited. In

---

[1] RAEX Ranking by Subject. (In Russian). Available at: https://best-edu.ru/ratings/national/predmetnyj-rejting-raex?group_mode_subject=1&name=&ugs=42&vedom=.

[2] Forbes Ranking of Best Russian Universities 2021. (In Russian). Available at: https://education.forbes.ru/authors/rating-vuzov-2021.

[3] Nacional'noe Priznanie Ranking of Russian Universities. (In Russian). Available at: https://univer.expert/akademicheskiye-reytingi/massovaya-kommunikatsiya-zhurnalistika-smi-2019/.

fact, only two Russian universities have launched such projects—Lomonosov Moscow State University and Udmurt State University.

Lomonosov Moscow State University offers Digital Journalism Master's program,[4] which is implemented jointly by the Faculty of Journalism and the Faculty of Computational Mathematics and Cybernetics. Students are trained to make textual, audio and video content of any complexity for digital platforms, as well as produce and promote content in the digital environment. The program also provides elective courses, allowing for an opportunity to plan an individual educational trajectory focused either on thematic or technological aspects. A list of disciplines taught on the course includes digital journalism in the Russian media system, content strategies of digital journalism, basics of web programming and machine learning, data journalism, digital journalism technologies, digital journalism research and analysis.

Udmurt State University offers a Digital Journalism Bachelor's program, which focuses on both traditional and new disciplines.[5] A range of innovative disciplines dealing with technological aspects of modern journalism includes courses on big data, internet journalism, social media, internet promotion of media content, and modern information technologies.

However, the area of digital journalism is not as poorly represented in Russian educational and academic field as it may seem. Though there are few Digital Journalism educational programs, most leading Russian universities offer corresponding programs featuring related disciplines, which are thematically similar to the area of digital journalism. Most of such programs are themed around digital, internet or electronic media, and are generally aimed at adapting journalism work to realities of the digital environment.

For instance, Kazan Federal University stands out due to the comprehensive and technologically sophisticated nature of its program on digital media. The academic institution offers Media Engineering: Digital Media and Digital Video Production Bachelor's program, which lays a systematic focus on the process of creating and promoting digital content in the modern media space.[6] Students master all stages of digital media production, and are presented with a wide range of innovative disciplines, such as adaptive strategies of digital media production, artificial intelligence and algorithms in media, mathematical modeling in digital media industry, digital manipulations, mobile app production, web design, blogging, AR and VR technologies, digital storytelling, and content strategies in digital media. Kazan Federal University has launched Digital Storytelling and Screenwriting Master's program, which is targeted at future journalists willing to engage with audio-visual and interactive content

---

[4] Digital Journalism Master's program. (In Russian). Available at: http://www.journ.msu.ru/education/magistrate/programmy/tsifrovaya-zhurnalistika.php.

[5] Institute of Udmurt Philology, Finno-Ugric Studies and Journalism. (In Russian). Available at: https://f-uffu.udsu.ru/abiturientam.

[6] Bachelor's Programs at the Department of TV production and digital communications. (In Russian). Available at: https://kpfu.ru/media-sociology/struktura/otdelenie-zhurnalistiki/tv-and-digital/bakalavriat.

production in the digital environment.[7] In line with the newest technological trends, it is well-adapted to the demands of the current digital media market.

The Peoples' Friendship University of Russia offers an English-language Master's program on digital media with an additional focus on globalization.[8] It addresses different aspects of the global digital media environment, with an aim to enhance students' digital competencies, thus training competitive experts capable of finding their niche at the regional, national and global media market. A list of disciplines includes theoretical courses on digital mass media and current trends of information market, as well as practical courses on multimedia storytelling, mobile journalism and social media, big data and infographics, etc.

National Research Tomsk State University offers Master's program aimed at training specialists in the field of digital media communications, prepared to work with new media and cross-platform projects.[9] The underlying idea of Journalism and Digital Media Platforms program is that the emergence of information society calls for new education trajectories, which will combine creative, technological, managing, and research skills.

National Research University Higher School of Economics offers no comprehensive programs focused specifically on digital journalism. However, educational trajectory of Bachelor´s program on journalism includes courses on digital marketing and digital memory.[10] Besides, there is a minor program titled Digital Media for the Future offered as part of Bachelor´s training.[11] It aims to adapt the journalism students to the new digitalized realities, and covers technological trends in media and new media methodologies, changing business models, as well as multimedia trends.

A range of journalism programs provided by Russian universities are focused specifically on multimedia formats and convergent media channels. For instance, Russian Presidential Academy of National Economy and Public Administration has a Master's program, which is aimed at training students to work with digital media, and lays key focus on new journalism methods and formats (e.g. longread, infographics, webcasting).[12] A list of disciplines includes convergent journalism, computer technologies in journalism, theory and practice of digital media, new technologies in PR and advertising. Moscow Polytechnic University offers Periodicals and Multimedia Journalism Bachelor's

---

[7] Master's Programs at the Department of TV production and digital communications. (In Russian). Available at: https://kpfu.ru/media-sociology/struktura/otdelenie-zhurnalistiki/tv-and-digital/magistratura.

[8] Global and Digital Media Master's Program. (In Russian). Available at: https://www.rudn.ru/education/educational-programs/51653.

[9] Journalism and Digital Media Platforms Master's Program. (In Russian). Available at: https://fj-tsu.ru/magistrate.

[10] Journalism Bachelor's Program. Available at: https://www.hse.ru/ba/journ/.

[11] Digital Media for the Future. (In Russian). Available at: https://www.hse.ru/edu/courses/346231379.

[12] Journalism and Media Technologies Master's Program. (In Russian). Available at: https://igsu.ranepa.ru/program/p75857/.

program, which builds its educational trajectory around multimedia information environment and different media platforms, with a focus on digital transformations in media.[13] Russian State University for the Humanities provides Bachelor's program on multimedia journalism and modern technologies, which centers on new technologies, multimedia formats and innovative approaches towards media production.[14] Ural Federal University offers Bachelor's program on media communications and multimedia technologies, which among other disciplines provides courses on digital communications and social media.[15] Chelyabinsk State University has a Bachelor's program titled Media Production on Different Platforms that partially addresses the field, in particular by including disciplines, such as web-design and internet media planning, as well as convergent journalism.[16] In 2022, Plekhanov Russian University of Economics is launching a Master's program on digital media branding.[17]

Yet another cluster of programs is focused on internet journalism, for instance Internet Journalism and Video Blogging Master's program[18] at North-Caucasus Federal University, Internet Journalism Bachelor's programs at Novgorod State University[19] and Moscow State University of Economics and Humanities.[20] Their educational trajectories involve all types of professional tasks related to the content production in the digital environment. They include technological disciplines, such as programming and data bases, technique and technology of web sources, desktop publishing, as well as courses on digital media, such as modern blogging technologies, economics and management of digital media, communicology of social media, language and discourse of electronic media, and so on.

A range of prominent Russian universities, for example Moscow State Institute of International Relations, Saint Petersburg State University, Moscow State Linguistic University, Novosibirsk State University, Voronezh State University, Kuban State University, still lack programs themed around digital journalism. Their educational trajectories are focused on other facets of

---

[13] 'Periodicals and Multimedia Journalism' Bachelor's program. (In Russian). Available at: https://mospolytech.ru/postupayushchim/programmy-obucheniya/bakalavriat/periodicheskie-izdaniya-i-multimediynaya-zhurnalistika/.

[14] Multimedia Journalism and Modern Media Technologies Bachelor's Program. (In Russian). Available at: https://www.rsuh.ru/media/bachelor/multimediynaya-zhurnalistika-i-sovremennye-mediatekhnologii.php.

[15] Media Communications and Multimedia Technologies Bachelor's Program. (In Russian). Available at: https://journ-urgi.urfu.ru/ru/abiturientu/bakalavriat/mediacom/.

[16] Bachelor Journalism Program at Chelyabinsk State University. (In Russian). Available at: https://www.csu.ru/faculties/DocLib1/bachelor.aspx.

[17] Cybernetics and Media: New Programs at PRUE. (In Russian). Available at: https://www.rea.ru/ru/news/Pages/novye-napravlenia-it-media.aspx.

[18] Journalism Department at the North-Caucasus Federal University. (In Russian). Available at: https://www.ncfu.ru/university/institutes/hum-inst/kafedra-istorii-i-teorii-zhurnalistiki/.

[19] Journalism Department at the Novgorod State University. (In Russian). Available at: https://portal.novsu.ru/dept/1588617/.

[20] Journalism Department at the Moscow State University of Economics and Humanities. (In Russian). Available at: https://mgei.ru/faculties/zhurnalistika/.

journalism, such as literary, linguistic, and international aspects, management, etc. However, some of these institutions have designated departments, which conduct research work in the area of digital journalism and electronic media. For instance, Department of Digital Media Communications[21] at Saint Petersburg State University prioritizes research on digital media and organizes thematic projects and courses, such as Day of Media Literacy aimed at increasing students' professional capabilities via new technologies, and a course on the convergence of press and digital channels.

To conclude, many leading Russian universities build their journalism programs around the thematic and problematic scope of digital journalism. Most of them, while not being dedicated entirely to the field, encompass areas of new media, multimedia technologies, digital communications and internet journalism. However, a number of leading Russian universities still lack corresponding programs.

As for specific digital journalism programs, it is worth noting that educational initiatives are launched by government institutions, major media outlets and online schools. State-supported 'Digital Journalism' all-Russian educational project is aimed at training skilled experts in advanced information and communication technologies.[22] The program combines the most essential aspects of several industries: prominent journalists give lectures and workshops on the best media practices, IT specialists share their knowledge on state-of-the-art technologies aiming to enhance the listeners' digital competencies, while key state officials provide details on digital government strategies. Digital Journalism educational program was also launched by TASS News Academy, an educational institution established by one of the oldest Russian information agencies. The program attendants are supposed to master digital tools and learn to create and promote multimedia cross-platform projects.[23] A number of Digital Journalism programs designed to provide new-level competencies for journalists are also organized by online schools, such as Skillcare,[24] MBA City Business Academy,[25] as well as by state-supported portals, such as Technograd.[26]

---

[21] Department of Digital Media Communications. (In Russian). Available at: http://jf.spbu.ru/press-dept/3804.html.

[22] 'Digital Journalism' All-Russian Educational Project. (In Russian). Available at: https://xn%2D%2D80aaafvjeashuizetqkm0b6o.xn%2D%2Dp1ai/.

[23] 'Digital Journalism' at TASS News Academy. (In Russian). Available at: https://academy.tass.ru/cifrovaya_zhurnalistika.html.

[24] 'Digital Journalism' at Skillcare. (In Russian). Available at: https://skillcare.ru/course/%D0%A6%D0%B8%D1%84%D1%80%D0%BE%D0%B2%D0%B0%D1%8F-%D0%B6%D1%83%D1%80%D0%BD%D0%B0%D0%BB%D0%B8%D1%81%D1%82%D0%B8%D0%BA%D0%B0/1.

[25] 'Blogger (Digital Journalism)' at MBA City Business Academy. (In Russian). Available at: https://mba-city.ru/journalism/online_journalism/.

[26] 'Digital Journalism: Journalist-Blogger' at Technograd. (In Russian). Available at: https://technograd.moscow/corps/online/distantsionnye_kursy/6723.html.

Digital Journalism Studies in Russian Academic Field: Evolving Practices and Trends

To diversify and deepen understanding of digital journalism and Digital Journalism Studies in Russian context (and beyond), we moved on from analyzing digital journalism through a broad theoretical lens and then looking at how it is represented in Russian educational system, to another important topic—digital journalism coverage in Russian academic literature. For this purpose, we conducted a meta-analytical study to analyze the place and discourse of Digital Journalism Studies in the Russian academic field. The materials of the study were research papers on digital journalism, included in to the digital library of Russia at www.elibrary.ru. This is the largest digital library of scientific publications in Russia, which supports tools for searching and analyzing the data. The library is integrated with the Russian Science Citation Index (RSCI), which is the official, created under the auspices of the Ministry of Education and Science of the Russian Federation, a free public tool for measuring the publication activity of scientists and organizations.

The keyword we used for searching was 'digital journalism'. The search area was the title of the publication, abstract and keywords. Types of publication were papers submitted to the journals, books, materials of conferences and dissertations. The maximum possible range was chosen as the publication period. As a result, a total of 44 publications were found, which is a very small number of publications. For comparison, there are 294 publications to be found by 'digital media' keyword.

In terms of the distribution of publications by type of publication, 18 publications are research papers, 26 publications are conferences abstracts. The publication period covered 5 years: from 2018 to 2022. Over the years, the most publications were published in 2021 (18 publications), followed by 2019 (12), 202 (11), 2022 (2) and 2018 (1). It is obvious that 2022 is not representative, as it is still ongoing.

The publications we have identified can be divided into four groups. Firstly, these are problem statement articles that are focused on posing a problem, describe it in the context of current development trends and put it in the context of existing theoretical approaches. There were identified 15 articles of a such type. The second group (24 articles) consisted of articles that explore the issues of digital journalism, primarily of practical importance, or devoted to the consideration of digital journalism issues in a very particular area, containing the results of an original empirical study. The third group (4 articles) includes papers that explore the educational practice of the Russian Federation and consider digital journalism as part of the educational process. Finally, one paper is a book review and is devoted to a critical review of a book on digital journalism.

Problem Statement Papers

In recent decades, due to significant transformations of the digital media and communication environment, their functioning has changed dramatically. Considering the changes in the field of journalism, including the innovative processes that characterize the profession, the researchers tried to find more relevant definitions of this concept. Network-, multimedia-, convergent-, Internet-, online-, computer-, algorithmic-, automated-, robotic-, data-, cloud-journalism—there have been many attempts to describe the new properties and even nature of the profession that arose in the world and in Russia more than three centuries ago (Vartanova, 2021). Many Russian researchers of digital journalism often refer to the phrase 'new media' or 'digital media' (Avdonina & Bogatyreva, 2020). This terminological confusion may explain the fact that a few publications devoted to 'digital journalism' were found.

The attention of research articles is drawn to the fact that Russian scholars have not yet been able to come to a consensus regarding the term used to describe journalism in the digital environment. The Russian academic community has not yet formulated unambiguous, universally supported definitions of the new term, but a description of the properties and characteristics of this phenomenon has been presented.

Digital journalism is often associated with more general issues of the functioning of the media space and journalism: digitalization, multimediatization, convergence, platformization and social networks expansion (Kurushkin, 2019). Another block of subtopics is the evolution of formats and genres of journalism, points to the growing role of visualization data, interactivity, data journalism, increasing demand for the analytical, opinionated journalism and user-generated content within the journalism materials (Solomin, 2022). The issue of new competencies and skills required for journalists working in the digital environment is being updated.

Media researchers note that digital journalism in the near future will become not only the dominant, but also the only form of existence of the profession. Therefore, by and large, everything that is now related to the current processes of the development of journalism can be attributed to digital journalism. It is characterized by the fact that it is a network production, distribution and consumption of news and analytics, that uses digital technologies and services such as websites, social platforms, mobile devices, big data and algorithms. It has multimedia characteristics, changes the role of a reporter, a professional journalist in his relationship with the audience, requires a new set of professional skills and abilities from journalists (Vodopetov & Mahmud, 2022). In addition, digital journalism is not only shaped by digital information and communication technologies, but also influences them, creating a special symbiotic relationship with the audience in the digital environment.

Fixing the features of digital journalism, almost all authors agree that the most important difference between a professional journalist and the "new professionals" media practice is the principle of responsibility for their texts and for the effects, they cause. This is a responsibility before the audience, editors, colleagues, and society. And that is why digital journalism is journalism with its traditional goals and values, but existing in technologically new conditions, which, while transforming its tools, cannot lose its socially significant nature and essence (Vartanova, 2021).

Empirical Evidence-Based Papers

Papers based on empirical research are devoted to different issues, such as professional journalism content in social media, the Telegram chatbot as a source of information for journalists, methods of creating and presenting text in Telegram, the influence of Instagram on editorial news agenda, measuring coverage and engagement of the audience of Internet resources, the technique of creating clickbait headlines, strategies for transforming the editorial work of a journalist in the digital environment in provincial newspapers, the potential of TikTok in creating journalistic content, etc. Much attention is paid to the journalism text in the digital environment. Many researches are focused on interactivity, efficiency, presentation, and style of text (Budnik, 2021).

Digital journalism exists in the context of an increased number of channels for broadcasting media texts (social networks, instant messengers, etc.). The proportion of users who access the Internet only from smartphones has significantly increased. As a result, the texts are adjusted to the requirements of news aggregators and other platforms. In modern media practice, new communication models are being built which destroy the canons of the so-called linear (verbal) text. Taking into account the specifics of the text in digital media, journalists are updating a number of new creative techniques aimed at keeping the attention of the audience.

Among the creative techniques inherent in digital journalism, the following are empirically confirmed (Gradyushko, 2018): (1) Visual elements. The digital age contributes to the fact that on the Internet the main information load falls on multimedia content (photos, collages, infographics, videos, etc.); (2) Alternate text and photo. One of the conducted studies revealed that every 2–3 paragraphs of text are broken up by visual elements. This is especially true in connection with the development of mobile journalism; (3) Structuring the material. In the context of the transformations of modern media, the division of the text into fragments is welcome. Important blocks of text and quotations emphasizing the main idea are highlighted in bold, italics, or taken out separately; (4) The special structure of paragraphs. It is noted that in the digital environment the optimal length of a paragraph usually does not exceed 5–7 lines. A paragraph with about 10 lines is already an array of text; (5) Font size. In a digital environment, it is important that text is easily readable both on a computer screen and on a smartphone display; (6) Interactive elements. Materials on some sites can be evaluated using special stickers using interactive elements; (7) Search engine optimization, adjustment to the requirements of news aggregators and recommendation services.

To improve the efficiency of work in the digital environment it is necessary: to work on the creation of full-fledged convergent editorial offices; produce special materials for the website and social networks; resolve the issue of remuneration of journalists who produce content for digital platforms; send employees to advanced training and retraining in the field of digital journalism; look for new ways to monetize Internet resources. There is no doubt that digital technologies have significantly transformed the work of regional media journalists, which poses new challenges for them in the struggle for the attention of the audience (ibid.).

Special attention is paid to creating an engaging headline and effective media text. Every year, competition between news sources for the attention of readers is growing. Since many headlines come to sites from social networks, news aggregators and recommender systems, there is an urgent need to create new types of headlines that generate the most clicks. It is noted that in digital journalism headlines often use a vivid statement, designed as a quote. Such headlines are longer than usual, but more informative (Gradyushko, 2020b).

The potential of the Telegram messenger for digital journalism is being explored, since it is this messenger that today becomes one of the key sources of news information for the global audience, primarily the Russian-speaking one (Bakeeva, 2021; Gradyushko, 2020a). Chatbots, which are used as a feedback tool in the Telegram interface, allow you to quickly receive user-generated content from the audience, as well as see the audience's reaction to a particular publication. Telegram news channels compete with professional media editorial staff in setting the agenda and analytics.

Papers Devoted to the Digital Journalism in the Educational Process

This block of articles explores the issues of transforming the professional competencies of a modern journalist. The authors focus on the structure of educational programs dedicated to digital journalism.

The specificity of such programs is the focus on the formation of fundamentally new, relevant competencies that ensure rapid adaptation to the new information demands of modern Russian society. These types of tasks of professional activity correspond to the following tasks of professional activity: implementation of authorial activity of any nature and level of complexity, taking into account the specifics of different types of media and other media; implementation of editorial activities of any level of complexity in different types of media and other media and coordination of the editorial process; creating a concept and planning the implementation of an individual and (or) collective project in the field of journalism; organization of work and management of an enterprise (division) in the modern media industry; systematic alignment of the production process of publishing a journalistic text and (or) product using modern editorial technologies (Larina & Gereykhanova, 2020).

Book Reviews

One of the articles found is a book review: Steensen S., & Westlund O. What Is Digital Journalism Studies? (London: Routledge 2021) (Kulchitskaya, 2021). Steensen and Westlund start from four structural assumptions when studying and describing digital journalism. The first of these prerequisites is that the media are looking for new ways to make money because the old advertising models have stopped working. The second premise is that journalism has begun to pay a lot of attention to the study of the audience and user behavior. Thirdly, the authors highlight the fact that companies that are not institutionally related to journalism now dominate the content distribution industry. For example, news articles can be found not only on the media website, but also in social networks, instant messengers and other digital platforms. Finally, authors point out that journalism today is more affected than ever by manipulation and misinformation, with the emergence of alternative media companies and the emergence of traditional media in a crisis of confidence.

As Steensen and Westlund note, although digital journalism is a new research field, the methods of analysis and theoretical approaches to its study remain quite traditional. Throughout the book, the authors convey the idea that digital journalism research is an interdisciplinary field that is not only focused on journalism, but is also open to research from related fields. Therefore, when studying this new direction, it is worth relying not only on the theory of journalism, but also using the tools and theoretical apparatus of other areas.

The academic discourse of digital journalism cannot be called solely focused on this term. In the Russian scientific tradition, other designations for the functioning of the journalistic profession in the digital environment are common. For comparison: Internet journalism is studied by 346 scientific publications, 1907 publications are devoted to new media as an umbrella term. Actually, the discourse of digital journalism is very limited, being presented by 44 publications only. However, even in this field, the qualitative diversity of approaches to digital journalism is obvious, taking into account both current trends in the development of the media in general and specific innovative tools for the professional activity of a journalist. Obviously, attention is paid to the education of modern journalists in the field of digital journalism and taking into account the foreign academic context.

Conclusion

Our chapter provided a systemic overview and classification of approaches to digital journalism and Digital Journalism Studies in the global academia, relying both on rich theoretical background (Molyneux et al., 2019; Steensen et al., 2019) and current empirical research (Bergström & Belfrage, 2018; Merten, 2021). We have shown that digital journalism and Digital Journalism Studies delve into the technologies, platforms, and audience relations that constitute Digital Journalism Studies' central objects of study, outlining its principal theories, the research methods being developed, its normative underpinnings, and possible futures for the academic field. We believe that ongoing transformations of journalism and communication, the growth of platform power and platform convergence, the rise of new business models and increasing role of audience participation and algorithms in news creation and dissemination make the topic of digital journalism as a theoretical area and as a social system timely and important—in different regions of the world, including Russia.

The study of digital journalism is overall highly relevant for journalism, media and communication fields: it explores a new and under-covered scholarly field of digital journalism, approached by scholars as a cross-disciplinary field that does not focus on journalism solely from the traditions of journalism studies, but is open to research from and conversations with related fields (Steensen & Westlund, 2021). We hope our chapter makes in this context contribution to journalism and communication studies, deepening our understanding of digital journalism as a new and rapidly developing field in the Russian academic and educational context, developing our outstanding of what digital journalism is in general, how it can be defined, how it operates, and what directions in may develop in the future. We have shown that while aspects of digital journalism are currently present in many study programs of Russian universities and higher education institutions in one way or another, there are only a few programs focused exclusively and solely on digital journalism. Although this chapter is not aimed at providing solid recommendations to educational institutions in Russia, we still believe closer attention to implementing full-fledged digital journalism programs in Russian Bachelor, Master, and PhD programs would be a good and promising idea in a long run, given ongoing digitalization of all aspects of everyday life.

Same goes for scholarly works on digital journalism: we found surprisingly limited number of publications approaching digital journalism and Digital Journalism Studies in Russian academic journals, something we did not expect we would face, thinking that overall number of relevant publications would be much higher. Guided by the idea of 'digital life', we think both of these aspects—representation of digital journalism in Russian education and academia—can contribute to developing digitalization of educational and research practices, as well as contribute to benefits scholarly community, students, educators, audience can receive from better attention to digital journalism and Digital Journalism Studies in different practices.

Concluding, we think further research in this area can possibly also approach digital journalism as part of broader national media systems with their specific characteristics (Hallin & Mancini, 2004), currently changing journalistic roles (Mellado & Hermida, 2021), specifics of media regulation in each country, including Russia (Vartanova, 2013), and many other aspects. Here more studies of professional journalistic practices in digital and traditional media outlets are needed in our view, examining challenges journalists face in their work (availability of ICTs and digital technologies in editorial offices, digital literacy issues, etc.), education/training of journalists working for ethnic media, as well best journalistic practices within digital journalism broader context.

REFERENCES

Avdonina, N., & Bogatyreva, V. (2020). Aktual'nyye tendentsii tsifrovoy zhurnalistiki i novykh media [Current trends in digital journalism and new media]. *Bulletin of Amur State University*, 2 (39), 9–18.

Bakeeva, D. (2021). Telegram-kanaly kak noveyshaya transformatsiya sotsial'nykh media: formirovaniye mediapovestki [Telegram channels as the latest transformation of social media: shaping the media agenda]. In: *MEDIAEducation: media inclusion vs media isolation. Proceedings of the VI International Scientific Conference*. Edited by A.A. Morozova. Chelyabinsk: 241–245.

Bergström, A., & Belfrage, M. J. (2018). News in social media. *Digital Journalism*, 6:5, 583–598, https://doi.org/10.1080/21670811.2018.1423625

Boczkowski, P. J. (2004). The processes of adopting multimedia and interactivity in three online newsrooms. *Journal of Communication*, 54(2), 197–213. https://doi.org/10.1111/j.1460-2466.2004.tb02624.x

Boczkowski, P. J. (2005). *Digitizing the News: Innovation in Online Newspapers*. Cambridge, MA: MIT Press.

Boczkowski, P. J. (2010). *News at Work: Imitation in an Age of Information Abundance*. Chicago: University of Chicago Press.

Bosch, T. (2010). Digital journalism and online public spheres in South Africa. *Communicatio*, 36:2, 265–275, https://doi.org/10.1080/02500167.2010.485374

Budnik, E. (2021). Tsifrovaya zhurnalistika: novyye praktiki, formy, metody, auditoria [Digital journalism: new practices, forms, methods, audiences]. In: *Mediation of Social and Individual Practices in the Digital Society: Journalism and Communication in an Age of Uncertainty. Abstracts the 13th International Media Readings in Moscow*: 133–134.

Carlson, D. (2003). The history of online journalism. In: Kawamoto, K. (ed.). *Digital Journalism: Emerging Media and the Changing Horizons of Journalism*. Lanham, MD: Rowman & Littlefield Publishers: 31–55.

Carlson, M., Robinson, S., Lewis, S. C., & Berkowitz, D. A. (2018). Journalism studies and its core commitments: The making of a communication field. *Journal of Communication*, 68(1), 6–25. https://doi.org/10.1093/joc/jqx006

Deuze, M. (2001). Online journalism: Modelling the first generation of news media on the World Wide Web. *First Monday*, 6(10). https://doi.org/10.5210/fm.v6i10.893

Deuze, M. (2004). What is multimedia journalism? *Journalism Studies*, 5(2), 139–152.

Dovbysh, O., Wijermars, M., & Makhortykh, M. (2022) How to reach Nirvana: Yandex, News personalisation, and the future of Russian journalistic media. *Digital Journalism*, https://doi.org/10.1080/21670811.2021.2024080

Duffy, A., & Ang, P. H. (2019). Digital journalism: Defined, refined, or re-defined. *Digital Journalism*, 7:3, 378–385, https://doi.org/10.1080/21670811.2019.1568899

Ekström, M., & Westlund, O. (2019). The dislocation of news journalism: a conceptual framework for the study of epistemologies of digital journalism. *Media and Communication*, 7, 259–270.

Eldridge II, S. A., Hess, K., Tandoc Jr., E. C., & Westlund, O. (2019). Navigating the scholarly terrain: Introducing the Digital Journalism Studies Compass. *Digital Journalism*, 7:3, 386–403, https://doi.org/10.1080/21670811.2019.1599724

Franklin, B., & Canter, L. (2019). *Digital Journalism Studies: The Key Concepts*. London, Routledge. ISBN: 1315406098

Ganter, S. A., & Paulino, F. O. (2021). Between attack and resilience: The ongoing institutionalization of independent digital journalism in Brazil. *Digital Journalism*, 9:2, 235–254, https://doi.org/10.1080/21670811.2020.1755331

Gladkova, A., & Mkrtycheva, Yu. (2021). Ethnicheskie SMI v usloviyakh tsifrovoi sredy: itogy ekspertnogo oprosa [Ethic media in the digital environment: Results of expert survey]. *Mediaalmanakh*, 3, 41–49.

Gradyushko, A. (2018). Novostnoye video dlya sotssetey kak novyy mediynyy format [News video for social networks as a new media format]. In: *Language and Speech on the Internet: Personality, Society, Communication, Culture*: 268–273.

Gradyushko, A. (2020a). Chat-bot v Telegram kak novyy istochnik informatsii dlya zhurnalistov [Chatbot in Telegram as a new source of information for journalists]. In: *Media Education: Media as a Total Everyday Life. Proceedings of the V International Scientific Conference*: 305–309.

Gradyushko, A. (2020b). Provokativnyye tekhniki sozdaniya zagolovkov v tsifrovoy zhurnalistike [Provocative headline techniques in digital journalism]. In: *Problems of Mass Communication. Materials of the International Scientific-Practical Conference of Researchers and Teachers of Journalism, Advertising and Public Relations*: 68–70.

Hallin, D. C., & Mancini, P. (2004). *Comparing Media Systems. Three Models of Media and Politics*. Cambridge University Press.

Jamil, S. (2020). Ethnic news media in the digital age: The impact of technological convergence in reshaping journalists' practices in Pakistan. *Journal of Multicultural Discourses*, 15 (2), 219–239. https://doi.org/10.1080/17447143.2020.1756305

Karlsson, M., & Sjøvaag, H. (2016) Introduction. *Digital Journalism*, 4:1, 1–7, https://doi.org/10.1080/21670811.2015.1096595

Kawamoto, K. (2003). *Digital Journalism: Emerging Media and the Changing Horizons of Journalism*. Lanham, MD: Rowman & Littlefield Publishers.

Kulchitskaya, D. (2021). Na puti k kontseptualizatsii tsifrovoy zhurnalistiki (retsenziya na knigu Steensen Steen, Westlund Oscar (2021). What is digital journalism studies? London; New York: Routledge, 2020) [Towards the Conceptualization of Digital Journalism (book review of Steensen Steen, Westlund Oscar (2021). What is digital journalism studies? London; New York: Routledge, 2020). *Mediascope*, 2.

Kurushkin, S. (2019) Zhurnalistika v tsifrovoy srede: tendentsii i problemy nauchnogo issledovaniya [Journalism in the digital environment: Trends and problems of scientific research]. *Age of Information*, 7(4), 11–18.

Larina, N., & Gereykhanova K. (2020). Razrabotka programmy magistratury Tsifrovaya zhurnalistika v ramkakh upravleniya deyatel'nost'yu vuza [Development of a Master's program Digital Journalism as part of the management of the university]. *The World of Science, Culture, Education*, 1 (80), 266–268.

Manovich, L. (2002). *The Language of New Media*. Cambridge, MA: MIT Press.

Mellado, C., & Hermida, A. (2021). A conceptual framework for journalistic identity on social media: How the personal and professional contribute to power and profit. *Digital Journalism*. https://doi.org/10.1080/21670811.2021.1907203

Merten, L. (2021). Block, hide or follow—Personal news curation practices on social media. *Digital Journalism*, 9:8, 1018–1039, https://doi.org/10.1080/21670811.2020.1829978

Molyneux, L., Lewis, S. C., & Holton, A. E. (2019). Media work, identity, and the motivations that shape branding practices among journalists: An explanatory framework. *New Media & Society*, 21(4), 836–855. https://doi.org/10.1177/1461444818809392

Mutsvairo, B., & Ragnedda, M. (eds.) (2019). *Mapping the Digital Divide in Africa. A Mediated Analysis*. Amsterdam University Press.

Napoli, P. M. (2021). The platform beat: Algorithmic watchdogs in the disinformation age. *European Journal of Communication*, 36(4), 376–390. https://doi.org/10.1177/02673231211028359

Ragnedda, M., & Gladkova, A. (eds). (2020). *Digital Inequalities in the Global South*. Palgrave Macmillan.

Salaverría, R. (2015). Ideas para renovar la investigación sobre medios digitales. *El Profesional de la Información*, 24(3), 223–226. https://doi.org/10.3145/epi.2015.may.01

Salaverría, R. (2019). Digital journalism: 25 years of research. Review article. *El Profesional de la Información*, 28(1). https://doi.org/10.3145/epi.2019.ene.01

Scolari, C. A. (2013). De las tablillas a las tablets: evolución de las emagazines. *El Profesional de la Información*, 22(1), 10–17. https://doi.org/10.3145/epi.2013.ene.02

Solomin, V. (2022). Trendy razvitiya mul'timediynoy (tsifrovoy) zhurnalistiki i novykh media [Trends in the development of multimedia (digital) journalism and new media]. In: *Media and Communications: State, Problems, Prospects*: 89–93.

Steensen, S., & Westlund, O. (2021). *What Is Digital Journalism Studies?* Routledge.

Steensen, S., Grøndahl Larsen, A. M., Benestad Hågvar, Y., & Kjos Fonn, B. (2019). What does Digital Journalism Studies look like? *Digital Journalism*, 7:3, 320–342. https://doi.org/10.1080/21670811.2019.1581071

Tandoc Jr., E., Hess, K., Eldridge II, S., & Westlund, O. (2020). Diversifying diversity in Digital Journalism Studies: Reflexive research, reviewing and publishing. *Digital Journalism*, 8:3, 301–309. https://doi.org/10.1080/21670811.2020.1738949

Vartanova, E. (2013). *Postsovetskie transformatsii rossiskikh SMI i zhurnalistiki* [Post-Soviet transformations of Russian mass media and journalism]. Moscow.

Vartanova, E. (2021). Tsifrovaya zhurnalistika kak novoye pole akademicheskikh issledovaniy [Digital journalism as a new field of academic research]. *Mediaalmanakh*, 6 (107), 8–14.

Vodopetov, S., & Mahmud, K.N.M. (2022). Transformatsiya zhurnalist·skoy deyatel'nosti v epokhu tsifrovykh tekhnologiy [Transformation of journalism in the digital age]. *Advances in the Humanities*, 6, 19–25.

Waisbord, S. (2019). The 5Ws and 1H of digital journalism. *Digital Journalism*, 7:3, 351–358, https://doi.org/10.1080/21670811.2018.1545592

Zelizer, B. (2019). Why journalism is about more than digital technology. *Digital Journalism*, 7:3, 343–350, https://doi.org/10.1080/21670811.2019.1571932

CHAPTER 24

Digital Climate Newsletters: The New Alternative for Climate Journalism?

Hanna E. Morris

INTRODUCTION

Across mainstream U.S. climate journalism, issues of climate justice are repeatedly sidestepped or superficially engaged with in favor of sensational stories and spectacular images of devastation following mega-storms and disasters. Editorial initiatives dedicated to improving climate reporting such as the Covering Climate Now initiative co-founded in 2019 by Kyle Pope from the *Columbia Journalism Review* and Mark Hertsgaard from *The Nation* in association with *The Guardian* and WNYC have, however, tended to focus on increasing the quantity and urgency of climate news stories as opposed to addressing the recurrent exclusions of people of color, Indigenous people, women, and people living in the Global South from reporting. Within the past couple of years, notable climate journalists and writers such as Emily Atkin, Eric Holthaus, Mary Annaïse Heglar and Amy Westervelt, among others, have begun to produce their own digital climate newsletters independent of mainstream publications to address these recurrent exclusions.

In this chapter, I will first outline key and fundamental shortcomings of mainstream U.S. climate journalism—in particular, the omission of climate justice perspectives and the marginalization of experiences and expertise from historically underrepresented groups. I will then review scholarship that explores the potential for alternative digital and social media to publish and include a more diverse set of positionalities from a more diverse set of

H. E. Morris (✉)
University of Toronto, Toronto, ON, Canada
e-mail: hanna.morris@utoronto.ca

© The Author(s), under exclusive license to Springer Nature Switzerland AG 2024
H. S. Dunn et al. (eds.), *The Palgrave Handbook of Everyday Digital Life*,
https://doi.org/10.1007/978-3-031-30438-5_24

media-makers. Following this, I will examine the self-presentation and stated mission of three prominent U.S. digital climate newsletters dedicated to issues of climate justice: *HEATED* (by Emily Atkin), *The Phoenix* (by Eric Holthaus), and *Hot Take* (by Mary Annaïse Heglar and Amy Westervelt). Through this examination, I will identify and assess the distinguishing characteristics, format, potential opportunities, and drawbacks of digital climate newsletters as an alternative to mainstream climate journalism amidst the rising threats of climate change and authoritarianism in everyday life.

Interrogating Mainstream Critiques of Mainstream Climate Journalism

Ahead of Earth Day 2022, the co-founders of Covering Climate Now, Mark Hertsgaard and Kyle Pope (2022), penned a special column for *Columbia Journalism Review*'s daily digest *The Media Today*, stating:

> It is tragic that, until very recently, the media's treatment of the environment story has gone backward from 50 years ago in every conceivable metric: less urgency, less space, fewer minutes on the air. The fact that journalism is finally beginning to give the story the attention it deserves probably says more about the state of the weather than it does about a newfound media commitment to chronicle what's happening.

This quote demonstrates a predominant critique of mainstream climate journalism repeatedly advanced in the public domain by high-profile figures from a largely male, white, and wealthy contingent of U.S. environmentalism (Taylor, 2002; Sze, 2020). Concerningly, this critique that climate journalism is not "urgent" enough and that there's not enough of it fails to consider the more fundamental issue at hand. Indeed, by totally sidestepping the necessary reflection of *who*, exactly, is doing the "chronicling," *how*, and *to what end?*—the "environment story" remains exclusionary and narrow to the detriment of an adequate understanding of the climate and other distinct environmental crises within context and with more nuance and depth.

Without an adequate investigation of the root causes of the climate crisis or a reckoning with the dynamics of power and privilege at the crux of the crisis, "urgent" stories of climate catastrophe tend to obscure different experiences of harm as well as exclude or belittle an array of different proposals for change (Callison, 2021). The consequences of this include a flurry of apocalyptic climate images and narratives that confuse as opposed to clarify how to respond. Apathy, inaction, or the hubris of an all-encompassing solution capable of "saving the world" follow (as often imagined and promoted by the very same high-profile figures calling for more "urgent" stories) (Morris, 2021). In turn, "the dominance of techno-managerial approaches and the marginalization of calls for addressing structural issues at the root of climate change" pervade across mainstream climate journalism and the mainstream climate movement (Carvalho, 2020, p. 104).

In critique of both climate reporting and high-profile commentary regarding it, climate justice activists and scholars contest an exclusionary mode of journalism and politics that promotes a one-size-fits-all "solution" to a very complex crisis (Sze, 2020). Climate justice advocates argue that top-down, so-called "global management" and "planetary security" projects led by Global North nation-states, totally sidestep key issues of justice and thus stall the necessary political work required to fundamentally challenge the status quo and foster more transformative climate politics (Sze, 2020). To this end, Carvalho (2020, p. 106) importantly points out how:

> Extant empirical research on dominant discourses on climate change and sustainability, such as the ones that are put forth by the most powerful political institutions and those that circulate in mainstream media, shows that those discourses are characterized by exclusionary mechanisms that reinforce the current distribution of power and foreclose alternative voices and views. The media, a vital element of the contemporary public sphere, have contributed mainly to reinforcing the symbolic power of certain social actors, such as top-level politicians, and reducing the scope for non-expert/non-elite participation in the politics of climate change. In contrast with mainstream media, alternative (non-commercial) media have been a significant venue for the expression of other worldviews and ideologies.

In this chapter, I examine the potential for alternative media online to provide a space for generating more robust and inclusive climate reporting. In particular, I focus on how climate justice perspectives and critiques are advanced (or not) through digital media and newsletters outside of the mainstream press.

Digital Media and Climate Justice

The potentially transformative role of counter-discourses and counter-visualities at the scale of everyday life and wider political movements for climate justice are important to consider. Climate justice activists produce their own media on blogs, podcasts, and social media including TikTok, Instagram, Twitter, and YouTube. Through these digital media productions, activists open-up avenues for imagining and building different futures beyond climate catastrophe and techno-managerialism (Sze, 2020; Carvalho, 2020). Different ways of addressing the climate crisis that belie managerial, militaristic, and hyper-capitalistic "solutions" are communicated and advanced through both grassroots movements and online media spaces.

Counter-discourses and activist-produced media can inspire profound movements for change. The Indigenous women and young people who led the #NoDAPL movement in 2016, for example, leveraged alternative digital and social media to build a powerful movement that ultimately inspired young

American climate activists and soon-to-be leaders such as Rep. Alexandria Ocasio-Cortez to run for office and to champion the Green New Deal (Estes and Dhillon, 2019). Despite the ultimate construction of the Dakota Access Pipeline (DAPL) following an executive order issued by Donald Trump promptly following his inauguration in 2017, the #NoDAPL movement sparked an unprecedented alliance between young Indigenous people and young climate activists around the concept of climate justice (Estes and Dhillon, 2019). It ignited a youth-led climate movement committed to social justice that centred Indigenous communities and rejected the exclusionary practices of an older, male-dominated, white, and wealthy stronghold of U.S. environmentalism.

In the words of Indigenous scholar Nick Estes and his co-author and co-editor Jaskiran Dhillon (2019, p. 5), the #NoDAPL movement:

> [...] points to the political possibilities of imagining and reimagining Indigenous decolonization and the political project of getting free—freedom for ourselves and the planet. In this sense, #NoDAPL wasn't a failure because DAPL was ultimately built. The movement reignited the fire of Indigenous liberation and reminded us that it is a fire that cannot be quelled. It provided, for a brief moment in time, a collective vision of what the future could be.

The #NoDAPL movement demonstrated the power of building this collective vision and solidarity through both on-the-ground actions *and* alternative digital media spaces. Social media, in particular, was understood as a pivotal and core organizing tool with tangible, material impacts—a key lesson that figures (like Ocasio-Cortez) took away from their experiences and participation in the #NoDAPL movement (Estes and Dhillon, 2019). To this end and in stride with the Black Lives Matter movement, videos of police violence taken on phones at Standing Rock and shared via social media though the #NoDAPL hashtag, generated a counter-narrative to mainstream media stories that portrayed protestors as dangerous and violent (Sze, 2020). In this way, social media and alternative digital media spaces allowed activists at Standing Rock to take more control over their narratives and to contest exclusionary and defamatory media representations.

Following the protests at Standing Rock, many young people a part of the U.S. climate movement adopted a more explicit and nuanced commitment to social justice as learned and practiced during the #NoDAPL movement (Estes and Dhillon, 2019). Notably, the movement for Black Lives aligned with Indigenous water defenders at Standing Rock and underscored the intersectionality of the lived experiences of Black, Indigenous, and People of Color (BIPOC) in the fight against an exploitative fossil fuel economy (Sze, 2020). A clear and strong counter-discourse that centered BIPOC perspectives gained immense traction within a youth-led climate justice movement through social media and alternative digital media spaces. This counter-discourse directly challenged the exclusions of a dominant mode of U.S. environmentalism led by predominantly older, white, and financially well-resourced men. Conversations about the climate crisis therefore gained a level of nuance, diversity, inclusion, and depth as well as widespread interest among Millennials and Gen Z in part due to the success of the #NoDAPL movement across social and digital media spaces (Estes and Dhillon, 2019). Critically, TallBear (2019) underscores how "the women-led condition"—in addition to the youth and BIPOC-led condition—of the contemporary climate movement and alternative climate media productions are especially striking and apparent. The larges-cale absence of both climate justice perspectives and women of color from mainstream media coverage is therefore all the more revealing of its profound oversights and exclusions.

As Estes and TallBear underscore, Sze (2020) also highlights how the counter-discourses emergent from the #NoDAPL movement flourished within social media and alternative digital media spaces. These counter-discourses were so influential and transformative not only because they centered the lived experiences of BIPOC, young people, and women, but also because they encouraged the imagining of many different possible futures and ways of living that previously seemed impossible or out of sight. Sze (2020, p. 44) writes:

> Making new identities was central to Standing Rock [...] That sense of community and optimism, the making of a temporary home in the face of violence and destruction, is why the details of how to live, eat, and shelter became a large part of media and activist accounts of Standing Rock. [...] Transformative politics, nonviolent direct action, and the solidarities—however fraught and temporary—offer a vision counterposed against the extractive one embodied by DAPL.

But despite this profound discursive shift and emergence of a more transformative form of climate politics, climate justice perspectives and counter-discourses continue to be marginalized and excluded from mainstream climate journalism in the U.S. Moreover, while social media and alternative digital media spaces have been incredibly productive terrain for building solidarity and a robust climate justice movement, digital media are not utopic or without issue. Asymmetries of power can be (and are) reproduced in alternative media spaces (Moernaut et al., 2018). As we've seen in recent years, conspiracy theories also thrive online as do practices like trolling and doxing of primarily female, nonbinary, and queer activists of color. Critically, the fact that digital media platforms are owned by large corporations more concerned with the bottom line than social justice and the climate crisis cannot be ignored. Digital media, therefore, require dedicated attention and close analysis to decipher the opportunities *and* drawbacks of alternative online media spaces for climate counter-discourses and climate justice movement-building.

Research Design

In this chapter, I specifically examine the self-presentation and distinguishing characteristics of three digital climate newsletters. In particular, I analyze how the authors of *HEATED* (by Emily Atkin), *The Phoenix* (by Eric Holthaus), and *Hot Take* (by Mary Annaïse Heglar and Amy Westervelt) position their publications in relation to mainstream climate journalism and high-profile critiques of it. These three newsletters are distinct from other climate newsletters produced by, for example, Bill McKibben for *The New Yorker*, because of the authors' stated alignment with the climate justice movement and their newsletters' independence from the legacy press.

Through my analysis, I seek to understand how each newsletter establishes its legitimacy and how, exactly, each of the authors seeks to align their publication with the climate justice movement. What critiques are advanced by the authors? What narratives, images, groups, and individuals do the newsletters feature, and how / in what manner? To grapple with these questions, I analyze the newsletters' "About" pages, mission statements, subscription pitches, logos, and other forms of self-presentation through the method of critical discourse analysis (CDA).

CDA's offer "productive tools" for "examining the discursive struggles between the proponents of alternative pathways to the future, analyzing the relation between discourse and socio-political contexts, and identifying the (potential) space for discourses of transformation" (Carvalho, 2020, p. 104). Through the method of CDA, I determine how each newsletter linguistically and conceptually distinguishes itself from mainstream climate journalism through an analysis of central appeals and allusions to certain controversies, events, contexts, groups, and people. Ultimately, I assess how the authors attempt to establish their publication's legitimacy. To this end and in the following section, I examine and detail how the newsletter authors seek to address (or not) the exclusions of mainstream climate journalism and also how the newsletter authors seek to align (or not) with the climate justice movement.

Purposefully Oppositional to the Mainstream

Across all three newsletters, the authors carve out their legitimacy through their publications' distinction from and purposeful opposition to mainstream climate journalism. This practice of establishing legitimacy through opposition to mainstream journalism is common for alternative media. Holt et al. (2019, p. 861, italics in original) underscore how:

> Often, the active positioning vis-à-vis, the challenge to and critique of legacy media and professional journalists have been a defining characteristic of various alternative media. Not surprising, alternative media have been practiced and understood primarily as alternative or even opposition to the *legacy* or *mainstream media*.

Indeed, "the term 'mainstream news media' [...] plays a crucial role in alternative news media's self-perception" (Holt et al., 2019, p. 861) and self-presentation. Cushion et al. (2021, p. 633) highlight how "it is the dominant characteristics of mainstream media in national media systems that help shape the editorial agenda of alternative media and the nature of criticism directed at professional journalism." It is here where the authors of all three digital climate newsletters clearly state their concerns about issues of climate justice and seek to cover what is actually happening in the everyday lives of readers on the ground and on the frontlines of the climate movement—the lives and experiences that mainstream publications consistently disregard.

To this end, each of the newsletter authors express deep emotion—anger and angst from Atkin, outrage and exhaustion from Westervelt and Heglar, grief and hope from Holthaus—to contest a detached and exclusionary mainstream press. Each of the authors repeatedly position themselves as "real" people with "real" emotions and "real" opinions. This self-presentation purposefully counters the traditional journalistic norms of objectivity and neutrality. The authors' "realness" is leveraged to effectively humanize the authors through a demonstrated sense of authenticity. As opposed to the typical journalist's self-presentation as an unattached observer, the newsletter authors here present themselves as emotionally attached and active participants in the struggle for climate justice. Each author therefore establishes their legitimacy precisely by claiming that they are *not* like the "typical" journalist.

The newsletter authors perform this "atypical" positionality through their informal style and language in addition to their emotional expressions and opinions. For example, through the use of hashtags, humor, memes, and also by embedding social media posts from vacations, weekends at home, and other aspects of their personal lives, the authors present themselves as just like you. Atkin, for instance, regularly expresses her "burn out"; Westervelt and Heglar share climate-themed cocktail recipes to help get through the stress of contemporary politics; Holthaus writes manifesto-like rants. Moreover, this informality, personability, and "alternativeness" as such are visually represented through the logos and graphical styles for each newsletter—e.g., the punky fire logo for *HEATED* harkening back to 1990s grunge culture; three tiny fire emojis as well as a hipster-esque cartoon logo portrait of Westervelt and Heglar for *Hot Take*; and psychedelic illustrations reminiscent of the 1960s counter-culture aesthetic for *The Phoenix*.

The newsletter authors' purposeful rejection of the cold, hard, and distanced realm of traditional journalism extends to their direct appeals to the readers themselves. Through "audience engagement," each author strives to establish a friendly, if not personal, relationship with their readers. Holthaus asks readers to "DM" him on Twitter and convenes "Tuesday Threads" where he polls readers with specific questions he then responds to; Atkin shares selfies and photos of her dogs and replies to comments on her personal Twitter profile; Westervelt and Heglar throw "subscriber-only virtual happy hours" and also encourage readers to interact with them on Twitter. This audience engagement, on the one hand, can be interpreted as in stride with celebrity Twitter (now X), Tik Tok, and Instagram accounts that seek to build a profitable fanbase of "followers." On the other hand, this interaction with readers can be understood as a corrective to the exclusions and distance of mainstream climate journalism from its readership. Indeed, publications like *The New York Times* and *The Wall Street Journal,* for instance, typically sideline the experiences and perspectives of the very same people each of the newsletter authors strive to connect with and center in their publications.

Building upon this personalized connection with people and their everyday lives, concerns, anxieties, and struggles, the newsletter authors also align themselves with the young and diverse activists on the "frontlines" of the climate justice movement to, in the words of Atkin's mission statement, "stop the forces that have been preventing climate action for the last 30 years." Holthaus's mission statement and "About" page similarly asserts:

> After centuries of systemic racism and colonialism and extractive capitalism, our world is at a turning point. You and I and everyone you know were born at exactly the right time to change everything. What we need isn't more stories about apocalypse; **what we need is justice**. (emphasis in the original text)

In stride with these appeals, Heglar's bio on the "About" page states: "Mary is an accomplished climate justice essayist whose work has been integral to getting the climate movement to understand climate change as a justice issue that intersects with every other justice issue." Westervelt's bio, notably, lists her journalistic credentials and accomplishments. These accolades effectively establish her as possessing "insider" knowledge of the journalism profession. Heglar, however, is positioned as solidly within the activist realm—establishing a direct link with the climate justice movement required to lend the newsletter its "street cred." Illustrating this, a common header repeatedly accompanying the *Hot Take* newsletter states:

> Hey Hot Cakes! Welcome to *Hot Take*! Your weekly (at least) newsletter surveying the state of the climate crisis and all the ways we're talking—and not talking about it! We give you a round up of the latest climate stories and articles of the week, plus exclusive original reporting and commentary from us. Oh, and who are we? Amy Westervelt, long-time climate journalist with more seasoning than an everything bagel, and Mary Annaïse Heglar, a literary writer known for her essays on climate, race, and emotion—and her enthusiasm for dad jokes!

The informal language and friendly appeal to readers (i.e., "Hot Cakes") and positioning of Westervelt as "seasoned" and Heglar as emotional, enthusiastic, and approachable with her "dad jokes" creates a sense of authenticity *and* expertise derived from direct *experience* within the ranks of both mainstream media and the activist frontlines.

Atkin's bio similarly establishes herself as, on the one hand, an angry and active part of the climate justice movement and on the other hand, a respected and accomplished journalist with years of experience. Atkin therefore portrays herself as possessing both non-traditional "street cred" and also more traditional journalistic credentials presented as evidence of her "insider" knowledge of the media industry. Westervelt's and Atkin's experience and command of the journalistic profession is, in this way, leveraged to show their expertise as well as their self-awareness and integrity that distinguishes them from their less-aware and "less-cool" counterparts still working for the legacy press.

Notably, all three of the newsletters directly and consistently critique mainstream climate journalism. These critiques, in particular, center-in on the exclusionary nature of mainstream climate media produced by wealthy, white, and older men. Holthaus, a self-identified white man himself, interestingly calls upon critiques made by Atkin (a young woman) and Heglar and Westervelt (both women of color) in his own newsletter. This reveals a notable function decipherable across these three digital climate newsletters: their role as curator / gatekeeper of the alternative digital climate media space. Indeed, Atkin has also featured both Heglar and Westervelt in her newsletter as has Heglar and Westervelt featured Atkin in their newsletter and podcast. There is a notable cross-promotion of each other's work. In this way, the curation and promotion of "good" climate journalism through weekly "digests" effectively serves an unofficial gatekeeping function. Absent of a more formal editor or content moderator of digital climate newsletters, this cross-promotion and curation by the authors in this emergent digital climate media space provides some structure to an otherwise amorphous terrain.

Affordances and Shortcomings of Digital Climate Newsletters

This ad hoc gatekeeping function, however, cannot always combat the power and reach of well-funded "bad actors" that propagate conspiracy theories and climate mis/dis-information online. Disinformation and false claims can go unchecked and proliferate across alternative digital media spaces absent of a more official content moderator or form of regulation. For example, a notable and revealing finding from my analysis demonstrates the significance of this lack of moderation through a controversy that unfolded in late 2020/early 2021 involving the subscription-based digital media platform that the newsletter authors each used prior to the controversy: Substack.

Substack came under fire beginning in 2020 due to the unchecked spread of COVID-19 misinformation and hate speech by platform-promoted and funded authors. *TechCrunch* (Ha, 2021) reported:

> Last week, the writer Jude Ellison Sady Doyle pointed to writers like Yglesias, Glenn Greenwald and Freddie deBoer (several of whom departed larger publications, supposedly turning to Substack for greater editorial independence) and suggested that the platform has become 'famous for giving massive advances […] to people who actively hate trans people and women, argue ceaselessly against our civil rights, and in many cases, have a public history of directly, viciously abusing trans people and/or cis women in their industry.'

Reporters at *Mashable* (Navlakha, 2022) also found that some high-profile (and therefore, highly profitable) Substack newsletters "promote anti-vaccine sentiments and COVID-19 misinformation, with writers like Dr. Joseph Mercola, Steve Kirsch, and Alex Berenson, each known for publishing a slew of misinformation surrounding the pandemic, finding a home on Substack after being deplatformed elsewhere."

To affirm their legitimacy as an "alternative" to the profit-logics of corporate media execs and the "tech-bros" behind Substack, *Hot Take* and *The Phoenix* along with a large contingent of other progressive newsletters migrated to a platform called Ghost in early 2021. *HEATED*, however, remained on Substack. Atkin did not weigh in on the controversy or provide reasons as to why she kept her newsletter at Substack. Holthaus as well as Westervelt and Heglar, however, dedicated entire editions of their newsletters to discuss the controversy and detailed their reasons for switching over to Ghost.

Holthaus (10/1/2021) wrote:

> I've been increasingly frustrated with Substack for many reasons over the past year, most importantly their refusal to take a stand to restrict harmful speech — on gender equality, COVID misinformation, and climate denial and delay — on their platform. I was under contract with Substack until yesterday. Today I left. I refuse to believe that any of us should have to accept a world where the status quo is trying to actively kill us. I also launched *The Phoenix* with this promise: 'We were born at exactly the right time to change everything.' I'm very excited about Ghost, but I'm even more excited about this chance to reboot *The Phoenix*.

Westervelt and Heglar wrote (4/2/2021):

> Hey Hot Cakes! After watching the various public and private conversations around Substack and its secret editorial policy play out, we decided to make the move to Ghost, a nonprofit, fully transparent platform that reinvests its revenue in technology and service updates. We know exactly where Ghost's money comes from and where it goes, because they post all of it online. So, yeah, you could say we're...um...ghosting Substack. (Mary's very proud of that one.)

But even with a move to Ghost, are these digital climate newsletters *really* "independent" from the mainstream? The profit-motive of start-up tech companies are not in-line with the stated commitments and values of the three digital climate newsletters under analysis in this chapter. Westervelt and Heglar explicitly acknowledge this disconnect and underscore the challenges they face as writers concerned with issues of climate justice within a hyper-capitalistic digital media sphere.

In particular, digital media companies and execs repeatedly remove themselves from any and all ethical and professional obligation to moderate content published on their platforms and refuse to clamp-down on disinformation and hate speech. Substack continues to deny any form of regulatory responsibility and continually defaults to its self-selected identity as a "neutral" tech company as opposed to a publisher or media company. This so-called "neutrality" as well as the company's stated commitment to "free speech," essentially equates informed critiques and investigative reporting with the so-called "research" of conspiracy theorists and disinformation campaigns. The refusal of Substack and other digital media companies to recognize their responsibility as publishers and to monitor and remove hate speech and disinformation from their platforms, reveals significant risks and potential drawbacks of digital climate newsletters within a hyper-capitalistic and unregulated digital media space.

Conclusion

The pointed critiques made by the authors of the three digital climate newsletters under analysis in this chapter underscore the oversights of the mainstream press and reveal the powerful potential of alternative digital climate media. As revealed by the disinformation and conspiracy theories that thrive on platforms like Substack, however, legitimate critiques of mainstream journalism are at risk of being co-opted by a reactionary right and climate deniers that use the very same digital platforms for very different (and contradicting) purposes (Rae, 2021; Cushion et al., 2021; Figenschou and Ihlebæk, 2019). This co-optation of legitimate critiques of the mainstream press among a reactionary right poses profound risks for climate justice-aligned publications within an unregulated alternative digital media space. Absent of a clear distinction between legitimate critiques and conspiracy theories, viable critiques can be appropriated, neutralized, and stripped of their potential capacity to foster a wider climate justice movement.

Moreover, the digital climate newsletter format is increasingly used by mainstream publications such as *The New Yorker*, *Washington Post*, *The New York Times*, and *The Atlantic*—presumably trying to capture a younger audience and profit from the appeal of a more personable format. Digital newsletters authored by one or two "authentic" individuals could increase accountability, inclusion, and trust in the legacy press or, concerningly, could further advance a dangerous cult of personality within an increasingly authoritarian culture. Further scholarly attention is required to attend to these affordances and risks of digital climate newsletters within the present contexts and conditions of the climate crisis, a hyper-capitalistic digital media sphere, and U.S. authoritarianism.

References

Callison, C. (2021) "Journalism, Indigenous knowing, and climate futures (and pasts)" in Bødker, H., & Morris, H.E. (Eds.) *Climate Change and Journalism: Negotiating Rifts of Time*. London, UK: Routledge, pp. 10–23.

Carvalho, A. (2020). "Discourses for transformation? Climate change, power and pathways," in Krippendorff, K., & Halibi, N. (Eds.) *Discourses in Action: What Language Enables Us to Do*. London, UK: Routledge, pp. 104–119.

Cushion, S., McDowell-Naylor, D., & Thomas, R. (2021) Why National Media Systems Matter: A Longitudinal Analysis of How UK Left-Wing and Right-Wing Alternative Media Critique Mainstream Media (2015–2018), *Journalism Studies*, (22)5, pp. 633–652.

Estes, N., & Dhillon, J. (Eds.) (2019). *Standing with Standing Rock*. Minnesota University Press.

Figenschou, T.U., & Ihlebæk, K.A. (2019) Challenging Journalistic Authority, *Journalism Studies*, (20)9, pp. 1221–1237.

Ha, A. (2021, March 18). "Substack faces backlash over the writes it supports with big advances," *TechCrunch*. Retrieved from: https://techcrunch.com/2021/03/18/substack-backlash/?guccounter=1

Hertsgaard, M., & Pope, K. (2022, April 21). "Earth Day, and the media's point of view," *The Media Today*.

Holt, K., Figenschou, T.C., & Frischlich, L. (2019). Key Dimensions of Alternative News Media, *Digital Journalism*, 7(7), pp. 860–869.

Holthaus, E. (2021, October 21). "Welcome to Phoenix 2.0," *The Phoenix*. Retrieved from: https://thephoenix.earth/welcome-to-the-phoenix-2-0/

Moernaut, R., Mast, J. and Pepermans, Y. (2018). Reversed positionality, reversed reality? The multimodal Environmental Justice frame in mainstream and alternative media, *International Communication Gazette*, 80(5), pp. 476–505.

Morris, H.E. (2021). Apocalypse Divided: Analyzing Power, Media, and Climate Change Before and After Trump. *Politique Américaine*, 36(1), 53–75.

Navlakha, M. (2022, March 9). "Why Substack creators are leaving the platform, again," *Mashable*. Retrieved from: https://mashable.com/article/substack-writers-leaving-misinformation

Rae, M. (2021). Hyperpartisan news: Rethinking the media for populist politics, *New Media & Society*, 23(5), pp. 117–1132.

Sze, J. (2020). *Environmental Justice in a Moment of Danger*. Oakland, CA: University of California Press.

TallBear, K. (2019). "Badass Indigenous Women Caretake Relations: #STANDINGROCK, #IDLENOMORE, #BLACKLIVESMATTER" in Estes, N., & Dhillon, J. (Eds.) *Standing with Standing Rock*. Minnesota University Press, pp. 1–10.

Taylor, D.E. (2002). Race, class, gender, and American environmentalism. Gen. Tech. Rep. PNW-GTR-534. Portland, OR: U.S. Department of Agriculture, Forest Service, Pacific Northwest Research Station. https://www.fs.fed.us/pnw/pubs/gtr534.pdf

Westervelt, A., & Heglar, M. (2021, April 2). "We're Ghosting Substack," *Hot Take*.

CHAPTER 25

Public Service Broadcasting in Transition: The Rise of Digital Non-State Public Service Media in Southern Africa

Khulekani Ndlovu and Peter Mutanda

Introduction

From its inception, public service broadcasting (PSB) in Southern Africa has been beset by challenges posed by a colonial heritage, partisan and state imposed editorial policies and compromised financial viability. Firstly, in post-colonial Southern Africa, public service broadcasting was naturally assumed to be the responsibility of state broadcasters. Given that broadcasting in Africa was introduced and owned by colonial governments, it advanced the racialised, imperial and capitalist interests of the colonial enterprise. Consequently, PSB fell short of the public service ideals of being an inclusive, egalitarian and robust portion of the public sphere. Upon political independence, these state broadcasters underwent a cosmetic change that did not go beyond renaming them to reflect the nationalist ethos of the newly independent states.

In principle, these broadcasters were supposed to be African incarnations of the BBC model of broadcasting. However, in practice, they remained partisan megaphones of the elites in power. Instead of being in the service of colonialism, they were now in the service of the hegemonic ambitions of the governing liberation parties. The upshot of this was that most state broadcasters in Southern Africa failed to be in the service of the public interest, civic education and deliberative democracy. Apart from narrow state control, many national

K. Ndlovu (✉) • P. Mutanda
University of Botswana, Gaborone, Botswana
e-mail: Ndlovukh@ub.ac.bw

© The Author(s), under exclusive license to Springer Nature Switzerland AG 2024
H. S. Dunn et al. (eds.), *The Palgrave Handbook of Everyday Digital Life*,
https://doi.org/10.1007/978-3-031-30438-5_25

broadcasters also had to contend with the challenge of inadequate capitalisation as most relied on government handouts or licensing fees. The cumulative effect of the above coupled with the pressure to commercialise meant that the public service mandate of the state broadcasters was and has been severely compromised. However, the technology transition from analogue to digital broadcasting and its reduction of the barriers of entry into the broadcasting sector has meant that non-state actors are able to help plug the gaps in conventional public service broadcasting. Civil society, commercial and philanthropic media initiatives and community stations have now taken up some of the public service broadcasting mandates. They are often seen to function as the locus of public discourse, perform civic education roles and advance community dialogue in the public interest. Using a desk review of illustrative cases drawn from South Africa, Zimbabwe and Botswana this chapter explores how these various online initiatives in Southern Africa act as quasi-public broadcasters by capitalising on the everyday affordances of digital media.

In the main, the chapter considers how these digital initiatives disrupt the gatekeeping function of mainstream media and compound the threats to the commercial media business model. Further, we advance the view that these initiatives have facilitated the formation of virtually fluid discourse publics and the creation of new media rituals. The chapter begins with an overview of public service broadcasting in southern Africa, followed by a discussion of the diffusion of digital media in Africa. The theory section discusses the concept of interloper media and the public sphere to make sense of the production and consumption of PSB genre content in digital spaces. This is followed by two sections which constitute the desk review of the cases under discussion. The desk review is succeeded by a section which explores the disruptive impacts of digital transformation on mainstream media and the everyday lives of the audiences who consume digital PSB genre content. The penultimate section concludes the chapter.

Overview of Public Service Broadcasters in Southern Africa

Broadcasting in the Southern Africa was introduced by colonial governments to service settler interests and racial minority rule. The foregoing was reflected in the exclusive use of European languages in broadcasting, racialised staffing requirements and the deliberate targeting of a predominantly white target audience (Mano, 2010).

The establishment of amateur radio stations in Cape Town, Durban and Johannesburg in South Africa signalled the advent of broadcasting services in Southern Africa. Broadcasting in South Africa was institutionalised in 1936 with the establishment of the South African Broadcasting Corporation (SABC). The Governor General was solely responsible for the appointment of the board members of the newly established corporation and broadcasting rights were the exclusive privilege of the SABC (Bevan, 2008).

Meanwhile across the Limpopo in Rhodesia, radio broadcasting was introduced in 1933 by the British colonial administration. As in other colonies, the Rhodesian broadcaster did not produce any programmes for black people but was a local incarnation of the BBC (Smith, 2021). 1960 is the year that Rhodesia Television (RTV) was established in Salisbury (Harare) as a private enterprise. It was subsequently taken over by the Rhodesian government in 1975. The colonial government renamed it the Rhodesia Broadcasting Corporation Television (RBC TV) and used it as its propaganda mouth piece (Melber et al., 2004). In post-independence Zimbabwe, the RBC became the Zimbabwe Broadcasting Corporation (ZBC) (Nkomo, 2018).

It is worth noting that while South Africa and Rhodesia experienced apartheid and colonialism, Britain declared Bechuanaland (Botswana) a 'protectorate' for military strategic interests but not necessarily for its economic resources (Mogalakwe, 2006). Lesitaokana (2013) notes that the first colonial radio broadcast signal in Bechuanaland was sent by the British Colonial Administration in Mafikeng. The broadcast mainly catered for the immediate community that fell within the twenty-mile radius of the radio signal. Radio broadcasting was extended to Lobatse village in 1965 with the establishment of Radio Bechuanaland. When Botswana gained independence in 1966, Radio Bechuanaland was relaunched as Radio Botswana. The attainment of independence saw the broadcaster adopt a more national outlook in its programming that comprised of civic education, agricultural shows, current affairs, news, announcements of cabinet decisions and the live broadcasting of parliamentary debates (Lesitaokana, 2013).

In July 2000, the state broadcaster launched Botswana Television (BTV), which according to its founding documents was supposed to live up to the ideals of a PSB (Balule, 2013). However, media scholars have highlighted that the PSB mandate has been compromised by partisan posturing. Mosanako was critical of the BTV as an effective PSB. She indicates that: "…there is a challenge that the national media may carry developmental messages framed within the government view, but limited in terms of empowering ordinary citizens. (Mosanako, 2016, p. 325)

Furthermore, Balule attributes state interference to the political economy of the state broadcaster thus:

> … Botswana's laws and policies compares favourably with international standards, there are no structural guarantees and rules to promote PSB in the country. The absence of these is attributable to the government's attitude that public media funded through public funds must serve the interests of the government. This is a clear abuse of national assets, which must be used to serve the public interest and not partisan interests. (Balule, 2013, p. 92)

Generally, in post-independence Africa, the newly established governments tasked the colonially inherited broadcasters with the PSB mandate and the need to help decolonise, develop and build the post-colonial nations (Taha, 2016). The evidence suggests that just like their colonial predecessors, the spectre of government bias still haunts state broadcasters in post-colonial Southern Africa. For example, the post-apartheid SABC has been criticised for being subject to undue political influence from the ruling ANC and thus falling short of being a true public service broadcaster (Barnett, 1999; Fourie, 2013).

Similarly, the Zimbabwean ZBC has been faulted for being biased towards the ruling ZANU-PF (Masuku, 2011). Overt partisanship has dispelled any pretence by the ZBC of being a public service broadcaster (Masuku, 2011). On the other hand, the Zimbabwean government has been enforcing draconian laws to clamp down on media freedom (Alfandika & Gwindingwe, 2021). Thus, the national broadcaster in Zimbabwe is both state-owned and state-controlled, and mandated to serve the state's interests. Government appoints the ZBC Board. There is no process of public nomination or any form of public involvement in the selection of the board. Editorial independence at the ZBC is non-existent (Mano, 2016).

It is worth noting that reliance on ever decreasing state funding, unappealing content that gives audiences no justifiable reason to pay licence fees, have meant that most state broadcasters are in a financially precarious position. Recent global economic shifts and weak national economies have only compounded the problem (Ndlela, 2007). In the main, there is a great deal of scepticism about the ability of state broadcasters in Southern Africa to deliver on PSB mandates. It is against this backdrop that new digital technologies were celebrated as facilitating the growth of alternative media that can compensate for the deficiencies of state broadcasters. Berger et al.'s (2009) observations about the democratising potential of satellite television, aptly describe the potential of digital media. They argue that "although unevenly distributed, more media means a change for state-owned broadcasters who no longer have the field to themselves" (Berger et al., 2009, p. 10).

Mapping the Transition and the Diffusion of Digital Media in Southern Africa

It is now a truism that the proliferation of smart mobile technologies, though not a magic bullet that solves the myriad of challenges facing media in Southern Africa, has leapfrogged Africa's transition into the digital media ecosystem. Data from Internet World Stats (2022) shows that Africa accounts for 11.5 per cent of global internet use. This generalised statistic does not do justice to country-specific realities but is useful for signposting the digital divide and inequities that subsist between the Global North and the Global South (Gillwald & Mothobi, 2018). A country-specific look at the level of internet diffusion and use of digital platforms in the Southern African countries discusses in this chapter, paints a more optimistic picture. Recent figures show that Botswana has 1 247 000 active internet users, which translates to 51.3 per cent of its 2 429 926 241 population (Internet World Stats 2022). Figures for Zimbabwe reveal that internet penetration stands at 55.2 per cent of its 15 220 009 population. Sixty-three per cent of South Africa's 60 million population use the internet (Internet World Stats 2022). The foregoing statistical summaries reveal that in these countries a significant portion of the population enjoys a digital media presence.

Of note, is the fact that in Southern Africa 7 out of 10 people access the internet via mobile smartphone devices (Gillwald & Mothobi, 2018). Such a statistic takes on greater importance in a context where traditional mainstream media is suffering from a crisis of trust, partisan capture and compromised viability. Moreover, most broadcasters in the region have failed to meet the International Telecommunications Union June 2015 digital migration deadline. On the production side, undercapitalisation of broadcasters means they cannot replace analogue equipment with digital broadcasting consoles and transmitters (Motsaathebe & Chiumbu, 2021).

On the reception side, digital setup boxes and high-definition televisions are a luxury that the economic underclasses cannot afford (ibid). In the case of Botswana, (Lesitaokana & Mosanako, 2021) have chronicled how logistical and unresolved supply side challenges have meant that digitally ready set-top boxes are not readily available in the Botswana market. Further, they reveal that those who can afford them see no reason for buying the set-top boxes and prefer to continue with Multichoice's DSTV. For the remainder of the population, the authors posit that it is highly unlikely that the poor will purchase the set-top boxes if the state does not provide or subsidise the devices. Similarly, Matsilele et al., (2021) found that the digitisation of broadcasting in Zimbabwe has stalled due to administrative bureaucracy, financial incapacitation, analogue infrastructure, limited internet access and connectivity.

As with the case of Botswana, the authors reveal that the supply of set-top boxes is a challenge, as one of the companies responsible for their procurement is yet to initiate the procurement process (273). They further predict that a hyperinflationary environment and lack of disposable income mean that the bulk of the population will not be able to afford the set-top boxes. (Motsaathebe & Chiumbu, 2021) note that while South Africa has the highest internet diffusion and usage in the region, it is not altogether exempt from the challenges that have deferred the transition to digital broadcasting. Economic inequalities have meant that there is a need for the state to subsidise the non-affluent classes. Additionally, Motsaathebe & Chiumbu emphasise that the South African state "has failed to distribute STB which had been promised to low-income groups [...] Those identified for this subsidy included households that depend on social grants and those with a monthly income of less than R3200 (approximately $200)" (Motsaathebe & Chiumbu, 2021, p. 147). In addition to the foregoing, digital migration in South Africa has been frustrated by a lethargic administrative process, conflicting commercial interests and limited publicity of the digital migration initiative.

Of significance to this chapter is that while state broadcaster's transition to digital terrestrial television has been beset by challenges and is yet to be fully implemented, significant portions of the population in Southern Africa are already digitally connected because of smart mobile technology. Notwithstanding the reality of the digital exclusion of low income, rural and marginalised communities, most people consume a lot of audio-visual content that is made within the ever-growing digital ecosystem. Significantly, social networks have become an avenue for broadcasting alternative content that counters the partisan and poor-quality programming of most broadcasters. YouTube and Facebook live streaming have emerged as popular forms of deinstitutionalised television. Podcasting and X spaces are gaining popularity as digital platforms for publishing audio content.

Moreover, there is a plethora of internet-hosted audio streaming sites, which have facilitated the proliferation of online radio. The diffusion of the internet and use of social media in the region has given rise to peripheral "interloper media" (Eldridge, 2014, p. 1) which while not public service broadcasters in the traditional institutionalised sense, produce content that falls within the "PSB genre" (Fourie, 2013, p. 13). Our observation is that the illustrative cases that are the subject of this chapter are consistent with what Fourie characterises as "distributed PSB" within the new media environment (Fourie, 2010, p. 1).

Theorising Digital-Peripheral, Interloper Media as Quasi PSBs

The proliferation of digital media has made it possible for non-professional, de-institutionalised, civic and citizen actors to produce media content that complements traditional journalistic media (Cheruiyot et al., 2021; Eldridge, 2014; Schapals et al., 2019). This development has been interpreted as blurring the boundaries of mainstream journalism and has generated professional and academic narratives that seek to do "boundary maintenance" (Eldridge, 2014, p. 2). Boundary work mainly deploys dichotomous labels of insiders and outsiders and the spatial metaphor of centre and periphery to distinguish between legacy/professional/institutionalised and emergent/fluid/marginal forms of media practice. Recently, the concept of interloper media has been advanced to conceptualise the encroachment of new actors into the domain of legacy journalistic media. "It captures the socially-constructed discursive boundaries which journalists use to define their space in society, and the ways in which new actors persist to see themselves as journalists in the face of such boundary work" (Eldridge, 2019, p. 11).

For Holton and Belair-Gagnon (2018, p. 73), content creators and platforms that lay claim to the title of being journalists or journalistic media, are "explicit interlopers". The authors also recognise the existence of "implicit interlopers" (Holton & Belair-Gagnon, 2018, p. 74). Implicit interlopers are actors who produce "para-journalistic work" motivated by the need to "improve civic discourse" (Schapals et al., 2019, p. 19, 21). Holton and Belair-Gagnon (2018, p. 75) point to the need to acknowledge the work of "intralopers". These are people who perform extra-journalistic roles in newsrooms, which are essential to the editorial aspects of journalism. These include various tasks that span the range of technical and administrative duties.

For present purposes, we find the categories of explicit and implicit interlopers productive for conceptualising the work of digital-peripheral actors who are producing "PSB genre" content in Southern Africa (Fourie, 2013, p. 13). Though these digital peripheral actors may not always identify or be identified as journalists in the professional and normative sense, they produce content that is "functionally equivalent" to public service broadcasters (Schapals et al., 2019, p. 20). It is against this backdrop that we find the concept of interloper media useful for capturing this reality. The political-economic and sociocultural context that has compromised the ability of state-funded broadcasters to live up to PSB ideals, has meant that most of these digital-peripheral interlopers play an interventionist and counterhegemonic role. They are interventionist in that they seek to compensate for the failings of captured state broadcasters. Further, they are interventionist in that their para-journalistic efforts are in the service of a predetermined civic mission. Their counterhegemonic orientation is occasioned by the need to challenge partisan narratives that find currency in mainstream media and that do not cater for subaltern social groupings. In this sense, these digital-peripheral, interloper spaces also function as (counter) public spherules.

Generally, the Habermasian public sphere is the default philosophical perspective that has been used to articulate the socio-political role of public service broadcasting. In its classical sense the public sphere entails:

> The realm of all our social life in which something approaching public opinion can be formed. Access is guaranteed to all citizens. A portion of the public sphere comes to being in every conversation in which private individuals assemble to form a public body…citizens behaves as public body when they confer in an unrestricted fashion-that is, with the guarantee of freedom of assembly and association and the freedom to express and publish their opinions-about matters of general interest. (Habermas, 1989, p. 136)

Considered from this perspective, public broadcasters are supposed to facilitate deliberative democracy by being conduits of public interest information and the locus of rational argumentation. However as indicated above, state broadcasters have failed to live up to the normative ideals of the public sphere and PSB. According to Dahlberg (2007, p. 49) the public sphere norm:

... involves rational-critical deliberation over disputed validity claims, aimed at reaching understanding and agreement. This rational-critical communication is ideally inclusive (formally); free (non-coercive); sincere (as far as this is possible); respectful (putting oneself in the position of the other); reasoned (framing arguments in terms of why particular claims ought to be accepted) and reflexive (identity reconstituting).

In most of Southern Africa, inclusivity eludes most state broadcasters. In the main, they pander to parochial ethno-political interests and churn propaganda that does not pass the test of being sincere, reasoned and reflexive. Thus, in their current form, they fall short of satisfying the structural, representational and interactional dimensions of the public sphere (Dahlberg, 2007, pp. 148–150). Structurally, their political economy means they are beholden to governments who fund them. Representationally, they fail to adequately capture the range of expressions and experiences that characterise these postcolonial societies. Interactionally, they disappoint in terms of facilitating dialogue and intercourse among citizens. It is against this backdrop that digital platforms hold the promise of modestly compensating for the above failings.

Given that the public sphere is not an *a priori* spatially and institutionally bounded communicative space, but is constituted in every instance of public communication. Interloper media function as public sphericules and come into being when private citizens exercise communicative citizenship on online platforms vis-à-vis public interest issues. The concept of public sphericules speaks to the reality that it is not feasible nor ideal for the public sphere to be a unitary or homogeneous discursive space (Fraser, 1990; Gitlin, 1998). Within the ever-increasing digital ecosystem, "distinct communities of information and participation are multiplying" (Gitlin, 1998, p. 170). Some of these communities are the product of the efforts of politically conscious individuals or civic society actors. They exist at the margins of or outside the mainstream journalistic public sphere. It bears acknowledging that these online public sphericules are found wanting in terms of being inclusive and non-coercive given extant digital and gender inequities, the incivility of cyberbullying and their susceptibility to disinformation tendencies. Moreover, given their loose, organic, non-commercial and de-institutionalised nature, they tend to be sporadic, episodic and ephemeral. Notwithstanding the above, they do produce PSB genre content and thus function as interloper media.

PSB Genre Content on Digital Platforms

Digital media platforms are enabling civil society actors to contribute to public discourse, produce and disseminate content about governance and public interest issues. In countries like Zimbabwe where civil liberties and civic space are constrained, critical and dissenting views do not find expression in the state broadcaster. Thus, non-governmental organisations, human rights organisations and political activists have started digital media initiatives that create civic education content that is meant to hold the state to account, inform the public and foster critical deliberation about social and political issues. A notable example is the *Open Parly* initiative by Magamba Network, whose digital presence spans Instagram, Facebook, X and YouTube (704,635 followers). *Open Parly's* self-description on Facebook reads:

> We believe in more engagement between decision-makers and citizens for a better society for young Zimbabweans. Follow us for live coverage of parliamentary sittings, press conferences, politics, national budgets among many other trending topics.

Open Parly has since expanded its work to the realm of local government and is filling an information void which ideally should be plugged by the national broadcaster, ZBC. *Open Parly* streams full length videos of parliamentary proceedings on Facebook and YouTube and gives video snippets and textual summaries of the same on the X platform. Evidently, the procedural and discursive aspects of parliamentary democracy are a public interest issue. Further, by facilitating the public's access to parliamentary debates and discussions about the governance of the Zimbabwean polity, initiatives like *Open Parly* make elected representatives accountable to the constituents who elected them. This it does by giving summaries of which members of parliament have never said anything in the deliberative chamber, including those who sleep through parliamentary proceedings and how parliamentarians contributed to or voted for tabled bills and motions. In sum, *Open Parly*, as its name suggests has made parliament, which is one of the sites of deliberative democracy, more transparent and has extended it to a digital gallery that would otherwise never be part of the physical gallery because of time and space constraints.

The positive upshot of this is that it enriches public discourse which has been hollowed out by the partisan nature of media coverage of politics in Zimbabwe. Similar initiatives exist within the South African digital sphere. *Polity SA* publishes content about political governance in South Africa and describes its mission as that of "deepening democracy through access to information" (Polity SA, 2021). *Polity SA* is active on Facebook, YouTube, Instagram and Twitter and posts videos and links to podcasts about current affairs on its multimedia website.

To date, its YouTube content has garnered 1 591 769 views. As discussed above, the commercialisation and politicisation of state broadcasters has turned them into entertainment and propaganda platforms. Against this backdrop, the quality of information available to the public has been compromised. By seeking to compensate for identified information deficits, organisations like *Polity SA* reinvigorate debates about the judiciary, political party manifestos, economics regional and international geopolitics.

Another similar South African initiative is the *Daily Friend*, which is a media project of the Institute of Race Relations. So far, *The Daily Friend's* videos have 1 159 937 views and is also available as a podcast on Google Podcasts, Apple

Podcasts, Spotify and other audio streaming services. Ideologically, its multimodal content:

> advocates classical liberalism as an effective way to defeat poverty and tyranny through a system of limited government, a market economy, private enterprise, freedom of speech, individual liberty, property rights, and the rule of law (Daily Friend 2022).

While explicitly ideologically positioned it contributes to the pluralisation of views within the South African media marketplace of ideas.

In Botswana, *Motheo o Musha: A new Social contract* uses Facebook Live to broadcast town hall meetings and deliberations that it convenes as part of its "towards a new constitution" advocacy efforts. Botswana is currently undergoing a constitutional review process and public deliberation and sentiment about the sections needing review are key to the process. The constitution as a document that contains the democratic procedures, mechanisms, values and rights, must itself be the outcome of a democratic process. It must be the expression of public opinion and collective will of the people. It is against this backdrop that the initiative simultaneously seeks to inform and solicit public input about the extent to which the doctrine of separation of powers is observed by the judiciary, legislature and executive. The town hall meetings facilitate deliberation about procedural fairness in the workings of constitutionally mandated institutions.

Further, the initiative inculcates awareness of constitutionally guaranteed freedoms among Batswana. Similarly, the *Botswana Centre for Public Integrity* uses its Facebook page to post and stream videos about the vulnerability of the public sector to corruption, as well as interstate illicit financial flows. Followed by 6 609 people, the centre states that "sharing information, educating the public about integrity, transparency & accountability is at the core of our work" (Botswana Centre for Public Integrity 2023). The centre's efforts are informed by Sustainable Development Goal 16 which seeks to "promote peaceful and inclusive societies for sustainable development, provide access to justice for all and build effective, accountable and inclusive institutions at all levels". On the environmental front, the *Sustain 267 Podcast* (2022) seeks to "share and amplify African Voices, African Actions, and African Solutions to climate change, so we may contribute to the pool of knowledge that already exists". The podcast is available on Google Podcasts, Apple Podcasts, Spotify and other podcast hosting services. It seeks to put environmentalism on the public agenda by disseminating information and expert discussions about climate change, biodiversity and ecological conservation. Environmentalism is a public interest issue given its entanglement with food security, natural disasters and African livelihoods.

The foregoing cases illustrate that online civic media produce PSB genre content, which while not supplanting traditional broadcasters, complements them by disseminating information and facilitating citizen deliberation about social, political, economic and environmental developments that have a bearing on the overall welfare of societies. By seeking to foster an informed and politically engaged citizenry such initiatives, as well as the actors and institutions that initiate them, engender a "civic culture" that is essential to the proper workings of democracy (Dahlgren, 2002, p. 20).

Structurally, the not-for-profit orientation of these digital media offerings puts them in good stead to pursue the public interest which traditional broadcasters have subordinated to commercial and partisan political interests. However, it should be noted that while they are free from state meddling at the editorial level, they are not entirely free of the agendas of civil society funders. Notwithstanding the above, some of the initiatives actively seek to maintain their editorial independence by running their own crowdfunding initiatives to offset the undue influence of corporate donors.

Representationally, such initiatives contribute to the plurality of views in the public sphere as they make possible the competition of ideas about state governance, democracy, rule of law, ecological risks and policy. When considered individually, such PSB genre case studies seem to be negligible in terms of fostering diversity but when such initiatives are considered in their multiplicity, they do foster diversity at macro level.

X Spaces as Emergent Public Sphericules

While the foregoing section foregrounded the agency of various social actors in harnessing the mass mediating potential of digital media, this section focuses on how the digital affordances of digital media enable the formation of online sphericules. In 2022 the micro blogging social media platform Twitter, which has since rebranded to X, introduced a functionality that allows users to convene and moderate an audio discussion with anyone who has an X (Twitter) account. According to the company (2022), this new service:

> Twitter Spaces is where live audio conversations happen. The conversation about you and your content is at its best on Twitter, and now you can Tweet and talk. Spaces unlocks conversations on Twitter with the depth and power only the human voice can bring. These ephemeral, live audio conversations allow for open, authentic, and unfiltered discussions, and there's a space for any and every topic and conversation, from small and intimate to millions of listeners.

Coincidentally, just like the public sphere the spatial metaphor of X spaces signifies a virtual communicative arena defined by conversational interaction. While X Spaces can be convened to discuss anything from the mundane, sensational to the socially significant as shown by the above descriptor, our focus is on how X Spaces are used for political talk. This functionality has afforded disenfranchised and politically conscious publics the opportunity to initiate or be part of public dialogue about extant socio-economic and political issues. Recorded X Spaces are now available for 30 days after the live session, thus extending their influence in time and space. For example, one X Space by South Africa politician Mmusi Maimane titled *Is South Africa a failed state* had 4 200 participants (4/4/2022). In Zimbabwe, documentary filmmaker Hopewell Chin'ono holds the highest record of 10 000 X space participants.

In Botswana, the *Global Shapers Gaborone Hub* and *Family Meeting Botswana* host X Spaces that discuss a variety of public interest topics that include the national budget and related public administration issues. The affordances of Twitter Spaces are consistent with the interactional dimensions of the public sphere as identified by Dahlberg (2007) above. The foregoing is important given that political talk is "is seen as constitutive of publics, which is both morally and functionally vital for democracy", which is always "in search of the talkative public" (Dahlgren, 2002, p. 6). Thus, Twitter spaces while limited in their reach and inclusivity, are the digital incarnation of traditional radio political talk shows and can be seen to be reviving deliberative citizenship.

THE DISRUPTIVE IMPACTS OF DIGITAL PSB GENRE MEDIA

From a journalistic point of view, the illustrative cases discussed above are indicative of the disruptive impact of digital media on the gatekeeping function and business model of commercial mainstream media. In terms of gatekeeping, civil society and ordinary citizens are bypassing the agenda-setting role that in the pre-digital era was the preserve of the state-funded and commercial media. Various digital platforms have facilitated the exercise of citizens' agency in identifying and deliberating public interest issues. In the classical sense, the gatekeeping and agenda-setting role of mainstream media developed from its exclusive access to the news public. By reducing the barriers to entry into the media sphere, digital media have extended the ability to initiate one-to-many and many-to-many communication to everyone who has a smart device and internet connectivity (Thompson, 2020). While not new this has magnified traditional debates about whether the journalism profession, education, and its institutionalised practice is still relevant given that it is now an open profession and industry (Carlson & Lewis, 2015; Eldridge, 2019; Holton & Belair-Gagnon, 2018).

Further, this has made possible the emergence of fluid, organic, discourse publics which coalesce on issues of mutual interest. They are fluid in the sense that they develop a temporal interest in various public discourses that resonate with their civic convictions and have no abiding attachment to a particular media outlet/product as was the case with analogue media. Of interest is the parallel emergence of what can be characterised as personality publics, which while informational and deliberative, converge around a social media opinion leader. These information celebrities can be vloggers, podcasters and X spaces conveners.

This is evident in descriptions like 'join me in my space' or I am going to so and so's space (on X). While traditionally, opinion leaders functioned as intermediaries between the media and public over which they wielded influence, the digital media ecosystem means opinion leaders are not necessarily amplifying or filtering media messages but mass disseminating their own. The indication is that these opinion leaders no longer play a secondary role but a primary one. There is a sense in which this inversion means opinion leaders no longer submit to media logic but media is now submitting to the social media logic of viral personalities.

The effect of the foregoing is the unfolding commercialisation of public discourse as those who attract large audiences monetise their following. This has compounded commercial media's problems of declining audiences, decreasing revenue and the platformisation of advertising (Chibuwe et al., 2022; Santos & Mare, 2021). In some instances, commercial media are now partnering with the conveners of these personally branded discourse publics in a bid to cash in on the audiences they attract.

Socially these developments are disrupting the spatio-temporal organisation of users' professional and social lives. The ensuing discussion will exclusively use the example of X spaces to tease out the foregoing. The consumption of and participation in digital PSB, genre media is giving rise to novel media rituals vis-a-vis their integration into day-to-day routines of their publics. Media rituals are "any actions organised around key media-related categories and boundaries, whose performance reinforces, indeed helps legitimate, the underlying 'value' expressed in the idea that the media is our access point to our social centre" (Couldry, 2003, p. 2 emphasis in original). Of note is the emergence of binge discussions on X spaces. Traditionally, radio and television talk shows barely exceed an hour. This was informed by assumptions of attention fatigue on the part of the audience and pragmatic considerations of the need to share time with other programs and advertisers.

The emergence of what we style the binge discussion ritual runs counter to the foregoing. For example, a *Why are South Africans now saying #sorry Jacob Zuma* by @MrTshewuMoleme (04/07/2022) lasted for seven hours and 32 minutes and had an audience of 15 200 listeners. An audience of this size and engaged for this long, would be envied by commercial media currently beset by sustainability challenges as signposted above. Similarly, a 13th of July 2022 OpenParlyZW X space titled *Kembo Mohadi's daughter appointed ZEC commissioner*, lasted for 3 hours and 24 minutes. These anecdotal examples illustrate what we call the emergence of a binge discussion ritual in the context of the consumption of this digitally delivered quasi PSB content.

Relatedly, given that they can be consumed in real time and as recordings, they allow for flexible and customised listening. Delayed listenership is to a certain extent a new ritual when compared to the fact that for the most part delayed listening to live radio is rare in Southern Africa. Replays of aired programs are most often occasioned by the need to fill dead air in contexts of limited content owing to undercapitalisation of most radio stations.

It should be noted that this binge discussion/listenership ritual is disruptive in terms of the fact that certain activities are either postponed or altogether abondoned to participate in the live discussions. While we acknowledge that the mobile nature of the smart devices used to join these spaces, means its possible for participants to multitask, the reality of selective attention means domestic or professional activities are somehow disrupted. Further, from a digital wellbeing point of view, these developments are disrupting interpersonal relationships where social media are making people anti-social. The fact that virtual relationships and spaces take precedence over familial and offline relationships has been found to have negative ramifications (Büchi et al., 2019). Against this backdrop, interventions like digital detoxing and digital fasting are suggested as solutions to the addictive, emotionally and psychologically disruptive impact of social media (Mutsvairo et al., 2022).

Conclusion

This chapter detailed how online civic media initiatives and the affordances of emergent social media platforms have made possible the production of PSB genre content by implicit interlopers. These interlopers are complementing the efforts of or compensating for the shortcomings of traditional state broadcasters in Southern Africa. Using the public sphere norm as a reference, and a desk review of purposively selected cases, the chapter illustrated how structurally, representationally, and interactionally these interloper media initiatives function as public sphericules as they facilitate public debate about public interest issues and engender a civic culture that is indispensable to the proper functioning of deliberative democracy. These interloper media are disrupting the gatekeeping function of mainstream media and their business model. The digital ecosystem has enabled the rise of information celebrities who command the attention of audiences that mainstream media would rather be theirs. The effect of the forgoing has been the emergence of diffuse and fluid discourse publics which coalesce around social media opinion leaders and topics of interest. There is evidence that new media rituals and practices are in their formative stages.

References

About Open Parly. (2022). About Open Parly ZW. Retrieved August, 7, 2022, from https://www.facebook.com/openparlyzw/about_details

Alfandika, L., & Gwindingwe, G. (2021). The Airwaves Belong to the People: A Critical Analysis of Radio Broadcasting and Licensing in Zimbabwe. *Communicatio, 47*(2), 44–60. https://doi.org/10.1080/02500167.2020.1796729

Balule, T.B. (2013). Public Service Broadcasters or Government Mouthpieces—An Appraisal Of Public Service Broadcasting in Botswana. *SCRIPTed, 10*(1), 77–92. https://doi.org/10.2966/scrip.100113.77

Barnett, C. (1999). Broadcasting the rainbow nation: Media, democracy, and nation-building in South Africa. https://clivebarnett.files.wordpress.com/2017/03/rainbow-nation.pdf

Berger, G., Banda, F., Duncan, J., & Mukundu, R. (2009). *Beyond Broadcasting: The future of state-owned broadcasters in Southern Africa*. https://www.comminit.

com/media-development/content/beyond-broadcasting-future-state-owned-broadcasters-southern-africa
Bevan, C. (2008). Putting up screens: A history of television in South Africa, 1929–1976. 219.
Botswana Centre for Public Integrity. (2023). *Who are we*. Retrieved September 5, 2023, from https://www.bcpi.org.bw/about
Büchi, M., Festic, N., & Latzer, M. (2019). Digital Overuse and Subjective Well-Being in a Digitized Society. *Social Media + Society*, 5(4), 205630511988603. https://doi.org/10.1177/2056305119886031
Carlson, M., & Lewis, S. C. (Eds.). (2015). *Boundaries of Journalism: Professionalism, Practices and Participation*. Routledge, Taylor & Francis Group.
Cheruiyot, D., Wahutu, j. S., Mare, A., Ogola, G., & Mabweazara, H. M. (2021). Making News Outside Legacy Media: Peripheral Actors within an African Communication Ecology. *African Journalism Studies*, 42(4), 1–14. https://doi.org/10.1080/23743670.2021.2046397
Chibuwe, A., Munoriyarwa, A., Motsaathebe, G., Chiumbu, S., & Lesitaokana, W. (2022). Newsroom Disruptions and Opportunities in Times of Crisis: Analysing Southern African Media During the COVID-19 Crisis. *African Journalism Studies*, 1–18. https://doi.org/10.1080/23743670.2022.2071961
Couldry, N. (2003). *Media rituals: A critical approach*. Routledge. https://biblioteca-uoc.idm.oclc.org/login?url=https://www.taylorfrancis.com/books/9780203986608
Dahlberg, L. (2007). The Internet, Deliberative Democracy, and Power: Radicalizing the Public Sphere. *International Journal of Media & Cultural Politics*, 3(1), 47–64. https://doi.org/10.1386/macp.3.1.47_1
Dahlgren, P. (2002). In Search of the Talkative Public: Media, Deliberative Democracy and Civic Culture. *Javnost—The Public*, 9(3), 5–25. https://doi.org/10.1080/13183222.2002.11008804
Eldridge, S. A. (2014). Boundary Maintenance and Interloper Media Reaction: Differentiating between Journalism's Discursive Enforcement Processes. *Journalism Studies*, 15(1), 1–16. https://doi.org/10.1080/1461670X.2013.791077
Eldridge, S. A. (2019). Where Do We Draw the Line? Interlopers, (Ant)agonists, and an Unbounded Journalistic Field. *Media and Communication*, 7(4), 8–18. https://doi.org/10.17645/mac.v7i4.2295
Fourie, P. (2010). Distributed public service broadcasting as an alternative model for public service broadcasting in South Africa. *Communicare: Journal for Communication Sciences in Southern Africa*, 29(2), 1–25.
Fourie, P. (2013). The Rise and Fall of Public Service Broadcasting in South Africa: A Motivation for a New Broadcasting Model (Television). *Communitas*, 18, 1–20.
Fraser, N. (1990). Rethinking the Public Sphere: A Contribution to the Critique of Actually Existing Democracy. *Social Text*, 25/26, 56. https://doi.org/10.2307/466240
Gillwald, A., & Mothobi, O. (2018). A demand-side view of mobile internet from 10 African countries. Research ICT Africa.
Gitlin, T. (1998). Public Sphere or Public Sphericules? In T. Liebes & J. Curran (Eds.), *Media, Ritual and Identity* (pp. 168–174). Routledge.
Habermas, J. (1989). The Public Sphere: An Encyclopedia Article. In S. E. Bronner & D. Kellner (Eds.), *Critical Theory and Society: A Reader* (pp. 136–142). Routledge.

Holton, A. E., & Belair-Gagnon, V. (2018). Strangers to the Game? Interlopers, Intralopers, and Shifting News Production. *Media and Communication*, 6(4), 70–78. https://doi.org/10.17645/mac.v6i4.1490

Internet World Stats. (2022). *Internet World Stats: Usage and Population*. Retrieved September 5, 2023, from https://www.internetworldstats.com/stats.htm

Lesitaokana, W. O. (2013). Radio in Botswana: A Critical Examination of its Growth and Dominance Across Botswana's Mass Media Landscape. *Journal of Radio & Audio Media*, 20(1), 197–211. https://doi.org/10.1080/19376529.2013.777340

Lesitaokana, William O., & Mosanako, S. (2021). Digital Terrestrial Television Broadcasting (DTTB) in Botswana: Prospects and Challenges. In G. Motsaathebe & S. H. Chiumbu (Eds.), *Television in Africa in the Digital Age* (pp. 241–256). Springer International Publishing. https://doi.org/10.1007/978-3-030-68854-7

Mano, W. (2010). Africa: Media Systems. In W. Donsbach (Ed.), *The International Encyclopedia of Communication* (p. wbieca033). John Wiley & Sons, Ltd. https://doi.org/10.1002/9781405186407.wbieca033

Mano, W. (2016). The State and Public Broadcasting: Continuity and Change in Zimbabwe. In T. Flew, P. Iosifidis, & J. Steemers (Eds.), *Global Media and National Policies* (pp. 190–205). Palgrave Macmillan UK. https://doi.org/10.1057/9781137493958_12

Masuku, J. (2011). *The public broadcaster model and the Zimbabwe Broadcasting Corporation (ZBC): An analytical study*. https://scholar.sun.ac.za/handle/10019.1/6527

Matsilele, T., Munganidze, G., & Ruhanya, P. (2021). Dilemmas in Zimbabwe's Public Broadcasting in the Era of Digitisation. In G. Motsaathebe & S. H. Chiumbu (Eds.), *Television in Africa in the Digital Age* (pp. 259–282). Springer International Publishing. https://doi.org/10.1007/978-3-030-68854-7

Melber, H., Melber, H., Chiumbu, S., & Nordiska Afrikainstitutet (Eds.). (2004). *Media, Public Discourse and Political Contestation in Zimbabwe*. NAI.

Mogalakwe, M. (2006). *How Britain Underdeveloped Bechuanaland Protectorate: A Brief Critique of the Political Economy of Colonial Botswana*. https://ubrisa.ub.bw/handle/10311/652

Mosanako, S. (2016). *The State of Coverage of Development Issues on National Television in Botswana*. https://journals.ub.bw/index.php/bnr/article/view/874

Motsaathebe, G., & Chiumbu, S. H. (Eds.). (2021). *Television in Africa in the Digital Age*. Springer International Publishing. https://doi.org/10.1007/978-3-030-68854-7

Mutsvairo, B., Ragnedda, M., & Mabvundwi, K. (2022). 'Our old pastor thinks the mobile phone is a source of evil.' Capturing contested and conflicting insights on digital wellbeing and digital detoxing in an age of rapid mobile connectivity. *Media International Australia*, 1329878X2210909. https://doi.org/10.1177/1329878X221090992

Ndlela, N. (2007). Broadcasting Reforms in Southern Africa: Continuity and Change in the Era of Globalisation. *Westminster Papers in Communication and Culture*, 4(3), 67. https://doi.org/10.16997/wpcc.99

Nkomo, L. (2018). *Public service broadcasting and the risk of state capture: The case of the zimbabwe broadcasting corporation*. https://hdl.handle.net/10646/3903

Polity SA. (2021). *Description*. Retrieved February, 20, 2022, from https://www.youtube.com/@PolitySA/about

Santos, P., & Mare, A. (2021). The Reconfiguration of News Work in Southern Africa during the COVID-19 Pandemic. *Digital Journalism*, 9(9), 1391–1410. https://doi.org/10.1080/21670811.2021.1974914

Schapals, A. K., Maares, P., & Hanusch, F. (2019). Working on the Margins: Comparative Perspectives on the Roles and Motivations of Peripheral Actors in Journalism. *Media and Communication*, 7(4), 19–30. https://doi.org/10.17645/mac.v7i4.2374

Smith, V. E. (2021). Radio and the Nation: Histories of Broadcasting, Conflict and Race in Southern Africa. *Canadian Journal of African Studies / Revue Canadienne Des Études Africaines*, 55(2), 393–399. https://doi.org/10.1080/00083968.2020.1829832

Sustain 267 Podcast. (2022). *About*. Retrieved September, 6, 2023, from https://open.spotify.com/show/2YwuzrIdvvvcsUlIwlcsRn

Taha, M. H. (2016). *Early Uses of Broadcast Media in Southern Africa: Recurring Themes and Concerns*. http://www.ijhssnet.com/journals/Vol_6_No_12_December_2016/15.pdf

The Daily Friend. (2022). *Description*. Retrieved August, 8, 2022 from https://www.youtube.com/@DailyFriendSA/about

Thompson, J. B. (2020). Mediated Interaction in the Digital Age. *Theory, Culture & Society*, 37(1), 3–28. https://doi.org/10.1177/0263276418808592

CHAPTER 26

A Typology of Digital Leaks as Journalistic Source Materials

Philip Di Salvo

INTRODUCTION

The 2010–2020 decade witnessed a series of prominent high-level leak cases that have had a profound impact in shaping contemporary journalism within the context of an overall skyrocketing level of information leaks (Briant & Wanless, 2018, p. 44). The influence of major leaks has been so compelling that the last ten years have been defined as "the age of big leaks" (Shane, 2019). Unsurprisingly, prominent whistleblowers such as Chelsea Manning or Edward Snowden and publishers of leaks such as WikiLeaks' Julian Assange have gained global exposure, visibility, and even celebrity status. In earnest, journalism based on leaks did not emerge for the first time in the last decade; various examples of the phenomenon have played a major role in the history of journalism, including prior to digitalization (Stone & Bollinger, 2021). However, some affordances and contextual sea changes made possible by digitalization have contributed to making the practice of leaking easier and more frequent and have expanded the array of possibilities for leaking (Di Salvo, 2016; Johnson et al., 2020). Consequently, leaks have taken different shapes and forms, sometimes involving new actors and practices, such as hackers as sources, and digital whistleblowing platforms as conduits for leaked information, making potential leaking scenarios more numerous and complex for journalists (Hintz, 2019; Di Salvo, 2020).

P. Di Salvo (✉)
School of Humanities and Social Sciences, University of St. Gallen, St. Gallen, Switzerland
e-mail: philip.disalvo@unisg.ch

© The Author(s), under exclusive license to Springer Nature Switzerland AG 2024
H. S. Dunn et al. (eds.), *The Palgrave Handbook of Everyday Digital Life*,
https://doi.org/10.1007/978-3-031-30438-5_26

Overall, the classic whistleblower–journalist relationship has now been juxtaposed with other potential situations that were not so much visible in the analogue era (Tiffen, 2018). In particular, anecdotal evidence shows that leaks are now increasingly occurring beyond traditional whistleblowing formats, which, despite still playing a crucial role, are now in parallel with other scenarios and occurrences of leaks, some of which are more controversial and lack clear definitions or do not necessarily involve journalists as primary recipients (Flynn, 2011). This shift also implies changes in how journalists are called to approach leaks as news sources. With leaks becoming more frequent and multi-formed, journalists also need to come to terms with potentially having to report on newsworthy materials made available by hacktivists who obtained them through cyberattacks aimed at exposing companies, governments, or other actors (Coleman, 2017). Whereas leaks still represent a form of "non-routine" channel of news sourcing, given their controversial and disruptive nature (Wheatley, 2020), they are undoubtedly becoming a peculiar element of the contemporary information ecosystem and an integral practice of the journalistic field. Moreover, leaks have gone through a process of progressive "normalization" in the journalistic field (Singer, 2005; Baack, 2016) as other digital practices and technologies before, such as blogging or the use of social media for reporting purposes. This has definitely not yet evolved into making the reporting on leaks a daily activity for most journalists, but on a more systemic level, digitalization has helped leaks in gaining the status of a more-than-ever "accepted" practice. This is visible, for instance, in the increase number of stories based on leaks of various kinds occurring in relation to different journalistic beats. A good example of this trend can be seen, among others, in the covering of social media companies and their scandals and controversies, which is increasingly made possible thanks to the contribution of whistleblowers coming from within Silicon Valley companies, such as for the recent "Facebook Files" (2021) and the "Uber Files" (2022) investigations. Even sports reporting has seen leaks taking an important role, as the "Football Leaks" (2016) investigation shows (Larrondo-Ureta & Ferreras-Rodríguez, 2021).

Taking an even broader look at the significance of leaks, they could also be considered as an integral component of digitalization and a theoretical lens to look at in order to interpret and criticize the effects of digitalization at large (Bory & Di Salvo, 2022). Starting from this perspective, mostly based on various forms of weaknesses, biases, and malfunctions as core traits of anything digital, leaks could be seen as a defining element of the digital culture and environment in which also journalism operates today. Whereas leaks would be considered as problematic by those organizations and individuals suffering them, they are at the same time a beneficial and crucial resource for journalists, who can gain incomparable informational value out of them. Overall, leaks are a defining phenomenon of digitlization at large and, as such, they have inevitably been integrated in the journalistic field as much as other, similarly defining, but less disruptive components of digitalization.

Despite their crucial role in investigative journalism and beyond, the phenomenon of leaks has received limited attention from journalism studies (Reich, 2008; Wahl-Jorgensen & Hunt, 2012). Furthermore, there is a dearth of research on the centrality of leaks in either exposing public-interest stories and cases or as a sourcing strategy for reporters. This chapter aims to narrow this gap by providing a framework for analyzing and understanding contemporary leaks. It also seeks to shed light on how leaks take place in the digital context, the practices and modes followed, the various actors involved, and the extent of their involvement. This theoretical article is based on a selection of case studies and contributes to the understanding of contemporary leaks and their relationship with journalism. This chapter is structured around four different sections. The first one will offer some theoretical takes on leaks, conceptualizing core differences among different forms of leaking scenario, including whistleblowing and hacks. The second section, will focus on the elements of the analytical framework at the core of the chapter. The third section, instead, will be based on the application of such framework to an array of case studies representing different instances of leaks. Finally, the outcomes of such application will be discussed in the final section of the chapter.

Leaks: Whistleblowing and Beyond

"Whistleblowing" and "leaking" carry different meanings and definitions, and some leaks even contradict the traditionally intended definition of whistleblowing (Zittrain, 2016). Whistleblowing is commonly defined as the "disclosure by organizational members of illegal, immoral or illegitimate practices under the control of their employers, to persons or organizations that may be able to affect action" (Miceli & Near, 1992, p. 15). Furthermore, it is a clearly identified practice and assumes a legal status in many jurisdictions and contexts that have adopted whistleblowing protection legislation. As such, whistleblowers have always been crucial and "accepted" assets for journalists when it comes to launching or supporting investigations, and they represent some of the potentially most proficuous and powerful sources for accessing public interest information (Wahl-Jorgensen & Hunt, 2012). Although sometimes used as a synonym of "whistleblowing," the term "leaking" actually carries a broader meaning, lacks an identified institutional definition, and may be used to refer to very different scenarios (Arnold, 2019).

For instance, as Touchton et al. (2020, p. 1) argued, "leaking" usually implies negative connotations, such as the fact that the information involved should not have been disclosed and that the "leaker" may be inspired by nefarious motives. Thus, the term "leaking" carries dual implications, as leaks can be the start of public interest-oriented transparency releases and beneficial disclosures. At the same time, they can also be used to serve political agendas, perform influence operations, or even further criminal goals (Hintz, 2019). Thus, following Hintz's definition (2019), the term "leaks" can also refer to a more neutral understanding of how information may reach the public or the attention of journalists. We define leaks as follows:

> the channels through which journalists receive relevant information from sources, and they typically encompass unauthorized disclosures of information that is transferred to the journalist from inside an institution or a closed group (such as a company or a government) and would otherwise not (or not in that form or at that moment) be available. (Hintz, 2019)

In light of this definition, this chapter will use the term "leaks" to refer to a vast array of contexts where journalists may come into possession of otherwise undisclosed information, documents, or data. This includes instances spanning from the traditional concept of whistleblowing up to other less institutionalized forms of leaking. The rationale for using "leaks" in such a loose way is connected to the fact that the term "leaks" itself has historically evolved and has progressively expanded in meaning to become an "umbrella-term for a wider variety of situations" (Reich, 2008, p. 556). Nevertheless, further clarification is needed: in journalistic *jargon*, the term "leak" can also be used to refer to source–journalist relationships that do not involve the disclosure of otherwise inaccessible information but, rather, only a cozy relationship with a powerful figure who is granted anonymity for opportunistic purposes, usually without actual security concerns. Historically, the practice of granting anonymity to individuals in high-power positions has been far from rare among journalists (Boeyink, 1990). Consequently, especially when politicians are involved, the condition of being unnamed in the press is frequently exploited as an instrument by "high-placed officials" to "carefully craft their message" or spin media coverage (Duffy & Freeman, 2011, p. 302). These instances will not be considered as "leaks" in the current analysis because, in order to be included in this typology, "leaks" need to involve actual inaccessible information provided by sources whose actions reflect a real act of disclosure of some kind.

Among the various forms and shapes that leaking can embody, only whistleblowing has been studied with a systematic theoretical approach based on a range of disciplines (Culiberg & Mihelič, 2017). In particular, Ceva and Bocchiola (2018) examined whistleblowing by decomposing the practice to its core six elements: "action," "object," "agent," "locus," "addressee," and "aim." Their framework can be effectively applied to assess and define instances involving leaks, as in the Snowden case (Ceva & Bocchiola, 2019). Regarding other less institutionalized forms of leaks, a systemic analysis has yet to be provided, and only certain types of leaks have been studied. Reich (2008), who focused on whistleblowing, proposed an "anatomy" of leaks based on their frequency, the initiatives of the sources, the diversity of sources, types of sources, their identities, and the technology involved. Reich and Barnoy (2016) later updated this framework, applying it to the phenomenon of "Megaleaks," that is, leaks based on "big package releases" in terms of the massive volume of information and the conglomeration of events and topics involved, such as the

2016 "Panama Papers" (Baack, 2016). Conversely, Coleman (2017) provided a definition and genealogy of "public interest hacks," defined as "computer infiltration(s) for the purpose of leaking documents that will have political consequence," and highlighted a series of cases where hacktivists cyberattacked organizations or individuals with the aim of releasing information about them.

Whereas these types of leaks constitute a significant part of how leaks occur today, they should be seen in a broader context of possibilities. Thus, in an attempt to cover the various forms of leaks today, this chapter will advance a broader taxonomy based on the elements of the aforementioned frameworks in order to contextualize how leaks can occur and engage with journalistic work without inductively including them in a predetermined casuistry. Such a typology will take into account the evolving and sometimes erratic nature of digital phenomena such as leaks, which are prone to hybridization, adaptation, and constant change. The next section will present the framework regarding how the statuary elements of leaks come together in different assemblages.

An "Assemblage" Framework for Analyzing Leaks

In seeking to respond to the need to examine how leaks can take shape, this chapter proposes a framework for analyzing different scenarios to frame the phenomenon according to different compositional elements. Employing Deleuze and Guattari's (2008) notion of "assemblage" in understanding social complexity, leaks are here considered as defined solely by their "relations of composition, mixture, and aggregation" (Nail, 2017, p. 23). Any encompassing definition would inevitably fail to include possible forms of leaks created by digitalization, its actors, and affordances. As such, the definition of a leak is better structured if it is offered according to its contingent and singular features and how they come together in a specific context—that is, according to how its own elements come together as an assemblage.

The idea of looking at leaks using "de-structuring" them is not new, as discussed in the previous section. Here, by relying on the previous work of Ceva and Bocchiola (2018), Reich (2008), and Reich and Barnoy (2016), this proposed "assemblage" framework will be structured around a broad and diverse set of leak scenarios while following anecdotal examples from the past decade. The proposed elements enable an examination of leaks as assemblages, produced by a combination of various elements and functions whose composition leads to the emergence of specific but not predetermined kinds of leaks. For instance, the involvement of a hacktivist using a cyberattack to obtain information later made available on the open Internet is a specific kind of leak, different from the one made possible by a whistleblower who decides to hand over insider information directly to a designated journalist.

As such, an (open) framework that includes as many potential "assemblages" as possible is required in order to grasp the potential outcomes of leaks today, starting from the assumption that the evolving shapes of leaks may require future adjustments and expansions of the said framework. Thus, and again following ideas and notions taken from Deleuze and Guattari (2008, p. 12), the framework is intended as a "map" and not a "tracing." It is based on the following five core elements, which ought to be viewed in continuity and connection with those previously advanced by Ceva and Bocchiola (2018), Reich (2008), and Reich and Barnoy (2016):

(a) Definition of the leak
(b) Actors responsible for the leak
(c) Purposes of the leak
(d) Journalist roles
(e) Practices and technologies involved in the leak

These five elements allow the analysis to focus on leaks without necessarily having whistleblowing and its classic components as the analytical starting point. As such, the framework will also be useful for the analysis of those instances of leaks involving various forms of hacktivism or hacking and that share only some traits (or none) with whistleblowing. The five elements are thrashed out below:

(a) Definition of the leak

This refers to the actions behind the leak and the disclosure of the information at its core. Leaks can occur because of whistleblowing, as per the traditional definition, or by other actions perpetuated by outsider actors, including cyberattacks and data dumps. The actions taken in the release of the leaked information by the authors responsible for the leaking are the first elements in defining leaks.

(b) Actors responsible for the leak

These are the individuals or groups who act as the sources of the leak or bear responsibility for the release of the information. An important dimension are the roles, status, or affiliations of these actors. They can be whistleblowers and other insiders or external actors disclosing information without authorization or who typically perform other actions.

(c) Purposes of the leak

This refers to the reasons why information is leaked. These purposes may refer to legitimate whistleblowing, political activism, hacktivism, or other less public interest-oriented aims, such as political influence at the state actor level. The purposes of leaks are also usaully directly connected with the actors' identities.

(d) Journalist roles

This refers to the involvement of journalists and media organizations in the publication and dissemination of the leak. In particular, it is connected to the level of engagement that journalists may have with the leaked information and the sources. Journalists can be designated recipients of the leaked information or may only be reporting on it secondarily in instances where the information is disclosed without their direct mediation (i.e., when the leak is released on the open Internet). Here, "journalists" refers to a broad definition of "journalism" that extends to the involvement of hybrid and "interloper" organizations whose belonging to the journalistic field is occasionally contested (Eldridge, 2017).

Additionally, the use of the term "journalists" here looks beyond normative and institutional understandings and debates regarding what journalism is and includes as many "acts of journalism" as possible in order to "encapsulate the vast array of journalism forms, formats and outlets present in today's information environment" (Schapals, 2022). As such, entities such as WikiLeaks and the Distributed Denial of Secrets (DDoS) collective will be included here in light of their clear journalistic traits and performance of journalistic acts (Thielman, 2019), such as the publication of information in the public interest, and their roles in what Benkler (2013) has defined as "the networked fourth estate."

(e) Practices and technologies involved in the leak

This refers to the practices involved in the leak or to how technologies may facilitate or shape the act of leaking, especially in relation to the actual release of information. In certain cases, the technology used can also be at the core of the emergence of new practices, as in the case of online whistleblowing platforms (i.e., WikiLeaks or those operated by other media organizations) based on encryption tools, among others.

APPLYING THE ASSEMBLAGE FRAMEWORK TO RECENT LEAKS

What follows is the application of the framework to a selection of recent case studies, selected for their journalistic value and potential representability of the widest possible set of leak scenarios. These case studies are considered "diverse cases," selected for "encompassing a full range of variation" (Seawright & Gerring, 2008, p. 300) in the possibilities of leaks. These case studies were selected following an approach of purposeful sampling aimed at choosing case studies that are "information rich" (Emmel, 2014) and potentially more explicative for this analysis. The case studies being examined are as follows (in chronological order):

The Hacking Team Leak (2015)

The Italian surveillance company Hacking Team suffered a leak after it was hacked by the hacktivist (or hacktivist group) Phineas Fisher in 2015. A total of 400 GB of data belonging to the company, including internal emails and the source code of some of its products and software, were released on the Internet by Phineas Fisher through file-sharing services (Franceschi-Bicchierai, 2016a). Later, the leaked information was also archived and re-published in searchable formats by WikiLeaks and Distributed Denial of Secrets (DDoS).

The Drone Papers (2015)

In 2015, the US-based news outlet *The Intercept* published an extensive investigation into US secret military drone programs. The publication was based on a cache of leaked documents obtained by a journalist at *The Intercept* (2015). In 2021, former intelligence contractor Daniel Hale was sentenced to 45 months in prison for leaking the materials. After being originally charged in 2019, Hale pleaded guilty to the retention and transmission of national defence information (Barnes, 2021).

The DNC Leaks (2016)

During the 2016 US presidential campaign, the servers of the Democratic National Committee (DNC), together with the email accounts of prominent figures in Hillary Clinton's presidential campaign, were hit by various cyberattacks. The attacks resulted in a large-scale leak of internal emails released through dedicated websites, direct communication with journalists and news outlets, and WikiLeaks, which published thousands of the leaked emails. Various sources, including a United States Department of Justice investigation, have attributed the operation to Russian hackers operating for the Kremlin intelligence agencies and who acted through various fake online personas (e.g., DCLeaks and Guccifer 2.0) to mask the real nature of the state actor level influence campaign (Rid, 2020, pp. 358–376).

The Panama Papers (2016)

The Panama Papers is a joint investigation into the offshore economy conducted by *Süddeutsche Zeitung* and the International Consortium of Investigative Journalists (ICIJ) in 2016. The investigation exposed the activities of Mossack Fonseca, a Panama-based company specialized in providing offshore services. The collaborative investigation was based on 1.5 million financial and legal records analyzed by a team of 370 international journalists under the coordination of the ICIJ (Cabra & Kissane, 2016). In 2017, the investigation won the Pulitzer Prize for Explanatory Reporting and is considered among the most defining examples of data journalism and cross-border collaborative investigations.

The Retina-X and FlexiSpy Leaks (2017)

In 2017, *VICE* technology magazine *Motherboard* published an investigation into "stalkerware," surveillance software that can be used to track and monitor devices and the communication of ordinary people, including employees and loved ones. The investigation revealed the existence of a wide market and the widespread use of stalkerware, together with the ease with which the technology can be purchased. *Motherboard* journalists were provided with internal information by hackers who had hacked US stalkerware companies Retina-X and FlexiSpy to expose their activities, going on to supply the journalists with needed source materials (Di Salvo & Porlezza, 2020).

BlueLeaks (2020)

BlueLeaks is the name given to a leak involving 269 GB of internal US law enforcement data obtained by the hacktivist collective Anonymous and released online by the transparency group DDoSecrets in 2020. The leak revealed previously unavailable insights about law enforcement operations in the US, together with personal information about officers (Lee, 2020).

The Facebook Papers (2021)

The Facebook Papers is the anecdotal name of a journalistic investigation based on a cache of internal Facebook documents released to the *Wall Street Journal*, a consortium of Western media, and the US Congress by Facebook whistleblower Frances Haugen in 2021 (Benton, 2021). The leak exposed the internal decision-making process of Facebook - now Meta - in regard to some of its most controversial activities, such as content moderation and relationships with state actors and governments around the world, among others.

These case studies are by no means meant to be exhaustive when it comes to representing the complexity and diversity of contemporary leaks. However, together, they form an extensive sample of how leaks have taken shape in recent years. For instance, they involve classic whistleblowing cases, controversial leaks emerging from cyberattacks, operations by state actors, financial megaleaks, and hacktivist exposés involving journalists, though not always. What follows is the analysis of these case studies according to the proposed framework. A summary of the results is also presented in Table 26.1.

(a) Definition of the leak

The overview of the selected case studies shows that leaks can occur following different modes and actions. The Drone Papers and The Facebook Papers, for instance, are explicit whistleblowing cases. Here, two whistleblowers—from the intelligence community and a private company, respectively—exposed insider information to highlight public interest cases to external third parties and inspire action. The Panama Papers case is characterized by the vast volume

Table 26.1 A summary of the case studies

Leak name	Definition of the leak	Actors responsible for the leak	Purposes of the leak	Journalist roles	Practices and technologies involving the leak
The Hacking Team leak	Public interest hack	Phineas Fisher (hacker)	Hacktivism	Secondary	Data dumping
The Drone Papers	Whistleblowing	Daniel Hale (whistleblower)	Whistleblowing	Primary	Direct communication (encryption)
DNC Leaks	Public interest hack	Russian intelligence hackers (state actor)	Political influence	Ambivalent	Whistleblowing platform + data dumping + direct communication
The Panama Papers	Megaleak	John Doe (whistleblower)	Whistleblowing	Primary	Direct communication (encryption)
The Retina-X and Flexispy leaks	Public interest hack	Unnamed and Leopard Boy hacktivists (hacker)	Hacktivism	Primary	Whistleblowing platform + direct communication
BlueLeaks	Public interest hack	Anonymous (hacker)	Hacktivism	Primary	Direct communication (encryption)
The Facebook Papers	Whistleblowing	Frances Haugen (whistleblower)	Whistleblowing	Primary but not exclusive	Direct communication (encryption)

of information involved and represents a clear instance of a "megaleak," including the fact that it was the subject of a large-scale international journalistic investigation. "Megaleaks" can be subsumed under whistleblowing (when the source is an insider), but the journalistic practices they normally involve—from data journalism to cross-border investigations—make them a clearly identifiable category in the leaking ecosystem (Baack, 2016; Woodall, 2018).

The origins of the Retina-X and FlexiSpy and Hacking Team leaks show that these cases do not constitute whistleblowing as they were both generated from the actions of outsiders. In the Hacking Team leak case, hacktivist(s) Phineas Phisher broke into the company's systems and later leaked internal files and information over the Internet; in the cases of Retina-X and Flexispy, the companies were hacked by unnamed hackers—with the exception of one, Leopard Boy—who shared the data directly with journalists. Similarly, in the BlueLeaks case, individuals claiming an affiliation with the hacktivist collective Anonymous claimed responsibility for the hack against a group of US law enforcement agencies and for forwarding the documents to the DDoSecrets group, which later released them (Lee, 2020).

All these instances fall under Coleman's (2017) label of "public interest hack" cases, all of which were perpetuated with the explicit goal of releasing information to the public. Finally, the DNC leak was also a public interest hack as internal DNC emails were stolen by outside hackers and later released through different strategies. The entire operation was part of a state-actor-level action of political influence whose aims were neither informational nor activist.

(b) Actors responsible for the leak

The selected case studies arguably present an overview of the kinds of actors behind leaks. In particular, a distinction between "insider" and "outsider" sources plays a major role in defining leak cases. In instances of whistleblowing, such as the Facebook Papers and the Drone Papers, leaks start from the actions of insiders who release information to the outside of the affected organizations. In these instances, the news organizations were explicitly sought after. In other instances, outsiders claimed responsibility for the release of information. Here, the array of actors can span from hacktivist hackers inspired by activist agendas (e.g., the Hacking Team, the Retina-X and Flexispy leaks, and BlueLeaks) to intelligence operatives serving the interests of state actors in the context of a broad influence campaign (DNC leak). In other instances, such as the Panama Papers, no identifiable details about the source were provided, and the individual is still today being referred to by the nickname "John Doe." Nevertheless, the source has stated on the record that they were not affiliated with "any government or intelligence agency, directly or as a contractor" and has made some references to other whistleblowers when expressing their rationales about leaking (Süddeutsche Zeitung, 2016). As such, it can be speculated that John Doe is a whistleblower operating from within.

(c) Purposes of the leak

Motivations related to starting a leak are difficult to speculate about or interpret, especially given the fact that they may not be publicly stated or reported. However, at least in the cases in focus here, some elements are available. Frances Haugen, the Facebook Papers source, self-defined as a whistleblower (Milmo, 2021). The alleged Drone Papers source, Daniel Hale, pleaded guilty to "retention and transmission of national defense information" to a reporter (United States Department of Justice, 2021), effectively affirming his role as a whistleblower. For the Hacking Team leak, hacktivist(s) Phineas Fisher claimed responsibility for the hack and leak and later expressed their motivations for targeting the company as "set them back a bit and give some breathing room to the people being targeted with their software," underlining an activist rationale (Franceschi-Bicchierai, 2016b). Similarly, the hackers responsible for the hack and leak of Retina-X and FlexiSpy told reporters about having hacked the companies to expose the unethical business of stalkerware, and to "send a warning to this sort of industry as a whole," and to shed light on the potential data misuses inherent in the technology (Franceschi-Bicchierai & Cox, 2017). For BlueLeaks, the source of the data was revealed as the Anonymous hacktivist collective; however, given the ephemeral and decentralized nature of the group, there are no official statements claiming responsibility. Nevertheless, some observers have included the BlueLeaks hack within a broader set of retaliatory digital actions perpetuated by Anonymous members in the wake of the killing of George Floyd (Beran, 2020).

Regarding the Panama Papers, whistleblower John Doe published a manifesto about their rationale for the leaks, claiming that they were motivated "not for any specific political purpose, but simply because I understood enough about their contents to realize the scale of the injustices they described" (Süddeutsche Zeitung, 2016). Finally, as the DNC leak was part of an undercover operation perpetrated by a state actor, no explicit details about motivations and rationales are available. However, it has been proven that Russian intelligence agents used a fake persona nicknamed Guccifer 2.0 to mimic a fake Romanian hacktivist as the actor responsible for the hack and leak so that the operation could have the appearance of a hacktivist attempt, thereby masking its geopolitical motivations (Gallagher, 2018; Rid, 2020, pp. 368–376).

(d) Journalist roles

In terms of how journalists may be involved as direct recipients of a leak or actors called to report on them, the case studies discussed here again offer a range of insights. For the clear whistleblowing instances, such as The Drone Papers and The Facebook Papers, the sources reached out directly to reporters and news outlets. Similarly, for the Panama Papers megaleak, journalists were directly involved with John Doe from the beginning. Such a straightforward arrangement was not necessarily replicated in leaks from outsider sources. For instance, Phineas Fisher released the Hacking Team's documents on the Internet without involving designated recipients. Journalists reported on the documents as they were made available through the Hacking Team's Twitter account, which was also hacked. Whistleblowing platforms such as WikiLeaks and DDoSecrets archived the material on their websites but were not directly addressed by the source. In other similar cases, outsider sources reached out to designated journalists or news organizations.

This was the case for the Retina-X and FlexiSpy leaks, whose documents were handed over to *Motherboard* journalists to trigger a journalistic investigation. Similarly, DDoSecrets was the designated recipient of the cache of BlueLeaks documents by an Anonymous representative(s). However, as the US authorities have concluded in their investigations into the case, hackers responsible for the DNC leak followed a dual approach by launching the dedicated website DCLeaks, where emails were initially dumped and published online, and later forwarding the materials to WikiLeaks through various methods of communication using the Guccifer 2.0 and DCLeaks personas. Other journalists and news organization were allegedly contacted with the same goal (United States Department of Justice, 2019).

(e) Practices and technologies involved in the leak

When it comes to particular practices or technologies involved in leaking, the case studies offer various insights into how leaks can be transferred to the designated recipients or published, especially in terms of the use of dedicated information security technologies or practices (AUTHOR, 2020; McGregor, 2021). Although insights of this kind were not provided in all the cases under study, some of them do shed light on how cryptography can be directly connected to leaks and how the use of encryption tools may come to support or even define certain instances of leaks. In other cases, whether encryption was used at all remained undisclosed. Facebook whistleblower Frances Haugen originally reached out to a *Wall Street Journal* reporter through an "encrypted text" (Horwitz, 2021), but it is unclear how the documents were originally transferred. A journalist involved in the consortium of news outlets that later analyzed the cache of documents declared that the data had been shared to the reporters through Google Drive, a commercial solution (Kantrowitz, 2021). Some of the instances included here involve the use of digital whistleblowing platforms (Di Salvo & Porlezza, 2020). In the Retina-X and Flexispy cases, for instance, the journalists stated that at least some of the documents involved in the leaks were obtained through the *Motherboard* SecureDrop (Franceschi-Bicchierai & Cox, 2017).

It is unclear whether The Drone Papers started from a leak via the whistleblowing platform of *The Intercept*, but the United States Department of Justice quoted in a statement a reference to an unspecified "encrypted messaging platform" through which the alleged source of the leak communicated with a reporter (2021). In the case of the Panama Papers, it is known that John Doe contacted the *Süddeutsche Zeitung* anonymously through unspecified encrypted channels and asked that journalists be willing to only communicate online and through secure channels (Obermayer & Obermaier, 2017). According to the United States Department of Justice (2019), WikiLeaks, the pioneer whistleblowing platform, obtained the emails involved in the DNC leaks "through encrypted channels, including possibly through WikiLeaks's private communication system," which—although not specified—could be a reference to WikiLeaks's anonymous encrypted submission system. Conversely, DDoSecrets did not release information about how they came to obtain the BlueLeaks documents, but the collective's website lists various forms of encrypted communication as potential sources.

Discussion

Several patterns emerged from the framework regarding how leaks may take shape in the current age of digitalization. Starting from the assumption that contemporary leaking goes well beyond classic whistleblowing, it is now possible to elaborate on how this is happening and the patterns followed. Different actors and groups are now using leaks as an effective informational strategy. Whether following a public interest-oriented agenda or a malicious one, leaking has been established as a powerful and effective strategy for informational purposes, particularly when it comes to exposing data and digital information that would otherwise have remained hidden.

Digitalization has influenced and facilitated the practice of leaking in various ways, as the case studies seem to suggest. First, digitalization has made information more accessible and easier to transfer through digital channels and tools. At the same time, the possibility of using cyberattacking strategies and practices has also connected hacking with information activism instances of various kinds. The use of hacks to disclose the information is now an identifiable—and undoubtedly controversial—hacktivist strategy (Chadiwick, 2017; Coleman, 2017). At the same time, in the context of investigative journalism practices, it is clear that digitalization is at the core of the investigation and coverage of megaleaks, such as the Panama Papers, which are deeply connected to data-driven and quantitative reporting practices such as data journalism (Coddington, 2015).

Finally, the characteristics and number of recipient individuals or groups have also multiplied, allowing more actors than journalists to become recipients and distributors of leaks. In some instances, whistleblowers or outsider sources have found effective strategies in the use of digital tools and practices and, consequently, have become first-person publishers of their leaks. In other instances, organizations explicitly devoted to the publications of leaks—such as WikiLeaks and the DDoS collective—have been launched with different journalistic traits and aims. Furthermore, instances of leaks generated by the actions of state actors also show the sometimes close connection between leaking and intelligence operations and political influence (Briant & Wanless, 2018). Overall, in this complex digital scenario, leaks appear divided between various axes. First, they can be distributed as "insider" or "outsider" leaks: on one side are those leaks that represent clear instances of whistleblowing, regardless of the quantity and nature of the documents exposed in this way. On the opposite side are leaks where the unauthorized release of information is the consequence of more disruptive—and illegal, if not criminal—actions, with cyberattacks being the most frequent. Here, hackers represent the most active social group, although the agendas and motivations can vary considerably, as shown in the cases under study here.

On the level of the practices and technologies involved, leaks may occur in contexts entailing specific digital practices or where practices traditionally connected to leaking—such as private communication between sources and journalists—are supplanted by their digital equivalents. In this sense, whistleblowing platforms capable of anonymizing these interactions and that offer a complete infrastructure for the transmission of leaks represent a clear innovation and, potentially, an advancement in the area of leaking in terms of security and empowerment. In other cases, where the exposure of leaks passed through a more traditional source–journalist relationship (Liebes & Blum-Kulka, 2004), an adaptation to digitally mediated practices was visible, although not a profound change in terms of roles and dynamics. Sources such as whistleblowers may have different skill and knowledge levels relating to information security, and journalists on the other side of the exchange may be in a similar position.

However, a learning curve in regards to the use of information security for source protection has been visible since the Snowden revelations, and a growing number of newsrooms, at least in Europe and the US, are now using various encryption tools to deal with their sources or attract potential leaks from the Internet. Since 2017, the adoption of dedicated information security practices by journalists has accelerated following years of neglect (McGregor, 2021, p. 104). As instantiated in some of the case studies, the tools used to communicate with whistleblowers can also become drop-boxes for other actors, such as hackers.

In certain instances, journalists or journalistic organizations are not directly involved in the process of leaking information provided by sources, neither as recipients nor as publishers of the leaks. Moreover, as instantiated in certain "public interest hacks," sources have been first to release the information in their possession. In these instances, journalists have had the opportunity to cover cases involving leaks only after they have reached the public sphere and without having the opportunity to break the news themselves. This is clearly a sign of the loss of exclusivity of journalism in regards to the opportunity to cover leaks. Nevertheless, this also confirms the central role of hybrid, nontraditional, and "interloper" organizations (Eldridge, 2017), such as WikiLeaks and DDoS; despite performing some journalistic functions, they do not follow publication strategies that would necessarily adhere to traditional journalistic standards, if not openly challenge or disrupt them. In all these contexts, journalists may find themselves involved in very disruptive reporting circumstances and potentially in direct communication with sources whose agendas and aims may be dramatically different and even hostile compared to theirs, or they may be asked to report on leaks with questionable ethical implications—a sign of what has been defined as "dysfunctional hybridity," that is, where older and newer media logics collide with the interdependence of journalism, politics, and hacking (Chadwick, 2017, pp. 272–281).

Conclusion

The evidence suggests that "the age of big leaks" is here to stay (Shane, 2019) and that leaks will continue to influence various power dynamics of the contemporary information ecosystem and journalism at the same time. The 2022 Russian attack on Ukraine underscores how, for instance, the practice of leaking connected to cyberattacks is an integral component of contemporary warfare (Faife, 2022), as much as the DNC leaks had demonstrated the centrality of the practice in the context of political interference. As discussed at the beginning of this chapter, leaks are increasingly reclaiming a central space in the most peculiar dynamics of digitalization, making them an even more natural resource for journalists.

Moreover, the variety and quantity of potential "assemblages" constituting the leaks described here are a sign of the expansion of possibilities for leaking. With journalists already under stress from an increased number of potential sources in the digital realm, leaks are adding themselves to this occasional cacophony of potential sources available to them, which extends well beyond whistleblowing. As such, leaks require new framing and new ethical approaches for journalists, together with the acknowledgement that at least for journalists covering certain beats, leaks are to be included among common reporting scenarios. Whereas dealing with a leak will probably not become a day-to-day newsroom practice in the same way as following newswires or conducting interviews, leaks are already a fundamental component of today's journalism, if not a defining one.

This chapter does have some limitations. As it was based on a selection of case studies, the results and consequent considerations are a direct reflection of the examples discussed here, which have inevitably failed to include all potential types of leaks. For instance, more research is needed in the gray areas between cybercrime and political hacking or data breaches caused by criminal cyberattacks that may still have some public interest traits or journalistic value. Moreover, as argued in the chapter, the term "leaks" is very broad, and its use can vary and be applied to an evolving set of reporting scenarios. To a certain extent, the term could even be applied to accidental leaks, such as those caused by malfunctions, human mistakes, or other similar incidents. One case in point is a 2021 BBC story based on data retrieved from a tablet on a battlefield in Libya (Ibrahim & Barabanov, 2021). For these reasons, the framework included here should be seen as a progression in the understanding of contemporary leaks and a contribution to their theoretical framing beyond whistleblowing to include a range of possible assemblages. At the same time, it can also be applied with the aim of further understanding the roles that journalists and newsrooms can have in the context of reporting on leaks and in their diffusion in the public sphere. The framework could have a double function: understanding leaks themselves and, at the same time, being a tool for shedding light on journalism's modes and functions in these contexts. As such, the framework offers various possibilities in terms of expansion, adaptation, and further use.

Moreover, it is only the starting point of potentially more "assemblages" constituting leaks in the digital era. Finally, all these instances are somehow connected to English-speaking or European and US contexts and their journalistic cultures. Whereas instances of leaks coming from these areas tend to obtain more international and global exposure, they are not the only ones. Also, further research is needed on these geographical and cultural issues to grasp, from a real global perspective, the various forms that leaks take. Again, the hope is that the proposed framework could inspire further inquiry into this area.

Acknowledgements This article generated within a mobility research fellowship funded by the Swiss National Science Foundation (SNSF), grant number P2TIP1_191492.

References

Arnold, J. R. (2019). *Whistleblowers, Leakers, and Their Network. From Snowden to Samizdat*. New York: Rowman & Littlefield.

Baack, S. (2016). What big data leaks tell us about the future of journalism—And its past. *Internet Policy Review*. https://policyreview.info/articles/news/what-big-data-leaks-tell-us-about-future-journalism-and-its-past/413.

Barnes, J.E. (2021). Ex-Intelligence Analyst Is Sentenced for Leaking to a Reporter. *The New York Times*, July 27th. https://www.nytimes.com/2021/07/27/us/politics/daniel-hale-leak-sentence.html.

Benkler, Y. (2013). WikiLeaks and the Networked Fourth Estate. In: Brevini, B., Hintz, A. & McCurdy, P. (Eds.). *Beyond WikiLeaks. Implications for the Future of Communications, Journalism and Society*. London: Palgrave Macmillan, 11–34.

Benton, J. (2021). In the ocean's worth of new Facebook revelations out today, here are some of the most important drops. *The Nieman Journalism Lab*, October 25th. https://www.niemanlab.org/2021/10/in-the-oceans-worth-of-new-facebook-revelations-out-today-here-are-some-of-most-important-drops/.

Beran, D. (2020). The Return of Anonymous. *The Atlantic*, August 11th. https://www.theatlantic.com/technology/archive/2020/08/hacker-group-anonymous-returns/615058/.

Boeyink, D. E. (1990). Anonymous sources in news stories: Justifying exceptions and limiting abuses. *Journal of Mass Media Ethics*, 5(4), 233–246.

Bory, P., & Di Salvo, P. (2022). Weak systems unveiling the vulnerabilities of digitization. *Tecnoscienza*, 12(2), 79–87.

Briant, E. L. & Wanless, A. (2018). A digital ménage à trois: Strategic leaks, propaganda and journalism. In: Bjola, C. & Pamment, J. (Eds.). *Countering Online Propaganda and Extremism. The Dark Side of Digital Diplomacy*. Abingdon-on-Thames: Routledge, 44–65.

Cabra, M. & Kissane, E. (2016). Wrangling 2.6TB of data: The people and the technology behind the Panama Papers. *ICIJ.org*, April 25th. https://www.icij.org/investigations/panama-papers/data-tech-team-icij/.

Ceva, E. & Bocchiola, M. (2018). *Is Whistleblowing a Duty?* Cambridge: Polity.

Ceva, E. & Bocchiola, M. (2019). Theories of whistleblowing. *Philosophy Compass*, 15(1). https://doi.org/10.1111/phc3.12642.

Chadwick, A. (2017). *The Hybrid Media System: Politics and Power (2nd edition)*. Oxford: Oxford University Press.

Coddington, M. (2015). Clarifying Journalism's Quantitative Turn. A typology for evaluating data journalism, computational journalism, and computer-assisted reporting. *Digital Journalism*, 3(3), 331–348.

Coleman, G. (2017). The Public Interest Hack. *Limn*, 8, 18–23.

Culiberg, B., & Mihelič, K. K. (2017). The Evolution of Whistleblowing Studies: A Critical Review and Research Agenda. *Journal of Business Ethics*, 146(4), 787–803.

Deleuze, G. & Guattari, F. (2008). *A Thousand Plateaus: Capitalism and Schizophrenia*. London: Continuum.

Di Salvo, P. (2016). Strategies of Circulation Restriction in Whistleblowing: The Pentagon Papers, WikiLeaks and Snowden Cases Authors. *Tecnoscienza*, 7(1), 67–86.

Di Salvo, P. (2020). *Digital Whistleblowing Platforms in Journalism. Encrypting Leaks*. London: Palgrave Macmillan.

Di Salvo, P. & Porlezza, C. (2020). Hybrid professionalism in journalism: Opportunities and risks of hacker sources. *SComS. Studies in Communication Sciences*, 20(2), 243–254.

Duffy, M. J., & Freeman, C. P. (2011). Unnamed sources: A utilitarian exploration of their justification and guidelines for limited use. *Journal of Mass Media Ethics*, 26(4), 297–315.

Eldridge, S. A. (2017). *Online Journalism from the Periphery. Interloper Media and the Journalistic Field*. London: Routledge.

Emmel, N. (2014). Purposeful Sampling. In: Emmel, N. (Ed.) *Sampling and Choosing Cases in Qualitative Research: A Realist Approach*. Thousand Oaks: Sage, 33–44.

Faife, C. (2022). In Ukraine, hacktivists fight back with data leaks. *The Verge*, March 11th. https://www.theverge.com/2022/3/11/22968049/anonymous-hacks-ukraine-russia-cybercrime-danger.

Flynn, K. (2011). The practice and politics of leaking. *Social Alternatives*, 30(1), 24–28.

Franceschi-Bicchierai, L. (2016a). The Vigilante Who Hacked Hacking Team Explains How He Did It. *Motherboard*, April 15th. https://www.vice.com/en/article/3dad3n/the-vigilante-who-hacked-hacking-team-explains-how-he-did-it-.

Franceschi-Bicchierai, L. (2016b). Hacker 'Phineas Fisher' Speaks on Camera for the First Time—Through a Puppet. *Motherboard*, July 20th. https://www.vice.com/en/article/78kwke/hacker-phineas-fisher-hacking-team-puppet.

Franceschi-Bicchierai, L. & Cox, J. (2017). Inside the 'Stalkerware' Surveillance Market, Where Ordinary People Tap Each Other's Phones. *Motherboard*, April 18th. https://www.vice.com/en/article/53vm7n/inside-stalkerware-surveillance-market-flexispy-retina-x.

Gallagher, S. (2018). DNC "lone hacker" Guccifer 2.0 pegged as Russian spy after opsec fail. *Ars Technica*, March 23th. https://arstechnica.com/tech-policy/2018/03/dnc-lone-hacker-guccifer-2-0-pegged-as-russian-spy-after-opsec-fail/.

Hintz, A. (2019). Leaks. In: T. P. Vos & F. Hanusch (Eds.). *The International Encyclopedia of Journalism Studies*. Hoboken: Wiley.

Horwitz, J. (2021). The Facebook Whistleblower, Frances Haugen, Says She Wants to Fix the Company, Not Harm It. *The Wall Street Journal*, October 3rd. https://www.wsj.com/articles/facebook-whistleblower-frances-haugen-says-she-wants-to-fix-the-company-not-harm-it-11633304122.

Ibrahim, N. & Barabanov, I. (2021). The lost tablet and the secret documents. BBC News, https://www.bbc.co.uk/news/extra/8iaz6xit26/the-lost-tablet-and-the-secret-documents.

Johnson, B. G., Bent, L., & Dade, C. (2020). An Ethic of Advocacy: Metajournalistic Discourse on the Practice of Leaks and Whistleblowing from Valerie Plame to the Trump Administration. *Journal of Media Ethics*, 35(1), 2–16.

Kantrowitz, A. (2021). I'm in the consortium possessing the leaked Facebook documents. Let's dissolve it. *The Nieman Journalism Lab*, October 26th. https://www.niemanlab.org/2021/10/im-in-the-consortium-possessing-the-leaked-facebook-documents-lets-dissolve-it/.

Larrondo-Ureta, A., & Ferreras-Rodríguez, E. M. (2021). The potential of investigative data journalism to reshape professional culture and values. A study of bellwether transnational projects. *Communication & Society, 34*(1), 41–56.

Lee, M. (2020). Hack of 251 Law Enforcement Websites Exposes Personal Data of 700,000 Cops. *The Intercept*, July 15th. https://theintercept.com/2020/07/15/blueleaks-anonymous-ddos-law-enforcement-hack/.

Liebes, T. & Blum-Kulka, S. (2004). It takes two to blow the whistle: Do journalists control the outbreak of scandal? *American Behavioral Scientist, 47*(9), 1153–1170.

McGregor, S. E. (2021). *Information Security Essentials: A Guide for Reporters, Editors, and Newsroom Leaders.* New York, NY: Columbia University Press.

Miceli, M. P. & Near, J. (1992). *Blowing the Whistle. The Organizational and Legal Implications for Companies and Employees.* New York: Lexington Books.

Milmo, D. (2021). Frances Haugen: 'I never wanted to be a whistleblower. But lives were in danger'. *The Guardian*, October 24th. https://www.theguardian.com/technology/2021/oct/24/frances-haugen-i-never-wanted-to-be-a-whistleblower-but-lives-were-in-danger.

Nail, T. (2017). What is an Assemblage? *SubStance, 142*(46), 21–37.

Obermayer, B. & Obermaier, F. (2017). *The Panama Papers. Breaking the Story of How the Rich and Powerful Hide Their Money.* London: Oneworld Publications.

Reich, Z. (2008). The anatomy of leaks. Tracing the path of unauthorized disclosure in the Israeli press. *Journalism, 9*(5), 555–581.

Reich, Z. & Barnoy, A. (2016). The Anatomy of Leaking in the Age of Megaleaks. New triggers, old news practices. *Digital Journalism, 4*, 886–898.

Rid, T. (2020). *Active measures: The secret history of disinformation and political warfare.* New York, NY: Farrar.

Schapals, A. K. (2022). *Peripheral Actors in Journalism Deviating from the Norm?* Abingdon-on-Thames: Routledge.

Seawright, J., & Gerring, J. (2008). Case selection techniques in case study research: A menu of qualitative and quantitative options. *Political Research Quarterly, 61*(2), 294–308.

Shane, S. (2019). The Age of Big Leaks. *The New York Times*, February 2nd. Available from: https://www.nytimes.com/2019/02/02/sunday-review/data-leaks-journalism.html.

Singer, J. B. (2005). The Political J-Blogger: 'Normalizing' a New Media Form to Fit Old Norms and Practices. *Journalism, 6*(2), 173–98. https://doi.org/10.1177/1464884905051009.

Stone, G. & Bollinger, L. (2021). *National Security, Leaks and Freedom of the Press: The Pentagon Papers Fifty Years On.* Oxford: Oxford University Press.

Süddeutsche Zeitung. (2016). John Doe's Manifesto. https://panamapapers.sueddeutsche.de/articles/572c897a5632a39742ed34ef/.

The Intercept. (2015). The Drone Papers. https://theintercept.com/drone-papers/.

Thielman, S. (2019). A new group devoted to transparency is exposing secrets Wikileaks chose to keep. *Columbia Journalism Review*, February 6th. https://www.cjr.org/tow_center/emma-best-ddosecrets.php.

Tiffen, R. (2018). The Era of Mega-Leaks. In: Schapals, A. K., Bruns, A., & McNair, B. (Eds.). *Digitizing democracy.* New York, NY: Routledge.

Touchton, M.R., Klofstad, C.A., West, J.P. & Uscinski, J.E. (2020). Whistleblowing or leaking? Public opinion toward Assange, Manning, and Snowden. *Research & Politics, 7*(1). https://doi.org/10.1177/2053168020904582.

United States Department of Justice. (2019). Report on the Investigation into Russian Interference in the 2016 Presidential Election. https://www.justice.gov/archives/sco/file/1373816/download.

United States Department of Justice. (2021). Former Intelligence Analyst Pleads Guilty to Disclosing Classified Information. https://www.justice.gov/usao-edva/pr/former-intelligence-analyst-pleads-guilty-disclosing-classified-information.

Wahl-Jorgensen, K. & Hunt, J. (2012). Journalism, accountability and the possibilities for structural critique: A case study of coverage of whistleblowing. *Journalism*, *13*(4), 399–416.

Wheatley, D. (2020). A typology of news sourcing: Routine and non-routine channels of production. *Journalism Practice*, *14*(3), 277–298.

Woodall, A. (2018). Media capture in the era of megaleaks. *Journalism*, *19*(8), 1182–1195.

Zittrain, J. (2016). Mass Hacks of Private Email Aren't Whistleblowing, They are at Odds With It. *Just Security*, October 19th. https://www.justsecurity.org/33677/mass-hacks-private-email-arent-whistleblowing-odds-it/.

CHAPTER 27

Gig Labour and the Future of Freelance Journalism in South Africa and Zimbabwe

Dumisani Moyo and Allen Munoriyarwa

INTRODUCTION

The rapid digitisation and technological convergence of the past few decades has had profound ramifications for various social, economic and political practices everywhere, complicating and altering forever, the ways in which we work, communicate and go about our everyday life. In the journalism industry, journalists and content creators have felt the impact of digitisation, which has upended traditional ways of work and forced some of them into 'freelancing' and short-term employment, with no prospect of stable jobs as media institutions struggle to survive. While freelancing in journalism has been a critical component of the profession for many years, the rapid digitisation over the past two decades has made it more fashionable. The rise in artificial intelligence, spurred by improved machine learning and algorithms, has led to the automation of certain roles in the media industry, with implications for jobs and the quality of journalism, among other things.

This has worsened the precarity of journalism labour in contexts where newsrooms already faced viability challenges, especially in the global South. Laying off journalists, or hiring them on short-term contracts as content

---

D. Moyo (✉)
North West University, Potchefstroom, South Africa

A. Munoriyarwa
Department of Media Studies, University of Botswana, Gaborone, Botswana
e-mail: munoriyarwaa@ub.ac.bw

providers have become the norm. For millions of journalists churned out from Journalism Schools, across many parts of the world, job stability has become elusive. Declining readership and viewership, coupled with the 'flight' of advertisers from traditional media to online platforms has meant little to no hope of professional advancement. Cost-conscious media managers are cutting into journalism labour to trim costs, leaving most journalists to fend for themselves with low-tier salaries, frozen benefits and vanishingly scarce allowances. Journalists thus bear the brunt of declining revenues in the media industry (Dolber et al., 2021), and continuously face threats of retrenchment as the traditional business model underpinned by advertising, circulation and viewership flounders in the face of proliferating digital news platforms.

These challenges, while heightened by the COVID-19 pandemic, have been years in the making. For the past decade or so, media organisations have been digitising, sending thousands of workers into informal labour and outright unemployment (Dolber et al., 2021). These developments have huge implications for democracy, as capacity to produce investigative and other public interest stories diminishes, and misinformation and disinformation increase on the digital platforms.

The logic is that as advertisers move to online platforms, so do jobs. Criticism has mounted that these platforms, which have taken on most of the traditional jobs, have radically redefined labour and exposed workers to uncertainty. Whereas in traditional journalism one could spend an entire career working for one media organisation, the new world of work, epitomosed by what is now referred to as the gig economy, has normalised short-termism, labour mobility, as well as concurrent work for multiple 'employers' as everday practices in the sector. Job design and the organisation of work is increasingly centred around the online environment, where all key practices—from identifying news leads to engagement with sources to distribution and consumption of news products—are transactred. Digital transformation has thus brought with it new ways of working for journalists and other content producers.

The proliferation of definitions and claims about what exactly is gig labour testifies to both its complexity and newness in academic studies. It has, in extant research, been used to refer to independent contract work in a number of practices—ranging from taxi-services, food delivery, programming and translation, news writing and dissemination online—generally, services that are traded via online platforms. In this chapter, we adopt the International Labour Organisation (ILO, 2018), definition of the practice as any labour activity that comprises of a variety of tasks, digitally-mediated or transacted through internet platforms and often delivered remotely or performed locally. We augment this with the definition proffered by Jabagi et al. (2019, p. 193), that, gig labour is, "… an emerging labour market wherein organizations engage independent workers for short-term contracts ("gigs") to create virtual jobs…" The foundations of gig labour is digital labour platforms. In this chapter, we limit ourselves to platforms on which journalism is performed by adopting

Esau et al. (2017) definition of journalism platforms as news forums, news blogs, online websites and Facebook news pages.

Our aim is to explore and examine the ways freelance journalism labour has been affected by the gig work culture in southern Africa. We draw on in-depth and semi-structured interviews with selected freelance journalists in South Africa and Zimbabwe in March 2022. Through these interviews, we sought to establish these journalists' understanding of freelancing in the era of digital technologies and convergence; the opportunities and constraints to freelance journalism; the financial suitability of freelancing; the desirability of (re-)joining as a full-time journalist for a news media organisation; the extent to which freelancing has prepared them for such a task; and their views about the sustainability of freelance journalism as a mode of journalism labour.

Responses from the interviewees were subjected to thematic analysis, which allowed us to draw common themes emerging from the data (Braun & Clark, 2012). Although some of our informants granted us consent to use their names, we decided to anonymise all of them for purposes of consistency. Altogether, we interviewed twelve free-lance journalists—six from South Africa and six from Zimbabwe. We acknowledge the limited nature of our data set. However, for research that is exploratory, and that seeks depth of meaning rather than representation, this limited set of data presents no challenges of validity.

There is no extant literature known to the authors that examines the implications of gig labour specifically on freelance journalism practice on the African continent. Research by Anwar and Graham (2021), for instance, has focused on the impact of gig labour on African workers generally, without focusing on specific nuances in the journalistic field. By focusing on how gig labour is impacting the specific field of journalism practice, our chapter moves away from anecdotal understanding of labour in the gig economy to problematising gig labour on a particular community of practice.

We argue that the precarious circumstances of journalism, especially in the global south contexts, render journalists to extreme forms of exploitation, and make it even more difficult for freelancers to position and identify themselves as journalists with a fixed occupational ideology because of the way they operate on the margins of the profession. Furthermore, we make an argument that the absence of visible unionism that caters for their professional interests, makes it difficult for freelancers to organise for their rights. In the process, their contribution to journalism work, whilst immense, is gradually and systemically invisibilised. We conclude by arguing for a stronger drive to get gig workers in journalism to belong to supportive associations that champion their causes—including fair and commensurate pay for their work to circumvent exploitation by unscrupulous platforms and other users of their content, precarity of their labour, and simultaneously improve their own welfare at an individual level. This, potentially, opens avenues through which freelancers can rise above the precarity that defines their current status.

In the next section, we provide a literature review of journalism labour in the gig economy. This is followed by the conceptual framework around gig labour. We then follow this with a presentation and discussion of findings, and then a conclusion.

Conceptualising Gig Labour in the Context of Online Freelance Journalism

The concept of gig labour asserts that digital convergence has created new forms of labour characterised by casualisation and informalisation of jobs (Anwar & Graham, 2021; Dolber et al., 2021). The consequence has been the mushrooming of new modes of production and resistance in a converged journalism/media ecosystem (Dolber et al., 2021). Gig labour has been described in many ways, ranging from 'crown work', to 'platform labour.' Ride-hailing services have dominated much scholarly research about gig labour, which explains why gig labour has often been misnamed as 'uberisation' of work. Most existing literature has tended to celebrate gig labour as revolutionising the labour market. Srnicek (2017), for instance, argues that gig labour drives down the cost of doing business by cutting the costs of wages for employees and eliminating related labour costs like payment of entitlements such as sick leave, superannuation, and so on. It is thus seen as providing a cheaper alternative for struggling media companies who can now contract freelance journalists and other content producers instead of hiring full-time journalists. In addition, free-lancing also benefits journalists, as it potentially entails an enriched lifestyle, with greater choice and flexibility at various levels, including flexible working hours, and not being tied to one employer. As Fahim (2020) writes,

> … journalists, reporters, content creators, possibly now have the opportunity to move into areas of journalism that they've always wanted to. In a gig journalism landscape, you can offer yourself to take up jobs that fully interest you, charge the 'client' what you believe you're worth, and work for various companies at the same time. It will no longer be moonlighting as a freelancer can legally work for a media house to write a news story, and at the same time produce an in-house content for a corporate client. Graduates and new blood joining the journalism industry can also have a hand in trying out producing content for various forms of media while figuring out what's best for them, and to build out that portfolio.

However, these 'emancipatory' claims have been challenged by other scholars. De Stefano (2016), and Dosen and Graham (2018), for instance, argue that gig labour leads to greater labour precarity, risk and poor working conditions. In a similar vein, Standing (2014) argues that the contemporary neoliberal era is witnessing, "the emergence of a new working class (the precariat') that lacks various forms of labour security, insufficient social income, lack of community benefits and lack of work-related identity" (in Anwar & Graham,

2021, p. 242)., The ILO (2016) concurs with this position, defining platform work as insecure, unprotected and non-standard.

Gig labour has also been linked directly to controversies around quality of work (Burchell et al., 2014). There is no consensus, however, as to what constitutes job quality. However, several key characteristics are important to job quality, including income, health and autonomy (Monteith & Giesbert, 2014). It is important to interrogate the position of gig workers in relation to these key job quality measures. Autonomy, for example, gives workers power to bargain for better working conditions and has implications for workers like freelance journalists producing content for platforms. Anwar and Graham (2021) for example, have noted that gig labour is a consequence of the restructuring of capitalist labour relations, which, as De Stefano (2016) notes, has led to increasing casualisation of labour. Notably, gig labour wages are low, and gig work is, "a continuum, of underpaid, mispaid and poorly paid human tasks" Casilli (2017, p. 3935). An additional complication is the customer evaluation that gig labourers are subjected to as part of the validation of their work (Healy et al., 2017). For example, a freelance journalist's contract is, more often than not, likely to be renewed if their stories receive high numbers of clicks and drive traffic to the platform.

There is also a widely shared perception that gig labour offers workers greater flexibility on who to work for, where, when, and how. Yet, as Rosenblat and Stark (2016) argue, platform labour renders workers subject to algorithmic control. While platform workers are liberated from the control of organised labour, they deliver themselves into the clutches of algorithms. Algorithms and automation processes, as Gregory (2021) argues, are not transparent. Much of their operations are hidden from the public, and they reproduce pre-existing biases embedded in their initial design. A major downside that comes with the platforms is the creation of disposable labour—labour that can easily be hired and fired. As Anwar and Graham argue, "…the burden of risk gets shifted from firms to workers, and the online labour markets are implicated in generating a disposable labour force." (p. 241). In addition, a general perception of freelance journalists as entrepreneurs—as "individual businesses that negotiate with clients rather than a class of workers" (Salamon, 2019) has meant that they do not enjoy the typical protections that journalists in traditional systems get from their unions and other media freedom watchdogs.

In this chapter, we draw on Koutsimpogiorgos et al.'s (2020) four-dimensional conceptualisation of gig labour, which looks at online platforms versus offline intermediation, independent contractors versus employee status, paid versus unpaid tasks, and delivery of services versus goods. First, we consider gig labour as platform-mediated (Koutsimpogiorgos et al., 2020). Gig labour is either mediated through an application-based platform or through a website (Stewart & Stanford, 2017), as a defining feature. This understanding helps us conceive freelance journalists as part of gig labour. As Hayes and Silke (2018) note, contemporary freelance journalism is increasingly being transacted on news websites, creating, in the process, variegated and contextually—defined forms of digital labour. Furthermore, this conceptualisation allows us to factor in journalists who are successfully carving careers as bloggers (Lennon, 2003) who still sell their labour on a platform in exchange for an income. Online platforms, furthermore, mediate supply (for example, the supply of news on a website by a news agency), and demand (for example, the demand for news by readers), at a lower transaction cost for the supplier.

The second dimension in this conceptualisation is the constitution of gig labour. In existing studies, (see Friedman, 2014; Kuhn & Maleki, 2017) gig labour is constituted by a plethora of players. These range from contract labourers, to freelancers, and self-employed workers. As Koutsimpogiorgos et al. (2020) note, these are not synonymous. There are distinctive features of each. But, freelancing has emerged as the most preferred name that explains gig work. Koutsimpogiorgos et al. (2020) define freelancing as work, "organised into specific tasks upon which gig work workers and requesters agree ex ante, that is, before completion of the task" (p. 530). For example, a freelance journalist can be hired to provide news along with a specific newsbeat, certain breaking events, or to cover a specific (geographical) community, or to cover a topical investigative story. Prassl and Risak (2015), however, hazards that there is a need as we distinguish the various dimensions of platform labour, to understand two broad manifestations of platform labour. These are internal platform labour, where an organisation uses its own internal fully-employed staff to perform labour for it. For instance, a news website can hire full time journalists to gather, write and disseminate news for it. But to supplement this internal workforce, it can hire external labour. Thus, there should be, according to Prassl and Risak (2015) conceptualisation, a distinction between internal and external platform labour.

The third dimension is a conceptualisation of gig labour as paid labour. This, arguably, brings freelancers to the bracket of employees because payment is a necessary condition of labour (De Stefano, 2015). But, the fact that they do not hold permanent tenure then pushes them to the opposite side of the employment equation, defined by precarity (Standing, 2014). Fourth, and lastly, we conceptualise gig labour narrowly as the selling of labour, and we, therefore, distinguish gig labour from those who sell capital goods, but are still classified in some literature as gig workers. For instance, we separate a freelance journalist from a gig worker who rents out accommodation through Airbnb (Prassl & Risak, 2015; Koutsimpogiorgos et al., 2020).

This is not easy to differentiate because there is always a conflation of both (Koutsimpogiorgos et al., 2020). For example, an Airbnb service provider requires reception services). But for conceptual clarity, we consider only freelancers as offering a labour service, not consumer goods like renting out services. This four-dimensional conceptualization helps us understand gig labour in a much narrow but focused way. Thus, we draw on a number of specificities about gig labour: it is platform or web-mediated; tasks are specified ex ante; tasks are paid for; people are not full-time employees, which means they can 'rent' their labour to different platforms. Evidently, gig labour has significantly contributed to the way digital transformation has disrupted the entire value chain of news/content production, distribution and consumption, in the process altering several other everyday practices, as we demonstrate below.

Findings

Drawing from our analysis of the data, we crystallised our findings under three broad themes, which directly respond to our research questions. First, we establish that our respondents found gig labour in journalism to be a mixed bag—a boon in terms of providing flexibility in relation to income and work routines on one hand, and a threat in the sense that it leaves them in a permanent sense of precarity on another. Second, they view gig journalism as robbing them of a professional identity, as they are no longer considered as fully belonging to the journalistic community. They feel alienated from their peers in the traditional media, and unable to form meaningful relations and collaborations with them. Finally, our respondents lament the lack of active unions to fight for their labour rights. Those who work for exploitative platforms find themselves trapped in what has been termed 'in-work poverty', with no recourse. We articulate these findings in detail below, followed by a discussion and conclusion.

Mixed Fortunes: Labour Precarity Versus Flexibility in Income and Work Routines

The first key finding in this study is that respondents find working for web-based news platforms a mixed bag of fortunes that juxtaposes precariousness of freelance journalism labour with, simultaneously, flexibility in terms of both work routines and multiple income sources. This precarity of journalism labour, as highlighted by the freelance journalists is manifested in three negative practices in the gig economy—exploitation, exclusion and commodification of labour. The lack of security of tenure and predictable income also adds to the precarity. For these freelance journalists, working for news platforms creates a labour condition of 'permanent impermanence,' as they cannot tie themselves down to a single platform. Respondent 1 from Zimbabwe explains the reason: "When you write for a digital platform, you would actually feel that there is no very close relationship with that platform. After all, it is a mere platform, not an institution with human beings on which permanent relationships can be formed. So, you rove from one platform to another and before you know it, you would have worked for many of them…" (Respondent 1, Zimbabwe).

Furthermore, platforms, on which freelance journalists work, have become potentate in journalism labour, as they have become the final arbiters of who gets assigned to write what, and where, and how much they get paid. Because of this overarching power, there is no 'binding loyalty' between the platforms and the journalists writing for them. What this means is that: "you can write up to twenty or even more stories for a particular web-based platform. But then, when you get a more rewarding opportunity, you leave, even without saying good-bye. But also, you can be 'fired' by the platform" (Respondent 1, Zimbabwe)

This element of free agency and flexibility on the part of the freelance journalist came out strongly from informants from both countries as something that they cherished, even as they knew that the platform reserved the right to 'fire' them. There are a few ways, according to our respondents, through which platforms fire freelance journalists, underscoring the precarity of platform labour in journalism. As another respondent notes, "You know you are fired when your stories are not being published, or when they put certain conditions on your work expectations, like giving you a huge number of stories to publish within a month…that is a sure way of chasing you away from their platform… (Respondent 1, South Africa). This makes the idea of 'freedom' embedded in 'freelancing' an oxymoron, as there is clearly a limit to the freedom that these journalists have. This also highlights a power relation that is heavily skewed in favour of the platforms, who wield the power to change the rules of engagement as they see fit. Every news platform brings with it its own set of demands. Thus, "the freelance journalist is a permanent job hunter…he is always looking for those platforms that give the greatest satisfaction…but they may not be easy to come by as platforms are exploitative" (Respondent 2, South Africa).

Exploitation of freelance journalism labour, while rampant, is not uniform across platforms. Some exploit freelance journalists more than others, suggesting that journalistic labour is even more precarious and prone to unbridled exploitation. On some news platforms, for instance, freelancers are rewarded per story published. On others, they are paid per number of words, or,

> You are paid per clicks that your story gets. I once freelanced for a news website where I could only get paid after the story has clicked 5 000 hits. This means all my stories were published, but I was not paid because none achieved that huge number of hits. (Respondent 2, South Africa)

Such freelance labour exploitation thrives on the skewed (or lack of clear) contractual obligations that bind the freelancer and the online platform. News platforms take advantage of this to maximise profit, or to frustrate journalists. As one respondent argued: "If you write a story, they may tell you that we are no longer able to pay you per word as agreed. We will now pay a lumpsum for the whole story. Most of the times, you will see that the lumpsum is far smaller than what you could have received if you had been paid per word. In some instances, they just cut the story. This reduces the number of words. And hence, cuts costs on their side." (Respondent 2, South Africa).

Because freelancers have no say on the conditions of their own labour, they often feel excluded and commodified as labourers. By commodification of labour, we adopt the common classical Marxist explanation of the process (cf Maddison, 2008) to mean a process that, "separate [the] direct production from ownership of the means of production and alienate producers from ownership of their labour" (Maddison, 2008, p. 238). This often happens when independent producers, like freelance journalists in this case, are expropriated and turned into wage labour (Maddison, 2008). In platform journalism labour, commodification manifests in different ways. For example, freelance journalists, as commodified labour, are forced to sell their creative and intellectual abilities for wages under the terms dictated by online platforms. The freelance journalists are thus insecure and keep searching for platforms that give better value for their labour. One respondent noted: "When you notice that a certain platform pays far much better than the other, you start making in-roads to write for it. After all, what you need when you have a passion and talent for writing, is an income." (Respondent 3, South Africa).

This suggests a considerable degree of agency on the part of the freelance journalist, because even though they do not have much say on the price of their stories (which is the prerogative of the website owners and editors), they can to some degree resist or circumvent exploitation and seek better prices. When a freelance journalist decides to ditch an online website because it pays less, as compared to the other, it is in itself an active contest of the commodification of their labour. Another respondent noted: "If there is an important news story to pursue in a distant place, I need to factor in several factors before pursuing it. First, how much does the commissioning website pay? Secondly, does the ultimate payment and the costs of my expenditures give me a living wage? If not, I would decline, or I pitch it with a better-paying news website." (Respondent 4, South Africa).

Commodification of journalism labour leads to alienation of producers of stories from their product. One respondent summed this consequence thus: "When you work for a website, you can write a whole feature story, or even a ground-breaking investigative piece of work and use a pseudonym. Even when the story trends, you do not feel like it is yours. Website allow that. But you do not mind as long as you get paid." (Respondent 1, South Africa). Works of intellectual labour are often associated with individuals. But in this case, payment trumps all other considerations. The precarity and subsequent commodification of journalism labour should be juxtaposed with benefits that journalists get. As much as freelance journalists feel aliened, commodified and oppressed by the precariousness of their labour, the financial rewards, according to respondents, are worth the while. This is more so, "when one is able to make it on mainstream websites that pay for the number of words that you write" (Respondent 5, South Africa).

However, the general consensus amongst respondents is that when one finds a big established outlet, one gets more certainty about a decent and steady income. In addition, getting an overseas-based contract is deemed to always bring better payment rates than what one gets from struggling local newsrooms whose advertising share has dwindled over the years. As one respondent put it, "Some organisations will go for a long time without having paid you…and yet you have bills to pay, and people to feed. You end up accepting whatever little is there." (Respondent 2, South Africa).

It was therefore evident that much as freelance journalists enjoyed the flexibility and multiple income streams that come with gig labour and serving as contributors to platforms, a strong sense of precarity, being exploited and living on the margins pervades.

Operating on the Periphery?: Gig Labour and Journalistic Identity

The second key finding, which is linked to the first, relates to the question of journalistic identity in the context of gig labour. The emerging precarity of freelance journalism labour has contributed to a crisis of identity amongst freelancers. Ibarra (1999), defines work identity as enactment of a work-related role. This is the question of who, exactly they identify themselves as, professionally. During significant moments of transition, individuals often change the ways they identify themselves as, from a professional/worker perspective (Ashforth & Schinoff, 2016). This is more so for newcomers, newly-promoted individuals, those exposed to new technologies and platforms to work on, and those in demanding circumstances (Ashforth & Schinoff, 2016). This rings true for freelancers because of their own individual doubts about whether they are valued working outside newsrooms, and whether the platforms they work for see them as contributing to a robust public sphere, or as 'flirting' labourers to be exploited. One informant notes that "most of the time, we feel alienated because we are not closely linked to the newsroom. It is hard to think exactly who you are when you work on the periphery of the profession. Beyond money, there is nothing else I really think I represent as a journalist." (Respondent 2, Zimbabwe).

This underlines a misalignment between freelance journalists' self-identity and how they are perceived and expected of by the platforms they work for. We argue that this results from their sense of dispensability as precarious and temporary labour. This reinforces freelance journalists' perception that they are not necessarily seen as central to the quotidian activities, and are treated as 'an afterthought' by traditional media. One informant notes: "We are just accepted as contributors who fill space and write, only. I do not think beyond this we are valued. We are just there to write, nothing else because we operate on the margins of real journalism." (Respondent 1, Zimbabwe).

As freelancers, they find it hard to, over time, create an identity based on the ethos, values, beliefs and practices of the journalism profession. This is because they often are 'flirting and fleeting labour'—only attracted to platforms that meet their financial needs at a time, and with no loyalty to institutions. This is how they are viewed in the mainstream, by editors and colleagues, who see them as 'space fillers' and not a group of professional journalists who are part of the guild and quotidian practices of the profession. One informant adds: "You can write for an online platform, which also has a hard copy presence (sic). But you may leave the news institutions without even knowing who works there. The luck freelancer interacts, rarely, with the mainstream (sic). Most of us almost often never do…" (Respondent 3, Zimbabwe).

For platform workers like freelance journalists, contracting with several news platforms to provide labour becomes in itself an indicator of their professionalism. One informant notes: "When you are a freelance, the number of platforms you write for and their quality become a measure of success" (Respondent 2, Zimbabwe).

Yet, on the other hand, institutions provide agency through which journalists can develop interactive and professional skills and master the demands of journalism. Thus, platform work, is not only defined by precarity of individual work, but the lack of a visible and stable environment, as in organisations—like mainstream newsrooms, where they can develop physical, psychological and social space—or 'holding environments' to deal with feelings of anxiety often associated with freelance and gig labour (Bauman, 2013, p. 249). They are, hence, disconnected from a typical mainstream work ethos that would ordinarily provide peer and other forms of support. Furthermore, they cannot learn about the interests of their audiences. Because of the de-institutionalised nature of gig work they perform, they have no opportunity to engage and understand what their audiences want. One informant indicates: "With freelance journalism, we have no feedback structure to understand if you are exciting an audience. The only way close to that is visiting the story and see how much clicks and hits it has recorded. But that is hardly enough to understand the audience." (Respondent 4, Zimbabwe).

It is this disconnection that makes it hard for freelance journalist to develop a professional identity. To understand this level of disconnection, there is need to grasp the nature of platform work. Freelance journalists working for news platforms, often work in a distributed context. Newsrooms are known for bringing journalists close together (Hollifield et al., 2001), allowing them to create a collective journalistic culture, share experiences, values identities through practices like collaboration, data sharing etc. Newsrooms also allow journalists to network and form professional connections and associations to defend their profession, and establish professional standards (Diedong, 2008). The same cannot be said of platforms and websites. They are too widely distributed, and not cohered enough to foster such a relationship amongst freelancers. After all, they focus on the bigger picture—the product form the journalists, not much about related issues of journalistic belonging, networking, wellbeing, relations, and so on. Working in such 'isolated environments' robs freelancers of a social and professional space which they can use to, "…derive ideal images of a possible or desirable self at work" (Bellesia et al., 2019, p. 248). News platforms do not provide them with role models to learn from, or derive professional cues from, or foster a professional identity. They are, hence, 'itinerant professionals." (Barley & Kunda, 2006, p. 50).

The fact that freelance journalists rarely come into contact with the rules of the mainstream media, which have often been taken for granted as representing the journalism profession (see Domingo & Le Cam, 2014), means that defining who they are is not a straightforward process. Identity construction is hence, made difficult, if not impossible, by their perceived non-integration in the mainstream. They, hence are a 'different selves' carving their own individual identities in a different working environment outside the mainstream-defining rules.

Un-unionised Gig Labour and 'In-work Poverty'

The identity crisis discussed above is exacerbated by the challenge of establishing and sustaining, in both South Africa and Zimbabwe, effective and inclusive unionised spaces through which freelance journalists' grievances can be channelled. One function of trade unions is to channel protests through formalised and recognised institutions. While there are associations such as the Southern African Freelancers' Association (SAFREA) and the Zimbabwe Freelance Journalist Association (ZFLJA), these are not widely known, according to our respondents. In South Africa, one informant said of SAFREA, "We hardly know it. We have no idea what it does and where. We would even be happy if we knew of its existence. These are organisations that should represent us… (Respondent 5, South Africa). Yet SAFREA has a well-developed official website and boasts over 500 members. Its study on the freelance media industry conducted in 2018/19 established that 26.9% of respondents belonged to SAFREA, while nearly 30% indicated that they did not belong to any organisation.

In Zimbabwe, an informant said of ZFLJA: "There used to be this organisation. But the founder passed on. That marked the end of the organisation. Now, it just exists in name…" (Respondent 3, Zimbabwe). This makes it difficult to organise and speak back to the continued casualisation of their labour, its precarity, and the exploitation that comes with all this (De Stefano, 2016; Pangrazio et al., 2021; Veen et al., 2020). This perpetuates 'in-work poverty'—which is defined as a situation where you work, but you remain very poor. Many freelancers see their profession as 'ununionisable', because of its unstructured nature, and the fact that most of the news platforms they write for compete, rather than complement each other. News platforms are, hence, disengaged from traditional forms of trade unions that always depended on and catered for institutionalised workforce. Not having affinal networks amongst freelancers erodes their ability to speak with a unified voice to improve their working conditions and earn the respect of the profession. Lazar and Sanchez (2019, p. 367), argued that, "precarisation has reconfigured traditional frontiers of (labour) solidarity". As one of our respondents notes that: "In the absence of a (trade) union to represent freelancers who write for online platforms, exploitation is bound to continue unabated… Wage inconsistencies and sometimes no payment at all or even less payment which is a violation of agreed contracts, will continue…" (Respondent 2, South Africa).

It is important to note, however, that SAFREA's work mostly focuses on making sure that freelance journalists and other content producers have decent working conditions and are fairly remunerated for their labour. SAFREA benchmarks rates used by freelancers in various media spaces to assist content producers and other freelancing service providers in coming up with fair and realistic charges for their labour.

Existing mainstream unions like South Africa Union of Journalists (SAUJ) and Zimbabwe Union of Journalists (ZUJ), mainly cater for journalists who are in the mainstream, leaving freelancer at the margins of the profession's labour movements. This means journalism is fractured as a class. Journalists have always been thought to belong to the middle class (Nixon & Day, 1968; Khorana, 2012), with economic gains and professional aspirations that define them as socially, economically and financially advanced middle class (Khorana, 2012). This has been because of strong unions within the profession that have always agitated for better working conditions for journalists, with some organisations even representing journalists at a global level. But, the absence of union agitation for freelancers working for platforms mean that some members of the journalism fraternity remain at the bottom rung of the ladder. The wage differences within platforms themselves means that freelance journalists cannot even aspire to be at the same level with their own counterparts. Thus, journalism becomes a tale of many professions serving the same public, but rewarded differently. There are particularly exploitative platforms that do not even value the labour of freelance journalists. One of the informants narrates such illogical treatment by some online news organisations thus:

> I worked for a platform that only paid when your story reached 5 000 hits. I wrote about 15 stories. None of them could reach that 5000 hits. When we started this was not agreed on. My stories are there online. But they do not have 5000 hits. I could not be paid.... (Respondent 1, South Africa)

There are three types of wage differentiation in journalism as a result of gig labour. There is a wage structure for mainstream, full-time employed journalists on permanent or long term contracts. Then there are different wage structures for freelances. As we noted, some platforms pay per word. Others per story, and yet others per hits on the story once it is published. This mismatch between the wage structures of institutionalised journalists, and freelance journalists means journalists cannot be considered a homogenous group, since some of them if not most, work for exploitative institutions on exploitative contracts. As most of our informants noted, working for platforms means that you can be working, but remain poor. This in-work poverty situation is worsened by the nature of online news platforms themselves. Some of them are ephemeral (Esau et al., 2017). This means they can disappear suddenly, leaving already precarious freelance journalists in an even more precarious situation.

Discussion: Platform Labour and the Systemic Invisibilisation of Freelance Journalism

This chapter examined how digital transformation has disrupted traditional journalism labour, focusing on freelance journalists in South Africa and Zimbabwe. With digitisation and automation becoming some of the preferred solutions to declining revenues in the traditional media sector, many journalists have been laid off, and are joining the growing legion of contract or gig workers as 'freelancers' and content producers, frequently enlarged by graduates from journalism schools. In both countries, freelance journalism on digital platforms is on the rise and has broadly affected journalism in three main ways. First, although freelance journalism has been around for decades now, it is evident that emergent gig workers in journalism now increasingly work on the margins of the profession, more so in a context where media industries are in decline and many journalists are laid off.

This has increased their precarity, even though some, especially those working for bigger and more successful news platforms find the financial rewards satisfactory. Secondly, we note that platform-based journalists struggle to form a professional identity. Gig practices in journalism have eroded the solidarity that always existed in the journalism profession and created a chasm that leaves many operating in isolation (Khorana, 2012). By their nature, news platforms do not provide support for contributors to develop new forms of professional identity, as they alienate freelance journalists from the online community that consumes their products. Contrary to the widely held view that online platforms in tech-intensive environments do offer maximum support for identity construction (Berlossi, 2018), we make an argument that for journalists, platforms do not foster socialisation and identity construction.

Further, gig workers in journalism remain largely un-unionised. This adds to their precarity, casualisation, exploitation and hence the prevalent in-work poverty amongst journalists. These three effects we note above, are a sign of the symbolic deterioration of the working conditions of journalists. Working standards for journalists are increasingly going down, at a time when staff-turnover in mainstream journalism institutions is increasing, in the process, sending more journalists into freelancing. Thus, the structural constraints of the labour market is increasing journalists' precarity.

Gig work for journalists has, therefore, led to the systematic invisibilisation of freelance journalism labour. This is a consequence of the intensified conditions of precarity in what used to be a stable profession. 'Formalised journalism' as embodied by fully employed journalists now stands in stark contrast with less formalised freelance journalism. This division between formalised and informalised journalism labour, gradually transforms the essential qualities of journalism. Freelance journalists can produce up to 15 stories a month in order to increase their levels of income by maximising on the economies of scale. This illustrates two important points. Firstly, freelance journalism still produces a highly efficient regime of journalists who write for a living. Yet, secondly, this highly efficient guild of freelance journalists are not involved in collective effort to challenge and improve their own working conditions. We argue that the "work for clicks" culture may, arguably jeopardise the monitory and watchdog role of the media. The danger is that this might erode the previously held sacrosanct role of the media in the public sphere.

Conclusion: Regulatory Dilemmas of Gig Labour in Journalism

While it is not easy to determine the size of the gig economy in southern Africa, there is enough evidence to suggest this it is a growing economy, and that the Covid-19 pandemic has spurred its growth between 2020 and 2021. With global trends moving decidedly towards freelancing, and as it becomes cheaper and faster to produce content and disseminate it online—and as Generation Z graduates into adulthood, it is safe to project that gig labour will soon overtake the traditional ways of doing journalism, to become the mainstay in the sector. Thus existing journalism support organisations could start making the shift to cater for gig workers in anticipation of the inevitable explosion in gig journalism—lest they become irrelevant. In addition, new support organisation could be established to protect freelance journalists from rampant exploitation.

Pioneering work by organisations such as SAFREA could be expanded and made more visible to increase membership and ensure that current and future gig workers in journalism are adequately supported. We argue that, considering that gig labour is the future of journalism work, and will undoubtedly surpass traditional forms of full-time employment of journalists and other content producers, it is time that meaningful investment be made in such associations—in the interest of sustaining public interest journalism.

At the same time, limited but enabling statutory regulation may be necessary to shield gig journalists from low social security and social protection contributions which are consequential to their low renumeration, and may affect the quality of their lives. For states and governments, statutory regulation may also present the benefit of fighting tax evasion which is highly likely in unregulated labour markets like platform work. The danger, however, is that in (semi) authoritarian regimes, statutory regulation of gig journalism may be used as a chance to restrict the work of freelance journalists, and this would need to be closely guarded against.

This chapter has added to critical literature on gig labour by focusing on the less-explored concept of gig labour in journalism in less-researched global south contexts of Zimbabwe and South Africa. It illustrates how digital transformation has had a lasting impact on everyday journalistic practices, particularly in the rise of gig journalism, which is characterised by flexibility, choice and cost-cutting on one hand, and job insecurity and precarity on the other. A limitation of this chapter is its reliance on a limited set of data. Yet, its major strength is that it is one of the emerging work that explores gig practices in the journalism profession. Future work in this area may focus on a large set of data, and expand the research beyond South Africa and Zimbabwe.

References

Anwar, M.A. & Graham, M. (2021). Between a rock and a hard place: Freedom, flexibility, precarity and vulnerability in the gig economy in Africa. *Competition & Change*, 25(2), 237–258.

Ashforth, B.E. & Schinoff, B.S. (2016). Identity under construction: How individuals come to define themselves in organizations. *Annual Review of Organizational Psychology and Organizational Behavior*, 3(1), 111–137.

Barley, S.R. & Kunda, G. (2006). Contracting: A new form of professional practice. *Academy of Management Perspectives*, 20(1), 45–66.

Bauman, Z. (2013). *Wasted Lives: Modernity and Its Outcasts*. London: Wiley.

Bellesia, F., Mattarelli, E., Bertolotti, F. & Sobrero, M. (2019). Platforms as entrepreneurial incubators? How online labor markets shape work identity. *Journal of Managerial Psychology*, 34(4), 246–268.

Berlossi, D. (2018). Online platforms and occurences. Accessible at:https://www.concurrences.com › dictionary › online-p. Accessed on 15 August 2021.

Braun, V., & Clarke, V. (2012). Thematic analysis. In H. Cooper, P. M. Camic, D. L. Long, A. T. Panter, D. Rindskopf, & K. J. Sher (Eds.), APA handbook of research methods in psychology, Vol. 2. Research designs: Quantitative, qualitative, neuropsychological, and biological (pp. 57–71). *American Psychological Association*. https://doi.org/10.1037/13620-004

Burchell, B., Sehnbruch, K., Piasna, A., et al. (2014). The quality of employment and decent work: Definitions, methodologies, and ongoing debates. *Cambridge Journal of Economics*, 38(2), 459–477.

Casilli, A. (2017). Global digital culture| Digital labor studies go global: Toward a digital decolonial turn. *International Journal of Communication*, 11, 3934–3954.

De Stefano, V. (2015). The rise of the just-in-time workforce: On-demand work, crowdwork, and labor protection in the gig economy. *Comparative Labour Law & Policy Journal*, 37(3), 471–504.

De Stefano, V. (2016). "The rise of the "just-in-time workforce" : on-demand work, crowdwork and labour protection in the "gig-economy"," ILO Working Papers 994899823402676, International Labour Organization.

Diedong, A. 2008. Establishing journalistic standards in the Ghanaian press. *African Communication Research*, 1(2), 207–231.

Dolber, B., Rodino-Colocino, M., Kumanyika, C. & Wolfson, T. eds. (2021). *The Gig Economy: Workers and Media in the Age of Convergence*. London: Routledge.

Domingo, D. & Le Cam, F. (2014). Journalism in dispersion: Exploring the blurring boundaries of newsmaking through a controversy. *Digital Journalism*, 2(3), 310–321.

Dosen, I., & Graham, M. (2018). Labour rights in the gig economy: An explainer, Research note (Victoria.Parliamentary Library and Information Service), no. 7, June 2018, Parliamentary Library and Information Service, Parliament of Victoria, Melbourne, viewed 26 Sep 2023 . https://www.parliament.vic.gov.au/publications/researchpapers/download/36-researchpapers/13869-labour-rights-in-the-gig-economy-an-explainer.

Esau, K., Friess, D. & Eilders, C. (2017). Design matters! An empirical analysis of online deliberation on different news platforms. *Policy & Internet*, 9(3), 321–342.

Fahim, H. (2020). 'The rise of gig economy: Is freelance journalism the future hiring model for the media?' Accessible at: https://www.linkedin.com/pulse/rise-gig-economy-freelance-journalism-future-hiring-model-fahim. Accessed 1 September 2022.

Friedman, G. (2014). Workers without employers: Shadow corporations and the rise of the gig economy. *Review of Keynesian Economics*, 2(2), 171–188.

Gregory, K. (2021). 'My Life Is More Valuable Than This': Understanding Risk among On-Demand Food Couriers in Edinburgh. *Work, Employment and Society*, 35(2), 316–331. https://doi.org/10.1177/0950017020969593.

Hayes, K. & Silke, H. (2018). The networked freelancer? Digital labour and freelance journalism in the age of social media. *Digital Journalism*, 6(8), 1018–1028.

Healy, J., Nicholson, D. & Pekarek, A. (2017). Should we take the gig economy seriously? *Labour & Industry: A journal of the social and economic relations of work*, 27(3), 232–248.

Hollifield, C.A., Kosicki, G.M. & Becker, L.B. (2001). Organizational vs. professional culture in the newsroom: Television news directors' and newspaper editors' hiring decisions. *Journal of Broadcasting & Electronic Media*, 45(1), 92–117.

Ibarra, H. (1999). Provisional selves: Experimenting with image and identity in professional adaptation. *Administrative Science Quarterly*, 44(4), 764–791.

ILO. (2016). Network on future of work. Accessible at: https://www.ilo.org/global/topics/future-of-work/network/lang-en/index.htm.

ILO. (2018). World Employment and Social Outlook: Trends 2018. Geneva: ILO. Accessible at: https://www.ilo.org/wcmsp5/groups/public/%2D%2D-dgreports/%2D%2D-dcomm/%2D%2Dpubl/documents/publication/wcms_615594.pdf. Accessed 10 October 2021.

Jabagi, N., Croteau, A.M., Audebrand, L.K. & Marsan, J. (2019). Gig-workers' motivation: Thinking beyond carrots and sticks. *Journal of Managerial Psychology*, 34(4), 192–213.

Khorana, S. (2012). The female journalist in Bollywood: Middle-class career woman or problematic national heroine? *Metro Magazine: Media & Education Magazine*, 171, 102–106.

Koutsimpogiorgos, N., Van Slageren, J., Herrmann, A.M. & Frenken, K. (2020). Conceptualizing the gig economy and its regulatory problems. *Policy & Internet*, 12(4), 525–545.

Kuhn, K.M. & Maleki, A. (2017). Micro-entrepreneurs, dependent contractors, and instaserfs: Understanding online labor platform workforces. *Academy of Management Perspectives*, 31(3), 183–200.

Lazar, S. & Sanchez, A. (2019). Understanding labour politics in an age of precarity. *Dialectical Anthropology*, 43(1), 3–14.

Lennon, S. (2003). Blogging journalists invite outsiders' reporting in. *Nieman Reports*, 57(3), 76. https://niemanreports.org/articles/blogging-journalists-invite-outsiders-reporting-in/. Accessed 2 September 2022.

Maddison, R. (2008). Labour commodification and classification: An illustrative case study of the New South Wales boilermaking trades, 1860–1920. https://ro.uow.edu.au/artspapers/1737. Accessed 2 September 2022.

Monteith, W. & Giesbert, L. (2014). Perceptions of 'Good Working the Informal Urban Economy: Evidence from Burkina Faso, Uganda and Sri Lanka. In *EADI 14th General Conference: Responsible Development in a Polycentric World: Inequality, Citizenship and the Middle Classes.*

Nixon, R.B. & Day, J.L. (1968). The Latin American journalist: A tentative profile. *Journalism Quarterly*, 45(3), 509–515.

Pangrazio, L., Bishop, C. & Lee, F. (2021). Old media, new gigs: The discursive construction of the gig economy in Australian news media. *Work, Employment and Society 4(2)*, 1–19.

Prassl, J. & Risak, M. (2015). Uber, taskrabbit, and co.: Platforms as employers-rethinking the legal analysis of crowdwork. *Comparative Labor Law and Policy Journal*, 37, 619.

Rosenblat, A. & Stark, L. (2016). Algorithmic labor and information asymmetries: A case study of Uber's drivers. *International Journal of Communication*, 10, 3758–3784.

Salamon, E. 2019. Digitising freelance media labour: A class of workers negotiates entrepreneurialism and activism. *New Media and Society*, 22(1), 105–122

Srnicek, N. (2017). *Platform Capitalism*. Malden, MA: Polity Press.

Standing, G. (2014). *The Precariat: The New Dangerous Class, Trade*. London; New York: Bloomsbury Academic.

Stewart, A., & Stanford, J. (2017). Regulating work in the gig economy: What are the options? *The Economic and Labour Relations Review*, 28(3), 420–437. https://doi.org/10.1177/1035304617722461

Veen, A., Barratt, T. & Goods, C. (2020). Platform-capital's 'appetite' for control: A labour process analysis of food-delivery work in Australia. *Work, Employment and Society*, 34(3), 388–406.

Index[1]

A

Africa, 207, 333, 363, 365, 366, 369, 371, 373, 374, 400, 405, 406, 451, 452, 454

Artificial intelligence (AI), vi, 5, 12, 114, 116, 125–131, 134, 136, 170, 171n1, 228, 233, 267, 272, 329, 330, 332–335, 337, 339, 392, 400, 425, 489

B

Brazil, 15, 16, 32, 119, 245–259, 347–353, 355–358, 424

C

Children, vii, 6, 9, 14, 87, 117, 118, 120, 125, 137, 199, 223–242, 246, 254, 261, 266, 269–271, 273–276, 307, 314, 315, 339, 401

China, 12, 13, 91–104, 112, 113, 116

Climate change, vii, 11, 114, 206, 213, 268, 399, 440, 441, 446, 460

Climate journalism, 17, 439–449

Climate newsletters, 17, 439–449

Contestations, vi, 8–9, 11, 13–14, 146, 178

Covid-19, vii, 16, 67, 91–104, 116, 119, 145, 146, 171, 181, 183, 207, 245–250, 252, 253, 259, 262, 307, 308, 311, 314, 320, 321, 327, 328, 331, 333–335, 337, 338, 347, 348, 350, 353–355, 357, 380–385, 383n4, 390, 397, 399–403, 406, 409, 410, 447, 448, 490, 503

Culture, vi, 4, 7, 8, 11, 15–16, 23, 28, 30, 62, 63, 80, 82–88, 96, 116–118, 121, 269, 349, 352, 357, 363–374, 382, 384, 385, 388, 389, 392, 393, 421, 424, 445, 449, 464, 470, 484, 491, 499, 503

Cybersecurity, 212, 217, 350

D

Deep fakes, 4

Development, vi, vii, 5, 7, 9–11, 14, 16, 26–28, 40, 45, 62, 63, 73, 77, 97, 98, 101–103, 114, 116, 127, 131, 134, 135, 170, 189, 206, 207, 209, 210, 214–217, 223–240, 251, 255, 262, 263, 269, 272, 274, 276, 283, 284, 286, 288, 291, 293, 298, 301, 310, 314, 322, 328, 329, 331, 336, 339, 341, 342, 347, 348, 351, 363–366, 369–374, 380, 390, 392, 397–410, 417, 419, 422, 423, 429–431, 433, 456, 460, 461, 463, 464, 490

[1] Note: Page numbers followed by 'n' refer to notes.

Digital abodes, 13, 109–122
Digital access, 3, 9–11, 217, 262, 271, 357, 405
Digital affordances, vi, 11, 13–14, 23, 461
Digital analytics, 4, 11, 210, 266, 341, 422, 423, 430
Digital business, vi, 4, 10, 13, 37, 61, 70–73, 112, 125, 130, 210, 227, 234, 328, 330, 334–336, 341, 350, 391, 423, 426, 434, 452, 462, 464
Digital Climate Effects, 206
Digital consumption, vi, 11, 15–16
Digital divide, vi, 7, 9, 14–15, 206, 208, 209, 214, 307–322, 331, 350, 366, 398, 399, 401, 403–410, 418, 454
Digital domain, 2, 116, 365, 367–369, 379–393
Digital education, 272
Digital empowerment, 210, 215, 216
Digital humanitarianism, 16, 397–410
Digital inclusion, 11, 206–211, 213–216, 318, 320, 321, 353, 365, 391
Digital inequalities, 10, 14, 15, 208, 209, 271, 272, 307, 308, 311, 313, 320, 321
Digital infrastructure, 28, 91, 114, 271, 358, 385, 392
Digitalisation, v, vii, viii, 11–16, 125, 328, 397, 401
Digital journalism, vi, vii, 16–18, 417–435
Digital labour, 490, 494
Digital leaks, 17, 469–484
Digital life, 1–4, 13, 37, 102, 143, 144, 148, 206, 207, 209, 211, 418, 434
Digital lifeworlds, vi, 9, 12–13
Digital literacies, 9, 11, 15, 261–276, 331, 389, 391, 392, 405, 406, 435
Digital media, 8, 77, 102, 112, 117, 118, 147, 259, 271, 335, 348–350, 389, 420, 421, 423, 425–431, 441–443, 447–449, 452, 454–456, 458, 461–463
Digital misinformation, 347–358
Digital news, 490
Digital platforms, vi, 5, 6, 28, 29, 72, 93, 119, 134, 148, 170, 179, 180, 183, 212, 330, 365, 374, 381, 388–390, 418, 425, 432, 433, 449, 454, 456, 458–462, 490, 495, 502
Digital revolution, 13, 125–138, 309
Digital Strategies, vii, 273
Digital technology, v–viii, 2, 7, 8, 11–17, 30, 77, 94, 95, 98, 103, 109, 121, 125, 133, 135, 190, 191, 205, 207, 209, 213, 215, 217, 223–242, 261–263, 268–275, 283–302, 307, 318, 320–322, 327, 328, 331, 335, 337–341, 347, 353, 355, 356, 373, 379, 384, 386–390, 392, 393, 397–401, 403, 404, 406–410, 418–420, 430, 432, 435, 454, 491
Digital transformation, vi, 37, 73, 130, 134, 197, 206, 207, 210, 211, 272, 273, 308, 347, 350, 392, 397–410, 427, 452, 490, 495, 502, 503
Digital work, 250–252, 334, 341
Digitization, 30, 93, 103, 205–217, 265, 270, 272, 273, 341, 372–374, 385
Din, 125–138

E
Education, vi, vii, 4, 10, 12–15, 51, 64, 72, 73, 125, 132, 133, 137, 197–200, 206, 208, 210, 223–225, 227, 230–234, 236, 237, 239–240, 245–259, 261–276, 287, 289, 293–295, 297, 300–302, 307–309, 313–315, 317, 318, 321, 322, 327, 328, 336, 340–342, 353, 356–358, 419, 424, 426, 433–435, 451–453, 459, 462
Equality, 174n15, 175, 178–181, 286
Europe, 208, 334, 398, 483
Everyday challenges, 12, 188, 190, 193, 197, 199, 273, 290, 308, 321, 337, 379
Everyday digital life, 37, 143, 148, 206, 207, 262
Everyday knowledge, 23–34
Everyday life, v–vii, 2–4, 7, 9, 11, 12, 23, 24, 27–30, 61, 62, 77–80, 83, 86, 87, 93, 109, 118, 121, 143, 145, 188, 190, 193–195, 206, 223, 227, 289, 301, 302, 308, 320, 321,

327–342, 364, 371, 379, 381, 393, 397, 434, 440, 441, 489

F
Facebook, 6, 12, 14, 29–31, 37–57, 113, 114, 116, 128, 147, 151, 159, 161, 169–184, 190, 193, 209, 349, 350, 356, 367, 369–374, 380, 381, 385–387, 392, 456, 459, 460, 477, 481, 491
Fourth Industrial Revolution (4IR), 5, 329, 340, 374
Freelance journalism, 17, 489–504
Future, vi, 5, 8, 11, 13, 17, 18, 37, 54, 82, 93, 94, 99, 103, 110, 114, 119, 120, 126, 129, 136, 137, 162, 173, 177, 179, 183, 184, 188, 197, 223–225, 227, 229, 231, 234, 236, 238–240, 242, 252, 259, 272–276, 317n2, 320, 327, 328, 330–331, 333, 335–339, 342, 365, 374, 380, 381, 386, 391–393, 410, 417, 422, 425, 430, 434, 441–444, 473, 489–504

G
Gamification, vii, 14, 245–259
Ghana, 14, 116, 121, 205–217, 370
Gig economy, 334, 335, 490–492, 495, 503
Globalisation, 4, 5, 8, 16, 63, 112, 134, 286, 310, 347, 349, 426
Global South, vi, 78, 110, 207, 253, 283, 307, 308, 331, 337, 398, 399, 402, 406, 418, 439, 454, 489, 491, 503

H
Hyderabad, 12, 61–74, 72n5

I
India, 12, 61, 63–65, 67, 70, 71, 112, 114, 116, 144, 187–200, 333, 349
Industry 5.0, 329–330, 340–342

Information and Communication Technology (ICT), 7, 10, 15, 18, 125, 131, 133, 205–217, 272, 301, 308–311, 313–322, 328, 331–333, 337, 338, 340, 342, 364, 365, 368–371, 373, 418, 428, 430, 435
Information society, 7, 190–192, 356, 426
Instagram, 6, 12, 29, 37–39, 45, 52–54, 77–88, 113, 171, 172, 178n19, 349, 356, 381, 385–387, 431, 441, 445, 459
Interactivity, 169–184, 212, 231, 269, 421, 430, 431
Internet, 1–4, 9–11, 14, 28, 29, 37, 38, 41, 42, 71, 92, 93, 95, 100, 101, 112–115, 125–127, 129, 150, 151, 172, 181, 183, 187–200, 205–213, 215, 246, 247, 253, 256, 259, 269, 271, 273, 285, 287, 288, 297–299, 307, 308, 310–317, 319–322, 328, 331, 333, 337–339, 348, 349, 352, 353, 356, 357, 365–367, 371, 373, 385, 387, 389, 391, 398, 400, 401, 404–406, 419–421, 425, 427, 428, 430–433, 454–456, 462, 473, 475, 476, 478, 480, 483, 490
Intimate image sharing, 14, 187–200
Iran, 12, 37–57, 144, 150

J
Jamaica, 187–200, 293, 296, 298, 299
Johannesburg, 12, 77–88, 452
Journalism, vii, 11, 16–18, 174, 178, 417–428, 430–434, 441, 444–446, 449, 456, 457, 462, 469–471, 475, 476, 478, 482–484, 489–504

K
Knowledge society, 7

L
Labour, vi, 13, 17, 63, 65, 73, 78, 86, 110, 120, 125, 129–135, 137, 138, 174, 300, 331, 334, 489–504

M

Media, v, vi, 3, 4, 6, 11, 16–18, 29, 38, 45, 46, 52, 53, 62, 68, 96, 97, 100, 102, 113, 121, 127, 128, 130, 144, 152, 159, 170, 175, 183, 184, 188, 205–207, 209, 211, 213, 253–255, 259, 309, 310, 314, 333, 347, 348, 367, 369, 381, 384, 385, 387, 390, 391, 402, 419–421, 423–428, 430–435, 440, 441, 443–449, 452–460, 462–464, 472, 475, 477, 483, 489–493, 495, 498–503

Me Too, 13, 169–184

N

Networked communities, 2
Networking, 4, 40, 169, 173, 499
News, 4, 25, 52, 111, 151, 152, 175, 177, 188, 193, 333, 348, 350, 354

P

Pandemic, vii, 11–16, 69, 71, 72, 91–104, 109, 110, 112, 114, 116, 119, 134, 136, 146, 171, 175, 181, 183, 245–250, 252–257, 262, 267, 270, 271, 307–322, 327, 328, 331–338, 341, 347, 348, 350, 353, 357, 380–385, 387, 390, 397–406, 409, 410, 448, 490, 503
Policy interventions, 14, 211, 307–322
Policy-making, 10, 188, 216, 272–274, 309
Public service, vii, 17, 121, 207, 209, 212, 311, 317–322, 336, 350, 451–464

R

Radio, 211, 213, 256, 364, 369, 373, 387, 388, 388n10, 419, 421, 452, 453, 456, 462, 463
Remote volunteering, 397–410
Revenge porn, 3, 187–190, 195, 198
Rural, 11, 114, 213, 214, 253, 294, 348, 349, 353, 405, 406, 456

S

Site Codes, 13, 91–104
Social inclusion, 207, 208, 285, 307–322
Social media, v–vii, 1, 3, 5, 6, 12–13, 24, 28, 30, 37–57, 77–88, 92, 99, 100, 102, 113, 114, 117, 144, 169–173, 175, 178, 178n19, 179, 181–184, 187, 188, 190, 194, 199, 209, 213, 266, 269, 270, 274, 319n6, 328, 333, 347–356, 358, 367–370, 372–374, 381, 385–391, 402, 418, 424–427, 431, 439, 441–443, 445, 456, 461–464, 470
South Africa, 12, 17, 77–88, 364, 369, 371, 452, 453, 455, 459, 462, 489–504
Spatial identifiers, 91–104
Stealth, 13, 125–138

T

Taxonomy, 13, 144, 147, 148, 148n1, 152, 153, 161, 180, 473
Technology transformations, 95, 213, 299, 409
Telegram, 13, 38, 39, 52–54, 57, 162, 431, 432
Television, 29, 71, 81, 115–117, 194, 206, 211, 213, 256, 308, 315, 316, 318n3, 319, 320, 369, 387, 388, 388n10, 391, 419–421, 454–456, 463

U

United States (US), 6, 8, 17, 38, 40, 48, 53, 112–115, 118, 133, 144, 151, 190, 192, 287, 293, 333, 334, 391, 420, 476–478, 480, 483, 484
Urban, 4, 11–13, 61–64, 66, 71, 73, 74, 77–79, 83–88, 91–104, 118, 253, 310, 313, 348, 349, 351, 355, 356

V

Volunteering, 397–410

W

WikiLeaks, 469, 475, 476, 480–483

Work, vi, vii, 3, 5, 10, 11, 15–16, 25, 31, 61–65, 67–73, 83, 92, 95, 96, 99, 100, 102, 103, 110, 116, 125, 130–138, 160, 179, 199, 205–208, 211, 213, 216, 224, 225, 227, 229, 230, 232, 233, 235, 239, 242, 245, 246, 250–259, 261–263, 265, 267, 270, 271, 275, 289, 292, 296–300, 308, 309, 311, 320, 322, 327–342, 356, 368, 370–374, 397–402, 404, 405, 407–410, 418, 422, 424–426, 428, 431, 432, 434, 441, 446, 447, 456, 457, 459, 460, 473, 489–504

Z

Zimbabwe, 17, 364, 452–455, 458, 459, 462, 489–504